The
COMPLEAT
FISH COOK

BARBARA GRUNES and PHYLLIS MAGIDA

CB
CONTEMPORARY
BOOKS
CHICAGO

Library of Congress Cataloging-in-Publication Data

Grunes, Barbara.
  The compleat fish cook : 100 delicious recipes for grilling,
sautéing, broiling, panfrying, smoking, and more / Barbara Grunes
and Phyllis Magida.
      p.   cm.
    ISBN 0-8092-4360-1
      1. Cookery (Fish)   2. Cookery (Shellfish)   I. Magida, Phyllis.
II. Title.
TX747.G834   1990
641.6′92—dc20   89-48146
                                                                    CIP

Published by Contemporary Books, Inc.
180 North Michigan Avenue, Chicago, Illinois 60601
Manufactured in the United States of America
International Standard Book Number: 0-8092-4360-1

This book is dedicated to our children:
Allen, Reba, Louis, Tina, Dorothy, and Andrew.

CONTENTS

INTRODUCTION

Fresh fish is the food of today. More and more supermarkets are featuring fresh fish counters, and fish markets and specialty shops all over the country are offering an increasing selection from the bounty produced by our oceans, lakes, rivers, and streams.

Besides being low in calories and low in cholesterol, fish is so good that no matter what method you use to cook it, if it's done properly, it will turn out delicious. For this reason, our recipes include very detailed instructions that practically guarantee success. And again and again, we stress checking fish for doneness at every turn. Overcooking is the enemy of good fish. If you cook your fish with care, you will be well rewarded. We advocate cooking fish until it's slightly underdone, as it will continue to cook for a moment or two after it's removed from the heat.

We are pleased to introduce two new methods of fish cookery. In our grilling chapter, we use herb stems such as rosemary, tarragon, and mint stems for skewers. The stems not only make pretty skewers (we remove all leaves except for a clump on one end) but impart a subtle flavor to the fish as well.

Another cooking method, in our broiling chapter, calls for arranging fish on slices of tomato, green and red peppers, and other vegetables to prevent the fish from sticking to the pan. And this too adds flavor to the final product.

We've organized the recipes in this book by cooking method, and each chapter opens with detailed instructions, including which fish types and cuts are appropriate for that method, the equipment and utensils you'll need, step-by-step directions, and tips for producing the best results using that method.

The recipes have been adapted from many cuisines, taken from our personal files, improvised from classic dishes, and created especially for this book. In the following pages you'll find everything from Salmon Tartare to Panfried Catfish coated with cornmeal, from Broiled Bluefish with Pimiento-Tarragon Sauce to Mahimahi Chow Mein, from Linguine with Sautéed Squid to Deep-Fried Smelt with Shallot Barbecue Sauce, from Cold Poached Red Snapper with Middle Eastern Accompaniments to Classic Pickled Herring.

We hope you enjoy cooking and eating these fish dishes as much as we enjoyed creating the recipes for you.

HOW TO BUY FISH

This is the most important technique you can master.

Go to a fish market with the largest possible turnover, then get to know your fishmonger. Ask him for the freshest possible fish. If you want to cook fresh trout, but the grouper is fresher, buy the grouper and change your recipe plans. Freshness is more important than anything else in buying fish.

To Choose a Fresh Whole Fish

Look for crystal-clear, bright eyes and gills that show a little bit of red underneath. If the eyes are cloudy, or if the gills are brown or darker underneath, the fish is too old. Also, the skin should look fresh and glistening; if it has begun to turn gray or fade, the fish is old. With your finger, push a small dent into the side of the fish. If the fish is fresh, the flesh will be elastic and firm enough to spring back, filling up the dent. If the dent remains, the fish is too old. Lastly, open the fish up and smell the inside, where the intestines have been removed. If the fish is fresh, it will have no odor beyond the faint smell of seaweed.

Fish steaks and fillets should feel firm and moist to the touch, not spongy or dry. The flesh should have a translucent, clear look and not be at all milky and white. If possible, ask the fishmonger to cut the fish steaks to order from a fish you have chosen. Fillets should be firm, translucent, and not white—whiteness is a sign of age. Run your finger over the surface of the fillet. If you get a slimy, sticky mucus on your finger, the fish is old.

Make friends with your fishmonger! Fresh fish are available at a number of places: supermarkets, specialty fish shops, and fish farms (where you catch your own). Wherever you buy, be sure to check the fish for freshness. Also, look first at the fish caught in your area—they are probably cheaper and fresher than imported varieties. In the past, fish and shellfish were always shipped frozen. This is only sometimes true today, and frozen does not necessarily mean tasteless. Check with your fishmonger. Ask him for the freshest and best.

When possible, buy fish with the head, the tail, and the backbone intact. Cooking a fish with the head and tail will seal in the juices, and the backbone acts as a heat conductor, which is important when cooking a large fish.

Be sure to always wash and pat fish dry when ready to use.

How Much Fish to Buy per Person
The chart below will tell you how much fish to allow per person. Although most dietitians recommend less protein per meal, we have upped the servings for three reasons: (1) We are referring to uncooked fish, which weighs more than cooked fish. (2) Fish eating is relatively new in this country, and since your guests are used to beef, you might want to serve them slightly larger portions of fish. (3) Americans are used to large amounts of animal protein, and you don't want your guests to feel that you are skimping on the entree.

HOW MUCH FISH TO BUY PER PERSON, PER SERVING

Fish (whole)	Buy small individual 1-lb. fish per person. Figure 1 lb. or slightly less per person when portions are part of a larger fish (3–3½ lb. stuffed fish will serve 3–4 people amply).
Fish Fillets	6–7 oz. per person
Fish Steaks	6–7 oz. per person
Fish Kabobs	6–7 oz. per person

FISH SPECIES

Fish come naturally in many guises: fatty, moderate, or lean; freshwater (more tiny bones) or saltwater (fewer small, annoying bones); coolwater fish (with richer flavor caused by higher fat content) and warm-water fish; and don't forget the textural differences, ranging from tender, delicately melting types to fish so firm and chewy that you'll feel as though you're eating beef.

The chart on pages 4–6 includes fat content, texture, and calories per 100 grams (about 3½ oz., raw) of the wide variety of fish you'll find in this book. Calorie and fat content charts are based on USDA figures. Textural comments are made by the authors and refer to cooked texture. When a fish is designated fatty, this means it contains over 10 percent fat; when a fish is designated moderate, it has 6–10 percent fat; when a fish is designated lean, this means it has less than 5 percent fat. While all fish species are relatively low in fat, for those on very low-fat, low-calorie diets, serve the portions designated in the preceding chart but choose one of the lean species listed on pages 4–6.

When you're beginning to experiment with fish, you may want to substitute a fish of similar flavor and texture in a recipe. Almost every fish is interchangeable in our recipes. Kabobs are the exception; soft-fleshed fish will not stay on the skewer. The chart shows which types are similar to others, as well as nutritional information.

FAT CONTENT, TEXTURE, FLAVOR, AND CALORIES IN FISH SPECIES

FISH	FAT CONTENT	TEXTURE & FLAVOR	CALORIES per 100 g	SUBSTITUTIONS
Bass, Black Sea	low	med. firm mild	100	red sea bass, striped sea bass, grouper, halibut, mahimahi, rockfish, snapper, tilefish, monkfish, porgy
Bass, Red Sea	low	med. firm mild	90	same as black sea bass
Bass, Striped	low	med. firm mild	90	red sea bass, black sea bass, grouper, halibut, orange roughy, ocean perch, rockfish, tilefish
Bluefish	mod. high	delicate distinctive	110	mackerel, kingfish, whitefish, lake trout, rainbow trout
Buffalofish	high	med. distinctive	215	red sea bass, black sea bass, snapper, yellowtail, butterfish
Catfish, Freshwater	mod. high	med. firm sweet	115	orange roughy, ocean perch, small rockfish, walleye pike
Cod	low	delicate mild	75	scrod (the same as cod), haddock, pollack, lingcod, black cod, flounder
Grouper	low	firm mild	95	black sea bass, red sea bass, snapper, halibut, walleye pike, tautog, tilefish
Halibut	mod. high	med. firm sweet	110	black sea bass, red sea bass, snapper, mahimahi, yellowtail, tilefish
Mackerel	high	med. distinctive	175	bluefish, rainbow trout, brook trout, whitefish, lake trout, yellowtail, sea trout
Mahimahi	mod. low	med. firm mild	90	black sea bass, red sea bass, snapper, ono (wahoo), salmon, yellowtail, sea trout
Ono	med.	firm mild	120	swordfish, shark, kingfish, rockfish, snapper, grouper, yellowtail, pompano
Orange Roughy	low	med. very mild	75	sole, catfish, scrod (cod), haddock, pollack, small rockfish, ocean perch, turbot, flounder, tilapia
Ocean Perch	mod. high	med. mild	105	walleye pike, orange roughy, flounder, turbot, small rockfish, tilapia, sea trout
Pompano	high	med. mildly distinct.	165	ono (wahoo), yellowtail, kingfish, swordfish, bluefish, mackerel
Redfish	low	med. firm mild	90	same as black sea bass
Rockfish	low	med. firm mild	90	snapper, grouper, catfish, ocean perch, sea bass, tilefish, monkfish, sea trout

FAT CONTENT, TEXTURE, FLAVOR, AND CALORIES IN FISH SPECIES

Salmon, Atlantic	high	med. firm mildly distinct.	220	All salmon can be substituted for one another, lake trout, whitefish, rainbow trout, brook trout
Salmon, Chinook	high	med. firm mildly distinct.	185	Same as Atlantic salmon
Salmon, Sockeye	high	med. firm mildly distinct.	155	Same as Atlantic salmon
Scrod	low	delicate mild	75	same as cod
Shark	mod. low	firm mildly distinct.	85	swordfish, ono (wahoo), tuna, marlin
Sole	low	delicate sweet	85	orange roughy, ocean perch, flounder, turbot, tilapia
Snapper, Red	mod. low	med. firm mild	110	same as black sea bass
Swordfish	mod. high	firm mildly distinct.	125	ono (wahoo), shark, tuna, marlin
Trout, Brook	mod. high	med. mildly distinct.	110	rainbow trout, lake trout, salmon, walleye pike, whitefish, crappie, sunfish, haddock, pollack
Trout, Rainbow	high	med. mildly distinct.	130	same as brook trout
Trout, Lake	high	med. mildly distinct.	165	same as brook trout
Tuna, Bluefin	high	firm mildly distinct.	160	swordfish, shark, ono (wahoo), any other tuna, marlin
Tuna, Yellowfin	mod. high	firm mildly distinct.	125	same as bluefin tuna
Yellowtail, Pacific Coast	mod. low	med. firm mild	100	snapper, grouper, kingfish, ono (wahoo), pompano, rockfish, tautog
Walleye Pike	low	med. firm mildly distinct.	90	flounder, rainbow trout, brook trout, ocean perch, catfish, lake perch, crappie, sunfish, tilapia
Whitefish, Lake	high	delicate mildly distinct.	165	same as brook trout

In general fish are not high in cholesterol.

FAT CONTENT, TEXTURE, FLAVOR, AND CALORIES IN SHELLFISH SPECIES

SHELLFISH	FAT CONTENT	TEXTURE & FLAVOR	CALORIES per 100 g
Clams	low	firm distinctive	63
Crab	mod. low	med. firm mildly distinct.	85
Lobster	low	firm mildly distinct.	100
Mussels	low	med. mildly distinct.	77
Oysters	mod. low	med. distinctive	80
Scallops	low	med. mild	80
Shrimp	low	med. firm mildly distinct.	95

Latest research indicates that the cholesterol levels of shellfish are negligible to moderate at most.

HOW TO STORE FISH

Try to use the fish the day you bring it home. But if you must store the fish overnight, begin by filling a pan with water and setting it in the freezer. While you wait for the water in the pan to freeze, rinse the fish in cold, salted water and pat it dry with paper towels. Rewrap it in clean wax paper, then place it in a clean plastic bag and secure it with a twister seal. Set it on a plate and cover both the plate and the fish with the plastic wrap; refrigerate temporarily.

When the water is frozen, remove the pan from the freezer. Place the plate with the fish on the ice and set it in the refrigerator overnight. It will stay extra-cold until you are ready to use it.

HOW TO TEST FISH FOR DONENESS

When fish is raw, the flesh appears translucent and has visible sheets of muscle fiber layered on top of each other, which resemble a stack of thin trays. When the fish is cooked, the tissue holding these together will have melted from the heat and the fish flesh will have a flaky appearance. To tell if fish is cooked through, insert fork tines into the fish flesh at a 45-degree angle and twist slightly, lifting up at the same time. If the fish flesh looks flaky and has lost its opaque appearance, the fish is cooked. For shellfish, you'll know it's done when it turns white. Don't overcook shellfish, especially shrimp and lobster, as it tends to turn tough.

Fish Stock with White Wine

The most satisfactory stock is made with a white, nonoily fish. Most fishmongers will give you the necessary heads and bones if you ask.

1. Place all ingredients in a soup kettle. Heat to a boil, reduce to a medium simmer over medium heat, and cover the pot, leaving a space so steam can escape. Simmer for 40 to 50 minutes.

2. Remove the pot from the heat, uncover it, and allow the stock to cool. Strain the stock in a colander or sieve lined with a double thickness of cheesecloth. Discard the solids and store in the refrigerator if you plan to use the stock in the next few days. Otherwise, a great way to use this is to freeze the stock in ice cube trays, adding a cube or two (depending on cube size) to recipes calling for fish stock.

Makes about 7½ cups

INGREDIENTS
1½ large onions, chopped coarse
⅓–½ cup chopped fresh parsley
¾ teaspoon dried thyme
¾ teaspoon salt
3 pounds fish heads and bones (from nonoily fish only)
9 cups cold water
1½ cups dry white wine

Basic Marinade

This basic marinade can be used for any kind of fish, whether dry or oily, since it adds flavor to oily fish and both moisture and flavor to the dry varieties. Refer to the tips below for marinating suggestions.

1. Mix all ingredients in a small bowl and use to marinate fish as directed in individual recipes.

Makes about 1⅓ cups

TIPS FOR MARINATING

• When marinating fillets and steaks, use a heavy, securely shut plastic bag, turning once or twice during marinating time to be sure all surfaces are covered. Marinating moistens and adds flavor to fish.
• Marinate for 10 to 30 minutes, depending on the thickness of the fish.
• Drain the fish before cooking and reserve the liquid to use for basting if you're broiling or grilling.

INGREDIENTS
1 cup vegetable oil
⅓ cup tarragon vinegar
2 tablespoons minced fresh parsley
2 scallions, minced
½ teaspoon salt
½ teaspoon dried tarragon
¼ teaspoon freshly ground pepper

BROILING

Broiling is a dry-heat method in which food is cooked by very high heat positioned above the food, in the form of either a red-hot heating element in the ceiling of an electric oven or an overhead flame in a gas oven. Most ovens designed for home use cannot produce the superb results of restaurant ovens, because restaurant ovens reach much higher temperatures. However, a gas oven will come closer than an electric oven; an overhead flame reaches about 3,000° F, while an overhead electric heating element reaches approximately 2,000° F.

Fish

Whole fish are better cooked by methods other than broiling. A whole fish is usually thick and would need to be broiled on both sides, and a heavy half-cooked fish tends to fall apart when turned. Broil only delicate fillets (on one side only), substantially textured fillets (on both sides), and fish steaks (on both sides).

Equipment

Broil fish in a shallow pan such as a jelly roll pan or a broiler pan. This will catch the juices and support the fish while it cooks.

A spatula is also necessary to turn some types of fish during broiling. Fish with thin, delicate textures should be broiled on one side only; if you attempt to turn these, they will fall apart.

A handy tool for basting is a pastry brush. It's especially good for thick fillets.

Method

Step 1: Position a rack in the oven so that there will be approximately three to six inches between the overhead heat source and the highest point of the fish. (Individual recipes will specify optimal distance from the heat source.) Turn on the broiler and allow it to preheat for 15 minutes. Lay the fish on a flat pan lined with aluminum foil. Brush the top surface of the fish with vegetable oil or dot with unsalted butter.

Step 2: When the oven is hot, slide the pan onto the center of the rack. Broil until the surface of the fish is no longer translucent but has turned white, is slightly crusty, and is lightly mottled with brown. If you're broiling a thin fillet, continue broiling until the fish is done. (See "How to Test Fish for Doneness.") If you're broiling a fish steak or a thick fillet, turn the fish carefully, using a spatula and another utensil such as a knife or fork to support it.

Step 3: Brush the newly exposed surface of the

fish with vegetable oil or dot with unsalted butter. Return the pan to the center of the rack under the broiler and let the fish cook until it has turned white and is lightly mottled with brown. Check for doneness. (See "How to Test Fish for Doneness.") Use a spatula to carefully transfer the fish to a serving platter. Serve immediately.

Tips for Successful Broiling
   1. If the fish is placed too close to the broiler,

the outside will burn, overcook, or dry out while the inside stays raw and cold. If the fish is placed too far from the broiler, the outside will not end up with a normal broiled appearance, which is slightly crusty and mottled with golden brown. You might have to experiment with your oven to determine the optimal rack position.
   2. Thin lemon, lime, or orange slices on top of fillets are a great way to keep the fish from drying out, as well as to add flavor.

Broiled Monkfish
with Lobster Butter and Lobster Roe

Monkfish is known as "poor man's lobster" because it has a meaty texture and delicate flavor that resemble this crustacean but is not nearly as costly. We've enhanced the lobster taste still further by adding Lobster Butter, which is made by drying out lobster shells in the oven, blender-pulverizing them with melted butter, then straining out the shell particles. The strained butter that results has a delicious lobster taste.

Ask your fishmonger for lobster shells when he has lobster available and, if necessary, freeze the shells in plastic bags until ready to use. In a pinch, substitute shrimp shells, drying them out and blender-pulverizing them with melted butter in the same way you make lobster butter.

Lobster roe is a specialty food and can be found in mail-order catalogs. See Appendix for sources.

INGREDIENTS
2¼ pounds monkfish fillets,
 cut into 6 serving pieces
2 pinches freshly grated
 nutmeg
Lobster Butter (recipe follows)
2 ounces lobster roe (optional)

1. Preheat the broiler and line a shallow pan with aluminum foil.

2. Place the fish in the pan and sprinkle with nutmeg. Brush with melted Lobster Butter.

3. Broil the fish about 6 inches from the heat source for about 5 minutes. Turn the fish over with a spatula and baste with Lobster Butter and more nutmeg. Broil it for 3 minutes or until it flakes easily when tested.

4. Place the monkfish pieces on individual plates, sprinkle with lobster roe, and serve with the remaining Lobster Butter, either melted or room temperature.

Makes 6 servings

Lobster Butter

INGREDIENTS
Shells from 2 cooked lobsters,
including feet
1 cup (½ pound) unsalted
butter or margarine, melted

1. Preheat the oven to 300° F. Arrange the shells on a cookie sheet and bake until the shells are crisp, about 15 minutes. Cool the shells.

2. Crumble the shells into a food processor fitted with the steel blade and add the melted butter. Process until the shells are chopped medium fine.

3. Strain through a colander or strainer lined with a double thickness of cheesecloth. Discard the shells and pour the butter into a crock. Freeze unused butter for later use.

Makes 6 servings

Broiled Red Snapper
Brushed with Chili Butter

This Chili Butter is good with any grilled fish. If desired, make it in large quantities, form into rolls, wrap in plastic wrap, and freeze until needed. Bring to room temperature before serving. You can use either regular or hot chili powder, depending on your taste.

1. Make the Chili Butter: Soften the butter in a bowl with the back of a wooden spoon or in a food processor fitted with the steel blade. Mix in the chili powder, cumin, cayenne, and garlic powder. Mound into a small bowl. Cover lightly and refrigerate. Remove the butter from the refrigerator 45 minutes before you use it or soften it to room temperature in the microwave.

2. Preheat the broiler and line a shallow pan with aluminum foil.

3. Place the red snapper fillets in the pan and brush with Chili Butter. Broil the fish 4 to 6 inches from the heat source for 5 to 8 minutes or until the fish flakes easily when tested. Using a spatula, transfer the fish to individual plates and serve hot. Goes well with warm tortillas, refried beans, and salad or with plenty of garlic bread.

Makes 6 servings

CHILI BUTTER
¾ cup unsalted butter or
   margarine at room
   temperature, cut into ½-inch
   pieces
1 teaspoon chili powder
½ teaspoon ground cumin
¼ teaspoon cayenne pepper
¼ teaspoon garlic powder

FISH
2¼–2½ pounds red snapper
   fillets, cut into 6 serving
   pieces

PISTACHIO-LIME BUTTER
¾ cup unsalted butter or
    margarine or a combination
    at room temperature, cut
    into ½-inch pieces
3 tablespoons minced shelled
    pistachio nuts
½ teaspoon grated lime zest

FISH
6- to 7-ounce salmon steaks
¼ cup extra-virgin olive oil
¼ cup freshly squeezed lime
    juice
1 teaspoon dried basil
2 limes, sliced, for garnish

Broiled Salmon Steaks with Pistachio-Lime Butter

Any kind of nut, from black walnuts to pine nuts, can be crushed and mixed with softened butter as a quick, delicious sauce for grilled fish. The nuts can be minced in a food processor, but don't overprocess, or the result will be a gooey mess.

1. Make the Pistachio-Lime Butter: Soften the butter in a bowl with the back of a wooden spoon or in a food processor fitted with the steel blade.

2. Mix in the nuts and lime zest. Spoon the butter into a crock, cover, and chill it until needed. Remove the butter from the refrigerator 45 minutes before you use it.

3. Preheat the broiler and line a shallow pan with aluminum foil.

4. Arrange the salmon steaks in the pan. Mix together the oil, lime juice, and basil. Brush the top surface of the salmon steaks with the oil mixture. Broil the salmon steaks 4 to 6 inches from the heat source for 4 to 5 minutes. Turn the salmon steaks over with a spatula. Brush the fish with the oil mixture and continue broiling until the fish flakes easily when tested.

5. Using a spatula, transfer the salmon steaks to individual plates. Garnish with lime slices and place a dollop of Pistachio-Lime Butter on top of each steak. Serve immediately.

Makes 6 servings

Broiled Whitefish Fillets with Whitefish Caviar Butter

If whitefish caviar isn't available, substitute any of the cheaper fish roes, either black or red. The taste will still be very good. Fresh lime wedges make a nice garnish for this dish.

1. Preheat the broiler and line a shallow pan with aluminum foil.

2. Make the Whitefish Caviar Butter: Soften the butter in a bowl with the back of a wooden spoon or in a food processor fitted with the steel blade. Mix the caviar into the soft butter. Mix in the lime juice. Taste and add more caviar if desired. Spoon the butter into a crock, cover, and refrigerate until needed. Remove the butter from the refrigerator 45 minutes before you use it.

3. Arrange the lime slices in groups of three slices each. Set a piece of whitefish on each group of lime slices. Dot the whitefish with soft butter. Sprinkle with pepper and garlic powder. Broil about 4 to 6 inches from the heat source for 6 to 8 minutes, checking after 5 minutes and basting the fish with Whitefish Caviar Butter once during broiling. Cooking time depends on the thickness of the fish and the precise distance from the heat source. When done, the fish should be opaque, slightly firm, and slightly browned on the edges.

4. Using a spatula, transfer the fish to a serving platter and garnish the platter with lime wedges. Spoon a dollop of the Whitefish Caviar Butter onto each hot fillet and serve immediately.

Makes 6 servings

WHITEFISH CAVIAR BUTTER
½ cup (¼ pound) unsalted butter or margarine or a combination at room temperature, cut into ½-inch pieces
2 tablespoons (or more to taste) whitefish caviar (see Appendix)
1 teaspoon freshly squeezed lime juice

FISH
2 limes, cut into slices
2¼ pounds whitefish fillets, cut into 6 serving pieces
2 tablespoons unsalted butter or margarine at room temperature
¼ teaspoon freshly ground white pepper
¼ teaspoon garlic powder
Lime wedges for garnish

INGREDIENTS

⅓ cup extra-virgin olive oil
3 tablespoons freshly squeezed
   lemon juice
1 tablespoon dried oregano
½ teaspoon dried rosemary
2¼–2½ pounds swordfish
   steaks, cut into 6 serving
   pieces
3 lemons, sliced paper-thin

Broiled Marinated Swordfish Steaks over Lemon Slices

Lemon, orange, and lime slices or any firm-textured vegetable slices, such as onion, function very well as tiny buffers between fish steaks or fillets and the pan, and allow the fish to be removed easily while adding extra flavor. Since most fillets are not turned, simply remove the cooked fillet carefully from its fruit or vegetable base and transfer it to a serving platter without the slices.

1. Preheat the broiler and line a shallow pan with aluminum foil.

2. Combine the oil, lemon juice, oregano, and rosemary in a small bowl. Drizzle the fish with the rosemary marinade. Place the fish in a large plastic bag, seal the bag, and place it in the refrigerator for 2½ hours, turning once and making sure all of the fish surfaces have been touched by the marinade.

3. Arrange the lemon slices in six groups in the pan and place each piece of swordfish on a group of lemon slices. Broil the fish 4 to 6 inches from the heat source for 7 to 9 minutes, basting it with the marinade once or twice. Broiling time depends on the precise distance from the heat source and the thickness of the fish. When done, the fish should be just turning opaque and should flake easily when tested.

4. Using a spatula, transfer the fish and lemon slices to a serving platter and serve immediately.

Makes 6 servings

Broiled Bluefish
with Pimiento-Tarragon Sauce

This is a wonderfully meaty, substantial fish and nicely balances the aromatic tarragon.

1. Preheat the broiler and line a shallow pan with aluminum foil.

2. Make the Pimiento-Tarragon Sauce: Stir the pimientos, vinegar, and shallots together in a small saucepan. Cook over medium heat, stirring almost continuously, until almost all liquid has evaporated. Remove from heat.

3. Whisk in the butter a few pieces at a time until incorporated. Season with the tarragon, cilantro, salt, and pepper. Keep the sauce warm while the fish is broiling.

4. Arrange the bell pepper rings in six groups in the pan and place one serving of bluefish on each group. Sprinkle with salt, pepper, and tarragon. Broil approximately 6 inches from the heat source for 5 to 7 minutes, basting the fish with oil once, until the fish flakes easily when tested.

5. Using a spatula, transfer each slice of fish to a serving plate. Pour the warm sauce over or around the bluefish and serve immediately.

Makes 6 servings

PIMIENTO-TARRAGON SAUCE
1-ounce jar pimientos, chopped, including juice
1 teaspoon tarragon vinegar
3 shallots, minced
½ cup (¼ pound) unsalted butter or margarine or a combination, cut into ½-inch pieces
½ teaspoon dried tarragon
½ teaspoon chopped cilantro
¼ teaspoon salt
¼ teaspoon freshly ground pepper

FISH
2 red bell peppers, seeded and sliced into thin rings
2¼–2½ pounds bluefish fillets, cut into 6 serving pieces
¼ teaspoon each salt, freshly ground pepper, and dried tarragon
3 tablespoons extra-virgin olive oil

INGREDIENTS

1 large red onion, cut into 12
   paper-thin slices
3 1-pound mackerel, cleaned,
   split, and heads discarded,
Salt and freshly ground pepper
   to taste
6 anchovy fillets, drained
6 tomatoes, halved
   horizontally
2 tablespoons seasoned bread
   crumbs
2 tablespoons unsalted butter
   or margarine
3 tablespoons extra-virgin
   olive oil
2 lemons, cut into wedges, for
   garnish

Mackerel Broiled over Red Onion Slices

Broiling this fish atop the onion allows a wonderful flavor to seep right into the fish.

1. Preheat the broiler and line a shallow pan with aluminum foil.

2. Arrange the onion slices in six pairs in the pan and set the split side of a mackerel over each pair. Sprinkle the mackerel with salt and pepper. Place 1 anchovy fillet on each piece of mackerel. Place the tomatoes in the pan around the mackerel. Sprinkle each tomato half with bread crumbs and dot with butter.

3. Broil the fish and tomatoes about 6 inches from the heat source for 5 to 7 minutes, basting the fish once with olive oil. Remove the tomatoes when they are done to your taste, about 5 minutes. When done, the fish will flake easily when tested and be slightly charred around the edges.

4. Using a spatula, transfer the fish, including onions, to individual serving plates. Serve hot with broiled tomatoes and lemon wedges.

Makes 6 servings

GRILLING

Grilling is a dry-heat method in which food is placed on a grid approximately 4 to 6 inches from burning coals. The heat from the coals cooks the food, which simultaneously takes on the smoky flavors given off by the coals. Leaving the cover on the grill during grilling intensifies the smoky flavor.

Fish

Fresh fish and shellfish of every kind are delicious when charcoal-grilled. Do not cook frozen fish on charcoal, hoping that the smoky aroma will neutralize the fishy smell; it won't.

Use marinades (such as Basic Marinade; see Index) to add flavor and moisture to fish, if desired, before grilling.

Equipment

Grills: Charcoal grills come in different sizes, shapes, and prices. Even the simplest one—made with just a deep fire pan for holding briquets plus a grid—will do the trick, although we feel that a cover is desirable because covering the grill intensifies the smoky flavor imparted to the food.

There are three basic models. The kettle, or covered cooker, has a deep fire pan, a cover, and two sets of dampers. This type is available in round, square, and rectangular shapes and ranges from slightly below dining table height to counter height.

The simple and inexpensive brazier consists of a round grill on legs with a shallow fire pan and grid. More elaborate braziers come with hoods, covers, or rotisserie attachments.

Portable or tabletop grills are small with short legs and may be made in the brazier fashion or more elaborately in the kettle fashion. They're terrific for taking to the beach or on picnics. Another type of grill with a short base comes from Japan and is called a *hibachi*. This tiny grill will cook enough for only two or three people but is ideal for use on a fire escape because it sits on a pedestal base rather than legs.

Gas and electric grills are also available, but we do not recommend these. Foods that are not cooked over charcoal will not have that characteristic grilled flavor.

Charcoal: Burning charcoal gives off a smoky

flavor that is delicious in food. Charcoal comes in two basic forms: pure hardwood charcoal, which is sold in lump form, and charcoal that has been compressed into briquet form. The smoke that comes from pure hardwood charcoal has a slightly more savory, woody scent and is superior to that from briquets.

Briquets may be made entirely of charred pieces of wood, or the wood may be compressed mechanically with charred paper and/or sawdust, all of which is held together with some kind of artificial mastic such as a petroleum product. Unfortunately there is no standard of identity for briquets, so the quality of the smoke they produce varies widely. The best briquets contain very little mastic—just enough to hold them together—and, in the bag, smell faintly of burnt wood. Avoid those that, in the bag, have an artificial odor such as motor oil; these may give off the same odor when they burn.

To increase smoky grilling flavor, you may want to add aromatics to the charcoal. Aromatics include such hardwood chips as mesquite, hickory, oak, apple, maple, and cherry wood chips, each of which has a different flavor. Hardwood chips should be soaked in cold water for 30 minutes, then drained and sprinkled onto the ashen coals immediately before grilling. When using aromatics, be sure to cover the grill.

Additional aromatics include stalks of fresh herbs such as thyme, tarragon, basil, fennel, bay leaves, rosemary, sage, and juniper twigs, which you can sprinkle over the hot coals just before setting the fish on the grill. In China barbecuers throw tea leaves or pieces of orange peel onto the hot coals. And in France they substitute grapevine cuttings or a handful of garlic cloves.

Starters: Several types of charcoal starters are on the market, including liquid starters, which are sprinkled on the briquets for easy lighting. To use liquid starters, arrange briquets in a pyramid in the fire pan, sprinkle them liberally with liquid starter, and let them sit for a moment. Then light the briquets in several places using a long-handled wooden match.

There are also instant-lighting briquets, which have been presprinkled with lighter fluid. To use these, arrange them in a single layer right next to each other on the floor of the fire pan; then use a long-handled wooden match to light them in several places.

Electric starters are also available. These can be laid right on the charcoal in the fire pan and plugged into a nearby outlet. Within minutes the starter is hot enough to begin igniting the charcoal.

Utensils: Utensils to have on hand for grilling include metal or Oriental wooden skewers, a grill basket for turning whole fish on the grill, and a spatula for turning fillets and fish steaks.

One particularly effective piece of equipment for grilling both fish and shellfish is a stainless-steel wire rack called a Griffo-grill. It fits directly on the grid but is made in such a close-meshed manner that it allows juices to drip through, meanwhile offering maximum support for delicate seafood. Lightly oil it before each use to prevent sticking. It's available in hardware shops and supermarkets. If you can't find it, send a check or money order for $11.95 to Griffo-grill, 301 Oak St., Quincy, IL 62301. Another Griffo-grill has two handles and an ultra-heavy-duty frame, measures 12 inches by 16 inches, and sells for $39.95, including shipping.

Method

Step 1: Have the table set and sauces made beforehand as fish grills quickly. Arrange charcoal as desired (depending on the starter you plan to use) in the bottom of the fire pan. Ignite the charcoal and let the coals burn until they turn ashen and gray.

Step 2: Oil the grid thoroughly. Arrange room-temperature fish on the grid over ashen charcoal and cover the grill. In general the grill should be 4 to 6 inches from the coals. Since fish cooks quickly, you must check it often to be sure it has not dried out. Turn the fish if necessary, using a long-handled wide spatula, and cover the grill again.

Step 3: When the fish is done, immediately transfer it to a platter or plates and serve.

Tips for Successful Charcoal Grilling

1. Lay delicate fillets on thin slices of lemon, orange, or onion on the grid. Cover and watch carefully. Do not turn thin fillets. When done, transfer the fish to a serving platter and discard the slices.

2. You'll have a better chance of removing delicate fillets from the grill if you cut them no larger than four inches square.

3. When grilling a fillet with the tail section, fold this section under; this will help even out the thickness of the fish and so make possible a more uniformly cooked fillet.

4. Today's trend is to undercook fish, rather than cook it until dry. Fish should be moist and have just lost its translucent quality. If you want to take extra precautions to keep a piece of fish moist, marinate it in several spoonfuls of oil in a plastic bag and turn it regularly before cooking. When it comes to grilling it, however, don't forget to give it your full attention. Marinating fish in oil will not ensure that it will not overcook.

HERB STEM SKEWERS FOR SHISH KABOBS

Instead of using the traditional wood or metal skewers, we suggest threading kabobs directly onto herb stems.

We've experimented with mint, rosemary, and tarragon stems but see no reason why other herb stems cannot be used, provided they complement the taste of the food.

Choose herb stems that are thick and strong enough to support the food and between 10 and 12 inches long. Remove all leaves, except for a clump at one end, which makes an attractive decoration. Wash the stem well and pat it dry with paper towels. Cut a point on the end opposite the clump of leaves so the food pieces will thread on easily. Cover the leafy end with a small piece of foil during grilling to prevent scorching.

MARINADE
½ cup vegetable oil
3 tablespoons freshly squeezed
  lemon juice
½ teaspoon salt
¼ teaspoon freshly ground
  pepper
2 bay leaves, crumbled
3 tablespoons chopped fresh
  mint leaves

SHELLFISH
36 large sea scallops (about
  2–2½ pounds)
6 thick, strong mint stems,
  each 10 to 12 inches long
  (make sure they have not
  been chemically sprayed)
18 baby pattypan squash,
  yellow or green, halved
  horizontally
3 lemons, quartered, for
  garnish

Scallops on Mint Stem Skewers

In this dish mint flavor is imparted to the scallops in two different ways: first through the chopped fresh mint in the marinade and then through the mint stem skewers.

1. Make the marinade: Combine the oil, lemon juice, salt, pepper, bay leaves, and mint in a large plastic bag and set the bag in a bowl. Add the scallops, seal the bag, and turn it several times. Return the bag to the bowl and let it sit at room temperature for 1 hour, turning it occasionally to make sure the marinade touches all the scallop surfaces.

2. Meanwhile, prepare the mint stems: Remove the leaves, leaving only a leafy cluster at one end. With a small sharp knife, cut a point at the opposite end of the stem.

3. Remove the scallops from the marinade. Brush the cut surfaces of the squash with the marinade. Thread the squash and scallops alternately on the mint stem skewers, using six squash halves and six scallops per skewer. Cover the leafy cluster at the end of each skewer with a small piece of aluminum foil.

4. Arrange the skewers on the oiled grids, about 6 inches from the ashen coals. Grill for about 2 minutes, then turn and grill for another 2 minutes or until done to taste. Transfer the skewers to a serving platter and remove the foil. Serve immediately, garnished with lemon wedges.

Makes 6 servings

Rolled Mackerel Fillets on Rosemary Skewers

Rosemary has a strong flavor, so we've chosen a fish with a substantial flavor—mackerel—to stand up to it. In this recipe the fillets are rolled before being placed on a rosemary stem skewer.

It is not necessary to marinate mackerel before grilling, as it is a fatty fish and will not dry out unless it is overcooked.

1. Make the Provençale Sauce: Heat the butter and oil in a medium, heavy saucepan. Add the onion and garlic and sauté them over medium heat, stirring often with a wooden spoon. Take care that the garlic does not burn.

2. Add the tomatoes, tomato paste, parsley, salt, black pepper, and bay leaf. Heat to a simmer and cook for 5 minutes, stirring often. Discard the bay leaf. Reserve the sauce in the saucepan at room temperature.

3. Remove the leaves from the rosemary stems, reserving a clump of leaves at one end. Cut a point at the opposite end with a small sharp knife.

4. Lay the fillets flat and brush each with oil. Roll each fillet around a strip of red pepper. Insert the pointed end of one herb skewer through the center of a mackerel roll and carefully push the roll to the far end of the skewer. Skewer four olives and push them close together near the fish roll. Repeat with the remaining skewers. Cover the leafy end of each skewer with a small piece of foil.

5. Arrange the skewers on the oiled grill screen, about 6 inches from the ashen coals, and cook for about 3 to 4 minutes on one side. Turn the skewers carefully and cook for 3 to 4 minutes or until the fish is completely cooked.

6. Transfer the skewers carefully to a serving platter, remove the foil, and garnish with lemon wedges. Serve with the Provençale Sauce.

Makes 6 servings

PROVENÇALE SAUCE

1 tablespoon unsalted butter
2 tablespoons good-quality imported olive oil
½ cup finely chopped onion
3 cloves garlic, minced fine
1 14½-ounce can crushed tomatoes, with liquid
2 tablespoons tomato paste
2 tablespoons chopped fresh parsley
¼ teaspoon salt
¼ teaspoon freshly ground black pepper
1 large bay leaf

FISH

6 rosemary stems with leaves, each 10 to 12 inches long (make sure they have not been chemically sprayed)
2¼ pounds mackerel fillets, cut into 6 serving pieces
Good-quality imported olive oil for brushing fillets
2 red bell peppers, cut into thirds lengthwise
24 large pimiento-stuffed green olives
2 lemons, quartered, for garnish

INGREDIENTS
1 recipe Basic Marinade (see Index)
½ teaspoon chopped fresh tarragon leaves
36 large shrimp (slightly over 2 pounds), peeled and deveined
6 tarragon stems with leaves, each 10 to 12 inches long (make sure they have not been chemically sprayed)
12 sun-dried tomatoes (either vacuum-packed or packed in oil)
18 zucchini slices ½ inch thick
3 lemons, quartered, for garnish

Shrimp on Tarragon Skewers

Shrimp on the grill are heavenly, especially with the aromatic tarragon imparted by the herb skewers.

1. Combine the Basic Marinade with the chopped tarragon and place in a large plastic bag set in a bowl. Add the shrimp, seal the bag, and turn it several times. Return the bag to the bowl and let it sit for 1 hour at room temperature, turning it several times to make sure the marinade touches all the shrimp surfaces.

2. Wash the tarragon stems and pat dry with paper towels. Remove the leaves, leaving a clump of leaves at one end. Cut a point at the opposite end of the skewer with a small sharp knife. Drain the sun-dried tomatoes if packed in oil. If vacuum-packed, brush each tomato with oil. Cut each tomato into three pieces.

3. Drain the shrimp, discarding the marinade. Thread three zucchini slices, six tomato pieces, and six shrimp alternately on each tarragon skewer. Wrap a piece of foil around the leafy section of each stem.

4. Arrange the skewers on the oiled grid, about 6 inches from the ashen coals. Grill for 3 minutes, then turn the stems carefully and grill them for another 2 to 3 minutes. Transfer the stems to a serving platter and remove the foil. Garnish the platter with lemon wedges.

Makes 6 servings

Tuna Chunks on Mint Skewers with Peach Chutney Butter

The mint flavor imparted by the stems marries well with the mild-flavored tuna and sweet peaches.

1. Combine marinade with mint and place in a large plastic bag set in a bowl. Add tuna, then seal the bag and turn it several times. Return the bag to the bowl and let sit at room temperature for 1 hour, turning it occasionally to make sure the marinade touches all fish surfaces.

2. Prepare the mint stems: Remove the leaves from the stems, leaving a clump of leaves at one end for decoration. Cut a point on the opposite stem end, using a small sharp knife.

3. Cut each peach half into three pieces, making a total of 36 pieces. Mix 4 tablespoons each of the butter and margarine with the peach chutney in a small bowl. Let sit at room temperature.

4. Melt the remaining 2 tablespoons each of the butter and margarine and brush the mixture on the cut side of each fruit piece with a pastry brush.

5. Drain the tuna, discarding the marinade. Divide the tuna pieces and thread them alternately with the peaches on each mint stem skewer. Cover the leafy ends with small pieces of aluminum foil.

6. Lay the skewers on a well-oiled grid, about 4 to 6 inches from ashen coals. Grill for about 2 to 3 minutes, then turn the skewers carefully and grill them for another 2 to 3 minutes or until the fish flakes easily. Transfer the skewers to a large serving platter and discard the foil. Spoon a dollop of chutney butter on the tuna and peaches and serve immediately.

Makes 6 servings

INGREDIENTS

1 recipe Basic Marinade (see Index)

2 tablespoons chopped fresh mint leaves

2¼ pounds tuna, sliced ¾ inch thick and cut into ¾-inch chunks

6 mint stems with leaves, each 10 to 12 inches long (make sure they have not been chemically sprayed)

6 ripe peaches or nectarines, halved and pits removed

6 tablespoons unsalted butter at room temperature

6 tablespoons margarine at room temperature

5 tablespoons prepared peach chutney

CRANBERRY BUTTER
¾ cup unsalted butter or margarine at room temperature
1 16-ounce can whole-berry cranberry sauce
1 teaspoon minced orange zest
½ teaspoon ground cinnamon

FISH
1 recipe Basic Marinade (see Index)
6 5- to 6-ounce cod steaks
Lemon wedges for garnish

Cod Steaks with Cranberry Butter

This butter is so good, you may want to double the recipe and serve the cod with heated French bread. Top both cod steaks and hot bread pieces with cranberry butter. If you make the butter ahead of time, be sure to take it out of the refrigerator 45 minutes before serving.

1. Make the Cranberry Butter: Stir the butter, ¼ cup of the canned cranberry sauce, the orange zest, and the cinnamon and mix well. Spoon it into a small serving bowl.

2. Pour the marinade into a large plastic bag set in a bowl. Add the cod steaks, seal the bag, and turn it a few times. Return the bag to the bowl and let it sit at room temperature for 1 hour, turning it occasionally to make sure the marinade touches all the fish surfaces.

3. Remove the cod from the marinade, discarding the marinade. Place the cod on the oiled grid, about 6 inches from the ashen coals, and grill for 3 to 4 minutes. Turn the cod carefully, using an oiled spatula, and grill it for another 3 to 4 minutes or until the steaks are cooked through and lightly browned.

4. Using a spatula, transfer the steaks to a serving platter. Spoon a small mound of room-temperature Cranberry Butter over each steak. Garnish the platter with lemon wedges and pass around the remaining Cranberry Butter at the table.

Makes 6 servings

Rainbow Trout with Italian Stuffing

The stuffing for this dish can easily be made ahead and refrigerated, covered, until it's time to stuff the fish for grilling. Use any type of rice, depending on your preference, from orzo to brown to white.

1. Make the Italian Stuffing: Combine all stuffing ingredients in a medium bowl and mix well.

2. Hold the fish under cool running water, letting the water run into the fish cavities as well as onto outside surfaces. Pat the fish dry with paper towels. Stuff each trout loosely with about ½ cup stuffing. Brush the outside of each fish with olive oil.

3. Use vegetable oil to oil the inside grids of two grill baskets. Arrange the fish in the baskets, then tuck lemon slices between the fish and the grids to prevent the fish from sticking to the grids.

4. Lay the baskets on the grid, about 6 inches from the ashen coals. Grill the trout for about 6 minutes or until brown on one side. Turn the baskets and grill for another 6 minutes or until the second side is browned.

5. Open the grill baskets and carefully remove the trout, discarding the lemon slices. Arrange the fish on a serving platter garnished with lemon quarters and serve immediately.

Makes 6 servings

ITALIAN STUFFING
3 cups cooked rice
3 sun-dried tomatoes, packed in oil or vacuum packed (drained if in oil), and diced
6 scallions, chopped
¼ cup freshly grated Parmesan cheese
½ teaspoon salt
½ teaspoon freshly ground pepper
Large pinch dried oregano

FISH
6 8- to 10-ounce rainbow trout, scaled and cleaned, head and tails left intact
Good-quality imported olive oil for brushing fish
Vegetable oil for brushing grill baskets
24 thin lemon slices
2 lemons, quartered, for garnish

FISH

1 recipe Basic Marinade (see Index)
2¼ pounds lemon sole fillets, cut into 6 serving pieces
12 thin lemon slices
2 lemons, cut into wedges for garnish
⅓ cup fresh parsley for garnish

LEMON SAUCE

2 tablespoons unsalted butter
2 tablespoons margarine
3 tablespoons all-purpose flour
1 cup chicken stock
¾ cup milk
¾ cup half-and-half
1 egg yolk
¼ cup freshly squeezed lemon juice
2 teaspoons finely chopped lemon zest
¼ teaspoon salt
¼ teaspoon paprika
¼ teaspoon thyme

Lemon Sole with "Old Thyme" Lemon Sauce

When serving white fish with light-colored sauces, add colorful side dishes such as broccoli or baked or broiled tomato halves.

1. Pour the marinade into a large plastic bag set in a bowl. Add the lemon sole, seal the bag, and turn it several times. Return the bag to the bowl and let it sit at room temperature for 1 hour, turning it occasionally to make sure the marinade touches all the fish surfaces.

2. Make the Lemon Sauce: Heat the butter and margarine in a saucepan over medium heat. Add the flour, stirring constantly with a wire whisk until well combined.

3. Mix the stock and milk in a bowl and add it to the saucepan a few tablespoons at a time, stirring well after each addition. Mix the half-and-half and egg yolk in another bowl. Spoon ½ cup of the hot broth mixture into the egg yolk mixture, stirring constantly.

4. Add remaining hot broth mixture to egg mixture in a thin, steady stream, stirring constantly. When everything is well combined, spoon mixture back into saucepan.

5. Stir the lemon juice, zest, salt, paprika, and thyme into the sauce and place the saucepan over medium heat for 1 minute, stirring constantly with the whisk. Transfer the sauce to a serving bowl.

6. Drain the sole, discarding the marinade. Arrange the lemon slices in pairs on the oiled grid, about 6 inches from the ashen coals. Place the fillets on the lemon slices and grill them for about 3 minutes. Transfer the fish to a serving platter, discarding the lemon slices.

7. Arrange lemon wedges and parsley on serving platter with fillets. Serve each fillet topped with warm Lemon Sauce.

Makes 6 servings

Mixed Grill with Tex-Mex Accompaniments and Corn Muffins with Sweet Peppers

This mixed fish grill is served with seven southwestern condiments, and we suggest adding a cold Mexican beer such as Tecate. Drinking Tecate involves a tequilalike ceremony:

Bring the Tecate cans to the table chilled and give one can to each guest. Place a small bowl or plate of salt, along with a plate of lime wedges, on the table with the Tecate. Sprinkle a pinch of salt onto the soft saddle of one hand (the webbed area between thumb and forefinger), then pick up a lime wedge and squeeze a few drops onto the salt. Take a lick of salt/lime and follow it immediately with a sip of Tecate.

1. Pour the marinade into a large plastic bag set in a bowl. Add the fish pieces, seal the bag, and turn it several times. Return the bag to the bowl and let it sit at room temperature for 1 hour, turning it occasionally to make sure the marinade touches all the fish surfaces.

2. Make the Guacamole and Corn Muffins. While the muffins bake, fill six bowls with lettuce, tomato, green onions, jalapeños, cheese, and sour cream. Spoon Guacamole into a seventh bowl. Put all bowls on the table.

3. Remove fillets from marinade, discarding marinade. Arrange lemon slices on oiled grill, about 5–6 inches from the ashen coals. Place fish over lemon slices and grill for about 5 to 6 minutes or until fish is no longer translucent.

4. Using a spatula, transfer the fish carefully to a serving platter, discarding the lemon slices. Serve one piece of each kind of fish to each guest. Pass the accompaniments so the toppings can be sprinkled on the fish in layers. Serve with the hot Corn Muffins and cold Mexican beer.

Makes 6 servings

INGREDIENTS

1 recipe Basic Marinade (see Index)

¾ pound each grouper fillets, red snapper fillets, and rockfish fillets, each type of fish cut into 6 pieces

1 recipe Guacamole (recipe follows)

1 recipe hot Corn Muffins with Sweet Peppers (recipe follows)

1 bowl of each of the following:

Shredded lettuce

Chopped tomato

2 green onions

1 4-ounce jar jalapeño peppers, drained and chopped

Shredded Longhorn cheddar or Monterey Jack cheese

Sour cream or sour half-and-half

18 thin lemon slices

Corn Muffins with Sweet Peppers

The sweet peppers add original crunch to these already tasty muffins.

1. Preheat the oven to 425° F. Grease a 12-cup muffin tin or line each cup with a paper liner. Combine flour, cornmeal, sugar, and baking powder in the large bowl of an electric mixer.

2. Add the milk and egg. Turn the beaters on for just long enough to mix, then turn them off. Add the vegetable shortening and turn the beaters on again until the shortening is just incorporated. Stir in chopped bell pepper.

3. Spoon the batter into 12 muffin cups, dividing it evenly. Bake the muffins for 14 to 18 minutes or until they are slightly browned on the edges and firm to the touch.

4. Immediately invert the pan carefully to remove the muffins. Arrange them on a serving platter and transfer them to the table. If necessary, reheat the muffins in a 250° F oven for a few minutes before serving. The muffins can be frozen.

Makes 12 muffins

INGREDIENTS
¾ cup all-purpose flour
1 cup yellow cornmeal
¾ cup sugar
1 tablespoon double-acting
   baking powder
1 cup milk
1 egg, slightly beaten
4 tablespoons vegetable
   shortening, melted
½ cup chopped red bell pepper

Guacamole

1. Halve the avocados, remove and reserve the pits, and peel. Cut the avocado into chunks and place in a food processor or blender container. Add the garlic, onion, salt, pepper, olive oil, lemon juice, and chili powder. Cut the jalapeños into quarters and add them to the other ingredients. Pulse until a coarse puree results.

2. Spoon the Guacamole into a container and add the pits (to help keep the avocado puree from turning brown). Cover with plastic wrap, pressing it over the top of the Guacamole, making it as airtight as possible. Store in the refrigerator until ready to serve.

Makes 1¾ cups

INGREDIENTS
3 large ripe avocados
2 cloves garlic, peeled and halved
1 small onion, quartered
¼ teaspoon salt
¼ teaspoon freshly ground pepper
1 tablespoon good-quality imported olive oil
1 tablespoon freshly squeezed lemon juice
½ teaspoon chili powder, either regular or hot
2–4 jarred jalapeño peppers, stems removed, halved

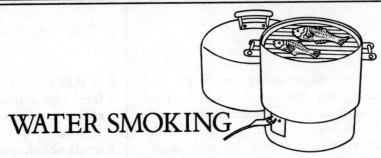

WATER SMOKING

Water smoking is a moist-heat method in which fish is cooked through a combination of elements: the hot smoke from the charcoal, the hot steam produced by the evaporating water, and the heat from the charcoal that builds up inside the closed smoker. Water smoking differs from true smoking in that it is faster and easier, doesn't use a brine, and doesn't take place in a smokehouse. Water smoking is done in a small, portable water smoker.

Fish
The fish best suited for water smoking are fatty fish—salmon, bluefish, and sturgeon are particularly good. We have also included commercially smoked fish (finnan haddie) as well as some shellfish (shrimp and crab legs) that lend themselves well to water smoking.

Equipment
Smokers: Water smokers are really covered cylindrical portable grills that consist of three sections: a fire pan at the bottom to hold burning charcoal, a water pan in the center to hold evaporating water, and a grid at the top to hold the food being smoked. The cylindrical shape of the smoker encourages smoke to rise toward the food.

Charcoal: Charcoal and aromatics are used in water smoking as they are in grilling (see Chapter 2). Since smoking can take many hours, however, you will need more briquets for water smoking.

Method
Step 1: If you are using wood chips for extra smoke, submerge them in cold water for about 30 minutes. Fill the fuel pan three-quarters full of briquets and light.

Step 2: When the coals are partly ashen, fill the water pan three-quarters full of boiling water. Place the fish on the ungreased grid at the top. Drain the wood chips and sprinkle them over the partly ashen charcoal. Cover the smoker.

Step 3: Smoke the fish for the minimum time stated in the recipe, making sure to check the water and charcoal pans every 30 to 45 minutes to be sure that the charcoal has not burned away and the water in the water pan has not evaporated. Add briquets—usually five or six are sufficient—throughout the smoking as needed. The evaporating water adds both heat and moisture. Also check the water pan every 30 to 45 minutes throughout the smoking process, adding water as needed. When the minimum time has elapsed, check the fish for doneness every 20 minutes thereafter. (See "How to Test Fish for Doneness.")

Step 4: Transfer the fish to a serving platter and serve it immediately or allow it to cool to room temperature. Chill it if desired. Smoked fish may be accompanied by a sauce or served as is.

Tips for Successful Smoking

1. Smoking adds such a delicious flavor to fish that it is not necessary to marinate fish beforehand.

2. If desired, add three or four bay leaves, cinnamon sticks, or other aromatic herbs or flavorings to the water pan. They will impart a subtle, delicate flavor to the smoked fish.

3. Smoked fish has a definite flavor. When storing it in the refrigerator, take care that it is wrapped carefully in foil or plastic wrap and then placed in a plastic bag and sealed; otherwise it will transfer its smoky flavor to everything around it.

BRINE
3 quarts water
1 cup salt
½ cup sugar
1 teaspoon freshly ground
    pepper
3 bay leaves, crumbled

FISH
6 ½- to ¾-inch-thick salmon
    steaks
Vegetable oil for brushing
    salmon
6 3-inch-long fresh tarragon
    sprigs *or* 6 pinches dried
    tarragon
Fresh parsley sprigs
3 lemons, cut into quarters
1 recipe Tartar Sauce
    (optional) (see Index)

**AROMATICS FOR WATER
PAN**
2 cloves garlic, crushed
2 stalks celery with leaves
2 bay leaves, crumbled

Smoked Salmon Steaks

These steaks are so delicious, we like them without any sauce at all. But if you wish to serve a sauce, add our homemade Tartar Sauce (see Index).

1. Combine the water, salt, sugar, pepper, and bay leaves in a deep ceramic or glass bowl. Add the salmon steaks, making certain they're completely submerged. Allow them to soak for 3 to 5 hours, refrigerated. Remove, drain, and pat dry.

2. Brush each piece of salmon lightly with oil on each side, then top each with a tarragon sprig.

3. Fill the fuel pan three-quarters full of charcoal briquets and light carefully. When the coals are partly ashen, arrange the steaks on the bottom rack in a single layer on the oiled rack in the smoker above the charcoal. Fill the water pan three-quarters full of water and add the aromatics. Place the water pan in the smoker and cover the smoker.

4. Smoke the steaks for 1½ to 3 hours or until the fish has lost its translucency and has a cooked, flaky appearance. Check the fuel and water pans every 45 minutes, adding charcoal briquets or water as needed. Check for doneness after 1½ hours by inserting fork tines into the fish at a 45-degree angle and twisting the tines gently, lifting the fork up slightly. If the fish is not flaky, brush it again with oil and continue smoking, checking every 30 minutes for doneness.

5. Arrange the smoked steaks on a serving platter and garnish them with parsley and lemon wedges. Serve hot or cold with Tartar Sauce, potato salad, corn, and a tart salad, if desired.

Makes 6 servings

Smoked Split King Crab Legs with Spicy Tartar Sauce

If you like to surprise your guests with unusual dishes, we suggest serving this smoked crab, as they will probably not have tasted it before. Make the Spicy Tartar Sauce with homemade mayonnaise if possible. Otherwise, use a good-quality commercially available variety.

1. Make the Spicy Tartar Sauce: In a small mixing bowl, combine the horseradish, onion, relish, mustard, and lemon juice. Whisk in the mayonnaise. Blend in the catsup. Cover loosely and refrigerate until ready to serve (can be made a day ahead). Stir before serving.

2. Mix together the butter, lemon juice, red pepper flakes, and Worcestershire sauce. Brush the butter sauce over the cut side of the crab legs.

3. Fill the fire pan three-quarters full of charcoal briquets and light carefully. When the coals are partly ashen, sprinkle them with the drained wood chips. Arrange the crab legs in a single layer on the grid in the smoker above the charcoal. Fill the water pan three-quarters full of boiling water. Place the water pan in the smoker and place the crab on the lowest rack in the smoker.

4. Smoke the crab legs for about 20 minutes or until the crab has lost its translucency and has a cooked, flaky appearance. Add extra charcoal briquets if needed. To check for doneness, insert the tines of a fork into a cut crab leg, checking the texture. If the crab leg is not done, cover and check again in 10 minutes.

5. Arrange the smoked crab legs on a serving platter and garnish with lemon wedges. Serve hot or cold with the Spicy Tartar Sauce.

Makes 6 servings

SPICY TARTAR SAUCE
1 tablespoon prepared white horseradish
1 small onion, minced
½ cup sweet pickle relish, drained
1 teaspoon prepared mustard
1 tablespoon freshly squeezed lemon juice
2½ cups mayonnaise
1 tablespoon catsup

SHELLFISH
4 tablespoons unsalted butter or margarine, melted
3 tablespoons freshly squeezed lemon juice
½ teaspoon red pepper flakes
1 teaspoon Worcestershire sauce
5–6 pounds split king crab legs
3 cups elder wood chips, soaked in cold water for 30 minutes and drained
Lemon wedges for garnish

FISH
**2 pounds smoked finnan
haddie**
Warm water to cover
**12 toast triangles, buttered and
crusts removed**
3 cups milk
6 sprigs parsley

SAUCE
**4 tablespoons butter or
margarine**
1 medium onion, minced
2 tablespoons all-purpose flour
**⅛ teaspoon freshly ground
white pepper**

Finnan Haddie

Finnan haddie was first made by accident in Findon, Scotland. Haddock was hanging on a line to dry when a fire swept through the area. After the fire, the haddock pieces were found to have turned a beautiful golden brown from the smoke. The smoked fish was pronounced absolutely delicious, if a trifle intense in flavor.

To dilute the intensity, smoked finnan haddie is first soaked in warm water, then poached in milk, which also removes some of the salt used in processing. Nowadays, smoked cod is often substituted for smoked haddock, since the haddock population is declining.

1. Examine fish carefully for bones, running fingertips lightly over whole length of fillets. Remove bones with tweezers or long-nose pliers. Cut fish into 2-inch pieces.

2. Put fish into a large heavy saucepan. Cover with warm tap water and let sit 30 minutes. Drain water and check fish again for bones. Make toast triangles.

3. Return pieces to saucepan. Add milk and heat to boil. Simmer uncovered 15 to 20 minutes or until fish flakes with a fork. Remove with slotted spoon and place in bowl. Use fork to break fish into bite-sized pieces. Strain milk and reserve for sauce. Arrange toast triangles on platter and garnish with parsley.

4. Make sauce: Melt butter in saucepan over medium heat, then add onion and sauté until soft. Add flour, a little at a time, whisking well after each addition. Add strained milk a little at a time, whisking well after each addition. Add pepper. Cook, stirring often, until milk thickens slightly. Continue cooking and stirring for a few moments, until sauce loses its floury taste.

5. Stir in finnan haddie pieces with wooden spoon, mixing carefully. When fish is heated through, spoon into large serving bowl and bring to table with platter of toast.

To serve, arrange 2 buttered toast triangles on each dinner plate, spoon a little finnan haddie with sauce over toast, and add a sprig of parsley.

Makes 6 servings

Smoked Shrimp with Chili Butter

This recipe calls for tarragon and oregano sprigs tied together at one end to make a basting brush. If you have no sprigs, substitute a pastry brush.

1. Fill the fire pan three-quarters full of briquets and light carefully. When the coals are partly ashen, sprinkle them with the drained wood chips. Fill the water pan three-quarters full of boiling water and place it in the smoker. Make a bouquet of tarragon and oregano sprigs and secure with a rubber band at one end to use as a basting brush.

2. Make the Chili Butter: Combine the melted butter with the chili powder in a small bowl. Lay a piece of metal screen or a Griffo-grill over the grid in the smoker on the lowest rack. Arrange the shrimp on the screen, then brush each with chili butter, using the tarragon and oregano sprigs as a brush.

3. Cover the smoker and smoke the shrimp for 45 minutes. Then check to see if additional briquets or water is needed. Cook for an additional 30 minutes for a total of 75 minutes. When the shrimp are done, they will turn a rich golden brown color. Check the inside of one shrimp to make sure that it is fully cooked. If it is ready to eat, it will have lost its translucency and turned white inside.

4. Transfer the shrimp to a serving platter and garnish with lemon wedges. Serve hot or cold.

Makes 6 servings

INGREDIENTS

2 cups hickory chips, soaked in cold water for 30 minutes and drained

3 sprigs tarragon stems with leaves, each about 7 inches long (make sure they have not been chemically sprayed)

3 sprigs oregano stems with leaves, each about 7 inches long (make sure they have not been chemically sprayed)

½ cup (¼ pound) butter or margarine, melted

1 tablespoon chili powder

1 piece metal screen, large enough to fit over the grid in smoker, *or* a Griffo-grill (see Appendix)

36 large shrimp (slightly over 2 pounds) peeled and deveined

3 lemons, cut into wedges, for garnish

SPICY CRANBERRY RELISH

2 tablespoons unsalted butter
   or margarine
2 cloves garlic, minced
4 scallions, minced
1 teaspoon good-quality curry
   powder, hot or mild
2 large tomatoes, peeled,
   seeded, and pureed (see
   below)
1 cup water
1½ tablespoons honey
1¼ cups whole-berry cranberry
   sauce
½ teaspoon Worcestershire
   sauce
½ cup golden raisins
½ cup red wine vinegar

FISH

3 cups maple wood chips,
   soaked in cold water for 30
   minutes and drained
2¼ pounds bluefish fillets, cut
   into 6 serving pieces

Smoked Bluefish with Spicy Cranberry Relish

Assertively flavored smoked fish need hearty-flavored sauces and relishes such as this one to stand up to them.

1. Make the Spicy Cranberry Relish: Melt the butter in a heavy saucepan over medium heat. Sauté the garlic and scallions in the butter for 2 minutes, stirring often. Mix in the curry powder, tomato puree, water, honey, cranberry sauce, Worcestershire sauce, raisins, and vinegar. Reduce the heat to a simmer and continue cooking for 10 to 15 minutes, stirring occasionally. Cool, place in a covered container, and chill until ready to serve.

2. Fill fire pan three-quarters full of charcoal briquets and light carefully. When coals are partly ashen, sprinkle them with drained wood chips. Fill water pan three-quarters full of boiling water and place it in the smoker.

3. Place fillets skin side down on oiled grid. Cover the smoker. Continue smoking fish for 20 minutes, then check fish for doneness; it should flake easily and be firm when tested. If not done, smoke the fish for 10 minutes longer and check again until the fish is smoked to your taste.

4. Remove fish and place on individual plates. Serve with Spicy Cranberry Relish. Good warm or cold.

Makes 6 servings

TIPS FOR SEEDING AND PUREEING TOMATOES

• We like to use this quick method. Remove skin from tomatoes by dipping into boiling water for 30 seconds; rub off skin under cold running water.

• To seed, cut an X at the blossom end of the tomatoes. Squeeze with moderate pressure and discard seeds. Puree in food processor fitted with steel blade.

Smoked Haddock Fillets

Haddock is particularly well suited to smoking, and the bacon gives this mild fish added flavor, as does the marinade. Smoked haddock fillets make an elegant picnic dish. Serve them fresh from the smoker or chill them before serving, as desired.

1. Place the marinade in a large plastic bag set in a bowl. Add the haddock fillets, seal the bag, and turn it several times. Return the bag to the bowl and let it sit at room temperature for 1 hour, turning it occasionally to make sure the marinade touches all the fish surfaces.

2. Fill the fire pan three-quarters full of charcoal briquets and light carefully. Fill the water pan three-quarters full of boiling water and place it in the smoker.

3. When the coals are partly ashen, sprinkle them with the hickory chips. Drain the fillets, discarding the marinade. Sprinkle each with a pinch of oregano and wrap a strip of bacon around each fillet. Arrange the bacon-wrapped fillets on the oiled grid on the lowest rack and cover the smoker.

4. Check the fuel and water pans every 45 minutes to see if additional briquets or water is needed. Let the fillets smoke for 1½ hours, then test with fork tines to see if they have lost their translucency. If not, continue smoking and check fillets every 30 minutes. The very thickest haddock fillets should take no more than 2½ hours.

5. Transfer the fillets to a serving platter garnished with lemon wedges. Serve the fish with potato salad, coleslaw, and heated French bread if desired.

Makes 6 servings

INGREDIENTS
1 recipe Basic Marinade (see Index)
6 6-ounce haddock fillets
2 handfuls hickory chips, soaked in cold water for 30 minutes and drained
6 pinches dried oregano
6 strips bacon
3 lemons, cut into wedges, for garnish

INGREDIENTS
1 3-pound whitefish (must be
    absolutely fresh), scaled and
    cleaned, head and tail left
    intact
½ cup vegetable oil
3 tablespoons freshly squeezed
    lime juice
¼ teaspoon salt
¼ teaspoon cracked pepper
2 tablespoons chopped fresh
    parsley
4 lime slices
4 chive stems
2 handfuls fruit wood sprigs
    or any aromatic wood chips,
    soaked in cold water for 30
    minutes and drained
Parsley sprigs for garnish
Lemon wedges for garnish

Whole Smoked Whitefish

A whole smoked whitefish makes an elegant presentation, whether on a buffet table or as a cold entree. But be sure that any fish you buy is very fresh. Smoking adds a delightful flavor of its own, but it will not mask the flavor or odor of fish that is not completely fresh. We've added a marinade here to make the smoked fish even more flavorful.

1. Hold the whitefish under cold running water so that both the inside and outside are rinsed. Pat it lightly with paper towels to dry it. Make two diagonal cuts on each side of the fish, each not more than ½ inch deep and 1½ inches long.

2. Combine the vegetable oil, lime juice, salt, pepper, and parsley in a plastic bag large enough to accommodate the whole whitefish. Place the fish in the bag and seal the bag tightly. Turn the bag several times so the marinade touches all the fish surfaces. Place the bag on a large platter and set it in the refrigerator for 4 hours, turning it several times during marinating.

3. Remove the fish from the marinade, reserving the marinade, and shake the fish to remove excess. Lay the fish on the counter and place the lime slices and chive stems in the cavity.

4. Fill the fuel pan three-quarters full of briquets and light carefully. Fill the water pan three-quarters full of boiling water and place it in the smoker. When the coals are partly ashen, drain the wood and sprinkle it on the charcoal. Place the whitefish on the ungreased grid (lowest rack) and cover the smoker.

5. You will need to check the fuel and water pans every 45 minutes, adding briquets and water as needed. Smoke the fish for 3 hours, then check for doneness by inserting fork tines into the fish and twisting slightly, lifting the tines upward. If the flesh has lost its translucent appearance and looks flaky, the fish is done. Otherwise, continue smoking and check for doneness every 30 minutes thereafter. Brush the fish with marinade each time you check it.

6. Transfer the fish to a serving platter and garnish it with parsley and lemon wedges. Serve the fish hot or cold.

Makes 6 servings

Smoked Sturgeon with Southwestern Dipping Sauce

Sturgeon is a meaty fish, often difficult to find—even frozen is not that common. Smoked sturgeon is delicious. Use either dried green peppercorns or peppercorns packed in water.

1. Make the Southwestern Dipping Sauce: Put the tomato puree, garlic, salt, cumin, ground pepper, red pepper flakes, and cilantro into a food processor fitted with the steel blade. Pulse four times to combine the ingredients. Place the sauce in a bowl, cover, and chill until ready to serve.

2. Fill the fire pan three-quarters full of charcoal briquets and light carefully. Fill the water pan three-quarters full of boiling water and set it into the smoker.

3. Press the peppercorns into the sturgeon and place the fish in a single layer on the oiled grid on the lowest rack.

4. Cover the smoker. Smoke the fish for 20 to 30 minutes, checking it for doneness after 20 minutes; the fish should flake easily when tested and will be opaque and firm. If the fish is not done, cover the smoker and continue smoking for 10 minutes or until done to taste.

5. Place the fish on a serving platter; serve warm or cold with Southwestern Dipping Sauce.

Makes 6 servings

SOUTHWESTERN DIPPING SAUCE
4 large tomatoes, peeled, seeded, and pureed (see tips on pages 38–39)
2 cloves garlic, minced
½ teaspoon salt
¼ teaspoon each ground cumin, freshly ground pepper, red pepper flakes
¼ cup chopped cilantro

FISH
3 tablespoons green peppercorns, drained if in water, and crushed
2¼ pounds sturgeon, cut into 6 steaks

STEAMING

Steaming is a moist-heat method in which food is cooked by moist vapor. The steam is produced by either water or seasoned liquid.

Fish

Steam only nonoily fish such as bass, halibut, monkfish, trout, cod and scrod, rockfish, red snapper, tilefish, salmon, tuna, whitefish, and pike. Steaming will not eliminate the oily quality of certain fish. Shellfish especially good for steaming are shrimp, mussels, and crawfish.

Equipment

To steam a whole fish, you'll need a pot large enough to accommodate it. Any of the pots, racks, or covers described for poaching in Chapter 6 will work equally well for steaming. And if you have a really large fish, you can try dishwasher cooking (see pages 43–44).

Racks are necessary because the food must be positioned well above the simmering water so that it steams rather than poaches. The ideal steaming rack has legs that adjust to different heights. Most steaming racks are perforated to allow steam to circulate on all sides of the food.

The Japanese substitute platters or plates for racks because these catch the juices, which are then served with the finished dish. Or you can put a foil cradle under the fish before laying it on the rack.

Colanders make good steaming racks for seafood. Or you can set cake cooling racks on tin cans (see Chapter 6). You can also make a cheesecloth hamper/sling (see Chapter 6) to substitute for a rack.

Stockpots or saucepans with covers and racks work well when steaming shellfish, small fish, fillets, fish steaks, or fish balls. Or you can use electric rice or shellfish steamers or Chinese bamboo baskets—the ones used for steaming dim sum. Relatively inexpensive aluminum rice steamers are sold in Vietnamese markets.

Frying pans with lids (electric or manual) can also be used, provided they're deep enough to hold water and a rack.

The Liquid

We suggest using water for steaming because the steam penetrates the fish flesh to such a limited extent that only a little flavor is gained by substituting seasoned liquid. Instead of flavoring the liquid, try adding flavorings to the fish or making a sauce to accompany it.

Steam does not conduct heat as well as water,

and although it is slightly hotter than boiling water (it absorbs an extra degree or two of heat when it vaporizes), the same fish will take slightly longer to steam than it will to poach.

Although steaming and poaching are similar, a properly steamed fish is slightly more delicate in texture than one that is poached. It is easy to overcook steamed fish, so check it regularly during cooking. (See "How to Test Fish for Doneness.")

Method

Step 1: Measure the thickness of the fish at the thickest point in the center. Place the pot on a burner (or, if you're steaming a whole fish, place a rectangular pan over two burners). Pour water into the pot or pan to a depth that will leave at least 1 inch of space between the water and the rack, and bring it to a boil. Then place the rack in the pan, and reduce the heat until the water is at a simmer.

Step 2: Season the fish and place it on the rack. Do not let the water boil, or it will create so much steam that it will recondense under the lid and drip down onto the food, poaching it instead of steaming it.

Step 3: Steam the fish for 8 to 10 minutes for each inch of thickness. Watch the water level carefully during cooking so the water does not boil. Check the fish for doneness often during steaming, as with the other cooking methods.

Step 4: Remove the lid as soon as the fish is cooked and immediately transfer the fish to a serving platter. Serve it with a seasoned sauce.

Tips for Successful Steaming

1. When you are steaming a whole fish, it's better to leave the head and tail intact; otherwise flavor and juiciness escape through both openings during cooking. However, some people prefer the look of a fish without the head and tail, which is fine.

2. If desired, cut diagonal slashes, no more than ½ inch deep and about 1 inch apart, on both sides of the fish to cut down on the cooking time.

3. If your pot is too small to accommodate a whole fish, remove the head and tail, cut the fish in half lengthwise, and lay the two fillets near each other on the rack. We've even heard of cooks who reassemble the fish on the serving platter and disguise the seams with sauce and slices of scored cucumber or other decorations.

4. Make fish salad from leftover steamed fish with mayonnaise, capers, and seasonings.

DISHWASHER COOKING

If your whole fish is too big for your poacher or your oven, you might want to do what midwesterners do when they catch a Great Lakes fish that's too big for standard equipment and utensils: steam/poach the fish in the dishwasher.

Tear off a large piece of heavy-duty aluminum foil, line it with plastic wrap, and liberally butter the inside of the wrap. Sprinkle herbs, onions, and other seasonings as desired onto the wrap. Then place a couple of bay leaves, a few sprinkles of lemon juice, and a quartered onion inside the whole fish. Feel free to place herbs inside the fish, too, if desired.

Lay the fish on the foil/plastic wrap and wrap it up tightly, securing it on either end by folding the foil several times. Place this package in the top rack of your dishwasher. Some cooks run it through a whole hot-water washing cycle—without soap of course—and then check it when the drying cycle comes on. If it's cooked, take it out. If not, let it steam in the drying cycle.

Other cooks turn to the drying cycle immediately and cook it this way, using two or even three drying-only cycles, as necessary depending on fish size. Whatever you do, be sure to stop the cycles often and check the fish to prevent overcooking.

Steamed Salmon Sausage with Two-Mustard Mayonnaise

These lovely steamed sausages are good hot or cold.

1. Make the Two-Mustard Mayonnaise: Mix the mayonnaise with the Dijon mustard and honey mustard. Refrigerate until needed.

2. Puree the salmon in a food processor fitted with the steel blade. Add the onion, butter, bell pepper, salt, white pepper, green peppercorns, and egg. Pulse two times.

3. With the machine running, add the cream through the feed tube.

4. Put the mixture into a mixing bowl and blend in the scallops. Cover and chill for 45 minutes.

5. Cut 12 pieces of aluminum foil into 5-inch squares. Shape the seafood mixture into sausages 3½ inches by 1 inch. Put each one in the center of a foil square. Roll up the foil, twisting the ends tightly.

6. Pour water into a large kettle and heat to a boil. Add the wine. Place a rack in the pan, making sure the rack sits at least 1 inch above the water.

7. Arrange the sausages on the rack and cover the pot. Bring the water to a simmer and steam the sausages for about 8 to 10 minutes or until they are slightly firm to the touch and the color has lightened slightly. Cool on the rack for 5 minutes.

8. Transfer the sausages to a platter, discarding the aluminum foil.

9. To serve, cut two salmon sausages into ½-inch slices and arrange on each plate. Serve with Two-Mustard Mayonnaise.

Makes 6 servings

TWO-MUSTARD MAYONNAISE
1½ cups mayonnaise
1 teaspoon Dijon mustard
1 teaspoon honey mustard

SEAFOOD
1½ pounds salmon fillets, skin and all bones removed, cut into 1-inch pieces
1 small onion, minced
2 tablespoons unsalted butter or margarine or a combination
¼ cup diced green bell pepper
¼ teaspoon salt
¼ teaspoon freshly ground white pepper
½ teaspoon green peppercorns, either dried or drained, crushed
1 egg, slightly beaten
¾ cup heavy cream
½ pound sea scallops
2 cups dry white wine

SAUCE
½ teaspoon light soy sauce
¾ cup chicken stock
1 teaspoon Oriental (dark)
  sesame oil
1 tablespoon cornstarch mixed
  with 2 tablespoons water
3 scallions, minced

STUFFING
3 tablespoons peanut oil
⅓ cup chopped celery
½ teaspoon grated fresh
  gingerroot
¼ cup chopped water chestnuts
¼ cup chopped bamboo shoots
4 dried mushrooms,
  reconstituted in hot water,
  drained, and rinsed
½ cup chopped cooked ham

SEASONING
1 teaspoon dry white wine
1 teaspoon light soy sauce
¼ teaspoon each salt, freshly
  ground pepper, and sugar
1 teaspoon cornstarch mixed
  with 1 tablespoon water

FISH
1 1¼-pound whole flounder,
  scaled and cleaned
2 tablespoons light soy sauce
1 tablespoon dry white wine

Oriental Steamed Stuffed Flounder

When you're making any dish with several ingredients, take them all out before starting, then arrange the ingredients in groups: a sauce group, a stuffing group, and a seasoning group with the fish.

1. Make the sauce: Mix all sauce ingredients in a small saucepan. Warm the sauce, stirring occasionally. Set aside.

2. Make the stuffing: Heat the oil in a wok or heavy frying pan over medium-high heat. Stir in the celery and ginger and stir-fry for 30 seconds. Add the water chestnuts, bamboo shoots, mushrooms, and ham and stir-fry for 1 minute.

3. Mix in the seasoning ingredients and stir for 1 minute.

4. Pour water into a large kettle and heat to a boil. Stuff the fish cavity loosely with the prepared stuffing. Place an oiled rack in the pan, making sure the rack sits at least 1 inch above the water, and place the stuffed flounder on the rack.

5. Rub the flounder with the soy sauce and wine.

6. Cover the pot and bring the water to a simmer. Steam the flounder for about 15 minutes (about 10 minutes per pound) or until it flakes easily when tested.

7. Uncover the pot and let the fish cool on the rack for 5 minutes. Transfer the fish carefully to a platter. Drizzle the warm sauce over it and serve immediately.

Makes 4 servings

Steamed Whitefish Fillets Oriental

In this low-calorie whitefish recipe steaming cuts the calories even further and the sauce adds optimal flavor with minimal calories.

1. Prepare the sauce: Heat the peanut oil in a small saucepan and add the remaining sauce ingredients. Heat until warmed through and set aside.

2. Pour water into a large kettle and heat it to a boil on the stove. Place a rack in the pan, making sure the rack sits at least 1 inch above the water. Reduce the heat so the water is at a simmer.

3. Place a heatproof plate on the steamer rack; put the fish pieces on the plate. Sprinkle the ginger and orange zest over the whitefish.

4. Cover and steam the fish for 8 to 10 minutes. The fish is done when it flakes easily. Drain off the juice. Using a spatula, transfer the fish to a serving platter. Arrange the cucumbers, cilantro, and scallions around the fish. Drizzle with the hot sauce.

5. Take the fish to the table immediately and serve with hot Chinese noodles or rice.

Makes 6 servings

SAUCE
¼ cup peanut oil
2 cloves garlic, chopped
¼ cup light soy sauce
¼ cup dry white wine
½ cup dark soy sauce
1 teaspoon Oriental (dark) sesame oil

FISH
2¼–2½ pounds whitefish fillets, cut into 6 serving pieces
1 teaspoon grated fresh gingerroot
¼ cup grated orange zest (about 1 large orange)
2 cucumbers, peeled and sliced thin
⅓ cup chopped cilantro
6 scallions, chopped

REFRIED BEANS
1 pound dry pinto beans
6 strips bacon, cut into 1-inch
   pieces
1 teaspoon salt
2 cloves garlic, minced
¼ teaspoon each freshly
   ground pepper, ground
   cumin, and ground ginger

FISH
2¼–2½ pounds ono fillets, cut
   into 6 serving pieces
12 flour or corn tortillas
¼ teaspoon salt
¼ teaspoon freshly ground
   pepper
¼ teaspoon cumin
1½ cups sour cream
¼ cup chopped fresh chives

Steamed Ono
with Refried Beans, Tortillas,
and Sour Cream with Chives

Mexican food is often high in calories. But here's a dish with Mexican flavors that keeps the calories down. We use lettuce to line the pan instead of greasing it, the way the Orientals do.

1. Make the Refried Beans: Sort through the beans, discarding any that are not perfect and any foreign matter such as twigs or stones. Wash the beans and put them into a large pot. Cover with water and bring to a boil. Reduce the heat to a simmer and continue cooking for 3 hours, uncovered, adding more water as necessary and stirring occasionally. The beans can be cooked the day before; reserve 1 cup of the cooking liquid along with the beans.

2. Fry the bacon in a heavy skillet. Stir in the beans, 1 cup of the cooking liquid, the salt, garlic, pepper, cumin, and ginger.

3. Mash the beans with a potato masher or use a food processor and process them in three batches. Return the beans to the heat and continue cooking over medium heat for 10 to 12 minutes, stirring often. The beans will thicken as they cook. Reserve.

4. Pour water into a large kettle and heat to boil. Place a greased rack in the pan, making sure the rack sits at least 1 inch above the water. Place the ono pieces and foil-wrapped tortillas on the rack. Sprinkle with salt, pepper, and cumin.

5. Cover the pot and steam the fish and tortillas for 10 minutes per inch of thickness, about 5 to 7 minutes, or until the fish flakes easily when tested and is slightly firm to the touch. Let cool in the pan for 5 minutes.

6. Meanwhile, mix the sour cream with the chives.

7. On each plate place a slice of ono, a portion of beans, and a dab of sour cream. Serve with tortillas and extra beans and sour cream.

Makes 6 servings

Steamed Shark and Mushrooms with Gazpacho Salsa

Shark is one of those meaty fish with tensile strength, which means it holds together well even when cooked and will not fall apart when you transfer it from the steaming rack to dinner plates. For color and variety, try red, yellow, or orange peppers.

1. Make the Gazpacho Salsa: Mix together the tomatoes, onion, peppers, cucumber, cilantro, lime juice, and oil. Season with salt, garlic, and pepper. Place in a covered container and refrigerate until ready to serve. Bring to room temperature before serving.

2. Soak the shark steaks in the milk for 20 minutes. Drain.

3. Meanwhile, pour water into a large kettle and heat to a boil. Place a rack in the pan, making sure the rack sits at least 1 inch above the water. Place the lime peel (can be in large pieces) in the water. Place the shark and mushrooms on the rack.

4. Bring the water to a simmer and steam the shark for about 8 to 10 minutes.

5. Place the shark steaks and mushrooms on plates; serve with the Gazpacho Salsa.

Makes 6 servings

GAZPACHO SALSA
3 tomatoes, peeled, seeded, and diced
1 onion, minced
2 small green bell peppers, seeded and chopped
1 small cucumber, peeled, seeded, and diced
⅓ cup minced cilantro
3 tablespoons freshly squeezed lime juice
¼ cup extra-virgin olive oil
½ teaspoon salt
½ teaspoon minced garlic
¼ teaspoon freshly ground pepper

FISH
2¼–2½ pounds shark steaks, cut into 6 serving pieces
1½ cups milk
Peel from 2 limes
1 pound large mushrooms

INGREDIENTS

3 cups (1½ pounds) unsalted
butter

6 1½-pound whole lobsters,
(fishmonger will kill them
quickly and humanely for
you)

Seaweed (if available) or
parsley sprigs, for garnish

3 lemons, cut into wedges, for
garnish

Steamed Whole Maine Lobsters

This dish can be presented spectacularly if you ask the fishmonger for seaweed to decorate the platter. Don't worry if the first batch of lobsters cools by the time the second batch is cooked; lobsters are just as delicious at room temperature or chilled. If you prefer, use two or three pots and steam all at the same time.

Don't worry about the large amount of butter called for here. Six sticks are necessary to make enough drawn butter for everyone to have an ample portion, but no one uses all that is served.

1. Make clarified butter: Fill a large, flat pan with raised sides with boiling water. Place six narrow glasses (juice glasses are fine) in the pan; then place ½ cup of the butter in each glass and wait 20 minutes or so for the butter to melt and separate into 3 layers: a top layer of foam, a middle layer of clear fat, and a thin bottom layer of milk solids. Let the butter sit this way without disturbing until you are ready to serve.

2. Meanwhile, pour water into a large kettle and heat to a boil. Place a rack in the pan, making sure the rack sits at least 1 inch above the water. Place two lobsters on the rack and cover the pot. Bring the water to a simmer and steam the lobsters for 15 minutes (or 10 minutes per pound). Repeat with remaining lobsters.

3. While lobsters are steaming, arrange a bed of seaweed or parsley on a platter. When lobsters are cooled, arrange them on platter and garnish with lemon wedges.

4. Use a spoon to skim foam off the top of glasses. Take the platter to table with glasses of clarified butter and serve one to each guest. Show guests how to pour clarified butter over the lobster, taking care not to disturb the sediment on the bottom. Serve with corn on the cob, coleslaw, and baked potatoes or heated French bread.

Makes 6 servings

TIPS FOR CRACKING LOBSTER SHELLS

• Pick the lobster up in one hand and locate a claw—one of the big arms that resembles a big red boxing glove. Use your other hand to twist this claw from the body. Then twist off the second claw in the same manner. Pick up a lobster cracker (a tool that resembles a nutcracker) in one hand, insert one of the lobster claws into it, and press down hard until the shell breaks. Use the lobster cracker on various sections of the claw until the shell is sufficiently broken. Then remove as much of the shell as possible with your fingers and eat the meat. Repeat with the other claw.

• Next, pick up the whole lobster, holding the tail in one hand and the body/head section in the other. Crack the lobster in half so that you have one section in each hand.

• Lay the tail section down and hold the body/head section belly side up in one hand. Stick the thumb of the other hand under the lobster meat and lift it out of the shell. Break off the tiny claw-legs and reserve for a moment. Remove the second, softer undershell called the *belly shell*.

• Next, remove the black vein that runs the length of the body meat. You should also remove the small sac at the base of the lobster's head called the *sand sac*. Everything else—including the tomalley (drab green-colored liver)—is safe to eat. You may even find some coral-colored roe (eggs) if your lobster is female. Both the tomalley and the roe are delicious.

• Finally, pick up the tail section in one hand. Use the other hand to bend the flippers back and break them off. Insert a lobster fork into the hole you've made and push gently; the tail meat will come out the wide end of the shell. When it does, remove the black vein that runs the length of the tail.

• To eat the small claw-legs, put the open end of each into your mouth and suck out the meat as if using a straw.

**LEMON-CARDAMOM
BUTTER**
½ cup (¼ pound) unsalted
butter or margarine or a
combination at room
temperature, cut into ½-inch
pieces
1 tablespoon grated lemon zest
½ teaspoon cardamom seed,
crushed

SHELLFISH
¼ cup freshly squeezed lemon
juice
Peel from 1 lemon
½ teaspoon ground cloves
½ teaspoon cardamom seed,
crushed
4 pounds crawfish, deveined
1 pound fresh asparagus,
woody ends broken off,
peeled if desired

Steamed Crawfish
with Lemon-Cardamom Butter
and Asparagus

*Serve a mound of cooked crawfish to a group of guests who don't
know each other. Guaranteed, they'll be good friends by the end of
the communal meal.*

1. Make the Lemon-Cardamom Butter: Soften the butter in a bowl with the back of a wooden spoon or in a food
processor. Mix in the lemon zest and cardamom seed. Pack
the butter into a small bowl. Cover lightly and refrigerate
until ready to use. Remove the butter from the refrigerator
45 minutes before serving.

2. Meanwhile, pour water into a large kettle. Add the
lemon juice, peel (can be in large pieces), cloves, and
crushed cardamom seed. Heat to a boil and place a rack in
the pan, making sure the rack sits at least 1 inch above the
water. Place the crawfish in the middle of the rack with
the asparagus surrounding it. Cover the pot, bring the
water to a simmer, and steam the crawfish for 7 minutes or
until the shells turn red.

3. Mound the crawfish in a large bowl in the center of
the table. Serve hot with asparagus and melted Lemon-
Cardamom Butter as a dipping sauce. Guests open their
own crawfish, so provide paper bibs and a bowl for shells.

4. To eat crawfish, hold the tail in one hand and the
head in the other hand. Twist your hands in opposite
directions and pull the crawfish apart. Hold the body to
your lips, drawing in the juices. Extract the meat from the
tail using your thumbs.

Serve with aquavit or beer, rye bread, and fresh berries
and cream.

Makes 4 to 5 servings

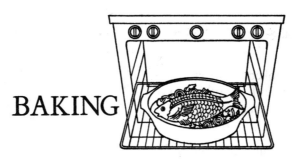

BAKING

Baking and roasting are both dry-heat methods in which food is placed in a pan and then cooked in the oven. Although there's really no difference between the two, *roasting* is the word used when a top round or similar cut of beef, poultry, or a leg of lamb is oven-cooked, and *baking* is the word used when meat loaf, a casserole, or fish is prepared in the same way. No matter how large the fish, it is always baked—never roasted.

Fish
Fish of all kinds and cuts—large whole fish, fish steaks, fillets, and shrimp—do well when baked. Butter, margarine, or oil should be used to grease any pan in which fish is placed for baking. Fish have a tendency to stick to pans that have not been oiled. Fish should always be arranged in a single layer in the pan, or they will cook unevenly, stick together, and break apart when lifted with a spatula.

Equipment
Any ovenproof baking pan or dish with at least slightly raised sides can be used for baking fish. If you use a glass dish, lower the baking temperature called for in the recipe by 25° F. Re-member to grease all pans. Because cooked fish is fragile, it should be baked and served in the same dish whenever possible. Too much lifting, even with a spatula, will cause a steak or fillet to fall apart.

One spatula for lifting will suffice, but two spatulas, used together to lift each piece of fish, are ideal. When baking a whole fish, never attempt to lift it from a baking dish to transfer it to a serving dish, or it will break into several pieces. Serve it right from the baking dish.

Method
Step 1: Preheat the oven to 350° F. If you are baking a whole fish, measure it at the thickest part in the center. Grease the pan thoroughly using oil, butter, or margarine. Arrange the fish in the center of the prepared pan. If you are baking fillets or steaks, simply lay them in the prepared pan in a single layer. They do not have to be far apart, but ideally they should not be touching.

Step 2: Place the baking dish or pan in the center of the oven. Bake a whole fish for 9 to 10 minutes per inch of thickness. For fillets and steaks, follow the recipe directions carefully and take care not to overcook them. (See "How to Test for Doneness.")

Step 3: When the fish is cooked, transfer steaks or fillets to serving dish with spatulas; serve whole fish directly from the baking dish.

Tips for Baking Fish

1. Increase the baking time 15 minutes for stuffed whole fish.

2. A whole fish to be baked should always have the head, tail, and backbone intact. Cooking a fish with the head and tail seals in the juices, and the backbone acts as a heat conductor, which shortens the cooking time.

Baked Redfish
with Marinated Roast Peppers

These peppers are so delicious you may wish to make a double portion and refrigerate the remainder, reserving them for use in salads.

1. Make Marinated Roast Red Peppers: Preheat the broiler. Arrange the peppers on a broiler pan 4 inches from the heat source. Broil the peppers, turning them often, until they are charred on all sides, about 5 to 7 minutes. One at a time, place them in a large, heavy plastic bag and seal it shut. When the peppers are cool, slip off the skins, cut them in half, and discard the seeds. Cut each pepper into strips and place them in a shallow bowl. Pour the ½ cup oil over the peppers and sprinkle them with the basil, oregano, garlic, salt, and pepper. Cover and refrigerate overnight.

2. Before cooking the fish, remove the peppers from the refrigerator to warm to room temperature and arrange the anchovy strips decoratively over the peppers. Preheat the oven to 375° F and line a cookie sheet with aluminum foil.

3. Brush the tomato halves with the 2 tablespoons oil and sprinkle them with the bread crumbs. Arrange them on the foil-lined cookie sheet.

4. Place the fillets in a large greased baking dish and sprinkle it with the wine. Put both the tomatoes and the fish in the oven; bake the fish for 6 to 8 minutes, the tomatoes for 10 minutes. The fish should flake easily when tested. Transfer the fish pieces with a slotted spoon to individual plates and add a tomato half to each plate. Serve hot with the roast peppers.

Makes 6 servings

MARINATED ROAST PEPPERS
3 large red bell peppers
½ cup extra-virgin olive oil
1 tablespoon dried basil
1 tablespoon dried oregano
6 cloves garlic, minced
½ teaspoon salt
¼ teaspoon freshly ground
    black pepper
6 anchovy fillets (or to taste)

FISH
3 large tomatoes, halved
    horizontally
2 tablespoons extra-virgin
    olive oil
½ cup seasoned bread crumbs
2¼–2½ pounds redfish fillets
    cut into 6 serving pieces
¾ cup dry white wine

PASTRY
1¾ cups all-purpose flour
¼ teaspoon salt
4 tablespoons unsalted butter
 or margarine, cut into
 ½-inch pieces
3 tablespoons vegetable
 shortening
5–7 tablespoons ice water

FILLING
2 tablespoons unsalted butter
 or margarine
4 shallots, minced
½-pound mushrooms, sliced
3 hard-cooked eggs, peeled
1½ cups cooked white rice
½ cup minced fresh parsley
½ cup fine bread crumbs
1 2-pound brook trout, cut
 into 2 fillets, skin and all
 bones removed
1 egg, slightly beaten and
 mixed with 1 tablespoon
 water
2 cups sour cream

Coulibiac

Nothing beats a pastry-covered fish for elegance. If desired, place overlapping flattened pastry circles on the pastry-covered fish to resemble scales. The fancier your decoration, the more elegant the presentation.

This was originally a Russian recipe and was later adapted by the French. We've further adapted it by substituting trout for the traditional salmon.

1. Make the pastry: Put the flour, salt, butter, and shortening in a food processor fitted with the steel blade. Pulse on and off until crumbled. With the machine running, pour the ice water through the feed tube in a slow, steady stream. Process only until a dough ball forms. Cover the dough with plastic wrap and chill it for 30 minutes.

2. Make the filling: Melt the butter in a frying pan over medium heat. Add the shallots and mushrooms and sauté them for 3 minutes, stirring often. Remove the pan from the heat and set aside.

3. Chop the eggs and toss them with the rice in a mixing bowl.

4. Toss the parsley and bread crumbs together and set aside.

5. Preheat the oven to 400° F. Cover a cookie sheet with aluminum foil.

6. To assemble: Roll out the dough on a lightly floured board to form a rectangle about 2½ times the size of the fish fillet. Move it to the foil-covered cookie sheet.

7. Sprinkle the bread crumb mixture lengthwise down the center of the pastry. Set the trout crosswise over the crumbs. Sprinkle the egg mixture over the fish and place the mushroom mixture on top, mounding it slightly. Set remaining fillet over mushrooms. Fold over the top and bottom of the pastry. Press the seams to seal completely and trim off the extra dough.

8. Make 2½-inch steam vents in the top crust. Roll out the dough scraps and cut them, free-form, into leaves if desired.

9. Brush the dough with the egg wash, decorate the crust with the leaves, and then gently brush the leaves with the egg wash. Bake the Coulibiac immediately for 45 minutes or until the crust is a golden brown.

10. With spatulas, place the Coulibiac on a serving tray. Take it to the table hot, slice it, and serve it with sour cream as a sauce.

Makes 4 to 6 servings

INGREDIENTS

3–4 tablespoons extra-virgin
  olive oil
3 cloves garlic, minced
1 large onion, sliced thin
6 medium tomatoes, peeled,
  seeded, and chopped
2 jalapeño peppers, seeded and
  chopped
1 cup pimiento-stuffed green
  olives
¼ teaspoon ground cinnamon
¼ teaspoon sugar
2 tablespoons freshly squeezed
  lime juice
½ teaspoon salt
3 large potatoes, peeled,
  quartered, and partially
  boiled (until fork tender—
  about 15–20 minutes)
1 2½- to 3-pound whole red
  snapper, scaled and cleaned,
  head and tail left intact

Baked Red Snapper Mexican Style

Whole snapper is baked with peppers, tomatoes, and potatoes for a complete Mexican feast.

1. Heat the olive oil in a heavy frying pan over medium heat. Add the garlic and onion and sauté for 5 minutes, stirring often. Stir in the tomatoes, peppers, olives, cinnamon, sugar, lime juice, salt, and potatoes. Reduce the heat to a simmer and continue cooking for 5 minutes.

2. Preheat the oven to 375° F. Arrange the red snapper in a greased baking dish and pour the vegetables around the fish.

3. Bake the red snapper on the middle rack for 12 to 15 minutes. To test for doneness, separate the fish at the thickest part with the tines of a fork to see if it is translucent and slightly firm. Serve this dish hot right in the baking pan, set over pads or trivets to protect your table.

Makes 5 to 6 servings

TIP FOR COOKING WITH JALAPEÑOS

• Jalapeños are extremely hot and can cause pain if you're not careful. Never touch your eyes when working with them. Either wear rubber gloves or wash your hands thoroughly when you finish.

Striped Bass Baked in Corn Husks

Corn husks are a wonderful way to keep the fish moist and they provide a fun way to serve fish to guests.

1. Preheat the oven to 450° F. Combine the apples, walnuts, and chopped celery. Pack the mixture loosely into each fish cavity. Soak the corn husks in cold water mixed with the sugar for 5 minutes; drain.

2. Place each fish in a corn husk. Brush each fish with the oil.

3. Use your hand to mold the fish inside the husk and tie the husks closed with string. Place the fish on a nonstick cookie sheet and bake on the middle rack for 8 to 10 minutes. To test for doneness, open the corn husk and test with the tines of a fork; the bass should be opaque and slightly firm in texture.

4. Using a spatula, place one corn husk with fish still inside it on each plate. Serve hot.

Makes 4 servings

INGREDIENTS

2 large apples, peeled, cored, and chopped
1 cup chopped black walnuts
2 large stalks celery, chopped
4 ½- to ¾-pound striped bass, scaled, cleaned, and heads discarded
4 outer green husks of corn
1 teaspoon sugar
4 teaspoons extra-virgin olive oil

INGREDIENTS

2 tablespoons unsalted butter
   or margarine
1 medium onion, minced
1 clove garlic, minced
1 large orange, peeled
½ cup seasoned bread crumbs
½ cup pine nuts
⅛ teaspoon salt
6 6- to 7-ounce flounder fillets
   (about 2–2½ pounds)
1¾ cups freshly squeezed
   orange juice
1½ tablespoons grated orange
   zest
1 teaspoon sugar
¼ teaspoon ground ginger
¼ teaspoon dry mustard
1 tablespoon cornstarch,
   dissolved in 2 tablespoons
   water

Flounder Rolls in Orange Sauce

Onion, garlic, and a bit of ginger are the perfect accompaniments to this delicately flavored fish.

1. Preheat the oven to 375° F. Melt the butter in a heavy frying pan over medium heat. Add the onion and garlic and sauté until tender, about 5 minutes, stirring often. Remove from the heat.

2. Chop the orange and discard the seeds. Mix the orange, bread crumbs, pine nuts, and salt into the onion and garlic.

3. Spoon the filling evenly over the thick end of each fillet. Roll up the flounder, jelly roll style. Set the rolls, seam side down, in an ovenproof dish such as a pie plate.

4. In a small saucepan, mix together the orange juice, zest, sugar, ginger, and mustard. Bring to a boil over medium heat. Stir the cornstarch mixture into the orange juice mixture and continue cooking, stirring often, until the sauce thickens slightly. Pour the sauce over the flounder rolls.

5. Place the baking dish on the middle rack and bake for 6 to 8 minutes or until the fish flakes easily when tested and has become slightly opaque.

6. Place a rolled fillet on each plate and drizzle it with the sauce. Serve hot.

Makes 6 servings

Baked Halibut Steaks with Toasted Almonds

This dish can be made almost impromptu if you remember to keep almonds in the pantry and stop and buy the fish on your way home from work. Order it at lunchtime to be sure the fishmonger has it in stock.

1. Preheat the oven to 375° F. Arrange the halibut steaks in a greased dish. Mix the lemon juice, salt, pepper, cumin, and cinnamon into the melted butter. Brush the seasoned butter over the fish. Sprinkle the fish with the toasted almonds.

2. Bake the fish on the middle rack for 10 minutes or until the fish flakes easily when tested and is slightly translucent. Place the halibut steaks on individual plates and serve with a salad and toasted tortilla chips if desired.

Makes 6 servings

INGREDIENTS

About 2¼–2½ pounds halibut, cut into 6 steaks

4 tablespoons freshly squeezed lemon juice

½ teaspoon salt

¼ teaspoon each freshly ground white pepper, ground cumin, and ground cinnamon

3 tablespoons unsalted butter or margarine, melted

¾ cup toasted slivered almonds

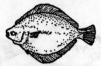

INGREDIENTS

Unsalted butter or margarine
   for greasing parchment or
   foil
2¼–2½ pounds orange roughy
   fillets, cut into 6 serving
   pieces
6 red bell pepper rings
6 large mushrooms, sliced thin
3 tablespoons chopped fresh
   parsley
¼ teaspoon freshly grated
   nutmeg
1 teaspoon dried tarragon
2 tablespoons extra-virgin
   olive oil
½ teaspoon salt

Orange Roughy in Parchment Paper

Place a child's scissors at each place so diners can open their own parchment packets and experience the aromas that will come out at them in a rush.

1. Preheat the oven to 425° F. Cut six pieces of parchment paper or aluminum foil into rectangles 3 inches longer than each piece of orange roughy. Liberally butter the paper. Arrange a piece of orange roughy on the buttered side of the paper on top of a red pepper ring. Arrange a sliced mushroom on each piece of fish. Sprinkle with parsley, nutmeg, and tarragon. Brush with oil, then sprinkle with salt.

2. Fold the sides, then the ends of the paper envelope around the fish. Arrange the fish packages on a nonstick cookie sheet. Bake the packages for 6 to 8 minutes or until the fish is cooked; the paper will brown lightly.

3. Place each package on a plate and serve it hot. Allow guests to open their own packages.

Makes 6 servings

Stuffed Shrimp

A very special appetizer, perfect for entertaining.

1. Butterfly the shrimp by cutting down the back almost all the way through the shrimp.

2. Preheat the oven to 400° F. Cover a cookie sheet with aluminum foil. Melt the butter and combine it in a bowl with the cracker crumbs, parsley, garlic, wine, pepper, and basil.

3. Place the shrimp cut side down on the prepared cookie sheet. Stuff each shrimp with a heaping tablespoon of the stuffing, patting the stuffing into a mound.

4. Bake the shrimp for 8 to 10 minutes or until done to taste. Place five stuffed shrimp on each plate and serve hot.

Makes 6 servings

INGREDIENTS

30 large shrimp (about 1¾ pounds), peeled and deveined, tails left intact

½ cup (¼ pound) unsalted butter or margarine or a combination

2 cups coarse cracker crumbs

¾ cup chopped fresh parsley

3 cloves garlic, minced

4 tablespoons dry white wine

½ teaspoon freshly ground black pepper

½ teaspoon dried basil

POACHING AND STEEPING

POACHING

Poaching is a moist-heat cooking method in which food is submerged in simmering water, either completely or with the bottom two-thirds under water and the top third above. The part of the food that is submerged completely cooks by convection, while the food that is positioned above the liquid is cooked by a combination of steam and the hot water that drips back onto the fish when the steam condenses under the pot lid.

Fish
Just about any fish or shellfish can be steamed. For poaching, however, thicker fillets, steaks, and whole fish are better; very thin, soft-textured fish tend to break up in the poaching liquid.

Equipment
You'll need a rectangular pot with a lid, a rack, and some cheesecloth for poaching whole fish. For poaching shellfish, fillets, and fish steaks you'll need a round pot with a lid, a rack, and some cheesecloth. A deep-frying thermometer will help you measure simmering temperatures.

A whole fish must be poached in a rectangular pot big enough to accommodate the length of the fish. Fish poachers, deep-sided oblong pans usually made of copper or aluminum with perforated racks and lids, are made especially for this purpose.

Poachers range from about 10 inches to 3 feet long, but 20 inches is the most common length. Both poachers and turkey roasters must sit on two burners on top of the stove, or they can be put in the oven. Poachers are always sold with perforated racks to support the fish during poaching.

Turkey roasters or any rectangular, deep-sided pot with a lid can be substituted for a fish poacher, provided you improvise a rack. Either use two vegetable steaming racks set next to each other inside the roaster or set a rectangular wire cake-cooling rack on two empty tin cans without the paper labels.

Whole fish, with or without heads and tails, become so fragile during poaching that they should be wrapped in two thicknesses of cheesecloth, or they will disintegrate. Since it's very hard to remove a poached fish from the rack—even using the cheesecloth—we suggest improvising a foil sling as well: Tear off two long sheets of aluminum foil and fold them in thirds lengthwise. Lay them on the counter parallel to each other, with about 6 inches of space between them. Lay the cheesecloth-wrapped fish across the strips so the fish is perpendicular to them. Then use these slings to set the fish on the rack. You won't really need them before the fish is cooked, but they will be a real help afterwards. If possible, enlist a friend to help by supporting the fish with a wide spatula as you remove it from the pot and place it on a serving platter.

Round pots of all sizes (including deep-sided frying pans) work fine for poaching fish steaks, small fish, or fillets. Round pots are fine for shellfish and fish balls too, but since these are hearty and will not fall apart in the broth, they don't have to be wrapped in cheesecloth. Shellfish and fish balls don't need a perforated rack either; they can be cooked on an improvised cheesecloth sling: Fold a long piece of cheesecloth in half lengthwise and tie each of its ends to the handle at either end of your pot so that it resembles a hammock. Arrange fish balls or shellfish in the hammock, then add the broth.

Using a lid prolongs the life of the liquid, which will recondense under the lid and drip back into the pot rather than boil away into the air. A lid is necessary only when the fish is two-thirds submerged and one-third above the liquid.

The Liquid
Although water will poach any fish or seafood satisfactorily, adding other ingredients to the poaching water imparts flavor to the fish. Flavorings include such things as onions, leeks, shallots, lemon and orange peel, peppercorns, parsley, and numerous other herbs and spices. Liquid seasonings include red and white wine, vinegar, and lemon juice.

Fish can also be poached in court bouillon, which is flavored liquid made by simmering various seasonings such as onions, wine, and bay leaves together. If fish heads and bones of non-oily fish are added, the liquid becomes fish stock. If you want your fish to have a faintly smoky flavor, you can add a tablespoon of liquid smoke for each 2 cups of broth.

The word *simmering*, which refers to liquid that trembles but stays below the boiling point, was an arbitrary culinary term until 1981, when author Howard Hillman published his *Kitchen Science* and came up with benchmark temperatures: low simmer, 180° F, where the water merely "smiles"; medium simmer, 195° F, where it trembles; and high simmer, 210° F, where it seems to shudder.

Method
Step 1: Place a rack in the pot, then set it over two burners on the stove or place it near the oven if you're oven-poaching. Measure the thickness of the fish in the center, at its thickest point. This will determine how long it should cook (see step 5).

Step 2: Wrap whole fish, fillets, or steaks in cheesecloth, then place them on the rack. Place shellfish or fish balls on the rack unwrapped. If the fish is large, add a foil sling before placing it on the rack.

Step 3: If you're using court bouillon, add solids to the bottom of the pot. Then carefully pour water into the pot to the desired depth. Otherwise, just pour in fish stock or water as desired. Fasten the deep-frying thermometer to the side of the pot and turn on the burners. Heat the liquid to a boil.

Step 4: Reduce the heat so that the water simmers at the desired level. Cover the pot loosely with the lid, allowing some steam to escape.

Step 5: Allow 4 to 6 minutes of poaching time for each ½ inch of fish thickness. Do not turn whole fish, which are very fragile, during poaching. And watch shellfish carefully, as they cook quickly and will toughen if overcooked for even a moment. Check the liquid level while poaching, adding water if needed.

Step 6: To remove shellfish, pour them quickly into a colander and run cool tap water over them to stop the cooking. Small cheesecloth-wrapped fillets and steaks can be removed from the pot with a spatula. Follow the recipe directions carefully, letting each poached whole fish cool somewhat before attempting to remove it.

Step 7: Place the poached fish on a platter and unwrap the cheesecloth carefully. Use paper towels to mop up any liquid that seeps out. Decorate whole fish if desired. Poached fillets and steaks should be unwrapped carefully once they're on the serving platter. Place poached shellfish on a platter and serve immediately.

Tips for Successful Poaching

1. If you find yourself with a fish too big for your poacher, one alternative is to cut off and discard its head and/or tail. Or some people even cut their fish in half, poach the two pieces, and then reassemble them before serving. This works very successfully if the fish is going to be decorated.

2. It's hard to know exactly how much fish stock or court bouillon you'll need when poaching, so make extra to have on hand if you need to add more to the pot. Freeze the remainder to use the next time. In a pinch, just add water.

3. Make fish salad from leftover poached fish, using mayonnaise, capers, salt, and pepper.

4. It's easy to overcook poached fish. Check it regularly during poaching. (See "How to Test Fish for Doneness.")

STEEPING

The Chinese have a method of cooking small pieces of chicken that they call *velvet chicken*. It consists of heating broth to a boil, letting it cool for a moment, then pouring it over small pieces of chicken to cover in a pan. The pan is then covered, and the chicken is steeped in this liquid until cooked, which results in an extremely delicate texture.

The same steeping technique can be used for shellfish and even for delicate fillets. To steep, arrange cheesecloth-wrapped fillets on the pan bottom in a single layer. Heat the liquid to a simmer, then pour it carefully and slowly over the fish. Cover the pot and let the fish or shellfish sit in the liquid for a minute, before removing the lid and checking the texture. Replace the lid and let the seafood sit for another minute or so before checking it for doneness. Continue checking until the fish has a firm texture and has lost its opaque appearance.

INGREDIENTS

¼ cup drained capers
2½ cups crème fraîche
6 large leaf lettuce or radicchio
   leaves
1 pound pike fillets, cut into
   2-inch pieces
½ teaspoon salt
¼ teaspoon freshly ground
   white pepper
¼ teaspoon freshly grated
   nutmeg
1 small handful fresh parsley,
   stems removed
⅓ cup whipping cream
2 large bay leaves

Miniature Quenelles

Quenelles are delicately packed, oval-shaped creamy fish balls. They are often served in good French restaurants.

1. Press the capers gently with paper towels to extract excess liquid. Combine them with the crème fraîche in a serving bowl and refrigerate. Lay six small dessert or salad plates on the counter and place a large lettuce leaf on each.

2. Place the pike, salt, pepper, nutmeg, and parsley in a food processor fitted with the steel blade. Process for about 30 seconds, then pulse on and off until a thick, fine puree results. Then, with the machine still running, add the cream and process for a few seconds to mix.

3. Fill a large, heavy skillet with 1 inch of water. Add the bay leaves, heat the water to a boil, and reduce the heat to a low simmer. Fill a small bowl with hot water and place it near the skillet.

4. Dip two teaspoons into the hot water, then use them to scoop up and shape a small fish paste oval. Slide the oval into the simmering water. Repeat, making nine more ovals and adding each to the pot.

5. When the last oval has been added, continue simmering for 2 minutes longer or until the bottom of the most recently added oval is firm. Remove them one by one from the pot with a slotted spoon and arrange them in a single layer on a serving platter.

6. Reheat the water to a low simmer and repeat with another 10 ovals. Continue cooking in batches of 10 until no fish paste remains.

7. Arrange one or two ovals on each lettuce-lined plate. Serve immediately with crème fraîche caper sauce.

Makes 6 servings

Mediterranean Fish Balls

These delicate 1-inch fish balls, similar to quenelles, are so good you'll find yourself popping them in your mouth like popcorn.

1. Cut the fillets into 1-inch pieces and process a few cupfuls at a time in a food processor fitted with a steel blade until the fish is finely pureed. Transfer the puree to a medium bowl. Combine the bread crumbs with the water in a separate bowl and let sit for 10 minutes. Squeeze the crumbs in your hands, discarding excess water. Add the crumbs to the fish, mixing well.

2. Place the parsley sprigs and scallions in a food processor fitted with the steel blade and pulse until finely chopped. Add the marjoram, salt, and cayenne pepper. Combine this mixture with the fish paste and mix very well. Set a bowl of cold water next to the fish paste.

3. Dip your hands in the water, then scoop up 2 tablespoons of the paste and shape it into a 1-inch ball. Repeat with the remaining paste.

4. Place the fish stock in a large kettle and heat to a boil. Reduce the heat to a medium simmer and let the stock simmer, covered, for 5 minutes. Carefully slide the balls, one at a time, into the simmering stock until the pot is full. Simmer them for 20 minutes, then remove them with a slotted spoon and arrange them over a platter of hot cooked rice or noodles. Serve immediately.

Makes 6 servings

INGREDIENTS

2 pounds red snapper fillets, skin removed
½ cup blender-made fresh bread crumbs
½ cup cold water
1 handful fresh parsley, stems removed
4 scallions, cut into 1-inch lengths
¾ teaspoon dried marjoram
½ teaspoon salt
½ teaspoon cayenne pepper
1 recipe Fish Stock with White Wine (see Index)
4½ cups hot cooked rice or noodles

POACHING LIQUID

1 pound trimmings from a
   light-flavored fish,
   including head, tail, and
   bones
2 very large onions, sliced,
   onion skin reserved
3 carrots, peeled and sliced
1 handful fresh parsley

FISH

1 pound each whitefish fillets,
   buffalofish fillets, and pike
   fillets
2 tablespoons matzo meal
¾ teaspoon salt
¼ teaspoon freshly ground
   black pepper
2 eggs, slightly beaten
4–5 tablespoons cold water
6–8 Boston or other attractive
   lettuce leaves
Prepared red horseradish

Gefilte Fish Balls

This is an old family recipe originally from Central Europe. It was traditionally reserved for special occasions, as the dish required chopping by hand for hours, but now with the aid of a food processor this can be made as often as you want!

1. Make the poaching liquid: Wash the fish trimmings under cold running water and place them in a large soup kettle. Add onion, onion skin, carrots, and parsley. Add enough water to half-fill the kettle and heat it to a boil over high heat. Reduce the heat until the water reaches a hard simmer, then cover and simmer for 20 minutes.

2. Cut the fillets into 2-inch pieces and place them in a food processor fitted with the steel blade. Process the fish, 2 cups at a time, until a fine puree results. Transfer the fish to a bowl and stir in the matzo meal, salt, and pepper. Add the eggs, mixing well. Sprinkle 4 tablespoons cold water over the fish and mix again. The mixture should be slightly sticky to the touch. If it is not, add another table-spoon of water. Place a small dish of cold water near the fish paste and lay a sheet of wax paper on the counter for the fish balls.

3. Wet your hands in the bowl of water and scoop up ¼ to ⅓ cup of the paste. Form the paste into an oval between your moistened palms. Lay the oval on the wax paper and repeat with the remaining paste.

4. Slide the ovals one at a time into the simmering poaching liquid. If the liquid does not cover the ovals, add hot water until all are submerged. Cover and simmer for 20 to 25 minutes or until the fish balls are completely cooked through. Check often to be sure you don't overcook them, as this causes the balls to become hard.

5. Let the ovals cool in the stock, then transfer them with a slotted spoon to a covered container and refrigerate them until ready to serve. Strain the broth through several thicknesses of cheesecloth and store it in a covered container in the refrigerator until it jells. Remove the carrots from the solids and discard the remaining solids. Garnish fish with the cooked carrots.

6. At serving time, line six to eight small salad plates with a lettuce leaf. Place two fish ovals on each leaf and top each with a couple of carrot circles. Add a few spoonfuls of jellied broth to each plate. Serve with a bowl of red horseradish.

Makes 6 to 8 servings (12 to 14 ovals)

INGREDIENTS
1 recipe Jujik (Turkish Cucumber-Yogurt Salad) (recipe follows)

1 recipe Tabbouleh (Cracked Wheat Salad) (recipe follows)

1 3½-pound whole red snapper, cleaned and scaled, head removed, tail left intact

3 quarts cold water

4 cups dry white wine

1 pound fish bones and cleaned fish heads (from nonoily fish only)

2 medium onions, chopped coarse

3 carrots, peeled and sliced

3 stalks celery with leaves, peeled and cut into chunks

1 large handful fresh parsley

¾ teaspoon dried tarragon

1 teaspoon salt

6 peppercorns

1 long, thin cucumber

12 whole-wheat pita bread loaves

7 whole lemons

Cold Poached Red Snapper with Middle Eastern Accompaniments

Red Snapper is a Mediterranean fish, but any firm-fleshed white fish such as salmon or trout will work as well in this three-dish feast. Be sure to read the poaching directions at the beginning of this chapter.

1. Make the jujik and tabbouleh, place them in serving bowls, cover, and refrigerate. Place the fish in a large turkey roaster or similar pot to make sure it fits. Then make a court bouillon: Combine the water, wine, fish bones and heads, onions, carrots, celery, parsley, tarragon, salt, and peppercorns in a large pot. Heat it to a boil and reduce the heat to a low simmer. Partially cover the pot and simmer the bouillon for 30 minutes. Then remove the pot from the heat, uncover it, and allow the bouillon to cool in the pot.

2. Place a rack large enough to support the fish in the bottom of the turkey roaster. Strain the cooled bouillon into the roaster. Hold the fish under cold running water to clean it inside and out.

3. Place the roaster over two burners and turn both on. Heat the bouillon to a boil, then reduce the heat to a medium simmer. Measure the fish at the thickest point.

4. Wrap the fish securely in two layers of cheesecloth and twist the ends to secure them. Place the snapper on the rack so that the ends of the cheesecloth hang over the pot edges. Check to be sure that the liquid covers the fish completely; if not, add equal parts water and wine. The bouillon will stop simmering when the fish is added. When it resumes simmering, begin the cooking, poaching the fish, uncovered, for 10 minutes per inch of thickness.

5. When the fish is done, turn off the burners. With pot holders, pick up the cheesecloth ends and carefully lift the fish out of the bouillon. Place the fish on a platter or tray and let it sit at room temperature until cooled. Remove the cheesecloth when the fish is at room temperature and use paper towels to wipe the fish and tray.

6. Preheat the oven to 350° F. Use a table knife to carefully scrape the top skin off the fish. Score the cucumber with fork tines by running the tines up and down the length of the cucumber several times. Cut the cucumber into thin rounds.

7. Wrap the pita loaves in foil and heat them in the oven for 10 to 15 minutes or until warmed. Meanwhile, arrange the cucumber slices in two overlapping rows down the center of the fish. Place a whole lemon at the upper end of the fish to approximate a head. Cut the remaining lemons into quarters and decorate the platter with them.

8. Place the bowls of jujik and tabbouleh on the table near the snapper. Remove the pita from the oven, arrange the loaves on a serving platter, and take them to the table. Serve immediately.

Note: After the fish has been poached, strain the bouillon, allow it to cool, then freeze it in an ice cube tray. Store the cubes in a plastic bag and use them to enrich fish sauces, aspics, or bouillons.

Makes 6 to 8 servings

Jujik (Turkish Cucumber-Yogurt Salad)

This delightfully cool Turkish cucumber-yogurt salad is a popular accompaniment to many Middle Eastern dishes.

1. Place the coarsely chopped cucumber in the center of a terry cloth or cotton kitchen towel and twist the towel tightly to extract as much liquid as possible. Place the cucumber in a serving bowl.

2. Add the yogurt, garlic to taste, and salt and mix well. Serve chilled.

Makes 6 to 8 servings (about 4½ cups)

INGREDIENTS

2 medium cucumbers, peeled, halved lengthwise, seeded, and chopped coarse
1 quart thick yogurt (pour off any visible liquid)
5–6 cloves garlic, minced fine
1 teaspoon salt

Tabbouleh (Cracked Wheat Salad)

This is a Middle Eastern treat that's especially fun to make for those lucky enough to grow mint in their herb gardens.

1. Place the bulgur in a large salad bowl (glass if possible) and cover it with the cold water. Let stand for 15 minutes or until all the water is absorbed.

2. Add the lemon juice, oil, salt, and mint and toss well to combine. Add the onion, tomatoes, and parsley and toss again thoroughly.

Makes 6 to 8 servings (about 4½ cups)

INGREDIENTS
1 cup bulgur wheat
3 cups cold water
¼ cup freshly squeezed lemon juice
¼ cup good-quality imported olive oil
1 teaspoon salt
⅓ cup finely chopped fresh mint *or* 3 tablespoons dried mint (optional)
1 large onion, chopped fine
2 large firm tomatoes, cored and cut into medium dice
¾ cup finely chopped fresh parsley

INSTANT AIOLI
1 cup prepared mayonnaise
4 cloves garlic, minced fine
¼ cup finely chopped fresh
parsley
Salt to taste (optional)

GARNISH
2 bunches fresh parsley sprigs
2 lemons, quartered

SHELLFISH
½ cup cold water
¼ cup white wine vinegar
1 teaspoon Old Bay Seasoning
or Chesapeake Bay Style
Seasoning
2 pounds medium to large
shrimp

Shirley's Baltimore Shrimp Boil with Aïoli

Shirley Sussman grew up in Baltimore, then moved to the Midwest 10 years ago. An excellent cook, she offered us the recipe for what she described as a typically Baltimore dish. "In Baltimore," she said, "when you don't know what else to make for supper, you make this."

Please note that the title is a misnomer. The shrimp isn't boiled; it's poached. And it's not wholly poached either; it's also steamed. Since very little water is used for poaching, the submerged shrimp poach for half the cooking time while the ones above the water steam. Midway through the cooking the positions of the shrimp are reversed so that all of the shrimp cook by the poach/steam method.

The recipe calls for a commercially available spice mixture sold either as Old Bay Seasoning (Baltimore Spice Co.) or Chesapeake Bay Style Seasoning (McCormick and Co.). The ingredients in both mixtures are similar and include such flavors and aromatics as celery salt or seeds, mustard or mustard flour, pepper, paprika, salt, and other spices.

1. Make the Instant Aïoli: Combine the mayonnaise, garlic, chopped parsley, and salt in a serving bowl and refrigerate.

2. Cover a large platter with the parsley sprigs and lemon quarters. Place the water, wine vinegar, and seasoning mix in a large saucepan and heat to a boil. Add the shrimp. Some will be submerged; some will sit above the liquid.

3. Cook the shrimp, uncovered, at a low simmer for about 3 to 4 minutes or until the shrimp begin to turn pink. Keep stirring the pot vigorously so those shrimp beneath the water are brought above to steam and vice versa.

4. Drain the shrimp and arrange them on the parsley-covered platter. Serve them with Instant Aïoli. Guests peel their own shrimp with their fingers, so provide extra napkins. If desired, add a large salad and French bread slices that have been buttered, sprinkled with freshly grated Parmesan cheese, and browned under the broiler.

Makes 6 servings

Steeped Flounder Fillets with Cider Sauce

This spicy sauce is the perfect accompaniment to the mildly flavored fish.

1. Make the Cider Sauce: Combine the cider, salt, and pepper in a saucepan. Bring the mixture to a boil and reduce the heat to a simmer. Continue cooking for 4 to 5 minutes.

2. Remove the pan from the heat. Cool slightly and whisk in the butter and egg yolks.

3. Transfer the sauce to the top of a double boiler over simmering water and stir until the sauce thickens. Serve hot.

4. Fill a heavy frying pan one-third full of water. Place the orange slices in the pan, cover the pan, and bring the water to a rolling boil over medium heat. Remove the pan from the heat, uncover it, place the flounder fillets over the orange slices, and cover the pan tightly. Steep the fish for 4 to 8 minutes or until it is firm and flakes easily when tested.

5. Drain the flounder, transfer it to individual plates, and serve it hot with Cider Sauce.

Makes 6 servings

CIDER SAUCE
¾ cup apple cider
¼ teaspoon salt
¼ teaspoon freshly ground pepper
4 tablespoons unsalted butter or margarine, cut into ½-inch pieces
2 egg yolks, well beaten

FISH
1 large orange, sliced paper-thin
1 tablespoon grated orange zest
2¼–2½ pounds flounder fillets, cut into 6 serving pieces

INGREDIENTS

1½ pounds baby squid

2 quarts cold water

2 bay leaves

¼ cup good-quality imported olive oil

¼ cup freshly squeezed lime juice

1 tablespoon finely minced lime zest

2 cloves garlic, minced

2 tablespoons minced fresh parsley

2 teaspoons dried oregano

Italian-Style Squid Salad

This delicious cold squid salad must be prepared several hours in advance of serving. Serve it as an appetizer, a luncheon dish, or a first course.

1. Clean the squid according to the directions in the box. Cut the squid into ½-inch rings using a sharp scissors.

2. Place the water in a large pot, uncovered, add the bay leaves, and heat to a boil. Reduce the heat to a low simmer. Slide the squid rings into the simmering water and poach them for 2 minutes, watching them constantly. As soon as the rings turn white and lose their opaque appearance, transfer them quickly to a bowl of cold water to stop the cooking.

3. When the squid rings are cool, drain them, pat them dry with paper towels, and place them in a large glass bowl. Mix olive oil, lime juice and zest, garlic, parsley, and oregano in a small bowl. Pour the dressing over the squid rings and toss to combine. Cover the bowl and place it in the refrigerator for 4 to 6 hours before serving.

Makes 6 servings

TIPS FOR CLEANING BABY OR MEDIUM-SIZE SQUID

• To separate the mantle (body) from the tentacles, hold the body in one hand and use the other hand to hold the tentacles just above the eyes. Gently pull the two sections apart. To clean the body portion, remove the transparent sword-shaped quill called the *pen*, a rudimentary bone in the back of the body that you'll be able to feel when you hold the body. Make a small cut at the top of the bony portion, then squeeze or pull the pen out and discard it.

- Next, insert a spoon or your finger into the mantle, scooping out any remaining matter. Rinse the body under cold running water and then peel off the outer membrane. The meat underneath will be snow white in color. Finally, pull the fins away from the body.
- If you wish to use the tentacles in any of the stuffed squid recipes, clean them as follows: Cut the eye section away from the arms and discard the eyes. In the center of the tentacles, at the base, you'll feel a small, hard bone. This is the beak. Squeeze it out by applying pressure with both thumbs. When the tentacle portion is cleaned, chop it finely and brown it in a little butter, then add it to the stuffing you've made.

INGREDIENTS

1¾ quarts water, or enough to cover fish
1½ cups dry white wine
1 large carrot, sliced
2 medium onions, sliced
¼ cup fresh chopped parsley
2 bay leaves
1 teaspoon salt
5 black peppercorns
6 ¾-inch-thick salmon steaks
2 egg whites, beaten to soft peaks
1 eggshell, broken into pieces
6 3-inch-long scallion stems, halved lengthwise
24 carrot slices, each the thickness of a quarter
Green or black olive slices, pickle slices, capers, and thin lemon slices, for garnish (optional)
4½ teaspoons unflavored gelatin
Boiled Potatoes with Dill (recipe follows)
Blueberry Pie with Lemon Crust (recipe follows)

Boston Red, White, and Blue Fourth of July Feast

In Boston on the Fourth of July many families insist on a red, white, and blue picnic, which consists traditionally of red salmon, white potatoes, and blueberry pie. You can simply grill the salmon beforehand, then serve it chilled, as is usually done. Or you can make this elegant version, which includes chilled poached salmon steaks covered with aspic and decorated with edible flowers.

1. In a fish poacher or large soup pot, bring the water, wine, carrot, onions, parsley, bay leaves, salt, and peppercorns to a boil over medium-high heat.

2. Reduce the heat to a hard simmer. Simmer the liquid for 15 minutes, partially covered, then carefully add three salmon steaks to the poaching liquid, sliding them off a spatula. Cook the steaks for 7 to 8 minutes and check for doneness by pulling up a corner of one steak to see if it's cooked through. Then check the remaining two steaks. If additional poaching is needed, check to see that you have enough liquid.

3. Transfer the steaks to a platter using a slotted spoon and let them cool to room temperature. Repeat with the remaining three steaks. Measure out 3 cups of the poaching liquid and reserve it for the aspic.

4. Make the aspic: Strain the poaching liquid into a medium saucepan. Heat it over medium heat and add the beaten egg whites and eggshell. Heat the liquid to a boil and immediately turn off the heat. Stir a few times until the foam comes to the surface.

5. Remove the pan from the heat and let it stand for 8 minutes. Strain through four thicknesses of cheesecloth set in a colander.

6. Decorate the tops of the salmon steaks, making flowers or other designs using the scallion stems and carrot slices and, if desired, olive and pickle slices and capers.

7. Return the aspic to a clean saucepan and heat over medium heat until boiling. Remove it from the heat and stir in the gelatin, mixing until it dissolves completely. Transfer the aspic to a larger metal bowl set in a pan of ice water. The aspic will begin to thicken. When it reaches the consistency of heavy egg whites, spoon it carefully over the salmon steaks.

8. Place the steaks in the refrigerator to set for at least 4 hours. Transport the salmon steaks to the picnic site in a single layer in a baking pan (make sure fish stays cold in transport). Serve with cold boiled potatoes and blueberry pie. (Recipes follow.)

Makes 6 servings

Boiled Potatoes with Dill

Fresh dill adds wonderful flavor to new potatoes.

1. Wash the potatoes well and cut a thin slice from the bottom and top of each potato. Put the potatoes into a medium saucepan and cover them with cold water. Sprinkle with the salt and pepper.

2. Bring the water to a boil over medium heat. Reduce the heat to a simmer and continue cooking until the potatoes are tender when pierced with a fork or the tip of a sharp knife. Strain the potatoes, discarding the water.

3. Toss the hot potatoes with the butter and place them in a serving dish. Sprinkle them with dill and serve immediately or chill them and serve them cold at a picnic.

Makes 6 servings

INGREDIENTS
1½ pounds small boiling
   potatoes
½ teaspoon salt
¼ teaspoon freshly ground
   pepper
2 tablespoons unsalted butter
   or margarine
3 tablespoons minced fresh
   dill

CRUST

1¾ cups all-purpose flour
½ teaspoon salt
1 teaspoon grated lemon zest
6 tablespoons unsalted butter,
    cut into ½-inch pieces
6 tablespoons vegetable
    shortening
5–7 tablespoons ice water

FILLING

4 cups fresh blueberries
2½ tablespoons tapioca or
    cornstarch
1 cup sugar
1 teaspoon grated lemon zest
2 teaspoons freshly squeezed
    lemon juice
3 tablespoons milk
2 tablespoons sugar

Blueberry Pie with Lemon Crust

Tart lemon in the crust makes this a blueberry pie with a twist.

1. Make the crust: Use a food processor fitted with the steel blade or make the crust in a bowl and use a pastry blender or two knives. Put the flour into the food processor or bowl. Add the salt, lemon zest, butter, and shortening. Process or use a pastry blender until the mixture is blended and the dough is in small pieces. With the machine running, add the water through the feed tube (or pour in the water and mix in with a pastry blender or fork); the pastry will form a dough ball. Wrap the dough ball in aluminum foil and chill it for 45 minutes before using it.

2. Divide the dough in half. On a lightly floured board, roll out each piece to a circle ½ inch larger than a 9½-inch pie plate. Fit one piece into the pie plate and set aside. Preheat the oven to 375° F.

3. Place the blueberries in a deep mixing bowl and top them with the tapioca, sugar, lemon zest, and juice. Mound the mixture in the pie shell. Fit the remaining dough circle over the pie. Seal the edges decoratively and cut a ½-inch steam vent in the top crust.

4. Mix the milk and sugar together and brush the mixture over the pie. Bake the pie for 35 to 40 minutes; it should be golden brown. Cool the pie on a rack and serve it warm or cold, with vanilla ice cream if desired.

Makes 1 9½-inch pie

SERVING RAW

SALTING

Salting was originally a method of food preservation. The salt drew out moisture by osmosis, making the food less receptive to bacteria; it also provided a harsh environment of its own, retarding the growth of surface bacteria as well.

Although we no longer need salt to preserve food, we're so used to the textures and flavors that salt-preserved dishes offer that we continue to enjoy them anyway. In our version of gravlax, however, the fish is not salted heavily enough or for a long enough time to preserve it. The salt merely adds character, flavor, and a textural change: the fish is firmer and chewier because the salt has drawn out some of the moisture.

ACID COOKING (PICKLING)

Foods like cucumbers were originally submerged in acidic liquids like vinegar to preserve them. Much of the moisture in pickles is vinegar, not cucumber juice.

Fish flesh, however, is so delicate that when it's submerged in acidic liquids like vinegar, lemon juice, or lime juice the acid "cooks" the fish, causing the protein to coagulate as surely as if it had been exposed to direct heat. In fact, you cannot tell by looking whether fish has been cooked over heat or "cooked" in lemon juice, except that the acid-cooked fish is not browned.

Since fish flesh varies from the very strong (e.g., shark) to the very delicate (e.g., whitefish), we do not recommend using our proportions of lemon juice or vinegar to fish for any variety other than what is called for in the recipe.

RAW FISH

The Japanese swear by raw fish, and so do Americans who develop the sushi or the Salmon Tartare habit. Our recipe for Salmon Tartare calls merely for absolutely fresh fish that has no discernible fishy odor (see "How to Buy Fish"). The raw fish is then chopped fine and mixed with other ingredients for flavor. Our Salmon Tartare recipe can also be made with other fish (see "Fish Species" for our chart of fish that will substitute for each other well). Note: Raw fish occasionally contains parasites that can cause illness. You can minimize this if you purchase the fish from a reputable, trusted fishmonger.

DRIED FISH

Along with salting and pickling, fish were also originally dried to preserve them. Removing the liquid from the fish flesh was an effective way of discouraging bacteria, which thrive in a moist environment.

Since so many delicious recipes evolved to accommodate dried fish, people are reluctant to give up the preservation method, even though the need for preserving the foods has long since been eliminated with refrigeration and freezers.

Although any type of dried fish will work in our recipe for Sea'nd Pollack, we recommend using only dried pollack, which is the original fish around which the recipe developed. Changing the type of dried fish will change the character of the dish.

Tips for Serving Raw

1. Serve fish in a chilled bowl or on chopped ice in a larger bowl to prevent spoilage.

2. Leftover fish is perfect as a garnish or as an addition to almost any salad.

Classic Pickled Herring

Herring is an inexpensive treat. It's also wonderfully versatile, as shown by the variations of this dish in the following two recipes.

1. Slice the herring into 1½-inch pieces. Arrange the herring and onions in layers in a 1- or 1½-quart jar and set aside.

2. Make the marinade: Mix together the vinegar, water, pickling spices, bay leaves, and sugar in a saucepan. Bring the marinade to a boil over medium heat. Remove the pan from the heat and cool the marinade completely.

3. Pour the cooled marinade over the herring. If more liquid is needed to cover the herring and onions, pack the herring more tightly into the jar and/or add water to just cover the fish.

4. Cover the jar and refrigerate it for 4 to 6 days before serving.

Makes 4 to 5 cups

FISH
1–1¼ pounds herring, cleaned
   and scaled, heads and tails
   discarded
1 large red or white onion,
   sliced thin

MARINADE
2½ cups white vinegar
1¼ cups cold water
2 tablespoons pickling spices
2 bay leaves
3 tablespoons sugar

INGREDIENTS
1 recipe Classic Pickled
   Herring (minus the onions)
2 cups sour cream
½ teaspoon celery seed
1 cup seedless grapes (any
   variety), washed, drained,
   and halved

INGREDIENTS
1 tablespoon sugar
3 tablespoons white vinegar
2 slices white bread
½ recipe Classic Pickled
   Herring
1 large apple, peeled, cored,
   and chopped
2 hard-cooked eggs, peeled
   and chopped

Herring Fillets with Sour Cream

*With thin slices of rye bread, this dish makes a superb appetizer
or buffet item.*

1. Drain the pickled herring and cut it into 1-inch
pieces. Arrange a single layer of herring in a bowl and
spread it with sour cream. Continue layering herring and
sour cream until all have been used. Sprinkle with celery seed.
Cover with wax paper and refrigerate the herring overnight.

2. To serve, toss the creamed herring and grapes in a
serving bowl or dish.

Makes 4 to 5 cups

Chopped Herring

Delicious with crackers or thin slices of dark rye bread.

1. Combine the sugar and vinegar in a small bowl. Soak
the bread in the sugar/vinegar mixture for 15 minutes.

2. Put the pickled herring, including onion rings, in a
food processor fitted with the steel blade and pulse for 15
seconds or until minced. Add the drained bread, apple, and
eggs. Pulse for 8 to 10 seconds. Place the chopped herring
in a serving bowl, cover, and chill until serving time.

Makes 3 cups

Rollmops

Herring roll-ups make a delightful first course or an interesting-looking dish on a buffet table. These must be refrigerated for four or five days, so plan ahead!

1. Cover the herring with water in a large ceramic bowl. Soak it overnight, changing the water once. Drain, rinse well, and pat dry. Remove all visible bones, using sterilized tweezers reserved for this purpose.

2. Combine the vinegar, water, juniper berries, peppercorns, and bay leaves in a saucepan. Bring to a boil over medium heat. Remove the pot from the heat and let the mixture cool.

3. Arrange the herring flesh side up on the counter. Spread it with mustard, sprinkle with onion, and put one slice of pickle on the end of each fillet. Roll up the herring and secure shut with a toothpick. Set the herring rolls in a ceramic dish, pour the marinade over them, and cover with wax paper or plastic wrap. Refrigerate for 4 to 5 days before serving. Serve two rollmops per person as a first course or on a buffet table.

Makes 6 servings

INGREDIENTS
12 small matjes herring
2½ cups cider vinegar
2½ cups cold water
1 teaspoon juniper berries, crushed
½ teaspoon peppercorns, crushed
2 bay leaves
3–5 tablespoons German mustard
1 large onion, chopped
3 medium dill pickles (any variety), quartered lengthwise

INGREDIENTS

2 pounds whitefish fillets
3 large onions, sliced thin
½ cup cold water
½ teaspoon ground ginger
2½ tablespoons freshly
squeezed lemon juice
1 cup sugar
2¼ cups cider vinegar
1 large lemon *or* 2 limes, sliced
thin
¾ teaspoon salt
¼ teaspoon freshly ground
pepper
¾ cup chopped pitted prunes
½ teaspoon whole cloves,
crushed
½ teaspoon black peppercorns,
crushed
¼ teaspoon red pepper flakes
3 bay leaves

Deli-Pickled Whitefish Strips

Trout would work just as well as whitefish in this tangy dish, which makes a perfect appetizer.

1. Cut the whitefish fillets into 2-inch strips. Arrange them in layers with the sliced onions in a heavy pot. Set aside.

2. Mix together the water, ginger, lemon juice, and sugar in a saucepan. Cook over medium heat for 5 minutes or until the liquid begins to brown. Add the vinegar and reduce the heat to a simmer. Add the lemon slices, salt, pepper, prunes, cloves, peppercorns, red pepper flakes, and bay leaves. Continue cooking for 4 minutes.

3. Pour the hot sauce over the fish and onions. Bring the mixture to a boil over medium heat, cover, and simmer for 20 minutes. Cool.

4. With a slotted spoon, place the fish in a ceramic dish. Pour the remaining liquid over the whitefish and discard the bay leaves.

5. Cover lightly and chill overnight before serving.

Makes 6 to 8 servings

Sweet and Sour Mackerel

Raisins add texture and interest to this Oriental-flavored dish. Serve it for brunch or as an entree with a crisp, green salad.

1. Arrange the onion and lemon slices in a large, heavy saucepan. Add the mackerel pieces. Sprinkle with crumbs, vinegar, raisins, and sugar. Add cold water to cover the fish.

2. Heat the mixture to a boil over medium heat. Reduce the heat to a simmer. Cover the pot and continue cooking until the fish is tender, about 40 to 45 minutes. Stir twice, gently, using a wooden spoon. Cool the mackerel.

3. Place the mackerel mixture in a heavy glass or ceramic dish. Cover with wax paper and chill until ready to serve.

Makes 6 to 8 servings

INGREDIENTS
3 onions, sliced thin
1 large lemon, sliced thin
2½–3 pounds mackerel, cleaned, head and tail discarded, cut into 1-inch rounds
1 cup gingersnap crumbs
2 tablespoons white vinegar
¾ cup dark raisins
½ cup sugar

INGREDIENTS

1½–1¾ pounds center-cut
  salmon fillet, cut into 1- to
  1½-inch chunks
3 cups milk
1 cup sugar
1 large red onion, sliced thin
2¼ cups white vinegar
½ cup cold water
2 bay leaves
½ teaspoon white peppercorns,
  crushed
2 teaspoons pickling spices
1½ cups sour cream

Sara Bluestein's Salmon Chunks in Cream Marinade

This is an old family recipe that has graced many a holiday table.

1. Check the salmon, removing any remaining bones with sterilized tweezers reserved for this purpose. Place the salmon in a deep ceramic bowl and cover it with the milk. Mix in ¼ cup of the sugar. Cover lightly with wax paper and chill overnight. Drain and rinse the salmon under cold running water.

2. Mix together the remaining sugar and the onions, vinegar, water, bay leaves, peppercorns, and pickling spices. Toss the marinade with the salmon. Cover lightly and refrigerate for 48 hours, tossing each day.

3. Drain and reserve the marinade. Blend ⅓ cup of the marinade with the sour cream. Toss the cream mixture with the salmon. Place in a serving bowl and serve with a green salad.

Makes 6 servings

Gravlax

Sugar- and salt-cured salmon Scandinavian style with lots of dill.
Slice it paper-thin, across the grain and serve with brown bread
and grainy mustard for a real treat. It will keep in the refrigerator
for 4 or 5 days.

1. Check the salmon for bones and remove any remaining with sterilized tweezers reserved for this purpose. Arrange one-third of the dill in the bottom of a large ceramic dish. Set one slice of salmon, skin side down, over the dill.

2. Mix together the salt, sugar, and peppercorns. Sprinkle half the mixture over the salmon. Lay another third of the dill over the salmon. Place the remaining salmon on top. Sprinkle with the remaining seasonings and the brandy or aquavit. Place the remaining third of the dill on top of the salmon.

3. Cover the fish with a sheet of aluminum foil. Place a weight, such as a clean brick reserved for this purpose or large cans of food, on the foil to press the fish. Refrigerate the salmon for 2 to 3 days; drain any liquid that accumulates. Turn the fish over once a day.

4. To serve, remove the dill and peppercorns and cut the salmon into thin slices off the skin. Serve with mustard and rye bread. You may want to garnish it with dill sprigs.

Makes 4 to 6 servings

INGREDIENTS
2 1- to 1½-pound center-cut
  salmon fillets, scaled, skin
  left intact
2 bunches fresh dill, trimmed
¼ cup kosher salt
¼ cup sugar
1 teaspoon white peppercorns,
  crushed
2 tablespoons brandy or
  aquavit

INGREDIENTS

1½ pounds center-cut salmon
   fillet (must be freshest
   available: explain to
   fishmonger that it's to be
   eaten raw)
Freshly squeezed juice of 4
   limes
2 red onions, minced
1¼ cups minced cilantro
¼ teaspoon each Tabasco
   sauce, Dijon mustard, and
   freshly ground pepper
½ teaspoon salt
2 tablespoons drained large
   capers
4 hard-cooked eggs, white and
   yolks chopped separately
1 red onion, minced

Salmon Steak Tartare

Ground salmon with spices on rye makes an excellent appetizer.

1. Hand chop or grind the salmon with the lime juice and one of the onions in a food processor until medium fine. Mix in the cilantro, Tabasco, mustard, pepper, and salt. Shape into a mound in the center of a serving plate.

2. Garnish the salmon mound with the capers, chopped egg yolks, chopped egg whites, and remaining red onion. Serve chilled with thin slices of rye bread or crackers.

Makes 6 servings

Seviche with Bay Scallops

The bay scallops gently "cook" in this fresh lime marinade.

1. Wash and pat the scallops dry with paper towels. Place the scallops in a large, deep glass or ceramic bowl and toss them with the lime juice, olive oil, tomatoes, avocado, onion, garlic, cilantro, salt, and cayenne. Cover with wax paper and chill for 48 hours, stirring twice daily.

2. When ready to serve, arrange a lettuce leaf on a chilled salad plate. Mound with seviche and serve immediately.

Makes 6 to 8 servings

INGREDIENTS
1¾ pounds bay scallops
Freshly squeezed juice of 4
   limes
6 tablespoons extra-virgin
   olive oil
2 medium tomatoes, peeled,
   seeded, and chopped
1 large avocado, peeled,
   pitted, and chopped
1 medium red onion, chopped
2 cloves garlic, minced
⅓ cup chopped cilantro
½ teaspoon salt
¼ teaspoon cayenne pepper (or
   to taste)
8 small lettuce leaves

INGREDIENTS

1 2¼-ounce package dried
  pollack, cut into the
  thinnest possible strips with
  scissors
½ cup Korean hot bean paste
4 teaspoons mild (Japanese)
  soy sauce
2 tablespoons water
2 teaspoons dark sesame oil
4 teaspoons sugar
½ teaspoon sesame seed, for
  garnish

Sea'nd Pollack

*This Korean delicacy, usually served as an appetizer, is most
unusual. It's made by combining Korean hot bean paste (a
piquant, bright red, delicious bean puree) with garlic, Oriental
sesame oil, a little sugar, and a package of dried pollack that has
been torn into shreds. Strange as the dish sounds, it is absolutely
delicious and a favorite Korean specialty.*

*Korean hot bean paste (do not confuse this with Oriental red
bean paste) and dried pollack are available at Korean food shops.
Or see our list of mail order sources in the Appendix.*

1. Place the shredded pollack in a bowl. Mix the hot
bean paste, soy sauce, water, sesame oil, and sugar in a
separate bowl and stir well.

2. Add ⅓ cup hot bean dressing to the pollack and toss to
combine. Taste and add up to 2 tablespoons more dressing
if desired.

3. Toast the sesame seeds: Place the seeds in a single
layer in a frying pan over medium heat and let sit for 30
seconds. As soon as the seeds are hot, shake the pan.
Continue shaking until the seeds begin to take on color.
Remove the pan from the heat. The seeds will continue to
darken as they cook from internal heat for a few moments.

4. Sprinkle the toasted sesame seeds over the pollack
mixture and serve on a platter.

Makes 4 to 6 servings

SAUTEING AND STIR-FRYING

SAUTEING

Sautéing is a dry-heat cooking method in which food pieces are shaken rapidly in a pan containing hot fat until they're lightly fried on all sides. The word *sauté* comes from the French verb *sauter*—to jump—and is so much a part of French cooking that some French restaurants even have a chef specializing in sautéed preparations.

Fish

Whatever the fish being sautéed, the most important thing is that it be cut into small, equal-size pieces so it will sauté quickly and all the pieces will be done at the same time. Before sautéing fish, dry it on both sides with paper towels. The drier the fish the less steam it will produce to interfere with the sautéing process.

Equipment

In France a special pan called a *sautoir* is specially designed for sautéing; it has sides that are higher than those of most frying pans to prevent the food from falling out during the constant motion. French chefs use attractive, tin-lined copper pans because copper is a superior heat conductor. But any frying pan can be used to sauté, provided it conducts heat evenly and has no hot spots—places in the pan bottom that conduct heat so fast that they cause sticking and burning.

The Fat

Since sautéing demands high heat—about 325° F—plain butter, which has a smoke point of 250° F, is not a good sautéing medium. Since vegetable oil has a higher smoke point than butter, many chefs use a combination of the two (either half and half or three parts butter to four parts oil), which puts the smoke point somewhere in between. Or you can clarify the butter (see Index), which will raise butter's smoke point to 350° F.

Method

Step 1: Cut ingredients to be sautéed into small pieces, taking care that they are as equal in size as possible. Add the fat to the pan and place it over high heat. When the fat is hot, add the ingredients.

Step 2: As soon as the food pieces hit the hot fat,

take hold of the pan handle and begin shaking the pan back and forth rapidly, but in a controlled way, while holding it over the burner. The movement should be so vigorous that the food jumps up into the air above the pan, but not so wild that it falls over the side.

Step 3: Once the food pieces are cooked, remove the pan from the heat. At this point additional foods and liquids may be added for further cooking. Or the food can be taken from the pan and the pan then deglazed (see below).

To Deglaze a Pan

When foods are sautéed, they often leave a flavorful residue in the pan that can be added to the sauce. While the pan stays hot, the food pieces scrape off easily. But once the pan begins cooling, its metal pores close and trap the food bits.

Add ¼ cup hot water or wine to the empty pan and place it over high heat. Use a wooden spoon or spatula to scrape up all the solids and bits from the pan bottom and sides. When this is done, add additional ingredients for the sauce. Or the bits and pan juices can be scraped into a bowl for later use.

STIR-FRYING

Stir-frying, a dry-heat cooking method, is similar to sautéing in that the food is kept in constant motion in the air above the pan. Stir-fried food, however, is tossed up into the air with a spatula and ladle or similar utensils. Stir-frying is an Oriental technique.

Fish

Fish with tensile strength (fish that is not so soft that it falls apart when handled) is perfect for stir-frying. Cooked pasta and rice as well as raw vegetables are also often stir-fried with the fish. In stir-frying vegetables and fish, though, the most important thing to remember is that the pieces should be cut small (usually no more than 1 inch) and evenly sized. Oriental chefs enjoy arranging small piles of ingredients to be stir-fried on a single tray for convenience and eye appeal. The tray can be brought to the table for stir-frying right in front of the guests.

Equipment

Stir-frying is usually done in a traditional Chinese pan called a *wok*, which usually has a rounded bottom. Made of thin metal, it conducts heat quickly. The rounded bottom also helps the food fall back into the center once it's been tossed into the air.

Woks with rounded bottoms sit more easily on stove tops if they rest in a wok ring that acts as a stabilizing collar. The ring supports the wok and holds it in place so it doesn't tip over.

Stir-frying can be done in a large frying pan, but it will take a little longer and use a little more oil than it would if done in a wok.

The spatula designed for stir-frying resembles a small shovel and conforms to the wok shape for maximum efficiency. Both the spatula and the ladle meant for stir-frying—which resembles a wide spoon—are long-handled. If you don't have a spatula and ladle designed for use with a wok, you can use a wooden or cooking spoon and a plain spatula.

The Fat: Peanut oil or vegetable oil is always used for stir-frying, probably because most stir-fried recipes are Oriental and oil is the preferred medium in Asia. Sometimes a few drops of Oriental sesame oil are added to the vegetable oil for flavor.

Method

Step 1: Cut the ingredients and place them on a tray near the wok along with the serving platter and serving utensils. Place the wok ring on the burner, then set the seasoned wok (see below for seasoning directions) in the wok ring.

Step 2: Add the oil to the pan and heat the burner underneath. As soon as the oil is hot, add the food as directed. A few seconds after the food has been put into the hot oil, begin the stir-frying motion.

Step 3: Holding the ladle in one hand and the spatula in the other, use the two together to pick up food from the bottom of the wok and toss it lightly in the air. Use a lift-and-drop motion, as if you were tossing a green salad. Continue tossing the food in this manner for as long as the recipe directs. Then transfer the cooked food to a serving platter.

To Season a Wok

Seasoning a wok will seal the metal pores and prevent food from sticking to the wok. For teflon woks, there is no need to season.

Begin by washing the new wok thoroughly with hot water and detergent. This is especially necessary with new woks because many manufacturers add a protective coating of oil before shipping.

Lay a wok ring over a stove burner. Then place the empty wok in the wok ring. Light the burner (either gas or electric burners are fine) and let the wok sit over medium heat for 15 to 20 minutes. It will get very hot. Turn off the burners and allow the wok to cool, then rub it inside with cooking oil, using paper towels to sponge off the excess.

Use a seasoned wok as needed to cook in; after cooking, rinse it (do not use soap), wipe it out with paper towels, and dry it over low heat for 30 to 60 seconds to prevent rusting. Some cooks add a thin coating of oil each time the wok is used.

Tips for Sautéing and Stir-Frying

1. Be sure that food for both sautéing and stir-frying is cut into equal-size pieces so they cook within the same few minutes.

2. Be sure that the oil is very hot, whether stir-frying or sautéing. Food pieces will absorb tepid oil rather than fry in it.

3. Use a long-handled spatula to avoid burns, as the oil can spatter.

INGREDIENTS

1 teaspoon salt
1 pound linguine
¼ cup extra-virgin olive oil
1 tablespoon unsalted butter
3 cloves garlic, minced
¼ teaspoon each red pepper flakes, salt, and dried oregano
⅛ teaspoon freshly ground black pepper
2 pounds baby squid, cleaned and squid arms separated from body by fishmonger
½ cup fine bread crumbs
2 teaspoons chopped fresh parsley

Linguine with Sautéed Squid

This is a workable recipe for people who need a good-tasting dish in a hurry, as it takes just minutes from kitchen to table. Serve it as an appetizer or side dish to six or as an entree to four.

This recipe uses only the arms of baby squid, not the main portion. Freeze unused portions for use in other dishes such as Stir Fried Squid (recipe follows).

1. Half-fill a large pot with water, add 1 teaspoon salt, and heat to a boil. Add the linguine and cook it until it's just tender but not mushy (use the package directions as a guide, but check it often while it's cooking).

2. When the pasta is cooked, pour it into a colander and quickly run cold water over it to stop the cooking. Let the pasta sit in the colander until ready to serve.

3. Half-fill a large pot with water and heat it to a boil. This will be poured over the pasta to reheat it immediately before serving.

4. Place the olive oil and the tablespoon of butter in a medium saucepan and heat it over medium heat. When the fat is hot, add the garlic, red pepper flakes, salt, oregano, and black pepper. Stir constantly with a wooden spoon, taking care that the mixture does not burn.

5. Add the squid arms and sauté, shaking the pan back and forth over the heat. After 2 minutes, add the bread crumbs and parsley and sauté for another 2 minutes, shaking the pan back and forth.

6. Immediately pour the pot of hot water over the linguine in the colander and shake the colander until the water has drained out. Pour the linguine into a serving platter and use a wooden spoon to make a flat bed. Spoon the squid arms and sauce over the pasta and toss lightly. Serve immediately.

Makes 6 servings

Stir-Fried Squid

Here is a wonderfully quick, low-fat method of preparing tender squid.

1. Heat the oil in a wok or heavy skillet. Add the garlic, ginger, onion, and pepper flakes and stir-fry for 2 to 3 minutes. Add the green pepper and carrots and stir-fry for 3 minutes. Mix in the squid rings and stir-fry until the squid turns white, about 2 minutes. Sprinkle with soy sauce, and serve over hot, fluffy rice noodles.

Makes 4 servings

INGREDIENTS
3 tablespoons peanut oil
2 cloves garlic, minced
2 ¼-inch slices peeled fresh gingerroot, minced
1 medium red onion, sliced thin
¼ teaspoon red pepper flakes
1 large green bell pepper, seeded and sliced into ½-inch strips
3 medium carrots, peeled and sliced thin
1 pound squid, cleaned and cut with scissors into ¼-inch rings
2 tablespoons light soy sauce

ZINFANDEL SAUCE
1¼ pounds bones from nonoily fish
1 small onion, minced
2 bay leaves
3 large mushrooms, trimmed
½ teaspoon dried thyme
1¾ cups zinfandel
2 cups heavy cream

SHELLFISH
1 medium zucchini
5 tablespoons unsalted butter or margarine
¼ teaspoon each salt, freshly ground pepper, and garlic powder
2¼ pounds sea scallops

Sautéed Sea Scallops with Zinfandel Sauce

Zinfandel adds a nice flavor to this rich cream sauce. This combination of fish and rosé is nontraditional, but delicious.

1. Make the Zinfandel Sauce: Place the bones in a stockpot. Add the onion, bay leaves, mushrooms, thyme, and zinfandel. Cook at medium heat for 5 to 10 minutes. Continue cooking until the mixture is reduced, leaving only ¼ cup of liquid. Strain the sauce, return the liquid to a medium saucepan, and discard the solids.

2. Stir the cream into the saucepan and simmer until the mixture is reduced slightly, about 5 minutes, stirring occasionally. Leave the sauce in the pan until ready to serve.

3. Shred the zucchini using a food processor fitted with the shredding disc. Blanch the zucchini in boiling salted water. Drain the zucchini, rinse it under cold running water, and drain it again.

4. Melt 2¼ tablespoons of the butter in a heavy frying pan. Stir in the zucchini and season it with the salt, pepper, and garlic powder. Continue cooking over medium heat for 3 to 4 minutes, stirring constantly. Divide the zucchini among six warmed plates.

5. Melt the remaining butter in a large frying pan. Sauté the scallops in two batches for about 2 minutes on both sides until they are opaque. Arrange the scallops over the bed of zucchini on each plate. Drizzle the warm sauce over and around the scallops and serve immediately.

Makes 6 servings

Stir-Fried Scallops with Oriental Sauce

Small, delicate bay scallops are heavenly in this Oriental-flavored dish. You'll find the fermented black beans in Oriental food stores or most large supermarkets.

1. Mix the sauce ingredients together and set aside.

2. Toss the scallops, wine, salt, and pepper in a shallow bowl; marinate the scallops in this mixture for 20 minutes.

3. Heat 4 tablespoons of the oil in a wok. Add the scallops and stir-fry until they are almost cooked; reserve.

4. Heat the remaining oil in the wok. Add the garlic and ginger and stir-fry for 10 seconds.

5. Add the scallions and black beans and stir-fry for 15 seconds. Add the pork and green pepper and stir-fry until cooked, about 2 minutes.

6. Add the sauce and cook until slightly thickened. Add the eggs, but do not stir. Cover the wok and cook the mixture for 1 minute. Remove the cover and stir to combine. Serve with hot, fluffy rice.

Makes 4 to 5 servings

ORIENTAL SAUCE
2 teaspoons cornstarch
1 tablespoon Oriental soy
  sauce
2 teaspoons light soy sauce
1 teaspoon dark sesame oil
½ cup chicken stock

SHELLFISH
1½ pounds bay scallops
2 tablespoons dry white wine
½ teaspoon salt
¼ teaspoon freshly ground
  pepper
6 tablespoons peanut oil
3 cloves garlic, minced
¼ teaspoon ground ginger
4 scallions, chopped
1½ tablespoons fermented
  black beans, washed, rinsed,
  and mashed
½ pound ground pork
1 green bell pepper, seeded
  and sliced
2 eggs, beaten

MARINADE
2 egg whites, slightly beaten
2 tablespoons cornstarch
2 teaspoons light soy sauce
2 tablespoons peanut oil
¼ teaspoon salt
¼ teaspoon freshly ground pepper

FISH
1¾ pounds pike fillet, cut into 1-inch strips
6 tablespoons peanut oil
½ teaspoon grated fresh gingerroot
3 tablespoons dry white wine
3 cloves garlic, minced
1 onion, sliced thin
½ cup chopped celery
1 pound bok choy, trimmed and cut into ½-inch pieces
½ teaspoon salt
¼ teaspoon freshly ground pepper
¼ cup chicken stock mixed with 2 teaspoons cornstarch
1 tablespoon light soy sauce
1 teaspoon Oriental sesame oil

Stir-Fried Pike with Bok Choy

Check the Appendix for information about Oriental ingredients. They are available by mail order and in most Chinese grocery stores or large food markets.

1. Mix the marinade ingredients together in a shallow dish. Add the fish and marinate it at room temperature for 1 hour, turning it after 30 minutes.

2. Heat 3 tablespoons of the oil in a wok or heavy frying pan over medium-high heat. Add the ginger and stir-fry it for 10 seconds. Drain the fish and discard the marinade. Add the fish to the wok and stir-fry it for 5 minutes. Add the wine and continue stir-frying until the fish is cooked, about 1 minute. Fish should be firm and flake easily when tested. Remove the fish from the wok and set it aside.

3. Heat the remaining oil in the wok over medium-high heat. Stir in the garlic and onion and stir-fry for 1 minute. Add the celery and bok choy and stir-fry for 3 minutes. Season with salt and pepper. Stir in the stock, soy sauce, and sesame oil. Mix in the fish and stir until the fish is heated. Serve hot with white rice.

Makes 5 to 6 servings

Mahimahi Chow Mein

The firm texture of this popular Hawaiian fish makes it ideal for sautéing as it won't fall apart. You can find oyster sauce in jars in Oriental food stores.

1. Mix the sauce ingredients together in a small bowl and set aside.

2. Heat 2 tablespoons of the oil in a wok or heavy frying pan over medium-high heat; sprinkle with salt. Add the eggs and stir-fry them until scrambled. Remove the eggs from the wok and reserve.

3. Heat the remaining oil in the wok, add the garlic, and stir-fry for 30 seconds. Add the bean sprouts, celery, and water chestnuts and stir-fry for 3 minutes. Add the mahimahi and stir-fry until the fish flakes easily when tested. Sprinkle with red pepper flakes. Mix in the noodles and stir-fry until hot. Serve immediately.

Makes 4 to 5 servings

SAUCE
1 tablespoon oyster sauce
1 tablespoon cornstarch
¼ cup chicken stock
¾ teaspoon Oriental sesame oil
¼ teaspoon salt
¼ teaspoon freshly ground
    pepper

FISH
4 tablespoons peanut oil
½ teaspoon salt
2 eggs, beaten
3 cloves garlic, minced
1 cup fresh bean sprouts,
    washed under hot running
    water and drained
1 cup sliced celery
¾ cup sliced water chestnuts
1¼ pounds mahimahi fillets,
    cut into ½-inch pieces
¼ teaspoon red pepper flakes
½ pound whole wheat
    noodles, cooked according
    to package directions and
    drained

MILD TOMATILLO SAUCE
3 tablespoons peanut oil
6 whole scallions, minced
1 10-ounce can tomatillos
¼ teaspoon each salt, freshly
   ground pepper, and garlic
   powder
1 4-ounce can mild green
   chilies, drained, and
   chopped
1 cup sour cream

FISH
2 cups all-purpose flour
½ teaspoon salt
½ teaspoon dried tarragon
¼ teaspoon freshly ground
   white pepper
1¼ cups milk
2¼–2½ pounds Dover sole
   fillets, cut into 6 serving
   pieces
1 tablespoon peanut oil
3 tablespoons unsalted butter

Sautéed Dover Sole with Mild Tomatillo Sauce

Tomatillos, small green fruits resembling tomatoes, are available at Mexican grocery stores and many supermarkets. Fresh tomatillos and chilies are even better than canned, so feel free to substitute for the canned ingredients below when fresh are available.

1. Make the Mild Tomatillo Sauce: Heat the oil in a saucepan, add the scallions, and sauté for 3 minutes, stirring often. Mix in the tomatillos, salt, pepper, garlic powder, and green chilies. Simmer the sauce, covered, for 5 minutes, stirring often. Cool.

2. Puree the sauce in a blender or food processor fitted with the steel blade. Pour the sauce into a bowl and mix in the sour cream. Cover and chill until needed. Serve fish with the sauce on the side.

3. Place the flour in a shallow bowl and mix in the salt, tarragon, and pepper. Put the milk in another shallow dish. Roll the fish in the milk and then dredge it in the seasoned flour.

4. Heat the oil and butter in a heavy frying pan and fry the fish until it is golden brown on both sides and flakes easily. Using a spatula, transfer the fish to a platter. Drizzle the sauce over the fish and serve hot.

Makes 6 servings

DEEP FRYING

Deep frying is a dry-heat method in which food is submerged and cooked in hot oil. Deep-fried food cooks quickly and is browned and crusty on the outside.

Fish
Almost any fish can be deep-fried, though firmer varieties tend to work better. We especially like shrimp, clams, and smelt.

Equipment
You can use an electric deep fryer, which needs only to be plugged in. Or you can use a metal pot with high sides heated on a stove burner. When food is dropped into hot fat, the water it contains is quickly converted into steam, which causes an agitated bubbling. Be sure to choose a pot large enough to accommodate the bubble-up. Choose a flat-bottomed pot that will sit securely on the burner, and if possible, avoid pots with handles during deep frying, as these increase the chance of spills.

You'll need a commercially available candy or deep-frying thermometer. Be sure to buy the kind that attaches to the side of the pot. If you don't own a deep-fat thermometer, throw a 1-inch bread cube into the oil when you think it's hot enough to fry and leave it there for 1 min-

ute. (If your clock doesn't have a second hand, just count slowly to 60.) If the bread isn't browned at the end of this time, the oil is not hot enough.

Deep-fry baskets are optional. Placed in the hot oil before the food is added, they're then used to remove all the food at once. Or substitute a slotted spoon. We find a spoon preferable, since each piece of food browns at its own rate and a slotted spoon can remove them one by one. Place just-fried food on paper towels to allow excess oil to drain off. Pat lightly if desired to remove excess oil on top or turn the food over to drain it.

The Oil
All oils have a different smoke point—the temperature at which they begin to burn and emit a dark smoke. Since an oil's smoke point is lowered each time it's used, choose oils with a high smoke point for economy's sake. Do not use margarine, butter, lard, or olive oil as they all have low smoke points. Safflower oil is ideal for frying, with a smoke point that exceeds 500° F. This is followed by soybean oil, which burns at about 490° F; corn oil, which smokes at about 475° F; peanut oil, which burns at about

440° F, and vegetable shortening, which smokes at about 375° F. Never heat oil to its flash point—the point at which it catches fire, about 600° F.

Some cookbooks suggest using enough oil to fill the pot to a depth of 2 inches, but we find that a 3-inch depth is preferable for effective deep frying. Whatever you do, don't fill the pot more than one-third full as the oil bubbles up when the food is added and may overflow onto the burner, which could cause a kitchen fire.

Method

Step 1: Pour enough oil into a heavy, high-sided kettle to measure 3 inches deep and never more than one-third full. Insert a deep-frying thermometer and place the kettle on a stove burner. Heat over medium heat until the thermometer reaches 375° F.

Step 2: Slide room-temperature food pieces one at a time into the hot oil, using a slotted spoon. When four or five pieces have been added, allow them to brown on both sides, turning them with a spoon if necessary. Never deep-fry more than a small amount of food at one time. Too much food will crowd the pan, lowering the oil temperature drastically and causing the food to become oil-logged and to brown unevenly.

Step 3: Watch the food carefully as it fries. When it's brown on both sides, remove each piece with a slotted spoon and lay it on a double or triple thickness of paper towels to drain.

Step 4: Allow the oil to return to 375° F before frying subsequent batches.

Tips for Successful Deep Frying

1. Make sure the oil is sufficiently hot so the food develops an outside crust immediately. This acts as a buffer to prevent the food from getting grease-soaked inside.

2. Don't salt food before deep-frying it as salt intensifies the bubble-up when the food is first placed in the oil.

3. Fish pieces should be as uniformly sized as possible so everything is done at around the same time.

4. Remove and discard any food particles left in the oil after each batch is cooked, as they will burn and affect the flavor of succeeding batches.

5. If you are frying several batches of food and want to serve everything at the same time, keep each batch of food hot, after draining, by placing it in a 200° F oven. Arrange well-drained food in a single layer on a cookie sheet lined with paper towels and place it in the oven until all the food has been fried.

6. Food should be fried immediately before serving. Deep-frying in advance cuts down considerably on the quality of the food.

7. Oil should be stored for reuse. Allow it to cool, then strain it through several thicknesses of cheesecloth and store it in a covered container in the refrigerator. If the oil solidifies or becomes cloudy from the heat, it can still be used again. As soon as it is heated, it will again become transparent and liquid. When you wish

to reuse it, you'll need to add more oil to achieve the needed depth. Any oil that begins to darken or to smoke should be discarded.

8. To clean an oily kettle, fill the kettle with very hot water and detergent, then allow it to sit overnight. Very hot water makes the oil more fluid, so it clings with less tenacity to the interior of the metal pot.

INGREDIENTS

1 recipe Tartar Sauce (see
   Index)
6 4- to 5-inch French bread or
   sourdough rolls
½ teaspoon cayenne pepper
¼ teaspoon garlic powder
¼ teaspoon freshly ground
   white pepper
1–2 eggs, beaten
24 large fresh oysters, shucked
2–3 cups safflower or peanut
   oil
4–6 tablespoons unsalted butter
   or margarine
Garlic salt
Salt
Tabasco sauce
Lemon wedges

Oysters Médiatrice

The word médiatrice is French for "peacemaker." In New Orleans these oyster-stuffed rolls were thought to be the only thing that would pacify an angry wife whose husband had been out carousing all night.

This dish can be served as an appetizer, a main course, with cornmeal Spoon Bread (recipe follows), or as a snack. It can also be made in one large hollowed-out French bread and cut into slices to serve.

1. Place the Tartar Sauce in a sauceboat and refrigerate it. Cut an oval from the top crust of a French roll and hollow out the roll with your fingers, taking care not to break through the crust. Repeat with the remaining rolls, reserving the cutout ovals as caps.

2. Make fine crumbs of the excess bread in a food processor fitted with the steel blade. Measure 1 cup packed crumbs and mix them with the cayenne, garlic powder, and white pepper. Place them in a flat dish.

3. Place the eggs in a bowl. Drain the oysters, pat them dry with paper towels, and place them in the bowl with the eggs.

4. Remove the oysters from the eggs, one at a time, shaking them to remove the excess egg. Roll the oysters in the bread crumbs and place the oysters in a single layer on sheets of wax paper on the counter to dry for about 20 minutes.

5. Pour oil into a high-sided pot to a depth of 3 inches. Fasten a deep-frying thermometer to the pot and heat the oil to 375° F. Preheat the oven to 250° F.

6. While the oil heats, melt the margarine and use it to paint the inside of the hollowed-out rolls liberally. Then sprinkle the insides with garlic salt (don't forget the little cutout ovals). Arrange the rolls and tops on a cookie sheet and let them heat in the oven until the oysters are fried.

7. Fry the oysters: Slide each oyster into the hot oil, frying no more than six at a time and turning them if necessary. Fry them for about 1 to 2 minutes, then remove them with a slotted spoon and place them on paper towels to drain. Allow the oil to return to 375° F before frying the next batch of oysters. Repeat until all oysters are fried, keeping the early batches warm in the oven if desired.

8. When all the oysters are fried, salt them lightly, topping each with a shake of Tabasco and a dab of Tartar Sauce. Stuff each hot roll with four oysters, place the rolls on a platter, and serve immediately. Pass additional Tartar Sauce and the lemon wedges.

Makes 6 servings

Spoon Bread

This corn bread gets its name from the way it is served from its round dish—it's spooned.

1. Preheat the oven to 350° F. Combine the cornmeal, sugar, salt, and baking powder in a bowl. Stir in the boiling water and melted butter, mixing well. Then add the eggs and buttermilk, stirring well to combine.

2. Spoon the batter into a well-greased 9-inch round baking pan or a well-greased 9-inch cast-iron skillet.

3. Bake the Spoon Bread in the oven for 35 minutes. Serve it warm, spooning it from the skillet onto your guests' dinner plates.

Makes 8 to 10 servings

INGREDIENTS
1½ cups yellow cornmeal
1 tablespoon sugar
¼ teaspoon salt
1 tablespoon double-acting
  baking powder
1½ cups boiling water
4 tablespoons unsalted butter
  or margarine, melted
5 eggs, beaten
2 cups buttermilk

INGREDIENTS
1 recipe Tartar Sauce (see
  following page)
1 recipe Shallot Barbecue
  Sauce (see Index)
2 lemons, quartered
3 cups oyster crackers
¼ cup minced fresh parsley
½ teaspoon cayenne pepper
¼ teaspoon freshly grated
  nutmeg
2 eggs
1½ quarts shucked and drained
  clams (Ipswich if possible)
2–3 cups safflower or peanut
  oil

Deep-Fried Clams with Two Sauces

*Make both sauces, and your guests can opt for either a traditional
tartar or a more unusual barbecue sauce with shallots—or they
may choose both!*

1. Make the two sauces and store them, covered, in the
refrigerator until ready to serve. Allow the sauces to come
to room temperature before placing them on the dinner
table. Arrange a dish of lemon wedges on a plate and take
them to the table with the sauces.

2. Crush the crackers between wax paper sheets with a
rolling pin or use a food processor fitted with the steel
blade. Place the crumbs in a large bowl and combine them
with the parsley, cayenne pepper, and nutmeg. Place the
eggs in a small bowl and beat them until well mixed.

3. Dip the clams in egg, then in the cracker mixture.
Place the coated clams in a single layer on paper towels and
let them sit at room temperature for 20 minutes to dry.

4. Pour the oil into a high-sided pot to a depth of 3
inches or more. Insert a deep-frying thermometer and heat
the oil until it reaches 375° F. Slide the clams into the hot
oil, no more than five or six at a time. Fry about 2 minutes
or until well browned on both sides, turning if necessary.
Remove with a slotted spoon and drain on paper towels.

5. When the oil returns to 375° F, fry the next batch.
Continue frying batches until all the clams are fried. (Keep
the fried clams warm in the oven until you are finished.)
Mound the clams on a serving platter and pass Tartar
Sauce, Shallot Barbecue Sauce, and lemon wedges at the
table. If desired, add coleslaw, heated French bread, and
corn on the cob.

Makes 6 servings

Deep-Fried Clam Patties

The Tartar Sauce isn't necessary, but it does add a nice tang to these delicious clams.

1. Make the Tartar Sauce if desired and refrigerate it in a sauceboat. Chop the clams coarsely and place them in a medium bowl. Stir in the flour, crumbs, egg, salt, and pepper. Let the mixture stand at room temperature for 30 minutes.

2. Pour the oil into a high-sided pot to a depth of 3 inches. Add a deep-frying thermometer and heat the oil to 375° F. While the oil heats, form the clam mixture into 12 small patties.

3. Preheat the oven to 200° F. Slide the patties into the hot oil, no more than six at a time, and fry them for about 2 minutes, turning them with a slotted spoon if necessary. Remove the patties and drain them on paper towels. Wait until the oil returns to 375° F before frying the second batch. Keep the first batch warm on a cookie sheet lined with paper towels in the oven.

4. Arrange the hot patties on a serving platter and serve with a tart green salad and dark bread and butter. Add Tartar Sauce if desired.

Makes 6 servings

Tartar Sauce

After tasting this homemade version you'll never again buy tartar sauce in a jar!

1. Spoon the mayonnaise into a bowl and stir in the pickle, onion, and capers. Cover lightly and chill until needed. Stir and serve.

Makes 1 cup

INGREDIENTS
Tartar Sauce (optional) (recipe follows)
3½ pounds littleneck clams, shucked and drained, liquid reserved
¼ cup all-purpose flour
¼ cup fine bread crumbs
1 egg, slightly beaten
¼ teaspoon salt
¼ teaspoon freshly ground pepper
Safflower oil for deep frying

INGREDIENTS
1 cup homemade or good-quality prepared mayonnaise
1 tablespoon minced sweet pickle
1 tablespoon minced onion
2 teaspoons minced capers

INGREDIENTS

½ teaspoon minced fresh
   gingerroot
½ pound raw shrimp, peeled
   and pureed in a food
   processor fitted with the
   steel blade
¼ cup vegetable shortening
1 egg white
⅛ teaspoon salt
½ tablespoon dry white wine
1 tablespoon cornstarch
6 slices white bread, crusts
   removed
2½–3 cups peanut oil for deep
   frying
¼ cup black sesame seeds, for
   decoration (optional)
4 lettuce leaves for garnish
¼ cup parsley for garnish

Shrimp Toast

A wonderful shrimp mixture is spread atop bread and then deep-fried. A classic Chinese appetizer.

1. Combine the ginger, shrimp, shortening, egg white, salt, white wine, and cornstarch in a mixing bowl.

2. Cut each bread slice into four triangular pieces. Place ½ tablespoon of the shrimp mixture on each triangle and spread it evenly to the edges.

3. Heat the oil to 375° F in a wok or heavy skillet. Fry the shrimp toast shrimp side down for 10 seconds, then turn them over with two forks and fry them for 5 seconds, or until golden brown. Fry only four toasts at a time. Remove them with a slotted spoon and drain them on paper towels. Serve hot.

4. Decorate by sprinkling the toasts with black sesame seeds. Arrange the toast on lettuce leaves and decorate them attractively with parsley. These freeze well. (Reheat them frozen on a cookie sheet at 375° F for about 12 minutes.)

Makes 6 servings

Caribbean Salt-Dried Cod Fritters

The Caribbeans originally salt-dried their fish as a way to keep it edible in the tropical climate. This dish is delicious with cool cole slaw.

1. Place the cod in a bowl, cover it with cold water, and let it stand for 1 hour. Repeat three more times, washing away excess salt, and drain.

2. Shred the fish with a fork and place it in a deep mixing bowl. Stir in the scallions, garlic, cilantro, lime juice, flour, water, and baking powder. Blend until lump-free. Let the batter stand for 20 minutes.

3. Heat the peanut oil, 1 inch deep, in a heavy frying pan to 375° F. Slide a tablespoon of cod batter into the oil eight at a time. Cook, turning once, for about 4 minutes or until golden brown.

4. Remove the fritters with a slotted spoon and drain them on paper towels. Serve hot.

Makes 6 to 8 servings

INGREDIENTS
½ pound salt-dried cod fillet
6 scallions, chopped
2 cloves garlic, minced
3 tablespoons minced cilantro
1 tablespoon freshly squeezed
   lime juice
1½ cups all-purpose flour
1½ cups cold water
2 teaspoons double-acting
   baking powder
3 cups peanut oil for deep
   frying

Fish and Chips

In England deep-fried fish and chips are served in a rolled-up cone made of yesterday's newspaper and lined with a wax paper cone of similar size. If you wish to serve fish and chips on a large platter, lay a sheet of newspaper over the platter, then arrange a sheet of wax paper over this. Pile the fish and chips on the wax paper and serve as suggested, with malt vinegar and salt. Add Tartar Sauce or Shallot Barbecue Sauce (see Index) if desired.

INGREDIENTS

1 recipe Tartar Sauce or
  Shallot Barbecue Sauce (see
  Index)
6 sheets tabloid-size
  newspaper sheets (about
  13½″ × 11½″)
6 sheets wax paper (11″ × 6½″)
1½ cups all-purpose flour
½ teaspoon each salt, paprika,
  and double-acting baking
  powder
¼ teaspoon freshly ground
  pepper
1½ cups light English beer
1½ pounds baking potatoes
2¼ pounds sole, flounder, or
  perch fillets
Safflower oil for deep frying
Salt
1 cup malt vinegar

1. Make the sauce of your choice and refrigerate it in a sauceboat. Make newspaper cones: Fold one newspaper sheet in half to measure 6¾ inches by 11½ inches. Lay a sheet of wax paper over the newspaper. Roll the two together into a cone and secure with staples or cellophane tape. Repeat with the remaining newspaper and wax paper until you have six cones.

2. Make the batter: Mix the flour, ½ teaspoon salt, paprika, baking powder, and pepper in a bowl. Stir in the beer. Let the batter stand at room temperature for 20 minutes.

3. Cut the potatoes into quarters, then cut each quarter in half to yield eight pieces. Cut the fish into 1½-inch pieces. Pat the potatoes and fish dry with paper towels.

4. Pour the oil into a high-sided pan to a depth of 3 inches. Insert a deep-fat thermometer and heat the oil to 375° F. Preheat the oven to 200° F.

5. Slide the potatoes one by one into the hot oil, frying only a few at a time. Watch them carefully—they will take about 60 seconds or less, depending on how thinly sliced they are. When the first batch is well browned on both sides, remove with a slotted spoon and drain them on paper towels.

6. Lay a double thickness of paper towels on a cookie sheet and arrange the hot potatoes on the paper towels in a single layer. Place them in the oven to keep them warm until the fish are fried. As each batch of potatoes is finished, add them to the cookie sheet.

7. Dip a piece of fish into the batter, then slide it into the hot oil. Repeat, adding no more than four pieces to the oil. Let the fish fry for about 2 to 3 minutes or until browned on both sides. Drain the fish on paper towels. Make sure the oil returns to 375° F before adding subsequent batches of fish. Keep the fried fish warm in the oven.

8. When the potatoes and fish are done, remove the cookie sheets from the oven and sprinkle everything with salt. Fill the paper cones with equal amounts of fish and chips. Serve one cone to each guest, passing salt and a shaker full of malt vinegar for sprinkling into the cone.
Note: When fish is fried in oil, the oil absorbs fish odors. Be sure you fry the potatoes before you fry the fish, or your potatoes will taste fishy.

Makes 6 servings

SHALLOT BARBECUE SAUCE
2 tablespoons vegetable oil
4 large shallots, minced fine
2 large cloves garlic, minced
¾ cup catsup
1¼ cups chili sauce
3 tablespoons cider vinegar
3 tablespoons light brown sugar
1 tablespoon chili powder
½ teaspoon liquid smoke

FISH
Safflower oil for deep frying
2¼–2½ pounds 4- to 5-inch-long fresh smelt, cleaned (see following page)
2 cups pancake mix
½ teaspoon onion salt
½ teaspoon dried thyme
¼ teaspoon freshly ground pepper
2 eggs, slightly beaten
½ cup milk

Deep-Fried Smelt with Shallot Barbecue Sauce

Midwestern families crowd the shores in spring, during smelting season, to net and take home dozens of these mild-flavored, 4- to 5-inch-long fish. The fish are then gutted, deep-fried, and served with such accompaniments as French fries, coleslaw, and tartar or barbecue sauce.

If you plan to serve French fries with smelt, fry the potatoes before you fry the smelt; otherwise the oil will impart a fish flavor to the potatoes.

And incidentally, don't say "smelts." The plural of smelt *is* smelt.

1. Make the Shallot Barbecue Sauce: Heat the vegetable oil in a large saucepan. When the oil is hot, add the shallots and garlic and sauté them for 2 minutes or until soft. Stir in the catsup, chili sauce, cider vinegar, brown sugar, and chili powder. Simmer for 5 minutes, stirring often. Remove the sauce from the heat and stir in the liquid smoke, mixing well. When the sauce is cool, spoon it into a covered container and refrigerate until ready to serve.

2. About 10 minutes before serving time, pour the safflower oil into a deep fryer or high-sided frying pan to a depth of 3 inches. Insert a deep-frying thermometer and heat the oil over medium heat to 375° F. Rinse the smelt under cold running water and pat them dry with paper towels.

3. Spoon the pancake mix, onion salt, thyme, and pepper into a shallow dish. Mix the eggs with the milk in a second dish. Dip the smelt in the pancake mix, then in the milk mixture, then again in the pancake mix. Preheat the oven to 250° F.

4. When the thermometer registers 375° F, slide the smelt into the oil one by one. Do not cook more than four or five at one time. When the smelt are browned on both sides, about 2 to 3 minutes, remove them from the oil with a slotted spoon and drain them on paper towels. Transfer them to an ovenproof serving dish and keep them warm in the oven.

5. When all the smelt have been fried, serve them with Shallot Barbecue Sauce for dipping. Serve with coleslaw, French fried potatoes, hot French bread, and beer.

Makes 6 servings

TIPS FOR CLEANING SMELT

● Snip off the head of each smelt with scissors and slit the belly open. Use a rounded spoon or fingers to remove the innards. If desired, snip off the back fin and tail of smelt more than 5 inches long.

DIPPING SAUCE
¾ cup Japanese (light) soy
sauce
¼ cup chicken stock
1 tablespoon grated fresh
peeled gingerroot

SHELLFISH
36 large shrimp, peeled, tails
left on, butterflied, and
deveined
1 large sweet potato, peeled
and cut into 12 ¼-inch-thick
slices
1 thin eggplant (Oriental
eggplants have a 1½-inch
diameter), cut into 12 ¼- to
½-inch-thick crosswise
slices
6 large flowerets broccoli
1 red bell pepper, cut into 6 ¾-
inch-thick rings
Safflower oil for deep frying

BATTER
1 cup cake flour, sifted
¼ teaspoon baking soda
¼ teaspoon salt
¼ cup cornstarch
1 cup ice water

Deep-Fried Shrimp, Tempura Style

When the Japanese make tempura, they put a chopstick in the hot oil to check the oil temperature. If the oil bubbles rapidly around the chopstick, the oil has reached 375° F, which is perfect for deep-frying tempura and other dishes. Our Japanese-style deep-fried shrimp are made using a deep-frying thermometer, which tells you when the oil is precisely 375° F.

1. Make the dipping sauce: Combine the soy sauce, chicken stock, and ginger, then ladle the sauce into six individual sauce dishes and take them to the table. If these bowls are not available, pour the sauce into a small pitcher.

2. Dry the shrimp and vegetables on all sides with paper towels, then arrange them in a single layer on a cookie sheet lined with paper towels. Refrigerate until needed; tempura ingredients should be very cold.

3. Make the batter: Mix the cake flour, baking soda, and salt in a large bowl and place the mixture in the freezer for 10 minutes. Place the cornstarch in a separate dish and place it in the freezer.

4. Pour the oil into a deep kettle to a depth of 3 inches. Insert a deep-frying thermometer and heat the oil over medium heat until it reaches 375° F.

5. Fill the bottom of a pie plate with ice cubes and place the plate on the counter next to the stove. Remove the large bowl of dry ingredients from the freezer and set it on the ice cubes. Quickly stir the ice water into the flour mixture, then sprinkle the cornstarch over the mixture, stirring quickly until just combined. Do not overmix; the batter should be lumpy.

6. Preheat the oven to 200° F. Pick up one shrimp by its tail, then dip it quickly into the batter, give it a good shake to remove excess, and quickly but carefully slide it into the hot oil. Repeat the process with five more shrimp. Fry the shrimp for about 2 minutes, turning each one with two forks as needed so that they are evenly browned on each side.

7. Remove the fried shrimp with a slotted spoon and drain them on paper towels. Arrange them in a single layer on a cookie sheet lined with paper towels and place them in the oven to keep them warm. Repeat with the remaining shrimp, frying only six at a time.

8. When all the shrimp have been fried, dip each vegetable piece into the batter in the same manner, frying no more than about ½ cup at one time. As the vegetables finish cooking, place them on the cookie sheet to keep them warm.

9. When everything has been cooked, immediately transfer the shrimp and vegetables to a serving platter and serve each guest six shrimp, two slices each of eggplant and sweet potato, one slice of pepper, and one piece of broccoli.

Makes 6 servings

VEGETABLE SALSA

1 large green bell pepper, cut
   into chunks
2 fresh jalapeño peppers,
   seeded and quartered
1 medium onion, cut into
   chunks
½ medium zucchini, cut into
   chunks
2 pounds firm tomatoes
½ teaspoon salt
½ teaspoon red pepper flakes

SEAFOOD

¾ pound medium shrimp,
   shelled and deveined
½ pound each monkfish,
   grouper, and squid steak,
   cut into 1¼-inch cubes
Lemon wedges and parsley
   sprigs, for garnish
Safflower oil for deep frying

Fish and Shellfish Fondue with Vegetable Salsa

Fondue pots are really high-sided chafing dishes filled with cheese, chocolate, or hot oil. When cheese is used, guests spear chunks of bread onto long-handled forks and dip them into the simmering cheese. When chocolate is used, guests dip cake or fruit chunks. And when the pot is filled with hot oil, guests spear pieces of fish, beef, or seafood and hold them in the hot oil until they're cooked.

Fondue pots come in two varieties: the seafood and beef type has a potbellied shape to hold the oil, a narrow opening at the top to prevent splatters, and is made of metal. It must be set over a flame high enough to keep the oil at deep-frying temperature.

The cheese/dessert type is made of heatproof crockery and has a wide opening at the top. This pot should be set over a low flame so the fragile sauce within stays warm but does not burn. Cheese fondue should be heated on the stove, then poured hot into the fondue pot before serving.

The best burners for all types of fondue pots have lids to smother the flames and handles to adjust the intensity of the flame. Dessert sauce fondues also do well over the minimal heat of a candle flame.

The feast in this and the following recipe includes a fish and shellfish fondue and a dessert fondue.

1. Make the Vegetable Salsa: Place the green pepper, jalapeño, onions, and zucchini chunks in a food processor fitted with the steel blade and pulse on and off until coarsely chopped. Add the tomatoes, salt, and red pepper flakes and pulse again until finely chopped but not pureed. Transfer the salsa to a serving bowl, cover, and refrigerate until serving time.

2. Arrange the shrimp, monkfish, grouper, and squid cubes on a large serving platter. Decorate the platter with lemon wedges and parsley and set the platter on the table with the bowl of salsa.

3. Pour enough oil to half-fill the fondue pot into a pot and heat it on the stove to 375° F. Wearing oven mitts, carefully pour the hot oil into a fondue pot and set it over a high flame on the fondue burner at the table. (You can heat the oil over the heating element under the fondue pot, but the oil will take a long time to get hot, and some people feel it never does get hot enough this way.)

4. When the oil is hot enough, guests spear fish or shellfish with long-handled fondue forks and hold the raw food in the simmering oil for about 2 minutes or until cooked through. Serve with salsa.

Makes 6 servings

Dessert Fondue

You won't need to show guests how to dunk the goodies into the dessert sauce—they'll be at this dessert long before the sauce is even heated. The only precaution to take is to be sure you don't run out of either sauce or dippers.

1. Empty the jars of sundae sauce into the fondue pot and allow the sauce to heat slowly over the fondue burner at the table. Bring platters of dipping ingredients to the table along with fondue forks or long wooden toothpicks.

Makes 6 servings

INGREDIENTS

4 8-ounce jars prepared sundae sauce such as hot fudge, caramel, or butterscotch

6 each of any or all of the following:

Tiny bunches of seedless grapes

Marshmallows

Maraschino or fresh cherries on stems

Caramels

Angel food cake chunks (do not use cake soft enough to fall apart when dipped in sauce)

Chunks of any of the following fruits: apple, pear, peach, plum, nectarine, orange, canned mandarin orange, mango, pineapple, fresh coconut

PANFRYING

Panfrying is a dry-heat cooking method in which food is placed in a shallow layer of hot fat in a frying pan and fried on both sides. Since this takes only a few moments, panfrying has a last-minute, improvisational quality.

Fish
Large whole fish and fish steaks do not do well when panfried, because they are so thick. You're apt to end up with a dried exterior and a raw interior. Panfry only small whole fish or fillets.

Equipment
Although any frying pan can be used for panfrying, the most effective is a cast-iron skillet, which conducts heat slowly and evenly and has no hot spots. Once heated, it provides the perfect intense, even heat needed for panfrying. Do not use a lid when panfrying, as food will not be as crisp.

The Oil
Fish is panfried most effectively in peanut oil that, because of its high smoke point, will be hot enough to seal the outside pores of the fish and stop it from absorbing too much oil.

Method
Step 1: Bread the fish as directed in the recipe. Let it sit at room temperature for 20 minutes to dry. Add enough vegetable oil to the pan to half cover, but not submerge the fish. Heat the oil until hot but not smoking.

Step 2: Add room-temperature fish to the hot oil, one piece at a time, filling the pan loosely with fish pieces in a single layer. The pieces should not touch each other.

Step 3: Watch the fish carefully as it fries, lowering the heat if needed. Use a spatula to lift one end of the fish occasionally to see whether it is ready to be turned.

Step 4: Turn the fish when the first side is well browned. Fry the fish on the other side and transfer it to paper towels to drain.

Step 5: Remove any crumbs or pieces of residue that remain in the pan. Leaving them in will cause subsequent batches to have a burned flavor. Add oil as before, allow it to heat, then add the next batch of fish. Cook as directed.

Step 6: Repeat as many times as necessary. If

desired, keep the fish warm by placing the fried fish in a single layer on a cookie sheet lined with paper towels and place it in a 200° F oven while the remaining batches cook.

Care of the Cast-Iron Skillet
New cast-iron skillets must be seasoned. But even when seasoned, these skillets are so prone to rust that they can't even sit a few hours with the remains of dinner in them. As soon as you've used your skillet, clean and dry it. We've found it helpful to dry it on a stove burner while we wash other pots—it's easier on the kitchen towels. Never put a cast-iron skillet in the dishwasher because it will rust badly. In fact, it may rust just from sitting in a humid kitchen for a few months without being used.

To Season a Cast-Iron Skillet:
1. Wash the skillet with a stiff brush and soapy water (do not use detergent). Then rinse well and dry.
2. Pour 1 tablespoon vegetable oil into the pan and spread it over the sides and bottom, inside and out, with paper towels. (You can substitute unsalted vegetable shortening or lard for the oil if desired.)
3. Add oil—enough to cover the bottom of the pan—and heat it over medium heat until the oil is very hot but not smoking. Remove the pan from the heat and tilt the pan, swirling the hot oil all over the inside of the pan so it covers the bottom and sides.
4. Add another tablespoon or 2 of oil and

place the pan in a 200–250° F oven. Turn the heat off after an hour and let the pan sit in the oven until cool. Remove the pan from the oven, wipe off excess oil with paper towels, and store.

To Clean a Rusted Cast-Iron Skillet:
1. Moisten fine steel wool pads with water, then rub them on a bar of Fels Naptha soap (or any similar type of soap). Rub the entire pan with steel wool, then rinse the pan in hot water.
2. Repeat step 1, rubbing the pan on all sides until it feels completely smooth and even on all surfaces, inside and out. Repeat several times if needed.
3. Dry the pan completely and reseason it.

Tips for Successful Panfrying
1. Food should be brought to room temperature before panfrying, or it will cause a drastic drop in the temperature of the oil and the food will absorb the oil rather than fry in it.
2. Do not salt food before frying. Salt draws moisture to the surface of the food and will cause splattering. It also lowers the smoke point of the oil.
3. All breaded coatings should be given a little time (no more than 20 minutes) to dry. Arrange breaded food in a single layer on a sheet of wax paper on the counter and let sit until ready to panfry.
4. Panfried fish should be turned only once, using as wide a spatula as is available, since cooked fish has a tendency to fall apart when lifted.

Breaded Coatings

Breaded coatings add flavor, texture, and variety to fried foods. There are endless possibilities, including cornmeal, fine bread crumbs, crushed potato chips, crushed crackers, whole-grain flours, crushed breakfast cereals, wheat germ, and dried herbs.

Although there's no way to make absolutely sure that breading won't fall off fish pieces, there are a few things you can do to discourage this from happening:

1. Use paper towels to wipe off each piece of fish on all sides. When moist fish is dipped into a coating, the moisture turns to steam as soon as it hits the hot oil. It is this steam that pushes the coating off the fish.

2. Once the food has been coated, arrange the pieces in a single layer on a plate and allow them to sit at room temperature (not in the refrigerator) for twenty minutes to dry as much as possible. When coatings include egg or other liquids such as buttermilk or milk, this step is especially important.

3. Make sure that any breading used is made of very fine crumbs and is dry when added to the fish surface. Large or dampened crumbs tend to fall off.

4. Make sure that the oil is hot. Otherwise the coating will not form a sealed protective coating and the fish will absorb too much oil.

INGREDIENTS

1 recipe Crème Fraîche (recipe
   follows)

½ cup (¼ pound) unsalted
   butter

¼ cup freshly squeezed lemon
   juice

¼ teaspoon each salt, cayenne
   pepper, garlic powder, and
   onion powder

½ teaspoon dried thyme

2¼–2½ pounds redfish or other
   firm fish fillets

INGREDIENTS

1 quart whipping cream

½ cup buttermilk

Blackened Redfish
with Crème Fraîche

Open a window during the cooking of this recipe as blackened redfish tends to be very smoky. The Crème Fraîche must be prepared at least one day ahead.

1. Melt the butter in a small saucepan over low heat. Stir in the lemon juice, salt, cayenne, garlic powder, onion powder, and thyme. Pour the seasoned butter into a shallow dish.

2. Heat a large, heavy frying pan over high heat. Roll the redfish in the seasoned butter and fry it quickly, turning it once, for about 2 minutes on each side. The redfish will char on the outside and be tender on the inside. With a spatula, transfer the fish to a heated platter.

3. Place the fish on individual plates and serve it hot with a dollop of crème fraîche.

Note: This dish may also be prepared using prepared blackening spices in place of the above seasonings.

Makes 6 servings

Crème Fraîche

This simple, rich topping beats canned whipped cream every time!

1. Bring the cream and buttermilk to room temperature and mix thoroughly. Allow to sit in a warm place (75 to 80° F) about 24 hours or until thick.

2. Refrigerate until ready to serve.

Makes 1 quart

Kippers and Onions

Butter and sautéed onions provide the flavor in this dish, which is perfect for breakfast or brunch.

1. Melt 3 tablespoons of the butter in a large, heavy frying pan over medium heat. Add the onions and sauté them for 5 minutes, stirring often. Remove the onions from the frying pan.

2. Add the remaining butter to the pan and fry the kippers in it for 3 minutes. Turn them with a spatula and continue cooking for 3 minutes.

3. To serve, place a kipper on each plate, top with onions, and serve hot. Good served with scrambled eggs and fried potatoes.

Makes 6 servings

INGREDIENTS
6 tablespoons unsalted butter
3 large onions, sliced thin
6 kippered herrings,
** wrappings and bones**
** removed**
¼ teaspoon salt
¼ teaspoon freshly ground
** pepper**

INGREDIENTS

6 tablespoons cornstarch

3 scallions, minced

7 tablespoons peanut oil

2¼–2½ pounds red snapper
    fillets, cut into 6 serving
    pieces

3 cloves garlic, minced

½ teaspoon ground ginger

½ teaspoon salt

1 medium green or red bell
    pepper, seeded and cut into
    1-inch pieces

3 tablespoons light soy sauce

1 teaspoon dark sesame oil

½ cup chicken stock, mixed
    with 2 teaspoons cornstarch

2 tomatoes, each cut into 8
    wedges

6 scallions, slit in half
    lengthwise and cut into
    1-inch pieces

Shanghai Red Snapper

This colorful fish is browned in oil and then served with sautéed onions, peppers, and tomatoes.

1. Mix the 6 tablespoons cornstarch with the minced scallions; place on a plate.

2. Heat 4 tablespoons of the peanut oil in a wok or heavy frying pan over medium-high heat. Add the snapper pieces and brown them on both sides until cooked; the outside will be brown, and the inside will flake easily when tested and be translucent (about 3 to 5 minutes). Drain the fish on paper towels.

3. Heat the remaining oil in the frying pan or wok over medium-high heat. Add the garlic, ginger, salt, and scallion mixture and stir-fry for 30 seconds. Mix in the bell pepper and stir-fry for 3 minutes. Stir in the soy sauce, sesame oil, and chicken stock mixture. Continue cooking for about 2 minutes or until the sauce is heated and thickens slightly. Add tomatoes and scallions.

4. Place the fish on a heated platter and drizzle it with the sauce. Serve with hot white rice.

Makes 5 to 6 servings

Perch Fried in Cornmeal with Mustard Sauce

Always measure the thickest part of fish and allow a total of 10 minutes of cooking per inch (5 minutes on each side).

1. Double-check that all bones have been removed from the perch. Place the bread crumbs in a shallow dish and mix in the salt, pepper, garlic powder, oregano, and mustard. Roll the perch fillets in the crumbs.

2. Heat the oil and butter in large, heavy frying pan. Add the onion and fry for 4 minutes over medium heat, stirring often. Push the onions to one side of the pan. Add the fish fillets and fry them until crusty on both sides, about 3 to 5 minutes per side, depending on the thickness of the fish fillets. The fish is done when it is crusty and flakes easily. Use more oil or butter as needed. You may have to fry the fish in two batches.

3. Remove the fish from the pan and keep it warm in a 250° F oven. Sprinkle the wine into the pan and cook until reduced by half. Stir to incorporate the pan drippings. Whisk in the grainy mustard, Dijon mustard, dry mustard, cloves, and half-and-half. Continue cooking and whisking until the sauce thickens slightly and is warm, about 4 to 5 minutes.

4. Arrange the fish on individual plates and drizzle with the sauce. Garnish with lemon wedges and serve immediately.

Makes 6 servings

FISH
2¼–2½ pounds perch fillets
2 cups fine dry bread crumbs
¼ teaspoon each salt, freshly ground pepper, garlic powder, dried oregano, and dry mustard
3 tablespoons peanut oil
2 tablespoons unsalted butter
1 large onion, sliced thin
2 lemons, cut into wedges, for garnish

MUSTARD SAUCE
½ cup dry white wine
1 teaspoon grainy mustard
1 teaspoon Dijon mustard
½ teaspoon dry mustard
Pinch ground cloves
1 cup half-and-half

MARINADE
1¼ cups cider vinegar
2 tablespoons freshly squeezed
lemon or lime juice
2 cloves garlic, minced
1 teaspoon dried oregano

FISH
2 pounds catfish fillets
2 cups mashed potatoes
3 scallions, minced
2 eggs, slightly beaten
1 tablespoon all-purpose flour
2 cups all-purpose flour
¼ teaspoon each freshly grated
nutmeg, dry mustard,
turmeric, and dried sage
¼ cup peanut oil

Mississippi Catfish Cakes

Try these fish cakes as a perfect late-night supper dish.

1. Make the marinade: Mix together the vinegar, lemon juice, garlic, and oregano in a shallow dish. Add the catfish, cover, and refrigerate overnight. Drain the fish and discard the marinade.

2. Shred the catfish and place it in a deep mixing bowl. Blend in the potatoes, scallions, eggs, and 1 tablespoon flour. Shape the mixture into 3-inch patties ½ inch thick.

3. Mix together the 2 cups flour, nutmeg, mustard, turmeric, and sage and place in a shallow bowl. Gently roll each patty in the seasoned flour.

4. Heat the oil in a heavy frying pan over medium heat. Panfry the patties for about 3 minutes per side, until golden brown on each side and cooked through.

Makes 6 servings

Panfried Catfish

A little Tabasco sauce jazzes up this southern favorite.

1. Make the Tartar Sauce and refrigerate it in a sauce-boat until serving time. Combine the buttermilk, Tabasco, and salt in a glass bowl and add the catfish fillets. Let sit at room temperature for 1 hour.

2. Place the cornmeal in a flat dish. Remove the fish from the marinade and shake it to remove excess. Dip the fillets in the cornmeal until evenly coated.

3. Pour the safflower oil into a large, heavy-bottomed skillet to a depth of ½ inch. Heat the oil until very hot, then add the fillets in a single layer. The fish may have to be fried in more than one batch, using additional oil if necessary. Fry the fish on one side for about 4 minutes, then turn it and fry it on the other side for 3 minutes or until well browned.

4. Transfer the fish to paper towels to drain. If necessary, lay the catfish on a baking pan and keep it warm in a 250° F oven until all fish are fried.

5. Arrange the fillets on a serving platter and decorate the platter with parsley sprigs and lemon wedges. Serve with Tartar Sauce.

Makes 6 servings

INGREDIENTS
Tartar Sauce (see Index)
2 cups buttermilk
1 tablespoon Tabasco sauce
2 teaspoons salt
2¼ pounds catfish fillets, cut
   into 6 serving pieces
2 cups yellow cornmeal
Safflower oil for panfrying
Parsley sprigs
Lemon wedges

INGREDIENTS
Oatmeal Muffins (recipe follows)
2 cups rolled oats
¼ teaspoon each salt, freshly ground pepper, and garlic powder
2 eggs, slightly beaten
6 tablespoons unsalted butter or margarine
6 8- to 10-ounce trout, bones removed

Panfried Brook Trout with Oatmeal Coating Served with Oatmeal Muffins

Oatmeal is ground with spices to make an unusual but delicious coating for this fine-tasting fish.

1. Prepare the Oatmeal Muffins up to 1 day ahead.
2. Grind the oats in a food processor fitted with the steel blade until fine. Mix in the salt, pepper, and garlic powder and place in a shallow bowl.
3. Pour the eggs into another shallow dish.
4. Heat 3 tablespoons of the butter in a large, heavy frying pan over medium heat. Roll the trout in eggs and then dust it with the seasoned oatmeal.
5. Panfry the trout in as many batches as necessary, or use two pans at a time, for about 6 minutes, turning after 3 minutes with a spatula. The fish will flake easily when done.
6. Serve the fish immediately with oatmeal muffins.

Makes 6 servings

Oatmeal Muffins

Buttermilk is the secret to these great-tasting muffins.

1. Preheat the oven to 400° F. Grease a 12-cup muffin pan.

2. Blend the oats and buttermilk in a deep mixing bowl and let stand for 5 minutes.

3. Mix in the eggs, brown sugar, butter, and vanilla. Add the flour, baking powder, baking soda, salt, cinnamon, and raisins. Blend until all ingredients are combined, but do not overmix the batter; it should be slightly lumpy.

4. Spoon the batter into the prepared pan, filling the cups half full. Bake the muffins on the middle rack for 18 to 20 minutes or until a cake tester inserted in a muffin comes out clean. Cool the muffins in the pan for 5 minutes, then transfer them to a rack. Serve warm or cold.

Makes 1 dozen

INGREDIENTS
1½ cups rolled oats
1½ cups buttermilk
2 eggs, slightly beaten
½ cup plus 2 tablespoons firmly packed light brown sugar
6 tablespoons unsalted butter or margarine or a combination, melted and cooled
1 teaspoon vanilla extract
1½ cups all-purpose flour
2 teaspoons double-acting baking powder
1½ teaspoons baking soda
½ teaspoon salt
½ teaspoon ground cinnamon
½ cup golden raisins

INGREDIENTS
18 soft-shell crabs
2 eggs, beaten
1½ cups seasoned bread crumbs
¼ teaspoon each salt, freshly ground pepper, and garlic powder
3 tablespoons extra-virgin olive oil
2 tablespoons unsalted butter
2 lemons, cut into wedges, for garnish

Soft-Shell Crabs

Soft-shell crabs are available between the months of May and October. The shell is soft at this time because the crabs have molted.

1. Wash the crabs under cold running water. Put the crabs one at a time on a cutting surface. Cut off the face portion of the crab. Lifting the shell easily on either side of the back, scrape off the gills. Lift the shell and remove the sand receptacle from under the mouth area. Discard all the portions removed from the crab. Wash the crab and pat it dry with paper towels. (Or ask your fishmonger to clean them for you.)

2. Place the eggs in a shallow bowl. Arrange the bread crumbs in another shallow dish. Mix in the salt, pepper, and garlic powder. Dip the crabs in the eggs and then dredge them in the crumbs.

3. Heat the oil and butter in a large, heavy frying pan. In batches, fry the crabs for 2 minutes on each side; drain them on paper towels.

4. Serve the crabs hot, garnished with lemon wedges.

Makes 6 servings

APPENDIX:
MAIL ORDER SOURCES OF INGREDIENTS

This information was accurate as of December 1988. Write or call these companies and request catalogs or price lists.

Anzen Pacific Imports
7750 N.E. 17th St.
PO Box 11401
Portland, OR 97211
(503) 283-1284
Japanese, Chinese, plus some Korean, Thai, and Vietnamese ingredients.

Bayview International Trading Co.
301 Oak St.
Quincy, IL 62301
(217) 222-0779
American caviar and lobster roe.

Conte di Savoia
555 W. Roosevelt Rd.
Jeffro Plaza-Store #7
Chicago, IL 60607
(312) 666-3471
Mostly Italian and European, some Middle Eastern and Japanese ingredients.

Food Stuffs
338 Park Ave.
Glencoe, IL 60022
(708) 835-5105
European and American gourmet and specialty ingredients.

Griffo-grill
301 Oak St.
Quincy, IL 62301
(217) 222-0779

Holy Land Grocery, Inc.
4806 N. Kedzie Ave.
Chicago, IL 60659
(312) 588-3306
Middle Eastern ingredients.

House of Spices
76-17 Broadway
Jackson Heights
Queens, NY 11373
(718) 476-1577
Indian ingredients and all spices.

Leonard Solomon's Wine & Spirits
1456 N. Dayton St.
Chicago, IL 60622
(312) 915-5911
Fancy foods, Australian and French wines.

The Oriental Food Market
2801 W. Howard St.
Chicago, IL 60645
(312) 274-2826
Chinese ingredients.

People's Woods
55 Mill St.
Cumberland, RI 02864
(401) 725-2700 or 1-800-729-5800
Pure hardwood charcoals, gourmet cooking
   woods.

Star Market
3349 N. Clark St.
Chicago, IL 60659
(312) 472-0599
Japanese ingredients.

Tekla, Inc.
1456 N. Dayton St.
Chicago, IL 60622
(312) 915-5914
Russian caviar, smoked fish products, oils,
   vinegars, mustards, and pâtés.

Uwajimaya, Inc.
519 6th Avenue S.
Seattle, WA 98104
(206) 624-6248
Japanese, Korean, Chinese, plus some
   Vietnamese and Thai ingredients.

INDEX

If you enjoyed *The Compleat Fish Cook*, try these other Contemporary culinary classics, which are available in your local bookstore or by mail. To order directly, return the coupon below with payment to: Best Publications, Department BSD, 180 North Michigan Avenue, Chicago, Illinois 60601. Or call (312) 782-9181 to order with your credit card.

Qty.	Title/Author	Price	Total
_____	*Fish on the Grill* by Barbara Grunes and Phyllis Magida (5033-0)	$7.95 ea.	$_____
_____	*Shellfish on the Grill* by Phyllis Magida and Barbara Grunes (4597-3)	$7.95 ea.	$_____
_____	*Gourmet Fish on the Grill* by Phyllis Magida and Barbara Grunes (4596-5)	$8.95 ea.	$_____
_____	*Glorious Fish in the Microwave* by Patricia Tennison (4480-2)	$13.95 ea.	$_____
		Subtotal	$_____

Add $1.50 postage for the first book ordered. $ _1.50_

Add $.75 postage for each additional book ordered. $_____

Illinois residents add 7% sales tax;
California residents add 6% sales tax. $_____

                                                        Total Price $_____

Name _____

Address _____

City/State/Zip _____

☐ Enclosed is my check/money order payable to Best Publications.
Bill my
☐ VISA   ⟍ Account No. _____
☐ MasterCard   ╱ Expiration Date _____

Signature _____

For quantity discount information, please call the sales department at (312) 782-9181. Allow four to six weeks for delivery.

Offer expires May 31, 1991.   FI490

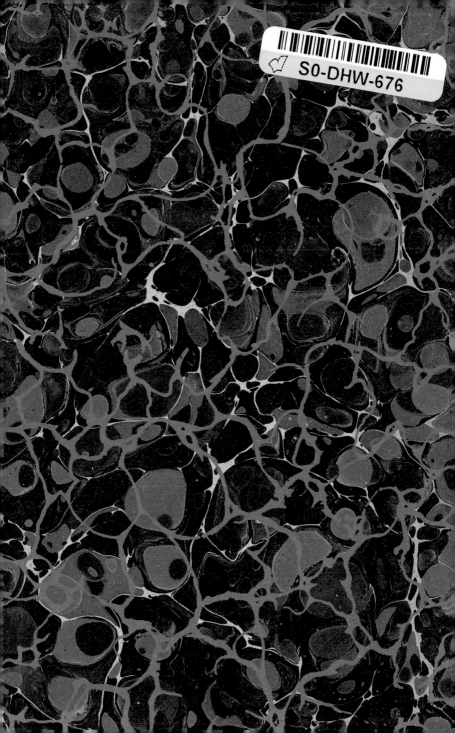

THE WORKS OF

GEORGE ELIOT

Foleshill Edition

FELIX HOLT

" Johnson, who had kept his
mentioned, now

FOLESHILL EDITION

FELIX HOLT
THE RADICAL
By GEORGE ELIOT

BOSTON · LITTLE, BROWN
AND COMPANY · MDCCCCV

UNIVERSITY PRESS · JOHN WILSON
AND SON · CAMBRIDGE, U.S.A.

FELIX HOLT, THE RADICAL.

INTRODUCTION.

FIVE-AND-THIRTY years ago the glory had not yet departed from the old coach-roads: the great roadside inns were still brilliant with well-polished tankards, the smiling glances of pretty barmaids, and the repartees of jocose ostlers; the mail still announced itself by the merry notes of the horn; the hedge-cutter or the rick-thatcher might still know the exact hour by the unfailing yet otherwise meteoric apparition of the pea-green Tally-ho or the yellow Independent; and elderly gentlemen in pony-chaises, quartering nervously to make way for the rolling swinging swiftness, had not ceased to remark that times were finely changed since they used to see the pack-horses and hear the tinkling of their bells on this very highway.

In those days there were pocket boroughs, a Birmingham unrepresented in Parliament and compelled to make strong representations out of it, unrepealed corn-laws, three-and-six-penny letters, a brawny and many-breeding pauperism, and other departed evils; but there were some pleasant things too, which have also departed. *Non omnia grandior ætas quæ fugiamus habet,* says the wise goddess: you have not the best of it in all things, O youngsters! the elderly man has his enviable memories, and not the least of them is the memory of a long journey in mid-spring or autumn on the outside of a stage-coach. Posterity may be shot, like a bullet through a tube, by atmospheric pressure from Winchester to Newcastle: that is a fine result to have among our hopes; but the slow old-fashioned way of getting from one end of our country to the other is the better thing to have in the memory. The tube-journey can never lend much to picture and narrative; it is as barren as an exclamatory O! Whereas the happy outside passenger seated on the box from the dawn to the gloaming gathered enough stories of English life, enough of English labors in town and country, enough aspects of earth and sky, to make episodes for a modern Odyssey. Suppose only that his journey took him through that central plain, watered at one extremity by the Avon, at the other by the Trent. As the morning silvered the meadows with their long lines of bushy willows marking the water-courses, or burnished the golden corn-ricks clustered near the long roofs of some midland homestead, he saw the full-uddered cows driven from their pasture to the early milking. Perhaps it was the shepherd, head servant of the farm, who drove them, his sheep-dog following with a heedless unofficial air as of a beadle in undress. The shepherd with a slow and slouching walk, timed by the walk of grazing beasts, moved aside, as if unwillingly, throwing out a monosyllabic hint to his cattle; his glance, accustomed to rest on things very near the earth, seemed to lift itself with difficulty to the coachman. Mail- or stage-coach for him belonged to that mysterious distant system of things called "Gover'ment," which, whatever it might be, was no business of his, any more than the most outlying nebula or the coal-sacks of the southern hemisphere: his solar system was the parish; the master's temper and the casualties of lambing-time were his region of storms. He cut his bread and bacon with his pocket-knife, and felt no bitterness except in the matter of pauper laborers and the bad luck that sent contrarious seasons and the sheep-rot. He and his cows were soon left behind, and the homestead too, with its pond overhung by elder-trees, its untidy kitchen-garden and cone-shaped yew-tree arbor. But everywhere the bushy hedgerows wasted the land with their straggling beauty, shrouded the grassy borders of the pastures with catkined hazels, and tossed their long blackberry branches on the corn-fields. Perhaps they were white with May, or starred with pale pink dog-roses; perhaps the urchins were already nutting amongst them, or gathering the plenteous crabs. It was worth the journey only to see those hedgerows, the liberal homes of unmarketable beauty—of the purple-blossomed ruby-berried nightshade, of the wild convolvulus climbing and spreading in tendrilled strength till it made a great curtain of pale-green hearts and white trumpets, of the many-tubed honeysuckle which, in its most delicate fragrance, hid a charm more subtle and penetrating than beauty. Even if it were winter the hedgerows showed their coral, the scarlet haws, the deep-crimson hips, with lingering brown leaves to make a resting-place for the jewels of the hoar-frost. Such hedgerows were often as tall as the laborers' cottages dotted along the lanes, or clustered into a small hamlet, their little dingy windows telling, like thick-filmed eyes, of nothing but the darkness within. The passenger on the coach-box, bowled along above such a hamlet, saw chiefly the roofs of it: probably turned its back on the road, and seemed to lie away from everything but its own patch of earth and sky, away from the parish church by long fields and green lanes, away from all intercourse except that of tramps. If its face could be seen, it was most likely dirty; but the dirt was Protestant dirt, and the big, bold, gin-breathing tramps were Protestant tramps. There was no sign of superstition near, no crucifix or image to indicate a misguided reverence: the inhabitants were probably so free from superstition that they were in much less awe of the parson than of the overseer. Yet they were saved from the excesses of Protestantism by not knowing how to read, and by the absence of hand-looms and mines to be the pioneers of Dissent: they were kept safely in the *via media* of indifference, and could have registered themselves in the census by a big black mark as members of the Church of England.

But there were trim cheerful villages too, with a neat or handsome parsonage and gray church set in the midst; there was the pleasant tinkle of the blacksmith's anvil, the patient cart-horses waiting at his door; the basket-maker peeling his willow wands in the sunshine; the wheelwright putting the last touch to a blue cart with red wheels; here and there a cottage with bright transparent windows showing pots full of blooming balsams or geraniums, and little gardens in front all double daisies or dark wallflowers; at the well clean and

comely women carrying yoked buckets, and toward the free
school small Britons dawdling on, and handling their marbles
in the pockets of unpatched corduroys adorned with brass
buttons. The land around was rich and marly, great corn-
stacks stood in the rick-yards—for the rick-burners had not
found their way hither; the homesteads were those of rich
farmers who paid no rent, or had the rare advantage of a
lease, and could afford to keep their corn till prices had risen.
The coach would be sure to overtake some of them on their
way to their outlying fields or to the market-town, sitting
heavily on their well-groomed horses, or weighing down one
side of an olive-green gig. They probably thought of the
coach with some contempt, as an accommodation for people
who had not their own gigs, or who, wanting to travel to London and such distant places, belonged to the trading and less
solid part of the nation. The passenger on the box could see
that this was the district of protuberant optimists, sure that
old England was the best of all possible countries, and that
if there were any facts which had not fallen under their own
observation, they were facts not worth observing: the district
of clean little market-towns without manufactures, of fat liv-
ings, an aristocratic clergy, and low poor-rates. But as the
day wore on the scene would change: the land would begin to
be blackened with coal-pits, the rattle of hand-looms to be
heard in hamlets and villages. Here were powerful men
walking queerly with knees bent outward from squatting in
the mine, going home to throw themselves down in their blackened flannel and sleep through the daylight, then rise and
spend much of their high wages at the ale-house with their
fellows of the Benefit Club; here the pale eager faces of hand-
loom weavers, men and women, haggard from sitting up late at
night to finish the week's work, hardly begun till the Wednesday. Everywhere the cottages and the small children were
dirty, for the languid mothers gave their strength to the loom;
pious Dissenting women, perhaps, who took life patiently, and
thought that salvation depended chiefly on predestination, and
not at all on cleanliness. The gables of Dissenting chapels
now made a visible sign of religion, and of a meeting-place to
counterbalance the ale-house, even in the hamlets; but if a

couple of old termagants were seen tearing each other's caps, it was a safe conclusion that, if they had not received the sacraments of the Church, they had not at least given in to schismatic rites, and were free from the errors of Voluntaryism. The breath of the manufacturing town, which made a cloudy day and a red gloom by night on the horizon, diffused itself over all the surrounding country, filling the air with eager unrest. Here was a population not convinced that old England was as good as possible; here were multitudinous men and women aware that their religion was not exactly the religion of their rulers, who might therefore be better than they were, and who, if better, might alter many things which now made the world perhaps more painful than it need be, and certainly more sinful. Yet there were the gray steeples too, and the churchyards, with their grassy mounds and venerable headstones, sleeping in the sunlight; there were broad fields and homesteads, and fine old woods covering a rising ground, or stretching far by the roadside, allowing only peeps at the park and mansion which they shut in from the working-day world. In these midland districts the traveller passed rapidly from one phase of English life to another: after looking down on a village dingy with coal-dust, noisy with the shaking of looms, he might skirt a parish all of fields, high hedges, and deep-rutted lanes; after the coach had rattled over the pavement of a manufacturing town, the scene of riots and trades-union meetings, it would take him in another ten minutes into a rural region, where the neighborhood of the town was only felt in the advantages of a near market for corn, cheese, and hay, and where men with a considerable banking account were accustomed to say that "they never meddled with politics themselves." The busy scenes of the shuttle and the wheel, of the roaring furnace, of the shaft and the pulley, seemed to make but crowded nests in the midst of the large-spaced slow-moving life of homesteads and far-away cottages and oak-sheltered parks. Looking at the dwellings scattered amongst the woody flats and the ploughed uplands, under the low gray sky which overhung them with an unchanging stillness as if Time itself were pausing, it was easy for the traveller to conceive that town and country had no pulse in common, except where the hand-looms made a far-reaching straggling fringe about the great centres of manufacture; that till the agitation about the Catholics in '29 rural Englishmen had hardly known more of Catholics than of the fossil mammals; and that their notion of Reform was a confused combination of rick-burners, trades-unions, Nottingham riots, and in general whatever required the calling out of the yeomanry. It was still easier to see that, for the most part, they resisted the rotation of crops and stood by their fallows: and the coachman would perhaps tell how in one parish an innovating farmer, who talked of Sir Humphry Davy, had been fairly driven out by popular dislike, as if he had been a confounded Radical; and how, the parson having one Sunday preached from the words, "Break up your fallow-ground," the people thought he had made the text out of his own head, otherwise it would never have come "so pat" on a matter of business; but when they found it in the Bible at home, some said it was an argument for fallows (else why should the Bible mention fallows?), but a few of the weaker sort were shaken, and thought it was an argument that fallows should be done away with, else the Bible would have said, "Let your fallows lie"; and the next morning the parson had a stroke of apoplexy, which, as coincident with a dispute about fallows, so set the parish against the innovating farmer and the rotation of crops, that he could stand his ground no longer, and transferred his lease.

The coachman was an excellent travelling companion and commentator on the landscape: he could tell the names of sites and persons, and explain the meaning of groups, as well as the shade of Virgil in a more memorable journey; he had as many stories about parishes, and the men and women in them, as the Wanderer in the "Excursion," only his style was different. His view of life had originally been genial, and such as became a man who was well warmed within and without, and held a position of easy, undisputed authority; but the recent initiation of Railways had imbittered him: he now, as in a perpetual vision, saw the ruined country strewn with shattered limbs, and regarded Mr. Huskisson's death as a proof of God's anger against Stephenson. "Why, every inn on the road would be shut up!" and at that word the coach-man looked before him with the blank gaze of one who had driven his coach to the outermost edge of the universe, and saw his leaders plunging into the abyss. Still he would soon relapse from the high prophetic strain to the familiar one of narrative. He knew whose the land was wherever he drove; what noblemen had half ruined themselves by gambling; who made handsome returns of rent; and who was at daggers drawn with his eldest son. He perhaps remembered the fathers of actual baronets, and knew stories of their extravagant or stingy housekeeping; whom they had married, whom they had horsewhipped, whether they were particular about pre-serving their game, and whether they had had much to do with canal companies. About any actual landed proprietor he could also tell whether he was a Reformer or an Anti-Re-former. That was a distinction which had "turned up" in latter times, and along with it the paradox, very puzzling to the coachman's mind, that there were men of old family and large estate who voted for the Bill. He did not grapple with the paradox; he let it pass, with all the discreetness of an experienced theologian or learned scholiast, preferring to point his whip at some object which could raise no questions.

No such paradox troubled our coachman when, leaving the town of Treby Magna behind him, he drove between the hedges for a mile or so, crossed the queer long bridge over the river Lapp, and then put his horses to a swift gallop up the hill by the low-nestled village of Little Treby, till they were on the fine level road, skirted on one side by grand larches, oaks, and wych elms, which sometimes opened so far as to let the trav-eller see that there was a park behind them.

How many times in the year, as the coach rolled past the neglected-looking lodges which interrupted the screen of trees, and showed the river winding through a finely timbered park, had the coachman answered the same questions, or told the same things without being questioned! That?—oh, that was Transome Court, a place there had been a fine sight of law-suits about. Generations back, the heir of the Transome name had somehow bargained away the estate, and it fell to the Durfeys, very distant connections, who only called them-

selves Transomes because they had got the estate. But the
Durfeys' claim had been disputed over and over again; and
the coachman, if he had been asked, would have said, though
he might have to fall down dead the next minute, that property didn't always get into the right hands. However, the
lawyers had found their luck in it; and people who inherited
estates that were lawed about often lived in them as poorly as
a mouse in a hollow cheese; and, by what he could make out,
that had been the way with these present Durfeys, or Transomes, as they called themselves. As for Mr. Transome, he
was as poor, half-witted a fellow as you'd wish to see; but
she was master, had come of a high family, and had a spirit
—you might see it in her eye and the way she sat her horse.
Forty years ago, when she came into this country, they said
she was a pictur'; but her family was poor, and so she took
up with a hatchet-faced fellow like this Transome. And the
eldest son had been just such another as his father, only worse
—a wild sort of half-natural, who got into bad company.
They said his mother hated him and wished him dead; for
she'd got another son, quite of a different cut, who had gone
to foreign parts when he was a youngster, and she wanted her
favorite to be heir. But heir or no heir, Lawyer Jermyn had
had *his* picking out of the estate. Not a door in his big
house but what was the finest polished oak, all got off the
Transome estate. If anybody liked to believe he paid for it,
they were welcome. However, Lawyer Jermyn had sat on
that box-seat many and many a time. He had made the wills
of most people thereabout. The coachman would not say that
Lawyer Jermyn was not the man he would choose to make his
own will some day. It was not so well for a lawyer to be
over-honest, else he might not be up to other people's tricks.
And as for the Transome business, there had been ins and
outs in time gone by, so that you couldn't look into it straight
backward. At this Mr. Sampson (everybody in North Loamshire knew Sampson's coach) would screw his features into
a grimace expressive of entire neutrality, and appear to aim
his whip at a particular spot on the horse's flank. If the
passenger was curious for further knowledge concerning the
Transome affairs, Sampson would shake his head and say

there had been fine stories in his time; but he never condescended to state what the stories were. Some attributed this
reticence to a wise incredulity, others to a want of memory,
others to a simple ignorance. But at least Sampson was right
in saying that there had been fine stories—meaning, ironi-
cally, stories not altogether creditable to the parties concerned.

And such stories often come to be fine in a sense that is not
ironical. For there is seldom any wrong-doing which does
not carry along with it some downfall of blindly climbing
hopes, some hard entail of suffering, some quickly satiated
desire that survives, with the life in death of old paralytic
vice, to see itself cursed by its woful progeny—some tragic
mark of kinship in the one brief life to the far-stretching life
that went before, and to the life that is to come after, such as
has raised the pity and terror of men ever since they began to
discern between will and destiny. But these things are often
unknown to the world; for there is much pain that is quite
noiseless; and vibrations that make human agonies are often
a mere whisper in the roar of hurrying existence. There are
glances of hatred that stab and raise no cry of murder; rob-
beries that leave man or woman forever beggared of peace and
joy, yet kept secret by the sufferer—committed to no sound
except that of low moans in the night, seen in no writing except that made on the face by the slow months of suppressed
anguish and early morning tears. Many an inherited sorrow
that has marred a life has been breathed into no human ear.

The poets have told us of a dolorous enchanted forest in the
under world. The thorn-bushes there, and the thick-barked
stems, have human histories hidden in them; the power of
unuttered cries dwells in the passionless-seeming branches,
and the red warm blood is darkly feeding the quivering nerves
of a sleepless memory that watches through all dreams. These
things are a parable.

CHAPTER I.

He left me when the down upon his lip
Lay like the shadow of a hovering kiss.
"Beautiful mother, do not grieve," he said:
"I will be great, and build our fortunes high,
And you shall wear the longest train at court,
And look so queenly, all the lords shall say,
'She is a royal changeling: there's some crown
Lacks the right head, since hers wears nought but braids.'"
O, he is coming now—but I am gray:
And he—

On the 1st of September, in the memorable year 1832, some one was expected at Transome Court. As early as two o'clock in the afternoon the aged lodge-keeper had opened the heavy gate, green as the tree-trunks were green with nature's powdery paint, deposited year after year. Already in the village of Little Treby, which lay on the side of a steep hill not far off the lodge gates, the elder matrons sat in their best gowns at the few cottage doors bordering the road, that they might be ready to get up and make their courtesy when a travelling carriage should come in sight; and beyond the village several small boys were stationed on the lookout, intending to run a race to the barn-like old church, where the sexton waited in the belfry ready to set the one bell in joyful agitation just at the right moment.

The old lodge-keeper had opened the gate and left it in the charge of his lame wife, because he was wanted at the Court to sweep away the leaves, and perhaps to help in the stables. For though Transome Court was a large mansion, built in the fashion of Queen Anne's time, with a park and grounds as fine as any to be seen in Loamshire, there were very few servants about it. Especially, it seemed, there must be a lack of gardeners; for, except on the terrace surrounded with a stone parapet in front of the house, where there was a parterre kept with some neatness, grass had spread itself over the gravel walks, and over all the low mounds once carefully cut as black beds for the shrubs and larger plants. Many of the windows had the shutters closed, and under the grand Scotch fir that stooped toward one corner the brown fir-needles of many years lay in a small stone balcony in front of two such darkened windows. All round, both near and far, there were grand trees, motionless in the still sunshine, and, like all large motionless things, seeming to add to the stillness. Here and there a leaf fluttered down; petals fell in a silent shower; a heavy moth floated by, and, when it settled, seemed to fall wearily; the tiny birds alighted on the walks, and hopped about in perfect tranquillity; even a stray rabbit sat nibbling a leaf that was to its liking, in the middle of a grassy space, with an air that seemed quite impudent in so timid a creature. No sound was to be heard louder than a sleepy hum, and the soft monotony of running water hurrying on to the river that divided the park. Standing on the south or east side of the house, you would never have guessed that an arrival was expected.

But on the west side, where the carriage entrance was, the gates under the stone archway were thrown open; and so was the double door of the entrance hall, letting in the warm light on the scagliola pillars, the marble statues, and the broad stone staircase, with its matting worn into large holes. And, stronger sign of expectation than all, from one of the doors which surrounded the entrance hall there came forth from time to time a lady, who walked lightly over the polished stone floor, and stood on the door-steps and watched and listened. She walked lightly, for her figure was slim and finely formed, though she was between fifty and sixty. She was a tall, proud-looking woman, with abundant gray hair, dark eyes and eyebrows, and a somewhat eagle-like yet not unfeminine face. Her tight-fitting black dress was much worn; the fine lace of her cuffs and collar, and of the small veil which fell backward over her high comb, was visibly mended; but rare jewels flashed on her hands, which lay on her folded black-clad arms like finely cut onyx cameos.

Many times Mrs. Transome went to the door-steps, watching and listening in vain. Each time she returned to the same room: it was a moderate-sized, comfortable room, with low ebony bookshelves round it, and it formed an anteroom to a large library, of which a glimpse could be seen through an open door-way, partly obstructed by a heavy tapestry curtain

drawn on one side. There was a great deal of tarnished gild-
ing and dinginess on the walls and furniture of this smaller
room, but the pictures above the bookcases were all of a cheerful kind: portraits in pastel of pearly-skinned ladies with
hair-powder, blue ribbons, and low bodices; a splendid portrait in oils of a Transome in the gorgeous dress of the Restoration; another of a Transome in his boyhood with his hand
on the neck of a small pony; and a large Flemish battle-piece,
where war seemed only a picturesque blue-and-red accident in
a vast sunny expanse of plain and sky. Probably such cheerful pictures had been chosen because this was Mrs. Transome's usual sitting-room: it was certainly for this reason
that, near the chair in which she seated herself each time she
re-entered, there hung a picture of a youthful face which
bore a strong resemblance to her own: a beardless but masculine face, with rich brown hair hanging low on the forehead,
and undulating beside each cheek down to the loose white
cravat. Near this same chair were her writing-table, with
vellum-covered account-books on it, the cabinet in which she
kept her neatly arranged drugs, her basket for her embroidery, a folio volume of architectural engravings from which
she took her embroidery patterns, a number of the *North
Loamshire Herald*, and the cushion for her fat Blenheim,
which was too old and sleepy to notice its mistress's restlessness. For, just now, Mrs. Transome could not abridge the
sunny tedium of the day by the feeble interest of her usual
indoor occupations. Her consciousness was absorbed by memories and prospects, and except when she walked to the entrance door to look out, she sat motionless with folded arms,
involuntarily from time to time turning toward the portrait
close by her, and as often, when its young brown eyes met
hers, turning away again with self-checking resolution.

At last, prompted by some sudden thought or by some
sound, she rose and went hastily beyond the tapestry curtain
into the library. She paused near the door without speaking:
apparently she only wished to see that no harm was being
done. A man nearer seventy than sixty was in the act of
ranging on a large library-table a series of shallow drawers,
some of them containing dried insects, others mineralogical

specimens. His pale mild eyes, receding lower jaw, and slight frame could never have expressed much vigor, either bodily or mental; but he had now the unevenness of gait and feebleness of gesture which tell of a past paralytic seizure. His threadbare clothes were thoroughly brushed; his soft white hair was carefully parted and arranged: he was not a neglected-looking old man; and at his side a fine black retriever, also old, sat on its haunches, and watched him as he went to and fro. But when Mrs. Transome appeared within the door-way, her husband paused in his work and shrank like a timid animal looked at in a cage where flight is impossible. He was conscious of a troublesome intention, for which he had been rebuked before—that of disturbing all his specimens with a view to a new arrangement.

After an interval, in which his wife stood perfectly still, observing him, he began to put back the drawers in their places in the row of cabinets which extended under the bookshelves at one end of the library. When they were all put back and closed, Mrs. Transome turned away, and the frightened old man seated himself with Nimrod the retriever on an ottoman. Peeping at him again, a few minutes after, she saw that he had his arm round Nimrod's neck, and was uttering his thoughts to the dog in a loud whisper, as little children do to any object near them when they believe themselves unwatched.

At last the sound of the church bell reached Mrs. Transome's ear, and she knew that before long the sound of wheels must be within hearing; but she did not at once start up and walk to the entrance door. She sat still, quivering and listening; her lips became pale, her hands were cold and trembling. Was her son really coming? She was far beyond fifty; and since her early gladness in this best-loved boy, the harvests of her life had been scanty. Could it be that now—when her hair was gray, when sight had become one of the day's fatigues, when her young accomplishments seemed almost ludicrous, like the tone of her first harpsichord and the words of the songs long browned with age—she was going to reap an assured joy?—to feel that the doubtful deeds of her life were justified by the result, since a kind Providence had sanctioned

them?—to be no longer tacitly pitied by her neighbors for her
lack of money, her imbecile husband, her graceless eldest-
born, and the loneliness of her life; but to have at her side
a rich, clever, possibly a tender, son? Yes; but there were
the fifteen years of separation, and all that had happened in
that long time to throw her into the background in her son's
memory and affection. And yet—did not men sometimes become more filial in their feeling when experience had mellowed
them, and they had themselves become fathers? Still, if Mrs.
Transome had expected only her son, she would have trembled
less; she expected a little grandson also: and there were reasons why she had not been enraptured when her son had written to her only when he was on the eve of returning that he
already had an heir born to him.

But the facts must be accepted as they stood, and, after all,
the chief thing was to have her son back again. Such pride,
such affection, such hopes as she cherished in this fifty-sixth
year of her life must find their gratification in him—or nowhere. Once more she glanced at the portrait. The young
brown eyes seemed to dwell on her pleasantly; but, turning
from it with a sort of impatience, and saying aloud, "Of
course he will be altered!" she rose almost with difficulty,
and walked more slowly than before across the hall to the
entrance door.

Already the sound of wheels was loud upon the gravel.
The momentary surprise of seeing that it was only a post-
chaise, without a servant or much luggage, that was passing
under the stone archway and then wheeling round against the
flight of stone steps, was at once merged in the sense that
there was a dark face under a red travelling-cap looking at
her from the window. She saw nothing else; she was not
even conscious that the small group of her own servants had
mustered, or that old Hickes the butler had come forward to
open the chaise door. She heard herself called "Mother!"
and felt a light kiss on each cheek; but stronger than all that
sensation was the consciousness which no previous thought
could prepare her for, that this son who had come back to her
was a stranger. Three minutes before, she had fancied that,
in spite of all changes wrought by fifteen years of separation,

she should clasp her son again as she had done at their parting; but in the moment when their eyes met, the sense of strangeness came upon her like a terror. It was not hard to understand that she was agitated, and the son led her across the hall to the sitting-room, closing the door behind them. Then he turned toward her and said, smiling,—

"You would not have known me, eh, mother?"

It was perhaps the truth. If she had seen him in a crowd, she might have looked at him without recognition—not, however, without startled wonder; for though the likeness to herself was no longer striking, the years had overlaid it with another likeness which would have arrested her. Before she answered him, his eyes, with a keen restlessness, as unlike as possible to the lingering gaze of the portrait, had travelled quickly over the room, alighting on her again as she said,—

"Everything is changed, Harold. I am an old woman, you see."

"But straighter and more upright than some of the young ones!" said Harold; inwardly, however, feeling that age had made his mother's face very anxious and eager. "The old women at Smyrna are like sacks. You've not got clumsy and shapeless. How is it I have the trick of getting fat?" (Here Harold lifted his arm and spread out his plump hand.) "I remember my father was as thin as a herring. How is my father? Where is he?"

Mrs. Transome just pointed to the curtained door-way, and let her son pass through it alone. She was not given to tears; but now, under the pressure of emotion that could find no other vent, they burst forth. She took care that they should be silent tears, and before Harold came out of the library again they were dried. Mrs. Transome had not the feminine tendency to seek influence through pathos; she had been used to rule in virtue of acknowledged superiority. The consciousness that she had to make her son's acquaintance, and that her knowledge of the youth of nineteen might help her little in interpreting the man of thirty-four, had fallen like lead on her soul; but in this new acquaintance of theirs she cared especially that her son, who had seen a strange world, should feel that he was come home to a mother who was to be con-

2

sulted on all things, and who could supply his lack of the local
experience necessary to an English landholder. Her part in
life had been that of the clever sinner, and she was equipped
with the views, the reasons, and the habits which belonged
to that character: life would have little meaning for her if
she were to be gently thrust aside as a harmless elderly
woman. And besides, there were secrets which her son must
never know. So, by the time Harold came from the library
again, the traces of tears were not discernible except to a very
careful observer. And he did not observe his mother carefully; his eyes only glanced at her on their way to the *North
Loamshire Herald* lying on the table near her, which he took
up with his left hand, as he said,—

"Gad! what a wreck poor father is! Paralysis, eh? Terribly shrunk and shaken—crawls about among his books and
beetles as usual, though. Well, it's a slow and easy death.
But he's not much over sixty-five, is he?"

"Sixty-seven, counting by birthdays; but your father was
born old, I think," said Mrs. Transome, a little flushed with
the determination not to show any unasked-for feeling.

Her son did not notice her. All the time he had been
speaking his eyes had been running down the columns of the
newspaper.

"But your little boy, Harold—where is he? How is it he
has not come with you?"

"Oh, I left him behind, in town," said Harold, still looking at the paper. "My man Dominic will bring him, with
the rest of the luggage. Ah, I see it is young Debarry, and
not my old friend, Sir Maximus, who is offering himself as
candidate for North Loamshire."

"Yes. You did not answer me when I wrote to you to
London about your standing. There is no other Tory candidate spoken of, and you would have all the Debarry interest."

"I hardly think that," said Harold, significantly.

"Why? Jermyn says a Tory candidate can never be got
in without it."

"But I shall not be a Tory candidate."

Mrs. Transome felt something like an electric shock.

"What then?" she said, almost sharply. "You will not call yourself a Whig?"

"God forbid! I'm a Radical."

Mrs. Transome's limbs tottered; she sank into a chair. Here was a distinct confirmation of the vague but strong feeling that her son was a stranger to her. Here was a revelation to which it seemed almost as impossible to adjust her hopes and notions of a dignified life as if her son had said that he had been converted to Mahometanism at Smyrna, and had four wives, instead of one son, shortly to arrive under the care of Dominic. For the moment she had a sickening feeling that it was all of no use that the long-delayed good fortune had come at last—all of no use though the unloved Durfey was dead and buried, and though Harold had come home with plenty of money. There were rich Radicals, she was aware, as there were rich Jews and Dissenters, but she had never thought of them as country people. Sir Francis Burdett had been generally regarded as a madman. It was better to ask no questions, but silently to prepare herself for anything else there might be to come.

"Will you go to your rooms, Harold, and see if there is anything you would like to have altered?"

"Yes, let us go," said Harold, throwing down the newspaper, in which he had been rapidly reading almost every advertisement while his mother had been going through her sharp inward struggle. "Uncle Lingon is on the bench still, I see," he went on, as he followed her across the hall; "is he at home—will he be here this evening?"

"He says you must go to the Rectory when you want to see him. You must remember you have come back to a family who have old-fashioned notions. Your uncle thought I ought to have you to myself in the first hour or two. He remembered that I had not seen my son for fifteen years."

"Ah, by Jove! fifteen years—so it is!" said Harold, taking his mother's hand and drawing it under his arm; for he had perceived that her words were charged with an intention. "And you are as straight as an arrow still; you will carry the shawls I have brought you as well as ever."

They walked up the broad stone steps together in silence.

Under the shock of discovering her son's Radicalism, Mrs. Transome had no impulse to say one thing rather than another; as in a man who had just been branded on the forehead all wonted motives would be uprooted. Harold, on his side, had no wish opposed to filial kindness, but his busy thoughts were imperiously determined by habits which had no reference to any woman's feeling; and even if he could have conceived what his mother's feeling was, his mind, after that momentary arrest, would have darted forward on its usual course.

"I have given you the south rooms, Harold," said Mrs. Transome, as they passed along a corridor lit from above, and lined with old family pictures. "I thought they would suit you best, as they all open into each other, and this middle one will make a pleasant sitting-room for you."

"Gad! the furniture is in a bad state," said Harold, glancing round at the middle room which they had just entered; "the moths seem to have got into the carpets and hangings."

"I had no choice except moths or tenants who would pay rent," said Mrs. Transome. "We have been too poor to keep servants for uninhabited rooms."

"What! you've been rather pinched, eh?"

"You find us living as we have been living these twelve years."

"Ah, you've had Durfey's debts as well as the lawsuits— confound them! It will make a hole in sixty thousand pounds to pay off the mortgages. However, he's gone now, poor fellow; and I suppose I should have spent more in buying an English estate some time or other. I always meant to be an Englishman, and thrash a lord or two who thrashed me at Eton."

"I hardly thought you could have meant that, Harold, when I found you had married a foreign wife."

"Would you have had me wait for a consumptive, lackadaisical Englishwoman, who would have hung all her relations round my neck? I hate English wives; they want to give their opinion about everything. They interfere with a man's life. I shall not marry again."

Mrs. Transome bit her lip, and turned away to draw up a

blind. She would not reply to words which showed how completely any conception of herself and her feelings was excluded from her son's inward world.

As she turned round again she said, "I suppose you have been used to great luxury; these rooms look miserable to you, but you can soon make any alteration you like."

"Oh, I must have a private sitting-room fitted up for myself downstairs. And the rest are bedrooms, I suppose," he went on, opening a side door. "Ah, I can sleep here a night or two. But there's a bedroom downstairs, with an ante-room, I remember, that would do for my man Dominic and the little boy. I should like to have that."

"Your father has slept there for years. He will be like a distracted insect, and never know where to go, if you alter the track he has to walk in."

"That's a pity. I hate going upstairs."

"There is the steward's room: it is not used, and it might be turned into a bedroom. I can't offer you my room, for I sleep upstairs." (Mrs. Transome's tongue could be a whip upon occasion, but the lash had not fallen on a sensitive spot.)

"No; I'm determined not to sleep upstairs. We'll see about the steward's room to-morrow, and I dare say I shall find a closet of some sort for Dominic. It's a nuisance he had to stay behind, for I shall have nobody to cook for me. Ah, there's the old river I used to fish in. I often thought, when I was at Smyrna, that I would buy a park with a river through it as much like the Lapp as possible. Gad, what fine oaks those are opposite! Some of them must come down, though."

"I've held every tree sacred on the demesne, as I told you, Harold. I trusted to your getting the estate some time, and releasing it; and I determined to keep it worth releasing. A park without fine timber is no better than a beauty without teeth and hair."

"Bravo, mother!" said Harold, putting his hand on her shoulder. "Ah, you've had to worry yourself about things that don't properly belong to a woman—my father being weakly. We'll set all that right. You shall have nothing to do now but to be grandmamma on satin cushions."

"You must excuse me from the satin cushions. That is part of the old woman's duty I am not prepared for. I am used to be chief bailiff, and to sit in the saddle two or three hours every day. There are two farms on our hands besides the Home Farm."

"Phew-ew! Jermyn manages the estate badly, then. That will not last under *my* reign," said Harold, turning on his heel and feeling in his pockets for the keys of his portmanteaus, which had been brought up.

"Perhaps when you've been in England a little longer," said Mrs. Transome, coloring as if she had been a girl, "you will understand better the difficulty there is in letting farms in these times."

"I understand the difficulty perfectly, mother. To let farms, a man must have the sense to see what will make them inviting to farmers; and to get sense supplied on demand is just the most difficult transaction I know of. I suppose if I ring there's some fellow who can act as valet and learn to attend to my hookah?"

"There is Hickes the butler, and there is Jabez the footman; those are all the men in the house. They were here when you left."

"Oh, I remember Jabez—he was a dolt. I'll have old Hickes. He was a neat little machine of a butler; his words used to come like the clicks of an engine. He must be an old machine now, though."

"You seem to remember some things about home wonderfully well, Harold."

"Never forget places and people—how they look and what can be done with them. All the country round here lies like a map in my brain. A deuced pretty country too; but the people were a stupid set of old Whigs and Tories. I suppose they are much as they were."

"I am, at least, Harold. You are the first of your family that ever talked of being a Radical. I did not think I was taking care of our old oaks for that. I always thought Radicals' houses stood staring above poor sticks of young trees and iron hurdles."

"Yes, but the Radical sticks are growing, mother, and half

the Tory oaks are rotting," said Harold, with gay carelessness. "You've arranged for Jermyn to be early to-morrow?"

"He will be here to breakfast at nine. But I leave you to Hickes now; we dine in an hour."

Mrs. Transome went away and shut herself in her own dressing-room. It had come to pass now—this meeting with the son who had been the object of so much longing; whom she had longed for before he was born, for whom she had sinned, from whom she had wrenched herself with pain at their parting, and whose coming again had been the one great hope of her years. The moment was gone by; there had been no ecstasy, no gladness even; hardly half an hour had passed, and few words had been spoken, yet with that quickness in weaving new futures which belongs to women whose actions have kept them in habitual fear of consequences, Mrs. Transome thought she saw with all the clearness of demonstration that her son's return had not been a good for her in the sense of making her any happier.

She stood before a tall mirror, going close to it and looking at her face with hard scrutiny, as if it were unrelated to herself. No elderly face can be handsome, looked at in that way; every little detail is startlingly prominent, and the effect of the whole is lost. She saw the dried-up complexion, and the deep lines of bitter discontent about the mouth.

"I am a hag!" she said to herself (she was accustomed to give her thoughts a very sharp outline), "an ugly old woman who happens to be his mother. That is what he sees in me, as I see a stranger in him. I shall count for nothing. I was foolish to expect anything else."

She turned away from the mirror and walked up and down her room.

"What a likeness!" she said, in a loud whisper; "yet, perhaps, no one will see it besides me."

She threw herself into a chair, and sat with a fixed look, seeing nothing that was actually present, but inwardly seeing with painful vividness what had been present with her a little more than thirty years ago—the little round-limbed creature that had been leaning against her knees, and stamping tiny feet, and looking up at her with gurgling laughter. She had thought that the possession of this child would give unity to her life, and make some gladness through the changing years that would grow as fruit out of these early maternal caresses. But nothing had come just as she had wished. The mother's early raptures had lasted but a short time, and even while they lasted there had grown up in the midst of them a hungry desire, like a black poisonous plant feeding in the sunlight,— the desire that her first, rickety, ugly, imbecile child should die, and leave room for her darling, of whom she could be proud. Such desires make life a hideous lottery, where every day may turn up a blank; where men and women who have the softest beds and the most delicate eating, who have a very large share of that sky and earth which some are born to have no more of than the fraction to be got in a crowded entry, yet grow haggard, fevered, and restless, like those who watch in other lotteries. Day after day, year after year, had yielded blanks; new cares had come, bringing other desires for results quite beyond her grasp, which must also be watched for in the lottery; and all the while the round-limbed pet had been grow- ing into a strong youth, who liked many things better than his mother's caresses, and who had a much keener consciousness of his independent existence than of his relation to her: the lizard's egg, that white rounded passive prettiness, had be- come a brown, darting, determined lizard. The mother's love is at first an absorbing delight, blunting all other sensibilities; it is an expansion of the animal existence; it enlarges the imagined range for self to move in: but in after years it can only continue to be joy on the same terms as other long-lived love—that is, by much suppression of self, and power of living in the experience of another. Mrs. Transome had darkly felt the pressure of that unchangeable fact. Yet she had clung to the belief that somehow the possession of this son was the best thing she lived for; to believe otherwise would have made her memory too ghastly a companion. Some time or other, by some means, the estate she was struggling to save from the grasp of the law would be Harold's. Somehow the hated Durfey, the imbecile eldest, who seemed to have become tena- cious of a despicable squandering life, would be got rid of; vice might kill him. Meanwhile the estate was burdened:

there was no good prospect for any heir. Harold must go and make a career for himself: and this was what he was bent on, with a precocious clearness of perception as to the conditions on which he could hope for any advantages in life. Like most energetic natures, he had a strong faith in his luck; he had been gay at their parting, and had promised to make his fortune; and in spite of past disappointments, Harold's possible fortune still made some ground for his mother to plant her hopes in. His luck had not failed him; yet nothing had turned out according to her expectations. Her life had been like a spoiled shabby pleasure-day, in which the music and the processions are all missed, and nothing is left at evening but the weariness of striving after what has been failed of. Harold had gone with the Embassy to Constantinople, under the patronage of a high relative, his mother's cousin; he was to be a diplomatist, and work his way upward in public life. But his luck had taken another shape: he had saved the life of an Armenian banker, who in gratitude had offered him a prospect which his practical mind had preferred to the problematic promises of diplomacy and high-born cousinship. Harold had become a merchant and banker at Smyrna; had let the years pass without caring to find the possibility of visiting his early home, and had shown no eagerness to make his life at all familiar to his mother, asking for letters about England, but writing scantily about himself. Mrs. Transome had kept up the habit of writing to her son, but gradually the unfruitful years had dulled her hopes and yearnings; increasing anxieties about money had worried her, and she was more sure of being fretted by bad news about her dissolute eldest son than of hearing anything to cheer her from Harold. She had begun to live merely in small immediate cares and occupations, and, like all eager-minded women who advance in life without any activity of tenderness or any large sympathy, she had contracted small rigid habits of thinking and acting, she had her " ways " which must not be crossed, and had learned to fill up the great void of life with giving small orders to tenants, insisting on medicines for infirm cottagers, winning small triumphs in bargains and personal economies, and parrying ill-natured remarks of Lady Debarry's by lancet-edged epigrams.

So her life had gone on till more than a year ago, when that desire which had been so hungry when she was a blooming young mother was at last fulfilled—at last, when her hair was gray, and her face looked bitter, restless, and unenjoying, like her life. The news came from Jersey that Durfey, the imbecile son, was dead. *Now* Harold was heir to the estate; now the wealth he had gained could release the land from its burthens; now he would think it worth while to return home. A change had at last come over her life, and the sunlight breaking the clouds at evening was pleasant, though the sun must sink before long. Hopes, affections, the sweeter part of her memories, started from their wintry sleep, and it once more seemed a great good to have had a second son who in some ways had cost her dearly. But again there were conditions she had not reckoned on. When the good tidings had been sent to Harold, and he had announced that he would return so soon as he could wind up his affairs, he had for the first time informed his mother that he had been married, that his Greek wife was no longer living, but that he should bring home a little boy, the finest and most desirable of heirs and grandsons. Harold, seated in his distant Smyrna home, considered that he was taking a rational view of what things must have become by this time at the old place in England, when he figured his mother as a good elderly lady, who would necessarily be delighted with the possession on any terms of a healthy grandchild, and would not mind much about the particulars of the long-concealed marriage.

Mrs. Transome had torn up that letter in a rage. But in the months which had elapsed before Harold could actually arrive, she had prepared herself as well as she could to suppress all reproaches or queries which her son might resent, and to acquiesce in his evident wishes. The return was still looked for with longing; affection and satisfied pride would again warm her later years. She was ignorant what sort of man Harold had become now, and of course he must be changed in many ways; but though she told herself this, still the image that she knew, the image fondness clung to, necessarily prevailed over the negatives insisted on by her reason.

And so it was, that when she had moved to the door to meet

him, she had been sure that she should clasp her son again, and feel that he was the same who had been her boy, her little one, the loved child of her passionate youth. An hour seemed to have changed everything for her. A woman's hopes are woven of sunbeams; a shadow annihilates them. The shadow which had fallen over Mrs. Transome in this first interview with her son was the presentiment of her powerlessness. If things went wrong, if Harold got unpleasantly disposed in a certain direction where her chief dread had always lain, she seemed to foresee that her words would be of no avail. The keenness of her anxiety in this matter had served as insight; and Harold's rapidity, decision, and indifference to any impressions in others which did not further or impede his own purposes had made themselves felt by her as much as she would have felt the unmanageable strength of a great bird which had alighted near her, and allowed her to stroke its wing for a moment because food lay near her.

Under the cold weight of these thoughts Mrs. Transome shivered. That physical reaction roused her from her revery, and she could now hear the gentle knocking at the door to which she had been deaf before. Notwithstanding her activity and the fewness of her servants, she had never dressed herself without aid; nor would that small, neat, exquisitely clean old woman who now presented herself have wished that her labor should be saved at the expense of such a sacrifice on her lady's part. The small old woman was Mrs. Hickes, the butler's wife, who acted as housekeeper, lady's maid, and superintendent of the kitchen—the large stony scene of inconsiderable cooking. Forty years ago she had entered Mrs. Transome's service, when that lady was beautiful Miss Lingon, and her mistress still called her Denner, as she had done in the old days.

"The bell has rung, then, Denner, without my hearing it?" said Mrs. Transome, rising.

"Yes, madam," said Denner, reaching from a wardrobe an old black velvet dress trimmed with much-mended point, in which Mrs. Transome was wont to look queenly of an evening.

Denner had still strong eyes of that short-sighted kind which sees through the narrowest chink between the eyelashes.

The physical contrast between the tall, eagle-faced, dark-eyed lady and the little peering waiting-woman, who had been round-featured and of pale mealy complexion from her youth up, had doubtless had a strong influence in determining Denner's feeling toward her mistress, which was of that worshipful sort paid to a goddess in ages when it was not thought necessary or likely that a goddess should be very moral. There were different orders of beings—so ran Denner's creed—and she belonged to another order than that to which her mistress belonged. She had a mind as sharp as a needle, and would have seen through and through the ridiculous pretensions of a born servant who did not submissively accept the rigid fate which had given her born superiors. She would have called such pretensions the wrigglings of a worm that tried to walk on its tail. There was a tacit understanding that Denner knew all her mistress's secrets, and her speech was plain and unflattering; yet with wonderful subtlety of instinct she never said anything which Mrs. Transome could feel humiliated by, as by a familiarity from a servant who knew too much. Denner identified her own dignity with that of her mistress. She was a hard-headed godless little woman, but with a character to be reckoned on as you reckon on the qualities of iron.

Peering into Mrs. Transome's face, she saw clearly that the meeting with the son had been a disappointment in some way. She spoke with a refined accent, in a low, quick, monotonous tone,—

"Mr. Harold is drest; he shook me by the hand in the corridor, and was very pleasant."

"What an alteration, Denner! No likeness to me now."

"Handsome, though, spite of his being so browned and stout. There's a fine presence about Mr. Harold. I remember you used to say, madam, there were some people you would always know were in the room though they stood round a corner, and others you might never see till you ran against them. That's as true as truth. And as for likenesses, thirty-five and sixty are not much alike, only to people's memories."

Mrs. Transome knew perfectly that Denner had divined her thoughts.

"I don't know how things will go on now; but it seems something too good to happen that they will go on well. I am afraid of ever expecting anything good again."

"That's weakness, madam. Things don't happen because they're bad or good, else all eggs would be addled or none at all, and at the most it is but six to the dozen. There's good chances and bad chances, and nobody's luck is pulled only by one string."

"What a woman you are, Denner! You talk like a French infidel. It seems to me you are afraid of nothing. I have been full of fears all my life—always seeing something or other hanging over me that I couldn't bear to happen."

"Well, madam, put a good face on it, and don't seem to be on the lookout for crows, else you'll set other people watching. Here you have a rich son come home, and the debts will all be paid, and you have your health and can ride about, and you've such a face and figure, and will have if you live to be eighty, that everybody is cap in hand to you before they know who you are—let me fasten up your veil a little higher: there's a good deal of pleasure in life for you yet."

"Nonsense! there's no pleasure for old women, unless they get it out of tormenting other people. What are your pleasures, Denner—besides being a slave to me?"

"Oh, there's pleasure in knowing one's not a fool, like half the people one sees about. And managing one's husband is some pleasure; and doing all one's business well. Why, if I've only got some orange flowers to candy, I shouldn't like to die till I see them all right. Then there's the sunshine now and then; I like that as the cats do. I look upon it, life is like our game at whist, when Banks and his wife come to the still-room of an evening. I don't enjoy the game much, but I like to play my cards well, and see what will be the end of it; and I want to see you make the best of your hand, madam, for your luck has been mine these forty years now. But I must go and see how Kitty dishes up the dinner, unless you have any more commands."

"No, Denner; I am going down immediately."

As Mrs. Transome descended the stone staircase in her old black velvet and point her appearance justified Denner's per-

sonal compliment.   She had that high-born imperious air
which would have marked her as an object of hatred and
reviling by a revolutionary mob.   Her person was too typical
of social distinctions to be passed by with indifference by any
one : it would have fitted an empress in her own right, who
had had to rule in spite of faction, to dare the violation of
treaties and dread retributive invasions, to grasp after new
territories, to be defiant in desperate circumstances, and to feel
a woman's hunger of the heart forever unsatisfied.   Yet Mrs.
Transome's cares and occupations had not been at all of an
imperial sort.   For thirty years she had led the monotonous,
narrowing life which used to be the lot of our poorer gentry;
who never went to town, and were probably not on speaking
terms with two out of the five families whose parks lay within
the distance of a drive.   When she was young she had been
thought wonderfully clever and accomplished, and had been
rather ambitious of intellectual superiority — had secretly
picked out for private reading the lighter parts of dangerous
French authors—and in company had been able to talk of Mr.
Burke's style, or of Chateaubriand's eloquence—had laughed
at the Lyrical Ballads and admired Mr. Southey's Thalaba.
She always thought that the dangerous French writers were
wicked and that her reading of them was a sin; but many
sinful things were highly agreeable to her, and many things
which she did not doubt to be good and true were dull and
meaningless.   She found ridicule of Biblical characters very
amusing, and she was interested in stories of illicit passion :
but she believed all the while that truth and safety lay in due
attendance on prayers and sermons, in the admirable doctrines
and ritual of the Church of England, equally remote from
Puritanism and Popery; in fact, in such a view of this world and
the next as would preserve the existing arrangements of English society quite unshaken, keeping down the obtrusiveness
of the vulgar and the discontent of the poor.   The history of
the Jews, she knew, ought to be preferred to any profane history; the Pagans, of course, were vicious, and their religions
quite nonsensical, considered as religions—but classical learning came from the Pagans; the Greeks were famous for sculp-
ture; the Italians for painting; the middle ages were dark

and Papistical; but now Christianity went hand in hand with civilization, and the providential government of the world, though a little confused and entangled in foreign countries, in our favored land was clearly seen to be carried forward on Tory and Church of England principles, sustained by the succession of the House of Brunswick, and by sound English divines. For Miss Lingon had had a superior governess, who held that a woman should be able to write a good letter, and to express herself with propriety on general subjects. And it is astonishing how effective this education appeared in a handsome girl, who sat supremely well on horseback, sang and played a little, painted small figures in water-colors, had a naughty sparkle in her eyes when she made a daring quotation, and an air of serious dignity when she recited something from her store of correct opinions. But however such a stock of ideas may be made to tell in elegant society, and during a few seasons in town, no amount of bloom and beauty can make them a perennial source of interest in things not personal; and the notion that what is true and, in general, good for mankind is stupid and drug-like is not a safe theoretic basis in circumstances of temptation and difficulty. Mrs. Transome had been in her bloom before this century began, and in the long painful years since then what she had once regarded as her knowledge and accomplishments had become as valueless as old-fashioned stucco ornaments, of which the substance was never worth anything, while the form is no longer to the taste of any living mortal. Crosses, mortifications, money-cares, conscious blameworthiness, had changed the aspect of the world for her: there was anxiety in the morning sunlight; there was unkind triumph or disapproving pity in the glances of greeting neighbors; there was advancing age, and a contracting prospect in the changing seasons as they came and went. And what could then sweeten the days to a hungry, much-exacting self like Mrs. Transome's? Under protracted ill every living creature will find something that makes a comparative ease, and, even when life seems woven of pain, will convert the fainter pang into a desire. Mrs. Transome, whose imperious will had availed little to ward off the great evils of her life, found the opiate for her discontent in the exertion of her will about smaller things. She was not cruel, and could not enjoy thoroughly what she called the old woman's pleasure of tormenting; but she liked every little sign of power her lot had left her. She liked that a tenant should stand bareheaded below her as she sat on horseback. She liked to insist that work done without her orders should be undone from beginning to end. She liked to be courtesied and bowed to by all the congregation as she walked up the little barn of a church. She liked to change a laborer's medicine fetched from the doctor, and substitute a prescription of her own. If she had only been more haggard and less majestic, those who had glimpses of her outward life might have said she was a tyrannical, griping harridan, with a tongue like a razor. No one said exactly that; but they never said anything like the full truth about her, or divined what was hidden under that outward life—a woman's keen sensibility and dread, which lay screened behind all her petty habits and narrow notions, as some quivering thing with eyes and throbbing heart may lie crouching behind withered rubbish. The sensibility and dread had palpitated all the faster in the prospect of her son's return; and now that she had seen him she said to herself, in her bitter way, "It is a lucky eel that escapes skinning. The best happiness I shall ever know will be to escape the worst misery."

CHAPTER II.

A jolly parson of the good old stock,
By birth a gentleman, yet homely too,
Suiting his phrase to Hodge and Margery
Whom he once christened, and has married since.
A little lax in doctrine and in life,
Not thinking God was captious in such things
As what a man might drink on holidays,
But holding true religion was to do
As you'd be done by—which could never mean
That he should preach three sermons in a week.

HAROLD TRANSOME did not choose to spend the whole evening with his mother. It was his habit to compress a great deal of effective conversation into a short space of time, asking rapidly all the questions he wanted to get answered, and diluting no subject with irrelevancies, paraphrase, or repetitions. He volunteered no information about himself and his past life at Smyrna, but answered pleasantly enough, though briefly, whenever his mother asked for any detail. He was evidently ill satisfied as to his palate, trying red pepper to everything, then asking if there were any relishing sauces in the house, and when Hickes brought various home-filled bottles, trying several, finding them failures, and finally falling back from his plate in despair. Yet he remained good-humored, saying something to his father now and then for the sake of being kind, and looking on with a pitying shrug as he saw him watch Hickes cutting his food. Mrs. Transome thought with some bitterness that Harold showed more feeling for her feeble husband, who had never cared in the least about him, than for her, who had given him more than the usual share of mother's love. An hour after dinner, Harold, who had already been turning over the leaves of his mother's account-books, said, —

"I shall just cross the park to the parsonage to see my uncle Lingon."

"Very well. He can answer more questions for you."

"Yes," said Harold, quite deaf to the innuendo, and accepting the words as a simple statement of the fact. "I want to hear all about the game and the North Loamshire hunt. I'm fond of sport; we had a great deal of it at Smyrna, and it keeps down my fat."

The Reverend John Lingon became very talkative over his second bottle of port, which was opened on his nephew's arrival. He was not curious about the manners of Smyrna, or about Harold's experience, but he unbosomed himself very freely as to what he himself liked and disliked, which of the farmers he suspected of killing the foxes, what game he had bagged that very morning, what spot he would recommend as a new cover, and the comparative flatness of all existing sport compared with cock-fighting, under which Old England had been prosperous and glorious, while, so far as he could see, it had gained little by the abolition of a practice which sharpened the faculties of men, gratified the instincts of the fowl, and carried out the designs of heaven in its admirable device of spurs. From these main topics, which made his points of

3

departure and return, he rambled easily enough at any new suggestion or query; so that when Harold got home at a late hour he was conscious of having gathered from amidst the pompous full-toned triviality of his uncle's chat some impressions which were of practical importance. Among the Rector's dislikes, it appeared, was Mr. Matthew Jermyn.

"A fat-handed, glib-tongued fellow, with a scented cambric handkerchief; one of your educated low-bred fellows; a foundling who got his Latin for nothing at Christ's Hospital; one of your middle-class upstarts who want to rank with gentlemen, and think they'll do it with kid gloves and new furniture."

But since Harold meant to stand for the county Mr. Lingon was equally emphatic as to the necessity of his not quarrelling with Jermyn till the election was over. Jermyn must be his agent; Harold must wink hard till he found himself safely returned; and even then it might be well to let Jermyn drop gently and raise no scandal. He himself had no quarrel with the fellow: a clergyman should have no quarrels, and he made it a point to be able to take wine with any man he met at table. And as to the estate, and his sister's going too much by Jermyn's advice, he never meddled with business: it was not his duty as a clergyman. That, he considered, was the meaning of Melchisedec and the tithe, a subject into which he had gone to some depth thirty years ago, when he preached the Visitation Sermon.

The discovery that Harold meant to stand on the liberal side —nay, that he boldly declared himself a Radical—was rather startling; but to his uncle's good humor, beatified by the sipping of port wine, nothing could seem highly objectionable, provided it did not disturb that operation. In the course of half an hour he had brought himself to see that anything really worthy to be called British Toryism had been entirely extinct since the Duke of Wellington and Sir Robert Peel had passed the Catholic Emancipation Bill; that Whiggery, with its rights of man stopping short at ten-pound householders, and its policy of pacifying a wild beast with a bite, was a ridiculous monstrosity; that therefore, since an honest man could not call himself a Tory, which it was, in fact, as impossible to be now as to fight for the old Pretender, and could still less become that execrable monstrosity a Whig, there remained but one course open to him. "Why, lad, if the world was turned into a swamp, I suppose we should leave off shoes and stockings, and walk about like cranes"—whence it followed plainly enough that, in these hopeless times, nothing was left to men of sense and good family but to retard the national ruin by declaring themselves Radicals, and take the inevitable process of changing everything out of the hands of beggarly demagogues and purse-proud tradesmen. It is true the Rector was helped to this chain of reasoning by Harold's remarks; but he soon became quite ardent in asserting the conclusion.

"If the mob can't be turned back, a man of family must try and head the mob, and save a few homes and hearths, and keep the country up on its last legs as long as he can. And you're a man of family, my lad—dash it! you're a Lingon, whatever else you may be, and I'll stand by you. I've no great interest; I'm a poor parson. I've been forced to give up hunting; my pointers and a glass of good wine are the only decencies becoming my station that I can allow myself. But I'll give you my countenance—I'll stick to you as my nephew. There's no need for me to change sides exactly. I was born a Tory, and I shall never be a bishop. But if anybody says you're in the wrong, I shall say, ' My nephew is in the right; he has turned Radical to save his country. If William Pitt had been living now, he'd have done the same; for what did he say when he was dying? Not "Oh, save my party!" but "Oh, save my country, heaven!"' That was what they dinned in our ears about Peel and the Duke; and now I'll turn it round upon them. They shall be hoist with their own petard. Yes, yes, I'll stand by you."

Harold did not feel sure that his uncle would thoroughly retain this satisfactory thread of argument in the uninspired hours of the morning; but the old gentleman was sure to take the facts easily in the end, and there was no fear of family coolness or quarrelling on this side. Harold was glad of it. He was not to be turned aside from any course he had chosen; but he disliked all quarrelling as an unpleasant expenditure of energy that could have no good practical result. He was at

once active and luxurious; fond of mastery, and good-natured
enough to wish that every one about him should like his mastery; not caring greatly to know other people's thoughts, and
ready to despise them as blockheads if their thoughts differed
from his, and yet solicitous that they should have no colorable
reason for slight thoughts about *him*. The blockheads must
be forced to respect him. Hence, in proportion as he foresaw
that his equals in the neighborhood would be indignant with
him for his political choice, he cared keenly about making a
good figure before them in every other way. His conduct as a
landholder was to be judicious, his establishment was to be
kept up generously, his imbecile father treated with careful
regard, his family relations entirely without scandal. He
knew that affairs had been unpleasant in his youth—that there
had been ugly lawsuits—and that his scapegrace brother Durfey had helped to lower still farther the depressed condition of
the family. All this must be retrieved, now that events had
made Harold the head of the Transome name.

Jermyn must be used for the election, and after that, if he
must be got rid of, it would be well to shake him loose quietly:
his uncle was probably right on both these points. But Harold's expectation that he should want to get rid of Jermyn
was founded on other reasons than his scented handkerchief
and his charity-school Latin.

If the lawyer had been presuming on Mrs. Transome's ignorance as a woman, and on the stupid rakishness of the original
heir, the new heir would prove to him that he had calculated
rashly. Otherwise, Harold had no prejudice against him. In
his boyhood and youth he had seen Jermyn frequenting Transome Court, but had regarded him with that total indifference
with which youngsters are apt to view those who neither deny
them pleasures nor give them any. Jermyn used to smile at
him, and speak to him affably; but Harold, half proud, half
shy, got away from such patronage as soon as possible: he
knew Jermyn was a man of business; his father, his uncle,
and Sir Maximus Debarry did not regard him as a gentleman
and their equal. He had known no evil of the man; but he
saw now that if he were really a covetous upstart there had
been a temptation for him in the management of the Transome

affairs; and it was clear that the estate was in a bad condition.

When Mr. Jermyn was ushered into the breakfast-room the next morning, Harold found him surprisingly little altered by the fifteen years. He was gray, but still remarkably handsome; fat, but tall enough to bear that trial to man's dignity. There was as strong a suggestion of toilet about him as if he had been five-and-twenty instead of nearly sixty. He chose always to dress in black, and was especially addicted to black satin waistcoats, which carried out the general sleekness of his appearance; and this, together with his white, fat, but beautifully shaped hands, which he was in the habit of rubbing gently on his entrance into a room, gave him very much the air of a lady's physician. Harold remembered with some amusement his uncle's dislike of those conspicuous hands: but as his own were soft and dimpled, and as he too was given to the innocent practice of rubbing those members, his suspicions were not yet deepened.

"I congratulate you, Mrs. Transome," said Jermyn, with a soft and deferential smile, "all the more," he added, turning toward Harold, "now I have the pleasure of actually seeing your son. I am glad to perceive that an Eastern climate has not been unfavorable to him."

"No," said Harold, shaking Jermyn's hand carelessly, and speaking with more than his usual rapid brusqueness, "the question is, whether the English climate will agree with me. It's deuced shifting and damp; and as for the food, it would be the finest thing in the world for this country if the southern cooks would change their religion, get persecuted, and fly to England, as the old silk-weavers did."

"There are plenty of foreign cooks for those who are rich enough to pay for them, I suppose," said Mrs. Transome, "but they are unpleasant people to have about one's house."

"Gad! I don't think so," said Harold.

"The old servants are sure to quarrel with them."

"That's no concern of mine. The old servants will have to put up with my man Dominic, who will show them how to cook and do everything else in a way that will rather astonish them."

"Old people are not so easily taught to change all their ways, Harold."

"Well, they can give up and watch the young ones," said Harold, thinking only at that moment of old Mrs. Hickes and Dominic. But his mother was not thinking of them only.

"You have a valuable servant, it seems," said Jermyn, who understood Mrs. Transome better than her son did, and wished to smoothen the current of their dialogue.

"Oh, one of those wonderful southern fellows that make one's life easy. He's of no country in particular. I don't know whether he's most of a Jew, a Greek, an Italian, or a Spaniard. He speaks five or six languages, one as well as another. He's cook, valet, major-domo, and secretary all in one; and, what's more, he's an affectionate fellow—I can trust to his attachment. That's a sort of human specimen that doesn't grow here in England, I fancy. I should have been badly off if I could not have brought Dominic."

They sat down to breakfast with such slight talk as this going on. Each of the party was preoccupied and uneasy. Harold's mind was busy constructing probabilities about what he should discover of Jermyn's mismanagement or dubious application of funds, and the sort of self-command he must in the worst case exercise in order to use the man as long as he wanted him. Jermyn was closely observing Harold with an unpleasant sense that there was an expression of acuteness and determination about him which would make him formidable. He would certainly have preferred at that moment that there had been no second heir of the Transome name to come back upon him from the East. Mrs. Transome was not observing the two men; rather, her hands were cold, and her whole person shaken by their presence; she seemed to hear and see what they said and did with preternatural acuteness, and yet she was also seeing and hearing what had been said and done many years before, and feeling a dim terror about the future. There were piteous sensibilities in this faded woman, who thirty-four years ago, in the splendor of her bloom, had been imperious to one of these men, and had rapturously pressed the other as an infant to her bosom, and now knew that she was of little consequence to either of them.

"Well, what are the prospects about the election?" said Harold, as the breakfast was advancing. "There are two Whigs and one Conservative likely to be in the field, I know. What is your opinion of the chances?"

Mr. Jermyn had a copious supply of words, which often led him into periphrase, but he cultivated a hesitating stammer, which, with a handsome impassiveness of face, except when he was smiling at a woman, or when the latent savageness of his nature was thoroughly roused, he had found useful in many relations, especially in business. No one could have found out that he was not at his ease. "My opinion," he replied, "is in a state of balance at present. This division of the county, you are aware, contains one manufacturing town of the first magnitude, and several smaller ones. The manufacturing interest is widely dispersed. So far—a—there is a presumption—a—in favor of the two Liberal candidates. Still, with a careful canvass of the agricultural districts, such as those we have round us at Treby Magna, I think—a—the auguries—a—would not be unfavorable to the return of a Conservative. A fourth candidate of good position, who should coalesce with Mr. Debarry—a——"

Here Mr. Jermyn hesitated for the third time, and Harold broke in.

"That will not be my line of action, so we need not discuss it. If I put up, it will be as a Radical; and I fancy in any county that would return Whigs there would be plenty of voters to be combed off by a Radical who offered himself with good pretensions."

There was the slightest possible quiver discernible across Jermyn's face. Otherwise he sat as he had done before, with his eyes fixed abstractedly on the frill of a ham before him and his hand trifling with his fork. He did not answer immediately, but when he did he looked round steadily at Harold.

"I'm delighted to perceive that you have kept yourself so thoroughly acquainted with English politics."

"Oh, of course," said Harold, impatiently. "I'm aware how things have been going on in England. I always meant to come back ultimately. I suppose I know the state of Europe as well as if I'd been stationary at Little Treby for the last fifteen years. If a man goes to the East, people seem to think he gets turned into something like the one-eyed calender in the 'Arabian Nights.'"

"Yet I should think there are some things which people who have been stationary at Little Treby could tell you, Harold," said Mrs. Transome. "It did not signify about your holding Radical opinions at Smyrna; but you seem not to imagine how your putting up as a Radical will affect your position here, and the position of your family. No one will visit you. And then—the sort of people who will support you! You really have no idea what an impression it conveys when you say you are a Radical. There are none of our equals who will not feel that you have disgraced yourself."

"Pooh!" said Harold, rising and walking along the room.

But Mrs. Transome went on with growing anger in her voice—"It seems to me that a man owes something to his birth and station, and has no right to take up this notion or the other, just as it suits his fancy; still less to work at the overthrow of his class. That was what every one said of Lord Grey, and my family at least is as good as Lord Grey's. You have wealth now, and might distinguish yourself in the county; and if you had been true to your colors as a gentleman, you would have had all the greater opportunity because the times are so bad. The Debarrys and Lord Wyvern would have set all the more store by you. For my part, I can't conceive what good you propose to yourself. I only entreat you to think again before you take any decided step."

"Mother," said Harold, not angrily or with any raising of his voice, but in a quick, impatient manner, as if the scene must be got through as quickly as possible; "it is natural that you should think in this way. Women, very properly, don't change their views, but keep to the notions in which they have been brought up. It doesn't signify what they think— they are not called upon to judge or to act. You must really leave me to take my own course in these matters, which properly belong to men. Beyond that, I will gratify any wish you choose to mention. You shall have a new carrriage and a pair of bays all to yourself; you shall have the house done up in first-rate style, and I am not thinking of marrying. But let us understand that there shall be no further collision between us on subjects on which I must be master of my own actions."

"And you will put the crown to the mortifications of my life, Harold. I don't know who would be a mother if she could foresee what a slight thing she will be to her son when she is old."

Mrs. Transome here walked out of the room by the nearest way—the glass door open toward the terrace. Mr. Jermyn had risen too, and his hands were on the back of his chair. He looked quite impassive: it was not the first time he had seen Mrs. Transome angry; but now, for the first time, he thought the outburst of her temper would be useful to him. She, poor woman, knew quite well that she had been unwise, and that she had been making herself disagreeable to Harold to no purpose. But half the sorrows of women would be averted if they could repress the speech they know to be useless—nay, the speech they have resolved not to utter. Harold continued his walking a moment longer, and then said to Jermyn,—

"You smoke?"

"No, I always defer to the ladies. Mrs. Jermyn is peculiarly sensitive in such matters, and doesn't like tobacco."

Harold, who, underneath all the tendencies which had made him a Liberal, had intense personal pride, thought, "Confound the fellow—with his Mrs. Jermyn! Does he think we are on a footing for me to know anything about his wife?"

"Well, I took my hookah before breakfast," he said aloud; "so, if you like, we'll go into the library. My father never gets up till mid-day, I find."

"Sit down, sit down," said Harold, as they entered the handsome, spacious library. But he himself continued to stand before a map of the county which he had opened from a series of rollers occupying a compartment among the bookshelves. "The first question, Mr. Jermyn, now you know my intentions, is, whether you will undertake to be my agent in this election, and help me through? There's no time to be lost, and I don't want to lose my chance, as I may not have another for seven years. I understand," he went on, flashing a look straight at Jermyn, "that you have not taken any conspicuous course in politics; and I know that Labron is agent for the Debarrys."

"Oh—a—my dear sir—a man necessarily has his political convictions, but of what use is it for a professional man—a— of some education, to talk of them in a little country town? There really is no comprehension of public questions in such places. Party feeling, indeed, was quite asleep here before the agitation about the Catholic Relief Bill. It is true that I concurred with our incumbent in getting up a petition against the Reform Bill, but I did not state my reasons. The weak points in that Bill are—a—too palpable, and I fancy you and I should not differ much on that head. The fact is, when I knew that you were to come back to us, I kept myself in reserve, though I was much pressed by the friends of Sir James Clement, the Ministerial candidate, who is——"

"However, you will act for me—that's settled?" said Harold.

"Certainly," said Jermyn, inwardly irritated by Harold's rapid manner of cutting him short.

"Which of the Liberal candidates, as they call themselves, has the better chance, eh?"

"I was going to observe that Sir James Clement has not so good a chance as Mr. Garstin, supposing that a third Liberal candidate presents himself. There are two senses in which a politician can be liberal"—here Mr. Jermyn smiled—"Sir James Clement is a poor baronet, hoping for an appointment, and can't be expected to be liberal in that wider sense which commands majorities."

"I wish this man were not so much of a talker," thought Harold; "he'll bore me. We shall see," he said aloud, "what can be done in the way of combination. I'll come down to your office after one o'clock if it will suit you?"

"Perfectly."

"Ah, and you'll have all the lists and papers and necessary information ready for me there. I must get up a dinner for the tenants, and we can invite whom we like besides the tenants. Just now, I'm going over one of the farms on hand with the bailiff. By the way, that's a desperately bad business, having three farms unlet—how comes that about, eh?"

"That is precisely what I wanted to say a few words about to you. You have observed already how strongly Mrs. Transome takes certain things to heart. You can imagine that she has been severely tried in many ways. Mr. Transome's want of health; Mr. Durfey's habits—a——"

"Yes, yes."

"She is a woman for whom I naturally entertain the highest respect, and she has had hardly any gratification for many years, except the sense of having affairs to a certain extent in her own hands. She objects to changes; she will not have a new style of tenants; she likes the old stock of farmers who milk their own cows, and send their younger daughters out to service: all this makes it difficult to do the best with the estate. I am aware things are not as they ought to be, for, in point of fact, an improved agricultural management is a matter in which I take considerable interest, and the farm which I myself hold on the estate you will see, I think, to be in a superior condition. But Mrs. Transome is a woman of strong feeling, and I would urge you, my dear sir, to make the changes which you have, but which I had not the right to insist on, as little painful to her as possible."

"I shall know what to do, sir, never fear," said Harold, much offended.

"You will pardon, I hope, a perhaps undue freedom of suggestion from a man of my age, who has been so long in a close connection with the family affairs—a—I have never considered that connection simply in the light of business—a——"

"Damn him, I'll soon let him know that *I* do," thought Harold. But in proportion as he found Jermyn's manners annoying, he felt the necessity of controlling himself. He despised all persons who defeated their own projects by the indulgence of momentary impulses.

"I understand, I understand," he said aloud. "You've had more awkward business on your hands than usually falls to the share of a family lawyer. We shall set everything right by degrees. But now as to the canvassing. I've made arrangements with a first-rate man in London, who understands these matters thoroughly—a solicitor, of course—he has carried no end of men into Parliament. I'll engage him to meet us at Duffield—say when?"

The conversation after this was driven carefully clear of all angles, and ended with determined amicableness. When Harold, in his ride an hour or two afterward, encountered his uncle shouldering a gun, and followed by one black and one liver-spotted pointer, his muscular person with its red eagle face set off by a velveteen jacket and leather leggings, Mr. Lingon's first question was,—

"Well, lad, how have you got on with Jermyn?"

"Oh, I don't think I shall like the fellow. He's a sort of amateur gentleman. But I must make use of him. I expect whatever I get out of him will only be something short of fair pay for what he has got out of us. But I shall see."

"Ay, ay, use his gun to bring down your game, and after that beat the thief with the butt-end. That's wisdom and justice and pleasure all in one—talking between ourselves as uncle and nephew. But I say, Harold, I was going to tell you, now I come to think of it, this is rather a nasty business, your calling yourself a Radical. I've been turning it over in after-dinner speeches, but it looks awkward—it's not what people are used to—it wants a good deal of Latin to make it go down. I shall be worried about it at the sessions, and I can think of nothing neat enough to carry about in my pocket by way of answer."

"Nonsense, uncle! I remember what a good speechifier you always were; you'll never be at a loss. You only want a few more evenings to think of it."

"But you'll not be attacking the Church and the institutions of the country—you'll not be going those lengths; you'll keep up the bulwarks, and so on, eh?"

"No, I sha'n't attack the Church, only the incomes of the bishops, perhaps, to make them eke out the incomes of the poor clergy."

"Well, well, I have no objection to that. Nobody likes our Bishop: he's all Greek and greediness; too proud to dine with his own father. You may pepper the bishops a little. But you'll respect the constitution handed down, etc.—and you'll rally round the throne—and the King, God bless him, and the usual toasts, eh?"

"Of course, of course. I am a Radical only in rooting out abuses."

"That's the word I wanted, my lad!" said the Vicar, slapping Harold's knee. "That's a spool to wind a speech on. Abuses is the very word; and if anybody shows himself offended, he'll put the cap on for himself."

"I remove the rotten timbers," said Harold, inwardly amused, "and substitute fresh oak, that's all."

"Well done, my boy! By George, you'll be a speaker! But I say, Harold, I hope you've got a little Latin left. This young Debarry is a tremendous fellow at the classics, and walks on stilts to any length. He's one of the new Conservatives. Old Sir Maximus doesn't understand him at all."

"That won't do at the hustings," said Harold. "He'll get knocked off his stilts pretty quickly there."

"Bless me! it's astonishing how well you're up in the affairs of the country, my boy. But rub up a few quotations—'*Quod turpe bonis decebat Crispinum*'—and that sort of thing—just to show Debarry what you could do if you liked. But you want to ride on?"

"Yes; I have an appointment at Treby. Good-by."

"He's a cleverish chap," muttered the Vicar, as Harold rode away. "When he's had plenty of English exercise, and brought out his knuckle a bit, he'll be a Lingon again as he used to be. I must go and see how Arabella takes his being a Radical. It's a little awkward; but a clergyman must keep peace in a family. Confound it! I'm not bound to love Toryism better than my own flesh and blood, and the manor I shoot over. That's a heathenish, Brutus-like sort of thing, as if Providence couldn't take care of the country without my quarrelling with my own sister's son!"

CHAPTER III.

'Twas town, yet country too; you felt the warmth
Of clustering houses in the wintry time;
Supped with a friend, and went by lantern home.
Yet from your chamber window you could hear
The tiny bleat of new-yeaned lambs, or see
The children bend beside the hedgerow banks
To pluck the primroses.

TREBY MAGNA, on which the Reform Bill had thrust the
new honor of being a polling-place, had been, at the beginning
of the century, quite a typical old market-town, lying in pleasant sleepiness among green pastures, with a rush-fringed river
meandering through them. Its principal street had various
handsome and tall-windowed brick houses with walled gardens
behind them; and at the end, where it widened into the market-place, there was the cheerful rough-stuccoed front of that
excellent inn, the Marquis of Granby, where the farmers put
up their gigs, not only on fair and market days, but on exceptional Sundays when they came to church. And the church
was one of those fine old English structures worth travelling
to see, standing in a broad churchyard with a line of solemn
yew-trees beside it, and lifting a majestic tower and spire far
above the red-and-purple roofs of the town. It was not large
enough to hold all the parishioners of a parish which stretched
over distant villages and hamlets; but then they were never so
unreasonable as to wish to be all in at once, and had never
complained that the space of a large side-chapel was taken up
by tombs of the Debarrys, and shut in by a handsome iron
screen. For when the black Benedictines ceased to pray and
chant in this church, when the Blessed Virgin and St. Greg-
ory were expelled, the Debarrys, as lords of the manor, naturally came next to Providence and took the place of the saints.
Long before that time, indeed, there had been a Sir Maximus
Debarry who had been at the fortifying of the old castle, which
now stood in ruins in the midst of the green pastures, and
with its sheltering wall toward the north made an excellent
strawyard for the pigs of Wace & Co., brewers of the celebrated Treby beer. Wace & Co. did not stand alone in the

town as prosperous traders on a large scale, to say nothing of those who had retired from business; and in no country town of the same small size as Treby was there a larger proportion of families who had handsome sets of china without handles, hereditary punch-bowls, and large silver ladles with a Queen Anne's guinea in the centre. Such people naturally took tea and supped together frequently; and as there was no professional man or tradesman in Treby who was not connected by business, if not by blood, with the farmers of the district, the richer sort of these were much invited, and gave invitations in their turn. They played at whist, ate and drank generously, praised Mr. Pitt and the war as keeping up prices and religion, and were very humorous about each other's property, having much the same coy pleasure in allusions to their secret ability to purchase, as blushing lasses sometimes have in jokes about their secret preferences. The Rector was always of the Debarry family, associated only with county people, and was much respected for his affability; a clergyman who would have taken tea with the townspeople would have given a dangerous shock to the mind of a Treby Churchman.

Such was the old-fashioned, grazing, brewing, wool-packing, cheese-loading life of Treby Magna, until there befell new conditions, complicating its relation with the rest of the world, and gradually awakening in it that higher consciousness which is known to bring higher pains. First came the canal; next, the working of the coal-mines at Sproxton, two miles off the town; and thirdly, the discovery of a saline spring, which suggested to a too constructive brain the possibility of turning Treby Magna into a fashionable watering-place. So daring an idea was not originated by a native Trebian, but by a young lawyer who came from a distance, knew the dictionary by heart, and was probably an illegitimate son of somebody or other. The idea, although it promised an increase of wealth to the town, was not well received at first; ladies objected to seeing "objects" drawn about in hand-carriages, the doctor foresaw the advent of unsound practitioners, and most retail tradesmen concurred with him that new doings were usually for the advantage of new people. The more unanswerable reasoners urged that Treby had prospered without

baths, and it was yet to be seen how it would prosper with
them; while a report that the proposed name for them was
Bethesda Spa threatened to give the whole affair a blasphemous aspect. Even Sir Maximus Debarry, who was to have
an unprecedented return for the thousands he would lay out on
a pump-room and hotel, regarded the thing as a little too new,
and held back for some time. But the persuasive powers of
the young lawyer, Mr. Matthew Jermyn, together with the
opportune opening of a stone-quarry, triumphed at last; the
handsome buildings were erected, an excellent guide-book and
descriptive cards, surmounted by vignettes, were printed, and
Treby Magna became conscious of certain facts in its own history of which it had previously been in contented ignorance.

But it was all in vain. The Spa, for some mysterious reason, did not succeed. Some attributed the failure to the coal-
mines and the canal; others to the peace, which had had ruin-
ous effects on the country; and others, who disliked Jermyn,
to the original folly of the plan. Among these last was Sir
Maximus himself, who never forgave the too persuasive attorney; it was Jermyn's fault not only that a useless hotel had
been built, but that he, Sir Maximus, being straitened for
money, had at last let the building, with the adjacent land lying on the river, on a long lease, on the supposition that it was
to be turned into a benevolent college, and had seen himself
subsequently powerless to prevent its being turned into a tape
manufactory—a bitter thing to any gentleman, and especially
to the representative of one of the oldest families in England.

In this way it happened that Treby Magna gradually passed
from being simply a respectable market-town—the heart of a
great rural district, where the trade was only such as had close
relations with the local landed interest—and took on the more
complex life brought by mines and manufactures, which belong
more directly to the great circulating system of the nation
than to the local system to which they have been superadded;
and in this way it was that Trebian Dissent gradually altered
its character. Formerly it had been of a quiescent, well-to-do
kind, represented architecturally by a small, venerable, dark-
pewed chapel, built by Presbyterians, but long occupied by a
sparse congregation of Independents, who were as little moved

by doctrinal zeal as their church-going neighbors, and did not feel themselves deficient in religious liberty, inasmuch as they were not hindered from occasionally slumbering in their pews, and were not obliged to go regularly to the weekly prayer-meeting. But when stone-pits and coal-pits made new hamlets that threatened to spread up to the very town, when the tape-weavers came with their news-reading inspectors and book-keepers, the Independent chapel began to be filled with eager men and women, to whom the exceptional possession of religious truth was the condition which reconciled them to a meagre existence, and made them feel in secure alliance with the unseen but supreme rule of a world in which their own visible part was small. There were Dissenters in Treby now who could not be regarded by the Church people in the light of old neighbors to whom the habit of going to chapel was an innocent, unenviable inheritance along with a particular house and garden, a tan-yard, or a grocery business—Dissenters who, in their turn, without meaning to be in the least abusive, spoke of the high-bred Rector as a blind leader of the blind. And Dissent was not the only thing that the times had altered; prices had fallen, poor-rates had risen, rent and tithe were not elastic enough, and the farmer's fat sorrow had become lean; he began to speculate on causes, and to trace things back to that causeless mystery, the cessation of one-pound notes. Thus, when political agitation swept in a great current through the country, Treby Magna was prepared to vibrate. The Catholic Emancipation Bill opened the eyes of neighbors, and made them aware how very injurious they were to each other and to the welfare of mankind generally. Mr. Tiliot, the Church spirit-merchant, knew now that Mr. Nuttwood, the obliging grocer, was one of those Dissenters, Deists, Socinians, Papists, and Radicals who were in league to destroy the Constitution. A retired old London tradesman, who was believed to understand politics, said that thinking people must wish George the Third alive again in all his early vigor of mind; and even the farmers became less materialistic in their view of causes, and referred much to the agency of the devil and the Irish Romans. The Rector, the Rev. Augustus Debarry, really a fine specimen of the old-fashioned aristocratic clergyman,

4

preaching short sermons, understanding business, and acting
liberally about his tithe, had never before found himself in
collision with Dissenters; but now he began to feel that these
people were a nuisance in the parish, that his brother Sir
Maximus must take care lest they should get land to build
more chapels, and that it might not have been a bad thing if
the law had furnished him as a magistrate with a power of
putting a stop to the political sermons of the Independent
preacher, which, in their way, were as pernicious sources of
intoxication as the beer-houses. The Dissenters, on their
side, were not disposed to sacrifice the cause of truth and freedom to a temporizing mildness of language; but they defended
themselves from the charge of religious indifference, and solemnly disclaimed any lax expectations that Catholics were
likely to be saved—urging, on the contrary, that they were not
too hopeful about Protestants who adhered to a bloated and
worldly Prelacy. Thus Treby Magna, which had lived quietly
through the great earthquakes of the French Revolution and
the Napoleonic wars, which had remained unmoved by the
"Rights of Man," and saw little in Mr. Cobbett's "Weekly
Register" except that he held eccentric views about potatoes,
began at last to know the higher pains of a dim political consciousness; and the development had been greatly helped by
the recent agitation about the Reform Bill. Tory, Whig, and
Radical did not perhaps become clearer in their definition of
each other; but the names seemed to acquire so strong a
stamp of honor or infamy, that definitions would only have
weakened the impression. As to the short and easy method
of judging opinions by the personal character of those who
held them, it was liable to be much frustrated in Treby. It
so happened in that particular town that the Reformers were
not all of them large-hearted patriots or ardent lovers of justice; indeed, one of them, in the very midst of the agitation,
was detected in using unequal scales—a fact to which many
Tories pointed with disgust as showing plainly enough, without further argument, that the cry for a change in the representative system was hollow trickery. Again, the Tories were
far from being all oppressors, disposed to grind down the
working classes into serfdom; and it was undeniable that the

inspector at the tape manufactory, who spoke with much eloquence on the extension of the suffrage, was a more tyrannical
personage than open-handed Mr. Wace, whose chief political
tenet was, that it was all nonsense giving men votes when
they had no stake in the country. On the other hand, there
were some Tories who gave themselves a great deal of leisure
to abuse hypocrites, Radicals, Dissenters, and atheism generally, but whose inflamed faces, theistic swearing, and frank-
ness in expressing a wish to borrow certainly did not mark
them out strongly as holding opinions likely to save society.

The Reformers had triumphed: it was clear that the wheels
were going whither they were pulling, and they were in fine
spirits for exertion. But if they were pulling toward the
country's ruin, there was the more need for others to hang on
behind and get the wheels to stick if possible. In Treby, as
elsewhere, people were told they must "rally" at the coming
election; but there was now a large number of waverers—men
of flexible, practical minds, who were not such bigots as to
cling to any views when a good tangible reason could be urged
against them; while some regarded it as the most neighborly
thing to hold a little with both sides, and were not sure that
they should rally or vote at all. It seemed an invidious thing
to vote for one gentleman rather than another.

These social changes in Treby parish are comparatively public matters, and this history is chiefly concerned with the private lot of a few men and women; but there is no private life
which has not been determined by a wider public life, from
the time when the primeval milkmaid had to wander with the
wanderings of her clan, because the cow she milked was one
of a herd which had made the pastures bare. Even in that
conservatory existence where the fair Camellia is sighed for
by the noble young Pineapple, neither of them needing to
care about the frost or rain outside, there is a nether appara-
tus of hot-water pipes liable to cool down on a strike of the
gardeners or a scarcity of coal. And the lives we are about to
look back upon do not belong to those conservatory species;
they are rooted in the common earth, having to endure all the
ordinary chances of past and present weather. As to the
weather of 1832, the Zadkiel of that time had predicted that

the electrical condition of the clouds in the political hemisphere would produce unusual perturbations in organic existence, and he would perhaps have seen a fulfilment of his
remarkable prophecy in that mutual influence of dissimilar
destinies which we shall see gradually unfolding itself. For if
the mixed political conditions of Treby Magna had not been
acted on by the passing of the Reform Bill, Mr. Harold Transome would not have presented himself as a candidate for
North Loamshire, Treby would not have been a polling-place,
Mr. Matthew Jermyn would not have been on affable terms
with a Dissenting preacher and his flock, and the venerable
town would not have been placarded with handbills, more or
less complimentary and retrospective—conditions in this case
essential to the "where," and the "what," without which, as
the learned know, there can be no event whatever.

For example, it was through these conditions that a young
man named Felix Holt made a considerable difference in the
life of Harold Transome, though nature and fortune seemed to
have done what they could to keep the lots of the two men
quite aloof from each other.   Felix was heir to nothing better
than a quack medicine; his mother lived up a back street in
Treby Magna, and her sitting-room was ornamented with her
best tea-tray and several framed testimonials to the virtues of
Holt's Cathartic Lozenges and Holt's Restorative Elixir.
There could hardly have been a lot less like Harold Transome's
than this of the quack doctor's son, except in the superficial
facts that he called himself a Radical, that he was the only
son of his mother, and that he had lately returned to his home
with ideas and resolves not a little disturbing to that mother's
mind.

But Mrs. Holt, unlike Mrs. Transome, was much disposed
to reveal her troubles, and was not without a counsellor into
whose ear she could pour them.   On this 2d of September,
when Mr. Harold Transome had had his first interview with
Jermyn, and when the attorney went back to his office with
new views of canvassing in his mind, Mrs. Holt had put on
her bonnet as early as nine o'clock in the morning, and had
gone to see the Rev. Rufus Lyon, minister of the Independent
Chapel usually spoken of as "Malthouse Yard."

CHAPTER IV.

"A pious and painful preacher."—FULLER.

MR. LYON lived in a small house, not quite so good as the parish clerk's, adjoining the entry which led to the Chapel Yard. The new prosperity of Dissent at Treby had led to an enlargement of the chapel, which absorbed all extra funds and left none for the enlargement of the minister's income. He sat this morning, as usual, in a low upstairs room, called his study, which, by means of a closet capable of holding his bed, served also as a sleeping-room. The book-shelves did not suffice for his store of old books, which lay about him in piles so arranged as to leave narrow lanes between them; for the minister was much given to walking about during his hours of meditation, and very narrow passages would serve for his small legs, unencumbered by any other drapery than his black silk stockings and the flexible, though prominent, bows of black ribbon that tied his knee-breeches. He was walking about now, with his hands clasped behind him, an attitude in which his body seemed to bear about the same proportion to his head as the lower part of a stone Hermes bears to the carven image that crowns it. His face looked old and worn, yet the curtain of hair that fell from his bald crown and hung about his neck retained much of its original auburn tint, and his large, brown, short-sighted eyes were still clear and bright. At the first glance, every one thought him a very odd-looking rusty old man; the free-school boys often hooted after him, and called him "Revelations"; and to many respectable Church people, old Lyon's little legs and large head seemed to make Dissent additionally preposterous. But he was too short-sighted to notice those who tittered at him—too absent from the world of small facts and petty impulses in which titterers live. With Satan to argue against on matters of vital experience as well as of church government, with great texts to meditate on, which seemed to get deeper as he tried to fathom them, it had never occurred to him to reflect what sort of image his small person made on the retina of a light-minded beholder. The good Rufus had his ire and his egoism; but they existed only as the red heat which gave force to his belief and his teaching. He was susceptible concerning the true office of deacons in the primitive Church, and his small nervous body was jarred from head to foot by the concussion of an argument to which he saw no answer. In fact, the only moments when he could be said to be really conscious of his body were when he trembled under the pressure of some agitating thought.

He was meditating on the text for his Sunday morning sermon, "And all the people said, Amen"—a mere mustard-seed of a text, which had split at first only into two divisions, "What was said," and "Who said it"; but these were growing into a many-branched discourse, and the preacher's eyes dilated, and a smile played about his mouth till, as his manner was, when he felt happily inspired, he had begun to utter his thoughts aloud in the varied measure and cadence habitual to him, changing from a rapid but distinct undertone to a loud emphatic *rallentando*.

"My brethren, do you think that great shout was raised in Israel by each man's waiting to say ' amen ' till his neighbors had said amen? Do you think there will ever be a great shout for the right—the shout of a nation as of one man, rounded and whole, like the voice of the archangel that bound together all the listeners of earth and heaven—if every Christian of you peeps round to see what his neighbors in good coats are doing, or else puts his hat before his face that he may shout and never be heard? But this is what you do: when the servant of God stands up to deliver his message, do you lay your souls beneath the Word as you set out your plants beneath the falling rain? No; one of you sends his eyes to all corners, he smothers his soul with small questions, 'What does brother Y. think?'—' Is this doctrine high enough for brother Z.?'—' Will the church members be pleased?' And another——"

Here the door was opened, and old Lyddy, the minister's servant, put in her head to say, in a tone of despondency, finishing with a groan, "Here is Mrs. Holt wanting to speak to you; she says she comes out of season, but she's in trouble."

"Lyddy," said Mr. Lyon, falling at once into a quiet conversational tone, "if you are wrestling with the enemy, let me refer you to Ezekiel the thirteenth and twenty-second, and beg of you not to groan. It is a stumbling-block and offence to my daughter; she would take no broth yesterday, because she said you had cried into it. Thus you cause the truth to be lightly spoken of, and make the enemy rejoice. If your faceache gives him an advantage, take a little warm ale with your meat—I do not grudge the money."

"If I thought my drinking warm ale would hinder poor dear Miss Esther from speaking light—but she hates the smell of it."

"Answer not again, Lyddy, but send up Mistress Holt to me."

Lyddy closed the door immediately.

"I lack grace to deal with these weak sisters," said the minister, again thinking aloud, and walking. "Their needs lie too much out of the track of my meditations, and take me often unawares. Mistress Holt is another who darkens counsel by words without knowledge, and angers the reason of the natural man. Lord, give me patience. My sins were heavier to bear than this woman's folly. Come in, Mrs. Holt—come in."

He hastened to disencumber a chair of Matthew Henry's Commentary, and begged his visitor to be seated. She was a tall elderly woman, dressed in black, with a light brown front and a black band over her forehead. She moved the chair a little and seated herself in it with some emphasis, looking fixedly at the opposite wall with a hurt and argumentative expression. Mr. Lyon had placed himself in the chair against his desk, and waited with the resolute resignation of a patient who is about to undergo an operation. But his visitor did not speak.

"You have something on your mind, Mrs. Holt?" he said, at last.

"Indeed I have, sir, else I shouldn't be here."

"Speak freely."

"It's well known to you, Mr. Lyon, that my husband, Mr. Holt, came from the north, and was a member in Malthouse Yard long before *you* began to be pastor of it, which was seven year ago last Michaelmas. It's the truth, Mr. Lyon, and I'm not that woman to sit here and say it if it wasn't true."

"Certainly, it is true."

"And if my husband had been alive when you'd come to preach upon trial, he'd have been as good a judge of your gifts as Mr. Nuttwood or Mr. Muscat, though whether he'd have agreed with some that your doctrine wasn't high enough, I can't say. For myself, I've my opinion about high doctrine."

"Was it my preaching you came to speak about?" said the minister, hurrying in the question.

"No, Mr. Lyon, I'm not that woman. But this I *will* say, for my husband died before your time, that he had a wonderful gift in prayer, as the old members well know, if anybody likes to ask 'em, not believing my words; and he believed himself that the receipt for the Cancer Cure, which I've sent out in bottles till this very last April before September as now is, and have bottles standing by me,—he believed it was sent to him in answer to prayer; and nobody can deny it, for he prayed most regular, and read out of the green baize Bible."

Mrs. Holt paused, appearing to think that Mr. Lyon had been successfully confuted, and should show himself convinced.

"Has any one been aspersing your husband's character?" said Mr. Lyon, with a slight initiative toward that relief of groaning for which he had reproved Lyddy.

"Sir, they daredn't. For though he was a man of prayer, he didn't want skill and knowledge to find things out for himself; and that was what I used to say to *my* friends when they wondered at my marrying a man from Lancashire, with no trade nor fortune but what he'd got in his head. But my husband's tongue 'ud have been a fortune to anybody, and there was many a one said it was as good as a dose of physic to hear him talk; not but what that got him into trouble in Lancashire, but he always said, if the worst came to the worst, he could go and preach to the blacks. But he did better than that, Mr. Lyon, for he married me; and this I *will* say, that for age, and conduct, and managing——"

"Mistress Holt," interrupted the minister, "these are not the things whereby we may edify one another. Let me beg of you to be as brief as you can. My time is not my own."

"Well, Mr. Lyon, I've a right to speak to my own character; and I'm one of your congregation, though I'm not a church member, for I was born in the General Baptist connection: and as for being saved without works, there's a many, I dare say, can't do without that doctrine; but I thank the Lord I never needed to put *my*self on a level with the thief on the cross. I've done *my* duty, and more, if anybody comes to that; for I've gone without my bit of meat to make broth for a sick neighbor: and if there's any of the church members say they've done the same, I'd ask them if they had the sinking at the stomach as I have; for I've ever strove to do the right thing, and more, for good-natured I always was; and I little thought, after being respected by everybody, I should come to be reproached by my own son. And my husband said when he was a-dying—' Mary,' he said, ' the Elixir, and the Pills, and the Cure will support you, for they've a great name in all the country round, and you'll pray for a blessing on them.' And so I have done, Mr. Lyon; and to say they're not good medicines, when they've been taken for fifty miles round by high and low, and rich and poor, and nobody speaking against 'em but Dr. Lukin, it seems to me it's a flying in the face of Heaven; for if it was wrong to take the medicines, couldn't the blessed Lord have stopped it?"

Mrs. Holt was not given to tears; she was much sustained by conscious unimpeachableness, and by an argumentative tendency which usually checks the too great activity of the lachrymal gland; nevertheless her eyes had become moist, her fingers played on her knee in an agitated manner, and she finally plucked a bit of her gown and held it with great nicety between her thumb and finger. Mr. Lyon, however, by listening attentively, had begun partly to divine the source of her trouble.

"Am I wrong in gathering from what you say, Mistress Holt, that your son has objected in some way to your sale of your late husband's medicines?"

"Mr. Lyon, he's masterful beyond everything, and he

talks more than his father did. I've got my reason, Mr. Lyon, and if anybody talks sense I can follow him; but Felix talks so wild, and contradicts his mother. And what do you think he says, after giving up his 'prenticeship, and going off to study at Glasgow, and getting through all the bit of money his father saved for his bringing-up—what has all his learning come to? He says I'd better never open my Bible, for it's as bad poison to me as the pills are to half the people as swallow 'em. You'll not speak of this again, Mr. Lyon—I don't think ill enough of you to believe *that*. For I suppose a Christian can understand the word o' God without going to Glasgow, and there's texts upon texts about ointment and medicine, and there's one as might have been made for a receipt of my husband's—it's just as if it was a riddle, and Holt's Elixir was the answer."

"Your son uses rash words, Mistress Holt," said the minister, "but it is quite true that we may err in giving a too private interpretation to the Scripture. The word of God has to satisfy the larger needs of His people, like the rain and the sunshine which no man must think to be meant for his own patch of seed-ground solely. Will it not be well that I should see your son, and talk with him on these matters? He was at chapel, I observed, and I suppose I am to be his pastor."

"That was what I wanted to ask you, Mr. Lyon. For perhaps he'll listen to you, and not talk you down as he does his poor mother. For after we'd been to chapel, he spoke better of you than he does of most: he said you was a fine old fellow, and an old-fashioned Puritan—he uses dreadful language, Mr. Lyon; but I saw he didn't mean you ill, for all that. He calls most folks' religion rottenness; and yet another time he'll tell me I ought to feel myself a sinner, and do God's will and not my own. But it's my belief he says first one thing and then another only to abuse his mother. Or else he's going off his head, and must be sent to a 'sylum. But if he writes to the *North Loamshire Herald* first, to tell everybody the medicines are good for nothing, how can I ever keep him and myself?"

"Tell him I shall feel favored if he will come and see me this evening," said Mr. Lyon, not without a little prejudice in favor of the young man, whose language about the preacher in Malthouse Yard did not seem to him to be altogether dreadful. "Meanwhile, my friend, I counsel you to send up a supplication, which I shall not fail to offer also, that you may receive a spirit of humility and submission, so that you may not be hindered from seeing and following the Divine guidance in this matter by any false lights of pride and obstinacy. Of this more when I have spoken with your son."

"I'm not proud or obstinate, Mr. Lyon. I never did say I was everything that was bad, and I never will. And why this trouble should be sent on me above everybody else—for I haven't told you all. He's made himself a journeyman to Mr. Prowd the watchmaker—after all this learning—and he says he'll go with patches on his knees, and he shall like himself the better. And as for his having little boys to teach, they'll come in all weathers with dirty shoes. If it's madness, Mr. Lyon, it's no use your talking to him."

"We shall see. Perhaps it may even be the disguised working of grace within him. We must not judge rashly. Many eminent servants of God have been led by ways as strange."

"Then I'm sorry for their mothers, that's all, Mr. Lyon; and all the more if they'd been well-spoken-on women. For not my biggest enemy, whether it's he or she, if they'll speak the truth, can turn round and say I've deserved this trouble. And when everybody gets their due, and people's doings are spoken of on the house-tops, as the Bible says they will be, it'll be known what I've gone through with those medicines— the pounding and the pouring, and the letting stand, and the weighing—up early and down late—there's nobody knows yet but One that's worthy to know; and the pasting o' the printed labels right side upward. There's few women would have gone through with it; and it's reasonable to think it'll be made up to me; for if there's promised and purchased blessings, I should think this trouble is purchasing 'em. For if my son Felix doesn't have a strait-waistcoat put on him, he'll have his way. But I say no more. I wish you good-morning, Mr. Lyon, and thank you, though I well know it's your duty to act as you're doing. And I never troubled you about

my own soul, as some do who look down on me for not being
a church member."

"Farewell, Mistress Holt, farewell. I pray that a more
powerful teacher than I am may instruct you."

The door was closed, and the much-tried Rufus walked
about again, saying aloud, groaningly,—

"This woman has sat under the Gospel all her life, and she
is as blind as a heathen, and as proud and stiff-necked as a
Pharisee; yet she is one of the souls I watch for. 'Tis true
that even Sara, the chosen mother of God's people, showed a
spirit of unbelief, and perhaps of selfish anger; and it is a
passage that bears the unmistakable signet, ' doing honor to
the wife or woman, as unto the weaker vessel.' For therein
is the greatest check put on the ready scorn of the natural
man."

CHAPTER V.

1ST CITIZEN.	Sir, there's a hurry in the veins of youth
	That makes a vice of virtue by excess.
2D CITIZEN.	What if the coolness of our tardier veins
	Be loss of virtue?
1ST CITIZEN.	All things cool with time—
	The sun itself, they say, till heat shall find
	A general level, nowhere in excess.
2D CITIZEN.	'Tis a poor climax, to my weaker thought,
	That future middlingness.

In the evening, when Mr. Lyon was expecting the knock at
the door that would announce Felix Holt, he occupied his
cushionless arm-chair in the sitting-room, and was skimming
rapidly, in his short-sighted way, by the light of one candle,
the pages of a missionary report, emitting occasionally a slight
"Hm-m" that appeared to be expressive of criticism rather
than of approbation. The room was dismally furnished, the
only objects indicating an intention of ornament being a book-
case, a map of the Holy Land, an engraved portrait of Dr.
Doddridge, and a black bust with a colored face, which for
some reason or other was covered with green gauze. Yet any
one whose attention was quite awake must have been aware,
even on entering, of certain things that were incongruous

with the general air of sombreness and privation. There was a delicate scent of dried rose-leaves; the light by which the minister was reading was a wax candle in a white earthenware candlestick, and the table on the opposite side of the fireplace held a dainty work-basket frilled with blue satin.

Felix Holt, when he entered, was not in an observant mood; and when, after seating himself, at the minister's invitation, near the little table which held the work-basket, he stared at the wax candle opposite to him, he did so without any wonder or consciousness that the candle was not of tallow. But the minister's sensitiveness gave another interpretation to the gaze which he divined rather than saw; and in alarm lest this inconsistent extravagance should obstruct his usefulness, he hastened to say,—

"You are doubtless amazed to see me with a wax-light, my young friend; but this undue luxury is paid for with the earnings of my daughter, who is so delicately framed that the smell of tallow is loathsome to her."

"I heeded not the candle, sir. I thank Heaven I am not a mouse to have a nose that takes note of wax or tallow."

The loud abrupt tones made the old man vibrate a little. He had been stroking his chin gently before, with a sense that he must be very quiet and deliberate in his treatment of the eccentric young man; but now, quite unreflectingly, he drew forth a pair of spectacles, which he was in the habit of using when he wanted to observe his interlocutor more closely than usual.

"And I myself, in fact, am equally indifferent," he said, as he opened and adjusted his glasses, "so that I have a sufficient light on my book." Here his large eyes looked discerningly through the spectacles.

"'Tis the quality of the page you care about, not of the candle," said Felix, smiling pleasantly enough at his inspector. "You're thinking that you have a roughly written page before you now."

That was true. The minister, accustomed to the respectable air of provincial townsmen, and especially to the sleek well-clipped gravity of his own male congregation, felt a slight shock as his glasses made perfectly clear to him the shaggy-headed, large-eyed, strong-limbed person of this questionable young man, without waistcoat or cravat. But the possibility, supported by some of Mrs. Holt's words, that a disguised work of grace might be going forward in the son of whom she complained so bitterly checked any hasty interpretations.

"I abstain from judging by the outward appearance only," he answered, with his usual simplicity. "I myself have experienced that when the spirit is much exercised it is difficult to remember neck-bands and strings and such small accidents of our vesture, which are nevertheless decent and needful so long as we sojourn in the flesh. And you, too, my young friend, as I gathered from your mother's troubled and confused report, are undergoing some travail of mind. You will not, I trust, object to open yourself fully to me, as to an aged pastor who has himself had much inward wrestling, and has especially known much temptation from doubt."

"As to doubt," said Felix, loudly and brusquely as before, "if it is those absurd medicines and gulling advertisements that my mother has been talking of to you—and I suppose it is—I've no more doubt about *them* than I have about pocket-picking. I know there's a stage of speculation in which a man may doubt whether a pickpocket is blameworthy—but I'm not one of your subtle fellows who keep looking at the world through their own legs. If I allowed the sale of those medicines to go on, and my mother to live out of the proceeds when I can keep her by the honest labor of my hands, I've not the least doubt that I should be a rascal."

"I would fain inquire more particularly into your objection to these medicines," said Mr. Lyon, gravely. Notwithstanding his conscientiousness and a certain originality in his own mental disposition, he was too little used to high principle quite dissociated from sectarian phraseology to be as immediately in sympathy with it as he would otherwise have been. "I know they have been well reported of, and many wise persons have tried remedies providentially discovered by those who are not regular physicians, and have found a blessing in the use of them. I may mention the eminent Mr. Wesley, who, though I hold not altogether with his Arminian doctrine, nor with the usages of his institution, was nevertheless a man of God; and the journals of various Christians whose names have left a sweet savor might be cited in the same sense. Moreover, your father, who originally concocted these medicines and left them as a provision for your mother, was, as I understand, a man whose walk was not unfaithful."

"My father was ignorant," said Felix, bluntly. "He knew neither the complication of the human system, nor the way in which drugs counteract each other. Ignorance is not so damnable as humbug, but when it prescribes pills it may happen to do more harm. I know something about these things. I was 'prentice for five miserable years to a stupid brute of a country apothecary—my poor father left money for that—he thought nothing could be finer for me. No matter: I know that the Cathartic Pills are a drastic compound which may be as bad as poison to half the people who swallow them; that the Elixir is an absurd farrago of a dozen incompatible things; and that the Cancer Cure might as well be bottled ditch-water."

Mr. Lyon rose, and walked up and down the room. His simplicity was strongly mixed with sagacity as well as sectarian prejudice, and he did not rely at once on a loud-spoken integrity—Satan might have flavored it with ostentation. Presently he asked, in a rapid low tone, "How long have you known this, young man?"

"Well put, sir," said Felix. "I've known it a good deal longer than I have acted upon it, like plenty of other things. But you believe in conversion?"

"Yea, verily."

"So do I. I was converted by six weeks' debauchery."

The minister started. "Young man," he said, solemnly, going up close to Felix and laying a hand on his shoulder, "speak not lightly of the Divine operations, and restrain unseemly words."

"I'm not speaking lightly," said Felix. "If I had not seen that I was making a hog of myself very fast, and that pig-wash, even if I could have got plenty of it, was a poor sort of thing, I should never have looked life fairly in the face to see what was to be done with it. I laughed out loud at last to think of a poor devil like me, in a Scotch garret, with my stockings out at heel and a shilling or two to be dissipated upon, with a smell of raw haggis mounting from below, and old women breathing gin as they passed me on the stairs— wanting to turn my life into easy pleasure. Then I began to see what else it could be turned into. Not much, perhaps. This world is not a very fine place for a good many of the people in it. But I've made up my mind it sha'n't be the worse for me, if I can help it. They may tell me I can't alter the world—that there must be a certain number of sneaks and robbers in it, and if I don't lie and filch somebody else will. Well, then, somebody else shall, for I won't. That's the upshot of my conversion, Mr. Lyon, if you want to know it."

Mr. Lyon removed his hand from Felix's shoulder and walked about again. "Did you sit under any preacher at Glasgow, young man?"

"No: I heard most of the preachers once, but I never wanted to hear them twice."

The good Rufus was not without a slight rising of resentment at this young man's want of reverence. It was not yet plain whether he wanted to hear twice the preacher in Malthouse Yard. But the resentful feeling was carefully repressed: a soul in so peculiar a condition must be dealt with delicately.

"And now, may I ask," he said, "what course you mean to take, after hindering your mother from making and selling these drugs? I speak no more in their favor after what you have said. God forbid that I should strive to hinder you from seeking whatsoever things are honest and honorable. But your mother is advanced in years; she needs comfortable sustenance; you have doubtless considered how you may make her amends? ' He that provideth not for his own——' I trust you respect the authority that so speaks. And I will not suppose that, after being tender of conscience toward strangers, you will be careless toward your mother. There be indeed some who, taking a mighty charge on their shoulders, must perforce leave their households to Providence, and to the care of humbler brethren, but in such a case the call must be clear."

"I shall keep my mother as well—nay, better—than she has kept herself. She has always been frugal. With my watch and clock cleaning, and teaching one or two little chaps that I've got to come to me, I can earn enough. As for me, I can live on bran porridge. I have the stomach of a rhinoceros."

"But for a young man so well furnished as you, who can questionless write a good hand and keep books, were it not well to seek some higher situation as clerk or assistant? I could speak to Brother Muscat, who is well acquainted with all such openings. Any place in Pendrell's Bank, I fear, is now closed against such as are not Churchmen. It used not to be so, but a year ago he discharged Brother Bodkin, although he was a valuable servant. Still, something might be found. There are ranks and degrees—and those who can serve in the higher must not unadvisedly change what seems to be a providential appointment. Your poor mother is not altogether——"

"Excuse me, Mr. Lyon; I've had all that out with my mother, and I may as well save you any trouble by telling you that my mind has been made up about that a long while ago. I'll take no employment that obliges me to prop up my chin with a high cravat, and wear straps, and pass the live-long day with a set of fellows who spend their spare money on shirt-pins. That sort of work is really lower than many handicrafts; it only happens to be paid out of proportion. That's why I set myself to learn the watchmaking trade. My father was a weaver first of all. It would have been better for him if he had remained a weaver. I came home through Lancashire and saw an uncle of mine who is a weaver still. I mean to stick to the class I belong to—people who don't follow the fashions."

Mr. Lyon was silent a few moments. This dialogue was far from plain sailing; he was not certain of his latitude and longitude. If the despiser of Glasgow preachers had been arguing in favor of gin and Sabbath-breaking, Mr. Lyon's course would have been clearer. "Well, well," he said, deliberately, "it is true that St. Paul exercised the trade of tent-making, though he was learned in all the wisdom of the Rabbis."

5

"St. Paul was a wise man," said Felix. "Why should I want to get into the middle class because I have some learning? The most of the middle class are as ignorant as the working people about everything that doesn't belong to their own Brummagem life. That's how the working men are left to foolish devices and keep worsening themselves: the best heads among them forsake their born comrades, and go in for a house with a high door-step and a brass knocker."

Mr. Lyon stroked his mouth and chin, perhaps because he felt some disposition to smile; and it would not be well to smile too readily at what seemed but a weedy resemblance of Christian unworldliness. On the contrary, there might be a dangerous snare in an unsanctified outstepping of average Christian practice.

"Nevertheless," he observed, gravely, "it is by such self-advancement that many have been enabled to do good service to the cause of liberty and to the public well-being. The ring and the robe of Joseph were no objects for a good man's ambition, but they were the signs of that credit which he won by his divinely inspired skill, and which enabled him to act as a savior to his brethren."

"Oh, yes, your ringed and scented men of the people!—I won't be one of them. Let a man once throttle himself with a satin stock, and he'll get new wants and new motives. Metamorphosis will have begun at his neck-joint, and it will go on till it has changed his likings first, and then his reasoning, which will follow his likings as the feet of a hungry dog follow his nose. I'll have none of your clerky gentility. I might end by collecting greasy pence from poor men to buy myself a fine coat and a glutton's dinner, on pretence of serving the poor men. I'd sooner be Paley's fat pigeon than a demagogue all tongue and stomach; though"—here Felix changed his voice a little—"I should like well enough to be another sort of demagogue, if I could."

"Then you have a strong interest in the great political movements of these times?" said Mr. Lyon, with a perceptible flashing of the eyes.

"I should think so. I despise every man who has not— or, having it, doesn't try to rouse it in other men."

"Right, my young friend, right," said the minister, in a deep cordial tone. Inevitably his mind was drawn aside from the immediate consideration of Felix Holt's spiritual interest by the prospect of political sympathy. In those days so many instruments of God's cause in the fight for religious and political liberty held creeds that were painfully wrong, and, indeed, irreconcilable with salvation! "That is my own view, which I maintain in the face of some opposition from brethren who contend that a share in public movements is a hindrance to the closer walk, and that the pulpit is no place for teaching men their duties as members of the commonwealth. I have had much puerile blame cast upon me because I have uttered such names as Brougham and Wellington in the pulpit. Why not Wellington as well as Rabshakeh? and why not Brougham as well as Balaam? Does God know less of men than He did in the days of Hezekiah and Moses?—is His arm shortened, and is the world become too wide for His providence? But, they say, there are no politics in the New Testament——"

"Well, they're right enough there," said Felix, with his usual unceremoniousness.

"What! you are of those who hold that a Christian minister should not meddle with public matters in the pulpit?" said Mr. Lyon, coloring. "I am ready to join issue on that point."

"Not I, sir," said Felix; "I should say, teach any truth you can, whether it's in the Testament or out of it. It's little enough anybody can get hold of, and still less what he can drive into the skulls of a pence-counting, parcel-tying generation, such as mostly fill your chapels."

"Young man," said Mr. Lyon, pausing in front of Felix. He spoke rapidly, as he always did, except when his words were specially weighted with emotion: he overflowed with matter, and in his mind matter was always completely organized into words. "I speak not on my own behalf, for not only have I no desire that any man should think of me above that which he seeth me to be, but I am aware of much that should make me patient under a disesteem resting even on too hasty a construction. I speak not as claiming reverence for my own age and office—not to shame you, but to warn you. It is good that you should use plainness of speech, and I am not of those who would enforce a submissive silence on the young, that they themselves, being elders, may be heard at large; for Elihu was the youngest of Job's friends, yet was there a wise rebuke in his words; and the aged Eli was taught by a revelation to the boy Samuel. I have to keep a special watch over myself in this matter, inasmuch as I have a need of utterance with makes the thought within me seem as a pent-up fire, until I have shot it forth, as it were, in arrowy words, each one hitting its mark. Therefore I pray for a listening spirit, which is a great mark of grace. Nevertheless, my young friend, I am bound, as I said, to warn you. The temptations that most beset those who have great natural gifts, and are wise after the flesh, are pride and scorn, more particularly toward those weak things of the world which have been chosen to confound the things which are mighty. The scornful nostril and the high head gather not the odors that lie on the track of truth. The mind that is too ready at contempt and reprobation is——"

Here the door opened, and Mr. Lyon paused to look round, but seeing only Lyddy with the tea-tray, he went on,—

"Is, I may say, as a clinched fist that can give blows, but is shut up from receiving and holding aught that is precious —though it were heaven-sent manna."

"I understand you, sir," said Felix, good-humoredly, putting out his hand to the little man, who had come close to him as he delivered the last sentence with sudden emphasis and slowness. "But I'm not inclined to clinch my fist at you."

"Well, well," said Mr. Lyon, shaking the proffered hand, "we shall see more of each other, and I trust shall have much profitable communing. You will stay and have a dish of tea with us: we take the meal late on Thursdays, because my daughter is detained by giving a lesson in the French tongue. But she is doubtless returned now, and will presently come and pour out tea for us."

"Thank you, I'll stay," said Felix, not from any curiosity to see the minister's daughter, but from a liking for the society of the minister himself—for his quaint looks and ways, and the transparency of his talk, which gave a charm even to his weaknesses. The daughter was probably some prim Miss, neat, sensible, pious, but all in a small feminine way, in which Felix was no more interested than in Dorcas meetings, biographies of devout women, and that amount of ornamental knitting which was not inconsistent with Nonconforming seriousness.

"I'm perhaps a little too fond of banging and smashing," he went on; "a phrenologist at Glasgow told me I had large veneration; another man there, who knew me, laughed out, and said I was the most blasphemous iconoclast living. 'That,' says my phrenologist, 'is because of his large Ideality, which prevents him from finding anything perfect enough to be venerated.' Of course I put my ears down and wagged my tail at that stroking."

"Yes, yes; I have had my own head explored with somewhat similar results. It is, I fear, but a vain show of fulfilling the heathen precept, 'Know thyself,' and too often leads to a self-estimate which will subsist in the absence of that fruit by which alone the quality of the tree is made evident. Nevertheless—— Esther, my dear, this is Mr. Holt, whose acquaintance I have even now been making with more than ordinary interest. He will take tea with us."

Esther bowed slightly as she walked across the room to fetch the candle and place it near her tray. Felix rose and bowed, also with an air of indifference, which was perhaps exaggerated by the fact that he was inwardly surprised. The minister's daughter was not the sort of person he expected. She was quite incongruous with his notion of ministers' daughters in general; and though he had expected something nowise delightful, the incongruity repelled him. A very delicate scent, the faint suggestion of a garden, was wafted as she went. He would not observe her, but he had a sense of an elastic walk, the tread of small feet, a long neck and a high crown of shining brown plaits with curls that floated backward—things, in short, that suggested a fine lady to him, and determined him to notice her as little as possible. A fine lady was always a sort of spun-glass affair—not natural, and with no beauty for him as art; but a fine lady as the daughter of this rusty old Puritan was especially offensive.

"Nevertheless," continued Mr. Lyon, who rarely let drop any thread of discourse, "that phrenological science is not irreconcilable with the revealed dispensations. And it is undeniable that we have our varying native dispositions which even grace will not obliterate. I myself, from my youth up, have been given to question too curiously concerning the truth —to examine and sift the medicine of the soul rather than to apply it."

"If your truth happens to be such medicine as Holt's Pills and Elixir, the less you swallow of it the better," said Felix. "But truth-venders and medicine-venders usually recommend swallowing. When a man sees his livelihood in a pill or a proposition, he likes to have orders for the dose, and not curious inquiries."

This speech verged on rudeness, but it was delivered with a brusque openness that implied the absence of any personal intention. The minister's daughter was now for the first time startled into looking at Felix. But her survey of this unusual speaker was soon made, and she relieved her father from the need to reply by saying,—

"The tea is poured out, father."

That was the signal for Mr. Lyon to advance toward the table, raise his right hand, and ask a blessing at sufficient length for Esther to glance at the visitor again. There seemed to be no danger of his looking at her: he was observing her father. She had time to remark that he was a peculiar-looking person, but not insignificant, which was the quality that most hopelessly consigned a man to perdition. He was massively built. The striking points in his face were large clear gray eyes and full lips.

"Will you draw up to the table, Mr. Holt?" said the minister.

In the act of rising Felix pushed back his chair too suddenly against the rickety table close by him, and down went the blue-frilled work-basket, flying open, and dispersing on the floor reels, thimble, muslin-work, a small sealed bottle of attar of rose, and something heavier than these—a duodecimo volume, which fell close to him between the table and the fender.

"Oh, my stars!" said Felix, "I beg your pardon." Esther had already started up, and with wonderful quickness had picked up half the small rolling things while Felix was lifting the basket and the book. This last had opened, and had its leaves crushed in falling; and, with the instinct of a bookish man, he saw nothing more pressing to be done than to flatten the corners of the leaves.

"Byron's Poems!" he said, in a tone of disgust, while Esther was recovering all the other articles. "'The Dream' —he'd better have been asleep and snoring. What! do you stuff your memory with Byron, Miss Lyon?"

Felix, on his side, was led at last to look straight at Esther, but it was with a strong denunciatory and pedagogic intention. Of course he saw more clearly than ever that she was a fine lady.

She reddened, drew up her long neck, and said, as she retreated to her chair again, —

"I have a great admiration for Byron."

Mr. Lyon had paused in the act of drawing his chair to the tea-table, and was looking on at this scene, wrinkling the corners of his eyes with a perplexed smile. Esther would not have wished him to know anything about the volume of Byron, but she was too proud to show any concern.

"He is a worldly and vain writer, I fear," said Mr. Lyon. He knew scarcely anything of the poet, whose books embodied the faith and ritual of many young ladies and gentlemen.

"A misanthropic debauchee," said Felix, lifting a chair with one hand, and holding the book open in the other, "whose notion of a hero was that he should disorder his stomach and despise mankind. His corsairs and renegades, his Alps and Manfreds, are the most paltry puppets that were ever pulled by the strings of lust and pride."

"Hand the book to me," said Mr. Lyon.

"Let me beg of you to put it aside till after tea, father," said Esther. "However objectionable Mr. Holt may find its pages, they would certainly be made worse by being greased with bread and butter."

"That is true, my dear," said Mr. Lyon, laying down the book on the small table behind him. He saw that his daughter was angry.

"Ho, ho!" thought Felix, "her father is frightened at her. How came he to have such a nice-stepping, long-necked peacock for his daughter? but she shall see that I am not frightened." Then he said aloud, "I should like to know how you will justify your admiration for such a writer, Miss Lyon."

"I should not attempt it with you, Mr. Holt," said Esther. "You have such strong words at command that they make the smallest argument seem formidable. If I had ever met the giant Cormoran, I should have made a point of agreeing with him in his literary opinions."

Esther had that excellent thing in woman, a soft voice with a clear fluent utterance. Her sauciness was always charming, because it was without emphasis, and was accompanied with graceful little turns of the head.

Felix laughed at her thrust with young heartiness.

"My daughter is a critic of words, Mr. Holt," said the minister, smiling complacently, "and often corrects mine on the ground of niceties, which I profess are as dark to me as if they were the reports of a sixth sense which I possess not. I am an eager seeker for precision, and would fain find language subtle enough to follow the utmost intricacies of the soul's pathways, but I see not why a round word that means some object, made and blessed by the Creator, should be branded and banished as a malefactor."

"Oh, your niceties—I know what they are," said Felix, in his usual *fortissimo*. "They all go on your system of make-believe. 'Rottenness' may suggest what is unpleasant, so you'd better say 'sugar-plums,' or something else such a long way off the fact that nobody is obliged to think of it. Those are your roundabout euphuisms that dress up swindling till it looks as well as honesty, and shoot with boiled pease instead of bullets. I hate your gentlemanly speakers."

"Then you would not like Mr. Jermyn, I think," said Esther. "That reminds me, father, that to-day, when I was giving Miss Louisa Jermyn her lesson, Mr. Jermyn came in and spoke to me with grand politeness, and asked me at what times you were likely to be disengaged, because he wished to make your better acquaintance, and consult you on matters of importance. He never took the least notice of me before. Can you guess the reason of his sudden ceremoniousness?"

"Nay, child," said the minister, ponderingly.

"Politics, of course," said Felix. "He's on some committee. An election is coming. Universal peace is declared, and the foxes have a sincere interest in prolonging the lives of the poultry. Eh, Mr. Lyon? Isn't that it?"

"Nay, not so. He is the close ally of the Transome family, who are blind hereditary Tories like the Debarrys, and will drive their tenants to the poll as if they were sheep. And it has even been hinted that the heir who is coming from the East may be another Tory candidate, and coalesce with the younger Debarry. It is said that he has enormous wealth, and could purchase every vote in the county that has a price."

"He is come," said Esther. "I heard Miss Jermyn tell her sister that she had seen him going out of her father's room."

"'Tis strange," said Mr. Lyon.

"Something extraordinary must have happened," said Esther, "for Mr. Jermyn to intend courting us. Miss Jermyn said to me only the other day that she could not think how I came to be so well educated and ladylike. She always thought Dissenters were ignorant, vulgar people. I said, So they were, usually, and Church people also in small towns. She considers herself a judge of what is ladylike, and she is vulgarity personified—with large feet, and the most odious scent on her handkerchief, and a bonnet that looks like ' The Fashion' printed in capital letters."

"One sort of fine ladyism is as good as another," said Felix.

"No, indeed. Pardon me," said Esther. "A real fine lady does not wear clothes that flare in people's eyes, or use importunate scents, or make a noise as she moves: she is something refined, and graceful, and charming, and never obtrusive."

"Oh, yes," said Felix, contemptuously. "And she reads Byron also, and admires Childe Harold—gentlemen of unspeakable woes, who employ a hairdresser, and look seriously at themselves in the glass."

Esther reddened, and gave a little toss. Felix went on triumphantly. "A fine lady is a squirrel-headed thing, with small airs, and small notions, about as applicable to the business of life as a pair of tweezers to the clearing of a forest. Ask your father what those old persecuted emigrant Puritans would have done with fine-lady wives and daughters."

"Oh, there is no danger of such misalliances," said Esther. "Men who are unpleasant companions and make frights of themselves are sure to get wives tasteless enough to suit them."

"Esther, my dear," said Mr. Lyon, "let not your playfulness betray you into disrespect toward those venerable pilgrims. They struggled and endured in order to cherish and plant anew the seeds of scriptural doctrine and of a pure discipline."

"Yes, I know," said Esther, hastily, dreading a discourse on the pilgrim fathers.

"Oh, they were an ugly lot!" Felix burst in, making Mr. Lyon start. "Miss Medora wouldn't have minded if they had all been put into the pillory and lost their ears. She would have said, ' Their ears did stick out so.' I shouldn't wonder if that's a bust of one of them." Here Felix, with sudden keenness of observation, nodded at the black bust with the gauze over its colored face.

"No," said Mr. Lyon; "that is the eminent George Whitefield, who, you well know, had a gift of oratory as of one on whom the tongue of flame had rested visibly. But Providence—doubtless for wise ends in relation to the inner man, for I would not inquire too closely into minutiæ which carry too many plausible interpretations for any one of them to be stable—Providence, I say, ordained that the good man should squint; and my daughter has not yet learned to bear with his infirmity."

"So she has put a veil over it. Suppose you had squinted yourself?" said Felix, looking at Esther.

"Then, doubtless, you could have been more polite to me, Mr. Holt," said Esther, rising and placing herself at her work-table. "You seem to prefer what is unusual and ugly."

"A peacock!" thought Felix. "I should like to come and

scold her every day, and make her cry and cut her fine hair off."

Felix rose to go, and said, "I will not take up more of your valuable time, Mr. Lyon. I know that you have not many spare evenings."

"That is true, my young friend; for I now go to Sproxton one evening in the week. I do not despair that we may some day need a chapel there, though the hearers do not multiply save among the women, and there is no work as yet begun among the miners themselves. I shall be glad of your company in my walk thither to-morrow at five o'clock, if you would like to see how that population has grown of late years."

"Oh, I've been to Sproxton already several times. I had a congregation of my own there last Sunday evening."

"What! do you preach?" said Mr. Lyon, with a brightened glance.

"Not exactly. I went to the ale-house."

Mr. Lyon started. "I trust you are putting a riddle to me, young man, even as Samson did to his companions. From what you said but lately, it cannot be that you are given to tippling and to taverns."

"Oh, I don't drink much. I order a pint of beer, and I get into talk with the fellows over their pots and pipes. Somebody must take a little knowledge and common sense to them in this way, else how are they to get it? I go for educating the non-electors, so I put myself in the way of my pupils—my academy is the beer-house. I'll walk with you to-morrow with great pleasure."

"Do so, do so," said Mr. Lyon, shaking hands with his odd acquaintance. "We shall understand each other better by and by, I doubt not."

"I wish you good-evening, Miss Lyon."

Esther bowed very slightly, without speaking.

"That is a singular young man, Esther," said the minister, walking about after Felix was gone. "I discern in him a love for whatsoever things are honest and true, which I would fain believe to be an earnest of further endowment with the wisdom that is from on high. It is true that, as the traveller in the desert is often lured, by a false vision of water and freshness, to turn aside from the track which leads to the tried and established fountains, so the Evil One will take advantage of a natural yearning toward the better to delude the soul with a self-flattering belief in a visionary virtue higher than the ordinary fruits of the Spirit. But I trust it is not so here. I feel a great enlargement in this young man's presence, notwithstanding a certain license in his language, which I shall use my efforts to correct."

"I think he is very coarse and rude," said Esther, with a touch of temper in her voice. "But he speaks better English than most of our visitors. What is his occupation?"

"Watch and clock making, by which, together with a little teaching, as I understand, he hopes to maintain his mother, not thinking it right that she should live by the sale of medicines whose virtues he distrusts. It is no common scruple."

"Dear me," said Esther, "I thought he was something higher than that." She was disappointed.

Felix, on his side, as he strolled out in the evening air, said to himself: "Now by what fine meshes of circumstance did that queer devout old man, with his awful creed, which makes this world a vestibule with double doors to hell, and a narrow stair on one side whereby the thinner sort may mount to heaven —by what subtle play of flesh and spirit did he come to have a daughter so little in his own likeness? Married foolishly, I suppose. I'll never marry, though I should have to live on raw turnips to subdue my flesh. I'll never look back and say, 'I had a fine purpose once—I meant to keep my hands clean and my soul upright, and to look truth in the face; but pray excuse me, I have a wife and children—I must lie and simper a little, else they'll starve'; or 'My wife is nice, she must have her bread well buttered, and her feelings will be hurt if she is not thought genteel.' That is the lot Miss Esther is preparing for some man or other. I could grind my teeth at such self-satisfied minxes, who think they can tell everybody what is the correct thing, and the utmost stretch of their ideas will not place them on a level with the intelligent fleas. I should like to see if she could be made ashamed of herself."

CHAPTER VI.

"Though she be dead, yet let me think she lives,
And feed my mind, that dies for want of her."
MARLOWE: *Tamburlaine the Great.*

HARDLY any one in Treby who thought at all of Mr. Lyon and his daughter had not felt the same sort of wonder about Esther as Felix felt. She was not much liked by her father's church and congregation. The less serious observed that she had too many airs and graces, and held her head much too high; the stricter sort feared greatly that Mr. Lyon had not been sufficiently careful in placing his daughter among God-fearing people, and that, being led astray by the melancholy vanity of giving her exceptional accomplishments, he had sent her to a French school, and allowed her to take situations where she had contracted notions not only above her own rank, but of too worldly a kind to be safe in any rank. But no one knew what sort of a woman her mother had been, for Mr. Lyon never spoke of his past domesticities. When he was chosen as pastor at Treby in 1825, it was understood that he had been a widower many years, and he had no companion but the tearful and much-exercised Lyddy, his daughter being still at school. It was only two years ago that Esther had come home to live permanently with her father, and take pupils in the town. Within that time she had excited a passion in two young Dissenting breasts that were clad in the best style of Treby waistcoat—a garment which at that period displayed much design both in the stuff and the wearer; and she had secured an astonished admiration of her cleverness from the girls of various ages who were her pupils; indeed, her knowledge of French was generally held to give a distinction to Treby itself as compared with other market-towns. But she had won little regard of any other kind. Wise Dissenting matrons were divided between fear lest their sons should want to marry her and resentment that she should treat those "undeniable" young men with a distant scorn which was hardly to be tolerated in a minister's daughter;

not only because that parentage appeared to entail an obligation to show an exceptional degree of Christian humility, but
because, looked at from a secular point of view, a poor minister must be below the substantial householders who kept him.
For at that time the preacher who was paid under the Voluntary system was regarded by his flock with feelings not less
mixed than the spiritual person who still took his tithe-pig or
his *modus*. His gifts were admired, and tears were shed under
best bonnets at his sermons; but the weaker tea was thought
good enough for him; and even when he went to preach a
charity sermon in a strange town he was treated with homemade wine and the smaller bedroom. As the good Churchman's reverence was often mixed with growling, and was apt
to be given chiefly to an abstract parson who was what a parson ought to be, so the good Dissenter sometimes mixed his
approval of ministerial gifts with considerable criticism and
cheapening of the human vessel which contained those treasures. Mrs. Muscat and Mrs. Nuttwood applied the principle
of Christian equality by remarking that Mr. Lyon had his
oddities, and that he ought not to allow his daughter to indulge in such unbecoming expenditure on her gloves, shoes,
and hosiery, even if she did pay for them out of her earnings.
As for the Church people who engaged Miss Lyon to give lessons in their families, their imaginations were altogether pros-
trated by the incongruity between accomplishments and Dissent, between weekly prayer-meetings and a conversance with
so lively and altogether worldly a language as the French.
Esther's own mind was not free from a sense of irreconcilable-
ness between the objects of her taste and the conditions of her
lot. She knew that Dissenters were looked down upon by
those whom she regarded as the most refined classes; her
favorite companions, both in France and at an English school
where she had been a junior teacher, had thought it quite
ridiculous to have a father who was a Dissenting preacher;
and when an ardently admiring school-fellow induced her
parents to take Esther as a governess to the younger children,
all her native tendencies toward luxury, fastidiousness, and
scorn of mock gentility were strengthened by witnessing the
habits of a well-born and wealthy family. Yet the position

of servitude was irksome to her, and she was glad at last to
live at home with her father; for though, throughout her girl-
hood, she had wished to avoid this lot, a little experience had
taught her to prefer its comparative independence. But she
was not contented with her life: she seemed to herself to be
surrounded with ignoble, uninteresting conditions, from which
there was no issue; for even if she had been unamiable enough
to give her father pain deliberately, it would have been no
satisfaction to her to go to Treby Church, and visibly turn her
back on Dissent. It was not religious differences, but social
differences, that Esther was concerned about, and her ambitious taste would have been no more gratified in the society of
the Waces than in that of the Muscats. The Waces spoke
imperfect English and played whist; the Muscats spoke the
same dialect and took in the 'Evangelical Magazine.' Esther
liked neither of these amusements. She had one of those exceptional organizations which are quick and sensitive without
being in the least morbid; she was alive to the finest shades
of manner, to the nicest distinctions of tone and accent; she
had a little code of her own about scents and colors, textures
and behavior, by which she secretly condemned or sanctioned
all things and persons. And she was well satisfied with herself for her fastidious taste, never doubting that hers was the
highest standard. She was proud that the best-born and
handsomest girls at school had always said that she might be
taken for a born lady. Her own pretty instep, clad in a silk
stocking, her little heel, just rising from a kid slipper, her
irreproachable nails and delicate wrist, were the objects of
delighted consciousness to her; and she felt that it was her
superiority which made her unable to use without disgust any
but the finest cambric handkerchiefs and freshest gloves. Her
money all went in the gratification of these nice tastes, and
she saved nothing from her earnings. I cannot say that she
had any pangs of conscience on this score; for she felt sure
that she was generous: she hated all meanness, would empty
her purse impulsively on some sudden appeal to her pity, and
if she found out that her father had a want she would supply it with some pretty device of a surprise. But then the
good man so seldom had a want—except the perpetual desire,

which she could never gratify, of seeing her under convictions, and fit to become a member of the church.

As for little Mr. Lyon, he loved and admired this unregenerate child more, he feared, than was consistent with the due preponderance of impersonal and ministerial regards: he prayed and pleaded for her with tears, humbling himself for her spiritual deficiencies in the privacy of his study; and then came downstairs to find himself in timorous subjection to her wishes, lest, as he inwardly said, he should give his teaching an ill savor by mingling it with outward crossing. There will be queens in spite of Salic or other laws of later date than Adam and Eve; and here, in this small dingy house of the minister in Malthouse Yard, there was a light-footed, sweet-voiced Queen Esther.

The stronger will always rule, say some, with an air of confidence which is like a lawyer's flourish, forbidding exceptions or additions. But what is strength? Is it blind wilfulness that sees no terrors, no many-linked consequences, no bruises and wounds of those whose cords it tightens? Is it the narrowness of a brain that conceives no needs differing from its own, and looks to no results beyond the bargains of to-day; that tugs with emphasis for every small purpose, and thinks it weakness to exercise the sublime power of resolved renunciation? There is a sort of subjection which is the peculiar heritage of largeness and of love; and strength is often only another name for willing bondage to irremediable weakness.

Esther had affection for her father: she recognized the purity of his character, and a quickness of intellect in him which responded to her own liveliness, in spite of what seemed a dreary piety, which selected everything that was least interesting and romantic in life and history. But his old clothes had a smoky odor, and she did not like to walk with him, because, when people spoke to him in the street, it was his wont, instead of remarking on the weather and passing on, to pour forth in an absent manner some reflections that were occupying his mind about the traces of the Divine government, or about a peculiar incident narrated in the life of the eminent Mr. Richard Baxter. Esther had a horror of appearing ridiculous even in the eyes of vulgar Trebians. She fancied that she should have loved her mother better than she was able to love her father; and she wished she could have remembered that mother more thoroughly.

But she had no more than a broken vision of the time before she was five years old—the time when the word oftenest on her lips was "Mamma"; when a low voice spoke caressing French words to her, and she in her turn repeated the words to her rag doll; when a very small white hand, different from any that came after, used to pat her, and stroke her, and tie on her frock and pinafore; and when at last there was nothing but sitting with a doll on a bed where mamma was lying, till her father once carried her away. Where distinct memory began, there was no longer the low caressing voice and the small white hand. She knew that her mother was a French-woman, that she had been in want and distress, and that her maiden name was Annette Ledru. Her father had told her no more than this; and once, in her childhood, when she had asked him some question, he had said, " My Esther, until you are a woman, we will only think of your mother: when you are about to be married and leave me, we will speak of her, and I will deliver to you her ring and all that was hers; but, without a great command laid upon me, I cannot pierce my heart by speaking of that which was and is not." Esther had never forgotten these words, and the older she became the more impossible she felt it that she should urge her father with questions about the past.

His inability to speak of that past to her depended on manifold causes. Partly it came from an initial concealment. He had not the courage to tell Esther that he was not really her father: he had not the courage to renounce that hold on her tenderness which the belief in his natural fatherhood must help to give him, or to incur any resentment that her quick spirit might feel at having been brought up under a false supposition. But there were other things yet more difficult for him to be quite open about—deep sorrows of his life as a Christian minister that were hardly to be told to a girl.

Twenty-two years before, when Rufus Lyon was no more than thirty-six years old, he was the admired pastor of a large Independent congregation in one of our southern seaport

6

towns. He was unmarried, and had met all exhortations of friends who represented to him that a bishop—*i.e.*, the overseer of an Independent church and congregation—should be the husband of one wife, by saying that St. Paul meant this particular as a limitation, and not as an injunction; that a minister was permitted to have one wife, but that he, Rufus Lyon, did not wish to avail himself of that permission, finding his studies and other labors of his vocation all-absorbing, and seeing that mothers in Israel were sufficiently provided by those who had not been set apart for a more special work. His church and congregation were proud of him: he was put forward on platforms, was made a "deputation," and was requested to preach anniversary sermons in far-off towns. Wherever noteworthy preachers were discussed, Rufus Lyon was almost sure to be mentioned as one who did honor to the Independent body; his sermons were said to be full of study, yet full of fire; and while he had more of human knowledge than many of his brethren, he showed in an eminent degree the marks of a true ministerial vocation. But on a sudden this burning and shining light seemed to be quenched: Mr. Lyon voluntarily resigned his charge and withdrew from the town.

A terrible crisis had come upon him; a moment in which religious doubt and newly awakened passion had rushed together in a common flood, and had paralyzed his ministerial gifts. His life of thirty-six years had been a story of purely religious and studious fervor; his passion had been for doctrines, for argumentative conquest on the side of right; the sins he had had chiefly to pray against had been those of personal ambition (under such forms as ambition takes in the mind of a man who has chosen the career of an Independent preacher), and those of a too restless intellect, ceaselessly urging questions concerning the mystery of that which was assuredly revealed, and thus hindering the due nourishment of the soul on the substance of the truth delivered. Even at that time of comparative youth his unworldliness and simplicity in small matters (for he was keenly awake to the larger affairs of this world) gave a certain oddity to his manners and appearance; and though his sensitive face had much beauty, his person altogether seemed so irrelevant to a fashionable view of things that well-dressed ladies and gentlemen usually laughed at him, as they probably did at Mr. John Milton after the Restoration and ribbons had come in, and still more at that apostle of weak bodily presence who preached in the back streets of Ephesus and elsewhere a new view of a new religion that hardly anybody believed in. Rufus Lyon was the singular-looking apostle of the Meeting in Skipper's Lane. Was it likely that any romance should befall such a man? Perhaps not; but romance did befall him.

One winter's evening in 1812 Mr. Lyon was returning from a village preaching. He walked at his usual rapid rate, with busy thoughts undistracted by any sight more distinct than the bushes and hedgerow trees, black beneath a faint moonlight, until something suggested to him that he had perhaps omitted to bring away with him a thin account-book in which he recorded certain subscriptions. He paused, unfastened his outer coat and felt in all his pockets, then he took off his hat and looked inside it. The book was not to be found, and he was about to walk on, when he was startled by hearing a low, sweet voice say, with a strong foreign accent, —

"Have pity on me, sir."

Searching with his short-sighted eyes, he perceived some one on a side bank; and, approaching, he found a young woman with a baby on her lap. She spoke again more faintly than before.

"Sir, I die with hunger; in the name of God take the little one."

There was no distrusting the pale face and the sweet low voice. Without pause, Mr. Lyon took the baby in his arms and said, "Can you walk by my side, young woman?"

She rose, but seemed tottering. "Lean on me," said Mr. Lyon. And so they walked slowly on, the minister for the first time in his life carrying a baby.

Nothing better occurred to him than to take his charge to his own house; it was the simplest way of relieving the woman's wants, and finding out how she could be helped further; and he thought of no other possibilities. She was too feeble for more words to be spoken between them till she was seated

by his fireside. His elderly servant was not easily amazed at
anything her master did in the way of charity, and at once
took the baby, while Mr. Lyon unfastened the mother's damp
bonnet and shawl, and gave her something warm to drink.
Then, waiting by her till it was time to offer her more, he
had nothing to do but to notice the loveliness of her face,
which seemed to him as that of an angel, with a benignity in
its repose that carried a more assured sweetness than any
smile. Gradually she revived, lifted up her delicate hands
between her face and the firelight, and looked at the baby,
which lay opposite to her on the old servant's lap, taking in
spoonfuls with much content, and stretching out naked feet
toward the warmth. Then, as her consciousness of relief
grew into contrasting memory, she lifted up her eyes to Mr.
Lyon, who stood close by her, and said, in her pretty broken
way, —

"I knew you had a good heart when you took your hat off.
You seemed to me as the image of the *bien-aimé Saint Jean.*"

The grateful glance of those blue-gray eyes, with their long
shadow-making eyelashes, was a new kind of good to Rufus
Lyon; it seemed to him as if a woman had never really looked
at him before. Yet this poor thing was apparently a blind
French Catholic—of delicate nurture, surely, judging from
her hands. He was in a tremor; he felt that it would be
rude to question her, and he only urged her now to take a
little food. She accepted it with evident enjoyment, looking
at the child continually, and then, with a fresh burst of gratitude, leaning forward to press the servant's hand, and say,
"Oh, you are good!" Then she looked up at Mr. Lyon again
and said, "Is there in the world a prettier *marmot?*"

The evening passed; a bed was made up for the strange
woman, and Mr. Lyon had not asked her so much as her
name. He never went to bed himself that night. He
spent it in misery, enduring a horrible assault of Satan.
He thought a frenzy had seized him. Wild visions of an
impossible future thrust themselves upon him. He dreaded
lest the woman had a husband; he wished that he might
call her his own, that he might worship her beauty, that
she might love and caress him. And what to the mass of

men would have been only one of many allowable follies—a transient fascination, to be dispelled by daylight and contact with those common facts of which common sense is the reflex —was to him a spiritual convulsion. He was as one who raved, and knew that he raved. These mad wishes were irreconcilable with what he was, and must be, as a Christian minister; nay, penetrating his soul as tropic heat penetrates the frame, and changes for it all aspects and all flavors, they were irreconcilable with that conception of the world which made his faith. All the busy doubts which had before been mere impish shadows flitting around a belief that was strong with the strength of an unswerving moral bias had now gathered blood and substance. The questioning spirit had become suddenly bold and blasphemous: it no longer insinuated scepticism—it prompted defiance; it no longer expressed cool inquisitive thought, but was the voice of a passionate mood. Yet he never ceased to regard it as the voice of the tempter: the conviction which had been the law of his better life remained within him as a conscience.

The struggle of that night was an abridgment of all the struggles that came after. Quick souls have their intensest life in the first anticipatory sketch of what may or will be, and the pursuit of their wish is the pursuit of that paradisiacal vision which only impelled them, and is left farther and farther behind, vanishing forever even out of hope in the moment which is called success.

The next morning Mr. Lyon heard his guest's history. She was the daughter of a French officer of considerable rank, who had fallen in the Russian campaign. She had escaped from France to England with much difficulty in order to rejoin her husband, a young Englishman, to whom she had become attached during his detention as a prisoner of war on parole at Vesoul, where she was living under the charge of some relatives, and to whom she had been married without the consent of her family. Her husband had served in the Hanoverian army, had obtained his discharge in order to visit England on some business, with the nature of which she was not acquainted, and had been taken prisoner as a suspected spy. A short time after their marriage he and his fellow prisoners had been moved to a town nearer the coast, and she had remained in wretched uncertainty about him, until at last a letter had come from him telling her that an exchange of prisoners had occurred, that he was in England, that she must use her utmost effort to follow him, and that on arriving on English ground she must send him word under a cover which he enclosed, bearing an address in London. Fearing the opposition of her friends, she started unknown to them, with a very small supply of money; and after enduring much discomfort and many fears in waiting for a passage, which she at last got in a small trading smack, she arrived at Southampton—ill. Before she was able to write, her baby was born; and before her husband's answer came, she had been obliged to pawn some clothes and trinkets. He desired her to travel to London, where he would meet her at the Belle Sauvage, adding that he was himself in distress, and unable to come to her: when once she was in London they would take ship and quit the country. Arrived at the Belle Sauvage, the poor thing waited three days in vain for her husband: on the fourth a letter came in a strange hand, saying that in his last moments he had desired this letter to be written to inform her of his death, and recommended her to return to her friends. She could choose no other course, but she had soon been reduced to walking, that she might save her pence to buy bread with; and on the evening when she made her appeal to Mr. Lyon she had pawned the last thing, over and above needful clothing, that she could persuade herself to part with. The things she had not borne to part with were her marriage-ring and a locket containing her husband's hair and bearing his baptismal name. This locket, she said, exactly resembled one worn by her husband on his watch-chain, only that his bore the name Annette, and contained a lock of her hair. The precious trifle now hung round her neck by a cord, for she had sold the small gold chain which formerly held it.

The only guaranty of this story, besides the exquisite candor of her face, was a small packet of papers which she carried in her pocket, consisting of her husband's few letters, the letter which announced his death, and her marriage certificate. It was not so probable a story as that of many an inventive vagrant; but Mr. Lyon did not doubt it for a moment. It was impossible to him to suspect this angelic-faced woman, but he had strong suspicions concerning her husband. He could not help being glad that she had not retained the address he had desired her to send to in London, as that removed any obvious means of learning particulars about him. But inquiries might have been made at Vesoul by letter, and her friends there might have been appealed to. A consciousness, not to be quite silenced, told Mr. Lyon that this was the course he ought to take; but it would have required an energetic self-conquest, and he was excused from it by Annette's own disinclination to return to her relatives, if any other acceptable possibility could be found.

He dreaded, with a violence of feeling which surmounted all struggles, lest anything should take her away, and place such barriers between them as would make it unlikely or impossible that she should ever love him well enough to become his wife. Yet he saw with perfect clearness that unless he tore up this mad passion by the roots his ministerial usefulness would be frustrated, and the repose of his soul would be destroyed. This woman was an unregenerate Catholic; ten minutes' listening to her artless talk made that plain to him: even if her position had been less equivocal, to unite himself to such a woman was nothing less than a spiritual fall. It was already a fall that he had wished there was no high purpose to which he owed an allegiance—that he had longed to fly to some backwoods where there was no church to reproach him, and where he might have this sweet woman to wife, and know the joys of tenderness. Those sensibilities which in most lives are diffused equally through the youthful years were aroused suddenly in Mr. Lyon, as some men have their special genius revealed to them by a tardy concurrence of conditions. His love was the first love of a fresh young heart full of wonder and worship. But what to one man is the virtue which he has sunk below the possibility of aspiring to is to another the backsliding by which he forfeits his spiritual crown.

The end was that Annette remained in his house. He had striven against himself so far as to represent her position to some chief matrons in his congregation, praying and yet dreading that they would so take her by the hand as to impose on him that denial of his own longing not to let her go out of his sight which he found it too hard to impose on himself. But they regarded the case coldly: the woman was, after all, a vagrant. Mr. Lyon was observed to be surprisingly weak on the subject—his eagerness seemed disproportionate and unbecoming; and this young Frenchwoman, unable to express herself very clearly, was no more interesting to those matrons and their husbands than other pretty young women suspiciously circumstanced. They were willing to subscribe something to carry her on her way, or if she took some lodgings they would give her a little sewing, and endeavor to convert her from Papistry. If, however, she was a respectable person, as she said, the only proper thing for her was to go back to her own country and friends. In spite of himself, Mr. Lyon exulted. There seemed a reason now that he should keep Annette under his own eyes. He told himself that no real object would be served by his providing food and lodging for her elsewhere—an expense which he could ill afford. And she was apparently so helpless, except as to the one task of attending to her baby, that it would have been folly to think of her exerting herself for her own support.

But this course of his was severely disapproved by his church. There were various signs that the minister was under some evil influence: his preaching wanted its old fervor, he seemed to shun the intercourse of his brethren, and very mournful suspicions were entertained. A formal remonstrance was presented to him, but he met it as if he had already determined to act in anticipation of it. He admitted that external circumstances, conjoined with a peculiar state of mind, were likely to hinder the fruitful exercise of his ministry, and he resigned it. There was much sorrowing, much expostulation, but he declared that for the present he was unable to unfold himself more fully; he only wished to state solemnly that Annette Ledru, though blind in spiritual things, was in a worldly sense a pure and virtuous woman. No more was to be said, and he departed to a distant town. Here he maintained himself, Annette, and the child with the remainder of his stipend, and with the wages he earned as a printer's reader. Annette was one of those angelic-faced helpless women who take all things as manna from heaven: the good image of the well-beloved Saint John wished her to stay with him, and there was nothing else that she wished for except the unattainable. Yet for a whole year Mr. Lyon never dared to tell Annette that he loved her: he trembled before this woman; he saw that the idea of his being her lover was too remote from her mind for her to have any idea that she ought not to live with him. She had never known, never asked, the reason why he gave up his ministry. She seemed to entertain as little concern about the strange world in which she lived as a bird in its nest; an avalanche had fallen over the past, but she sat warm and uncrushed—there was food for many morrows, and her baby flourished. She did not seem even to care about a priest, or about having her child baptized; and on the subject of religion Mr. Lyon was as timid, and shrank as much from speaking to her, as on the subject of his love. He dreaded anything that might cause her to feel a sudden repulsion toward him. He dreaded disturbing her simple gratitude and content. In these days his religious faith was not slumbering; it was awake and achingly conscious of having fallen in a struggle. He had had a great treasure committed to him, and had flung it away: he held himself a backslider. His unbelieving thoughts never gained the full ear and consent of his soul. His prayers had been stifled by the sense that there was something he preferred to complete obedience: they had ceased to be anything but intermittent cries and confessions, and a submissive presentiment, rising at times even to an entreaty, that some great discipline might come, that the dulled spiritual sense might be roused to full vision and hearing as of old, and the supreme facts become again supreme in his soul. Mr. Lyon will perhaps seem a very simple personage, with pitiably narrow theories; but none of our theories are quite large enough for all the disclosures of time, and to the end of men's struggles a penalty will remain for those who sink from the ranks of the heroes into the crowd for whom the heroes fight and die.

One day, however, Annette learned Mr. Lyon's secret. The

baby had a tooth coming, and, being large and strong now, was noisily fretful. Mr. Lyon, though he had been working extra hours and was much in need of repose, took the child from its mother immediately on entering the house and walked about with it, patting and talking soothingly to it. The stronger grasp, the new sensations, were a successful anodyne, and baby went to sleep on his shoulder. But fearful lest any movement should disturb it, he sat down, and endured the bondage of holding it still against his shoulder.

"You do nurse baby well," said Annette, approvingly. "Yet you never nursed before I came?"

"No," said Mr. Lyon. "I had no brothers and sisters."

"Why were you not married?" Annette had never thought of asking that question before.

"Because I never loved any woman—till now. I thought I should never marry. Now I wish to marry."

Annette started. She did not see at once that she was the woman he wanted to marry; what had flashed on her mind was that there might be a great change in Mr. Lyon's life. It was as if the lightning had entered into her dream and half awaked her.

"Do you think it foolish, Annette, that I should wish to marry?"

"I did not expect it," she said, doubtfully. "I did not know you thought about it."

"You know the woman I should like to marry?"

"I know her?" she said, interrogatively, blushing deeply.

"It is you, Annette—you whom I have loved better than my duty. I forsook everything for you."

Mr. Lyon paused: he was about to do what he felt would be ignoble—to urge what seemed like a claim.

"Can you love me, Annette? Will you be my wife?" Annette trembled and looked miserable.

"Do not speak—forget it," said Mr. Lyon, rising suddenly and speaking with loud energy. "No, no—I do not want it —I do not wish it."

The baby awoke as he started up; he gave the child into Annette's arms, and left her.

His work took him away early the next morning and the

next again. They did not need to speak much to each other. The third day Mr. Lyon was too ill to go to work. His frame had been overwrought; he had been too poor to have sufficiently nourishing food, and under the shattering of his long-deferred hope his health had given way. They had no regular servant—only occasional help from an old woman, who lit the fires and put on the kettles. Annette was forced to be the sick-nurse, and this sudden demand on her shook away some of her torpor. The illness was a serious one, and the medical man one day hearing Mr. Lyon in his delirium raving with an astonishing fluency in Biblical language, suddenly looked round with increased curiosity at Annette, and asked if she were the sick man's wife, or some other relative.

"No—no relation," said Annette, shaking her head. "He has been good to me."

"How long have you lived with him?"

"More than a year."

"Was he a preacher once?"

"Yes."

"When did he leave off being a preacher?"

"Soon after he took care of me."

"Is that his child?"

"Sir," said Annette, coloring indignantly, "I am a widow."

The doctor, she thought, looked at her oddly, but he asked no more questions.

When the sick man was getting better, and able to enjoy invalid's food, he observed one day, while he was taking some broth, that Annette was looking at him; he paused to look at her in return, and was struck with a new expression in her face, quite distinct from the merely passive sweetness which usually characterized it. She laid her little hand on his, which was now transparently thin, and said, "I am getting very wise; I have sold some of the books to make money— the doctor told me where; and I have looked into the shops where they sell caps and bonnets and pretty things, and I can do all that, and get more money to keep us. And when you are well enough to get up, we will go out and be married— shall we not? See! and *la petite*" (the baby had never been named anything else) "shall call you Papa—and then we shall never part."

Mr. Lyon trembled. This illness—something else, perhaps —had made a great change in Annette. A fortnight after that they were married. The day before he had ventured to ask her if she felt any difficulty about her religion, and if she would consent to have *la petite* baptized and brought up as a Protestant. She shook her head and said very simply,—

"No: in France, in other days, I would have minded; but all is changed. I never was fond of religion, but I knew it was right. *J'aimais les fleurs, les bals, la musique, et mon mari qui était beau.* But all that is gone away. There is nothing of my religion in this country. But the good God must be here, for you are good; I leave all to you."

It was clear that Annette regarded her present life as a sort of death to the world—an existence on a remote island where she had been saved from wreck. She was too indolent mentally, too little interested, to acquaint herself with any secrets of the isle. The transient energy, the more vivid consciousness and sympathy, which had been stirred in her during Mr. Lyon's illness had soon subsided into the old apathy to everything except her child. She withered like a plant in strange air, and the three years of life that remained were but a slow and gentle death. Those three years were to Mr. Lyon a period of such self-suppression and life in another as few men know. Strange! that the passion for this woman, which he felt to have drawn him aside from the right as much as if he had broken the most solemn vows—for that only was right to him which he held the best and highest—the passion for a being who had no glimpse of his thoughts induced a more thorough renunciation than he had ever known in the time of his complete devotion to his ministerial career. He had no flattery now, either from himself or the world; he knew that he had fallen, and *his* world had forgotten him, or shook their heads at his memory. The only satisfaction he had was the satisfaction of his tenderness—which meant untiring work, untiring patience, untiring wakefulness even to the dumb signs of feeling in a creature whom he alone cared for.

The day of parting came, and he was left with little Esther

as the one visible sign of that four years' break in his life. A year afterward he entered the ministry again, and lived with the utmost sparingness, that Esther might be so educated as to be able to get her own bread in case of his death. Her probable facility in acquiring French naturally suggested his sending her to a French school, which would give her a special advantage as a teacher. It was a Protestant school, and French Protestantism had the high recommendation of being non-Prelatical. It was understood that Esther would contract no Papistical superstitions; and this was perfectly true; but she contracted, as we see, a good deal of non-Papistical vanity.

Mr. Lyon's reputation as a preacher and devoted pastor had revived; but some dissatisfaction beginning to be felt by his congregation at a certain laxity detected by them in his views as to the limits of salvation, which he had in one sermon even hinted might extend to unconscious recipients of mercy, he had found it desirable seven years ago to quit this ten years' pastorate and accept a call from the less important church in Malthouse Yard, Treby Magna.

This was Rufus Lyon's history, at that time unknown in its fulness to any human being besides himself. We can perhaps guess what memories they were that relaxed the stringency of his doctrine on the point of salvation. In the deepest of all senses his heart said,—

> " Though she be dead, yet let me think she lives,
> And feed my mind, that dies for want of her."

------◆------

CHAPTER VII.

M. It was but yesterday you spoke him well—
    You've changed your mind so soon?
N.   Not I—'tis he
    That, changing to my thought, has changed my mind.
    No man puts rotten apples in his pouch
    Because their upper side looked fair to him.
    Constancy in mistake is constant folly.

THE news that the rich heir of the Transomes was actually come back, and had been seen at Treby, was carried to some one else who had more reasons for being interested in it than the Reverend Rufus Lyon was yet conscious of having. It was owing to this that at three o'clock, two days afterward, a carriage and pair, with coachman and footman in crimson and drab, passed through the lodge gates of Transome Court. Inside there was a hale, good-natured-looking man of sixty, whose hands rested on a knotted stick held between his knees; and a blue-eyed, well-featured lady, fat and middle-aged—a mountain of satin, lace, and exquisite muslin embroidery. They were not persons of highly remarkable appearance, but to most Trebians they seemed absolutely unique, and likely to be known anywhere. If you had looked down on them from the box of Sampson's coach, he would have said, after lifting his hat, "Sir Maximus and his lady—did you see?" thinking it needless to add the surname.

"We shall find her greatly elated, doubtless," Lady Debarry was saying. "She has been in the shade so long."

"Ah, poor thing!" said Sir Maximus. "A fine woman she was in her bloom. I remember the first county ball she attended we were all ready to fight for the sake of dancing with her. I always liked her from that time—I never swallowed the scandal about her myself."

"If we are to be intimate with her," said Lady Debarry, "I wish you would avoid making such allusions, Sir Maximus. I should not like Selina and Harriet to hear them."

"My dear, I should have forgotten all about the scandal, only you remind me of it sometimes," retorted the Baronet, smiling and taking out his snuff-box.

"These sudden turns of fortune are often dangerous to an excitable constitution," said Lady Debarry, not choosing to notice her husband's epigram. "Poor Lady Alicia Methurst got heart-disease from a sudden piece of luck—the death of her uncle, you know. If Mrs. Transome were wise she would go to town—she can afford it now—and consult Dr. Truncheon. I should say myself he would order her digitalis: I have often guessed exactly what a prescription would be. But it certainly was always one of her weak points to think that she understood medicine better than other people."

"She's a healthy woman enough, surely: see how upright she is, and she rides about like a girl of twenty."

"She is so thin that she makes me shudder."

"Pooh! she's slim and active: women are not bid for by the pound."

"Pray don't be so coarse."

Sir Maximus laughed and showed his good teeth, which made his laughter very becoming. The carriage stopped, and they were soon ushered into Mrs. Transome's sitting-room, where she was working at her worsted embroidery. A little daily embroidery had been a constant element in Mrs. Transome's life; that soothing occupation of taking stitches to produce what neither she nor any one else wanted was then the resource of many a well-born and unhappy woman.

She received much warm congratulation and pressure of her hand with perfect composure of manner; but she became paler than usual, and her hands turned quite cold. The Debarrys did not yet know what Harold's politics were.

"Well, our lucky youngster is come in the nick of time," said Sir Maximus: "if he'll stand, he and Philip can run in harness together and keep out both the Whigs."

"It is really quite a providential thing—his returning just now," said Lady Debarry. "I couldn't help thinking that something would occur to prevent Philip from having such a man as Peter Garstin for his colleague."

"I call my friend Harold a youngster," said Sir Maximus, "for, you know, I remember him only as he was when that portrait was taken."

"That is a long while ago," said Mrs. Transome. "My son is much altered, as you may imagine."

There was a confused sound of voices in the library while this talk was going on. Mrs. Transome chose to ignore that noise, but her face, from being pale, began to flush a little.

"Yes, yes, on the outside, I dare say. But he was a fine fellow—I always liked him. And if anybody had asked me what I should choose for the good of the county, I couldn't have thought of anything better than having a young Transome for a neighbor who will take an active part. The Transomes and the Debarrys were always on the right side together in old days. Of course he'll stand—he has made up his mind to it?"

The need for an answer to this embarrassing question was deferred by the increase of inarticulate sounds accompanied by a bark from the library, and the sudden appearance at the tapestry-hung door-way of old Mr. Transome with a cord round his waist, playing a very poor-paced horse for a black-maned little boy about three years old, who was urging him on with loud encouraging noises and occasional thumps from a stick which he wielded with some difficulty. The old man paused with a vague gentle smile at the door-way, while the Baronet got up to speak to him. Nimrod snuffed at his master's legs to ascertain that he was not hurt, and the little boy, finding something new to be looked at, let go the cord and came round in front of the company, dragging his stick, and standing at a safe war-dancing distance as he fixed his great black eyes on Lady Debarry.

"Dear me, what a splendid little boy, Mrs. Transome! why—it cannot be—can it be—that you have the happiness to be a grandmamma?"

"Yes; that is my son's little boy."

"Indeed!" said Lady Debarry, really amazed. "I never heard you speak of his marriage. He has brought you home a daughter-in-law, then?"

"No," said Mrs. Transome, coldly; "she is dead."

"O—o—oh!" said Lady Debarry, in a tone ludicrously undecided between condolence, satisfaction, and general mistiness. "How very singular—I mean that we should not have heard of Mr. Harold's marriage. But he's a charming little fellow: come to me, you round-cheeked cherub."

The black eyes continued fixed as if by a sort of fascination on Lady Debarry's face, and her affable invitation was unheeded. At last, putting his head forward and pouting his lips, the cherub gave forth with marked intention the sounds, "Nau-o-oom," many times repeated: apparently they summed up his opinion of Lady Debarry, and may perhaps have meant "naughty old woman," but his speech was a broken lisping polyglot of hazardous interpretation. Then he turned to pull at the Blenheim spaniel, which, being old and peevish, gave a little snap.

"Go, go, Harry; let poor Puff alone—he'll bite you," said Mrs. Transome, stooping to release her aged pet.

Her words were too suggestive, for Harry immediately laid hold of her arm with his teeth, and bit with all his might. Happily the stuffs upon it were some protection, but the pain forced Mrs. Transome to give a low cry; and Sir Maximus, who had now turned to reseat himself, shook the little rascal off, whereupon he burst away and trotted into the library again.

"I fear you are hurt," said Lady Debarry, with sincere concern. "What a little savage! Do have your arm attended to, my dear—I recommend fomentation—don't think of me."

"Oh, thank you, it is nothing," said Mrs. Transome, biting her lip and smiling alternately; "it will soon go off. The pleasures of being a grandmamma, you perceive. The child has taken a dislike to me; but he makes quite a new life for Mr. Transome; they were playfellows at once."

"Bless my heart!" said Sir Maximus, "it is odd to think of Harold having been a family man so long. I made up my mind he was a young bachelor. What an old stager I am, to be sure! And whom has he married? I hope we shall soon have the pleasure of seeing Mrs. Harold Transome." Sir Maximus, occupied with old Mr. Transome, had not overheard the previous conversation on that subject.

"She is no longer living," Lady Debarry hastily interposed; "but now, my dear Sir Maximus, we must not hinder Mrs. Transome from attending to her arm. I am sure she is in pain. Don't say another word, my dear—we shall see you again—you and Mr. Harold will come and dine with us on Thursday—say yes, only yes. Sir Maximus is longing to see him; and Philip will be down."

"Yes, yes!" said Sir Maximus; "he must lose no time in making Philip's acquaintance. Tell him Philip is a fine fellow—carried everything before him at Oxford. And your son must be returned along with him for North Loamshire. You said he meant to stand?"

"I will write and let you know if Harold has any engagement for Thursday; he would of course be happy otherwise," said Mrs. Transome, evading the question.

7

"If not Thursday, the next day—the very first day he can."

The visitors left, and Mrs. Transome was almost glad of the painful bite which had saved her from being questioned further about Harold's politics. "This is the last visit I shall receive from them," she said to herself as the door closed behind them, and she rang for Denner.

"That poor creature is not happy, Sir Maximus," said Lady Debarry as they drove along. "Something annoys her about her son. I hope there is nothing unpleasant in his character. Either he kept his marriage a secret from her, or she was ashamed of it. He is thirty-four at least by this time. After living in the East so long he may have become a sort of person one would not care to be intimate with, and that savage boy—he doesn't look like a lady's child."

"Pooh, my dear," said Sir Maximus, "women think so much of those minutiæ. In the present state of the country it is our duty to look at a man's position and politics. Philip and my brother are both of that opinion, and I think they know what's right, if any man does. We are bound to regard every man of our party as a public instrument, and to pull all together. The Transomes have always been a good Tory family, but it has been a cipher of late years. This young fellow coming back with a fortune to give the family a head and a position is a clear gain to the county; and with Philip he'll get into the right hands—of course he wants guiding, having been out of the country so long. All we have to ask is, whether a man's a Tory, and will make a stand for the good of the country?—that's the plain English of the matter. And I do beg of you, my dear, to set aside all these gossiping niceties, and exert yourself, like a woman of sense and spirit as you are, to bring the right people together."

Here Sir Maximus gave a deep cough, took out his snuff-box, and tapped it: he had made a serious marital speech, an exertion to which he was rarely urged by anything smaller than a matter of conscience. And this outline of the whole duty of a Tory was matter of conscience with him; though the *Duffield Watchman* had pointed expressly to Sir Maximus Debarry, amongst others, in branding the co-operation of the Tories as a conscious selfishness and reckless immorality, which, however, would be defeated by the co-operation of all the friends of truth and liberty, who, the *Watchman* trusted, would subordinate all non-political differences in order to return representatives pledged to support the present Government.

"I am sure, Sir Maximus," Lady Debarry answered, "you could not have observed that anything was wanting in my manners to Mrs. Transome."

"No, no, my dear; but I say this by way of caution. Never mind what was done at Smyrna, or whether Transome likes to sit with his heels tucked up. We may surely wink at a few things for the sake of the public interest, if God Almighty does; and if He didn't, I don't know what would have become of the country—Government could never have been carried on, and many a good battle would have been lost. That's the philosophy of the matter, and the common sense too."

Good Sir Maximus gave a deep cough and tapped his box again, inwardly remarking that if he had not been such a lazy fellow he might have made as good a figure as his son Philip.

But at this point the carriage, which was rolling by a turn toward Treby Magna, passed a well-dressed man, who raised his hat to Sir Maximus, and called to the coachman to stop.

"Excuse me, Sir Maximus," said this personage, standing uncovered at the carriage door, "but I have just learned something of importance at Treby, which I thought you would like to know as soon as possible."

"Ah! what's that? Something about Garstin or Clement?" said Sir Maximus, seeing the other draw a poster from his pocket.

"No; rather worse, I fear you will think. A new Radical candidate. I got this by a stratagem from the printer's boy. They're not posted yet."

"A Radical!" said Sir Maximus, in a tone of incredulous disgust, as he took the folded bill. "What fool is he?—he'll have no chance."

"They say he's richer than Garstin."

"Harold Transome!" shouted Sir Maximus, as he read the name in three-inch letters. "I don't believe it—it's a trick —it's a squib: why—why—we've just been to his place—eh?

do you know any more? Speak, sir—speak; don't deal out
your story like a damned mountebank, who wants to keep
people gaping."

"Sir Maximus, pray don't give way so," said Lady Debarry.

"I'm afraid there's no doubt about it, sir," said Christian.
"After getting the bill, I met Mr. Labron's clerk, and he said
he had just had the whole story from Jermyn's clerk. The
Ram Inn is engaged already, and a committee is being made
up. He says Jermyn goes like a steam-engine, when he has
a mind, although he makes such long-winded speeches."

"Jermyn be hanged for a two-faced rascal! Tell Mitchell
to drive on. It's of no use to stay chattering here. Jump
up on the box and go home with us. I may want you."

"You see I was right, Sir Maximus," said the Baronet's
wife. "I had an instinct that we should find him an unpleasant person."

"Fudge! if you had such a fine instinct, why did you let us
go to Transome Court and make fools of ourselves?"

"Would you have listened to me? But of course you will
not have him to dine with you?"

"Dine with me? I should think not. I'd sooner he
should dine off me. I see how it is clearly enough. He has
become a regular beast among those Mahometans—he's got
neither religion nor morals left. He can't know anything
about English politics. He'll go and cut his own nose off as a
landholder, and never know. However, he won't get in—
he'll spend his money for nothing."

"I fear he is a very licentious man," said Lady Debarry.
"We know now why his mother seemed so uneasy. I should
think she reflects a little, poor creature."

"It's a confounded nuisance we didn't meet Christian on our
way, instead of coming back; but better now than later.
He's an uncommonly adroit, useful fellow, that factotum of
Philip's. I wish Phil would take my man and give me Christian. I'd make him house-steward; he might reduce the
accounts a little."

Perhaps Sir Maximus would not have been so sanguine as
to Mr. Christian's economical virtues if he had seen that gentleman relaxing himself the same evening among the other dis-

tinguished dependents of the family and frequenters of the steward's room. But a man of Sir Maximus's rank is like those antediluvian animals whom the system of things condemned to carry such a huge bulk that they really could not inspect their bodily appurtenance, and had no conception of their own tails: their parasites doubtless had a merry time of it, and often did extremely well when the high-bred saurian himself was ill at ease. Treby Manor, measured from the front saloon to the remotest shed, was as large as a moderate-sized village, and there were certainly more lights burning in it every evening, more wine, spirits, and ale drunk, more waste and more folly, than could be found in some large villages. There was fast revelry in the steward's room, and slow revelry in the Scotch bailiff's room; short whist, costume, and flirtation in the housekeeper's room, and the same at a lower price in the servants' hall; a select Olympian feast in the private apartment of the cook, who was a much grander person than her ladyship, and wore gold and jewelry to a vast amount of suet; a gambling group in the stables, and the coachman, perhaps the most innocent member of the establishment, tippling in majestic solitude by a fire in the harness-room. For Sir Maximus, as every one said, was a gentleman of the right sort, condescended to no mean inquiries, greeted his head servants with a "Good-evening, gentlemen," when he met them in the Park, and only snarled in a subdued way when he looked over the accounts, willing to endure some personal inconvenience in order to keep up the institutions of the country, to maintain his hereditary establishment, and do his duty in that station of life—the station of the long-tailed saurian—to which it had pleased Providence to call him.

The focus of brilliancy at Treby Manor that evening was in no way the dining-room, where Sir Maximus sipped his port under some mental depression, as he discussed with his brother, the Reverend Augustus, the sad fact that one of the oldest names in the county was to be on the wrong side—not in the drawing-room, where Miss Debarry and Miss Selina, quietly elegant in their dress and manners, were feeling rather dull than otherwise, having finished Mr. Bulwer's "Eugene Aram," and being thrown back on the last great prose work of Mr.

Southey, while their mamma slumbered a little on the sofa. No; the centre of eager talk and enjoyment was the steward's room, where Mr. Scales, house-steward and head butler, a man most solicitous about his boots, wrist-bands, the roll of his whiskers, and other attributes of a gentleman, distributed cigars, cognac, and whiskey to various colleagues and guests who were discussing, with that freedom of conjecture which is one of our inalienable privileges as Britons, the probable amount of Harold Transome's fortune, concerning which fame had already been busy long enough to have acquired vast magnifying power.

The chief part in this scene was undoubtedly Mr. Christian's, although he had hitherto been comparatively silent; but he occupied two chairs with so much grace, throwing his right leg over the seat of the second, and resting his right hand on the back; he held his cigar and displayed a splendid seal-ring with such becoming nonchalance, and had his gray hair arranged with so much taste, that experienced eyes would at once have seen even the great Scales himself to be but a secondary character.

" Why," said Mr. Crowder, an old respectable tenant, though much in arrear as to his rent, who condescended frequently to drink in the steward's room for the sake of the conversation; "why, I suppose they get money so fast in the East—it's wonderful. Why," he went on, with a hesitating look toward Mr. Scales, "this Transome has p'raps got a matter of a hundred thousand."

" A hundred thousand, my dear sir! fiddlestick's end of a hundred thousand," said Mr. Scales, with a contempt very painful to be borne by a modest man.

" Well," said Mr. Crowder, giving way under torture, as the all-knowing butler puffed and stared at him, " perhaps not so much as that."

"Not so much, sir! I tell you that a hundred thousand pounds is a bagatelle."

" Well, I know it's a big sum," said Mr. Crowder, deprecatingly.

Here there was a general laugh. All the other intellects present were more cultivated than Mr. Crowder's.

"Bagatelle is the French for trifle, my friend," said Mr. Christian. "Don't talk over people's heads so, Scales. I shall have hard work to understand you myself soon."

"Come, that's a good one," said the head gardener, who was a ready admirer; "I should like to hear the thing you don't understand, Christian."

"He's a first-rate hand at sneering," said Mr. Scales, rather nettled.

"Don't be waspish, man. I'll ring the bell for lemons, and make some punch. That's the thing for putting people up to the unknown tongues," said Mr. Christian, starting up, and slapping Scales's shoulder as he passed him.

"What I mean, Mr. Crowder, is this." Here Mr. Scales paused to puff, and pull down his waistcoat in a gentlemanly manner, and drink. He was wont in this way to give his hearers time for meditation.

"Come, then, speak English; I'm not against being taught," said the reasonable Crowder.

"What I means is, that in a large way of trade a man turns his capital over almost as soon as he can turn himself. Bless your soul! I know something about these matters, eh, Brent?"

"To be sure you do—few men more," said the gardener, who was the person appealed to.

"Not that I've had anything to do with commercial families myself. I've those feelings that I look to other things besides lucre. But I can't say that I've not been intimate with parties who have been less nice than I am myself; and knowing what I know, I shouldn't wonder if Transome had as much as five hundred thousand. Bless your soul, sir! people who get their money out of land are as long scraping five pounds together as your trading men are in turning five pounds into a hundred."

"That's a wicked thing, though," said Mr. Crowder, meditatively. "However," he went on, retreating from his difficult ground, "trade or no trade, the Transomes have been poor enough this many a long year. I've a brother a tenant on their estate—I ought to know a little bit about that."

"They've kept up no establishment at all," said Mr. Scales,

with disgust. "They've even let their kitchen-gardens. I suppose it was the eldest son's gambling. I've seen something of that. A man who has always lived in first-rate families is likely to know a thing or two on that subject."

"Ah, but it wasn't gambling did the first mischief," said Mr. Crowder, with a slight smile, feeling that it was his turn to have some superiority. "Newcomers don't know what happened in this country twenty and thirty years ago. I'm turned fifty myself, and my father lived under Sir Maxum's father. But if anybody from London can tell me more than I know about this country-side, I'm willing to listen."

"What was it, then, if it wasn't gambling?" said Mr. Scales, with some impatience. "*I* don't pretend to know."

"It was law—law—that's what it is. Not but what the Transomes always won."

"And always lost," said the too-ready Scales. "Yes, yes; I think we all know the nature of law."

"There was the last suit of all made the most noise, as I understood," continued Mr. Crowder; "but it wasn't tried hereabout. They said there was a deal o' false swearing. Some young man pretended to be the true heir—let me see—I can't justly remember the names—he'd got two. *He* swore he was one man, and *they* swore he was another. However, Lawyer Jermyn won it—they say he'd win a game against the Old One himself—and the young fellow turned out to be a scamp. Stop a bit—his name was Scaddon—Henry Scaddon."

Mr. Christian here let a lemon slip from his hand into the punch-bowl with a plash which sent some of the nectar into the company's faces.

"Hallo! What a bungler I am!" he said, looking as if he were quite jarred by this unusual awkwardness of his. "Go on with your tale, Mr. Crowder—a scamp named Henry Scaddon."

"Well, that's the tale," said Mr. Crowder. "He was never seen nothing of any more. It was a deal talked of at the time —and I've sat by; and my father used to shake his head; and always when this Mrs. Transome was talked of he used to shake his head, and say she carried things with a high hand once. But, Lord! it was before the battle of Waterloo, and I'm a poor hand at tales; I don't see much good in 'em myself—but if anybody'll tell me a cure for the sheep-rot I'll thank him."

Here Mr. Crowder relapsed into smoking and silence, a little discomfited that the knowledge of which he had been delivered had turned out rather a shapeless and insignificant birth.

"Well, well, bygones should be bygones; there are secrets in most good families," said Mr. Scales, winking, "and this young Transome, coming back with a fortune to keep up the establishment, and have things done in a decent and gentlemanly way—it would all have been right if he'd not been this sort of Radical madman. But now he's done for himself. I heard Sir Maximus say at dinner that he would be excommunicated; and that's a pretty strong word, I take it."

"What does it mean, Scales?" said Mr. Christian, who loved tormenting.

"Ay, what's the meaning?" insisted Mr. Crowder, encouraged by finding that even Christian was in the dark.

"Well, it's a law term—speaking in a figurative sort of way—meaning that a Radical was no gentleman."

"Perhaps it's partly accounted for by his getting his money so fast, and in foreign countries," said Mr. Crowder, tentatively. "It's reasonable to think he'd be against the land and this country—eh, Sircome?"

Sircome was an eminent miller who had considerable business transactions at the Manor, and appreciated Mr. Scales's merits at a handsome percentage on the yearly account. He was a highly honorable tradesman, but in this and in other matters submitted to the institutions of his country; for great houses, as he observed, must have great butlers. He replied to his friend Crowder sententiously.

"I say nothing. Before I bring words to market, I should like to see 'em a bit scarcer. There's the land and there's trade—I hold with both. I swim with the stream."

"Hey-day, Mr. Sircome! that's a Radical maxim," said Mr. Christian, who knew that Mr. Sircome's last sentence was his favorite formula. "I advise you to give it up, else it will injure the quality of your flour."

"A Radical maxim!" said Mr. Sircome, in a tone of angry astonishment. "I should like to hear you prove that. It's as old as my grandfather, anyhow."

"I'll prove it in one minute," said the glib Christian. "Reform has set in by the will of the majority—that's the rabble, you know; and the respectability and good sense of the country, which are in the minority, are afraid of Reform running on too fast. So the stream must be running toward Reform and Radicalism; and if you swim with it, Mr. Sircome, you're a Reformer and a Radical, and your flour is objectionable, and not full weight—and being tried by Scales, will be found wanting."

There was a roar of laughter. This pun upon Scales was highly appreciated by every one except the miller and the butler. The latter pulled down his waistcoat, and puffed and stared in rather an excited manner. Mr. Christian's wit, in general, seemed to him a poor kind of quibbling.

"What a fellow you are for fence, Christian," said the gardener. "Hang me if I don't think you're up to everything."

"That's a compliment you might pay Old Nick, if you come to that," said Mr. Sircome, who was in the painful position of a man deprived of his formula.

"Yes, yes," said Mr. Scales; "I'm no fool myself, and could parry a thrust if I liked, but I shouldn't like it to be said of me that I was up to everything. I'll keep a little principle, if you please."

"To be sure," said Christian, ladling out the punch. "What would justice be without Scales?"

The laughter was not quite so full-throated as before. Such excessive cleverness *was* a little Satanic.

"A joke's a joke among gentlemen," said the butler, getting exasperated; "I think there has been quite liberties enough taken with my name. But if you must talk about names, I've heard of a party before now calling himself a Christian, and being anything *but* it."

"Come, that's beyond a joke," said the surgeon's assistant, a fast man, whose chief scene of dissipation was the Manor. "Let it drop, Scales."

"Yes, I dare say it's beyond a joke. I'm not a harlequin

to talk nothing but jokes. I leave that to other Christians, who are up to everything, and have been everywhere—to the hulks, for what I know; and more than that, they come from nobody knows where, and try to worm themselves into gentlemen's confidence, to the prejudice of their betters."

There was a stricter sequence in Mr. Scales's angry eloquence than was apparent—some chief links being confined to his own breast, as is often the case in energetic discourse. The company were in a state of expectation. There was something behind worth knowing, and something before them worth seeing. In the general decay of other fine British pugnacious sports, a quarrel between gentlemen was all the more exciting, and though no one would himself have liked to turn on Scales, no one was sorry for the chance of seeing him put down. But the amazing Christian was unmoved. He had taken out his handkerchief and was rubbing his lips carefully. After a slight pause, he spoke with perfect coolness.

"I don't intend to quarrel with you, Scales. Such talk as this is not profitable to either of us. It makes you purple in the face—you *are* apoplectic, you know—and it spoils good company. Better tell a few fibs about me behind my back—it will heat you less, and do me more harm. I'll leave you to it; I shall go and have a game at whist with the ladies."

As the door closed behind the questionable Christian, Mr. Scales was in a state of frustration that prevented speech. Every one was rather embarrassed.

"That's a most uncommon sort o' fellow," said Mr. Crowder, in an undertone, to his next neighbor, the gardener. "Why, Mr. Philip picked him up in foreign parts, didn't he?"

"He was a courier," said the gardener. "He's had a deal of experience. And I believe, by what I can make out—for he's been pretty free with me sometimes—there was a time when he was in that rank of life that he fought a duel."

"Ah! that makes him such a cool chap," said Mr. Crowder.

"He's what I call an overbearing fellow," said Mr. Sircome, also *sotto voce*, to his next neighbor, Mr. Filmore, the surgeon's assistant. "He runs you down with a sort of talk that's neither here nor there. He's got a deal too many samples in his pocket for me."

"All I know is, he's a wonderful hand at cards," said Mr. Filmore, whose whiskers and shirt-pin were quite above the average. "I wish I could play *écarté* as he does; it's beautiful to see him; he can make a man look pretty blue—he'll empty his pocket for him in no time."

"That's none to his credit," said Mr. Sircome.

The conversation had in this way broken up into *tête-à-tête*, and the hilarity of the evening might be considered a failure. Still the punch was drunk, the accounts were duly swelled, and, notwithstanding the innovating spirit of the time, Sir Maximus Debarry's establishment was kept up in a sound hereditary British manner.

CHAPTER VIII.

"Rumor doth double like the voice and echo."
SHAKESPEARE.

The mind of a man is as a country which was once open to squatters, who have bred and multiplied and become masters of the land. But then happeneth a time when new and hungry comers dispute the land; and there is trial of strength, and the stronger wins. Nevertheless the first squatters be they who have prepared the ground, and the crops to the end will be sequent (though chiefly on the nature of the soil, as of light sand, mixed loam, or heavy clay, yet) somewhat on the primal labor and sowing.

THAT talkative maiden Rumor, though in the interest of art she is figured as a youthful winged beauty with flowing garments, soaring above the heads of men, and breathing world-thrilling news through a gracefully curved trumpet, is in fact a very old maid, who puckers her silly face by the fireside, and really does no more than chirp a wrong guess or a lame story into the ear of a fellow-gossip; all the rest of the work attributed to her is done by the ordinary working of those passions against which men pray in the Litany, with the help of a plentiful stupidity against which we have never yet had any authorized form of prayer.

When Mr. Scales's strong need to make an impressive figure in conversation, together with his very slight need of any other premise than his own sense of his wide general knowledge and probable infallibility, led him to specify five hundred thousand as the lowest admissible amount of Harold Transome's commercially acquired fortune, it was not fair to put this down to poor old Miss Rumor, who had only told Scales that the fortune was considerable. And again, when the curt Mr. Sircome found occasion at Treby to mention the five hundred thousand as a fact that folks seemed pretty sure about, this expansion of the butler into "folks" was entirely due to Mr. Sircome's habitual preference for words which could not be laid hold of or give people a handle over him. It was in this simple way that the report of Harold Transome's fortune spread and was magnified, adding much lustre to his opinions in the eyes of Liberals, and compelling even men of the opposite party to admit that it increased his eligibility as a member for North Loamshire. It was observed by a sound thinker in these parts that property was ballast; and when once the aptness of that metaphor had been perceived, it followed that a man was not fit to navigate the sea of politics without a great deal of such ballast; and that, rightly understood, whatever increased the expense of election, inasmuch as it virtually raised the property qualification, was an unspeakable boon to the country.

Meanwhile the fortune that was getting larger in the imagination of constituents was shrinking a little in the imagination of its owner. It was hardly more than a hundred and fifty thousand; and there were not only the heavy mortgages to be paid off, but also a large amount of capital was needed in order to repair the farm-buildings all over the estate, to carry out extensive draining, and make allowances to incoming tenants, which might remove the difficulty of newly letting the farms in a time of agricultural depression. The farms actually tenanted were held by men who had begged hard to succeed their fathers in getting a little poorer every year, on land which was also getting poorer, where the highest rate of increase was in the arrears of rent, and where the master, in crushed hat and corduroys, looked pitiably lean and careworn by the side of pauper laborers, who showed that superior assimilating power often observed to attend nourishment by the public money. Mr. Goffe, of Rabbit's End, had never had it explained to him that, according to the true theory of rent, land must inevitably be given up when it would not yield

a profit equal to the ordinary rate of interest; so that from
want of knowing what was inevitable, and not from a Titanic
spirit of opposition, he kept on his land. He often said of
himself, with a melancholy wipe of his sleeve across his brow,
that he "didn't know which-a-way to turn"; and he would
have been still more at a loss on the subject if he had quitted
Rabbit's End with a wagonful of furniture and utensils, a file
of receipts, a wife with five children, and a shepherd-dog in
low spirits.

It took no long time for Harold Transome to discover this
state of things, and to see, moreover, that, except on the demesne immediately around the house, the timber had been mis-
managed. The woods had been recklessly thinned, and there
had been insufficient planting. He had not yet thoroughly in-
vestigated the various accounts kept by his mother, by Jermyn,
and by Banks the bailiff; but what had been done with the
large sum which had been received for timber was a suspicious
mystery to him. He observed that the farm held by Jermyn
was in first-rate order, that a good deal had been spent on the
buildings, and that the rent had stood unpaid. Mrs. Transome had taken an opportunity of saying that Jermyn had had
some of the mortgage-deeds transferred to him, and that his
rent was set against so much interest. Harold had only said,
in his careless yet decisive way, "Oh, Jermyn be hanged! It
seems to me, if Durfey hadn't died and made room for me,
Jermyn would have ended by coming to live here, and you
would have had to keep the lodge and open the gate for his
carriage. But I shall pay him off—mortgages and all—by and
by. I'll owe him nothing—not even a curse." Mrs. Transome said no more. Harold did not care to enter fully into
the subject with his mother. The fact that she had been
active in the management of the estate—had ridden about it
continually, had busied herself with accounts, had been head
bailiff of the vacant farms, and had yet allowed things to go
wrong—was set down by him simply to the general futility of
women's attempts to transact men's business. He did not
want to say anything to annoy her: he was only determined
to let her understand, as quietly as possible, that she had better cease all interference.

Mrs. Transome did understand this; and it was very little that she dared to say on business, though there was a fierce struggle of her anger and pride with a dread which was nevertheless supreme. As to the old tenants, she only observed, on hearing Harold burst forth about their wretched condition, "that with the estate so burthened the yearly loss by arrears could better be borne than the outlay and sacrifice necessary in order to let the farms anew."

"I was really capable of calculating, Harold," she ended, with a touch of bitterness. "It seems easy to deal with farmers and their affairs when you only see them in print, I dare say; but it's not quite so easy when you live among them. You have only to look at Sir Maximus's estate: you will see plenty of the same thing. The times have been dreadful, and old families like to keep their old tenants. But I dare say that is Toryism."

"It's a hash of odds and ends, if that is Toryism, my dear mother. However, I wish you had kept three more old tenants; for then I should have had three more fifty-pound voters. And, in a hard run, one may be beaten by a head. But," Harold added, smiling and handing her a ball of worsted which had fallen, "a woman ought to be a Tory, and graceful, and handsome, like you. I should hate a woman who took up my opinions, and talked for me. I'm an Oriental, you know. I say, mother, shall we have this room furnished with rosecolor? I notice that it suits your bright gray hair."

Harold thought it was only natural that his mother should have been in a sort of subjection to Jermyn throughout the awkward circumstances of the family. It was the way of women, and all weak minds, to think that what they had been used to was inalterable, and any quarrel with a man who managed private affairs was necessarily a formidable thing. He himself was proceeding very cautiously, and preferred not even to know too much just at present, lest a certain personal antipathy he was conscious of toward Jermyn, and an occasional liability to exasperation, should get the better of a calm and clear-sighted resolve not to quarrel with the man while he could be of use. Harold would have been disgusted with himself if he had helped to frustrate his own purpose. And his strongest purpose now was to get returned for Parliament, to make figure there as a Liberal member, and to become on all grounds a personage of weight in North Loamshire.

How Harold Transome came to be a Liberal in opposition to all the traditions of his family was a more subtle inquiry than he had ever cared to follow out. The newspapers undertook to explain it. The *North Loamshire Herald* witnessed, with a grief and disgust certain to be shared by all persons who were actuated by wholesome British feeling, an example of defection in the inheritor of a family name which in times past had been associated with attachment to right principle, and with the maintenance of our constitution in Church and State; and pointed to it as an additional proof that men who had passed any large portion of their lives beyond the limits of our favored country usually contracted not only a laxity of feeling toward Protestantism, nay, toward religion itself—a latitudinarian spirit hardly distinguishable from atheism—but also a levity of disposition inducing them to tamper with those institutions by which alone Great Britain had risen to her pre-eminence among the nations. Such men, infected with outlandish habits, intoxicated with vanity, grasping at momentary power by flattery of the multitude, fearless because godless, liberal because un-English, were ready to pull one stone from under another in the national edifice, till the great structure tottered to its fall. On the other hand, the *Duffield Watchman* saw in this signal instance of self-liberation from the trammels of prejudice a decisive guaranty of intellectual pre-eminence, united with a generous sensibility to the claims of man as man, which had burst asunder, and cast off, by a spontaneous exertion of energy, the cramping outworn shell of hereditary bias and class interest.

But these large-minded guides of public opinion argued from wider data than could be furnished by any knowledge of the particular case concerned. Harold Transome was neither the dissolute cosmopolitan so vigorously sketched by the Tory *Herald*, nor the intellectual giant and moral lobster suggested by the liberal imagination of the *Watchman*. Twenty years ago he had been a bright, active, good-tempered lad, with sharp eyes and a good aim; he delighted in success and in

predominance; but he did not long for an impossible predom·
inance, and become sour and sulky because it was impossible.
He played at the games he was clever in, and usually won;
all other games he let alone, and thought them of little worth.
At home and at Eton he had been side by side with his stupid
elder brother Durfey, whom he despised; and he very early
began to reflect that, since this Caliban in miniature was older
than himself, he must carve out his own fortune. That was
a nuisance; and on the whole the world seemed rather ill
arranged, at Eton especially, where there were many reasons
why Harold made no great figure. He was not sorry the
money was wanting to send him to Oxford; he did not see the
good of Oxford; he had been surrounded by many things during his short life of which he had distinctly said to himself
that he did not see the good, and he was not disposed to venerate on the strength of any good that others saw. He turned
his back on home very cheerfully, though he was rather fond
of his mother, and very fond of Transome Court, and the river
where he had been used to fish; but he said to himself as he
passed the lodge gates, "I'll get rich somehow, and have an
estate of my own, and do what I like with it." This determined aiming at something not easy, but clearly possible,
marked the direction in which Harold's nature was strong; he
had the energetic will and muscle, the self-confidence, the
quick perception, and the narrow imagination which make
what is admiringly called the practical mind.

Since then his character had been ripened by a various experience, and also by much knowledge which he had set himself deliberately to gain. But the man was no more than the
boy writ large, with an extensive commentary. The years had
nourished an inclination to as much opposition as would enable him to assert his own independence and power without
throwing himself into that tabooed condition which robs power
of its triumph. And this inclination had helped his shrewd-
ness in forming judgments which were at once innovating and
moderate. He was addicted at once to rebellion and to conformity, and only an intimate personal knowledge could enable
any one to predict where his conformity would begin. The
limit was not defined by theory, but was drawn in an irregular

8

zigzag by early disposition and association; and his resolution, of which he had never lost hold, to be a thorough Englishman again some day had kept up the habit of considering all his conclusions with reference to English politics and English social conditions. He meant to stand up for every change that the economical condition of the country required, and he had an angry contempt for men with coronets on their coaches, but too small a share of brains to see when they had better make a virtue of necessity. His respect was rather for men who had no coronets, but who achieved a just influence by furthering all measures which the common sense of the country, and the increasing self-assertion of the majority, peremptorily demanded. He could be such a man himself.

In fact, Harold Transome was a clever, frank, good-natured egoist; not stringently consistent, but without any disposition to falsity; proud, but with a pride that was moulded in an individual rather than an hereditary form; unspeculative, unsentimental, unsympathetic; fond of sensual pleasures, but disinclined to all vice, and attached as a healthy, clear-sighted person to all conventional morality, construed with a certain freedom, like doctrinal articles to which the public order may require subscription. A character is apt to look but indifferently, written out in this way. Reduced to a map, our premises seem insignificant, but they make, nevertheless, a very pretty freehold to live in and walk over; and so, if Harold Transome had been among your acquaintances, and you had observed his qualities through the medium of his agreeable person, bright smile, and a certain easy charm which accompanies sensuousness when unsullied by coarseness—through the medium also of the many opportunities in which he would have made himself useful or pleasant to you—you would have thought him a good fellow, highly acceptable as a guest, a colleague, or a brother-in-law. Whether all mothers would have liked him as a son is another question.

It is a fact perhaps kept a little too much in the background that mothers have a self larger than their maternity, and that when their sons have become taller than themselves, and are gone from them to college or into the world, there are wide spaces of their time which are not filled with praying for their boys, reading old letters, and envying yet blessing those who are attending to their shirt-buttons. Mrs. Transome was certainly not one of those bland, adoring, and gently tearful women. After sharing the common dream that when a beautiful man-child was born to her her cup of happiness would be full, she had travelled through long years apart from that child, to find herself at last in the presence of a son of whom she was afraid, who was utterly unmanageable by her, and to whose sentiments in any given case she possessed no key. Yet Harold was a kind son: he kissed his mother's brow, offered her his arm, let her choose what she liked for the house and garden, asked her whether she would have bays or grays for her new carriage, and was bent on seeing her make as good a figure in the neighborhood as any other woman of her rank. She trembled under this kindness: it was not enough to satisfy her; still, if it should ever cease and give place to something else—she was too uncertain about Harold's feelings to imagine clearly what that something would be. The finest threads, such as no eye sees, if bound cunningly about the sensitive flesh, so that the movement to break them would bring torture, may make a worse bondage than any fetters. Mrs. Transome felt the fatal threads about her, and the bitterness of this helpless bondage mingled itself with the new elegancies of the dining and drawing rooms, and all the household changes which Harold had ordered to be brought about with magical quickness. Nothing was as she had once expected it would be. If Harold had shown the least care to have her stay in the room with him—if he had really cared for her opinion—if he had been what she had dreamed he would be in the eyes of those people who had made her world—if all the past could be dissolved, and leave no solid trace of itself— mighty *ifs* that were all impossible—she would have tasted some joy; but now she began to look back with regrets to the days when she sat in loneliness among the old drapery, and still longed for something that might happen. Yet, save in a bitter little speech, or in a deep sigh heard by no one besides Denner, she kept all these things hidden in her heart, and went out in the autumn sunshine to overlook the alterations in the pleasure-grounds very much as a happy woman might have

done.   One day, however, when she was occupied in this way
an occasion came on which she chose to express indirectly a
part of her inward care.

She was standing on the broad gravel in the afternoon; the
long shadows lay on the grass; the light seemed the more glorious because of the reddened and golden trees.   The gardeners
were busy at their pleasant work; the newly turned soil gave
out an agreeable fragrance; and little Harry was playing with
Nimrod round old Mr. Transome, who sat placidly on a low
garden-chair.   The scene would have made a charming picture
of English domestic life, and the handsome, majestic, gray-
haired woman (obviously grandmamma) would have been especially admired.   But the artist would have felt it requisite to
turn her face toward her husband and little grandson, and to
have given her an elderly amiability of expression which would
have divided remark with his exquisite rendering of her Indian
shawl.   Mrs. Transome's face was turned the other way, and
for this reason she only heard an approaching step, and did
not see whose it was; yet it startled her: it was not quick
enough to be her son's step, and, besides, Harold was away at
Duffield.   It was Mr. Jermyn's.

CHAPTER IX.

"A woman, naturally born to fears."—*King John.*

" Methinks
Some unborn sorrow, ripe in fortune's womb,
Is coming toward me; and my inward soul
With nothing trembles."—*King Richard II.*

MATTHEW JERMYN approached Mrs. Transome, taking off his
hat and smiling.   She did not smile, but said,—

"You knew Harold was not at home?"

"Yes; I came to see you, to know if you had any wishes
that I could further, since I have not had an opportunity of
consulting you since he came home."

"Let us walk toward the Rookery, then."

They turned together, Mr. Jermyn still keeping his hat off
and holding it behind him; the air was so soft and agreeable

that Mrs. Transome herself had nothing but a large veil over her head.

They walked for a little while in silence till they were out of sight, under tall trees, and treading noiselessly on fallen leaves. What Jermyn was really most anxious about was to learn from Mrs. Transome whether anything had transpired that was significant of Harold's disposition toward him, which he suspected to be very far from friendly. Jermyn was not naturally flinty-hearted; at five-and-twenty he had written verses, and had got himself wet through in order not to disappoint a dark-eyed woman whom he was proud to believe in love with him; but a family man with grown-up sons and daughters, a man with a professional position and complicated affairs that make it hard to ascertain the exact relation between property and liabilities, necessarily thinks of himself and what may be impending.

"Harold is remarkably acute and clever," he began at last, since Mrs. Transome did not speak. "If he gets into Parliament I have no doubt he will distinguish himself. He has a quick eye for business of all kinds."

"That is no comfort to me," said Mrs. Transome. To-day she was more conscious than usual of that bitterness which was always in her mind in Jermyn's presence, but which was carefully suppressed:—suppressed because she could not endure that the degradation she inwardly felt should ever become visible or audible in acts or words of her own—should ever be reflected in any word or look of his. For years there had been a deep silence about the past between them: on her side, because she remembered; on his, because he more and more forgot.

"I trust he is not unkind to you in any way. I know his opinions pain you; but I trust you find him in everything else disposed to be a good son."

"Oh, to be sure—good as men are disposed to be to women, giving them cushions and carriages, and recommending them to enjoy themselves, and then expecting them to be contented under contempt and neglect. I have no power over him— remember that—none."

Jermyn turned to look in Mrs. Transome's face: it was

long since he had heard her speak to him as if she were losing her self-command.

"Has he shown any unpleasant feeling about your management of the affairs?"

"*My* management of the affairs!" Mrs. Transome said, with concentrated rage, flashing a fierce look at Jermyn. She checked herself: she felt as if she were lighting a torch to flare on her own past folly and misery. It was a resolve which had become a habit that she would never quarrel with this man—never tell him what she saw him to be. She had kept her woman's pride and sensibility intact: through all her life there had vibrated the maiden need to have her hand kissed and be the object of chivalry. And so she sank into silence again, trembling.

Jermyn felt annoyed—nothing more. There was nothing in his mind corresponding to the intricate meshes of sensitiveness in Mrs. Transome's. He was anything but stupid; yet he always blundered when he wanted to be delicate or magnanimous; he constantly sought to soothe others by praising himself. Moral vulgarity cleaved to him like an hereditary odor. He blundered now.

"My dear Mrs. Transome," he said, in a tone of bland kindness, "you are agitated—you appear angry with me. Yet I think, if you consider, you will see that you have nothing to complain of in me, unless you will complain of the inevitable course of man's life. I have always met your wishes both in happy circumstances and in unhappy ones. I should be ready to do so now, if it were possible."

Every sentence was as pleasant to her as if it had been cut in her bared arm. Some men's kindness and love-making are more exasperating, more humiliating, than others' derision; but the pitiable woman who has once made herself secretly dependent on a man who is beneath her in feeling must bear that humiliation for fear of worse. Coarse kindness is at least better than coarse anger; and in all private quarrels the duller nature is triumphant by reason of its dulness. Mrs. Transome knew in her inmost soul that those relations which had sealed her lips on Jermyn's conduct in business matters had been with him a ground for presuming that he should have impunity in any lax dealing into which circumstances had led him. She knew that she herself had endured all the more privation because of his dishonest selfishness. And now Harold's long-deferred heirship, and his return with startlingly unexpected penetration, activity, and assertion of mastery, had placed them both in the full presence of a difficulty which had been prepared by the years of vague uncertainty as to issues. In this position, with a great dread hanging over her, which Jermyn knew, and ought to have felt that he had caused her, she was inclined to lash him with indignation, to scorch him with the words that were just the fit names for his doings—inclined all the more when he spoke with an insolent blandness, ignoring all that was truly in her heart. But no sooner did the words " You have brought it on me " rise within her than she heard within also the retort, " You brought it on yourself." Not for all the world beside could she bear to hear that retort uttered from without. What did she do? With strange sequence to all that rapid tumult, after a few moments' silence she said, in a gentle and almost tremulous voice,—

" Let me take your arm."

He gave it immediately, putting on his hat and wondering. For more than twenty years Mrs. Transome had never chosen to take his arm.

" I have but one thing to ask you.   Make me a promise."

" What is it? "

" That you will never quarrel with Harold."

" You must know that it is my wish not to quarrel with him."

" But make a vow—fix it in your mind as a thing not to be done. Bear anything from him rather than quarrel with him."

" A man can't make a vow not to quarrel," said Jermyn, who was already a little irritated by the implication that Harold might be disposed to use him roughly.   " A man's temper may get the better of him at any moment.   I am not prepared to bear *anything*."

" Good God! " said Mrs. Transome, taking her hand from his arm, " is it possible you don't feel how horrible it would be? "

As she took away her hand Jermyn let his arm fall, put both his hands in his pockets, and, shrugging his shoulders, said, "I shall use him as he uses me."

Jermyn had turned round his savage side, and the blandness was out of sight. It was this that had always frightened Mrs. Transome: there was a possibility of fierce insolence in this man who was to pass with those nearest to her as her indebted servant, but whose brand she secretly bore. She was as powerless with him as she was with her son.

This woman, who loved rule, dared not speak another word of attempted persuasion. They were both silent, taking the nearest way into the sunshine again. There was a half-formed wish in both their minds—even in the mother's—that Harold Transome had never been born.

"We are working hard for the election," said Jermyn, recovering himself, as they turned into the sunshine again. "I think we shall get him returned, and in that case he will be in high good-humor. Everything will be more propitious than you are apt to think. You must persuade yourself," he added, smiling at her, "that it is better for a man of his position to be in Parliament on the wrong side than not to be in at all."

"Never," said Mrs. Transome. "I am too old to learn to call bitter sweet and sweet bitter. But what I may think or feel is of no consequence now. I am as unnecessary as a chimney ornament."

And in this way they parted on the gravel, in that pretty scene where they had met. Mrs. Transome shivered as she stood alone: all around her, where there had once been brightness and warmth, there were white ashes, and the sunshine looked dreary as it fell on them.

Mr. Jermyn's heaviest reflections in riding homeward turned on the possibility of incidents between himself and Harold Transome which would have disagreeable results, requiring him to raise money, and perhaps causing scandal, which in its way might also help to create a monetary deficit. A man of sixty, with a wife whose Duffield connections were of the highest respectability, with a family of tall daughters, an expensive establishment, and a large professional business, owed a great deal more to himself as the mainstay of all those solidities than to feelings and ideas which were quite unsubstantial. There were many unfortunate coincidences which placed Mr. Jermyn in an uncomfortable position just now; he had not been much to blame, he considered; if it had not been for a sudden turn of affairs no one would have complained. He defied any man to say that he had intended to wrong people; he was able to refund, to make reprisals, if they could be fairly demanded. Only he would certainly have preferred that they should not be demanded.

A German poet was intrusted with a particularly fine sausage, which he was to convey to the donor's friend at Paris. In the course of a long journey he smelt the sausage; he got hungry, and desired to taste it; he pared a morsel off, then another, and another, in successive moments of temptation, till at last the sausage was, humanly speaking, at an end. The offence had not been premeditated. The poet had never loved meanness, but he loved sausage; and the result was undeniably awkward.

So it was with Matthew Jermyn. He was far from liking that ugly abstraction rascality, but he had liked other things which had suggested nibbling. He had had to do many things in law and in daily life which, in the abstract, he would have condemned; and indeed he had never been tempted by them in the abstract. Here, in fact, was the inconvenience; he had sinned for the sake of particular concrete things, and particular concrete consequences were likely to follow.

But he was a man of resolution, who, having made out what was the best course to take under a difficulty, went straight to his work. The election must be won: that would put Harold in good-humor, give him something to do, and leave himself more time to prepare for any crisis.

He was in anything but low spirits that evening. It was his eldest daughter's birthday, and the young people had a dance. Papa was delightful—stood up for a quadrille and a country-dance, told stories at supper, and made humorous quotations from his early readings: if these were Latin, he apologized, and translated to the ladies; so that a deaf lady visitor from Duffield kept her trumpet up continually, lest she should lose any of Mr. Jermyn's conversation, and wished that her niece Maria had been present, who was young and had a good memory.

Still the party was smaller than usual, for some families in Treby refused to visit Jermyn now that he was concerned for a Radical candidate.

CHAPTER X.

"He made love neither with roses, nor with apples, nor with locks of hair."—THE OCRITUS.

ONE Sunday afternoon Felix Holt rapped at the door of Mr. Lyon's house, although he could hear the voice of the minister preaching in the chapel. He stood with a book under his arm, apparently confident that there was some one in the house to open the door for him. In fact, Esther never went to chapel in the afternoon: that "exercise" made her head ache.

In these September weeks Felix had got rather intimate with Mr. Lyon. They shared the same political sympathies; and though, to Liberals who had neither freehold nor copyhold nor leasehold, the share in a county election consisted chiefly of that prescriptive amusement of the majority known as "looking on," there was still something to be said on the occasion, if not to be done. Perhaps the most delightful friendships are those in which there is much agreement, much disputation, and yet more personal liking; and the advent of the public-spirited, contradictory, yet affectionate Felix into Treby life had made a welcome epoch to the minister. To talk with this young man, who, though hopeful, had a singularity which some might at once have pronounced heresy, but which Mr. Lyon persisted in regarding as orthodoxy "in the making," was like a good bite to strong teeth after a too-plentiful allowance of spoon-meat. To cultivate his society with a view to checking his erratic tendencies was a laudable purpose; but perhaps if Felix had been rapidly subdued and reduced to conformity little Mr. Lyon would have found the conversation much flatter.

Esther had not seen so much of their new acquaintance as her father had. But she had begun to find him amusing, and also rather irritating to her woman's love of conquest. He always opposed and criticised her; and, besides that, he looked at her as if he never saw a single detail about her person— quite as if she were a middle-aged woman in a cap. She did not believe that he had ever admired her hands, or her long neck, or her graceful movements, which had made all the girls at school call her Calypso (doubtless from their familiarity with "Télémaque"). Felix ought properly to have been a little in love with her—never mentioning it, of course, because that would have been disagreeable, and his being a regular lover was out of the question. But it was quite clear that, instead of feeling any disadvantage on his side, he held himself to be immeasurably her superior: and, what was worse, Esther had a secret consciousness that he was her superior. She was all the more vexed at the suspicion that he thought slightly of her; and wished in her vexation that she could have found more fault with him—that she had not been obliged to admire more and more the varying expressions of his open face and his deliciously good-humored laugh, always loud at a joke against himself. Besides, she could not help having her curiosity roused by the unusual combinations both in his mind and in his outward position, and she had surprised herself as well as her father one day by suddenly starting up and proposing to walk with him when he was going to pay an afternoon visit to Mrs. Holt, to try and soothe her concerning Felix. "What a mother he has!" she said to herself when they came away again; "but, rude and queer as he is, I cannot say there is anything vulgar about him. Yet—I don't know—if I saw him by the side of a finished gentleman." Esther wished that finished gentleman were among her acquaintances: he would certainly admire her, and make her aware of Felix's inferiority.

On this particular Sunday afternoon, when she heard the knock at the door, she was seated in the kitchen corner between the fire and the window reading "Réné." Certainly in her well-fitting light-blue dress—she almost always wore some shade of blue—with her delicate sandalled slipper stretched toward the fire, her little gold watch, which had cost her nearly a quarter's earnings, visible at her side, her slender fingers playing with a shower of brown curls, and a coronet of shining plaits at the summit of her head, she was a remarkable Cinderella. When the rap came, she colored, and was going to shut her book and put it out of the way on the window-ledge behind her; but she desisted with a little toss, laid it open on the table beside her, and walked to the outer door, which opened into the kitchen. There was rather a mischievous gleam in her face: the rap was not a small one; it came probably from a large personage with a vigorous arm.

"Good-afternoon, Miss Lyon," said Felix, taking off his cloth cap: he resolutely declined the expensive ugliness of a hat, and in a poked cap and without a cravat made a figure at which his mother cried every Sunday, and thought of with a slow shake of the head at several passages in the minister's prayer.

"Dear me, it is you, Mr. Holt! I fear you will have to wait some time before you can see my father. The sermon is not ended yet, and there will be the hymn and the prayer, and perhaps other things to detain him."

"Well, will you let me sit down in the kitchen? I don't want to be a bore."

"Oh, no," said Esther, with her pretty light laugh, "I always give you credit for not meaning it. Pray come in, if you don't mind waiting. I was sitting in the kitchen: the kettle is singing quite prettily. It is much nicer than the parlor—not half so ugly."

"There I agree with you."

"How very extraordinary! But if you prefer the kitchen, and don't want to sit with me, I can go into the parlor."

"I came on purpose to sit with you," said Felix, in his blunt way, "but I thought it likely you might be vexed at seeing me. I wanted to talk to you, but I've got nothing pleasant to say. As your father would have it, I'm not given to prophesy smooth things—to prophesy deceit."

"I understand," said Esther, sitting down. "Pray be seated. You thought I had no afternoon sermon, so you came to give me one."

"Yes," said Felix, seating himself sideways in a chair not far off her, and leaning over the back to look at her with his large clear gray eyes, "and my text is something you said the other day. You said you didn't mind about people having right opinions so that they had good taste. Now I want you to see what shallow stuff that is."

"Oh, I don't doubt it if you say so. I know you are a person of right opinions."

"But by opinions you mean men's thoughts about great subjects, and by taste you mean their thoughts about small ones : dress, behavior, amusements, ornaments."

"Well—yes—or, rather, their sensibilities about those things."

"It comes to the same thing; thoughts, opinions, knowledge, are only a sensibility to facts and ideas. If I understand a geometrical problem, it is because I have a sensibility to the way in which lines and figures are related to each other; and I want you to see that the creature who has the sensibilities that you call taste, and not the sensibilities that you call opinions, is simply a lower, pettier sort of being—an insect that notices the shaking of the table, but never notices the thunder."

"Very well, I am an insect; yet I notice that you are thundering at me."

"No, you are not an insect. That is what exasperates me at your making a boast of littleness. You have enough understanding to make it wicked that you should add one more to the women who hinder men's lives from having any nobleness in them."

Esther colored deeply : she resented this speech, yet she disliked it less than many Felix had addressed to her.

"What is my horrible guilt?" she said, rising and standing, as she was wont, with one foot on the fender, and looking at the fire. If it had been any one but Felix who was near her, it might have occurred to her that this attitude showed her to advantage; but she had only a mortified sense that he was quite indifferent to what others praised her for.

"Why do you read this mawkish stuff on a Sunday, for

example?" he said, snatching up "Réné," and running his eye over the pages.

"Why don't you always go to chapel, Mr. Holt, and read Howe's 'Living Temple,' and join the Church?"

"There's just the difference between us—I know why I don't do those things. I distinctly see that I can do something better. I have other principles, and should sink myself by doing what I don't recognize as the best."

"I understand," said Esther, as lightly as she could, to conceal her bitterness. "I am a lower kind of being, and could not so easily sink myself."

"Not by entering into your father's ideas. If a woman really believes herself to be a lower kind of being, she should place herself in subjection: she should be ruled by the thoughts of her father or husband. If not, let her show her power of choosing something better. You must know that your father's principles are greater and worthier than what guides your life. You have no reason but idle fancy and selfish inclination for shirking his teaching and giving your soul up to trifles."

"You are kind enough to say so. But I am not aware that I have ever confided my reasons to you."

"Why, what worth calling a reason could make any mortal hang over this trash?—idiotic immorality dressed up to look fine, with a little bit of doctrine tacked to it, like a hare's foot on a dish, to make believe the mess is not cat's flesh. Look here! 'Est-ce ma faute, si je trouve partout les bornes, si ce qui est fini n'a pour moi aucune valeur?' Yes, sir, distinctly your fault, because you're an ass. Your dunce who can't do his sums always has a taste for the infinite. Sir, do you know what a rhomboid is? Oh, no, I don't value these things with limits. 'Cependant, j'aime la monotonie des sentimens de la vie, et si j'avais encore la folie de croire au bonheur——'"

"Oh, pray, Mr. Holt, don't go on reading with that dreadful accent; it sets one's teeth on edge." Esther, smarting helplessly under the previous lashes, was relieved by this diversion of criticism.

"There it is!" said Felix, throwing the book on the table,

and getting up to walk about. "You are only happy when you can spy a tag or a tassel loose to turn the talk, and get rid of any judgment that must carry grave action after it."

"I think I have borne a great deal of talk without turning it."

"Not enough, Miss Lyon—not all that I came to say. I want you to change. Of course I am a brute to say so. I ought to say you are perfect. Another man would, perhaps. But I say I want you to change."

"How am I to oblige you? By joining the Church?"

"No; but by asking yourself whether life is not as solemn a thing as your father takes it to be—in which you may be either a blessing or a curse to many. You know you have never done that. You don't care to be better than a bird trimming its feathers, and pecking about after what pleases it. You are discontented with the world because you can't get just the small things that suit your pleasure, not because it's a world where myriads of men and women are ground by wrong and misery, and tainted with pollution."

Esther felt her heart swelling with mingled indignation at this liberty, wounded pride at this depreciation, and acute consciousness that she could not contradict what Felix said. He was outrageously ill bred; but she felt that she should be lowering herself by telling him so, and manifesting her anger; in that way she would be confirming his accusation of a littleness that shrank from severe truth; and, besides, through all her mortification there pierced a sense that this exasperation of Felix against her was more complimentary than anything in his previous behavior. She had self-command enough to speak with her usual silvery voice.

"Pray go on, Mr. Holt. Relieve yourself of these burning truths. I am sure they must be troublesome to carry unuttered."

"Yes, they are," said Felix, pausing, and standing not far off her. "I can't bear to see you going the way of the foolish women who spoil men's lives. Men can't help loving them, and so they make themselves slaves to the petty desires of petty creatures. That's the way those who might do better spend their lives for naught—get checked in every great effort

—toil with brain and limb for things that have no more to do with a manly life than tarts and confectionery. That's what makes women a curse; all life is stunted to suit their little- ness. That's why I'll never love, if I can help it; and if I love, I'll bear it, and never marry."

The tumult of feeling in Esther's mind—mortification, anger, the sense of a terrible power over her that Felix seemed to have as his angry words vibrated through her—was getting almost too much for her self-control. She felt her lips quiv- ering; but her pride, which feared nothing so much as the betrayal of her emotion, helped her to a desperate effort. She pinched her own hand hard to overcome her tremor, and said, in a tone of scorn,—

"I ought to be very much obliged to you for giving me your confidence so freely."

"Ah! now you are offended with me, and disgusted with me. I expected it would be so. A woman doesn't like a man who tells her the truth."

"I think you boast a little too much of your truth-telling, Mr. Holt," said Esther, flashing out at last. "That virtue is apt to be easy to people when they only wound others and not themselves. Telling the truth often means no more than tak- ing a liberty."

"Yes, I suppose I should have been taking a liberty if I had tried to drag you back by the skirt when I saw you run- ning into a pit."

"You should really found a sect. Preaching is your voca- tion. It is a pity you should ever have an audience of only one."

"I see; I have made a fool of myself. I thought you had a more generous mind—that you might be kindled to a better ambition. But I've set your vanity aflame—nothing else. I'm going. Good-by."

"Good-by," said Esther, not looking at him. He did not open the door immediately. He seemed to be adjusting his cap and pulling it down. Esther longed to be able to throw a lasso round him and compel him to stay, that she might say what she chose to him; her very anger made this departure irritating, especially as he had the last word, and that a very bitter one. But soon the latch was lifted and the door closed behind him. She ran up to her bedroom and burst into tears. Poor maiden! There was a strange contradiction of impulses in her mind in those first moments. She could not bear that Felix should not respect her, yet she could not bear that he should see her bend before his denunciation. She revolted against his assumption of superiority, yet she felt herself in a new kind of subjection to him. He was ill bred, he was rude, he had taken an unwarrantable liberty; yet his indignant words were a tribute to her: he thought she was worth more pains than the women of whom he took no notice. It was excessively impertinent in him to tell her of his resolving not to love—not to marry—as if she cared about that; as if he thought himself likely to inspire an affection that would incline any woman to marry him after such eccentric steps as he had taken. Had he ever for a moment imagined that she had thought of him in the light of a man who would make love to her? . . . But did he love her one little bit, and was that the reason why he wanted her to change? Esther felt less angry at that form of freedom; though she was quite sure that she did not love him, and that she could never love any one who was so much of a pedagogue and a master, to say nothing of his oddities. But he wanted her to change. For the first time in her life Esther felt herself seriously shaken in her self-contentment. She knew there was a mind to which she appeared trivial, narrow, selfish. Every word Felix had said to her seemed to have burned itself into her memory. She felt as if she should forevermore be haunted by self-criticism, and never do anything to satisfy those fancies on which she had simply piqued herself before without being dogged by inward questions. Her father's desire for her conversion had never moved her; she saw that he adored her all the while, and he never checked her unregenerate acts as if they degraded her on earth, but only mourned over them as unfitting her for heaven. Unfitness for heaven (spoken of as "Jerusalem" and "glory"), the prayers of a good little father, whose thoughts and motives seemed to her like the "Life of Dr. Doddridge," which she was content to leave unread, did not attack her self-respect and self-satisfaction.

9

But now she had been stung—stung even into a new consciousness concerning her father. Was it true that his life
was so much worthier than her own? She could not change
for anything Felix said, but she told herself he was mistaken
if he supposed her incapable of generous thoughts.

She heard her father coming into the house. She dried her
tears, tried to recover herself hurriedly, and went down to
him.

"You want your tea, father; how your forehead burns!"
she said gently, kissing his brow, and then putting her cool
hand on it.

Mr. Lyon felt a little surprise; such spontaneous tenderness
was not quite common with her; it reminded him of her
mother.

"My sweet child," he said gratefully, thinking with wonder of the treasures still left in our fallen nature.

CHAPTER XI.

> Truth is the precious harvest of the earth.
> But once, when harvest waved upon a land,
> The noisome cankerworm and caterpillar,
> Locusts, and all the swarming foul-born broods,
> Fastened upon it with swift, greedy jaws,
> And turned the harvest into pestilence,
> Until men said, What profits it to sow?

FELIX was going to Sproxton that Sunday afternoon. He
always enjoyed his walk to that outlying hamlet; it took him
(by a short cut) through a corner of Sir Maximus Debarry's
park; then across a piece of common, broken here and there
into red ridges below dark masses of furze; and for the rest
of the way alongside the canal, where the Sunday peaceful-
ness that seemed to rest on the bordering meadows and pastures was hardly broken if a horse pulled into sight along the
towing-path, and a boat, with a little curl of blue smoke issu-
ing from its tin chimney, came slowly gliding behind. Felix
retained something of his boyish impression that the days in
a canal-boat were all like Sundays; but the horse, if it had
been put to him, would probably have preferred a more Ju-

daic or Scotch rigor with regard to canal-boats, or at least that the Sunday towing should be done by asses, as a lower order.

This canal was only a branch of the grand trunk, and ended among the coal-pits, where Felix, crossing a network of black tram-roads, soon came to his destination—that public institute of Sproxton, known to its frequenters chiefly as Chubb's, but less familiarly as the Sugar Loaf, or the New Pits; this last being the name for the more modern and lively nucleus of the Sproxton hamlet. The other nucleus, known as the Old Pits, also supported its "public," but it had something of the forlorn air of an abandoned capital; and the company at the Blue Cow was of an inferior kind—equal, of course, in the fundamental attributes of humanity, such as desire for beer, but not equal in ability to pay for it.

When Felix arrived, the great Chubb was standing at the door. Mr. Chubb was a remarkable publican; none of your stock Bonifaces, red, bloated, jolly, and joking. He was thin and sallow, and was never, as his constant guests observed, seen to be the worse (or the better) for liquor; indeed, as among soldiers an eminent general was held to have a charmed life, Chubb was held by the members of the Benefit Club to have a charmed sobriety, a vigilance over his own interest that resisted all narcotics. His very dreams, as stated by himself, had a method in them beyond the waking thoughts of other men. Pharaoh's dream, he observed, was nothing to them; and, as lying so much out of ordinary experience, they were held particularly suitable for narration on Sunday evenings, when the listening colliers, well washed and in their best coats, shook their heads with a sense of that peculiar edification which belongs to the inexplicable. Mr. Chubb's reasons for becoming landlord of the Sugar Loaf were founded on the severest calculation. Having an active mind, and being averse to bodily labor, he had thoroughly considered what calling would yield him the best livelihood with the least possible exertion, and in that sort of line he had seen that a "public" amongst miners who earned high wages was a fine opening. He had prospered according to the merits of such judicious calculation, was already a forty-shilling freeholder, and was conscious of a vote for the county. He was not one of those mean-spirited men who found the franchise embarrassing and would rather have been without it: he regarded his vote as part of his investment, and meant to make the best of it. He called himself a straightforward man, and at suitable moments expressed his views freely; in fact, he was known to have one fundamental division for all opinion—"my idee" and "humbug."

When Felix approached, Mr. Chubb was standing, as usual, with his hands nervously busy in his pockets, his eyes glancing round with a detective expression at the black landscape, and his lipless mouth compressed, yet in constant movement. On a superficial view it might be supposed that so eager-seeming a personality was unsuited to the publican's business; but in fact it was a great provocative to drinking. Like the shrill biting talk of a vixenish wife, it would have compelled you to "take a little something" by way of dulling your sensibility.

Hitherto, notwithstanding Felix drank so little ale, the publican had treated him with high civility. The coming election was a great opportunity for applying his political "idee," which was, that society existed for the sake of the individual, and that the name of that individual was Chubb. Now, from a conjunction of absurd circumstances inconsistent with that idea, it happened that Sproxton had been hitherto somewhat neglected in the canvass. The head member of the Company that worked the mines was Mr. Peter Garstin, and the same company received the rent for the Sugar Loaf. Hence, as the person who had the most power of annoying Mr. Chubb, and being of detriment to him, Mr. Garstin was naturally the candidate for whom he had reserved his vote. But where there is this intention of ultimately gratifying a gentleman by voting for him in an open British manner on the day of the poll, a man, whether Publican or Pharisee (Mr. Chubb used this generic classification of mankind as one that was sanctioned by Scripture), is all the freer in his relations with those deluded persons who take him for what he is not, and imagine him to be a waverer. But for some time opportunity had seemed barren. There were but three dubious votes besides Mr. Chubb's in the small district of which the

Sugar Loaf could be regarded as the centre of intelligence and inspiration: the colliers, of course, had no votes, and did not need political conversion; consequently, the interests of Sproxton had only been tacitly cherished in the breasts of candidates. But ever since it had been known that a Radical candidate was in the field, that in consequence of this Mr. Debarry had coalesced with Mr. Garstin, and that Sir James Clement, the poor baronet, had retired, Mr. Chubb had been occupied with the most ingenious mental combinations in order to ascertain what possibilities of profit to the Sugar Loaf might lie in this altered state of the canvass.

He had a cousin in another county, also a publican, but in a larger way, and resident in a borough, and from him Mr. Chubb had gathered more detailed political information than he could find in the Loamshire newspapers. He was now enlightened enough to know that there was a way of using voteless miners and navvies at Nominations and Elections. He approved of that; it entered into his political "idee"; and indeed he would have been for extending the franchise to this class—at least in Sproxton. If any one had observed that you must draw a line somewhere, Mr. Chubb would have concurred at once, and would have given permission to draw it at a radius of two miles from his own tap.

From the first Sunday evening when Felix had appeared at the Sugar Loaf, Mr. Chubb had made up his mind that this 'cute man who kept himself sober was an electioneering agent. That he was hired for some purpose or other there was not a doubt; a man didn't come and drink nothing without a good reason. In proportion as Felix's purpose was not obvious to Chubb's mind, it must be deep; and this growing conviction had even led the publican on the last Sunday evening privately to urge his mysterious visitor to let a little ale be chalked up for him—it was of no consequence. Felix knew his man, and had taken care not to betray too soon that his real object was so to win the ear of the best fellows about him as to induce them to meet him on a Saturday evening in the room where Mr. Lyon, or one of his deacons, habitually held his Wednesday preachings. Only women and children, three old men, a journeyman tailor, and a consumptive youth attended those preachings; not a collier had been won from the strong ale of the Sugar Loaf, not even a navvy from the muddier drink of the Blue Cow. Felix was sanguine; he saw some pleasant faces among the miners when they were washed on Sundays; they might be taught to spend their wages better. At all events, he was going to try: he had great confidence in his powers of appeal, and it was quite true that he never spoke without arresting attention. There was nothing better than a dame school in the hamlet; he thought that if he could move the fathers, whose blackened week-day persons and flannel caps, ornamented with tallow candles by way of plume, were a badge of hard labor for which he had a more sympathetic fibre than for any ribbon in the button-hole—if he could move these men to save something from their drink, and pay a schoolmaster for their boys, a greater service would be done them than if Mr. Garstin and his company were persuaded to establish a school.

"I'll lay hold of them by their fatherhood," said Felix; "I'll take one of their little fellows and set him in the midst. Till they can show there's something they love better than swilling themselves with ale, extension of the suffrage can never mean anything for them but extension of boozing. One must begin somewhere: I'll begin at what is under my nose. I'll begin at Sproxton. That's what a man would do if he had a red-hot superstition. Can't one work for sober truth as hard as for megrims?"

Felix Holt had his illusions, like other young men, though they were not of a fashionable sort; referring neither to the impression his costume and horsemanship might make on beholders, nor to the ease with which he would pay the Jews when he gave a loose to his talents and applied himself to work. He had fixed his choice on a certain Mike Brindle (not that Brindle was his real name—each collier had his *sobriquet*) as the man whom he would induce to walk part of the way home with him this very evening, and get to invite some of his comrades for the next Saturday. Brindle was one of the head miners; he had a bright good-natured face, and had given especial attention to certain performances with a magnet which Felix carried in his pocket.

Mr. Chubb, who had also his illusions, smiled graciously as the enigmatic customer came up to the door-step.

"Well, sir, Sunday seems to be your day: I begin to look for you on a Sunday now."

"Yes, I'm a working man; Sunday is my holiday," said Felix, pausing at the door since the host seemed to expect this.

"Ah, sir, there's many ways of working. I look at it you're one of those as work with your brains. That's what I do myself."

"One may do a good deal of that and work with one's hands too."

"Ah, sir," said Mr. Chubb, with a certain bitterness in his smile, "I've that sort of head that I've often wished I was stupider. I use things up, sir; I see into things a deal too quick. I eat my dinner, as you may say, at breakfast-time. That's why I hardly ever smoke a pipe. No sooner do I stick a pipe in my mouth than I puff and puff till it's gone before other folks' are well lit; and then where am I? I might as well have let it alone. In this world it's better not to be too quick. But you know what it is, sir."

"Not I," said Felix, rubbing the back of his head, with a grimace. "I generally feel myself rather a blockhead. The world's a largish place, and I haven't turned everything inside out yet."

"Ah, that's your deepness. I think we understand one another. And about this here election, I lay two to one we should agree if we was to come to talk about it."

"Ah!" said Felix, with an air of caution.

"You're none of a Tory, eh, sir? You won't go to vote for Debarry? That was what I said at the very first go-off. Says I, he's no Tory. I think I was right, sir—eh?"

"Certainly; I'm no Tory."

"No, no, you don't catch me wrong in a hurry. Well, between you and me, I care no more for the Debarrys than I care for Johnny Groats. I live on none o' their land, and not a pot's worth did they ever send to the Sugar Loaf. I'm not frightened at the Debarrys: there's no man more independent than me. I'll plump or I'll split for them as treat

me the handsomest and are the most of what I call gentlemen;
that's my idee. And in the way of hacting for any man,
them are fools that don't employ me."

We mortals sometimes cut a pitiable figure in our attempts
at display. We may be sure of our own merits, yet fatally
ignorant of the point of view from which we are regarded by
our neighbor. Our fine patterns in tattooing may be far from
throwing him into a swoon of admiration, though we turn
ourselves all round to show them. Thus it was with Mr.
Chubb.

"Yes," said Felix, dryly; "I should think there are some
sorts of work for which you are just fitted."

"Ah, you see that? Well, we understand one another.
You're no Tory; no more am I. And if I'd got four hands
to show at a nomination, the Debarrys shouldn't have one of
'em. My idee is, there's a deal too much of their scutchins
and their moniments in Treby Church. What's their scutchins mean? They're a sign with little liquor behind 'em;
that's how I take it. There's nobody can give account of 'em,
as I ever heard."

Mr. Chubb was hindered from further explaining his views
as to the historical element in society by the arrival of new
guests, who approached in two groups. The foremost group
consisted of well-known colliers, in their good Sunday beavers
and colored handkerchiefs serving as cravats, with the long
ends floating. The second group was a more unusual one, and
caused Mr. Chubb to compress his mouth and agitate the muscles about it in rather an excited manner.

First came a smartly dressed personage on horseback, with
a conspicuous expansive shirt-front and figured satin stock.
He was a stout man, and gave a strong sense of broadcloth.
A wild idea shot through Mr. Chubb's brain: could this
grand visitor be Harold Transome? Excuse him: he had
been given to understand by his cousin from the distant borough that a Radical candidate in the condescension of canvassing had even gone the length of eating bread and treacle with
the children of an honest freeman, and declaring his preference for that simple fare. Mr. Chubb's notion of a Radical
was that he was a new and agreeable kind of lick spittle who

fawned on the poor instead of on the rich, and so was likely
to send customers to a "public"; so that he argued well
enough from the premises at his command.

The mounted man of broadcloth had followers: several
shabby-looking men, and Sproxton boys of all sizes, whose
curiosity had been stimulated by unexpected largesse. A
stranger on horseback scattering halfpence on a Sunday was
so unprecedented that there was no knowing what he might
do next; and the smallest hindmost fellows in sealskin caps
were not without hope that an entirely new order of things
had set in.

Every one waited outside for the stranger to dismount, and
Mr. Chubb advanced to take the bridle.

"Well, Mr. Chubb," were the first words when the great
man was safely out of the saddle, "I've often heard of your
fine tap, and I'm come to taste it."

"Walk in, sir—pray walk in," said Mr. Chubb, giving the
horse to the stable-boy. "I shall be proud to draw for you.
If anybody's been praising me, I think my ale will back
him."

All entered in the rear of the stranger except the boys, who
peeped in at the window.

"Won't you please to walk into the parlor, sir?" said
Chubb, obsequiously.

"No, no, I'll sit down here. This is what I like to see,"
said the stranger, looking round at the colliers, who eyed him
rather shyly—"a bright hearth where working men can enjoy
themselves. However, I'll step into the other room for three
minutes, just to speak half a dozen words with you."

Mr. Chubb threw open the parlor door, and then, stepping
back, took the opportunity of saying, in a low tone, to Felix,
"Do you know this gentleman?"

"Not I; no."

Mr. Chubb's opinion of Felix Holt sank from that moment.
The parlor door was closed, but no one sat down or ordered
beer.

"I say, master," said Mike Brindle, going up to Felix,
"don't you think that's one o' the 'lection men?"

"Very likely."

"I heared a chap say they're up and down everywhere," said Brindle; "and now's the time, they say, when a man can get beer for nothing."

"Ay, that's sin' the Reform," said a big, red-whiskered man called Dredge. "That's brought the 'lections and the drink into these parts; for afore that it was all kep up the Lord knows wheer."

"Well, but the Reform's niver come anigh Sprox'on," said a gray-haired but stalwart man called Old Sleck. "I don't believe nothing about'n, I don't."

"Don't you?" said Brindle, with some contempt. "Well, I do. There's folks won't believe beyond the end o' their own pickaxes. You can't drive nothing into 'em, not if you split their skulls. I know for certain sure, from a chap in the cartin' way, as he's got money and drink too only for holler-ing. Eh, master, what do *you* say?" Brindle ended, turning with some deference to Felix.

"Should you like to know all about the Reform?" said Felix, using his opportunity. "If you would, I can tell you."

"Ay, ay—tell's; you know, I'll be bound," said several voices at once.

"Ah, but it will take some little time. And we must be quiet. The cleverest of you—those who are looked up to in the Club—must come and meet me at Peggy Button's cottage next Saturday, at seven o'clock, after dark. And, Brindle, you must bring that little yellow-haired lad of yours. And anybody that's got a little boy—a very little fellow, who won't understand what is said—may bring him. But you must keep it close, you know. We don't want fools there. But every-body who hears me may come. I shall be at Peggy But-ton's."

"Why, that's where the Wednesday preachin' is," said Dredge. "I've been aforced to give my wife a black eye to hinder her from going to the preachin'. Lors-a-massy, she thinks she knows better nor me, and I can't make head nor tail of her talk."

"Why can't you let the woman alone?" said Brindle, with some disgust. "I'd be ashamed to beat a poor crawling thing 'cause she likes preaching."

"No more I did beat her afore, not if she scrat' me," said Dredge, in vindication; "but if she jabbers at me, I can't abide it. Howsomever, I'll bring my Jack to Peggy's o' Saturday. His mother shall wash him. He is but four year old, and he'll swear and square at me a good un, if I set him on."

"There you go blatherin'," said Brindle, intending a mild rebuke

This dialogue, which was in danger of becoming too personal, was interrupted by the reopening of the parlor door, and the reappearance of the impressive stranger with Mr. Chubb, whose countenance seemed unusually radiant.

"Sit you down here, Mr. Johnson," said Chubb, moving an arm-chair. "This gentleman is kind enough to treat the company," he added, looking round; "and, what's more, he'll take a cup with 'em; and I think there's no man but what'll say that's a honor."

The company had nothing equivalent to a "hear, hear," at command, but they perhaps felt the more, as they seated themselves with an expectation unvented by utterance. There was a general satisfactory sense that the hitherto shadowy Reform had at length come to Sproxton in a good round shape, with broadcloth and pockets. Felix did not intend to accept the treating, but he chose to stay and hear, taking his pint as usual.

"Capital ale, capital ale," said Mr. Johnson, as he set down his glass, speaking in a quick, smooth treble. "Now," he went on, with a certain pathos in his voice, looking at Mr. Chubb, who sat opposite, "there's some satisfaction to me in finding an establishment like this at the Pits. For what would higher wages do for the working man if he couldn't get a good article for his money? Why, gentlemen"—here he looked round—"I've been into ale-houses where I've seen a fine fellow of a miner or a stone-cutter come in and have to lay down money for beer that I should be sorry to give to my pigs!" Here Mr. Johnson leaned forward with squared elbows, hands placed on his knees, and a defiant shake of the head.

"Aw, like at the Blue Cow," fell in the irrepressible

Dredge, in a deep bass; but he was rebuked by a severe nudge from Brindle.

"Yes, yes, you know what it is, my friend," said Mr. Johnson, looking at Dredge, and restoring his self-satisfaction. "But it won't last much longer, that's one good thing. Bad liquor will be swept away with other bad articles. Trade will prosper—and what's trade now without steam? and what is steam without coal? And mark you this, gentlemen —there's no man and no government can make coal."

A brief loud "Haw, haw," showed that this fact was appreciated.

"Nor freeston' nayther," said a wide-mouthed wiry man called Gills, who wished for an exhaustive treatment of the subject, being a stone-cutter.

"Nor freestone, as you say; else, I think, if coal could be made above ground, honest fellows who are the pith of our population would not have to bend their backs and sweat in a pit six days out of the seven. No, no: I say, as this country prospers it has more and more need of you, sirs. It can do without a pack of lazy lords and ladies, but it can never do without brave colliers. And the country *will* prosper. I pledge you my word, sirs, this country will rise to the tip-top of everything, and there isn't a man in it but what shall have his joint in the pot, and his spare money jingling in his pocket, if we only exert ourselves to send the right men to Parliament—men who will speak up for the collier, and the stone-cutter, and the navvy" (Mr. Johnson waved his hand liberally), "and will stand no nonsense. This is a crisis, and we must exert ourselves. We've got Reform, gentlemen, but now the thing is to make Reform work. It's a crisis—I pledge you my word it's a crisis."

Mr. Johnson threw himself back as if from the concussion of that great noun. He did not suppose that one of his audience knew what a crisis meant; but he had large experience in the effect of uncomprehended words; and in this case the colliers were thrown into a state of conviction concerning they did not know what, which was a fine preparation for "hitting out," or any other act carrying a due sequence to such a conviction.

Felix felt himself in danger of getting into a rage. There is hardly any mental misery worse than that of having our own serious phrases, our own rooted beliefs, caricatured by a charlatan or a hireling. He began to feel the sharp lower edge of his tin pint-measure, and to think it a tempting missile.

Mr. Johnson certainly had some qualifications as an orator. After this impressive pause he leaned forward again, and said, in a lowered tone, looking round,—

"I think you all know the good news."

There was a movement of shoe-soles on the quarried floor, and a scrape of some chair-legs, but no other answer.

"The good news I mean is, that a first-rate man, Mr. Transome of Transome Court, has offered himself to represent you in Parliament, sirs. I say you in particular, for what he has at heart is the welfare of the working man—of the brave fellows that wield the pickaxe, and the saw, and the hammer. He's rich—has more money than Garstin—but he doesn't want to keep it to himself. What he wants is, to make a good use of it, gentlemen. He's come back from foreign parts with his pockets full of gold. He could buy up the Debarrys if they were worth buying, but he's got something better to do with his money. He means to use it for the good of the working men in these parts. I know there are some men who put up for Parliament and talk a little too big. They may say they want to befriend the colliers, for example. But I should like to put a question to them I should like to ask them, 'What colliers?' There are colliers up at Newcastle, and there are colliers down in Wales. Will it do any good to honest Tom, who is hungry in Sproxton, to hear that Jack at Newcastle has his bellyful of beef and pudding?"

"It ought to do him good," Felix burst in, with his loud abrupt voice, in odd contrast with glib Mr. Johnson's. "If he knows it's a bad thing to be hungry and not have enough to eat, he ought to be glad that another fellow, who is not idle, is not suffering in the same way."

Every one was startled. The audience was much impressed with the grandeur, the knowledge, and the power of Mr. Johnson. His brilliant promises confirmed the impression that Reform had at length reached the New Pits; and Reform, if it were good for anything, must at last resolve itself into spare money—meaning "sport" and drink, and keeping away from work for several days in the week. These "brave" men of Sproxton liked Felix as one of themselves, only much more knowing—as a working man who had seen many distant parts, but who must be very poor, since he never drank more than a pint or so. They were quite inclined to hear what he had got to say on another occasion, but they were rather irritated by his interruption at the present moment. Mr. Johnson was annoyed, but he spoke with the same glib quietness as before, though with an expression of contempt.

"I call it a poor-spirited thing to take up a man's straightforward words and twist them. What I meant to say was plain enough—that no man can be saved from starving by looking on while others eat. I think that's common sense, eh, sirs?"

There was again an approving "Haw, haw." To hear anything said, and understand it, was a stimulus that had the effect of wit. Mr. Chubb cast a suspicious and viperous glance at Felix, who felt that he had been a simpleton for his pains.

"Well, then," continued Mr. Johnson, "I suppose I may go on. But if there is any one here better able to inform the company than I am, I give way—I give way."

"Sir," said Mr. Chubb, magisterially, "no man shall take the words out of *your* mouth in this house. And," he added, looking pointedly at Felix, "company that's got no more orders to give, and wants to turn up rusty to them that has, had better be making room than filling it. Love an' 'armony's the word on our Club's flag, an' love an' 'armony's the meaning of ' The Sugar Loaf, William Chubb.' Folks of a different mind had better seek another house of call."

"Very good," said Felix, laying down his money and taking his cap. "I'm going." He saw clearly enough that if he said more, there would be a disturbance which could have no desirable end.

When the door had closed behind him, Mr. Johnson said, "What is that person's name?"

"Does anybody know it?" said Mr. Chubb.

A few noes were heard.

"I've heard him speak like a downright Reformer, else I should have looked a little sharper after him. But you may see he's nothing partic'lar."

"It looks rather bad that no one knows his name," said Mr. Johnson. "He's most likely a Tory in disguise—a Tory spy. You must be careful, sirs, of men who come to you and say they're Radicals, and yet do nothing for you. They'll stuff you with words—no lack of words—but words are wind. Now, a man like Transome comes forward and says to the working men of this country: 'Here I am, ready to serve you and to speak for you in Parliament, and to get the laws made all right for you; and in the mean while, if there's any of you who are my neighbors who want a day's holiday, or a cup to drink with friends, or a copy of the King's likeness—why, I'm your man. I'm not a paper handbill—all words and no substance—nor a man with land and nothing else; I've got bags of gold as well as land.' I think you know what I mean by the King's likeness?"

Here Mr. Johnson took a half-crown out of his pocket and held the head toward the company.

"Well, sirs, there are some men who like to keep this pretty picture a great deal too much to themselves. I don't know whether I'm right, but I think I've heard of such a one not a hundred miles from here. I think his name was Spratt, and he managed some company's coal-pits."

"Haw, haw! Spratt—Spratt's his name," was rolled forth to an accompaniment of scraping shoe-soles.

"A screwing fellow, by what I understand—a domineering fellow—who would expect men to do as he liked without paying them for it. I think there's not an honest man who wouldn't like to disappoint such an upstart."

There was a murmur which was interpreted by Mr. Chubb. "I'll answer for 'em, sir."

"Now, listen to me. Here's Garstin: he's one of the Company you work under. What's Garstin to you? who sees him? and when they do see him they see a thin miserly fellow who keeps his pockets buttoned. He calls him·

self a Whig, yet he'll split votes with a Tory—he'll drive with the Debarrys. Now, gentlemen, if I said I'd got a vote, and anybody asked me what I should do with it, I should say, 'I'll plump for Transome.' You've got no votes, and that's a shame. But you *will* have some day, if such men as Transome are returned; and then you'll be on a level with the first gentleman in the land, and if he wants to sit in Parliament, he must take off his hat and ask your leave. But though you haven't got a vote you can give a cheer for the right man, and Transome's not a man like Garstin; if you lost a day's wages by giving a cheer for Transome, he'll make you amends. That's the way a man who has no vote can yet serve himself and his country; he can lift up his hand and shout 'Transome forever!'—'Hurray for Transome!' Let the working men—let colliers and navvies and stone-cutters, who between you and me have a good deal too much the worst of it, as things are now—let them join together and give their hands and voices for the right man, and they'll make the great people shake in their shoes a little; and wher you shout for Transome, remember you shout for more wages, and more of your rights, and you shout to get rid of rats and *sprats* and such small animals, who are the tools the rich make use of to squeeze the blood out of the poor man."

"I wish there'd be a row—I'd pommel him," said Dredge, who was generally felt to be speaking to the question.

"No, no, my friend—there you're a little wrong. No pommelling—no striking first. There you have the law and the constable against you. A little rolling in the dust and knocking hats off, a little pelting with soft things that'll stick and not bruise—all that doesn't spoil the fun. If a man is to speak when you don't like to hear him, it is but fair you should give him something he doesn't like in return. And the same if he's got a vote and doesn't use it for the good of the country; I see no harm in splitting his coat in a quiet way. A man must be taught what's right if he doesn't know it. But no kicks, no knocking down, no pommelling."

"It 'ud be good fun, though, if so-*be*," said Old Sleck, allowing himself an imaginative pleasure.

"Well, well, if a Spratt wants you to say Garstin, it's some pleasure to think you can say Transome. Now, my notion is this. You are men who can put two and two together—I don't know a more solid lot of fellows than you are; and what I say is, let the honest men in this country who've got no vote show themselves in a body when they have the chance. Why, sirs, for every Tory sneak that's got a vote, there's fifty-five fellows who must stand by and be expected to hold their tongues. But I say, let 'em hiss the sneaks, let 'em groan at the sneaks, and the sneaks will be ashamed of themselves. The men who've got votes don't know how to use them. There's many a fool with a vote who is not sure in his mind whether he shall poll, say for Debarry, or Garstin, or Transome—whether he'll plump or whether he'll split; a straw will turn him. Let him know your mind if he doesn't know his own. What's the reason Debarry gets returned? Because people are frightened at the Debarrys. What's that to you? You don't care for the Debarrys. If people are frightened at the Tories, we'll turn round and frighten *them*. You know what a Tory is—one who wants to drive the working men as he'd drive cattle. That's what a Tory is; and a Whig is no better, if he's like Garstin. A Whig wants to knock the Tory down and get the whip, that's all. But Transome's neither Whig nor Tory; he's the working man's friend, the collier's friend, the friend of the honest navvy. And if he gets into Parliament, let me tell you, it will be the better for you. I don't say it will be the better for overlookers and screws, and rats and *sprats;* but it will be the better for every good fellow who takes his pot at the Sugar Loaf."

Mr. Johnson's exertions for the political education of the Sproxton men did not stop here, which was the more disinterested in him as he did not expect to see them again, and could only set on foot an organization by which their instruction could be continued without him. In this he was quite successful. A man known among the "butties" as Pack, who had already been mentioned by Mr. Chubb, presently joined the party, and had a private audience of Mr. Johnson, that he might be instituted as the "shepherd" of this new flock.

"That's a right down genelman," said Pack, as he took the seat vacated by the orator, who had ridden away.

10

"What's his trade, think you?" said Gills, the wiry stone-cutter.

"Trade?" said Mr. Chubb. "He's one of the top-sawyers of the country. He works with his head, you may see that.'

"Let's have our pipes, then," said Old Sleck; "I'm pretty well tired o' jaw."

"So am I," said Dredge. "It's wriggling work—like following a stoat. It makes a man dry. I'd as lief hear preaching, on'y there's nought to be got by't. I shouldn't know which end I stood on if it wasn't for the tickets and the treatin'.'"

CHAPTER XII.

"Oh, sir, 'twas that mixture of spite and overfed merriment which passes for humor with the vulgar. In their fun they have much resemblance to a turkey-cock. It has a cruel beak, and a silly iteration of ugly sounds; it spreads its tail in self-glorification, but shows you the wrong side of that ornament—liking admiration, but knowing not what is admirable."

THIS Sunday evening, which promised to be so memorable in the experience of the Sproxton miners, had its drama also for those unsatisfactory objects to Mr. Johnson's moral sense, the Debarrys. Certain incidents occurring at Treby Manor caused an excitement there which spread from the dining-room to the stables; but no one underwent such agitating transitions of feeling as Mr. Scales. At six o'clock that superior butler was chuckling in triumph at having played a fine and original practical joke on his rival Mr. Christian. Some two hours after that time, he was frightened, sorry, and even meek; he was on the brink of a humiliating confession; his cheeks were almost livid; his hair was flattened for want of due attention from his fingers; and the fine roll of his whiskers, which was too firm to give way, seemed only a sad reminiscence of past splendor and felicity. His sorrow came about in this wise.

After service on that Sunday morning, Mr. Philip Debarry had left the rest of the family to go home in the carriage, and had remained at the Rectory to lunch with his uncle Augustus, that he might consult him touching some letters of importance. He had returned the letters to his pocket-book, but had not returned the book to his pocket, and he finally walked away leaving the enclosure of private papers and bank-notes on his uncle's escritoire. After his arrival at home he was reminded of his omission, and immediately despatched Christian with a note begging his uncle to seal up the pocket-book and send it by the bearer. This commission, which was given between three and four o'clock, happened to be very un-welcome to the courier. The fact was that Mr. Christian, who had been remarkable through life for that power of adapting himself to circumstances which enables a man to fall safely on all-fours in the most hurried expulsions and escapes, was not exempt from bodily suffering—a circumstance to which there is no known way of adapting one's self so as to be perfectly comfortable under it, or to push it off on to other people's shoul-ders. He did what he could: he took doses of opium when he had an access of nervous pains, and he consoled himself as to future possibilities by thinking that if the pains ever be-came intolerably frequent a considerable increase in the dose might put an end to them altogether. He was neither Cato nor Hamlet, and though he had learned their soliloquies at his first boarding-school, he would probably have increased his dose without reciting those masterpieces. Next to the pain itself, he disliked that any one should know of it: defec-tive health diminished a man's market value; he did not like to be the object of the sort of pity he himself gave to a poor devil who was forced to make a wry face or "give in" alto-gether.

He had felt it expedient to take a slight dose this after-noon, and still he was not altogether relieved at the time he set off to the Rectory. On returning with the valuable case safely deposited in his hind pocket, he felt increasing bodily uneasiness, and took another dose. Thinking it likely that he looked rather pitiable, he chose not to proceed to the house by the carriage-road. The servants often walked in the park on a Sunday, and he wished to avoid any meeting. He would make a circuit, get into the house privately, and after deliv-ering his packet to Mr. Debarry, shut himself up till the ringing of the half-hour bell. But when he reached an elbowed seat under some sycamores, he felt so ill at ease that he yielded to the temptation of throwing himself on it to rest a little. He looked at his watch: it was but five; he had done his errand quickly hitherto, and Mr. Debarry had not urged haste. But in less than ten minutes he was in a sound sleep. Certain conditions of his system had determined a stronger effect than usual from the opium.

As he had expected, there were servants strolling in the park, but they did not all choose the most frequented part. Mr. Scales, in pursuit of a slight flirtation with the younger lady's maid, had preferred a more sequestered walk in the company of that agreeable nymph. And it happened to be this pair, of all others, who alighted on the sleeping Christian—a sight which at the very first moment caused Mr. Scales a vague pleasure as at an incident that must lead to something clever on his part. To play a trick, and make some one or other look foolish, was held the most pointed form of wit throughout the back regions of the Manor, and served as a constant substitute for theatrical entertainment: what the farce wanted in costume or "make up" it gained in the reality of the mortification which excited the general laughter. And lo! here was the offensive, the exasperatingly cool and superior, Christian caught comparatively helpless, with his head hanging on his shoulder, and one coat-tail hanging out heavily below the elbow of the rustic seat. It was this coat-tail which served as a suggestion to Mr. Scales's genius. Putting his finger up in warning to Mrs. Cherry, and saying, "Hush—be quiet—I see a fine bit of fun"—he took a knife from his pocket, stepped behind the unconscious Christian, and quickly cut off the pendent coat-tail. Scales knew nothing of the errand to the Rectory; and as he noticed that there was something in the pocket, thought it was probably a large cigar-case. So much the better—he had no time to pause. He threw the coat-tail as far as he could, and noticed that it fell among the elms under which they had been walking. Then, beckoning to Mrs. Cherry, he hurried away with her toward the more open part of the park, not daring to explode in laughter until it was safe from the chance of waking the sleeper. And then the vision of the graceful, well-appointed Mr. Christian, who

sneered at Scales about his "get up," having to walk back to
the house with only one tail to his coat, was a source of so
much enjoyment to the butler that the fair Cherry began to
be quite jealous of the joke. Still she admitted that it really
was funny, tittered intermittently, and pledged herself to se-
crecy. Mr. Scales explained to her that Christian would try
to creep in unobserved, but that this must be made impossible;
and he requested her to imagine the figure this interloping
fellow would cut when everybody was asking what had happened. "Hallo, Christian! where's your coat-tail?" would
become a proverb at the Manor, where jokes kept remarkably
well without the aid of salt; and Mr. Christian's comb would
be cut so effectually that it would take a long time to grow
again. Exit Scales, laughing, and presenting a fine example
of dramatic irony to any one in the secret of Fate.

When Christian awoke, he was shocked to find himself in
the twilight. He started up, shook himself, missed something, and soon became aware what it was he missed. He
did not doubt that he had been robbed, and he at once foresaw that the consequences would be highly unpleasant. In
no way could the cause of the accident be so represented to
Mr. Philip Debarry as to prevent him from viewing his hitherto unimpeachable factotum in a new and unfavorable light.
And though Mr. Christian did not regard his present position
as brilliant, he did not see his way to anything better. A
man nearly fifty who is not always quite well is seldom ardently hopeful: he is aware that this is a world in which
merit is often overlooked. With the idea of robbery in full
possession of his mind, to peer about and search in the dimness, even if it had occurred to him, would have seemed a preposterous waste of time and energy. He knew it was likely
that Mr. Debarry's pocket-book had important and valuable
contents, and that he should deepen his offence by deferring
his announcement of the unfortunate fact. He hastened
back to the house, relieved by the obscurity from that mortification of his vanity on which the butler had counted. Indeed, to Scales himself the affair had already begun to appear
less thoroughly jocose than he had anticipated. For he observed that Christian's non-appearance before dinner had

caused Mr. Debarry some consternation; and he had gathered
that the courier had been sent on a commission to the Rectory. "My uncle must have detained him for some reason or
other," he heard Mr. Philip say; "but it is odd. If he were
less trusty about commissions, or had ever seemed to drink
too much, I should be uneasy." Altogether the affair was not
taking the turn Mr. Scales had intended. At last, when dinner had been removed, and the butler's chief duties were at
an end, it was understood that Christian had entered without
his coat-tail, looking serious and even agitated; that he had
asked leave at once to speak to Mr. Debarry; and that he was
even then in parley with the gentlemen in the dining-room.
Scales was in alarm; it must have been some property of Mr.
Debarry's that had weighted the pocket. He took a lantern,
got a groom to accompany him with another lantern, and with
the utmost practicable speed reached the fatal spot in the
park. He searched under the elms—he was certain that the
pocket had fallen there—and he found the pocket; but he
found it empty, and, in spite of further search, did not find
the contents, though he had at first consoled himself with
thinking that they had fallen out, and would be lying not far
off. He returned with the lanterns and the coat-tail, and a
most uncomfortable consciousness in that great seat of a butler's emotion, the stomach. He had no sooner re-entered
than he was met by Mrs. Cherry, pale and anxious, who drew
him aside to say that if he didn't tell everything she would;
that the constables were to be sent for; that there had been
no end of bank-notes and letters and things in Mr. Debarry's
pocket-book, which Christian was carrying in that very pocket
Scales had cut off; that the Rector was sent for, the constable
was coming, and they should all be hanged. Mr. Scales'
own intellect was anything but clear as to the possible issues.
Crestfallen, and with the coat-tail in his hands as an attesta-
tion that he was innocent of anything more than a joke, he
went and made his confession. His story relieved Christian
a little, but did not relieve Mr. Debarry, who was more annoyed at the loss of the letters, and their chance of getting
into hands that might make use of them, than at the loss of
the bank-notes. Nothing could be done for the present, but

that the Rector, who was a magistrate, should instruct the constables, and that the spot in the park indicated by Scales should again be carefully searched. This was done, but in vain; and many of the family at the Manor had disturbed sleep that night.

CHAPTER XIII.

" Give sorrow leave awhile, to tutor me
To this submission."—*Richard II.*

MEANWHILE Felix Holt had been making his way back from Sproxton to Treby in some irritation and bitterness of spirit. For a little while he walked slowly along the direct road, hoping that Mr. Johnson would overtake him, in which case he would have the pleasure of quarrelling with him, and telling him what he thought of his intentions in coming to cant at the Sugar Loaf. But he presently checked himself in this folly, and turned off again toward the canal that he might avoid the temptation of getting into a passion to no purpose.

"Where's the good," he thought, "of pulling at such a tangled skein as this electioneering trickery? As long as three-fourths of the men in this country see nothing in an election but self-interest, and nothing in self-interest but some form of greed, one might as well try to purify the proceedings of the fishes, and say to a hungry codfish—'My good friend, abstain; don't goggle your eyes so, or show such a stupid, gluttonous mouth, or think the little fishes are worth nothing except in relation to your own inside.' He'd be open to no argument short of crimping him. I should get into a rage with this fellow, and perhaps end by thrashing him. There's some reason in me as long as I keep my temper, but my rash humor is drunkenness without wine. I shouldn't wonder if he upsets all my plans with these colliers. Of course he's going to treat them for the sake of getting up a posse at the nomination and speechifyings. They'll drink double, and never come near me on a Saturday evening. I don't know what sort of man Transome really is. It's no use my speaking to anybody else, but if I could get at him, he might put a veto on this thing. Though, when once the men have been promised and set agoing, the mischief is likely to be past mending. Hang the Liberal codfish! I shouldn't have minded so much if he'd been a Tory!"

Felix went along in the twilight, struggling in this way with the intricacies of life, which would certainly be greatly simplified if corrupt practices were the invariable mark of wrong opinions. When he had crossed the common and had entered the park, the overshadowing trees deepened the gray gloom of the evening; it was useless to try and keep the blind path, and he could only be careful that his steps should be bent in the direction of the park gate. He was striding along rapidly now, whistling " Bannockburn " in a subdued way as an accompaniment to his inward discussion, when something smooth and soft on which his foot alighted arrested him with an unpleasant, startling sensation, and made him stoop to examine the object he was treading on. He found it to be a large leather pocket-book, swelled by its contents, and fastened with a sealed ribbon as well as a clasp. In stooping, he saw about a yard off something whitish and square lying on the dark grass. This was an ornamental note-book of pale leather stamped with gold. Apparently it had burst open in falling, and out of the pocket formed by the cover there protruded a small gold chain about four inches long, with various seals and other trifles attached to it by a ring at the end. Felix thrust the chain back; and finding that the clasp of the note-book was broken, he closed it and thrust it into his side pocket, walking along under some annoyance that fortune had made him the finder of articles belonging most probably to one of the family at Treby Manor. He was much too proud a man to like any contact with the aristocracy, and he could still less endure coming within speech of their servants. Some plan must be devised by which he could avoid carrying these things up to the Manor himself: he thought at first of leaving them at the lodge, but he had a scruple against placing property, of which the ownership was after all uncertain, in the hand of persons unknown to him. It was possible that the large pocket-book contained papers of high importance, and that it did not belong to any of the Debarry family. He resolved at last to carry his findings to Mr. Lyon, who would perhaps be good-natured enough to save him from the necessary transactions with the people at the Manor by undertaking those transactions himself. With this determination he walked straight to Malthouse Yard, and waited outside the chapel until the congregation was dispersing, when he passed along the aisle to the vestry in order to speak to the minister in private.

But Mr. Lyon was not alone when Felix entered. Mr. Nuttwood, the grocer, who was one of the deacons, was complaining to him about the obstinate demeanor of the singers, who had declined to change the tunes in accordance with a change in the selection of hymns, and had stretched short metre into long out of pure wilfulness and defiance, irreverently adapting the most sacred monosyllables to a multitude of wandering quavers, arranged, it was to be feared, by some musician who was inspired by conceit rather than by the true spirit of psalmody.

"Come in, my friend," said Mr. Lyon, smiling at Felix, and then continuing in a faint voice, while he wiped the perspiration from his brow and bald crown, "Brother Nuttwood, we must be content to carry a thorn in our sides while the necessities of our imperfect state demand that there should be a body set apart and called a choir, whose special office it is to lead the singing, not because they are more disposed to the devout uplifting of praise, but because they are endowed with better vocal organs and have attained more of the musician's art. For all office, unless it be accompanied by peculiar grace, becomes, as it were, a diseased organ, seeking to make itself too much of a centre. Singers, specially so called, are, it must be confessed, an anomaly among us who seek to reduce the Church to its primitive simplicity, and to cast away all that may obstruct the direct communion of spirit with spirit."

"They are so headstrong," said Mr. Nuttwood, in a tone of sad perplexity, "that if we dealt not warily with them, they might end in dividing the church, even now that we have had the chapel enlarged. Brother Kemp would side with them, and draw the half part of the members after him. I cannot but think it a snare when a professing Christian has a bass voice like Brother Kemp's. It makes him desire to be heard of men; but the weaker song of the humble may have more power in the ear of God."

"Do you think it any better vanity to flatter yourself that God likes to hear you, though men don't?" said Felix, with unwarrantable bluntness.

The civil grocer was prepared to be scandalized by anything that came from Felix. In common with many hearers in Malthouse Yard, he already felt an objection to a young man who was notorious for having interfered in a question of wholesale and retail which should have been left to Providence. Old Mr. Holt, being a church-member, had probably had "leadings" which were more to be relied on than his son's boasted knowledge. In any case, a little visceral disturbance and inward chastisement to the consumers of questionable medicines would tend less to obscure the divine glory than a show of punctilious morality in one who was not a "professor." Besides, how was it to be known that the medicines would not be blessed, if taken with due trust in a higher influence? A Christian must consider not the medicines alone in their relation to our frail bodies (which are dust), but the medicines with Omnipotence behind them. Hence a pious vender will look for "leadings," and he is likely to find them in the cessation of demand and the disproportion of expenses and returns. The grocer was thus on his guard against the presumptuous disputant.

"Mr. Lyon may understand you, sir," he replied. "He seems to be fond of your conversation. But you have too much of the pride of human learning for me. I follow no new lights."

"Then follow an old one," said Felix, mischievously disposed toward a sleek tradesman. "Follow the light of the old-fashioned Presbyterians that I've heard sing at Glasgow. The preacher gives out the psalm, and then everybody sings a different tune, as it happens to turn up in their throats. It's a domineering thing to set a tune and expect everybody else to follow it. It's a denial of private judgment."

"Hush, hush, my young friend," said Mr. Lyon, hurt by

this levity, which glanced at himself as well as at the deacon. "Play not with paradoxes. That caustic which you handle in order to scorch others may happen to sear your own fingers and make them dead to the quality of things. 'Tis difficult enough to see our way and keep our torch steady in this dim labyrinth: to whirl the torch and dazzle the eyes of our fellow-seekers is a poor daring, and may end in total darkness. You yourself are a lover of freedom, and a bold rebel against usurping authority. But the right to rebellion is the right to seek a higher rule, and not to wander in mere lawlessness. Wherefore, I beseech you, seem not to say that liberty is license. And I apprehend—though I am not endowed with an ear to seize those earthly harmonies, which to some devout souls have seemed, as it were, the broken echoes of the heavenly choir—I apprehend that there is a law in music, disobedience whereunto would bring us in our singing to the level of shrieking maniacs or howling beasts: so that herein we are well instructed how true liberty can be nought but the transfer of obedience from the will of one or of a few men to that will which is the norm or rule for all men. And though the transfer may sometimes be but an erroneous direction of search, yet is the search good and necessary to the ultimate finding. And even as in music, where all obey and concur to one end, so that each has the joy of contributing to a whole whereby he is ravished and lifted up into the courts of heaven, so will it be in that crowning time of the millennial reign, when our daily prayer will be fulfilled, and one law shall be written on all hearts, and be the very structure of all thought, and be the principle of all action."

Tired, even exhausted, as the minister had been when Felix Holt entered, the gathering excitement of speech gave more and more energy to his voice and manner; he walked away from the vestry table, he paused, and came back to it; he walked away again, then came back, and ended with his deepest-toned largo, keeping his hands clasped behind him, while his brown eyes were bright with the lasting youthfulness of enthusiastic thought and love. But to any one who had no share in the energies that were thrilling his little body, he would have looked queer enough. No sooner had he finished his eager speech, than he held out his hand to the deacon, and said, in his former faint tone of fatigue,—

"God be with you, brother. We shall meet to-morrow, and we will see what can be done to subdue these refractory spirits."

When the deacon was gone, Felix said, "Forgive me, Mr. Lyon; I was wrong, and you are right."

"Yes, yes, my friend; you have that mark of grace within you, that you are ready to acknowledge the justice of a rebuke. Sit down; you have something to say—some packet there."

They sat down at a corner of the small table, and Felix drew the note-book from his pocket to lay it down with the pocket-book, saying,—

"I've had the ill-luck to be the finder of these things in the Debarrys' Park. Most likely they belong to one of the family at the Manor, or to some grandee who is staying there. I hate having anything to do with such people. They'll think me a poor rascal, and offer me money. You are a known man, and I thought you would be kind enough to relieve me by taking charge of these things, and writing to Debarry, not mentioning me, and asking him to send some one for them. I found them on the grass in the park this evening about half-past seven, in the corner we cross going to Sproxton."

"Stay," said Mr. Lyon, "this little book is open; we may venture to look in it for some sign of ownership. There be others who possess property, and might be crossing that end of the park, besides the Debarrys."

As he lifted the note-book close to his eyes, the chain again slipped out. He arrested it and held it in his hand, while he examined some writing, which appeared to be a name on the inner leather. He looked long, as if he were trying to decipher something that was partly rubbed out; and his hands began to tremble noticeably. He made a movement in an agitated manner, as if he were going to examine the chain and seals, which he held in his hand. But he checked himself, closed his hand again, and rested it on the table, while with the other hand he pressed the sides of the note-book together.

Felix observed his agitation, and was much surprised; but

with a delicacy of which he was capable under all his abrupt-
ness, he said, "You are overcome with fatigue, sir. I was
thoughtless to tease you with these matters at the end of Sunday, when you have been preaching three sermons."

Mr. Lyon did not speak for a few moments, but at last he
said,—

"It is true. I am overcome. It was a name I saw—a
name that called up a past sorrow. Fear not; I will do what
is needful with these things. You may trust them to me."

With trembling fingers he replaced the chain, and tied both
the large pocket-book and the note-book in his handkerchief.
He was evidently making a great effort over himself. But
when he had gathered the knot of the handkerchief in his
hand, he said,—

"Give me your arm to the door, my friend. I feel ill.
Doubtless I am over-wearied."

The door was already open, and Lyddy was watching for
her master's return. Felix therefore said good-night and
passed on, sure that this was what Mr. Lyon would prefer.
The minister's supper of warm porridge was ready by the
kitchen-fire, where he always took it on a Sunday evening,
and afterward smoked his weekly pipe up the broad chimney
—the one great relaxation he allowed himself. Smoking, he
considered, was a recreation of the travailed spirit, which, if
indulged in, might endear this world to us by the ignoble
bonds of mere sensuous ease. Daily smoking might be lawful, but it was not expedient. And in this Esther concurred
with a doctrinal eagerness that was unusual in her. It was
her habit to go to her own room, professedly to bed, very early
on Sundays—immediately on her return from chapel—that she
might avoid her father's pipe. But this evening she had remained at home, under a true plea of not feeling well; and
when she heard him enter, she ran out of the parlor to meet
him.

"Father, you are ill," she said, as he tottered to the wicker-
bottomed arm-chair, while Lyddy stood by, shaking her
head.

"No, my dear," he answered feebly, as she took off his hat
and looked in his face inquiringly; "I am weary."

"Let me lay these things down for you," said Esther, touching the bundle in the handkerchief.

"No; they are matters which I have to examine," he said, laying them on the table, and putting his arm across them. "Go you to bed, Lyddy."

"Not me, sir. If ever a man looked as if he was struck with death, it's you, this very night as here is."

"Nonsense, Lyddy," said Esther, angrily. "Go to bed when my father desires it. I will stay with him."

Lyddy was electrified by surprise at this new behavior of Miss Esther's. She took her candle silently and went.

"Go you too, my dear," said Mr. Lyon, tenderly, giving his hand to Esther when Lyddy was gone. "It is your wont to go early. Why are you up?"

"Let me lift your porridge from before the fire, and stay with you, father. You think I'm so naughty that I don't like doing anything for you," said Esther, smiling rather sadly at him.

"Child, what has happened? you have become the image of your mother to-night," said the minister, in a loud whisper. The tears came and relieved him, while Esther, who had stooped to lift the porridge from the fender, paused on one knee and looked up at him.

"She was very good to you?" asked Esther, softly.

"Yes, dear. She did not reject my affection. She thought not scorn of my love. She would have forgiven me, if I had erred against her, from very tenderness. Could you forgive me, child?"

"Father, I have not been good to you; but I will be, I will be," said Esther, laying her head on his knee.

He kissed her head. "Go to bed, my dear; I would be alone."

When Esther was lying down that night, she felt as if the little incidents between herself and her father on this Sunday had made it an epoch. Very slight words and deeds may have a sacramental efficacy, if we can cast our self-love behind us, in order to say or do them. And it has been well believed through many ages that the beginning of compunction is the beginning of a new life; that the mind which sees

itself blameless may be called dead in trespasses—in trespasses
on the love of others, in trespasses on their weakness, in trespasses on all those great claims which are the image of our
own need.

But Esther persisted in assuring herself that she was not
bending to any criticism from Felix. She was full of resentment against his rudeness, and yet more against his too harsh
conception of her character. She was determined to keep as
much at a distance from him as possible.

* * *

CHAPTER XIV.

This man's metallic; at a sudden blow
His soul rings hard. I cannot lay my palm,
Trembling with life, upon that jointed brass.
I shudder at the cold unanswering touch;
But if it press me in response, I'm bruised.

THE next morning, when the Debarrys, including the Rector, who had ridden over to the Manor early, were still seated
at breakfast, Christian came in with a letter, saying that it
had been brought by a man employed at the chapel in Malthouse Yard, who had been ordered by the minister to use all
speed and care in the delivery.

The letter was addressed to Sir Maximus.

"Stay, Christian, it may possibly refer to the lost pocket-
book," said Philip Debarry, who was beginning to feel rather
sorry for his factotum, as a reaction from previous suspicions
and indignation.

Sir Maximus opened the letter and felt for his glasses, but
then said, "Here, you read it, Phil: the man writes a hand
like small print."

Philip cast his eyes over it, and then read aloud in a tone
of satisfaction:

SIR,—I send this letter to apprise you that I have now in my possession certain articles which, last evening, at about half-past seven o'clock,
were found lying on the grass at the western extremity of your park.
The articles are—1°, a well-filled pocket-book, of brown leather, fastened
with a black ribbon and with a seal of red wax; 2°, a small note-book,
covered with gilded vellum, whereof the clasp was burst, and from out
whereof had partly escaped a small gold chain, with seals and a locket

attached, the locket bearing on the back a device, and round the face a female name.

Wherefore I request that you will further my effort to place these articles in the right hands, by ascertaining whether any person within your walls claims them as his property, and by sending that person to me (if such be found); for I will on no account let them pass from my care save into that of one who, declaring himself to be the owner, can state to me what is the impression on the seal, and what the device and name upon the locket.

I am, sir, yours to command in all right dealing,

RUFUS LYON.

MALTHOUSE YARD, Oct. 3, 1832.

"Well done, old Lyon," said the Rector; "I didn't think that any composition of his would ever give me so much pleasure."

"What an old fox it is!" said Sir Maximus. "Why couldn't he send the things to me at once along with the letter?"

"No, no, Max; he uses a justifiable caution," said the Rector, a refined and rather severe likeness of his brother, with a ring of fearlessness and decision in his voice which startled all flaccid men and unruly boys. "What are you going to do, Phil?" he added, seeing his nephew rise.

"To write, of course. Those other matters are yours, I suppose?" said Mr. Debarry, looking at Christian.

"Yes, sir."

"I shall send you with a letter to the preacher. You can describe your own property. And the seal, uncle—was it your coat-of-arms?"

"No, it was this head of Achilles. Here, I can take it off the ring, and you can carry it, Christian. But don't lose that, for I've had it ever since eighteen hundred. I should like to send my compliments with it," the Rector went on, looking at his brother, "and beg that since he has so much wise caution at command, he would exercise a little in more public matters, instead of making himself a firebrand in my parish, and teaching hucksters and tape-weavers that it's their business to dictate to statesmen."

"How did Dissenters, and Methodists, and Quakers, and people of that sort first come up, uncle?" said Miss Selina, a radiant girl of twenty, who had given much time to the harp.

"Dear me, Selina," said her elder sister, Harriet, whose forte was general knowledge, "don't you remember 'Woodstock'? They were in Cromwell's time."

"Oh! Holdenough, and those people? Yes; but they preached in the churches; they had no chapels. Tell me, uncle Gus; I like to be wise," said Selina, looking up at the face which was smiling down on her with a sort of severe benignity. "Phil says I'm an ignorant puss."

"The seeds of Nonconformity were sown at the Reformation, my dear, when some obstinate men made scruples about surplices and the place of the communion-table, and other trifles of that sort. But the Quakers came up about Cromwell's time, and the Methodists only in the last century. The first Methodists were regular clergymen, the more's the pity."

"But all those wrong things—why didn't government put them down?"

"Ah, to be sure," fell in Sir Maximus, in a cordial tone of corroboration.

"Because error is often strong, and government is often weak, my dear. Well, Phil, have you finished your letter?"

"Yes, I will read it to you," said Philip, turning and leaning over the back of his chair with the letter in his hand.

There is a portrait of Mr. Philip Debarry still to be seen at Treby Manor, and a very fine bust of him at Rome, where he died fifteen years later, a convert to Catholicism. His face would have been plain but for the exquisite setting of his hazel eyes, which fascinated even the dogs of the household. The other features, though slight and irregular, were redeemed from triviality by the stamp of gravity and intellectual preoccupation in his face and bearing. As he read aloud, his voice was what his uncle's might have been if it had been modulated by delicate health and a visitation of self-doubt.

Sir,—In reply to the letter with which you have favored me this morning, I beg to state that the articles you describe were lost from the pocket of my servant, who is the bearer of this letter to you, and is the claimant of the vellum note-book and the gold chain. The large leathern pocket-book is my own property, and the impression on the wax, a helmeted head of Achilles, was made by my uncle, the Rev. Augustus

11

Debarry, who allows me to forward his seal to you in proof that I am not making a mistaken claim.

I feel myself under deep obligation to you, sir, for the care and trouble you have taken in order to restore to its right owner a piece of property which happens to be of particular importance to me. And I shall consider myself doubly fortunate if at any time you can point out to me some method by which I may procure you as lively a satisfaction as I am now feeling, in that full and speedy relief from anxiety which I owe to your considerate conduct.

I remain, sir, your obliged and faithful servant,

PHILIP DEBARRY.

" You know best, Phil, of course," said Sir Maximus, pushing his plate from him, by way of interjection. " But it seems to me you exaggerate preposterously every little service a man happens to do for you. Why should you make a general offer of that sort? How do you know what he will be asking you to do? Stuff and nonsense! Tell Willis to send him a few head of game. You should think twice before you give a blank check of that sort to one of these quibbling, meddlesome Radicals."

" You are afraid of my committing myself to 'the bottomless perjury of an et cetera,'" said Philip, smiling, as he tunred to fold his letter. " But I think I am not doing any mischief; at all events, I could not be content to say less. And I have a notion that he would regard a present of game just now as an insult. I should, in his place."

" Yes, yes, you; but you don't make yourself a measure of Dissenting preachers, I hope," said Sir Maximus, rather wrathfully. " What do you say, Gus?"

" Phil is right," said the Rector, in an absolute tone. " I would not deal with a Dissenter, or put profits into the pocket of a Radical which I might put into the pocket of a good Churchman and a quiet subject. But if the greatest scoundrel in the world made way for me, or picked my hat up, I would thank him. So would you, Max."

" Pooh! I didn't mean that one shouldn't behave like a gentleman," said Sir Maximus, in some vexation. He had great pride in his son's superiority even to himself; but he did not enjoy having his own opinion argued down as it always was, and did not quite trust the dim vision opened by

Phil's new words and new notions. He could only submit in silence while the letter was delivered to Christian, with the order to start for Malthouse Yard immediately.

Meanwhile, in that somewhat dim locality the possible claimant of the note-book and the chain was thought of and expected with palpitating agitation. Mr. Lyon was seated in his study, looking haggard and already aged from a sleepless night. He was so afraid lest his emotion should deprive him of the presence of mind necessary to the due attention to particulars in the coming interview, that he continued to occupy his sight and touch with the objects which had stirred the depths, not only of memory, but of dread. Once again he unlocked a small box which stood beside his desk, and took from it a little oval locket, and compared this with one which hung with the seals on the stray gold chain. There was the same device in enamel on the back of both: clasped hands surrounded with blue flowers. Both had round the face a name in gold italics on a blue ground: the name on the locket taken from the drawer was *Maurice ;* the name on the locket which hung with the seals was *Annette,* and within the circle of this name there was a lover's knot of light-brown hair, which matched a curl that lay in the box. The hair in the locket which bore the name of Maurice was of a very dark brown, and before returning it to the drawer Mr. Lyon noted the color and quality of this hair more carefully than ever. Then he recurred to the note-book: undoubtedly there had been something, probably a third name, beyond the names *Maurice Christian,* which had themselves been rubbed and slightly smeared as if by accident; and from the very first examination in the vestry, Mr. Lyon could not prevent himself from transferring the mental image of the third name in faint lines to the rubbed leather. The leaves of the note-book seemed to have been recently inserted; they were of fresh white paper, and only one bore some abbreviations in pencil with a notation of small sums. Nothing could be gathered from the comparison of the writing in the book with that of the yellow letters which lay in the box: the smeared name had been carefully printed, and so bore no resemblance to the signature of those letters; and the pencil abbreviations and figures had been made too hurriedly to bear any decisive witness. "I will ask him to write—to write a description of the locket," had been one of Mr. Lyon's thoughts; but he faltered in that intention. His power of fulfilling it must depend on what he saw in this visitor, of whose coming he had a horrible dread, at the very time he was writing to demand it. In that demand he was obeying the voice of his rigid conscience, which had never left him perfectly at rest under his one act of deception—the concealment from Esther that he was not her natural father, the assertion of a false claim upon her. "Let my path be henceforth simple," he had said to himself in the anguish of that night; "let me seek to know what is, and if possible to declare it." If he was really going to find himself face to face with the man who had been Annette's husband, and who was Esther's father—if that wandering of his from the light had brought the punishment of a blind sacrilege as the issue of a conscious transgression,—he prayed that he might be able to accept all consequences of pain to himself. But he saw other possibilities concerning the claimant of the book and chain. His ignorance and suspicions as to the history and character of Annette's husband made it credible that he had laid a plan for convincing her of his death as a means of freeing himself from a burthensome tie; but it seemed equally probable that he was really dead, and that these articles of property had been a bequest, or a payment, or even a sale, to their present owner. Indeed, in all these years there was no knowing into how many hands such pretty trifles might have passed. And the claimant might, after all, have no connection with the Debarrys; he might not come on this day or the next. There might be more time left for reflection and prayer.

All these possibilities, which would remove the pressing need for difficult action, Mr. Lyon represented to himself, but he had no effective belief in them; his belief went with his strongest feeling, and in these moments his strongest feeling was dread. He trembled under the weight that seemed already added to his own sin; he felt himself already confronted by Annette's husband and Esther's father. Perhaps the father was a gentleman on a visit to the Debarrys. There was no hindering the pang with which the old man said to himself,—

"The child will not be sorry to leave this poor home, and I shall be guilty in her sight."

He was walking about among the rows of books when there came a loud rap at the outer door. The rap shook him so that he sank into his chair, feeling almost powerless. Lyddy presented herself.

"Here's ever such a fine man from the Manor wants to see you, sir. Dear heart, dear heart! shall I tell him you're too bad to see him?"

"Show him up," said Mr. Lyon, making an effort to rally. When Christian appeared, the minister half rose, leaning on an arm of his chair, and said, "Be seated, sir," seeing nothing but that a tall man was entering.

"I've brought you a letter from Mr. Debarry," said Christian, in an off-hand manner. This rusty little man, in his dismal chamber, seemed to the Ulysses of the steward's room a pitiable sort of human curiosity, to whom a man of the world would speak rather loudly, in accommodation to an eccentricity which was likely to be accompanied with deafness. One cannot be eminent in everything; and if Mr. Christian had dispersed his faculties in study that would have enabled him to share unconventional points of view, he might have worn a mistaken kind of boot, and been less competent to win at *écarté*, or at betting, or in any other contest suitable to a person of figure.

As he seated himself, Mr. Lyon opened the letter, and held it close to his eyes, so that his face was hidden. But at the word "servant" he could not avoid starting, and looking off the letter toward the bearer. Christian, knowing what was in the letter, conjectured that the old man was amazed to learn that so distinguished-looking a personage was a servant; he leaned forward with his elbows on his knees, balanced his cane on his fingers, and began a whispering whistle. The minister checked himself, finished the reading of the letter, and then slowly and nervously put on his spectacles to survey this man, between whose fate and his own there might be a terrible collision. The word "servant" had been a fresh caution to him. He must do nothing rashly. Esther's lot was deeply concerned.

"Here is the seal mentioned in the letter," said Christian.

Mr. Lyon drew the pocket-book from his desk, and after comparing the seal with the impression, said, "It is right, sir: I deliver the pocket-book to you."

He held it out with the seal, and Christian rose to take them, saying, carelessly, "The other things—the chain and the little book—are mine."

"Your name then is——"

"Maurice Christian."

A spasm shot through Mr. Lyon. It had seemed possible that he might hear another name, and be freed from the worse half of his anxiety. His next words were not wisely chosen, but escaped him impulsively.

"And you have no other name?"

"What do you mean?" said Christian sharply.

"Be so good as to reseat yourself."

Christian did not comply. "I'm rather in a hurry, sir," he said, recovering his coolness. "If it suits you to restore to me those small articles of mine, I shall be glad; but I would rather leave them behind than be detained." He had reflected that the minister was simply a punctilious old bore. The question meant nothing else. But Mr. Lyon had wrought himself up to the task of finding out, then and there, if possible, whether or not this were Annette's husband. How could he lay himself and his sin before God if he wilfully declined to learn the truth?

"Nay, sir, I will not detain you unreasonably," he said, in a firmer tone than before. "How long have these articles been your property?

"Oh, for more than twenty years," said Christian, carelessly.

He was not altogether easy under the minister's persistence, but for that very reason he showed no more impatience.

"You have been in France and in Germany?"

"I have been in most countries on the Continent."

"Be so good as to write me your name," said Mr. Lyon, dipping a pen in the ink, and holding it out with a piece of paper.

Christian was much surprised, but not now greatly alarmed. In his rapid conjectures as to the explanation of the minister's curiosity, he had alighted on one which might carry advantage rather than inconvenience. But he was not going to commit himself.

"Before I oblige you there, sir," he said, laying down the pen, and looking straight at Mr. Lyon, "I must know exactly the reasons you have for putting these questions to me. You are a stranger to me—an excellent person, I dare say—but I have no concern about you farther than to get from you those small articles. Do you still doubt that they are mine? You wished, I think, that I should tell you what the locket is like. It has a pair of hands and blue flowers on one side, and the name Annette round the hair on the other side. That is all I have to say. If you wish for anything more from me, you will be good enough to tell me why you wish it. Now then, sir, what is your concern with me?"

The cool stare, the hard challenging voice, with which these words were uttered, made them fall like the beating, cutting chill of heavy hail on Mr. Lyon. He sank back in his chair in utter irresolution and helplessness. How was it possible to lay bare the sad and sacred past in answer to such a call as this? The dread with which he had thought of this man's coming, the strongly confirmed suspicion that he was really Annette's husband, intensified the antipathy created by his gestures and glances. This sensitive little minister knew instinctively that words which would cost him efforts as painful as the obedient footsteps of a wounded bleeding hound that wills a foreseen throe, would fall on this man as the pressure of tender fingers falls on a brazen glove. And Esther—if this man was her father—every additional word might help to bring down irrevocable, perhaps cruel, consequences on her. A thick mist seemed to have fallen where Mr. Lyon was looking for the track of duty: the difficult question, how far he was to care for consequences in seeking and avowing the truth, seemed anew obscured. All these things, like the vision of a coming calamity, were compressed into a moment of consciousness. Nothing could be done to-day; everything must be deferred. He answered Christian in a low, apologetic tone.

"It is true, sir; you have told me all I can demand. I have no sufficient reason for detaining your property further.'

He handed the note-book and chain to Christian, who had been observing him narrowly, and now said, in a tone of indifference, as he pocketed the articles,—

"Very good, sir. I wish you a good-morning."

"Good-morning," said Mr. Lyon, feeling, while the door closed behind his guest, that mixture of uneasiness and relief which all procrastination of difficulty produces in minds capable of strong forecast. The work was still to be done. He had still before him the task of learning everything that could be learned about this man's relation to himself and Esther. Christian, as he made his way back along Malthouse Lane, was thinking, "This old fellow has got some secret in his head. It's not likely he can know anything about me: it must be about Bycliffe. But Bycliffe was a gentleman: how should he ever have had anything to do with such a seedy old ranter as that?"

CHAPTER XV.

And doubt shall be as lead upon the feet
Of thy most anxious will.

Mr. Lyon was careful to look in at Felix as soon as possible after Christian's departure, to tell him that his trust was discharged. During the rest of the day he was somewhat relieved from agitating reflections by the necessity of attending to his ministerial duties, the rebuke of rebellious singers being one of them; and on his return from the Monday evening prayer-meeting he was so overcome with weariness that he went to bed without taking note of any objects in his study. But when he rose the next morning, his mind, once more eagerly active, was arrested by Philip Debarry's letter, which still lay open on his desk, and was arrested by precisely that portion which had been unheeded the day before: "*I shall consider myself doubly fortunate if at any time you can point out to me some method by which I can procure you as lively a*

satisfaction as I am now feeling, in that full and speedy relief
from anxiety which I owe to your considerate conduct."

To understand how these words would carry the suggestion
they actually had for the minister in a crisis of peculiar personal anxiety and struggle, we must bear in mind that for
many years he had walked through life with the sense of having for a space been unfaithful to what he esteemed the highest trust ever committed to man—the ministerial vocation.
In a mind of any nobleness, a lapse into transgression against
an object still regarded as supreme, issues in a new and purer
devotedness, chastised by humility and watched over by a
passionate regret. So it was with that ardent spirit which
animated the little body of Rufus Lyon. Once in his life he
had been blinded, deafened, hurried along by rebellious impulse; he had gone astray after his own desires, and had let
the fire die out on the altar; and as the true penitent, hating
his self-besotted error, asks from all coming life duty instead
of joy, and service instead of ease, so Rufus was perpetually
on the watch lest he should ever again postpone to some private affection a great public opportunity which to him was
equivalent to a command.

Now here was an opportunity brought by a combination
of that unexpected incalculable kind which might be regarded
as the Divine emphasis invoking especial attention to trivial
events—an opportunity of securing what Rufus Lyon had
often wished for as a means of honoring truth, and exhibiting error in the character of a stammering, halting, short-
breathed usurper of office and dignity. What was more exasperating to a zealous preacher, with whom copious speech
was not a difficulty but a relief—who never lacked argument,
but only combatants and listeners—than to reflect that there
were thousands on thousands of pulpits in this kingdom, supplied with handsome sounding-boards, and occupying an ad-
vantageous position in buildings far larger than the chapel in
Malthouse Yard—buildings sure to be places of resort, even
as the markets were, if only from habit and interest; and that
these pulpits were filled, or rather made vacuous, by men
whose privileged education in the ancient centres of instruction
issued in twenty minutes' formal reading of tepid exhortation

or probably infirm deductions from premises based on rotten
scaffolding?   And it is in the nature of exasperation gradually
to concentrate itself.   The sincere antipathy of a dog toward
cats in general necessarily takes the form of indignant bark-
ing at the neighbor's black cat which makes daily trespass;
the bark at imagined cats, though a frequent exercise of the
canine mind, is yet comparatively feeble.   Mr. Lyon's sar-
casm was not without an edge when he dilated in general on an
elaborate education for teachers which issued in the minimum
of teaching, but it found a whetstone in the particular example of that bad system known as the Rector of Treby Magna.
There was nothing positive to be said against the Rev. Augustus Debarry; his life could not be pronounced blameworthy
except for its negatives.   And the good Rufus was too pure-
minded not to be glad of that.   He had no delight in vice as
discrediting wicked opponents; he shrank from dwelling on
the images of cruelty or of grossness, and his indignation was
habitually inspired only by those moral and intellectual mistakes which darken the soul but do not injure or degrade the
temple of the body.   If the Rector had been a less respectable
man, Rufus would have more reluctantly made him an object
of antagonism; but as an incarnation of self-destroying error,
dissociated from those baser sins which have no good repute
even with the worldly, it would be an argumentative luxury to
get into close quarters with him, and fight with a dialectic
short-sword in the eyes of the Treby world (sending also a
written account thereof to the chief organs of Dissenting opinion).   Vice was essentially stupid—a deaf and eyeless mon-
ster, insusceptible to demonstration: the Spirit might work
on it by unseen ways, and the unstudied sallies of sermons
were often as the arrows which pierced and awakened the
brutified conscience; but illuminated thought, finely dividing
speech, were the choicer weapons of the Divine armory, which
whoso could wield must be careful not to leave idle.

Here, then, was the longed-for opportunity.   Here was an
engagement—an expression of a strong wish—on the part of
Philip Debarry, if it were in his power, to procure a satisfaction to Rufus Lyon.   How had that man of God and exem-
plary Independent minister, Mr. Ainsworth, of persecuted

sanctity, conducted himself when a similar occasion had befallen him at Amsterdam? He had thought of nothing but the glory of the highest cause, and had converted the offer of recompense into a public debate with a Jew on the chief mysteries of the faith. Here was a model: the case was nothing short of a heavenly indication, and he, Rufus Lyon, would seize the occasion to demand a public debate with the Rector on the Constitution of the true Church.

What if he were inwardly torn by doubt and anxiety concerning his own private relations and the facts of his past life? That danger of absorption within the narrow bounds of self only urged him the more toward action which had a wider bearing, and might tell on the welfare of England at large. It was decided. Before the minister went down to his breakfast that morning he had written the following letter to Mr. Philip Debarry:

SIR,—Referring to your letter of yesterday, I find the following words: "I shall consider myself doubly fortunate if at any time you can point out to me some method by which I may procure you as lively a satisfaction as I am now feeling, in that full and speedy relief from anxiety which I owe to your considerate conduct."

I am not unaware, sir, that, in the usage of the world, there are words of courtesy (so called) which are understood, by those amongst whom they are current, to have no precise meaning, and to constitute no bond or obligation. I will not now insist that this is an abuse of language, wherein our fallible nature requires the strictest safeguards against laxity and misapplication, for I do not apprehend that in writing the words I have above quoted, you were open to the reproach of using phrases which, while seeming to carry a specific meaning, were really no more than what is called a polite form. I believe, sir, that you used these words advisedly, sincerely, and with an honorable intention of acting on them as a pledge, should such action be demanded. No other supposition on my part would correspond to the character you bear as a young man who aspires (albeit mistakenly) to engraft the finest fruits of public virtue on a creed and institutions whereof the sap is composed rather of human self-seeking than of everlasting truth.

Wherefore I act on this my belief in the integrity of your written word; and I beg you to procure for me (as it is doubtless in your power) that I may be allowed a public discussion with your near relative, the rector of this parish, the Reverend Augustus Debarry, to be held in the large room of the Free School, or in the Assembly Room of the Marquis of Granby, these being the largest covered spaces at our command. For I presume he would neither allow me to speak within his church, nor

would consent himself to speak within my chapel; and the probable in-clemency of the approaching season forbids an assured expectation that we could discourse in the open air. The subjects I desire to discuss are, —first, the Constitution of the true Church; and, secondly, the bearing thereupon of the English Reformation. Confidently expecting that you will comply with this request, which is the sequence of your expressed desire, I remain, sir, yours, with the respect offered to a sincere with-stander,   RUFUS LYON.
MALTHOUSE YARD.

After writing this letter, the good Rufus felt that serenity and elevation of mind which is infallibly brought by a preoc-cupation with the wider relations of things. Already he was beginning to sketch the course his argument might most judi-ciously take in the coming debate; his thoughts were running into sentences, and marking off careful exceptions in paren-theses; and he had come down and seated himself at the break-fast-table quite automatically, without expectation of toast or coffee, when Esther's voice and touch recalled him to an in-ward debate of another kind, in which he felt himself much weaker. Again there arose before him the image of that cool, hard-eyed, worldly man, who might be this dear child's father, and one against whose rights he had himself grievously of-fended. Always as the image recurred to him Mr. Lyon's heart sent forth a prayer for guidance, but no definite guid-ance had yet made itself visible for him. It could not be guidance—it was a temptation—that said, "Let the matter rest: seek to know no more; know only what is thrust upon you." The remembrance that in his time of wandering he had wilfully remained in ignorance of facts which he might have inquired after, deepened the impression that it was now an imperative duty to seek the fullest attainable knowledge. And the inquiry might possibly issue in a blessed repose, by putting a negative on all his suspicions. But the more vividly all the circumstances became present to him, the more unfit he felt himself to set about any investigation concerning this man who called himself Maurice Christian. He could seek no confidant or helper among "the brethren"; he was obliged to admit to himself that the members of his church, with whom he hoped to go to heaven, were not easy to converse with on earth touching the deeper secrets of his experience, and were still less able to advise him as to the wisest procedure, in a case of high delicacy, with a worldling who had a carefully trimmed whisker and a fashionable costume. For the first time in his life it occurred to the minister that he should be glad of an adviser who had more worldly than spiritual experience, and that it might not be inconsistent with his principles to seek some light from one who had studied human law. But it was a thought to be paused upon, and not followed out rashly; some other guidance might intervene.

Esther noticed that her father was in a fit of abstraction, that he seemed to swallow his coffee and toast quite unconsciously, and that he vented from time to time a low guttural interjection, which was habitual with him when he was absorbed by an inward discussion. She did not disturb him by remarks, and only wondered whether anything unusual had occurred on Sunday evening. But at last she thought it needful to say, " You recollect what I told you yesterday, father? "

" Nay, child; what? " said Mr. Lyon, rousing himself.

" That Mr. Jermyn asked me if you would probably be at home this morning before one o'clock."

Esther was surprised to see her father start and change color as if he had been shaken by some sudden collision before he answered,—

" Assuredly; I do not intend to move from my study after I have once been out to give this letter to Zachary."

" Shall I tell Lyddy to take him up at once to your study if he comes? If not, I shall have to stay in my own room, because I shall be at home all this morning, and it is rather cold now to sit without a fire."

" Yes, my dear, let him come up to me; unless, indeed, he should bring a second person, which might happen, seeing that in all likelihood he is coming, as hitherto, on electioneering business. And I could not well accommodate two visitors upstairs."

While Mr. Lyon went out to Zachary, the pew-opener, to give him a second time the commission of carrying a letter to Treby Manor, Esther gave her injunction to Lyddy that if one gentleman came he was to be shown upstairs—if two, they were to be shown into the parlor. But she had to resolve

various questions before Lyddy clearly saw what was expected
of her,—as that, "if it was the gentleman as came on Thursday in the pepper-and-salt coat, was he to be shown upstairs?
And the gentleman from the Manor yesterday as went out
whistling—had Miss Esther heard about him? There seemed
no end of these great folks coming to Malthouse Yard since
there was talk of the election; but they might be poor lost
creatures the most of 'em." Whereupon Lyddy shook her
head and groaned, under an edifying despair as to the future
lot of gentlemen callers.

Esther always avoided asking questions of Lyddy, who
found an answer as she found a key, by pouring out a pocket-
ful of miscellanies. But she had remarked so many indications that something had happened to cause her father unusual
excitement and mental preoccupation, that she could not help
connecting with them the fact of this visit from the Manor,
which he had not mentioned to her.

She sat down in the dull parlor and took up her netting;
for since Sunday she had felt unable to read when she was
alone, being obliged, in spite of herself, to think of Felix Holt
—to imagine what he would like her to be, and what sort of
views he took of life so as to make it seem valuable in the
absence of all elegance, luxury, gayety, or romance. Had he
yet reflected that he had behaved very rudely to her on Sunday? Perhaps not. Perhaps he had dismissed her from his
mind with contempt. And at that thought Esther's eyes
smarted unpleasantly. She was fond of netting, because it
showed to advantage both her hand and her foot; and across
this image of Felix Holt's indifference and contempt there
passed the vaguer image of a possible somebody who would
admire her hands and feet, and delight in looking at their
beauty, and long, yet not dare, to kiss them. Life would be
much easier in the presence of such a love. But it was precisely this longing after her own satisfaction that Felix had
reproached her with. Did he want her to be heroic? That
seemed impossible without some great occasion. Her life was
a heap of fragments, and so were her thoughts: some great
energy was needed to bind them together. Esther was beginning to lose her complacency at her own wit and criticism;

to lose the sense of superiority in an awakening need for reliance on one whose vision was wider, whose nature was purer and stronger than her own. But then, she said to herself, that "one" must be tender to her, not rude and predominating in his manners. A man with any chivalry in him could never adopt a scolding tone toward a woman—that is, toward a charming woman. But Felix had no chivalry in him. He loved lecturing and opinion too well ever to love any woman.

In this way Esther strove to see that Felix was thoroughly in the wrong—at least, if he did not come again expressly to show that he was sorry.

CHAPTER XVI.

TRUEBLUE. These men have no votes. Why should I court them?
GREYFOX. No votes, but power.
TRUEBLUE. What! over charities?
GREYFOX. No, over brains; which disturbs the canvass. In a natural state of things the average price of a vote at Paddlebrook is nine-and-sixpence, throwing the fifty-pound tenants, who cost nothing, into the divisor. But these talking men cause an artificial rise of prices.

THE expected important knock at the door came about twelve o'clock, and Esther could hear that there were two visitors. Immediately the parlor door was opened and the shaggy-haired, cravatless image of Felix Holt, which was just then full in the mirror of Esther's mind, was displaced by the highly contrasted appearance of a personage whose name she guessed before Mr. Jermyn had announced it. The perfect morning costume of that day differed much from our present ideal: it was essential that a gentleman's chin should be well propped, that his collar should have a voluminous roll, that his waistcoat should imply much discrimination, and that his buttons should be arranged in a manner which would now expose him to general contempt. And it must not be forgotten that at the distant period when Treby Magna first knew the excitements of an election, there existed many other anomalies now obsolete, besides short-waisted coats and broad stiffeners.

But we have some notions of beauty and fitness which with

stand the centuries; and quite irrespective of dates, it would be pronounced that at the age of thirty-four Harold Transome was a striking and handsome man. He was one of those people, as Denner had remarked, to whose presence in the room you could not be indifferent: if you do not hate or dread them, you must find the touch of their hands, nay, their very shadows, agreeable.

Esther felt a pleasure quite new to her as she saw his finely embrowned face and full bright eyes turned toward her with an air of deference by which gallantry must commend itself to a refined woman who is not absolutely free from vanity. Harold Transome regarded women as slight things, but he was fond of slight things in the intervals of business; and he held it among the chief arts of life to keep these pleasant diversions within such bounds that they should never interfere with the course of his serious ambition. Esther was perfectly aware, as he took a chair near her, that he was under some admiring surprise at her appearance and manner. How could it be otherwise? She believed that in the eyes of a high-bred man no young lady in Treby could equal her: she felt a glow of delight at the sense that she was being looked at.

"My father expected you," she said to Mr. Jermyn. "I delivered your letter to him yesterday. He will be down immediately."

She disentangled her foot from her netting and wound it up.

"I hope you are not going to let us disturb you," said Harold, noticing her action. "We come to discuss election affairs, and we particularly desire to interest the ladies."

"I have no interest with any one who is not already on the right side," said Esther, smiling.

"I am happy to see at least that you wear the Liberal colors."

"I fear I must confess that it is more from love of blue than from love of Liberalism. Yellow opinions could only have brunettes on their side." Esther spoke with her usual pretty fluency, but she had no sooner uttered the words than she thought how angry they would have made Felix.

"If my cause is to be recommended by the becomingness of

my colors, then I am sure you are acting in my interest by wearing them."

Esther rose to leave the room.

"Must you really go?" said Harold, preparing to open the door for her.

"Yes; I have an engagement—a lesson at half-past twelve," said Esther, bowing and floating out like a blue-robed Naïad, but not without a suffused blush as she passed through the doorway.

It was a pity the room was so small, Harold Transome thought: this girl ought to walk in a house where there were halls and corridors. But he had soon dismissed this chance preoccupation with Esther; for before the door was closed again Mr. Lyon had entered, and Harold was entirely bent on what had been the object of his visit. The minister, though no elector himself, had considerable influence over Liberal electors, and it was the part of wisdom in a candidate to cement all political adhesion by a little personal regard, if possible. Garstin was a harsh and wiry fellow; he seemed to suggest that sour whey, which some say was the original meaning of Whig in the Scottish, and it might assist the theoretic advantages of Radicalism if it could be associated with a more generous presence. What would conciliate the personal regard of old Mr. Lyon became a curious problem to Harold, now the little man made his appearance. But canvassing makes a gentleman acquainted with many strange animals, together with the ways of catching and taming them; and thus the knowledge of natural history advances amongst the aristocracy and the wealthy commoners of our land.

"I am very glad to have secured this opportunity of making your personal acquaintance, Mr. Lyon," said Harold, putting out his hand to the minister when Jermyn had mentioned his name. "I am to address the electors here, in the Market-Place, to-morrow; and I should have been sorry to do so without first paying my respects privately to my chief friends, as there may be points on which they particularly wish me to explain myself."

"You speak civilly, sir, and reasonably," said Mr. Lyon, with a vague short-sighted gaze, in which a candidate's ap-

12

pearance evidently went for nothing. "Pray be seated, gentlemen. It is my habit to stand."

He placed himself at a right angle with his visitors, his worn look of intellectual eagerness, slight frame, and rusty attire making an odd contrast with their flourishing persons, unblemished costume, and comfortable freedom from excitement. The group was fairly typical of the difference between the men who are animated by ideas and the men who are expected to apply them. Then he drew forth his spectacles, and began to rub them with the thin end of his coat-tail. He was inwardly exercising great self-mastery—suppressing the thought of his personal needs, which Jermyn's presence tended to suggest, in order that he might be equal to the larger duties of this occasion.

"I am aware—Mr. Jermyn has told me," said Harold, "what good service you have done me already, Mr. Lyon. The fact is, a man of intellect like you was especially needed in my case. The race I am running is really against Garstin only, who calls himself a Liberal, though he cares for nothing, and understands nothing, except the interests of the wealthy traders. And you have been able to explain the difference between Liberal and Liberal, which, as you and I know, is something like the difference between fish and fish."

"Your comparison is not unapt, sir," said Mr. Lyon, still holding his spectacles in his hand, "at this epoch, when the mind of the nation has been strained on the passing of one measure. Where a great weight has to be moved, we require not so much selected instruments as abundant horse-power. But it is an unavoidable evil of these massive achievements that they encourage a coarse undiscriminatingness obstructive of more nicely wrought results, and an exaggerated expectation inconsistent with the intricacies of our fallen and struggling condition. I say not that compromise is unnecessary, but it is an evil attendant on our imperfection; and I would pray every one to mark that, where compromise broadens, intellect and conscience are thrust into narrower room. Wherefore it has been my object to show our people that there are many who have helped to draw the car of Reform whose ends are but partial, and who forsake not the ungodly principle of selfish alliances, but would only substitute Syria for Egypt—thinking chiefly of their own share in peacocks, gold, and ivory."

"Just so," said Harold, who was quick at new languages, and still quicker at translating other men's generalities into his own special and immediate purposes, "men who will be satisfied if they can only bring in a plutocracy, buy up the land, and stick the old crests on their new gateways. Now the practical point to secure against these false Liberals at present is, that our electors should not divide their votes. As it appears that many who vote for Debarry are likely to split their votes in favor of Garstin, it is of the first consequence that my voters should give me plumpers. If they divide their votes they can't keep out Debarry, and they may help to keep out me. I feel some confidence in asking you to use your influence in this direction, Mr. Lyon. We candidates have to praise ourselves more than is graceful; but you are aware that, while I belong by my birth to the classes that have their roots in tradition and all the old loyalties, my experience has lain chiefly among those who make their own career, and depend on the new rather than the old. I have had the advantage of considering national welfare under varied lights: I have wider views than those of a mere cotton lord. On questions connected with religious liberty I would stop short at no measure that was not thorough."

"I hope not, sir—I hope not," said Mr. Lyon, gravely; finally putting on his spectacles and examining the face of the candidate, whom he was preparing to turn into a catechumen. For the good Rufus, conscious of his political importance as an organ of persuasion, felt it his duty to catechise a little, and also to do his part toward impressing a probable legislator with a sense of his responsibility. But the latter branch of duty somewhat obstructed the catechising, for his mind was so urged by considerations which he held in danger of being overlooked, that the questions and answers bore a very slender proportion to his exposition. It was impossible to leave the question of church-rates without noting the grounds of their injustice, and without a brief enumeration of reasons why Mr. Lyon, for his own part, would not present that passive resistance to a legal imposition which had been adopted by the Friends (whose heroism in this regard was nevertheless worthy of all honor).

Comprehensive talkers are apt to be tiresome when we are not athirst for information, but, to be quite fair, we must admit that superior reticence is a good deal due to the lack of matter. Speech is often barren; but silence also does not necessarily brood over a full nest. Your still fowl, blinking at you without remark, may all the while be sitting on one addled nest-egg; and when it takes to cackling, will have nothing to announce but that addled delusion.

Harold Transome was not at all a patient man, but in matters of business he was quite awake to his cue, and in this case it was perhaps easier to listen than to answer questions. But Jerymn, who had plenty of work on his hands, took an opportunity of rising, and saying, as he looked at his watch,—

"I must really be at the office in five minutes. You will find me there, Mr. Transome; you have probably still many things to say to Mr. Lyon."

"I beseech you, sir," said the minister, changing color, and by a quick movement laying his hand on Jermyn's arm—"I beseech you to favor me with an interview on some private business—this evening, if it were possible."

Mr. Lyon, like others who are habitually occupied with impersonal subjects, was liable to this impulsive sort of action. He snatched at the details of life as if they were darting past him—as if they were like the ribbons at his knees, which would never be tied all day if they were not tied on the instant. Through these spasmodic leaps out of his abstractions into real life, it constantly happened that he suddenly took a course which had been the subject of too much doubt with him ever to have been determined on by continuous thought. And if Jermyn had not startled him by threatening to vanish just when he was plunged in politics, he might never have made up his mind to confide in a worldly attorney.

("An odd man," as Mrs. Muscat observed, "to have such a gift in the pulpit. But there's one knows better than we do——" which, in a lady who rarely felt her judgment at a loss, was a concession that showed much piety.)

Jermyn was surprised at the little man's eagerness. "By all means," he answered, quite cordially. "Could you come to my office at eight o'clock?"

"For several reasons, I must beg you to come to me."

"Oh, very good. I'll walk out and see you this evening, if possible. I shall have much pleasure in being of any use to you." Jermyn felt that in the eyes of Harold he was appearing all the more valuable when his services were thus in request. He went out, and Mr. Lyon easily relapsed into politics, for he had been on the brink of a favorite subject on which he was at issue with his fellow-Liberals.

At that time, when faith in the efficacy of political change was at fever-heat in ardent Reformers, many measures which men are still discussing with little confidence on either side were then talked about and disposed of like property in near reversion. Crying abuses — "bloated paupers," "bloated pluralists," and other corruptions hindering men from being wise and happy—had to be fought against and slain. Such a time is a time of hope. Afterward, when the corpses of those monsters have been held up to the public wonder and abhorrence, and yet wisdom and happiness do not follow, but rather a more abundant breeding of the foolish and unhappy, comes a time of doubt and despondency. But in the great Reform year Hope was mighty : the prospect of Reform had even served the voters instead of drink; and in one place, at least, there had been "a dry election." And now the speakers at Reform banquets were exuberant in congratulation and promise : Liberal clergymen of the Establishment toasted Liberal Catholic clergymen without any allusion to scarlet, and Catholic clergymen replied with a like tender reserve. Some dwelt on the abolition of all abuses, and on millennial blessedness generally; others, whose imaginations were less suffused with exhalations of the dawn, insisted chiefly on the ballot-box.

Now on this question of the ballot the minister strongly took the negative side. Our pet opinions are usually those which place us in a minority of a minority amongst our own party :—very happily, else those poor opinions, born with no silver spoon in their mouths—how would they get nourished and fed? So it was with Mr. Lyon and his objection to the ballot. But he had thrown out a remark on the subject which was not quite clear to his hearer, who interpreted it according to his best calculation of probabilities.

"I have no objection to the ballot," said Harold, "but I think that is not the sort of a thing we have to work at just now. We shouldn't get it. And other questions are imminent."

"Then, sir, you would vote for the ballot?" said Mr. Lyon, stroking his chin.

"Certainly, if the point came up. I have too much respect for the freedom of the voter to oppose anything which offers a chance of making that freedom more complete."

Mr. Lyon looked at the speaker with a pitying smile and a subdued "h'm—m—m," which Harold took for a sign of satisfaction. He was soon undeceived.

"You grieve me, sir; you grieve me much. And I pray you to reconsider this question, for it will take you to the root, as I think, of political morality. I engage to show to any impartial mind, duly furnished with the principles of public and private rectitude, that the ballot would be pernicious, and that if it were not pernicious it would still be futile. I will show, first, that it would be futile as a preservative from bribery and illegitimate influence; and, secondly, that it would be in the worst kind pernicious, as shutting the door against those influences whereby the soul of a man and the character of a citizen are duly educated for their great functions. Be not alarmed if I detain you, sir. It is well worth the while."

"Confound this old man," thought Harold. "I'll never make a canvassing call on a preacher again, unless he has lost his voice from a cold." He was going to excuse himself as prudently as he could, by deferring the subject till the morrow, and inviting Mr. Lyon to come to him in the committee-room before the time appointed for his public speech; but he was relieved by the opening of the door. Lyddy put in her head to say,—

"If you please, sir, here's Mr. Holt wants to know if he may come in and speak to the gentleman. He begs your pardon, but you're to say 'no' if you don't like him to come."

"Nay, show him in at once, Lyddy. A young man," Mr. Lyon went on, speaking to Harold, "whom a representative ought to know—no voter, but a man of ideas and study."

"He is thoroughly welcome," said Harold, truthfully enough, though he felt little interest in the voteless man of ideas except as a diversion from the subject of the ballot. He had been standing for the last minute or two, feeling less of a victim in that attitude, and more able to calculate on means of escape.

"Mr. Holt, sir," said the minister, as Felix entered, "is a young friend of mine, whose opinions on some points I hope to see altered, but who has a zeal for public justice which I trust he will never lose."

"I am glad to see Mr. Holt," said Harold, bowing. He perceived from the way in which Felix bowed to him and turned to the most distant spot in the room that the candidate's shake of the hand would not be welcome here. "A formidable fellow," he thought, "capable of mounting a cart in the market-place to-morrow and cross-examining me, if I say anything that doesn't please him."

"Mr. Lyon," said Felix, "I have taken a liberty with you in asking to see Mr. Transome when he is engaged with you. But I have to speak to him on a matter which I shouldn't care to make public at present, and it is one on which I am sure you will back me. I heard that Mr. Transome was here, so I ventured to come. I hope you will both excuse me, as my business refers to some electioneering measures which are being taken by Mr. Transome's agents."

"Pray go on," said Harold, expecting something unpleasant.

"I'm not going to speak against treating voters," said Felix; "I suppose buttered ale, and grease of that sort to make the wheels go, belong to the necessary humbug of Representation. But I wish to ask you, Mr. Transome, whether it is with your knowledge that agents of yours are bribing rough fellows who are no voters—the colliers and navvies at Sproxton—with the chance of extra drunkenness, that they may make a posse on your side at the nomination and polling?"

"Certainly not," said Harold. "You are aware, my dear

sir, that a candidate is very much at the mercy of his agents as to the means by which he is returned, especially when many years' absence has made him a stranger to the men actually conducting business. But are you sure of your facts?"

"As sure as my senses can make me," said Felix, who then briefly described what had happened on Sunday. "I believed that you were ignorant of all this, Mr. Transome," he ended, "and that was why I thought some good might be done by speaking to you. If not, I should be tempted to expose the whole affair as a disgrace to the Radical party. I'm a Radical myself, and mean to work all my life long against privilege, monopoly, and oppression. But I would rather be a livery-servant proud of my master's title, than I would seem to make common cause with scoundrels who turn the best hopes of men into by-words for cant and dishonesty."

"Your energetic protest is needless here, sir," said Harold, offended at what sounded like a threat, and was certainly premature enough to be in bad taste. In fact, this error of behavior in Felix proceeded from a repulsion which was mutual. It was a constant source of irritation to him that the public men on his side were, on the whole, not conspicuously better than the public men on the other side; that the spirit of innovation, which with him was a part of religion, was in many of its mouthpieces no more of a religion than the faith in rotten boroughs; and he was thus predisposed to distrust Harold Transome. Harold, in his turn, disliked impracticable notions of loftiness and purity—disliked all enthusiasm; and he thought he saw a very troublesome, vigorous incorporation of that nonsense in Felix. But it would be foolish to exasperate him in any way.

"If you choose to accompany me to Jermyn's office," he went on, "the matter shall be inquired into in your presence. I think you will agree with me, Mr. Lyon,·that this will be the most satisfactory course?"

"Doubtless," said the minister, who liked the candidate very well, and believed that he would be amenable to argument; "and I would caution my young friend against a too great hastiness of words and action. David's cause against

Saul was a righteous one; nevertheless not all who clave unto David were righteous men."

"The more was the pity, sir," said Felix. "Especially if he winked at their malpractices."

Mr. Lyon smiled, shook his head, and stroked his favorite's arm deprecatingly.

"It is rather too much for any man to keep the consciences of all his party," said Harold. "If you had lived in the East, as I have, you would be more tolerant. More tolerant, for example, of an active industrious selfishness, such as we have here, though it may not always be quite scrupulous: you would see how much better it is than an idle selfishness. I have heard it said, a bridge is a good thing—worth helping to make, though half the men who worked at it were rogues."

"Oh, yes!" said Felix, scornfully, "give me a handful of generalities and analogies, and I'll undertake to justify Burke and Hare, and prove them benefactors of their species. I'll tolerate no nuisances but such as I can't help; and the question now is, not whether we can do away with all the nuisances in the world, but with a particular nuisance under our noses."

"Then we had better cut the matter short, as I propose, by going at once to Jermyn's," said Harold. "In that case, I must bid you good-morning, Mr. Lyon."

"I would fain," said the minister, looking uneasy—"I would fain have had a further opportunity of considering that question of the ballot with you. The reasons against it need not be urged lengthily; they only require complete enumeration to prevent any seeming hiatus, where an opposing fallacy might thrust itself in."

"Never fear, sir," said Harold, shaking Mr. Lyon's hand cordially, "there will be opportunities. Shall I not see you in the committee-room to-morrow?"

"I think not," said Mr. Lyon, rubbing his brow, with a sad remembrance of his personal anxieties. "But I will send you, if you will permit me, a brief writing, on which you can meditate at your leisure."

"I shall be delighted. Good-by."

Harold and Felix went out together; and the minister,

going up to his dull study, asked himself whether, under the pressure of conflicting experience, he had faithfully discharged the duties of the past interview?

If a cynical sprite were present, riding on one of the motes in that dusty room, he may have made himself merry at the illusions of the little minister who brought so much conscience to bear on the production of so slight an effect. I confess to smiling myself, being sceptical as to the effect of ardent appeals and nice distinctions on gentlemen who are got up, both inside and out, as candidates in the style of the period; but I never smiled at Mr. Lyon's trustful energy without falling to penitence and veneration immediately after. For what we call illusions are often, in truth, a wider vision of past and present realities—a willing movement of a man's soul with the larger sweep of the world's forces—a movement toward a more assured end than the chances of a single life. We see human heroism broken into units and say, this unit did little—might as well not have been. But in this way we might break up a great army into units; in this way we might break the sunlight into fragments, and think that this and the other might be cheaply parted with. Let us rather raise a monument to the soldiers whose brave hearts only kept the ranks unbroken, and met death—a monument to the faithful who were not famous, and who are precious as the continuity of the sunbeams is precious, though some of them fall unseen and on barrenness.

At present, looking back on that day at Treby, it seems to me that the sadder illusion lay with Harold Transome, who was trusting in his own skill to shape the success of his own morrows, ignorant of what many yesterdays had determined for him beforehand.

CHAPTER XVII.

It is a good and soothfast saw:
Half-roasted never will be raw;
No dough is dried once more to meal,
No crock new-shapen by the wheel;
You can't turn curds to milk again,
Nor Now, by wishing back to Then;
And having tasted stolen honey,
You can't buy innocence for money.

JERMYN was not particularly pleased that some chance had apparently hindered Harold Transome from making other canvassing visits immediately after leaving Mr. Lyon, and so had sent him back to the office earlier than he had been expected to come. The inconvenient chance he guessed at once to be represented by Felix Holt, whom he knew very well by Trebian report to be a young man with so little of the ordinary Christian motives as to making an appearance and getting on in the world, that he presented no handle to any judicious and respectable person who might be willing to make use of him.

Harold Transome, on his side, was a good deal annoyed at being worried by Felix into an inquiry about electioneering details. The real dignity and honesty there was in him made him shrink from this necessity of satisfying a man with a troublesome tongue; it was as if he were to show indignation at the discovery of one barrel with a false bottom, when he had invested his money in a manufactory where a larger or smaller number of such barrels had always been made. A practical man must seek a good end by the only possible means; that is to say, if he is to get into Parliament he must not be too particular. It was not disgraceful to be neither a Quixote nor a theorist, aiming to correct the moral rules of the world; but whatever actually was, or might prove to be, disgraceful, Harold held in detestation. In this mood he pushed on unceremoniously to the inner office without waiting to ask questions; and when he perceived that Jermyn was not alone, he said, with haughty quickness,—

"A question about the electioneering at Sproxton. Can you

give your attention to it at once? Here is Mr. Holt, who has come to me about the business."

"A—yes—a—certainly," said Jermyn, who, as usual, was the more cool and deliberate because he was vexed. He was standing, and, as he turned round, his broad figure concealed the person who was seated writing at the bureau. "Mr. Holt —a—will doubtless—a—make a point of saving a busy man's time. You can speak at once. This gentleman"—here Jermyn make a slight backward movement of the head—"is one of ourselves; he is a true-blue."

"I have simply to complain," said Felix, "that one of your agents has been sent on a bribing expedition to Sproxton— with what purpose you, sir, may know better than I do. Mr. Transome, it appears, was ignorant of the affair, and does not approve it."

Jermyn, looking gravely and steadily at Felix while he was speaking, at the same time drew forth a small sheaf of papers from his side-pocket, and then, as he turned his eyes slowly on Harold, felt in his waistcoat pocket for his pencil-case.

"I don't approve it at all," said Harold, who hated Jermyn's calculated slowness and conceit in his own impenetrability. "Be good enough to put a stop to it, will you?"

"Mr. Holt, I know, is an excellent Liberal," said Jermyn, just inclining his head to Harold, and then alternately looking at Felix and docketing his bills; "but he is perhaps too inexperienced to be aware that no canvass—a—can be conducted without the action of able men, who must—a—be trusted, and not interfered with. And as to any possibility of promising to put a stop—a—to any procedure—a—that depends. If he had ever held the coachman's ribbons in his hands, as I have in my younger days—a—he would know that stopping is not always easy."

"I know very little about holding ribbons," said Felix; "but I saw clearly enough at once that more mischief had been done than could be well mended. Though I believe, if it were heartily tried, the treating might be reduced, and something might be done to hinder the men from turning out in a body to make a noise, which might end in worse."

"They might be hindered from making a noise on our side,"

said Jermyn, smiling. "That is perfectly true. But if they made a noise on the other—would your purpose be answered better, sir?"

Harold was moving about in an irritated manner while Felix and Jermyn were speaking. He preferred leaving the talk to the attorney, of whose talk he himself liked to keep as clear as possible.

"I can only say," answered Felix, "that if you make use of those heavy fellows when the drink is in them, I shouldn't like your responsibility. You might as well drive bulls to roar on our side as bribe a set of colliers and navvies to shout and groan."

"A lawyer may well envy your command of language, Mr. Holt," said Jermyn, pocketing his bills again, and shutting up his pencil; "but he would not be satisfied with the accuracy—a—of your terms. You must permit me to check your use of the word 'bribery.' The essence of bribery is, that it should be legally proved; there is not such a thing—a—*in rerum natura*—a—as unproved bribery. There has been no such thing as bribery at Sproxton, I'll answer for it. The presence of a body of stalwart fellows on—a—the Liberal side will tend to preserve order; for we know that the benefit clubs from the Pitchley district will show for Debarry. Indeed, the gentleman who has conducted the canvass at Sproxton is experienced in Parliamentary affairs, and would not exceed—a—the necessary measures that a rational judgment would dictate."

"What! you mean the man who calls himself Johnson?" said Felix, in a tone of disgust.

Before Jermyn chose to answer, Harold broke in, saying, quickly and peremptorily, "The long and the short of it is this, Mr. Holt: I shall desire and insist that whatever can be done by way of remedy shall be done. Will that satisfy you? You see now some of a candidate's difficulties?" said Harold, breaking into his most agreeable smile. "I hope you will have some pity for me."

"I suppose I must be content," said Felix, not thoroughly propitiated. "I bid you good-morning, gentlemen."

When he was gone out, and had closed the door behind

him, Harold, turning round and flashing, in spite of himself, an angry look at Jermyn, said,—

"And who is Johnson? an *alias*, I suppose. It seems you are fond of the name."

Jermyn turned perceptibly paler, but disagreeables of this sort between himself and Harold had been too much in his anticipations of late for him to be taken by surprise. He turned quietly round and just touched the shoulder of the person seated at the bureau, who now rose.

"On the contrary," Jermyn answered, "the Johnson in question is this gentleman, whom I have the pleasure of introducing to you as one of my most active helpmates in electioneering business—Mr. Johnson, of Bedford Row, London. I am comparatively a novice—a—in these matters. But he was engaged with James Putty in two hardly contested elections, and there could scarcely be a better initiation. Putty is one of the first men of the country as an agent—a—on the Liberal side—a—eh, Johnson? I think Makepiece is—a—not altogether a match for him, not quite of the same calibre—a— *haud consimili ingenio*—a—in tactics—a—and in experience?"

"Makepiece is a wonderful man, and so is Putty," said the glib Johnson, too vain not to be pleased with an opportunity of speaking, even when the situation was rather awkward. "Makepiece for scheming, but Putty for management. Putty knows men, sir," he went on, turning to Harold; "it's a thousand pities that you have not had his talents employed in your service. He's beyond any man for saving a candidate's money—does half the work with his tongue. He'll talk of anything, from the Areopagus, and that sort of thing, down to the joke about 'Where are you going, Paddy?'—you know what I mean, sir! 'Back again, says Paddy'—an excellent electioneering joke. Putty understands these things. He has said to me, 'Johnson, bear in mind there are two ways of speaking an audience will always like: one is, to tell them what they don't understand; and the other is, to tell them what they're used to.' I shall never be the man to deny that I owe a great deal to Putty. I always say it was a most providential thing in the Mugham election last year that Putty was not on the Tory side. He managed the women; and, if you'll believe me, sir, one-fourth of the men would never have voted if their wives hadn't driven them to it for the good of their families. And as for speaking—it's currently reported in our London circles that Putty writes regularly for the *Times*. He has that kind of language; and I needn't tell you, Mr. Transome, that it's the apex, which, I take it, means the tip-top—and nobody can get higher than that, I think. I've belonged to a political debating society myself; I've heard a little language in my time; but when Mr. Jermyn first spoke to me about having the honor to assist in your canvass of North Loamshire"—here Johnson played with his watch-seals and balanced himself a moment on his toes—"the very first thing I said was, 'And there's Garstin has got Putty! No Whig could stand against a Whig,' I said, 'who had Putty on his side: I hope Mr. Transome goes in for something of a deeper color.' I don't say that, as a general rule, opinions go for much in a return, Mr. Transome; it depends on who are in the field before you, and on the skill of your agents. But as a Radical, and a moneyed Radical, you are in a fine position, sir; and with care and judgment—with care and judgment——"

It had been impossible to interrupt Johnson before, without the most impolitic rudeness. Jermyn was not sorry that he should talk, even if he made a fool of himself; for in that solid shape, exhibiting the average amount of human foibles, he seemed less of the *alias* which Harold had insinuated him to be, and had all the additional plausibility of a lie with a circumstance.

Harold had thrown himself with contemptuous resignation into a chair, had drawn off one of his buff gloves, and was looking at his hand. But when Johnson gave his iteration with a slightly slackened pace, Harold looked up at him and broke in,—

"Well, then, Mr. Johnson, I shall be glad if you will use your care and judgment in putting an end, as well as you can, to this Sproxton affair; else it may turn out an ugly business."

"Excuse me, sir; I must beg you to look at the matter a little more closely. You will see that it is impossible to take a single step backward at Sproxton. It was a matter of ne-

cessity to get the Sproxton men; else I know to a certainty
the other side would have laid hold of them first, and now
I've undermined Garstin's people. They'll use their authority, and give a little shabby treating, but I've taken all the
wind out of their sails. But if, by your orders, I or Mr.
Jermyn here were to break promise with the honest fellows,
and offend Chubb the publican, what would come of it?
Chubb would leave no stone unturned against you, sir; he
would egg on his customers against you; the colliers and navvies would be at the nomination and at the election all the
same, or rather not all the same, for they would be there
against us; and instead of hustling people good-humoredly by
way of a joke, and counterbalancing Debarry's cheers, they'd
help to kick the cheering and the voting out of our men, and
instead of being, let us say, half a dozen ahead of Garstin,
you'd be half a dozen behind him, that's all. I speak plain
English to you, Mr. Transome, though I've the highest respect
for you as a gentleman of first-rate talents and position. But,
sir, to judge of these things a man must know the English
voter and the English publican; and it would be a poor tale
indeed"—here Mr. Johnson's mouth took an expression at
once bitter and pathetic—"that a gentleman like you, to say
nothing of the good of the country, should have gone to the
expense and trouble of a canvass for nothing but to find himself out of Parliament at the end of it. I've seen it again and
again; it looks bad in the cleverest man to have to sing small."

Mr. Johnson's argument was not the less stringent because
his idioms were vulgar. It requires a conviction and resolution amounting to heroism not to wince at phrases that class
our foreshadowed endurance among those common and igno-
minious troubles which the world is more likely to sneer at than
to pity. Harold remained a few moments in angry silence
looking at the floor, with one hand on his knee and the other
on his hat, as if he were preparing to start up.

"As to undoing anything that's been done down there," said
Johnson, throwing in this observation as something into the
bargain, "I must wash my hands of it, sir. I couldn't work
knowingly against your interest. And that young man who
has just gone out,—you don't believe that he need be listened

to, I hope? Chubb, the publican, hates him. Chubb would guess he was at the bottom of your having the treating stopped, and he'd set half a dozen of the colliers to duck him in the canal, or break his head by mistake. I'm an experienced man, sir. I hope I've put it clear enough."

"Certainly, the exposition befits the subject," said Harold, scornfully, his dislike of the man Johnson's personality being stimulated by causes which Jermyn more than conjectured. "It's a damned, unpleasant, ravelled business that you and Mr. Jermyn have knit up between you. I've no more to say."

"Then, sir, if you've no more commands, I don't wish to intrude. I shall wish you good-morning, sir," said Johnson, passing out quickly.

Harold knew that he was indulging his temper, and he would probably have restrained it as a foolish move if he had thought there was great danger in it. But he was beginning to drop much of his caution and self-mastery where Jermyn was concerned, under the growing conviction that the attorney had very strong reasons for being afraid of him; reasons which would only be re-enforced by any action hostile to the Transome interest. As for a sneak like this Johnson, a gentleman had to pay him, not to please him. Harold had smiles at command in the right place, but he was not going to smile when it was neither necessary nor agreeable. He was one of those good-humored, yet energetic men, who have the gift of anger, hatred, and scorn upon occasion, though they are too healthy and self-contented for such feelings to get generated in them without external occasion. And in relation to Jermyn the gift was coming into fine exercise.

"A—pardon me, Mr. Harold," said Jermyn, speaking as soon as Johnson went out, "but I am sorry—a—you should behave disobligingly to a man who has it in his power to do much service—who, in fact, holds many threads in his hands. I admit that—a—*nemo mortalium omnibus horis sapit*, as we say—a——"

"Speak for yourself," said Harold. "I don't talk in tags of Latin, which might be learned by a schoolmaster's footboy. I find the King's English express my meaning better."

"In the King's English, then," said Jermyn, who could be

13

idiomatic enough when he was stung, "a candidate should keep his kicks till he's a member."

"Oh, I suppose Johnson will bear a kick if you bid him. You're his principal, I believe."

"Certainly, thus far—a—he is my London agent. But he is a man of substance, and——"

"I shall know what he is if it's necessary, I dare say. But I must jump into the carriage again. I've no time to lose; I must go to Hawkins at the factory. Will you go?"

When Harold was gone, Jermyn's handsome face gathered blackness. He hardly ever wore his worst expression in the presence of others, and but seldom when he was alone, for he was not given to believe that any game would ultimately go against him. His luck had been good. New conditions might always turn up to give him new chances; and if affairs threatened to come to an extremity between Harold and himself, he trusted to finding some sure resource.

"He means to see to the bottom of everything if he can, that's quite plain," said Jermyn to himself. "I believe he has been getting another opinion; he has some new light about those annuities on the estate that are held in Johnson's name. He has inherited a deuced faculty for business—there's no denying that. But I shall beg leave to tell him that I've propped up the family. I don't know where they would have been without me; and if it comes to balancing, I know into which scale the gratitude ought to go. Not that he's likely to feel any—but he can feel something else; and if he make signs of setting the dogs on me, I shall make him feel it. The people named Transome owe me a good deal more than I owe them."

In this way Mr. Jermyn inwardly appealed against an unjust construction which he foresaw that his old acquaintance the Law might put on certain items in his history.

I have known persons who have been suspected of undervaluing gratitude, and excluding it from the list of virtues; but on closer observation it has been seen that, if they have never felt grateful, it has been for want of an opportunity; and that, far from despising gratitude, they regard it as the virtue most of all incumbent—on others toward them.

CHAPTER XVIII.

The little, nameless, unremembered acts
Of kindness and of love.
WORDSWORTH: *Tintern Abbey.*

JERMYN did not forget to pay his visit to the minister in Malthouse Yard that evening. The mingled irritation, dread, and defiance which he was feeling toward Harold Transome in the middle of the day, depended on too many and far-stretching causes to be dissipated by eight o'clock; but when he left Mr. Lyon's house he was in a state of comparative triumph in the belief that he, and he alone, was now in possession of facts which, once grouped together, made a secret that gave him new power over Harold.

Mr. Lyon, in his need for help from one who had that wisdom of the serpent which, he argued, is not forbidden, but is only of hard acquirement to dove-like innocence, had been gradually led to pour out to the attorney all the reasons which made him desire to know the truth about the man who called himself Maurice Christian: he had shown all the precious relics, the locket, the letters, and the marriage certificate. And Jermyn had comforted him by confidently promising to ascertain, without scandal or premature betrayals, whether this man were really Annette's husband, Maurice Christian Bycliffe.

Jermyn was not rash in making this promise, since he had excellent reasons for believing that he had already come to a true conclusion on the subject. But he wished both to know a little more of this man himself, and to keep Mr. Lyon in ignorance—not a difficult precaution—in an affair which it cost the minister so much pain to speak of. An easy opportunity of getting an interview with Christian was sure to offer itself before long—might even offer itself to-morrow. Jermyn had seen him more than once, though hitherto without any reason for observing him with interest; he had heard that Philip Debarry's courier was often busy in the town, and it seemed especially likely that he would be seen there when the

Market was to be agitated by politics, and the new candidate was to show his paces.

The world of which Treby Magna was the centre was naturally curious to see the young Transome, who had come from the East, was as rich as a Jew, and called himself a Radical; characteristics all equally vague in the minds of various excellent ratepayers, who drove to market in their taxed carts, or in their hereditary gigs. Places at convenient windows had been secured beforehand for a few best bonnets; but, in general, a Radical candidate excited no ardent feminine partisanship, even among the Dissenters in Treby, if they were of the prosperous and long-resident class. Some chapel-going ladies were fond of remembering that "their family had been Church"; others objected to politics altogether as having spoiled old neighborliness, and sundered friends who had kindred views as to cowslip wine and Michaelmas cleaning; others, of the melancholy sort, said it would be well if people would think less of reforming Parliament and more of pleasing God. Irreproachable Dissenting matrons, like Mrs. Muscat, whose youth had been passed in a short-waisted bodice and tight skirt, had never been animated by the struggle for liberty, and had a timid suspicion that religion was desecrated by being applied to the things of this world. Since Mr. Lyon had been in Malthouse Yard there had been far too much mixing up of politics with religion; but, at any rate, these ladies had never yet been to hear speechifying in the marketplace, and they were not going to begin that practice.

Esther, however, had heard some of her feminine acquaintances say that they intended to sit at the druggist's upper window, and she was inclined to ask her father if he could think of a suitable place where she also might see and hear. Two inconsistent motives urged her. She knew that Felix cared earnestly for all public questions, and she supposed that he held it one of her deficiencies not to care about them: well, she would try to learn the secret of this ardor, which was so strong in him that it animated what she thought the dullest form of life. She was not too stupid to find it out. But this self-correcting motive was presently displaced by a motive of a different sort. It had been a pleasant variety in her monot-

onous days to see a man like Harold Transome, with a distinguished appearance and polished manners, and she would like
to see him again: he suggested to her that brighter and more
luxurious life on which her imagination dwelt without the
painful effort it required to conceive the mental condition
which would place her in complete sympathy with Felix Holt.
It was this less unaccustomed prompting of which she was
chiefly conscious when she awaited her father's coming down
to breakfast? Why, indeed, should she trouble herself so
much about Felix?

Mr. Lyon, more serene now that he had unbosomed his
anxieties and obtained a promise of help, was already swim-
ming so happily in the deep water of polemics in expectation
of Philip Debarry's answer to his challenge, that, in the occupation of making a few notes lest certain felicitous inspira-
tions should be wasted, he had forgotten to come down to
breakfast. Esther, suspecting his abstraction, went up to his
study, and found him at his desk looking up with wonder at
her interruption.

"Come, father, you have forgotten your breakfast."

"It is true, child; I will come," he said, lingering to make
some final strokes.

"Oh, you naughty father!" said Esther, as he got up from
his chair, "your coat-collar is twisted, your waistcoat is buttoned all wrong, and you have not brushed your hair. Sit
down and let me brush it again as I did yesterday."

He sat down obediently, while Esther took a towel, which
she threw over his shoulders, and then brushed the thick long
fringe of soft auburn hair. This very trifling act, which she
had brought herself to for the first time yesterday, meant a
great deal in Esther's little history. It had been her habit to
leave the mending of her father's clothes to Lyddy; she had
not liked even to touch his cloth garments; still less had it
seemed a thing she would willingly undertake to correct his
toilet and use a brush for him. But having once done this
under her new sense of faulty omission, the affectionateness
that was in her flowered so pleasantly, as she saw how much
her father was moved by what he thought a great act of tenderness, that she quite longed to repeat it. This morning, as

he sat under her hands, his face had such a calm delight in it
that she could not help kissing the top of his bald head; and
afterward, when they were seated at breakfast, she said, merrily,—

"Father, I shall make a *petit maître* of you by and by;
your hair looks so pretty and silken when it is well brushed."

"Nay, child, I trust that while I would willingly depart
from my evil habit of a somewhat slovenly forgetfulness in
my attire, I shall never arrive at the opposite extreme. For
though there is that in apparel which pleases the eye, and I
deny not that your neat gown and the color thereof—which is
that of certain little flowers that spread themselves in the
hedgerows, and make a blueness there as of the sky when it is
deepened in the water,—I deny not, I say, that these minor
strivings after a perfection which is, as it were, an irrecover-
able yet haunting memory, are a good in their proportion.
Nevertheless, the brevity of our life, and the hurry and crush
of the great battle with error and sin, often oblige us to an
advised neglect of what is less momentous. This, I conceive,
is the principle on which my friend Felix Holt acts; and I
cannot but think the light comes from the true fount, though
it shines through obstructions."

"You have not seen Mr. Holt since Sunday, have you,
father?"

"Yes; he was here yesterday. He sought Mr. Transome,
having a matter of some importance to speak upon with him.
And I saw him afterward in the street, when he agreed that I
should call for him this morning before I go into the market-
place. He will have it," Mr. Lyon went on, smiling, "that I
must not walk about in the crowd without him to act as my
special constable."

Esther felt vexed with herself that her heart was suddenly
beating with unusual quickness, and that her last resolution
not to trouble herself about what Felix thought had trans-
formed itself with magic swiftness into mortification that he
evidently avoided coming to the house when she was there,
though he used to come on the slightest occasion. He knew
that she was always at home until the afternoon on market-
days; that was the reason why he would not call for her

father. Of course, it was because he attributed such littleness to her that he supposed she would retain nothing else than a feeling of offence toward him for what he had said to her. Such distrust of any good in others, such arrogance of immeasurable superiority, was extremely ungenerous. But presently she said,—

"I should have liked to hear Mr. Transome speak, but I suppose it is too late to get a place now."

"I am not sure; I would fain have you go if you desire it, my dear," said Mr. Lyon, who could not bear to deny Esther any lawful wish. "Walk with me to Mistress Holt's, and we will learn from Felix, who will doubtless already have been out, whether he could lead you in safety to Friend Lambert's."

Esther was glad of the proposal, because, if it answered no other purpose, it would be an easy way of obliging Felix to see her, and of showing him that it was not she who cherished offence. But when, later in the morning, she was walking toward Mrs. Holt's with her father, they met Mr. Jermyn, who stopped them to ask, in his most affable manner, whether Miss Lyon intended to hear the candidate, and whether she had secured a suitable place. And he ended by insisting that his daughters, who were presently coming in an open carriage, should call for her, if she would permit them. It was impossible to refuse this civility, and Esther turned back to await the carriage, pleased with the certainty of hearing and seeing, yet sorry to miss Felix. There was another day for her to think of him with unsatisfied resentment, mixed with some longings for a better understanding; and in our springtime every day has its hidden growths in the mind, as it has in the earth when the little folded blades are getting ready to pierce the ground.

CHAPTER XIX.

Consistency ?—I never changed my mind,
Which is, and always was, to live at ease.

It was only in the time of the summer fairs that the
market-place had ever looked more animated than it did under
that autumn mid-day sun. There were plenty of blue cockades
and streamers, faces at all the windows, and a crushing buzz-
ing crowd, urging each other backward and forward round
the small hustings in front of the Ram Inn, which showed its
more plebeian sign at right angles with the venerable Marquis
of Granby. Sometimes there were scornful shouts, sometimes a rolling cascade of cheers, sometimes the shriek of a
penny whistle; but above all these fitful and feeble sounds,
the fine old church-tower, which looked down from above the
trees on the other side of the narrow stream, sent vibrating,
at every quarter, the sonorous tones of its great bell, the Good
Queen Bess.

Two carriages, with blue ribbons on the harness, were conspicuous near the hustings. One was Jermyn's, filled with
the brilliantly attired daughters, accompanied by Esther,
whose quieter dress helped to mark her out for attention as
the most striking of the group. The other was Harold Transome's; but in this there was no lady—only the olive-skinned
Dominic, whose acute yet mild face was brightened by the
occupation of amusing little Harry and rescuing from his
tyrannies a King Charles puppy, with big eyes, much after
the pattern of the boy's.

This Trebian crowd did not count for much in the political
force of the nation, but it was not the less determined as to
lending or not lending its ears. No man was permitted to
speak from the platform except Harold and his uncle Lingon,
though, in the interval of expectation, several Liberals had
come forward. Among these ill-advised persons the one whose
attempt met the most emphatic resistance was Rufus Lyon.
This might have been taken for resentment at the unreasonableness of the cloth, that, not content with pulpits, from

whence to tyrannize over the ears of men, wishes to have the larger share of the platforms; but it was not so, for Mr. Lingon was heard with much cheering, and would have been welcomed again.

The Rector of Little Treby had been a favorite in the neighborhood since the beginning of the century. A clergyman thoroughly unclerical in his habits had a piquancy about him which made him a sort of practical joke. He had always been called Jack Lingon, or Parson Jack—sometimes, in older and less serious days, even "Cock-fighting Jack." He swore a little when the point of a joke seemed to demand it, and was fond of wearing a colored bandana tied loosely over his cravat, together with large brown leather leggings; he spoke in a pithy familiar way that people could understand, and had none of that frigid mincingness called dignity, which some have thought a peculiar clerical disease. In fact, he was "a character"—something cheerful to think of, not entirely out of connection with Sunday and sermons. And it seemed in keeping that he should have turned sharp round in politics, his opinions being only part of the excellent joke called Parson Jack. When his red eagle face and white hair were seen on the platform, the Dissenters hardly cheered this questionable Radical; but to make amends, all the Tory farmers gave him a friendly "hurray." "Let's hear what old Jack will say for himself," was the predominant feeling among them; "he'll have something funny to say, I'll bet a penny."

It was only Lawyer Labron's young clerks and their hangers-on who were sufficiently dead to Trebian traditions to assail the parson with various sharp-edged interjections, such as broken shells, and cries of "Cock-a-doodle-doo."

"Come now, my lads," he began, in his full, pompous, yet jovial tones, thrusting his hands into the stuffed-out pockets of his greatcoat, "I'll tell you what; I'm a parson, you know; I ought to return good for evil. So here are some good nuts for you to crack in return for your shells."

There was a roar of laughter and cheering as he threw handfuls of nuts and filberts among the crowd.

"Come now, you'll say I used to be a Tory; and some of you, whose faces I know as well as I know the head of my own crab-stick, will say that's why I'm a good fellow. But now I'll tell you something else. It's for that very reason— that I used to be a Tory, and am a good fellow—that I go along with my nephew here, who is a thorough-going Liberal. For will anybody here come forward and say, 'A good fellow has no need to tack about and change his road'? No, there's not one of you such a Tom-noddy. What's good for one time is bad for another. If anybody contradicts that, ask him to eat pickled pork when he's thirsty, and to bathe in the Lapp there when the spikes of ice are shooting. And that's the reason why the men who are the best Liberals now are the very men who used to be the best Tories. There isn't a nastier horse than your horse that'll jib and back and turn round when there is but one road for him to go, and that's the road before him.

"And my nephew here—he comes of a Tory breed, you know—I'll answer for the Lingons. In the old Tory times there was never a pup belonging to a Lingon but would howl if a Whig came near him. The Lingon blood is good, rich, old Tory blood—like good rich milk—and that's why, when the right time comes, it throws up a Liberal cream. The best sort of a Tory turns to the best sort of Radical. There's plenty of Radical scum—I say, beware of the scum, and look out for the cream. And here's my nephew—some of the cream if there is any: none of your Whigs, none of your painted water that looks as if it ran, and it's standing still all the while; none of your spinning-jenny fellows. A gentle- man; but up to all sorts of business. I'm no fool myself; I'm forced to wink a good deal, for fear of seeing too much, for a neighborly man must let himself be cheated a little. But though I've never been out of my own country, I know less about it than my nephew does. You may tell what he is, and only look at him. There's one sort of fellow sees nothing but the end of his own nose, and another sort that sees noth- ing but the hinder side of the moon; but my nephew Harold is of another sort; he sees everything that's at hitting dis- tance, and he's not one to miss his mark. A good-looking man in his prime! Not a greenhorn; not a shrivelled old fellow, who'll come to speak to you and find he's left his teeth

t home by mistake.   Harold Transome will do you credit; if
anybody says the Radicals are a set of sneaks, Brummagem
halfpennies, scamps who want to play pitch-and-toss with the
property of the country, you can say, ' Look at the member
for North Loamshire!'   And mind what you'll hear him say;
he'll go in for making everything right—Poor-laws and Charities and Church—he wants to reform 'em all.   Perhaps you'll
say, 'There's that Parson Lingon talking about Church Reform—why, he belongs to the Church himself—he wants reforming too.'   Well, well, wait a bit, and you'll hear by and
by that old Parson Lingon is reformed—shoots no more, cracks
his joke no more, has drunk his last bottle : the dogs, the old
pointers, will be sorry; but you'll hear that the Parson at
Little Treby is a new man.   That's what the Church Reform
is sure to come to before long.   So now here are some more
nuts for you, lads, and I leave you to listen to your candidate.
Here he is—give him a good hurray; wave your hats, and I'll
begin.   Hurray!"

Harold had not been quite confident beforehand as to the
good effect of his uncle's introduction; but he was soon reas-
sured.   There was no acrid partisanship among the old-fashioned Tories who mustered strong about the Marquis of
Granby, and Parson Jack had put them in a good humor.
Harold's only interruption came from his own party.   The
oratorical clerk at the Factory, acting as the tribune of the
Dissenting interest, and feeling bound to put questions, might
have been troublesome; but his voice being unpleasantly sharp,
while Harold's was full and penetrating, the questioning was
cried down.   Harold's speech " did " : it was not of the glib-
nonsensical sort, not ponderous, not hesitating—which is as
much as to say, that it was remarkable among British speeches.
Read in print the next day, perhaps it would be neither preg-
nant nor conclusive, which is saying no more than that its
excellence was not of an abnormal kind, but such as is usually
found in the best efforts of eloquent candidates.   Accordingly
the applause drowned the opposition, and content predominated.

But, perhaps, the moment of most diffusive pleasure from
public speaking is that in which the speech ceases and the

audience can turn to commenting on it. The one speech, sometimes uttered under great responsibility as to missiles and other consequences, has given a text to twenty speakers who are under no responsibility. Even in the days of duelling a man was not challenged for being a bore, nor does this quality apparently hinder him from being much invited to dinner, which is the great index of social responsibility in a less barbarous age.

Certainly the crowd in the market-place seemed to experience this culminating enjoyment when the speaking on the platform in front of the Ram had ceased, and there were no less than three orators holding forth from the elevation of chance vehicles, not at all to the prejudice of the talking among those who were on a level with their neighbors. There was little ill-humor among the listeners, for Queen Bess was striking the last quarter before two, and a savory smell from the inn kitchens inspired them with an agreeable consciousness that the speakers were helping to trifle away the brief time before dinner.

Two or three of Harold's committee had lingered talking to each other on the platform, instead of re-entering; and Jermyn, after coming out to speak to one of them, had turned to the corner near which the carriages were standing, that he might tell the Transomes' coachman to drive round to the side door, and signal to his own coachman to follow. But a dialogue which was going on below induced him to pause, and, instead of giving the order, to assume the air of a careless gazer. Christian, whom the attorney had already observed looking out of a window at the Marquis of Granby, was talking to Dominic. The meeting appeared to be one of new recognition, for Christian was saying, —

"You've not got gray as I have, Mr. Lenoni; you're not a day older for the sixteen years. But no wonder you didn't know me; I'm bleached like a dried bone."

"Not so. It is true I was confused a meenute—I could put your face nowhere; but after that, Naples came behind it, and I said, Mr. Creestian. And so you reside at the Manor, and I am at Transome Court."

"Ah! it's a thousand pities you're not on our side, else we

might have dined together at the Marquis," said Christian. "Eh, could you manage it?" he added, languidly, knowing there was no chance of a yes.

"No—much obliged—couldn't leave the leetle boy. Ahi! Arry, Arry, pinch not poor Moro."

While Dominic was answering, Christian had stared about him, as his manner was when he was being spoken to, and had had his eyes arrested by Esther, who was leaning forward to look at Mr. Harold Transome's extraordinary little gypsy of a son. But happening to meet Christian's stare, she felt annoyed, drew back, and turned away her head, coloring.

"Who are those ladies?" said Christian, in a low tone, to Dominic, as if he had been startled into a sudden wish for this information.

"They are Meester Jermyn's daughters," said Dominic, who knew nothing either of the lawyer's family or of Esther.

Christian looked puzzled a moment or two, and was silent.

"Oh, well—*au revoir*," he said, kissing the tips of his fingers, as the coachman, having had Jermyn's order, began to urge on the horses.

"Does he see some likeness in the girl?" thought Jermyn, as he turned away. "I wish I hadn't invited her to come in the carriage, as it happens."

CHAPTER XX.

"Good earthenware pitchers, sir!—of an excellent quaint pattern and sober color."

THE market dinner at "the Marquis" was in high repute in Treby and its neighborhood. The frequenters of this three-and-sixpenny ordinary like to allude to it, as men allude to anything which implies that they move in good society, and habitually converse with those who are in the secret of the highest affairs. The guests were not only such rural residents as had driven to market, but some of the most substantial townsmen, who had always assured their wives that business required this weekly sacrifice of domestic pleasure. The

poorer farmers, who put up at the Ram or the Seven Stars,
where there was no fish, felt their disadvantage, bearing it
modestly or bitterly, as the case might be; and although the
Marquis was a Tory house, devoted to Debarry, it was too
much to expect that such tenants of the Transomes as had always been used to dine there should consent to eat a worse
dinner, and sit with worse company, because they suddenly
found themselves under a Radical landlord, opposed to the
political party known as Sir Maxim's. Hence the recent
political divisions had not reduced the handsome length of
the table at the Marquis; and the many gradations of dignity
—from Mr. Wace, the brewer, to the rich butcher from Leek
Malton, who always modestly took the lowest seat, though
without the reward of being asked to come up higher—had
not been abbreviated by any secessions.

To-day there was an extra table spread for expected super-
numeraries, and it was at this that Christian took his place
with some of the younger farmers, who had almost a sense of
dissipation in talking to a man of his questionable station and
unknown experience. The provision was especially liberal,
and on the whole the presence of a minority destined to vote
for Transome was a ground for joking which added to the
good-humor of the chief talkers. A respectable old acquaintance turned Radical rather against his will was rallied with
even greater gusto than if his wife had had twins twice over.
The best Trebian Tories were far too sweet-blooded to turn
against such old friends, and to make no distinction between
them and the Radical, Dissenting, Papistical, Deistical set
with whom they never dined, and probably never saw except
in their imagination. But the talk was necessarily in abeyance until the more serious business of dinner was ended, and
the wine, spirits, and tobacco raised mere satisfaction into
beatitude.

Among the frequent though not regular guests, whom every
one was glad to see, was Mr. Nolan, the retired London
hosier, a wiry old gentleman past seventy, whose square tight
forehead, with its rigid hedge of gray hair, whose bushy eyebrows, sharp dark eyes, and remarkable hooked nose, gave a
handsome distinction to his face in the midst of rural physi-

ognomies. He had married a Miss Pendrell early in life, when he was a poor young Londoner, and the match had been thought as bad as ruin by her family; but fifteen years ago he had had the satisfaction of bringing his wife to settle amongst her own friends, and of being received with pride as a brother-in-law, retired from business, possessed of unknown thousands, and of a most agreeable talent for anecdote and conversation generally. No question had ever been raised as to Mr. Nolan's extraction on the strength of his hooked nose, or of his name being Baruch. Hebrew names " ran " in the best Saxon families; the Bible accounted for them; and no one among the uplands and hedgerows of that district was suspected of having an Oriental origin unless he carried a pedlar's jewel-box. Certainly, whatever genealogical research might have discovered, the worthy Baruch Nolan was so free from any distinctive marks of religious persuasion—he went to church with so ordinary an irregularity, and so often grumbled at the sermon—that there was no ground for classing him otherwise than with good Trebian Churchmen. He was generally regarded as a good-looking old gentleman, and a certain thin eagerness in his aspect was attributed to the life of the metropolis, where narrow space had the same sort of effect on men as on thickly planted trees. Mr. Nolan always ordered his pint of port, which, after he had sipped it a little, was wont to animate his recollections of the Royal Family, and the various ministries which had been contemporary with the successive stages of his prosperity. He was always listened to with interest: a man who had been born in the year when good old King George came to the throne—who had been acquainted with the nude leg of the Prince Regent, and hinted at private reasons for believing that the Princess Charlotte ought not to have died—had conversational matter as special to his auditors as Marco Polo could have had on his return from Asiatic travel.

"My good sir," he said to Mr. Wace, as he crossed his knees and spread his silk handkerchief over them, " Transome may be returned, or he may not be returned—that's a question for North Loamshire; but it makes little difference to the kingdom. I don't want to say things which may put younger men out of spirits, but I believe this country has seen its best days—I do indeed."

"I am sorry to hear it from one of your experience, Mr. Nolan," said the brewer, a large, happy-looking man. "I'd make a good fight myself before I'd leave a worse world for my boys than I've found for myself. There isn't a greater pleasure than doing a bit of planting, and improving one's buildings, and investing one's money in some pretty acres of land, when it turns up here and there—land you've known from a boy. It's a nasty thought that these Radicals are to turn things round so as one can calculate on nothing. One doesn't like it for one's self, and one doesn't like it for one's neighbors. But somehow I believe it won't do: if we can't trust the Government just now, there's Providence and the good sense of the country; and there's a right in things—that's what I've always said—there's a right in things. The heavy end will get downmost. And if Church and King, and every man being sure of his own, are things good for this country, there's a God above will take care of 'em."

"It won't do, my dear sir," said Mr. Nolan—"it won't do. When Peel and the Duke turned round about the Catholics in '29, I saw it was all over with us. We could never trust ministers any more. It was to keep off a rebellion, they said; but I say it was to keep their places. They're monstrously fond of place, both of them—that I know." Here Mr. Nolan changed the crossing of his legs, and gave a deep cough, conscious of having made a point. Then he went on—"What we want is a king with a good will of his own. If we'd had that, we shouldn't have heard what we've heard to-day; Reform would never have come to this pass. When our good old King George the Third heard his ministers talking about Catholic Emancipation, he boxed their ears all round. Ah, poor soul! he did indeed, gentlemen," ended Mr. Nolan, shaken by a deep laugh of admiration.

"Well, now, that's something like a king," said Mr. Crowder, who was an eager listener.

"It was uncivil, though. How did they take it?" said Mr. Timothy Rose, a "gentleman farmer" from Leek Malton, against whose independent position nature had provided the safeguard of a spontaneous servility. His large porcine cheeks, round twinkling eyes, and thumbs habitually twirling expressed a concentrated effort not to get into trouble, and to speak everybody fair except when they were safely out of hearing.

"Take it! they'd be obliged to take it," said the impetuous young Joyce, a farmer of superior information. "Have you ever heard of the king's prerogative?"

"I don't say but what I have," said Rose, retreating. "I've nothing against it—nothing at all."

"No, but the Radicals have," said young Joyce, winking. "The prerogative is what they want to clip close. They want us to be governed by delegates from the trades-unions, who are to dictate to everybody, and make everything square to their mastery."

"They're a pretty set, now, those delegates," said Mr. Wace, with disgust. "I once heard two of 'em spouting away. They're a sort of fellow I'd never employ in my brewery, or anywhere else. I've seen it again and again. If a man takes to tongue-work it's all over with him. 'Everything's wrong,' says he. That's a big text. But does he want to make everything right? Not he. He'd lose his text. 'We want every man's good,' say they. Why, they never knew yet what a man's good is. How should they? It's working for his victual—not getting a slice of other people's."

"Ay, ay," said young Joyce, cordially. "I should just have liked all the delegates in the country mustered for our yeomanry to go into — that's all. They'd see where the strength of Old England lay then. You may tell what it is for a country to trust to trade when it breeds such spindling fellows as those."

"That isn't the fault of trade, my good sir," said Mr. Nolan, who was often a little pained by the defects of provincial culture. "Trade, properly conducted, is good for a man's constitution. I could have shown you, in my time, weavers past seventy, with all their faculties as sharp as a penknife, doing without spectacles. It's the new system of trade that's to blame: a country can't have too much trade if it's properly managed. Plenty of sound Tories have made their fortune by

14

trade. You've heard of Calibut & Co.—everybody has hear
of Calibut. Well, sir, I knew old Mr. Calibut as well as
know you. He was once a crony of mine in a city warehouse
and now, I'll answer for it, he has a larger rent-roll than Lor
Wyvern. Bless your soul! his subscriptions to charities woul
make a fine income for a nobleman. And he's as good a Tor
as I am. And as for his town establishment—why, hov
much butter do you think is consumed there annually?"

Mr. Nolan paused, and then his face glowed with triumpl
as he answered his own question. "Why, gentlemen, no
less than two thousand pounds of butter during the few month
the family is in town! Trade makes property, my good sir
and property is Conservative, as they say now. Calibut'
son-in-law is Lord Fortinbras. He paid me a large debt o
his marriage. It's all one web, sir. The prosperity of th
country is one web."

"To be sure," said Christian, who, smoking his cigar wit
his chair turned away from the table, was willing to mak
himself agreeable in the conversation. "We can't do withou
nobility. Look at France. When they got rid of the ol
nobles they were obliged to make new."

"True, very true," said Mr. Nolan, who thought Christia
a little too wise for his position, but could not resist the rar
gift of an instance in point. "It's the French Revolutio
that has done us harm here. It was the same at the end o
the last century, but the war kept it off—Mr. Pitt saved us
I knew Mr. Pitt. I had a particular interview with hin
once. He joked me about getting the length of his foot
'Mr. Nolan,' said he, 'there are those on the other side o
the water whose name begins with N. who would be glad t
know what you know.' I was recommended to send an ac
count of that to the newspapers after his death, poor man
but I'm not fond of that kind of show myself." Mr. Nola
swung his upper leg a little, and pinched his lip betwee
his thumb and finger, naturally pleased with his own mod
eration.

"No, no—very right," said Mr. Wace, cordially. "Bu
you never said a truer word than that about property. If a
man's got a bit of property, a stake in the country, he'll wan

to keep things square. Where Jack isn't safe, Tom's in danger. But that's what makes it such an uncommonly nasty thing that a man like Transome should take up with these Radicals. It's my belief he does it only to get into Parliament; he'll turn round when he gets there. Come, Dibbs, there's something to put you in spirits," added Mr. Wace, raising his voice a little and looking at a guest lower down. "You've got to vote for a Radical with one side of your mouth, and make a wry face with the other; but he'll turn round by and by. As Parson Jack says, he's got the right sort of blood in him."

"I don't care two straws who I vote for," said Dibbs, sturdily. "I'm not going to make a wry face. It stands to reason a man should vote for his landlord. My farm's in good condition, and I've got the best pasture on the estate. The rot's never come nigh me. Let them grumble as are on the wrong side of the hedge."

"I wonder if Jermyn 'll bring him in, though," said Mr. Sircome, the great miller. "He's an uncommon fellow for carrying things through. I know he brought me through that suit about my weir; it cost a pretty penny, but he brought me through."

"It's a bit of a pill for him, too, having to turn Radical," said Mr. Wace. "They say he counted on making friends with Sir Maximus by this young one coming home and joining with Mr. Philip."

"But I'll bet a penny he brings Transome in," said Mr. Sircome. "Folks say he hasn't got many votes hereabout; but toward Duffield, and all there, where the Radicals are, everybody's for him. Eh, Mr. Christian? Come—you're at the fountain-head—what do they say about it now at the Manor?"

When general attention was called to Christian, young Joyce looked down at his own legs and touched the curves of his own hair, as if measuring his own approximation to that correct copy of a gentleman. Mr. Wace turned his head to listen for Christian's answer with that tolerance of inferiority which becomes men in places of public resort.

"They think it will be a hard run between Transome and

Garstin," said Christian. "It depends on Transome's getting plumpers."

"Well, I know I shall not split for Garstin," said Mr. Wace. "It's nonsense for Debarry's voters to split for a Whig. A man's either a Tory or not a Tory."

"It seems reasonable there should be one of each side," said Mr. Timothy Rose. "I don't like showing favor either way. If one side can't lower the poor's rates and take off the tithe, let the other try."

"But there's this in it, Wace," said Mr. Sircome. "I'm not altogether against the Whigs. For they don't want to go so far as the Radicals do, and when they find they've slipped a bit too far they'll hold on all the tighter. And the Whigs have got the upper hand now, and it's no use fighting with the current. I run with the——"

Mr. Sircome checked himself, looked furtively at Christian, and, to divert criticism, ended with—"eh, Mr. Nolan?"

"There have been eminent Whigs, sir. Mr. Fox was a Whig," said Mr. Nolan. "Mr. Fox was a great orator. He gambled a good deal. He was very intimate with the Prince of Wales. I've seen him, and the Duke of York too, go home by daylight with their hats crushed. Mr. Fox was a great leader of Opposition: Government requires an Opposition. The Whigs should always be in opposition, and the Tories on the ministerial side. That's what the country used to like. 'The Whigs for salt and mustard, the Tories for meat,' Mr. Gottlib the banker used to say to me. Mr. Gottlib was a worthy man. When there was a great run on Gottlib's bank in '16, I saw a gentleman come in with bags of gold, and say, 'Tell Mr. Gottlib there's plenty more where that came from.' It stopped the run, gentlemen—it did indeed."

This anecdote was received with great admiration, but Mr. Sircome returned to the previous question.

"There, now, you see, Wace—it's right there should be Whigs as well as Tories—Pitt and Fox—I've always heard them go together."

"Well, I don't like Garstin," said the brewer. "I didn't like his conduct about the Canal Company. Of the two, I like Transome best. If a nag is to throw me, I say, let him have some blood."

"As for blood, Wace," said Mr. Salt, the wool-factor, a bilious man, who only spoke when there was a good opportunity of contradicting, "ask my brother-in-law Labron a little about that. These Transomes are not the old blood."

"Well, they're the oldest that's forthcoming, I suppose," said Mr. Wace, laughing. "Unless you believe in mad old Tommy Trounsem. I wonder where that old poaching fellow is now."

"I saw him half drunk the other day," said young Joyce. "He'd got a flag basket with handbills in it over his shoulder."

"I thought the old fellow was dead," said Mr. Wace. "Hey! why, Jermyn," he went on merrily, as he turned round and saw the attorney entering; "you Radical! how dare you show yourself in this Tory house? Come, this is going a bit too far. We don't mind Old Harry managing our law for us—that's his proper business from time immemorial; but——"

"But—a—" said Jermyn, smiling, always ready to carry on a joke, to which his slow manner gave the piquancy of surprise, "if he meddles with politics he must be a Tory."

Jermyn was not afraid to show himself anywhere in Treby. He knew many people were not exactly fond of him, but a man can do without that if he is prosperous. A provincial lawyer in those old-fashioned days was as independent of personal esteem as if he had been a Lord Chancellor.

There was a good-humored laugh at this upper end of the room as Jermyn seated himself at about an equal angle between Mr. Wace and Christian.

"We were talking about old Tommy Trounsem; you remember him? They say he's turned up again," said Mr. Wace.

"Ah?" said Jermyn, indifferently. "But—a—Wace—I'm very busy to-day—but I wanted to see you about that bit of land of yours at the corner of Pod's End. I've had a handsome offer for you—I'm not at liberty to say from whom—but an offer that ought to tempt you."

"It won't tempt me," said Mr. Wace, peremptorily; "if

I've got a bit of land, I'll keep it. It's hard enough to get hereabouts."

"Then I'm to understand that you refuse all negotiation?" said Jermyn, who had ordered a glass of sherry, and was looking round slowly as he sipped it, till his eyes seemed to rest for the first time on Christian, though he had seen him at once on entering the room.

"Unless one of the confounded railways should come. But then I'll stand out and make 'em bleed for it."

There was a murmur of approbation; the railways were a public wrong much denunciated in Treby.

"A—Mr. Philip Debarry at the Manor now?" said Jermyn, suddenly questioning Christian, in a haughty tone of superiority which he often chose to use.

"No," said Christian; "he is expected to-morrow morning."

"Ah!" Jermyn paused a moment or two, and then said, "You are sufficiently in his confidence, I think, to carry a message to him with a small document?"

"Mr. Debarry has often trusted me so far," said Christian, with much coolness; "but if the business is yours, you can probably find some one you know better."

There was a little winking and grimacing among those of the company who heard this answer.

"A—true—a," said Jermyn, not showing any offence; "if you decline. But I think, if you will do me the favor to step round to my residence on your way back, and learn the business, you will prefer carrying it yourself. At my residence, if you please—not my office."

"Oh, very well," said Christian. "I shall be very happy." Christian never allowed himself to be treated as a servant by any one but his master, and his master treated a servant more deferentially than an equal.

"Will it be five o'clock? what hour shall we say?" said Jermyn.

Christian looked at his watch and said, "About five I can be there."

"Very good," said Jermyn, finishing his sherry.

"Well—a—Wace—a—so you will hear nothing about Pod's End?"

"Not I."

"A mere pocket-handkerchief, not enough to swear by—a—" here Jermyn's face broke into a smile—"without a magnifying-glass."

"Never mind. It's mine into the bowels of the earth and up to the sky. I can build the Tower of Babel on it if I like—eh, Mr. Nolan?"

"A bad investment, my good sir," said Mr. Nolan, who enjoyed a certain flavor of infidelity in this smart reply, and laughed much at it in his inward way.

"See, now, how blind you Tories are," said Jermyn, rising; "if I had been your lawyer, I'd have had you make another forty-shilling freeholder with that land, and all in time for this election. But—a—the *verbum sapientibus* comes a little too late now."

Jermyn was moving away as he finished speaking, but Mr. Wace called out after him, "We're not so badly off for votes as you are—good sound votes, that'll stand the Revising Barrister. Debarry at the top of the poll!"

The lawyer was already out of the door-way.

———◆———

CHAPTER XXI.

'Tis grievous, that with all amplification of travel both by sea and land, a man can never separate himself from his past history.

MR. JERMYN's handsome house stood a little way out of the town, surrounded by garden and lawn and plantations of hopeful trees. As Christian approached it he was in a perfectly easy state of mind: the business he was going on was none of his, otherwise than as he was well satisfied with any opportunity of making himself valuable to Mr. Philip Debarry. As he looked at Jermyn's length of wall and iron railing he said to himself, "These lawyers are the fellows for getting on in the world with the least expense of civility. With this cursed conjuring secret of theirs called Law they think everybody is frightened at them. My Lord Jermyn seems to have his insolence as ready as his soft sawder. He's as sleek as a rat, and has as vicious a tooth. I know the sort of vermin well enough. I've helped to fatten one or two."

In this mood of conscious, contemptuous penetration, Christian was shown by the footman into Jermyn's private room, where the attorney sat surrounded with massive oaken bookcases, and other furniture to correspond, from the thickest-legged library-table to the calendar-frame and card-rack. It was the sort of room a man prepares for himself when he feels sure of a long and respectable future. He was leaning back in his leather chair, against the broad window opening on the lawn, and had just taken off his spectacles and let the newspaper fall on his knees, in despair of reading by the fading light.

When the footman opened the door and said, "Mr. Christian," Jermyn said, "Good-evening, Mr. Christian. Be seated," pointing to a chair opposite himself and the window. "Light the candles on the shelf, John, but leave the blinds alone."

He did not speak again till the man was gone out, but appeared to be referring to a document which lay on the bureau before him. When the door was closed he drew himself up again, began to rub his hands, and turned toward his visitor, who seemed perfectly indifferent to the fact that the attorney was in shadow, and that the light fell on himself.

"A—your name—a—is Henry Scaddon."

There was a start through Christian's frame, which he was quick enough, almost simultaneously, to try and disguise as a change of position. He uncrossed his legs and unbuttoned his coat. But before he had time to say anything Jermyn went on with slow emphasis.

"You were born on the 16th of December, 1782, at Blackheath. Your father was a cloth-merchant in London: he died when you were barely of age, leaving an extensive business; before you were five-and-twenty you had run through the greater part of the property, and had compromised your safety by an attempt to defraud your creditors. Subsequently you forged a check on your father's elder brother, who had intended to make you his heir."

Here Jermyn paused a moment and referred to the document. Christian was silent.

"In 1808 you found it expedient to leave this country in a military disguise, and were taken prisoner by the French. On the occasion of an exchange of prisoners you had the opportunity of returning to your own country, and to the bosom of your own family. You were generous enough to sacrifice that prospect in favor of a fellow-prisoner, of about your own age and figure, who had more pressing reasons than yourself for wishing to be on this side of the water. You exchanged dress, luggage, and names with him, and he passed to England instead of you as Henry Scaddon. Almost immediately afterward you escaped from your imprisonment, after feigning an illness which prevented your exchange of names from being discovered; and it was reported that you—that is, you under the name of your fellow-prisoner—were drowned in an open boat, trying to reach a Neapolitan vessel bound for Malta. Nevertheless I have to congratulate you on the falsehood of that report, and on the certainty that you are now, after the lapse of more than twenty years, seated here in perfect safety."

Jermyn paused so long that he was evidently awaiting some answer. At last Christian replied, in a dogged tone,—

"Well, sir, I've heard much longer stories than that told quite as solemnly when there was not a word of truth in them. Suppose I deny the very peg you hang your statement on. Suppose I say I am not Henry Scaddon."

"A—in that case—a," said Jermyn, with wooden indifference, "you would lose the advantage which—a—may attach to your possession of Henry Scaddon's knowledge. And at the same time, if it were in the least—a—inconvenient to you that you should be recognized as Henry Scaddon, your denial would not prevent me from holding the knowledge and evidence which I possess on that point; it would only prevent us from pursuing the present conversation."

"Well, sir, suppose we admit, for the sake of the conversation, that your account of the matter is the true one: what advantage have you to offer the man named Henry Scaddon?"

"The advantage—a—is problematical; but it may be considerable. It might, in fact, release you from the necessity of acting as courier, or—a—valet, or whatever other office you may occupy which prevents you from being your own master. On the other hand, my acquaintance with your secret is not necessarily a disadvantage to you. To put the matter in a nutshell, I am not inclined—a—gratuitously—to do you any harm, and I may be able to do you a considerable service."

"Which you want me to earn somehow?" said Christian. "You offer me a turn in a lottery?"

"Precisely. The matter in question is of no earthly interest to you, except—a—as it may yield you a prize. We lawyers have to do with complicated questions, and—a—legal subtleties, which are never—a—fully known even to the parties immediately interested, still less to the witnesses. Shall we agree, then, that you continue to retain two-thirds of the name which you gained by exchange, and that you oblige me by answering certain questions as to the experience of Henry Scaddon?"

"Very good. Go on."

"What articles of property, once belonging to your fellow-prisoner, Maurice Christian Bycliffe, do you still retain?"

"This ring," said Christian, twirling round the fine seal-ring on his finger, "his watch and the little matters that hung with it, and a case of papers. I got rid of a gold snuff-box once when I was hard up. The clothes are all gone, of course. We exchanged everything; it was all done in a hurry. Bycliffe thought we should meet again in England before long, and he was mad to get there. But that was impossible—I mean that we should meet soon after. I don't know what's become of him, else I would give him up his papers and the watch, and so on—though, you know, it was I who did *him* the service, and he felt that."

"You were at Vesoul together before being moved to Verdun?"

"Yes."

"What else do you know about Bycliffe?"

"Oh, nothing very particular," said Christian, pausing, and rapping his boot with his cane. "He'd been in the Hanoverian army—a high-spirited fellow, took nothing easily; not over-strong in health. He made a fool of himself with marrying at Vesoul; and there was the devil to pay with the girl's relations; and then, when the prisoners were ordered off, they had to part. Whether they ever got together again I don't know."

"Was the marriage all right, then?"

"Oh, all on the square—civil marriage, church—everything. Bycliffe was a fool—a good-natured, proud, headstrong fellow."

"How long did the marriage take place before you left Vesoul?"

"About three months. I was a witness to the marriage."

"And you know no more about the wife?"

"Not afterward. I knew her very well before—pretty Annette—Annette Ledru was her name. She was of a good family, and they had made up a fine match for her. But she was one of your meek little diablesses, who have a will of their own once in their lives—the will to choose their own master."

"Bycliffe was not open to you about his other affairs?"

"Oh, no—a fellow you wouldn't dare ask a question of. People told him everything, but he told nothing in return. If Madame Annette ever found him again, she found her lord and master with a vengeance; but she was a regular lapdog. However, her family shut her up—made a prisoner of her—to prevent her running away."

"Ah—good. Much of what you have been so obliging as to say is irrelevant to any possible purpose of mine, which, in fact, has to do only with a mouldy law-case that might be aired some day. You will doubtless, on your own account, maintain perfect silence on what has passed between us, and with that condition duly preserved—a—it is possible that—a —the lottery you have put into—as you observe—may turn up a prize."

"This, then, is all the business you have with me?" said Christian, rising.

"All. You will, of course, preserve carefully all the papers and other articles which have so many—a—recollections—a— attached to them?"

"Oh, yes. If there's any chance of Bycliffe turning up again, I shall be sorry to have parted with the snuff-box; but I was hard up at Naples. In fact, as you see, I was obliged at last to turn courier."

"An exceedingly agreeable life for a man of some—a—accomplishments and—a—no income," said Jermyn, rising, and reaching a candle, which he placed against his desk.

Christian knew this was a sign that he was expected to go, but he lingered standing, with one hand on the back of his chair. At last he said rather sulkily,—

"I think you're too clever, Mr. Jermyn, not to perceive that I'm not a man to be made a fool of."

"Well—a—it may perhaps be a still better guaranty for you," said Jermyn, smiling, "that I see no use in attempting that—a—metamorphosis."

"The old gentleman, who ought never to have felt himself injured, is dead now, and I'm not afraid of creditors after more than twenty years."

"Certainly not;—a—there may indeed be claims which can't assert themselves—a—legally which yet are molesting to a man of some reputation. But you may perhaps be happily free from such fears."

Jermyn drew round his chair toward the bureau, and Christian, too acute to persevere uselessly, said "Good-day," and left the room.

After leaning back in his chair to reflect a few minutes Jermyn wrote the following letter :—

DEAR JOHNSON,—I learn from your letter, received this morning, that you intend returning to town on Saturday.

While you are there, be so good as to see Medwin, who used to be with Batt & Cowley, and ascertain from him indirectly, and in the course of conversation on other topics, whether in that old business in 1810–11 Scaddon *alias* Bycliffe, or Bycliffe *alias* Scaddon, before his imprisonment, gave Batt & Cowley any reason to believe that he was married and expected to have a child. The question, as you know, is of no practical importance ; but I wish to draw up an abstract of the Bycliffe case, and the exact position in which it stood before the suit was closed by the death of the plaintiff, in order that, if Mr. Harold Transome desires it, he may see how the failure of the last claim has secured the Durfey-Transome title, and whether there is a hair's breadth of chance that another claim should be set up.

Of course there is not a shadow of such a chance. For even if Batt & Cowley were to suppose that they had alighted on a surviving representative of the Bycliffes, it would not enter into their heads to set up a new claim, since they brought evidence that the last life which suspended the Bycliffe remainder was extinct before the case was closed, a good twenty years ago.

Still, I want to show the present heir of the Durfey-Transomes the exact condition of the family title to the estates. So get me an answer from Medwin on the above-mentioned point. I shall meet you at Duffield next week. We must get Transome returned. Never mind his having been a little rough the other day, but go on doing what you know is necessary for his interest. His interest is mine, which I need not say is John Johnson's.

Yours faithfully,

MATTHEW JERMYN.

When the attorney had sealed this letter and leaned back in his chair again, he was inwardly saying,—

"Now, Mr. Harold, I shall shut up this affair in a private drawer till you choose to take any extreme measures which will force me to bring it out. I have the matter entirely in my own power. No one but old Lyon knows about the girl's birth. No one but Scaddon can clinch the evidence about Bycliffe, and I've got Scaddon under my thumb. No soul except myself and Johnson, who is a limb of myself, knows that there is one half-dead life which may presently leave the girl a new claim to the Bycliffe heirship. I shall learn through Methurst whether Batt & Cowley knew, through Bycliffe, of this woman having come to England. I shall hold all the threads between my thumb and finger. I can use the evidence or I can nullify it.

"And so, if Mr. Harold pushes me to extremity, and threatens me with Chancery and ruin, I have an opposing threat, which will either save me or turn into a punishment for him."

He rose, put out his candles, and stood with his back to the fire, looking out on the dim lawn, with its black twilight fringe of shrubs, still meditating. Quick thought was gleaming over five-and-thirty years filled with devices more or less clever, more or less desirable to be avowed. Those which might be avowed with impunity were not always to be distinguished as innocent by comparison with those which it was advisable to conceal. In a profession where much that is noxious may be done without disgrace, is a conscience likely to be without balm when circumstances have urged a man to overstep the line where his good technical information makes him aware that (with discovery) disgrace is likely to begin?

With regard to the Transome affairs, the family had been in pressing need of money, and it had lain with him to get it for them: was it to be expected that he would not consider his own advantage where he had rendered services such as are never fully paid? If it came to a question of right and wrong instead of law, the least justifiable things he had ever done had been done on behalf of the Transomes. It had been a deucedly unpleasant thing for him to get Bycliffe arrested and thrown into prison as Henry Scaddon—perhaps hastening the man's death in that way. But if it had not been done by dint of his (Jermyn's) exertions and tact, he would like to know where the Durfey-Transomes might have been by this time. As for right or wrong, if the truth were known, the very possession of the estate by the Durfey-Transomes was owing to law-tricks that took place nearly a century ago, when the original old Durfey got his base fee.

But inward argument of this sort now, as always, was merged in anger, in exasperation, that Harold, precisely Harold Transome, should have turned out to be the probable instrument of a visitation which would be bad luck, not justice; for is there any justice where ninety-nine out of a hundred escape? He felt himself beginning to hate Harold as he had never——

Just then Jermyn's third daughter, a tall slim girl, wrapped in a white woollen shawl, which she had hung over her blanket-wise, skipped across the lawn toward the greenhouse to get a flower. Jermyn was startled, and did not identify the figure, or rather he identified it falsely with another tall white-wrapped figure which had sometimes set his heart beating quickly more than thirty years before. For a moment he was fully back in those distant years when he and another bright-eyed person had seen no reason why they should not indulge their passion and their vanity, and determine for themselves how their lives should be made delightful in spite of unalterable external conditions. The reasons had been un-folding themselves gradually ever since through all the years which had converted the handsome, soft-eyed, slim young Jermyn (with a touch of sentiment) into a portly lawyer of sixty, for whom life had resolved itself into the means of keeping up his head among his professional brethren and main-taining an establishment—into a gray-haired husband and fa-ther, whose third affectionate and expensive daughter now rapped at the window and called to him, "Papa, papa, get ready for dinner; don't you remember that the Lukyns are coming?"

CHAPTER XXII.

Her gentle looks shot arrows, piercing him
As gods are pierced, with poison of sweet pity.

THE evening of the market-day had passed, and Felix had not looked in at Malthouse Yard to talk over the public events with Mr. Lyon. When Esther was dressing the next morn-ing, she had reached a point of irritated anxiety to see Felix at which she found herself devising little schemes for attain-ing that end in some way that would be so elaborate as to seem perfectly natural. Her watch had a long-standing ailment of losing; possibly it wanted cleaning; Felix would tell her if it merely wanted regulating, whereas Mr. Prowd might detain it unnecessarily, and cause her useless inconvenience. Or could she not get a valuable hint from Mrs. Holt about the home-made bread, which was something as "sad" as Lyddy herself? Or, if she came home that way at twelve o'clock, Felix might be going out, she might meet him and not be obliged to call. Or—but it would be very much beneath her to take any steps of this sort. Her watch had been losing for the last two months—why should it not go on losing a little longer? She could think of no devices that were not so transparent as to be undignified. All the more undignified because Felix chose to live in a way that would prevent any one from classing him according to his education and mental refinement—"which

certainly are very high," said Esther inwardly, coloring, as if
in answer to some contrary allegation, " else I should not think
his opinion of any consequence." But she came to the conclusion that she could not possibly call at Mrs. Holt's.

It followed that up to a few minutes past twelve, when she
reached the turning toward Mrs. Holt's, she believed that she
should go home the other way; but at the last moment there
is always a reason not existing before—namely, the impossibility of further vacillation. Esther turned the corner without any visible pause, and in another minute was knocking
at Mrs. Holt's door, not without an inward flutter, which she
was bent on disguising.

"It's never you, Miss Lyon! who'd have thought of seeing
you at this time? Is the minister ill? I thought he looked
creechy. If you want help, I'll put my bonnet on."

"Don't keep Miss Lyon at the door, mother; ask her to
come in," said the ringing voice of Felix, surmounting various small shufflings and babbling voices within.

"It's my wish for her to come in, I'm sure," said Mrs.
Holt, making way; " but what is there for her to come in to?
a floor worse than any public. But step in, pray, if you're
so inclined. When I've been forced to take my bit of carpet
up, and have benches, I don't see why I need mind nothing
no more."

"I only came to ask Mr. Holt if he would look at my watch
for me," said Esther, entering, and blushing a general rosecolor.

"He'll do that fast enough," said Mrs. Holt, with emphasis; "that's one of the things he *will* do."

"Excuse my rising, Miss Lyon," said Felix; "I'm binding
up Job's finger."

Job was a small fellow about five, with a germinal nose,
large round blue eyes, and red hair that curled close to his
head like the wool on the head of an infantine lamb. He had
evidently been crying, and the corners of his mouth were still
dolorous. Felix held him on his knee as he bound and tied
up very cleverly a tiny fore finger. There was a table in front
of Felix and against the window, covered with his watchmaking implements and some open books. Two benches stood at

right angles on the sanded floor, and six or seven boys of various ages up to twelve were getting their caps and preparing to go home. They huddled themselves together and stood still when Esther entered. Felix could not look up till he had finished his surgery, but he went on speaking.

"This is a hero, Miss Lyon. This is Job Tudge, a bold Briton, whose finger hurts him, but who doesn't mean to cry. Good-morning, boys. Don't lose your time. Get out into the air."

Esther seated herself on the end of the bench near Felix, much relieved that Job was the immediate object of attention; and the other boys rushed out behind her with a brief chant of "Good-morning!"

"Did you ever see," said Mrs. Holt, standing to look on, "how wonderful Felix is at that small work with his large fingers? And that's because he learnt doctoring. It isn't for want of cleverness he looks like a poor man, Miss Lyon. I've left off speaking, else I should say it's a sin and a shame."

"Mother," said Felix, who often amused himself and kept good-humored by giving his mother answers that were unintelligible to her, "you have an astonishing readiness in the Ciceronian antiphrasis, considering you have never studied oratory. There, Job—thou patient man—sit still if thou wilt; and now we can look at Miss Lyon."

Esther had taken off her watch and was holding it in her hand. But he looked at her face, or rather at her eyes, as he said, "You want me to doctor your watch?"

Esther's expression was appealing and timid, as it had never been before in Felix's presence; but when she saw the perfect calmness, which to her seemed coldness, of his clear gray eyes, as if he saw no reason for attaching any emphasis to this first meeting, a pang swift as an electric shock darted through her. She had been very foolish to think so much of it. It seemed to her as if her inferiority to Felix made a great gulf between them. She could not at once rally her pride and self-command, but let her glance fall on her watch, and said, rather tremulously, "It loses. It is very troublesome. It has been losing a long while."

Felix took the watch from her hand; then, looking round

15

and seeing that his mother was gone out of the room, he said, very gently,—

"You look distressed, Miss Lyon. I hope there's no trouble at home" (Felix was thinking of the minister's agitation on the previous Sunday). "But I ought perhaps to beg your pardon for saying so much."

Poor Esther was quite helpless. The mortification which had come like a bruise to all the sensibilities that had been in keen activity insisted on some relief. Her eyes filled instantly, and a great tear rolled down while she said in a loud sort of whisper, as involuntary as her tears,—

"I wanted to tell you that I was not offended—that I am not ungenerous—I thought you might think—but you have not thought of it."

Was there ever more awkward speaking?—or any behavior less like that of the graceful, self-possessed Miss Lyon, whose phrases were usually so well turned, and whose repartees were so ready?

For a moment there was silence. Esther had her two little delicately gloved hands clasped on the table. The next moment she felt one hand of Felix covering them both and pressing them firmly; but he did not speak. The tears were on both her cheeks now, and she could look up at him. His eyes had an expression of sadness in them, quite new to her. Suddenly little Job, who had his mental exercises on the occasion, called out, impatiently,—

"She's tut her finger!"

Felix and Esther laughed, and drew their hands away; and as Esther took her handkerchief to wipe the tears from her cheeks she said,—

"You see, Job, I am a naughty coward. I can't help crying when I've hurt myself."

"Zoo soodn't kuy," said Job, energetically, being much impressed with a moral doctrine which had come to him after a sufficient transgression of it.

"Job is like me," said Felix, "fonder of preaching than of practice. But let us look at this same watch," he went on, opening and examining it. "These little Geneva toys are cleverly constructed to go always a little wrong. But if you wind them up and set them regularly every night, you may know at least that it's not noon when the hand points there."

Felix chatted, that Esther might recover herself; but now Mrs. Holt came back and apologized.

"You'll excuse my going away, I know, Miss Lyon. But there were the dumplings to see to, and what little I've got left on my hands now I like to do well. Not but what I've more cleaning to do than ever I had in my life before, as you may tell soon enough if you look at this floor. But when you've been used to doing things, and they've been taken away from you, it's as if your hands had been cut off, and you felt the fingers as are of no use to you."

"That's a great image, mother," said Felix, as he snapped the watch together, and handed it to Esther; "I never heard you use such an image before."

"Yes, I know you've always some fault to find with what your mother says. But if ever there was a woman could talk with the open Bible before her, and not be afraid, it's me. I never did tell stories, and I never will—though I know it's done, Miss Lyon, and by church-members too, when they have candles to sell, as I could bring you the proof. But I never was one of 'em, let Felix say what he will about the printing on the tickets. His father believed it was gospel truth, and it's presumptuous to say it wasn't. For as for curing, how can anybody know? There's no physic'll cure without a blessing, and *with* a blessing I know I've seen a mustard-plaster work when there was no more smell nor strength in the mustard than so much flour. And reason good—for the mustard had lain in paper nobody knows how long—so I'll leave you to guess."

Mrs. Holt looked hard out of the window and gave a slight inarticulate sound of scorn.

Felix had leaned back in his chair with a resigned smile, and was pinching Job's ears.

Esther said, "I think I had better go now," not knowing what else to say, yet not wishing to go immediately, lest she should seem to be running away from Mrs. Holt. She felt keenly how much endurance there must be for Felix. And

she had often been discontented with her father, and called
him tiresome!

"Where does Job Tudge live?" she said, still sitting, and
looking at the droll little figure, set off by a ragged jacket
with a tail about two inches deep sticking out above the fun-
niest of corduroys.

"Job has two mansions," said Felix. "He lives here
chiefly; but he has another home, where his grandfather, Mr.
Tudge, the stone-breaker, lives. My mother is very good to
Job, Miss Lyon. She has made him a little bed in a cup-
board, and she gives him sweetened porridge."

The exquisite goodness implied in these words of Felix impressed Esther the more because in her hearing his talk had
usually been pungent and denunciatory. Looking at Mrs.
Holt, she saw that her eyes had lost their bleak northeasterly
expression, and were shining with some mildness on little
Job, who had turned round toward her, propping his head
against Felix.

"Well, why shouldn't I be motherly to the child, Miss
Lyon?" said Mrs. Holt, whose strong powers of argument
required the file of an imagined contradiction, if there were
no real one at hand. "I never was hard-hearted, and I never
will be. It was Felix picked the child up and took to him,
you may be sure, for there's nobody else master where he is;
but I wasn't going to beat the orphan child and abuse him
because of that, and him as straight as an arrow when he's
stripped, and me so fond of children, and only had one of my
own to live. I'd three babies, Miss Lyon, but the blessed
Lord only spared Felix, and him the masterfullest and the
brownest of 'em all. But I did my duty by him, and I said,
he'll have more schooling than his father, and he'll grow up
a doctor, and marry a woman with money to furnish—as I
was myself, spoons and everything—and I shall have the
grandchildren to look up to me, and be drove out in the gig
sometimes, like old Mrs. Lukyn. And you see what it's all
come to, Miss Lyon: here's Felix made a common man of
himself, and says he'll never be married—which is the most
unreasonable thing, and him never easy but when he's got the
child on his lap, or when——"

"Stop, stop, mother," Felix burst in; "pray don't use that limping argument again—that a man should marry because he's fond of children. That's a reason for not marrying. A bachelor's children are always young: they're immortal children—always lisping, waddling, helpless, and with a chance of turning out good."

"The Lord above may know what you mean! And haven't other folks' children a chance of turning out good?"

"Oh, they grow out of it very fast. Here's Job Tudge, now," said Felix, turning the little one round on his knee, and holding his head by the back—"Job's limbs will get lanky; this little fist, that looks like a puff-ball and can hide nothing bigger than a gooseberry, will get large and bony, and perhaps want to clutch more than its share; these wide blue eyes, that tell me more truth than Job knows, will narrow and narrow and try to hide truth that Job would be better without knowing; this little negative nose will become long and self-asserting; and this little tongue—put out thy tongue, Job"—Job, awe-struck under this ceremony, put out a little red tongue very timidly—"this tongue, hardly bigger than a rose-leaf, will get large and thick, wag out of season, do mischief, brag and cant for gain or vanity, and cut as cruelly, for all its clumsiness, as if it were a sharp-edged blade. Big Job will perhaps be naughty——" As Felix, speaking with the loud emphatic distinctness habitual to him, brought out this terribly familiar word, Job's sense of mystification became too painful: he hung his lip and began to cry.

"See there," said Mrs. Holt, "you're frightening the innicent child with such talk—and it's enough to frighten them that think themselves the safest."

"Look here, Job, my man," said Felix, setting the boy down and turning him toward Esther; "go to Miss Lyon, ask her to smile at you, and that will dry up your tears like the sunshine."

Job put his two brown fists on Esther's lap, and she stooped to kiss him. Then, holding his face between her hands, she said, "Tell Mr. Holt we don't mean to be naughty, Job. He should believe in us more. But now I must really go home."

Esther rose and held out her hand to Mrs. Holt, who kept it while she said, a little to Esther's confusion,—

"I am very glad it's took your fancy to come here some-times, Miss Lyon. I know you're thought to hold your head high, but I speak of people as I find 'em. And I'm sure any-body had need be humble that comes where there's a floor like this—for I've put by my best tea-trays, they're so out of all charicter—I must look Above for comfort now; but I don't say I'm not worthy to be called on for all that."

Felix had risen and moved toward the door that he might open it and shield Esther from more last words on his mother's part.

"Good-by, Mr. Holt."

"Will Mr. Lyon like me to sit with him an hour this even-ing, do you think?"

"Why not? He always likes to see you."

"Then I will come. Good-by."

"She's a very straight figure," said Mrs. Holt. "How she carries herself! But I doubt there's some truth in what our people say. If she won't look at young Muscat, it's the bet-ter for *him*. He'd need have a big fortune that marries her."

"That's true, mother," said Felix, sitting down, snatching up little Job, and finding a vent for some unspeakable feeling in the pretence of worrying him.

Esther was rather melancholy as she went home, yet hap-pier withal than she had been for many days before. She thought, "I need not mind having shown so much anxiety about his opinion. He is too clear-sighted to mistake our mutual position; he is quite above putting a false interpre-tation on what I have done. Besides, he had not thought of me at all—I saw that plainly enough. Yet he was very kind. There is something greater and better in him than I had im-agined. His behavior to-day—to his mother and me too—I should call it the highest gentlemanliness, only it seems in him to be something deeper. But he has chosen an intoler-able life; though I suppose, if I had a mind equal to his, and if he loved me very dearly, I should choose the same life."

Esther felt that she had prefixed an impossible "if" to that result. But now she had known Felix, her conception of what a happy love must be had become like a dissolving view, in which the once-clear images were gradually melting into new forms and new colors. The favorite Byronic heroes were beginning to look something like last night's decorations seen in the sober dawn. So fast does a little leaven spread within us —so incalculable is the effect of one personality on another. Behind all Esther's thoughts, like an unacknowledged yet constraining presence, there was the sense that if Felix Holt were to love her her life would be exalted into something quite new—into a sort of difficult blessedness, such as one may imagine in beings who are conscious of painfully growing into the possession of higher powers.

It was quite true that Felix had not thought the more of Esther because of that Sunday afternoon's interview which had shaken her mind to the very roots. He had avoided intruding on Mr. Lyon without special reason, because he believed the minister to be preoccupied with some private care. He had thought a great deal of Esther with a mixture of strong disapproval and strong liking, which both together made a feeling the reverse of indifference; but he was not going to let her have any influence on his life. Even if his determination had not been fixed, he would have believed that she would utterly scorn him in any other light than that of an acquaintance, and the emotion she had shown to-day did not change that belief. But he was deeply touched by this manifestation of her better qualities, and felt that there was a new tie of friendship between them. That was the brief history Felix would have given of his relation to Esther. And he was accustomed to observe himself. But very close and diligent looking at living creatures, even through the best microscope, will leave room for new and contradictory discoveries.

Felix found Mr. Lyon particularly glad to talk to him. The minister had never yet disburthened himself about his letter to Mr. Philip Debarry concerning the public conference; and as by this time he had all the heads of his discussion thoroughly in his mind, it was agreeable to recite them, as well as to express his regret that time had been lost by Mr. Debarry's absence from the Manor, which had prevented the immediate fulfilment of his pledge.

"I don't see how he can fulfil it if the Rector refuses," said Felix, thinking it well to moderate the little man's confidence.

"The Rector is of a spirit that will not incur earthly impeachment, and he cannot refuse what is necessary to his nephew's honorable discharge of an obligation," said Mr. Lyon. "My young friend, it is a case wherein the prearranged conditions tend by such a beautiful fitness to the issue I have sought that I should have forever held myself a traitor to my charge had I neglected the indication."

----------◆---------- *

CHAPTER XXIII.

"I will not excuse you; you shall not be excused; excuses shall not be admitted; there's no excuse shall serve; you shall not be excused."—*Henry IV*.

WHEN Philip Debarry had come home that morning and read the letters which had not been forwarded to him, he laughed so heartily at Mr. Lyon's that he congratulated himself on being in his private room. Otherwise his laughter would have awakened the curiosity of Sir Maximus, and Philip did not wish to tell any one the contents of the letter until he had shown them to his uncle. He determined to ride over to the Rectory to lunch; for, as Lady Mary was away, he and his uncle might be *tête-à-tête*.

The Rectory was on the other side of the river, close to the church of which it was the fitting companion: a fine old brick-and-stone house, with a great bow-window opening from the library onto the deep-turfed lawn, one fat dog sleeping on the door-stone, another fat dog waddling on the gravel, the autumn leaves duly swept away, the lingering chrysanthemums cherished, tall trees stooping or soaring in the most picturesque variety, and a Virginian creeper turning a little rustic hut into a scarlet pavilion. It was one of those rectories which are among the bulwarks of our venerable institutions—which arrest disintegrating doubt, serve as a double embankment against Popery and Dissent, and rally feminine instinct and affection to re-enforce the decisions of masculine thought.

" What makes you look so merry, Phil? " said the Rector, as his nephew entered the pleasant library.

" Something that concerns you," said Philip, taking out the letter. " A clerical challenge. Here's an opportunity for you to emulate the divines of the sixteenth century and have a theological duel. Read this letter."

" What answer have you sent the crazy little fellow?" said the Rector, keeping the letter in his hand and running over it again and again, with brow knit, but eyes gleaming without any malignity.

" Oh, I sent no answer. I awaited yours."

" Mine! " said the Rector, throwing down the letter on the table. " You don't suppose I'm going to hold a public debate with a schismatic of that sort? I should have an infidel shoe-maker next expecting me to answer blasphemies delivered in bad grammar."

" But you see how he puts it," said Philip. With all his gravity of nature he could not resist a slightly mischievous prompting, though he had a serious feeling that he should not like to be regarded as failing to fufil his pledge. " I think if you refuse, I shall be obliged to offer myself."

" Nonsense! Tell him he is himself acting a dishonorable part in interpreting your words as a pledge to do any prepos-terous thing that suits his fancy. Suppose he had asked you to give him land to build a chapel on; doubtless that would have given him a ' lively satisfaction.' A man who puts a non-natural strained sense on a promise is no better than a robber."

" But he has not asked for land. I dare say he thinks you won't object to his proposal. I confess there's a simplicity and quaintness about the letter that rather pleases me."

" Let me tell you, Phil, he's a crazy little firefly, that does a great deal of harm in my parish. He inflames the Dis-senters' minds on politics. There's no end to the mischief done by these busy prating men. They make the ignorant multitude the judges of the largest questions, both political and religious, till we shall soon have no institution left that is not on a level with the comprehension of a huckster or a drayman. There can be nothing more retrograde—losing all the results of civilization, all the lessons of Providence—letting the windlass run down after men have been turning at it painfully for generations. If the instructed are not to judge for the uninstructed, why, let us set Dick Stubbs to make our almanacs, and have a President of the Royal Society elected by universal suffrage."

The Rector had risen, placed himself with his back to the fire, and thrust his hands in his pockets, ready to insist further on this wide argument. Philip sat nursing one leg, listening respectfully, as he always did, though often listening to the sonorous echo of his own statements, which suited his uncle's needs so exactly that he did not distinguish them from his old impressions.

"True," said Philip, "but in special cases we have to do with special conditions. You know I defend the casuists. And it may happen that, for the honor of the Church in Treby and a little also for my honor, circumstances may demand a concession even to some notions of a Dissenting preacher."

"Not at all. I should be making a figure which my brother clergy might well take as an affront to themselves. The character of the Establishment has suffered enough already through the Evangelicals, with their extempore incoherence and their pipe-smoking piety. Look at Wimple, the man who is vicar of Shuttleton—without his gown and bands, anybody would take him for a grocer in mourning."

"Well, I shall cut a still worse figure, and so will you, in the Dissenting magazines and newspapers. It will go the round of the kingdom. There will be a paragraph headed, 'Tory Falsehood and Clerical Cowardice,' or else 'The Meanness of the Aristocracy and the Incompetence of the Beneficed Clergy.'"

"There would be a worse paragraph if I were to consent to the debate. Of course it would be said that I was beaten hollow, and that, now the question had been cleared up at Treby Magna, the Church had not a sound leg to stand on. Besides," the Rector went on, frowning and smiling, "it's all very well for you to talk, Phil, but this debating is not so easy when a man's close upon sixty. What one writes or says must be something good and scholarly; and after all had been done this little Lyon would buzz about one like a wasp, and cross-question and rejoin. Let me tell you, a plain truth may be so worried and mauled by fallacies as to get the worst of it. There's no such thing as tiring a talking machine like Lyon."

"Then you absolutely refuse?"

"Yes, I do."

"You remember that when I wrote my letter of thanks to Lyon you approved my offer to serve him if possible."

"Certainly I remember it. But suppose he had asked you to vote for civil marriage, or to go and hear him preach every Sunday?"

"But he has not asked that."

"Something as unreasonable, though."

"Well," said Philip, taking up Mr. Lyon's letter and looking graver—looking even vexed, "it is rather an unpleasant business for me. I really felt obliged to him. I think there's a sort of worth in the man beyond his class. Whatever may be the reason of the case, I shall disappoint him instead of doing him the service I offered."

"Well, that's a misfortune; we can't help it."

"The worst of it is, I should be insulting him to say, ' I will do anything else, but not just this that you want.' He evidently feels himself in company with Luther and Zwingle and Calvin, and considers our letters part of the history of Protestantism."

"Yes, yes. I know it's rather an unpleasant thing, Phil. You are aware that I would have done anything in reason to prevent you from becoming unpopular here. I consider your character a possession to all of us."

"I think I must call on him forthwith and explain and apologize."

"No, sit still; I've thought of something," said the Rector, with a sudden revival of spirits. "I've just seen Sherlock coming in. He is to lunch with me to-day. It would do no harm for him to hold the debate—a curate and a young man —he'll gain by it; and it would release you from any awkwardness, Phil. Sherlock is not going to stay here long, you know; he'll soon have his title. I'll put the thing to him.

He won't object if I wish it. It's a capital idea. It will do Sherlock good. He's a clever fellow, but he wants confidence."

Philip had not time to object before Mr. Sherlock appeared —a young divine of good birth and figure, of sallow complexion and bashful address.

"Sherlock, you have come in most opportunely," said the Rector. "A case has turned up in the parish in which you can be of eminent use. I know that is what you have desired ever since you have been with me. But I'm about so much myself that there really has not been sphere enough for you. You are a studious man, I know; I dare say you have all the necessary matter prepared—at your finger-ends, if not on paper."

Mr. Sherlock smiled with rather a trembling lip, willing to distinguish himself, but hoping that the Rector only alluded to a dialogue on Baptism by Aspersion, or some other pamphlet suited to the purposes of the Christian Knowledge Society. But as the Rector proceeded to unfold the circumstances under which his eminent service was to be rendered, he grew more and more nervous.

"You'll oblige me very much, Sherlock," the Rector ended, "by going into this thing zealously. Can you guess what time you will require? because it will rest with us to fix the day."

"I should be rejoiced to oblige you, Mr. Debarry, but I really think I am not competent to——"

"That's your modesty, Sherlock. Don't let me hear any more of that. I know Filmore of Corpus said you might be a first-rate man if your diffidence didn't do you injustice. And you can refer anything to me, you know. Come, you will set about the thing at once. But, Phil, you must tell the preacher to send a scheme of the debate—all the different heads—and he must agree to keep rigidly within the scheme. There, sit down at my desk and write the letter now; Thomas shall carry it."

Philip sat down to write, and the Rector, with his firm ringing voice, went on at his ease, giving "indications" to his agitated Curate.

"But you can begin at once preparing a good, cogent, clear statement, and considering the probable points of assault. You can look into Jewel, Hall, Hooker, Whitgift, and the rest: you'll find them all here. My library wants nothing in English divinity. Sketch the lower ground taken by Usher and those men, but bring all your force to bear on marking out the true High-Church doctrine. Expose the wretched cavils of the Nonconformists, and the noisy futility that belongs to schismatics generally. I will give you a telling passage from Burke on the Dissenters, and some good quotations which I brought together in two sermons of my own on the Position of the English Church in Christendom. How long do you think it will take you to bring your thoughts together? You can throw them afterward into the form of an essay; we'll have the thing printed; it will do you good with the Bishop."

With all Mr. Sherlock's timidity, there was fascination for him in this distinction. He reflected that he could take coffee and sit up late, and perhaps produce something rather fine. It might be a first step toward that eminence which it was no more than his duty to aspire to. Even a polemical fame like that of a Philpotts must have had a beginning. Mr. Sherlock was not insensible to the pleasure of turning sentences successfully, and it was a pleasure not always unconnected with preferment. A diffident man likes the idea of doing something remarkable, which will create belief in him without any immediate display of brilliancy. Celebrity may blush and be silent, and win a grace the more. Thus Mr. Sherlock was constrained, trembling all the while, and much wishing that his essay were already in print.

"I think I could hardly be ready under a fortnight."

"Very good. Just write that, Phil, and tell him to fix the precise day and place. And then we'll go to lunch."

The Rector was quite satisfied. He had talked himself into thinking that he should like to give Sherlock a few useful hints, look up his own earlier sermons, and benefit the Curate by his criticism, when the argument had been got into shape. He was a healthy-natured man, but that was not at all a reason why he should not have those sensibilities to the

odor of authorship which belong to almost everybody who is
not expected to be a writer—and especially to that form of
authorship which is called suggestion, and consists in telling
another man that he might do a great deal with a given subject by bringing a sufficient amount of knowledge, reasoning,
and wit to bear upon it.

Philip would have had some twinges of conscience about
the Curate if he had not guessed that the honor thrust upon
him was not altogether disagreeable. The Church might perhaps have had a stronger supporter; but, for himself, he had
done what he was bound to do: he had done his best toward
fulfilling Mr. Lyon's desire.

CHAPTER XXIV.

If he come not, the play is marred.—*Midsummer Night's Dream.*

Rufus Lyon was very happy on that mild November morning appointed for the great conference, in the larger room at
the Free School, between himself and the Rev. Theodore Sherlock, B.A. The disappointment of not contending with the
Rector in person, which had at first been bitter, had been
gradually lost sight of in the positive enjoyment of an opportunity for debating on any terms. Mr. Lyon had two grand
elements of pleasure on such occasions: confidence in the
strength of his case, and confidence in his own power of advo-
cacy. Not—to use his own phrase—not that he "glorified
himself herein"; for speech and exposition were so easy to
him that if he argued forcibly he believed it to be simply
because the truth was forcible. He was not proud of moving
easily in his native medium. A panting man thinks of himself as a clever swimmer; but a fish swims much better, and
takes his performance as a matter of course.

Whether Mr. Sherlock were that panting, self-gratulating
man remained a secret. Philip Debarry, much occupied with
his electioneering affairs, had only once had an opportunity
of asking his uncle how Sherlock got on, and the Rector had
said, curtly, "I think he'll do. I've supplied him well with

references. I advise him to read only and decline everything else as out of order. Lyon will speak to a point, and then Sherlock will read: it will be all the more telling. It will give variety." But on this particular morning peremptory business connected with the magistracy called the Rector away.

Due notice had been given, and the feminine world of Treby Magna was much more agitated by the prospect than by that of any candidate's speech. Mrs. Pendrell at the Bank, Mrs. Tiliot, and the Church ladies generally, felt bound to hear the Curate, who was known, apparently by an intuition concerning the nature of curates, to be a very clever young man; and he would show them what learning had to say on the right side. One or two Dissenting ladies were not without emotion at the thought that, seated on the front benches, they should be brought near to old Church friends, and have a longer greeting than had taken place since the Catholic Emancipation. Mrs. Muscat, who had been a beauty, and was as nice in her millinery as any Trebian lady belonging to the Establishment, reflected that she should put on her best large embroidered collar, and that she should ask Mrs. Tiliot where it was in Duffield that she once got her bed-hangings dyed so beautifully. When Mrs. Tiliot was Mary Salt, the two ladies had been bosom friends; but Mr. Tiliot had looked higher and higher since his gin had become so famous; and in the year '29 he had, in Mr. Muscat's hearing, spoken of Dissenters as sneaks—a personality which could not be overlooked.

The debate was to begin at eleven, for the Rector would not allow the evening to be chosen, when low men and boys might want to be admitted out of mere mischief. This was one reason why the female part of the audience outnumbered the males. But some chief Trebians were there, even men whose means made them as independent of theory as Mr. Pendrell and Mr. Wace; encouraged by reflecting that they were not in a place of worship, and would not be obliged to stay longer than they chose. There was a muster of all Dissenters who could spare the morning time, and on the back benches were all the aged Churchwomen who shared the remnants of the sacrament wine, and who were humbly anxious to neglect nothing ecclesiastical or connected with "going to a better place."

At eleven the arrival of listeners seemed to have ceased. Mr. Lyon was seated on the school tribune or daïs at his particular round table; another round table, with a chair, awaited the Curate, with whose superior position it was quite in keeping that he should not be first on the ground. A couple of extra chairs were placed farther back, and more than one important personage had been requested to act as chairman; but no Churchman would place himself in a position so equivocal as to dignity of aspect, and so unequivocal as to the obligation of sitting out the discussion; and the Rector had beforehand put a veto on any Dissenting chairman.

Mr. Lyon sat patiently absorbed in his thoughts, with his notes in minute handwriting lying before him, seeming to look at the audience, but not seeing them. Every one else was contented that there should be an interval in which there could be a little neighborly talk.

Esther was particularly happy, seated on a side-bench near her father's side of the tribune, with Felix close behind her, so that she could turn her head and talk to him. He had been very kind ever since that morning when she had called at his home, more disposed to listen indulgently to what she had to say, and less blind to her looks and movements. If he had never railed at her or ignored her, she would have been less sensitive to the attention he gave her; but as it was the prospect of seeing him seemed to light up her life, and to disperse the old dulness. She looked unusually charming to-day from the very fact that she was not vividly conscious of anything but of having a mind near her that asked her to be something better than she actually was. The consciousness of her own superiority amongst the people around her was superseded, and even a few brief weeks had given a softened expression to her eyes, a more feminine beseechingness and self-doubt to her manners. Perhaps, however, a little new defiance was rising in place of the old contempt—defiance of the Trebian views concerning Felix Holt.

"What a very nice-looking young woman your minister's daughter is!" said Mrs. Tiliot in an undertone to Mrs. Mus-

cat, who, as she had hoped, had found a seat next to her quon-
dam friend—"quite the lady."

"Rather too much so, considering," said Mrs. Muscat.
"She's thought proud, and that's not pretty in a girl, even
if there was anything to back it up. But now she seems to
be encouraging that young Holt, who scoffs at everything, as
you may judge by his appearance. She has despised his betters before now; but I leave you to judge whether a young
man who has taken to low ways of getting his living can pay
for fine cambric handkerchiefs and light kid gloves."

Mrs. Muscat lowered her blond eyelashes and swayed her
neat head just perceptibly from side to side, with a sincere
desire to be moderate in her expressions, notwithstanding any
shock that facts might have given her.

"Dear, dear," said Mrs. Tiliot. "What! that is young
Holt leaning forward now without a cravat? I've never seen
him before to notice him, but I've heard Tiliot talking about
him. They say he's a dangerous character, and goes stirring
up the working men at Sproxton. And—well, to be sure,
such great eyes and such a great head of hair—it is enough
to frighten one. What can she see in him? Quite below
her."

"Yes, and brought up a governess," said Mrs. Muscat;
"you'd have thought she'd know better how to choose. But
the minister has let her get the upper hand sadly too much.
It's a pity in a man of God. I don't deny he's *that*."

"Well, I am sorry," said Mrs. Tiliot, "for I meant her to
give my girls lessons when they came from school."

Mr. Wace and Mr. Pendrell meanwhile were standing up
and looking round at the audience, nodding to their fellow-
townspeople with the affability due from men in their position.

"It's time he came now," said Mr. Wace, looking at his
watch and comparing it with the schoolroom clock. "This
debating is a new-fangled sort of thing; but the Rector
would never have given in to it if there hadn't been good reasons. Nolan said he wouldn't come. He says this debating
is an atheistical sort of thing; the Atheists are very fond of
it. Theirs is a bad book to take a leaf out of. However, we

16

shall hear nothing but what's good from Mr. Sherlock.   He preaches a capital sermon—for such a young man."

"Well, it was our duty to support him—not to leave him alone among the Dissenters," said Mr. Pendrell.   "You see, everybody hasn't felt that.   Labron might have shown himself, if not Lukyn.   I could have alleged business myself if I had thought proper."

"Here he comes, I think," said Mr. Wace, turning round on hearing a movement near the small door on a level with the platform.   "By George! it's Mr. Debarry.   Come, now, this is handsome."

Mr. Wace and Mr. Pendrell clapped their hands, and the example was followed even by most of the Dissenters.   Philip was aware that he was doing a popular thing, of a kind that Treby was not used to from the elder Debarrys; but his appearance had not been long premeditated.   He was driving through the town toward an engagement at some distance, but on calling at Labron's office he had found that the affair which demanded his presence had been deferred, and so had driven round to the Free School.   Christian came in behind him.

Mr. Lyon was now roused from his abstraction, and, stepping from his slight elevation, begged Mr. Debarry to act as moderator or president on the occasion.

"With all my heart," said Philip.   "But Mr. Sherlock has not arrived, apparently?"

"He tarries somewhat unduly," said Mr. Lyon.   "Nevertheless there may be a reason of which we know not.   Shall I collect the thoughts of the assembly by a brief introductory address in the interval?"

"No, no, no," said Mr. Wace, who saw a limit to his powers of endurance.   "Mr. Sherlock is sure to be here in a minute or two."

"Christian," said Philip Debarry, who felt a slight misgiving, "just be so good—but stay, I'll go myself.   Excuse me, gentlemen: I'll drive round to Mr. Sherlock's lodgings.   He may be under a little mistake as to the time.   Studious men are sometimes rather absent.   You needn't come with me, Christian."

As Mr. Debarry went out, Rufus Lyon stepped on to the

tribune again in rather an uneasy state of mind. A few ideas had occurred to him, eminently fitted to engage the audience profitably, and so to wrest some edification out of an unforeseen delay. But his native delicacy made him feel that in this assembly the Church people might fairly decline any "deliverance" on his part which exceeded the programme, and Mr. Wace's negative had been energetic. But the little man suffered from imprisoned ideas, and was as restless as a racer held in. He could not sit down again, but walked backward and forward, stroking his chin, emitting his low guttural interjection under the pressure of clauses and sentences which he longed to utter aloud, as he would have done in his own study. There was a low buzz in the room, which helped to deepen the minister's sense that the thoughts within him were as divine messengers unheeded or rejected by a trivial generation. Many of the audience were standing; all, except the old Churchwomen on the back seats, and a few devout Dissenters who kept their eyes shut and gave their bodies a gentle oscillating motion, were interested in chat.

"Your father is uneasy," said Felix to Esther.

"Yes; and now, I think, he is feeling for his spectacles. I hope he has not left them at home: he will not be able to see anything two yards before him without them;—and it makes him so unconscious of what people expect or want."

"I'll go and ask him whether he has them," said Felix, striding over the form in front of him, and approaching Mr. Lyon, whose face showed a gleam of pleasure at this relief from his abstracted isolation.

"Miss Lyon is afraid that you are at a loss for your spectacles, sir," said Felix.

"My dear young friend," said Mr. Lyon, laying his hand on Felix Holt's forearm, which was about on a level with the minister's shoulder, "it is a very glorious truth, albeit made somewhat painful to me by the circumstances of the present moment, that as a counterpoise to the brevity of our mortal life (wherein, as I apprehend, our powers are being trained not only for the transmission of an improved heritage, as I have heard you insist, but also for our own entrance into a higher initiation in the Divine scheme)—it is, I say, a very

glorious truth that even in what are called the waste minutes
of our time, like those of expectation, the soul may soar and
range, as in some of our dreams which are brief as a broken
rainbow in duration, yet seem to comprise a long history of
terror or of joy. And again, each moment may be a beginning of a new spiritual energy; and our pulse would doubtless
be a coarse and clumsy notation of the passage from that
which was not to that which is, even in the finer processes of
the material world—and how much more——"

Esther was watching her father and Felix, and though she
was not within hearing of what was being said, she guessed
the actual state of the case—that the inquiry about the spectacles had been unheeded, and that her father was losing himself and embarrassing Felix in the intricacies of a dissertation.
There was not the stillness around her that would have made
a movement on her part seem conspicuous, and she was impelled by her anxiety to step on the tribune and walk up to
her father, who paused, a little startled.

"Pray see whether you have forgotten your spectacles, father. If so, I will go home at once and look for them."

Mr. Lyon was automatically obedient to Esther, and he
began immediately to feel in his pockets.

"How is it that Miss Jermyn is so friendly with the Dissenting parson?" said Christian to Quorlen, the Tory printer,
who was an intimate of his. "Those grand Jermyns are not
Dissenters surely?"

"*What* Miss Jermyn?"

"Why—don't you see?—that fine girl who is talking to
him."

"Miss Jermyn! Why, that's the little parson's daughter."

"His daughter!" Christian gave a low brief whistle, which
seemed a natural expression of surprise that "the rusty old
ranter" should have a daughter of such distinguished appearance.

Meanwhile the search for the spectacles had proved vain.
"'Tis a grievous fault in me, my dear," said the little man,
humbly; "I become thereby sadly burthensome to you."

"I will go at once," said Esther, refusing to let Felix go
instead of her. But she had scarcely stepped off the tribune

when Mr. Debarry re-entered, and there was a commotion which made her wait. After a low-toned conversation with Mr. Pendrell and Mr. Wace, Philip Debarry stepped on to the tribune with his hat in his hand, and said, with an air of much concern and annoyance,—

"I am sorry to have to tell you, ladies and gentlemen, that —doubtless owing to some accidental cause which I trust will soon be explained as nothing serious—Mr. Sherlock is absent from his residence, and is not to be found. He went out early, his landlady informs me, to refresh himself by a walk on this agreeable morning, as is his habit, she tells me, when he has been kept up late by study; and he has not returned. Do not let us be too anxious. I shall cause inquiry to be made in the direction of his walk. It is easy to imagine many accidents, not of a grave character, by which he might nevertheless be absolutely detained against his will. Under these circumstances, Mr. Lyon," continued Philip, turning to the minister, "I presume that the debate must be adjourned."

"The debate, doubtless," began Mr. Lyon; but his further speech was drowned by a general rising of the Church people from their seats, many of them feeling that, even if the cause were lamentable, the adjournment was not altogether disagreeable.

"Good gracious me!" said Mrs. Tiliot, as she took her husband's arm, "I hope the poor young man hasn't fallen into the river or broken his leg."

But some of the more acrid Dissenters, whose temper was not controlled by the habits of retail business, had begun to hiss, implying that in their interpretation the Curate's absence had not depended on any injury to life or limb.

"He's turned tail, sure enough," said Mr. Muscat to the neighbor behind him, lifting his eyebrows and shoulders, and laughing in a way that showed that, deacon as he was, he looked at the affair in an entirely secular light.

But Mrs. Muscat thought it would be nothing but right to have all the waters dragged, agreeing in this with the majority of the Church ladies.

"I regret sincerely, Mr. Lyon," said Philip Debarry, addressing the minister with politeness, "that I must say good-

morning to you, with the sense that I have not been able at
present to contribute to your satisfaction as I had wished."

"Speak not of it in the way of apology, sir," said Mr. Lyon,
in a tone of depression. "I doubt not that you yourself have
acted in good faith. Nor will I open any door of egress to
constructions such as anger often deems ingenious, but which
the disclosure of the simple truth may expose as erroneous
and uncharitable fabrications. I wish you good-morning, sir."

When the room was cleared of the Church people, Mr. Lyon
wished to soothe his own spirit and that of his flock by a few
reflections introductory to a parting prayer. But there was a
general resistance to this effort. The men mustered round
the minister, and declared their opinion that the whole thing
was disgraceful to the Church. Some said the Curate's absence had been contrived from the first. Others more than
hinted that it had been a folly in Mr. Lyon to set on foot any
procedure in common with Tories and clergymen, who, if they
ever aped civility to Dissenters, would never do anything but
laugh at them in their sleeves. Brother Kemp urged in his
heavy bass that Mr. Lyon should lose no time in sending an
account of the affair to the *Patriot;* and Brother Hawkins, in
his high tenor, observed that it was an occasion on which
some stinging things might be said with all the extra effect of
an *apropos.*

The position of receiving a many-voiced lecture from the
members of his church was familiar to Mr. Lyon; but now he
felt weary, frustrated, and doubtful of his own temper. Felix,
who stood by and saw that this man of sensitive fibre was suffering from talkers whose noisy superficiality cost them nothing, got exasperated. "It seems to me, sirs," he burst in, with
his predominant voice, "that Mr. Lyon has hitherto had the
hard part of the business, while you of his congregation have
had the easy one. Punish the Church clergy, if you like—
they can take care of themselves. But don't punish your own
minister. It's no business of mine, perhaps, except so far as
fair play is everybody's business; but it seems to me the time
to ask Mr. Lyon to take a little rest, instead of setting on him
like so many wasps."

By this speech Felix raised a displeasure which fell on the

minister as well as on himself; but he gained his immediate end. The talkers dropped off after a slight show of persistence, and Mr. Lyon quitted the field of no combat with a small group of his less imperious friends, to whom he confided his intention of committing his argument fully to paper, and forwarding it to a discriminating editor.

"But regarding personalities," he added, "I have not the same clear showing. For, say that this young man was pusillanimous—I were but ill provided with arguments if I took my stand even for a moment on so poor an irrelevancy as that because one curate is ill furnished therefore Episcopacy is false. If I held up any one to just obloquy, it would be the well-designated Incumbent of this parish, who, calling himself one of the Church militant, sends a young and weak-kneed substitute to take his place in the fight."

Mr. Philip Debarry did not neglect to make industrious inquiry concerning the accidents which had detained the Rev. Theordore Sherlock on his morning walk. That well-intentioned young divine was seen no more in Treby Magna. But the river was not dragged, for by the evening coach the Rector received an explanatory letter. The Rev. Theodore's agitation had increased so much during his walk that the passing coach had been a means of deliverance not to be resisted; and, literally at the eleventh hour, he had hailed and mounted the cheerful Tally-ho! and carried away his portion of the debate in his pocket.

But the Rector had subsequently the satisfaction of receiving Mr. Sherlock's painstaking production in print, with a dedication to the Rev. Augustus Debarry, a motto from St. Chrysostom, and other additions, the fruit of ripening leisure. He was "sorry for poor Sherlock, who wanted confidence"; but he was convinced that for his own part he had taken the course which under the circumstances was the least compromising to the Church. Sir Maximus, however, observed to his son and brother that he had been right and they had been wrong as to the danger of vague, enormous expressions of gratitude to a Dissenting preacher, and on any differences of opinion seldom failed to remind them of that precedent.

CHAPTER XXV.

Your fellow-man ?—Divide the epithet:
Say rather, you're the fellow, he the man.

WHEN Christian quitted the Free School with the discovery
that the young lady whose appearance had first startled him
with an indefinable impression in the market-place was the
daughter of the old Dissenting preacher who had shown so
much agitated curiosity about his name, he felt very much
like an uninitiated chess-player, who sees that the pieces are
in a peculiar position on the board, and might open the way
for him to give checkmate, if he only knew how. Ever since
his interview with Jermyn, his mind had been occupied with
the charade it offered to his ingenuity. What was the real
meaning of the lawyer's interest in him, and in his relations
with Maurice Christian Bycliffe? Here was a secret; and
secrets were often a source of profit, of that agreeable kind
which involved little labor. Jermyn had hinted at profit
which might possibly come through him; but Christian said
inwardly, with well-satisfied self-esteem, that he was not so
pitiable a nincompoop as to trust Jermyn. On the contrary,
the only problem before him was to find out by what combination of independent knowledge he could outwit Jermyn,
elude any purchase the attorney had on him through his past
history, and get a handsome bonus, by which a somewhat
shattered man of pleasure might live well without a master.
Christian, having early exhausted the more impulsive delights
of life, had become a sober calculator; and he had made up
his mind that, for a man who had long ago run through his
own money, servitude in a great family was the best kind of
retirement after that of a pensioner; but if a better chance
offered, a person of talent must not let it slip through his fingers. He held various ends of threads, but there was danger
in pulling at them too impatiently. He had not forgotten the
surprise which had made him drop the punch-ladle, when Mr.
Crowder, talking in the steward's room, had said that a scamp
named Henry Scaddon had been concerned in a lawsuit about

the Transome estate. Again, Jermyn was the family lawyer of the Transomes; he knew about the exchange of names between Scaddon and Bycliffe; he clearly wanted to know as much as he could about Bycliffe's history. The conclusion was not remote that Bycliffe had had some claim on the Transome property, and that a difficulty had arisen from his being confounded with Henry Scaddon. But hitherto the other incident which had been apparently connected with the interchange of names—Mr. Lyon's demand that he should write down the name Maurice Christian, accompanied with the question whether that were his whole name—had had no visible link with the inferences arrived at through Crowder and Jermyn.

The discovery made this morning at the Free School that Esther was the daughter of the Dissenting preacher at last suggested a possible link. Until then, Christian had not known why Esther's face had impressed him so peculiarly; but the minister's chief association for him was with Bycliffe, and that association served as a flash to show him that Esther's features and expression, and still more her bearing, now she stood and walked, revived Bycliffe's image. Daughter? There were various ways of being a daughter. Suppose this were a case of adoption: suppose Bycliffe were known to be dead, or thought to be dead. "Begad, if the old parson had fancied the original father was come to life again, it was enough to frighten him a little. "Slow and steady," Christian said to himself; "I'll get some talk with the old man again. He's safe enough: one can handle him without cutting one's self. I'll tell him I knew Bycliffe, and was his fellow-prisoner. I'll worm out the truth about this daughter. Could pretty Annette have married again, and married this little scarecrow? There's no knowing what a woman will not do."

Christian could see no distinct result for himself from his industry: but if there were to be any such result, it must be reached by following out every clew; and to the non-legal mind there are dim possibilities in law and heirship which prevent any issue from seeming too miraculous.

The consequence of these meditations was, that Christian

hung about Treby more than usual in his leisure time, and that on the first opportunity he accosted Mr. Lyon in the street with suitable civility, stating that since the occasion which had brought them together some weeks before, he had often wished to renew their conversation, and, with Mr. Lyon's permission, would now ask to do so. After being assured, as he had been by Jermyn, that this courier, who had happened by some accident to possess the memorable locket and pocket-book, was certainly not Annette's husband, and was ignorant whether Maurice Christian Bycliffe were living or dead, the minister's mind had become easy again; his habitual lack of interest in personal details rendering him gradually oblivious of Jermyn's precautionary statement that he was pursuing inquiries, and that if anything of interest turned up, Mr. Lyon should be made acquainted with it. Hence, when Christian addressed him, the minister, taken by surprise and shaken by the recollections of former anxieties, said, helplessly,—

"If it is business, sir, you would perhaps do better to address yourself to Mr. Jermyn."

He could not have said anything that was a more valuable hint to Christian. He inferred that the minister had made a confidant of Jermyn, and it was needful to be wary.

"On the contrary, sir," he answered, "it may be of the utmost importance to you that what passes between us should not be known to Mr. Jermyn."

Mr. Lyon was perplexed, and felt at once that he was no more in clear daylight concerning Jermyn than concerning Christian. He dared not neglect the possible duty of hearing what this man had to say, and he invited him to proceed to Malthouse Yard, where they could converse in private.

Once in Mr. Lyon's study, Christian opened the dialogue by saying that since he was in this room before it had occurred to him that the anxiety he had observed in Mr. Lyon might be owing to some acquaintance with Maurice Christian Bycliffe—a fellow-prisoner in France, whom he, Christian, had assisted in getting freed from his imprisonment, and who, in fact, had been the owner of the trifles which Mr. Lyon recently had in his possession and had restored. Christian hastened to say that he knew nothing of Bycliffe's history since they had parted in France, but that he knew of his marriage with Annette Ledru, and had been acquainted with Annette herself. He would be very glad to know what became of Bycliffe, if he could, for he liked him uncommonly.

Here Christian paused; but Mr. Lyon only sat changing color and trembling. This man's bearing and tone of mind were made repulsive to him by being brought in contact with keenly felt memories, and he could not readily summon the courage to give answers or ask questions.

"May I ask if you knew my friend Bycliffe?" said Christian, trying a more direct method.

"No, sir; I never saw him."

"Ah! well—you have seen a very striking likeness of him. It's wonderful—unaccountable; but when I saw Miss Lyon at the Free School the other day, I could have sworn she was Bycliffe's daughter."

"Sir!" said Mr. Lyon, in his deepest tone, half rising, and holding by the arms of his chair, "these subjects touch me with too sharp a point for you to be justified in thrusting them on me out of mere levity. Is there any good you seek or any injury you fear in relation to them?"

"Precisely, sir. We shall come now to an understanding. Suppose I believed that the young lady who goes by the name of Miss Lyon was the daughter of Bycliffe?"

Mr. Lyon moved his lips silently.

"And suppose I had reason to suspect that there would be some great advantage for her if the law knew who was her father?"

"Sir!" said Mr. Lyon, shaken out of all reticence, "I would not conceal it. She believed herself to be my daughter. But I will bear all things rather than deprive her of a right. Nevertheless I appeal to the pity of any fellow-man, not to thrust himself between her and me, but to let me disclose the truth to her myself."

"All in good time," said Christian. "We must do nothing rash. Then Miss Lyon is Annette's child?"

The minister shivered as if the edge of a knife had been drawn across his hand. But the tone of this question, by the very fact that it intensified his antipathy to Christian, enabled

him to collect himself for what must be simply the endurance
of a painful operation. After a moment or two he said more
coolly, "It is true, sir. Her mother became my wife. Proceed with any statement which may concern my duty."

"I have no more to say than this: If there's a prize that
the law might hand over to Bycliffe's daughter, I am much
mistaken if there isn't a lawyer who'll take precious good care
to keep the law hoodwinked. And that lawyer is Mat Jermyn.
Why, my good sir, if you've been taking Jermyn into your
confidence, you've been setting the fox to keep off the weasel.
It strikes me that when you were made a little anxious about
those articles of poor Bycliffe's, you put Jermyn on making
inquiries of me. Eh? I think I am right?"

"I do not deny it."

"Ah!—it was very well you did, for by that means I've
found out that he's got hold of some secrets about Bycliffe
which he means to stifle. Now, sir, if you desire any justice
for your daughter—step-daughter, I should say—don't so
much as wink to yourself before Jermyn; and if you've got
any papers or things of that sort that may come in evidence,
as these confounded rascals the lawyers call it, clutch them
tight, for if they get into Jermyn's hands they may soon fly
up the chimney. Have I said enough?"

"I had not purposed any further communication with Mr.
Jermyn, sir; indeed, I have nothing further to communicate.
Except that one fact concerning my daughter's birth, which
I have erred in concealing from her, I neither seek disclosures
nor do I tremble before them."

"Then I have your word that you will be silent about this
conversation between us? It is for your daughter's interest,
mind."

"Sir, I shall be silent," said Mr. Lyon, with cold gravity.
"Unless," he added, with an acumen as to possibilities rather
disturbing to Christian's confident contempt for the old man—
"unless I were called upon by some tribunal to declare the
whole truth in this relation; in which case I should submit
myself to that authority of investigation which is a requisite
of social order."

Christian departed, feeling satisfied that he had got the utmost to be obtained at present out of the Dissenting preacher, whom he had not dared to question more closely. He must look out for chance lights, and perhaps, too, he might catch a stray hint by stirring the sediment of Mr. Crowder's memory. But he must not venture on inquiries that might be noticed. He was in awe of Jermyn.

When Mr. Lyon was alone he paced up and down among his books, and thought aloud, in order to relieve himself after the constraint of this interview. "I will not wait for the urgency of necessity," he said, more than once. "I will tell the child without compulsion. And then I shall fear nothing. And an unwonted spirit of tenderness has filled her of late. She will forgive me."

CHAPTER XXVI.

Consideration like an angel came
And whipped the offending Adam out of her;
Leaving her body as a paradise
To envelop and contain celestial spirits.
SHAKESPEARE: *Henry V.*

THE next morning, after much prayer for the needful strength and wisdom, Mr. Lyon came downstairs with the resolution that another day should not pass without the fulfilment of the task he had laid on himself; but what hour he should choose for his solemn disclosure to Esther must depend on their mutual occupations. Perhaps he must defer it till they sat up alone together, after Lyddy was gone to bed. But at breakfast Esther said,—

"To-day is a holiday, father. My pupils are all going to Duffield to see the wild beasts. What have you got to do to-day? Come, you are eating no breakfast. Oh, Lyddy, Lyddy, the eggs are hard again. I wish you would not read Alleyne's 'Alarm' before breakfast; it makes you cry and forget the eggs."

"They *are* hard, and that's the truth; but there's hearts as are harder, Miss Esther," said Lyddy.

"I think not," said Esther. "This is leathery enough for

the heart of the most obdurate Jew.   Pray give it little Zach-ary for a football."

"Dear, dear, don't you be so light, miss.   We may all be dead before night."

"You speak out of season, my good Lyddy," said Mr. Lyon, wearily; "depart into the kitchen."

"What have you got to do to-day, father?" persisted Esther.   "I have a holiday."

Mr. Lyon felt as if this were a fresh summons not to delay. "I have something of great moment to do, my dear; and since you are not otherwise demanded, I will ask you to come and sit with me upstairs."

Esther wondered what there could be on her father's mind more pressing than his morning studies.

She soon knew.   Motionless, but mentally stirred as she had never been before, Esther listened to her mother's story, and to the outpouring of her step-father's long-pent-up expe-rience.   The rays of the morning sun which fell athwart the books, the sense of the beginning day, had deepened the so-lemnity more than night would have done.   All knowledge which alters our lives penetrates us more when it comes in the early morning: the day that has to be travelled with some-thing new and perhaps forever sad in its light is an image of the life that spreads beyond.   But at night the time of rest is near.

Mr. Lyon regarded his narrative as a confession—as a reve-lation to this beloved child of his own miserable weakness and error.   But to her it seemed a revelation of another sort: her mind seemed suddenly enlarged by a vision of passion and struggle, of delight and renunciation, in the lot of beings who had hitherto been a dull enigma to her.   And in the act of unfolding to her that he was not her real father, but had only striven to cherish her as a father, had only longed to be loved as a father, the odd, wayworn, unworldly man became the ob-ject of a new sympathy in which Esther felt herself exalted. Perhaps this knowledge would have been less powerful within her but for the mental preparation that had come during the last two months from her acquaintance with Felix Holt, which had taught her to doubt the infallibility of her own standard, and raised a presentiment of moral depths that were hidden from her.

Esther had taken her place opposite to her father, and had not moved even her clasped hands while he was speaking. But after the long outpouring in which he seemed to lose the sense of everything but the memories he was giving utterance to, he paused a little while and then said timidly,—

"This is a late retrieval of a long error, Esther. I make not excuses for myself, for we ought to strive that our affections be rooted in the truth. Nevertheless you——"

Esther had risen, and had glided on to the wooden stool on a level with her father's chair, where he was accustomed to lay books. She wanted to speak, but the floodgates could not be opened for words alone. She threw her arms round the old man's neck and sobbed out with a passionate cry, "Father, father! forgive me if I have not loved you enough. I will—I will!"

The old man's little delicate frame was shaken by a surprise and joy that were almost painful in their intensity. He had been going to ask forgiveness of her who asked it for herself. In that moment of supreme complex emotion one ray of the minister's joy was the thought, "Surely the work of grace is begun in her—surely here is a heart that the Lord hath touched."

They sat so, enclasped in silence, while Esther relieved her full heart. When she raised her head, she sat quite still for a minute or two looking fixedly before her, and keeping one little hand in the minister's. Presently she looked at him and said,—

"Then you lived like a working man, father; you were very, very poor. Yet my mother had been used to luxury. She was well born—she was a lady."

"It is true, my dear; it was a poor life that I could give her."

Mr. Lyon answered in utter dimness as to the course Esther's mind was taking. He had anticipated before his disclosure, from his long-standing discernment of tendencies in her which were often the cause of silent grief to him, that the discovery likely to have the keenest interest for her would

be that her parents had a higher rank than that of the poor
Dissenting preacher; but she had shown that other and better
sensibilities were predominant. He rebuked himself now for
a hasty and shallow judgment concerning the child's inner
life, and waited for new clearness.

"But that must be the best life, father," said Esther, suddenly rising, with a flush across her paleness, and standing
with her head thrown a little backward, as if some illumination had given her a new decision. "That must be the best
life."

"What life, my dear child?"

"Why, that where one bears and does everything because
of some great and strong feeling—so that this and that in one's
circumstances don't signify."

"Yea, verily; but the feeling that should be thus supreme
is devotedness to the Divine Will."

Esther did not speak; her father's words did not fit on to
the impressions wrought in her by what he had told her. She
sat down again, and said, more quietly,—

"Mamma did not speak much of my—first father?"

"Not much, dear. She said he was beautiful to the eye,
and good and generous; and that his family was of those who
have been long privileged among their fellows. But now I
will deliver to you the letters, which, together with a ring and
locket, are the only visible memorials she retained of him."

Mr. Lyon reached and delivered to Esther the box containing the relics. "Take them, and examine them in privacy,
my dear. And that I may no more err by concealment, I will
tell you some late occurrences that bear on these memorials,
though to my present apprehension doubtfully and confusedly."

He then narrated to Esther all that had passed between
himself and Christian. The possibility—to which Mr. Lyon's
alarms had pointed—that her real father might still be living,
was a new shock. She could not speak about it to her present
father, but it was registered in silence as a painful addition
to the uncertainties which she suddenly saw hanging over her
life.

"I have little confidence in this man's allegations," Mr.

Lyon ended. "I confess his presence and speech are to me as the jarring of metal. He bears the stamp of one who has never conceived aught of more sanctity than the lust of the eye and the pride of life. He hints at some possible inheritance for you, and denounces mysteriously the devices of Mr. Jermyn. All this may or may not have a true foundation. But it is not my part to move in this matter save on a clearer showing."

"Certainly not, father," said Esther, eagerly. A little while ago, these problematic prospects might have set her dreaming pleasantly; but now, for some reasons that she could not have put distinctly into words, they affected her with dread.

CHAPTER XXVII.

To hear with eyes is part of love's rare wit.
SHAKESPEARE: *Sonnets*

Custom calls me to't:
What custom wills, in all things should we do't,
The dust on antique time would lie unswept,
And mountainous error be too highly heaped
For truth to over-peer.—*Coriolanus.*

In the afternoon Mr. Lyon went out to see the sick amongst his flock, and Esther, who had been passing the morning in dwelling on the memories and the few remaining relics of her parents, was left alone in the parlor amidst the lingering odors of the early dinner, not easily got rid of in that small house. Rich people, who know nothing of these vulgar details, can hardly imagine their significance in the history of multitudes of human lives in which the sensibilities are never adjusted to the external conditions. Esther always felt so much discomfort from those odors that she usually seized any possibility of escaping from them, and to-day they oppressed her the more because she was weary with long-continued agitation. Why did she not put on her bonnet as usual and get out into the open air? It was one of those pleasant November afternoons—pleasant in the wide country—when the sunshine is on the clinging brown leaves of the young oaks, and

17

the last yellow leaves of the elms flutter down in the fresh
but not eager breeze. But Esther sat still on the sofa—pale
and with reddened eyelids, her curls all pushed back carelessly, and her elbow resting on the ridgy black horsehair,
which usually almost set her teeth on edge if she pressed it
even through her sleeve—while her eyes rested blankly on the
dull street. Lyddy had said, "Miss, you look sadly; if you
can't take a walk, go and lie down." She had never seen the
curls in such disorder, and she reflected that there had been
a death from typhus recently. But the obstinate Miss only
shook her head.

Esther was waiting for the sake of—not a probability, but
—a mere possibility, which made the brothy odors endurable.
Apparently, in less than a half an hour, the possibility came
to pass, for she changed her attitude, almost started from her
seat, sat down again, and listened eagerly. If Lyddy should
send him away, could she herself rush out and call him back?
Why not? Such things were permissible where it was understood, from the necessity of the case, that there was only
friendship. But Lyddy opened the door and said, "Here's
Mr. Holt, miss, wants to know if you'll give him leave to
come in. I told him you was sadly."

"Oh, yes, Lyddy, beg him to come in."

"I should not have persevered," said Felix, as they shook
hands, "only I know Lyddy's dismal way. But you do look
ill," he went on, as he seated himself at the other end of the
sofa. "Or rather—for that's a false way of putting it—you
look as if you had been very much distressed. Do you mind
about my taking notice of it?"

He spoke very kindly, and looked at her more persistently
than he had ever done before, when her hair was perfect.

"You are quite right. I am not at all ill. But I have
been very much agitated this morning. My father has been
telling me things I never heard before about my mother, and
giving me things that belonged to her. She died when I was
a very little creature."

"Then it is no new pain or trouble for you and Mr. Lyon?
I could not help being anxious to know that."

Esther passed her hand over her brow before she answered.

"I hardly know whether it is pain, or something better than pleasure. It has made me see things I was blind to before—depths in my father's nature."

As she said this, she looked at Felix, and their eyes met very gravely.

"It is such a beautiful day," he said, "it would do you good to go into the air. Let me take you along the river toward Little Treby, will you?"

"I will put my bonnet on," said Esther, unhesitatingly, though they had never walked out together before.

It is true that to get into the fields they had to pass through the street; and when Esther saw some acquaintances, she reflected that her walking alone with Felix might be a subject of remark—all the more because of his cap, patched boots, no cravat, and thick stick. Esther was a little amazed herself at what she had come to. So our lives glide on: the river ends we don't know where, and the sea begins, and then there is no more jumping ashore.

When they were in the streets Esther hardly spoke. Felix talked with his usual readiness, as easily as if he were not doing it solely to divert her thoughts, first about Job Tudge's delicate chest, and the probability that the little white-faced monkey would not live long: and then about a miserable beginning of a night-school, which was all he could get together at Sproxton; and the dismalness of that hamlet, which was a sort of lip to the coal-pit on one side and the "public" on the other—and yet a paradise compared with the wynds of Glasgow, where there was little more than a chink of daylight to show the hatred in women's faces.

But soon they got into the fields, where there was a right of way toward Little Treby, now following the course of the river, now crossing toward a lane, and now turning into a cart-track through a plantation.

"Here we are!" said Felix, when they had crossed the wooden bridge, and were treading on the slanting shadows made by the elm-trunks. "I think this is delicious. I never feel less unhappy than in these late autumn afternoons when they are sunny."

"Less unhappy! There now!" said Esther, smiling at him

with some of her habitual sauciness, " I have caught you in self-contradiction. I have heard you quite furious against puling, melancholy people. If I had said what you have just said, you would have given me a long lecture, and told me to go home and interest myself in the reason of the rule of three."

"Very likely," said Felix, beating the weeds, according to the foible of our common humanity when it has a stick in its hand. "But I don't think myself a fine fellow because I'm melancholy. I don't measure my force by the negations in me, and think my soul must be a mighty one because it is more given to idle suffering than to beneficent activity. That's what your favorite gentlemen do, of the Byronic-bilious style."

" I don't admit that those are my favorite gentlemen."

" I've heard you defend them—gentlemen like your Rénés, who have no particular talent for the finite, but a general sense that the infinite is the right thing for them. They might as well boast of nausea as a proof of a strong inside."

"Stop, stop! You run on in that way to get out of my reach. I convicted you of confessing that you are melancholy."

" Yes," said Felix, thrusting his left hand into his pocket, with a shrug; "as I could confess to a great many other things I'm not proud of. The fact is, there are not many easy lots to be drawn in the world at present; and such as they are I am not envious of them. I don't say life is not worth having: it is worth having to a man who has some sparks of sense and feeling and bravery in him. And the finest fellow of all would be the one who could be glad to have lived because the world was chiefly miserable, and his life had come to help some one who needed it. He would be the man who had the most powers and the fewest selfish wants. But I'm not up to the level of what I see to be best. I'm often a hungry, discontented fellow."

" Why have you made your life so hard then?" said Esther, rather frightened as she asked the question. "It seems to me you have tried to find just the most difficult task."

"Not at all," said Felix, with curt decision. " My course was a very simple one. It was pointed out to me by conditions that I saw as clearly as I see the bars of this stile. It's a difficult stile too," added Felix, striding over. "Shall I help you, or will you be left to yourself?"

"I can do without help, thank you."

"It was all simple enough," continued Felix, as they walked on. "If I meant to put a stop to the sale of those drugs, I must keep my mother, and of course at her age she would not leave the place she had been used to. And I had made up my mind against what they call genteel businesses."

"But suppose every one did as you do? Please to forgive me for saying so; but I cannot see why you could not have lived as honorably with some employment that presupposes education and refinement."

"Because you can't see my history or my nature," said Felix, bluntly. "I have to determine for myself, and not for other men. I don't blame them, or think I am better than they; their circumstances are different. I would never choose to withdraw myself from the labor and common burthen of the world; but I do choose to withdraw myself from the push and the scramble for money and position. Any man is at liberty to call me a fool, and say that mankind are benefited by the push and the scramble in the long run. But I care for the people who live now and will not be living when the long run comes. As it is, I prefer going shares with the unlucky."

Esther did not speak, and there was silence between them for a minute or two, till they passed through a gate into a plantation where there was no large timber, but only thin-stemmed trees and underwood, so that the sunlight fell on the mossy spaces which lay open here and there.

"See how beautiful those stooping birch-stems are with the light on them!" said Felix. "Here is an old felled trunk they have not thought worth carrying away. Shall we sit down a little while?"

"Yes; the mossy ground with the dry leaves sprinkled over it is delightful to one's feet." Esther sat down and took off her bonnet, that the light breeze might fall on her head. Felix, too, threw down his cap and stick, lying on the ground with his back against the felled trunk.

"I wish I felt more as you do," she said, looking at the

point of her foot, which was playing with a tuft of moss. "I can't help caring very much what happens to me. And you seem to care so little about yourself."

"You are thoroughly mistaken," said Felix. "It is just because I'm a very ambitious fellow, with very hungry passions, wanting a great deal to satisfy me, that I have chosen to give up what people call worldly good. At least that has been one determining reason. It all depends on what a man gets into his consciousness—what life thrusts into his mind, so that it becomes present to him as remorse is present to the guilty, or a mechanical problem to an inventive genius. There are two things I've got present in that way: one of them is the picture of what I should hate to be. I'm determined never to go about making my face simpering or solemn, and telling professional lies for profit; or to get tangled in affairs where I must wink at dishonesty and pocket the proceeds, and justify that knavery as part of a system that I can't alter. If I once went into that sort of struggle for success, I should want to win—I should defend the wrong that I had once identified myself with. I should become everything that I see now beforehand to be detestable. And what's more, I should do this, as men are doing it every day, for a ridiculously small prize—perhaps for none at all—perhaps for the sake of two parlors, a rank eligible for the churchwardenship, a discontented wife, and several unhopeful children."

Esther felt a terrible pressure on her heart—the certainty of her remoteness from Felix—the sense that she was utterly trivial to him.

"The other thing that's got into my mind like a splinter," said Felix, after a pause, "is the life of the miserable—the spawning life of vice and hunger. I'll never be one of the sleek dogs. The old Catholics are right, with their higher rule and their lower. Some are called to subject themselves to a harder discipline, and renounce things voluntarily which are lawful to others. It is the old word—'necessity is laid upon me.'"

"It seems to me you are stricter than my father is."

"No. I quarrel with no delight that is not base or cruel, but one must sometimes accommodate one's self to a small share. That is the lot of the majority. I would wish the minority joy, only they don't want my wishes."

Again there was silence. Esther's cheeks were hot in spite of the breeze that sent her hair floating backward. She felt an inward strain, a demand on her to see things in a light that was not easy or soothing. When Felix had asked her to walk, he had seemed so kind, so alive to what might be her feelings, that she had thought herself nearer to him than she had ever been before; but since they had come out he had appeared to forget all that. And yet she was conscious that this impatience of hers was very petty. Battling in this way with her own little impulses, and looking at the birch-stems opposite till her gaze was too wide for her to see anything distinctly, she was unaware how long they had remained without speaking. She did not know that Felix had changed his attitude a little, and was resting his elbow on the tree-trunk, while he supported his head, which was turned toward her. Suddenly he said, in a lower tone than was habitual to him,—

"You are very beautiful."

She started and looked round at him, to see whether his face would give some help to the interpretation of this novel speech. He was looking up at her quite calmly, very much as a reverential Protestant might look at a picture of the Virgin, with a devoutness suggested by the type rather than by the image. Esther's vanity was not in the least gratified: she felt that, somehow or other, Felix was going to reproach her.

"I wonder," he went on, still looking at her, "whether the subtle measuring of forces will ever come to measuring the force there would be in one beautiful woman whose mind was as noble as her face was beautiful—who made a man's passion for her rush in one current with all the great aims of his life."

Esther's eyes got hot and smarting. It was no use trying to be dignified. She had turned away her head, and now said, rather bitterly, "It is difficult for a woman ever to try to be anything good when she is not believed in—when it is always supposed that she must be contemptible."

"No, dear Esther,"—it was the first time Felix had been prompted to call her by her Christian name, and as he did so he laid his large hand on her two little hands, which were clasped on her knees. "You don't believe that I think you contemptible. When I first saw you——"

"I know, I know," said Esther, interrupting him impetuously, but still looking away. "You mean you did think me contemptible then. But it was very narrow for you to judge me in that way, when my life had been so different from yours. I have great faults. I know I am selfish, and think too much of my own small tastes and too little of what affects others. But I am not stupid. I am not unfeeling. I can see what is better."

"But I have not done you injustice since I knew more of you," said Felix, gently.

"Yes, you have," said Esther, turning and smiling at him through her tears. "You talk to me like an angry pedagogue. Were *you* always wise? Remember the time when you were foolish or naughty."

"That is not far off," said Felix, curtly, taking away his hand, and clasping it with the other at the back of his head. The talk, which seemed to be introducing a mutual understanding, such as had not existed before, seemed to have undergone some check.

"Shall we get up and walk back now?" said Esther, after a few moments.

"No," said Felix, entreatingly. "Don't move yet. I dare say we shall never walk together or sit here again."

"Why not?"

"Because I am a man who am warned by visions. Those old stories of visions and dreams guiding men have their truth: we are saved by making the future present to ourselves."

"I wish I could get visions, then," said Esther, smiling at him, with an effort at playfulness, in resistance to something vaguely mournful within her.

"That is what I want," said Felix, looking at her very earnestly. "Don't turn your head. Do look at me, and then I shall know if I may go on speaking. I do believe in you; but I want you to have such a vision of the future that you may never lose your best self. Some charm or other may be flung about you—some of your attar-of-rose fascinations—and nothing but a good strong terrible vision will save you. And if it did save you, you might be that woman I was thinking of a little while ago when I looked at your face: the woman whose beauty makes a great task easier to men instead of turning them away from it. I am not likely to see such fine issues; but they may come where a woman's spirit is finely touched. I should like to be sure they would come to you."

"Why are you not likely to know what becomes of me?" said Esther, turning away her eyes in spite of his command. "Why should you not always be my father's friend and mine?"

"Oh, I shall go away as soon as I can to some large town," said Felix, in his more usual tone,—"some ugly, wicked, misesable place. I want to be a demagogue of a new sort; an honest one, if possible, who will tell the people they are blind and foolish, and neither flatter them nor fatten on them. I have my heritage—an order I belong to. I have the blood of a line of handicraftsmen in my veins, and I want to stand up for the lot of the handicraftsman as a good lot, in which a man may be better trained to all the best functions of his nature than if he belonged to the grimacing set who have visiting-cards, and are proud to be thought richer than their neighbors."

"Would nothing ever make it seem right to you to change your mind?" said Esther (she had rapidly woven some possibilities out of the new uncertainties in her own lot, though she would not for the world have had Felix know of her weaving). "Suppose, by some means or other, a fortune might come to you honorably—by marriage, or in any other unexpected way—would you see no change in your course?"

"No," said Felix, peremptorily; "I will never be rich. I don't count that as any peculiar virtue. Some men do well to accept riches, but that is not my inward vocation: I have no fellow-feeling with the rich as a class; the habits of their lives are odious to me. Thousands of men have wedded poverty because they expect to go to heaven for it; I don't expect to go to heaven for it, but I wed it because it enables me to do what I most want to do on earth. Whatever the hopes for the world may be—whether great or small—I am a man of this generation; I will try to make life less bitter for a few within my reach. It is held reasonable enough to toil for the fortunes of a family, though it may turn to imbecility in the third generation. I choose a family with more chances in it."

Esther looked before her dreamily till she said, "That seems a hard lot; yet it is a great one." She rose to walk back.

"Then you don't think I'm a fool," said Felix, loudly, starting to his feet, and then stooping to gather up his cap and stick.

"Of course you suspected me of that stupidity."

"Well—women, unless they are Saint Theresas or Elizabeth Frys, generally think this sort of thing madness, unless when they read of it in the Bible."

"A woman can hardly ever choose in that way; she is dependent on what happens to her. She must take meaner things, because only meaner things are within her reach."

"Why, can you imagine yourself choosing hardship as the better lot?" said Felix, looking at her with a sudden question in his eyes.

"Yes, I can," she said, flushing over neck and brow.

Their words were charged with a meaning dependent entirely on the secret consciousness of each. Nothing had been said which was necessarily personal. They walked a few yards along the road by which they had come, without further speech, till Felix said gently, "Take my arm." She took it, and they walked home so, entirely without conversation. Felix was struggling as a firm man struggles with a temptation, seeing beyond it and disbelieving its lying promise. Esther was struggling as a woman struggles with the yearning for some expression of love, and with vexation under that subjection to a yearning which is not likely to be satisfied. Each was conscious of a silence which each was unable to break, till they entered Malthouse Lane, and were within a few yards of the minister's door.

"It is getting dusk," Felix then said; "will Mr. Lyon be anxious about you?"

"No, I think not. Lyddy would tell him that I went out

with you, and that you carried a large stick," said Esther, with her light laugh.

Felix went in with Esther to take tea, but the conversation was entirely between him and Mr. Lyon about the tricks of canvassing, the foolish personality of the placards, and the probabilities of Transome's return, as to which Felix declared himself to have become indifferent. This scepticism made the minister uneasy: he had great belief in the old political watchwords, had preached that universal suffrage and no ballot were agreeable to the will of God, and liked to believe that a visible "instrument" was forthcoming in the Radical Candidate who had pronounced emphatically against Whig finality. Felix, being in a perverse mood, contended that universal suffrage would be equally agreeable to the devil; that he would change his politics a little, have a larger traffic, and see himself more fully represented in Parliament.

"Nay, my friend," said the minister, "you are again sporting with paradox; for you will not deny that you glory in the name of Radical, or Root-and-branch man, as they said in the great times when Nonconformity was in its giant youth."

"A Radical—yes; but I want to go to some roots a good deal lower down than the franchise."

"Truly there is a work within which cannot be dispensed with; but it is our preliminary work to free men from the stifled life of political nullity, and bring them into what Milton calls ' the liberal air,' wherein alone can be wrought the final triumphs of the Spirit."

"With all my heart. But while Caliban is Caliban, though you multiply him by a million, he'll worship every Trinculo that carries a bottle. I forget, though—you don't read Shakespeare, Mr. Lyon."

"I am bound to confess that I have so far looked into a volume of Esther's as to conceive your meaning; but the fantasies therein were so little to be reconciled with a steady contemplation of that divine economy which is hidden from sense and revealed to faith that I forbore the reading, as likely to perturb my ministrations."

Esther sat by in unusual silence. The conviction that Felix willed her exclusion from his life was making it plain that something more than friendship between them was not so thoroughly out of the question as she had always inwardly asserted. In her pain that his choice lay aloof from her, she was compelled frankly to admit to herself the longing that it had been otherwise, and that he had entreated her to share his difficult life. He was like no one else to her: he had seemed to bring at once a law and the love that gave strength to obey the law. Yet the next moment, stung by his independence of her, she denied that she loved him; she had only longed for a moral support under the negations of her life. If she were not to have that support, all effort seemed useless.

Esther had been so long used to hear the formulas of her father's belief without feeling or understanding them that they had lost all power to touch her. The first religious experience of her life—the first self-questioning, the first voluntary subjection, the first longing to acquire the strength of greater motives and obey the more strenuous rule—had come to her through Felix Holt. No wonder that she felt as if the loss of him were inevitable backsliding.

But was it certain that she should lose him? She did not believe that he was really indifferent to her.

* * *

CHAPTER XXVIII.

> TITUS. But what says Jupiter, I ask thee?
> CLOWN. Alas, sir, I know not Jupiter:
>   I never drank with him in all my life.
>   *Titus Andronicus.*

THE multiplication of uncomplimentary placards noticed by Mr. Lyon and Felix Holt was one of several signs that the days of nomination and election were approaching. The presence of the Revising Barrister in Treby was not only an opportunity for all persons not otherwise busy to show their zeal for the purification of the voting-lists, but also to reconcile private ease and public duty by standing about the streets and lounging at doors.

It was no light business for Trebians to form an opinion; the mere fact of a public functionary with an unfamiliar title was enough to give them pause, as a premise that was not to be quickly started from. To Mr. Pink, the saddler, for example, until some distinct injury or benefit had accrued to him, the existence of the Revising Barrister was like the existence of the young giraffe which Wombwell had lately brought into those parts—it was to be contemplated, and not criticised. Mr. Pink professed a deep-dyed Toryism; but he regarded all fault-finding as Radical and somewhat impious, as disturbing to trade, and likely to offend the gentry or the servants through whom their harness was ordered: there was a Nemesis in things which made objection unsafe, and even the Reform Bill was a sort of electric eel which a thriving tradesman had better leave alone. It was only the "Papists" who lived far enough off to be spoken of uncivilly.

But Mr. Pink was fond of news, which he collected and retailed with perfect impartiality, noting facts and rejecting comments. Hence he was well pleased to have his shop so constant a place of resort for loungers that to many Trebians there was a strong association between the pleasures of gossip and the smell of leather. He had the satisfaction of chalking and cutting, and of keeping his journeymen close at work, at the very time that he learned from his visitors who were those whose votes had been called in question before His Honor, how Lawyer Jermyn had been too much for Lawyer Labron about Todd's cottages, and how, in the opinion of some townsmen, this looking into the value of people's property, and swearing it down below a certain sum, was a nasty inquisitorial kind of thing; while others observed that being nice to a few pounds was all nonsense—they should put the figure high enough, and then never mind if a voter's qualification was thereabouts. But, said Mr. Sims the auctioneer, everything was done for the sake of the lawyers. Mr. Pink suggested impartially that lawyers must live; but Mr. Sims, having a ready auctioneering wit, did not see that so many of them need live, or that babies were born lawyers. Mr. Pink felt that this speculation was complicated by the ordering of side-saddles for lawyers' daughters, and, returning to the firm ground of fact, stated that it was getting dusk.

The dusk seemed deepened the next moment by a tall figure

obstructing the door-way, at sight of whom Mr. Pink rubbed his hands and smiled and bowed more than once, with evident solicitude to show honor where honor was due, while he said,—

"Mr. Christian, sir, how do you do, sir?"

Christian answered with the condescending familiarity of a superior. "Very badly, I can tell you, with these confounded braces that you were to make such a fine job of. See, old fellow, they've burst out again."

"Very sorry, sir. Can you leave them with me?"

"Oh, yes, I'll leave them. What's the news, eh?" said Christian, half seating himself on a high stool, and beating his boot with a hand-whip.

"Well, sir, we look to you to tell us that," said Mr. Pink, with a knowing smile. "You're at headquarters—eh, sir? That was what I said to Mr. Scales the other day. He came for some straps, Mr. Scales did, and he asked that question in pretty near the same terms that you've done, sir, and I answered him, as I may say, ditto. Not meaning any disrespect to you, sir, but a way of speaking."

"Come, that's gammon, Pink," said Christian. "You know everything. You can tell me, if you will, who is the fellow employed to paste up Transome's handbills?"

"What do *you* say, Mr. Sims?" said Pink, looking at the auctioneer.

"Why, you know and I know well enough. It's Tommy Trounsem—an old, crippling, half-mad fellow. Most people know Tommy. I've employed him myself for charity."

"Where shall I find him?" said Christian.

"At the Cross-Keys, in Pollard's End, most likely," said Mr. Sims. "I don't know where he puts himself when he isn't at the public."

"He was a stoutish fellow fifteen year ago, when he carried pots," said Mr. Pink.

"Ay, and has snared many a hare in his time," said Mr. Sims. "But he was always a little cracked. Lord bless you! he used to swear he had a right to the Transome estate."

"Why, what put that notion into his head?" said Christian, who had learned more than he expected.

"The lawing, sir—nothing but the lawing about the estate.

There was a deal of it twenty year ago," said Mr. Pink. " Tommy happened to turn up hereabout at that time; a big, lungeous fellow, who would speak disrespectfully of hany-body."

"Oh, he meant no harm," said Mr. Sims. " He was fond of a drop to drink, and not quite right in the upper story, and he could hear no difference between Trounsem and Tran-some. It's an odd way of speaking they have in that part where he was born,—a little north'ard. You'll hear it in his tongue now, if you talk to him."

" At the Cross-Keys I shall find him, eh? " said Christian, getting off his stool. " Good-day, Pink—good-day."

Christian went straight from the saddler's to Quorlen's, the Tory printer's, with whom he had contrived a political spree. Quorlen was a new man in Treby, who had so reduced the trade of Dow, the old hereditary printer, that Dow had lapsed to Whiggery and Radicalism and opinions in general, so far as they were contented to express themselves in a small stock of types. Quorlen had brought his Duffield wit with him, and insisted that religion and joking were the handmaids of politics; on which principle he and Christian undertook the joking, and left the religion to the Rector. The joke at present in question was a practical one. Christian, turning into the shop, merely said, " I've found him out—give me the placards"; and, tucking a thickish flat bundle, wrapped in a black glazed cotton bag, under his arm, walked out into the dusk again.

"Suppose, now," he said to himself, as he strode along— "suppose there should be some secret to be got out of this old scamp, or some notion that's as good as a secret to those who know how to use it? That would be virtue rewarded. But I'm afraid the old tosspot is not likely to be good for much. There's truth in wine, and there may be some in gin and muddy beer; but whether it's truth worth my knowing is another question. I've got plenty of truth in my time out of men who were half-seas over, but never any that was worth a sixpence to me."

The Cross-Keys was a very old-fashioned "public": its bar was a big rambling kitchen, with an undulating brick floor; the small-paned windows threw an interesting obscurity over the far-off dresser, garnished with pewter and tin, and with large dishes that seemed to speak of better times; the two settles were half pushed under the wide-mouthed chimney; and the grate, with its brick hobs, massive iron crane, and various pothooks, suggested a generous plenty possibly existent in all moods and tenses except the indicative present. One way of getting an idea of our fellow-countrymen's miseries is to go and look at their pleasures. The Cross-Keys had a fungous-featured landlord and a yellow sickly landlady, with a large white kerchief bound round her cap, as if her head had recently required surgery; it had doctored ale, an odor of bad tobacco, and remarkably strong cheese. It was not what Astræa, when come back, might be expected to approve as the scene of ecstatic enjoyment for the beings whose special prerogative it is to lift their sublime faces toward heaven. Still, there was ample space on the hearth—accommodation for narrative bagmen or boxmen—room for a man to stretch his legs; his brain was not pressed upon by a white wall within a yard of him, and the light did not stare in mercilessly on bare ugliness, turning the fire to ashes. Compared with some beerhouses of this more advanced period, the Cross-Keys of that day represented a high standard of pleasure.

But though this venerable "public" had not failed to share in the recent political excitement of drinking, the pleasures it offered were not at this early hour of the evening sought by a numerous company. There were only three or four pipes being smoked by the firelight; but it was enough for Christian when he found that one of these was being smoked by the billsticker, whose large flat basket, stuffed with placards, leaned near him against the settle. So splendid an apparition as Christian was not a little startling at the Cross-Keys, and was gazed at in expectant silence; but he was a stranger in Pollard's End, and was taken for the highest style of traveller when he declared that he was deucedly thirsty, ordered sixpennyworth of gin and a large jug of water, and, putting a few drops of the spirit into his own glass, invited Tommy Trounsem, who sat next him, to help himself. Tommy was not slower than a shaking hand obliged him to be in accepting this invitation. He was a tall broad-shouldered old fellow, who had once been good-looking; but his cheeks and chest were both hollow now, and his limbs were shrunken.

"You've got some bills there, master, eh?" said Christian, pointing to the basket. "Is there an auction coming on?"

"Auction? no," said Tommy, with a gruff hoarseness, which was the remnant of a jovial bass, and with an accent which differed from the Trebian fitfully, as an early habit is wont to reassert itself. "I've nought to do wi' auctions; I'm a pol'tical charicter. It's me am getting Trounsem into Parl'ment."

"Trounsem, says he," the landlord observed, taking out his pipe with a low laugh. "It's Transome, sir. Maybe you don't belong to this part. It's the candidate 'ull do most for the working men, and's proved it too, in the way o' being open-handed and wishing 'em to enjoy themselves. If I'd twenty votes, I'd give one for Transome, and I don't care who hears me."

The landlord peeped out from his fungous cluster of features with a beery confidence that the high figure of twenty had somehow raised the hypothetic value of his vote.

"Spilkins, now," said Tommy, waving his hand to the landlord, "you let one genelman speak to another, will you? This genelman wants to know about my bills. Does he, or doesn't he?"

"What then? I spoke according," said the landlord, mildly holding his own.

"You're all very well, Spilkins," returned Tommy, "but y'aren't me. I know what the bills are. It's public business. I'm none o' your common bill-stickers, master: I've left off sticking up ten guineas reward for a sheep-stealer, or low stuff like that. These are Trounsem's bills; and I'm the rightful family, and so I give him a lift. A Trounsem I am, and a Trounsem I'll be buried; and if Old Nick tries to lay hold on me for poaching, I'll say, ' You be hanged for a law-yer, Old Nick; every hare and pheasant on the Trounsems' land is mine '; and what rises the family, rises old Tommy; and we're going to get into Parl'ment—that's the long and the short on't, master. And I'm the head o' the family, and I

18

stick the bills. There's Johnsons, and Thomsons, and Jacksons, and Billsons; but I'm a Trounsem, I am. What do you say to that, master?"

This appeal, accompanied by a blow on the table, while the landlord winked at the company, was addressed to Christian, who answered, with severe gravity,—

"I say there isn't any work more honorable than bill-sticking."

"No, no," said Tommy, wagging his head from side to side. "I thought you'd come in to that. I thought you'd know better than say contrairy. But I'll shake hands wi' you; I don't want to knock any man's head off. I'm a good chap—a sound crock—an old family kep' out o' my rights. I shall go to heaven, for all Old Nick."

As these celestial prospects might imply that a little extra gin was beginning to tell on the bill-sticker, Christian wanted to lose no time in arresting his attention. He laid his hand on Tommy's arm and spoke emphatically.

"But I'll tell you what you bill-stickers are not up to. You should be on the lookout when Debarry's side have stuck up fresh bills, and go and paste yours over them. I know where there's a lot of Debarry's bills now. Come along with me, and I'll show you. We'll paste them over, and then we'll come back and treat the company."

"Hooray!" said Tommy. "Let's be off, then."

He was one of the thoroughly inured, originally hale drunkards, and did not easily lose his head or legs or the ordinary amount of method in his talk. Strangers often supposed that Tommy was tipsy when he had only taken what he called "one blessed pint," chiefly from that glorious contentment with himself and his adverse fortunes which is not usually characteristic of the sober Briton. He knocked the ashes out of his pipe, seized his paste-vessel and his basket, and prepared to start with a satisfactory promise that he could know what he was about.

The landlord and some others had confidently concluded that they understood all about Christian now. He was a Transome's man, come to see after the bill-sticking in Transome's interest. The landlord, telling his yellow wife snappishly to open the door for the gentleman, hoped soon to see him again.

"This is a Transome's house, sir," he observed, "in respect of entertaining customers of that color. I do my duty as a publican, which, if I know it, is to turn back no genelman's money. I say, give every genelman a chanch, and the more the merrier, in Parl'ment and out of it. And if anybody says they want but two Parl'ment men, I say it 'ud be better for trade if there was six of 'em, and voters according."

"Ay, ay," said Christian; "you're a sensible man, land-lord. You don't mean to vote for Debarry, then, eh?"

"Not nohow," said the landlord, thinking that where nega-tives were good the more you had of them the better.

As soon as the door had closed behind Christian and his new companion, Tommy said,—

"Now, master, if you're to be my lantern, don't you be a Jacky Lantern, which I take to mean one as leads you the wrong way. For I tell you what—if you've had the luck to fall in wi' Tommy Trounsem, don't you let him drop."

"No, no—to be sure not," said Christian. "Come along here. We'll go to the Back Brewery wall first."

"No, no; don't you let me drop. Give me a shilling any day you like, and I'll tell you more nor you'll hear from Spil-kins in a week. There isna many men like me. I carried pots for fifteen year off and on—what do you think o' that, now, for a man as might ha' lived up there at Trounsem Park, and snared his own game? Which I'd ha' done," said Tommy, wagging his head at Christian in the dimness undisturbed by gas. "None o' your shooting for me—it's two to one you'll miss. Snaring's more fishing-like. You bait your hook, and if it isna the fishes' good will to come, that's nothing again' the sporting genelman. And that's what I say by snaring."

"But if you'd a right to the Transome estate, how was it you were kept out of it, old boy? It was some foul shame or other, eh?"

"It's the law—that's what it is. You're a good sort o' chap; I don't mind telling you. There's folks born to prop-erty, and there's folks catch hold on it; and the law's made

for them as catch hold. I'm pretty deep; I see a good deal
further than Spilkins. There was Ned Patch, the pedler,
used to say to me, ' You canna read, Tommy,' says he. ' No;
thank you,' says I; ' I'm not going to crack my headpiece to
make myself as big a fool as you.' I was fond o' Ned.
Many's the pot we've had together."

"I see well enough you're deep, Tommy. How came you
to know you were born to property?"

"It was the regester—the parish regester," said Tommy,
with his knowing wag of the head, "that shows as you was
born. I allays felt it inside me as I was somebody, and I
could see other chaps thought it on me too; and so one day at
Littleshaw, where I kep' ferrets and a little bit of a public,
there comes a fine man looking after me, and walking me up
and down wi' questions. And I made out from the clerk as
he'd been at the regester; and I gave the clerk a pot or two,
and he got it off our parson as the name o' Trounsem was a great
name hereabout. And I waits a bit for my fine man to come
again. Thinks I, if there's property wants a right owner, I
shall be called for; for I didn't know the law then. And I
waited and waited, till I see'd no fun i' waiting. So I parted
wi' my public and my ferrets—for she was dead a'ready, my
wife was, and I hadn't no cumbrance. And off I started a
pretty long walk to this country-side, for I could walk for a
wager in them days."

"Ah! well, here we are at the Back Brewery wall. Put
down your paste and your basket now, old boy, and I'll help
you. You paste, and I'll give you the bills, and then you can
go on talking."

Tommy obeyed automatically, for he was now carried away
by the rare opportunity of talking to a new listener, and was
only eager to go on with his story. As soon as his back was
turned, and he was stooping over his paste-pot, Christian,
with quick adroitness, exchanged the placards in his own bag
for those in Tommy's basket. Christian's placards had not
been printed at Treby, but were a new lot which had been
sent from Duffield that very day—"highly spiced," Quorlen
had said, "coming from a pen that was up to that sort of
thing." Christian had read the first of the sheet, and sup-

posed they were all alike. He proceeded to hand one to Tommy, and said,—

"Here, old boy, paste this over the other. And so, when you got into this country-side, what did you do?"

"Do? Why, I put up at a good public and ordered the best, for I'd a bit o' money in my pocket; and I axed about, and they said to me, if it's Trounsem business you're after, you go to Lawyer Jermyn. And I went; and says I, going along, he's maybe the fine man as walked me up and down. But no such thing. I'll tell you what Lawyer Jermyn was. He stands you there, and holds you away from him wi' a pole three yards long. He stares at you, and says nothing, till you feel like a Tomfool; and then he threats you to set the justice on you; and then he's sorry for you, and hands you money, and preaches you a sarmint, and tells you you're a poor man, and he'll give you a bit of advice—and you'd better not be meddling wi' things belonging to the law, else you'll be catched up in a big wheel and fly to bits. And I went of a cold sweat, and I wished I might never come i' sight o' Lawyer Jermyn again. But he says, if you keep i' this neighborhood, behave yourself well, and I'll pertect you. I were deep enough, but it's no use being deep, 'cause you can never know the law. And there's times when the deepest fellow's worst frightened."

"Yes, yes. There! Now for another placard. And so that was all?"

"All?" said Tommy, turning round and holding the paste-brush in suspense. "Don't you be running too quick. Thinks I, 'I'll meddle no more. I've got a bit o' money—I'll buy a basket, and be a potman. It's a pleasant life. I shall live at publics and see the world, and pick up 'quaintance, and get a chanch penny.' But when I'd turned into the Red Lion, and got myself warm again wi' a drop o' hot, something jumps into my head. Thinks I, Tommy, you've done finely for yourself: you're a rat as has broke up your house to take a journey, and show yourself to a ferret. And then it jumps into my head: I'd once two ferrets as turned on one another, and the little un killed the big un. Says I to the landlady, 'Missis, could you tell me of a lawyer,' says I,

'not very big or fine, but a second size—a pig-potato, like?'
—'That I can,' says she; 'there's one now in the bar parlor.'
—'Be so kind as to bring us together,' says I. And she
cries out—I think I hear her now—'Mr. Johnson!' And
what do you think?"

At this crisis in Tommy's story the gray clouds, which had
been gradually thinning, opened sufficiently to let down the
sudden moonlight, and show his poor battered old figure and
face in the attitude and with the expression of a narrator sure
of the coming effect on his auditor; his body and neck stretched
a little on one side, and his paste-brush held out with an
alarming intention of tapping Christian's coat-sleeve at the
right moment. Christian started to a safe distance, and
said,—

"It's wonderful. I can't tell what to think."

"Then never do you deny Old Nick," said Tommy, with
solemnity. "I've believed in him more ever since. Who
was Johnson? Why, Johnson was the fine man as had
walked me up and down with questions. And I out with it
to him then and there. And he speaks me civil, and says,
'Come away wi' me, my good fellow.' And he told me a
deal o' law. And he says, Whether you're a Tommy Trounsem or no, it's no good to you, but only to them as have got
hold o' the property. If you was a Tommy Trounsem twenty
times over, it 'ud be no good, for the law's bought you out;
and your life's no good, only to them as have catched hold o'
the property. The more you live, the more they'll stick in.
Not as they want you now, says he—you're no good to anybody, and you might howl like a dog for iver, and the law
'ud take no notice on you. Says Johnson, I'm doing a kind
thing by you to tell you. For that's the law. And if you
want to know the law, master, you ask Johnson. I heard
'em say after as he was an understrapper at Jermyn's.
I've never forgot it from that day to this. But I saw clear
enough, as if the law hadn't been again' me, the Trounsem
estate 'ud ha' been mine. But folks are fools hereabouts, and
I've left off talking. The more you tell 'em the truth, the
more they'll niver believe you. And I went and bought my
basket and the pots and——"

"Come, then, fire away," said Christian. "Here's another placard."

"I'm getting a bit dry, master."

"Well, then, make haste, and you'll have something to drink all the sooner."

Tommy turned to his work again, and Christian, continuing his help, said, "And how long has Mr. Jermyn been employing you?"

"Oh, no particular time—off and on; but a week or two ago he sees me upo' the road, and speaks to me uncommon civil, and tells me to go up to his office, and he'll give me employ. And I was no ways unwilling to stick the bills to get the family into Parl'ment. For there's no man can help the law. And the family's the family, whether you carry pots or no. Master, I'm uncommon dry; my head's a-turning round; it's talking so long on end."

The unwonted excitement of poor Tommy's memory was producing a reaction.

"Well, Tommy," said Christian, who had just made a discovery among the placards which altered the bent of his thoughts, "you may go back to the Cross-Keys now, if you like; here's a half-crown for you to spend handsomely. I can't go back there myself just yet; but you may give my respects to Spilkins, and mind you paste the rest of the bills early to-morrow morning."

"Ay, ay. But don't you believe too much i' Spilkins," said Tommy, pocketing the half-crown, and showing his gratitude by giving this advice—"he's no harm much—but weak. He thinks he's at the bottom o' things because he scores you up. But I bear him no ill-will. Tommy Trounsem's a good chap; and any day you like to give me half a crown, I'll tell you the same story over again. Not now; I'm dry. Come, help me up wi' these things; you're a younger chap than me. Well, I'll tell Spilkins you'll come again another day."

The moonlight which had lit up poor Tommy's oratorical attitude had served to light up for Christian the print of the placards. He had expected the copies to be various, and had turned them half over at different depths of the sheaf before drawing out those he offered to the bill-sticker. Suddenly

the clearer light had shown him on one of them a name which
was just then especially interesting to him, and all the more
when occurring in a placard intended to dissuade the electors
of North Loamshire from voting for the heir of the Transomes.
He hastily turned over the bills that preceded and succeeded,
that he might draw out and carry away all of this pattern! for
it might turn out to be wiser for him not to contribute to the
publicity of handbills which contained allusions to Bycliffe
versus Transome.   There were about a dozen of them; he
pressed them together and thrust them into his pocket, returning all the rest to Tommy's basket.   To take away this dozen
might not be to prevent similar bills from being posted up elsewhere, but he had reason to believe that these were all of the
same kind which had been sent to Treby from Duffield.

Christian's interest in his practical joke had died out like
a morning rushlight.   Apart from this discovery in the placards, old Tommy's story had some indications in it that were
worth pondering over.   Where was that well-informed Johnson now?   Was he still an understrapper of Jermyn's?

With this matter in his thoughts, Christian only turned in
hastily at Quorlen's, threw down the black bag which contained the captured Radical handbills, said he had done the
job, and hurried back to the Manor that he might study his
problem.

CHAPTER XXIX.

I doe believe that, as the gall has severall receptacles in several creatures, soe there's
scarce any creature but hath that emunctorye somewhere.—Sir Thomas Browne.

Fancy what a game at chess would be if all the chessmen
had passions and intellects, more or less small and cunning: if
you were not only uncertain about your adversary's men, but
a little uncertain also about your own; if your knight could
shuffle himself on to a new square by the sly; if your bishop,
in disgust at your castling, could wheedle your pawns out of
their places; and if your pawns, hating you because they are
pawns, could make away from their appointed posts that you
might get checkmate on a sudden.   You might be the longest-

headed of deductive reasoners, and yet you might be beaten by your own pawns. You would be especially likely to be beaten if you depended arrogantly on your mathematical imagination, and regarded your passionate pieces with contempt.

Yet this imaginary chess is easy compared with the game a man has to play against his fellow-men with other fellow-men for his instruments. He thinks himself sagacious, perhaps, because he trusts no bond except that of self-interest; but the only self-interest he can safely rely on is what seems to be such to the mind he would use or govern. Can he ever be sure of knowing this?

Matthew Jermyn was under no misgivings as to the fealty of Johnson. He had "been the making of Johnson"; and this seems to many men a reason for expecting devotion, in spite of the fact that they themselves, though very fond of their own persons and lives, are not at all devoted to the Maker they believe in. Johnson was a most serviceable subordinate. Being a man who aimed at respectability, a family man, who had a good church-pew, subscribed for engravings of banquet pictures where there were portraits of political celebrities, and wished his children to be more unquestionably genteel than their father, he presented all the more numerous handles of worldly motive by which a judicious superior might keep a hold on him. But this useful regard to respectability had its inconvenience in relation to such a superior: it was a mark of some vanity and some pride, which, if they were not touched just in the right handling-place, were liable to become raw and sensitive. Jermyn was aware of Johnson's weaknesses, and thought he had flattered them sufficiently. But on the point of knowing when we are disagreeable our human nature is fallible. Our lavender-water, our smiles, our compliments, and other polite falsities, are constantly offensive, when in the very nature of them they can only be meant to attract admiration and regard. Jermyn had often been unconsciously disagreeable to Johnson, over and above the constant offence of being an ostentatious patron. He would never let Johnson dine with his wife and daughters; he would not himself dine at Johnson's house when he was in town. He often did what was equivalent to poohpoohing his conversation by not even appearing to listen, and by suddenly cutting it short with a query on a new subject. Jermyn was able and politic enough to have commanded a great deal of success in his life, but he could not help being handsome, arrogant, fond of being heard, indisposed to any kind of comradeship, amorous and bland toward women, cold and self-contained toward men. You will hear very strong denials that an attorney's being handsome could enter into the dislike he excited; but conversation consists a good deal in the denial of what is true. From the British point of view masculine beauty is regarded very much as it is in the drapery business:—as good solely for the fancy department—for young noblemen, artists, poets, and the clergy. Some one who, like Mr. Lingon, was disposed to revile Jermyn (perhaps it was Sir Maximus) had called him "a cursed, sleek, handsome, long-winded, overbearing sycophant"; epithets which expressed, rather confusedly, the mingled character of the dislike he excited. And serviceable John Johnson, himself sleek, and mindful about his broadcloth and his cambric fronts, had what he considered "spirit" enough within him to feel that dislike of Jermyn gradually gathering force through years of obligation and subjection, till it had become an actuating motive disposed to use an opportunity, if not to watch for one.

It was not this motive, however, but rather the ordinary course of business, which accounted for Johnson's playing a double part as an electioneering agent. What men do in elections is not to be classed either among sins or marks of grace: it would be profane to include business in religion, and conscience refers to failure, not to success. Still, the sense of being galled by Jermyn's harness was an additional reason for cultivating all relations that were independent of him; and pique at Harold Transome's behavior to him in Jermyn's office perhaps gave all the more zest to Johnson's use of his pen and ink when he wrote a handbill in the service of Garstin, and Garstin's incomparable agent, Putty, full of innuendoes against Harold Transome, as a descendant of the Durfey-Transomes. It is a natural subject of self-congratulation to a man when special knowledge, gained long ago without any forecast, turns out to afford a special inspiration in the present; and Johnson felt a new pleasure in the consciousness that he of all people in the world next to Jermyn had the most intimate knowledge of the Transome affairs.   Still better—some of these affairs were secrets of Jermyn's.   If in an uncomplimentary spirit he might have been called Jermyn's "man of straw," it was a satisfaction to know that the unreality of the man John Johnson was confined to his appearance in annuity deeds, and that elsewhere he was solid, locomotive, and capable of remembering anything for his own pleasure and benefit. To act with doubleness toward a man whose own conduct was double was so near an approach to virtue that it deserved to be called by no meaner name than Diplomacy.

By such causes it came to pass that Christian held in his hands a bill in which Jermyn was playfully alluded to as Mr. German Cozen, who won games by clever shuffling and odd tricks without any honor, and backed Durfey's crib against Bycliffe,—in which it was adroitly implied that the so-called head of the Transomes was only the tail of the Durfeys,—and that some said the Durfeys would have died out and left their nest empty if it had not been for their German Cozen.

Johnson had not dared to use any recollections except such as might credibly exist in other minds besides his own.   In the truth of the case, no one but himself had the prompting to recall these outworn scandals; but it was likely enough that such foul-winged things should be revived by election heats for Johnson to escape all suspicion.

Christian could gather only dim and uncertain inferences from this flat irony and heavy joking; but one chief thing was clear to him.   He had been right in his conjecture that Jermyn's interest about Bycliffe had its source in some claim of Bycliffe's on the Transome property.   And then there was that story of the old bill-sticker's, which, closely considered, indicated that the right of the present Transomes depended, or at least had depended, on the continuance of some other lives.   Christian in his time had gathered enough legal notions to be aware that possession by one man sometimes depended on the life of another; that a man might sell his own interest in property, and the interest of his descendants, while a claim on that property would still remain to some one else than the purchaser, supposing the descendants became extinct, and the interest they had sold were at an end. But under what conditions the claim might be valid or void in any particular case was all darkness to him. Suppose Bycliffe had any such claim on the Transome estates: how was Christian to know whether at the present moment it was worth anything more than a bit of rotten parchment? Old Tommy Trounsem had said that Johnson knew all about it. But even if Johnson were still above-ground—and all Johnsons are mortal—he might still be an understrapper of Jermyn's, in which case his knowledge would be on the wrong side of the hedge for the purposes of Henry Scaddon. His immediate care must be to find out all he could about Johnson. He blamed himself for not having questioned Tommy further while he had him at command; but on this head the bill-sticker could hardly know more than the less dilapidated denizens of Treby.

Now it had happened that during the weeks in which Christian had been at work in trying to solve the enigma of Jermyn's interest about Bycliffe, Johnson's mind also had been somewhat occupied with suspicion and conjecture as to new information on the subject of the old Bycliffe claims which Jermyn intended to conceal from him. The letter which, after his interview with Christian, Jermyn had written with a sense of perfect safety to his faithful ally Johnson was, as we know, written to a Johnson who had found his self-love incompatible with that faithfulness of which it was supposed to be the foundation. Anything that the patron felt it inconvenient for his obliged friend and servant to know became by that very fact an object of peculiar curiosity. The obliged friend and servant secretly doted on his patron's inconvenience, provided that he himself did not share it; and conjecture naturally became active.

Johnson's legal imagination, being very differently furnished from Christian's, was at no loss to conceive conditions under which there might arise a new claim on the Transome estates. He had before him the whole history of the settlement of those estates made a hundred years ago by John Justus Transome, entailing them, whilst in his possession, on his son Thomas and his heirs male, with remainder to the Bycliffes in fee. He knew that Thomas, son of John Justus, proving a prodigal, had, without the knowledge of his father, the tenant in possession, sold his own and his descendants' right to a lawyer-cousin named Durfey; that, therefore, the title of the Durfey-Transomes, in spite of that old Durfey's tricks to show the contrary, depended solely on the purchase of the "base fee" thus created by Thomas Transome; and that the Bycliffes were the "remainder-men" who might fairly oust the Durfey-Transomes if ever the issue of the prodigal Thomas went clean out of existence, and ceased to represent a right which he had bargained away from them.

Johnson, as Jermyn's subordinate, had been closely cognizant of the details concerning the suit instituted by successive Bycliffes, of whom Maurice Christian Bycliffe was the last, on the plea that the extinction of Thomas Transome's line had actually come to pass—a weary suit, which had eaten into the fortunes of two families, and had only made the canker-worms fat. The suit had closed with the death of Maurice Christian Bycliffe in prison; but before his death, Jermyn's exertions to get evidence that there was still issue of Thomas Transome's line surviving, as a security of the Durfey title, had issued in the discovery of a Thomas Transome at Littleshaw, in Stonyshire, who was the representative of a pawned inheritance. The death of Maurice had made this discovery useless—had made it seem the wiser part to say nothing about it; and the fact had remained a secret known only to Jermyn and Johnson. No other Bycliffe was known or believed to exist, and the Durfey-Transomes might be considered safe, unless—yes, there was an "unless" which Johnson could conceive: an heir or heiress of the Bycliffes—if such a personage turned out to be in existence—might some time raise a new and valid claim when once informed that wretched old Tommy Trounsem the bill-sticker, tottering drunkenly on the edge of the grave, was the last issue remaining above-ground from that dissolute Thomas who played his Esau part a century before. While the poor old bill-sticker breathed, the Durfey-Transomes could legally keep their possession in spite of a possible Bycliffe proved real; but not when the parish had buried the bill-sticker.

Still, it is one thing to conceive conditions, and another to see any chance of proving their existence. Johnson at present had no glimpse of such a chance; and even if he ever gained the glimpse, he was not sure that he should ever make any use of it. His inquiries of Medwin, in obedience to Jermyn's letter, had extracted only a negative as to any information possessed by the lawyers of Bycliffe concerning a marriage, or expectation of offspring on his part. But Johnson felt not the less stung by curiosity to know what Jermyn had found out: that he had found something in relation to a possible Bycliffe Johnson felt pretty sure. And he thought with satisfaction that Jermyn could not hinder him from knowing what he already knew about Thomas Transome's issue. Many things might occur to alter his policy and give a new value to facts. Was it certain that Jermyn would always be fortunate?

When greed and unscrupulousness exhibit themselves on a grand historical scale, and there is question of peace or war or amicable partition, it often occurs that gentlemen of high diplomatic talents have their minds bent on the same object from different points of view. Each, perhaps, is thinking of a certain duchy or province, with a view to arranging the ownership in such a way as shall best serve the purposes of the gentleman with high diplomatic talents in whom each is more especially interested. But these select minds in high office can never miss their aims from ignorance of each other's existence or whereabouts. Their high titles may be learned even by common people from every pocket almanac.

But with meaner diplomatists, who might be mutually useful, such ignorance is often obstructive. Mr. John Johnson and Mr. Christian, otherwise Henry Scaddon, might have had a concentration of purpose and an ingenuity of device fitting them to make a figure in the parcelling of Europe, and yet they might never have met, simply because Johnson knew nothing of Christian, and because Christian did not know where to find Johnson.

CHAPTER XXX.

His nature is too noble for the world:
He would not flatter Neptune for his trident,
Or Jove for his power to thunder. His heart's his mouth:
What his breast forges, that his tongue must vent;
And, being angry, doth forget that ever
He heard the name of death.—*Coriolanus.*

CHRISTIAN and Johnson did meet, however, by means that were quite incalculable. The incident which brought them into communication was due to Felix Holt, who of all men in the world had the least affinity either for the industrious or the idle parasite.

Mr. Lyon had urged Felix to go to Duffield on the 15th of December, to witness the nomination of the candidates for North Loamshire. The minister wished to hear what took place; and the pleasure of gratifying him helped to outweigh some opposing reasons.

"I shall get into a rage at something or other," Felix had said. "I've told you one of my weak points. Where I have any particular business, I must incur the risks my nature brings. But I've no particular business at Duffield. However, I'll make a holiday and go. By dint of seeing folly, I shall get lessons in patience."

The weak point to which Felix referred was his liability to be carried completely out of his own mastery by indignant anger. His strong health, his renunciation of selfish claims, his habitual preoccupation with large thoughts and with purposes independent of every-day casualties, secured him a fine and even temper, free from moodiness or irritability. He was full of long-suffering toward his unwise mother, who "pressed him daily with her words and urged him, so that his soul was vexed"; he had chosen to fill his days in a way that required the utmost exertion of patience, that required those little rill-like outflowings of goodness which in minds of great energy must be fed from deep sources of thought and passionate devotedness. In this way his energies served to make him gentle; and now, in this twenty-sixth year of his life,

they had ceased to make him angry, except in the presence of
something that roused his deep indignation.   When once exasperated, the passionateness of his nature threw off the yoke of
a long-trained consciousness in which thought and emotion
had been more and more completely mingled, and concentrated
itself in a rage as ungovernable as that of boyhood.   He was
thoroughly aware of the liability, and knew that in such circumstances he could not answer for himself.   Sensitive people with feeble frames have often the same sort of fury within
them; but they are themselves shattered, and shatter nothing.
Felix had a terrible arm: he knew that he was dangerous; and
he avoided the conditions that might cause him exasperation
as he would have avoided intoxicating drinks if he had been
in danger of intemperance.

The nomination day was a great epoch of successful trickery, or, to speak in a more parliamentary manner, of war-
stratagem, on the part of skilful agents.   And Mr. Johnson
had his share of inward chuckling and self-approval, as one
who might justly expect increasing renown, and be some day
in as general request as the great Putty himself.   To have
the pleasure and the praise of electioneering ingenuity, and
also to get paid for it, without too much anxiety whether the
ingenuity will achieve its ultimate end, perhaps gives to some
select persons a sort of satisfaction in their superiority to their
more agitated fellow-men that is worthy to be classed with
those generous enjoyments of having the truth chiefly to yourself, and of seeing others in danger of drowning while you
are high and dry, which seem to have been regarded as unmixed privileges by Lucretius and Lord Bacon.

One of Mr. Johnson's great successes was this.   Spratt, the
hated manager of the Sproxton Colliery, in careless confidence
that the colliers and other laborers under him would follow
his orders, had provided carts to carry some loads of voteless
enthusiasm to Duffield on behalf of Garstin; enthusiasm which,
being already paid for by the recognized benefit of Garstin's
existence as a capitalist with a share in the Sproxton mines,
was not to cost much in the form of treating.   A capitalist was
held worthy of pious honor as the cause why working men existed.   But Mr. Spratt did not sufficiently consider that a cause

which has to be proved by argument or testimony is not an object of passionate devotion to colliers: a visible cause of beer acts on them much more strongly.   And even if there had been any love of the far-off Garstin, hatred of the too-immediate Spratt would have been the stronger motive.   Hence Johnson's calculations, made long ago with Chubb, the remarkable publican, had been well founded, and there had been diligent care to supply treating at Duffield in the name of Transome. After the election was over, it was not improbable that there would be much friendly joking between Putty and Johnson as to the success of this trick against Putty's employer, and Johnson would be conscious of rising in the opinion of his celebrated senior.

For the show of hands and the cheering, the hustling and the pelting, the roaring and the hissing, the hard hits with small missiles, and the soft hits with small jokes, were strong enough on the side of Transome to balance the similar "demonstrations" for Garstin, even with the Debarry interest in his favor.   And the inconvenient presence of Spratt was early got rid of by a dexterously managed accident, which sent him bruised and limping from the scene of action.   Mr. Chubb had never before felt so thoroughly that the occasion was up to a level with his talents, while the clear daylight in which his virtue would appear when at the election he voted, as his duty to himself bound him, for Garstin only, gave him thorough repose of conscience.

Felix Holt was the only person looking on at the senseless exhibitions of this nomination day who knew from the beginning the history of the trick with the Sproxton men.   He had been aware all along that the treating at Chubb's had been continued, and that so far Harold Transome's promise had produced no good fruits; and what he was observing to-day, as he watched the uproarious crowd, convinced him that the whole scheme would be carried out just as if he had never spoken about it.   He could be fair enough to Transome to allow that he might have wished, and yet have been unable, with his notions of success, to keep his promise; and his bitterness toward the candidate only took the form of contemptuous pity; for Felix was not sparing in his contempt for men

19

who put their inward honor in pawn by seeking the prizes of
the world. His scorn fell too readily on the fortunate. But
when he saw Johnson passing to and fro, and speaking to Jermyn on the hustings, he felt himself getting angry, and jumped
off the wheel of the stationary cart on which he was mounted,
that he might no longer be in sight of this man, whose vitiat-
ing cant had made his blood hot and his fingers tingle on the
first day of encountering him at Sproxton. It was a little too
exasperating to look at this pink-faced rotund specimen of
prosperity, to witness the power for evil that lay in his vulgar
cant, backed by another man's money, and to know that such
stupid iniquity flourished the flags of Reform, and Liberalism,
and justice to the needy. While the roaring and the scuffling
were still going on, Felix, with his thick stick in his hand,
made his way through the crowd, and walked on through the
Duffield streets, till he came out on a grassy suburb, where
the houses surrounded a small common. Here he walked about
in the breezy air, and ate his bread and apples, telling himself
that this angry haste of his about evils that could only be
remedied slowly could be nothing else than obstructive, and
might some day—he saw it so clearly that the thought seemed
like a presentiment—be obstructive of his own work.

"Not to waste energy, to apply force where it would tell, to
do small work close at hand, not waiting for speculative chances
of heroism, but preparing for them"—these were the rules he
had been constantly urging on himself. But what could be a
greater waste than to beat a scoundrel who had law and opo-
deldoc at command? After this meditation, Felix felt cool
and wise enough to return into the town, not, however, intending to deny himself the satisfaction of a few pungent words
wherever there was place for them. Blows are sarcasms turned
stupid: wit is a form of force that leaves the limbs at rest.

Anything that could be called a crowd was no longer to be
seen. The show of hands having been pronounced to be in
favor of Debarry and Transome, and a poll having been demanded for Garstin, the business of the day might be considered at an end. But in the street where the hustings were
erected, and where the great hotels stood, there were many
groups, as well as strollers and steady walkers to and fro.

Men in superior greatcoats and well-brushed hats were awaiting with more or less impatience an important dinner, either
at the Crown, which was Debarry's house, or at the Three
Cranes, which was Garstin's, or at the Fox and Hounds, which
was Transome's. Knots of sober retailers, who had already
dined, were to be seen at some shop doors; men in very shabby
coats and miscellaneous head-coverings, inhabitants of Duffield
and not county voters, were lounging about in dull silence, or
listening, some to a grimy man in a flannel shirt, hatless and
with turbid red hair, who was insisting on political points with
much more ease than had seemed to belong to the gentlemen
speakers on the hustings, and others to a Scotch vender of articles useful to sell, whose unfamiliar accent seemed to have a
guaranty of truth in it wanting as an association with every-
day English. Some rough-looking pipe-smokers, or distinguished cigar-smokers, chose to walk up and down in isolation and silence. But the majority of those who had shown a
burning interest in the nomination had disappeared, and cockades no longer studded a close-pressed crowd, like, and also
very unlike, meadow-flowers among the grass. The street
pavement was strangely painted with fragments of perishable
missiles ground flat under heavy feet: but the workers were
resting from their toil, and the buzz and tread and the fitfully
discernible voices seemed like stillness to Felix after the roar
with which the wide space had been filled when he left it.

The group round the speaker in the flannel shirt stood at
the corner of a side street, and the speaker himself was elevated by the head and shoulders above his hearers, not because he was tall, but because he stood on a projecting stone.
At the opposite corner of the turning was the great inn of the
Fox and Hounds, and this was the ultra-Liberal quarter of the
High Street. Felix was at once attracted by this group; he
liked the look of the speaker, whose bare arms were powerfully
muscular, though he had the pallid complexion of a man who
lives chiefly amidst the heat of furnaces. He was leaning
against the dark stone building behind him with folded arms,
the grimy paleness of his shirt and skin standing out in high
relief against the dark stone building behind him. He lifted
up one fore finger, and marked his emphasis with it as he

spoke. His voice was high and not strong, but Felix recognized the fluency and the method of a habitual preacher or lecturer.

"It's the fallacy of all monopolists," he was saying. "We know what monopolists are: men who want to keep a trade all to themselves, under the pretence that they'll furnish the public with a better article. We know what that comes to: in some countries a poor man can't afford to buy a spoonful of salt, and yet there's salt enough in the world to pickle every living thing in it. That's the sort of benefit monopolists do to mankind. And these are the men who tell us we're to let politics alone; they'll govern us better without our knowing anything about it. We must mind our business; we are ignorant; we've no time to study great questions. But I tell them this: the greatest question in the world is, how to give every man a man's share in what goes on in life——"

"Hear, hear!" said Felix in his sonorous voice, which seemed to give a new impressiveness to what the speaker had said. Every one looked at him: the well-washed face and its educated expression, along with a dress more careless than that of most well-to-do workmen on a holiday, made his appearance strangely arresting.

"Not a pig's share," the speaker went on, "not a horse's share, not the share of a machine fed with oil only to make it work and nothing else. It isn't a man's share just to mind your pin-making, or your glass-blowing, and higgle about your own wages, and bring up your family to be ignorant sons of ignorant fathers, and no better prospect; that's a slave's share; we want a freeman's share, and that is to think and speak and act about what concerns us all, and see whether these fine gentlemen who undertake to govern us are doing the best they can for us. They've got the knowledge, say they. Very well, we've got the wants. There's many a one would be idle if hunger didn't pinch him; but the stomach sets us to work. There's a fable told where the nobles are the belly and the people the members. But I make another sort of fable. I say, we are the belly that feels the pinches, and we'll set these aristocrats, these great people who call themselves our brains, to work at some way of satisfying us a bit better. The aris-

tocrats are pretty sure to try and govern for their own benefit;
but how are we to be sure they'll try and govern for ours?
They must be looked after, I think, like other workmen. We
must have what we call inspectors, to see whether the work's
well done for us. We want to send our inspectors to Parliament. Well, they say—you've got the Reform Bill; what
more can you want? Send your inspectors. But I say, the
Reform Bill is a trick—it's nothing but swearing in special
constables to keep the aristocrats safe in their monopoly; it's
bribing some of the people with votes to make them hold their
tongues about giving votes to the rest. I say, if a man doesn't
beg or steal, but works for his bread, the poorer and the more
miserable he is, the more he'd need have a vote to send an
inspector to Parliament—else the man who is worst off is likely
to be forgotten; and I say, he's the man who ought to be first
remembered. Else what does their religion mean? Why do
they build churches and endow them that their sons may get
paid well for preaching a Saviour, and making themselves as
little like Him as can be? If I want to believe in Jesus Christ,
I must shut my eyes for fear I should see a parson. And
what's a bishop? A bishop's a parson dressed up, who sits
in the House of Lords to help and throw out Reform Bills.
And because it's hard to get anything in the shape of a man
to dress himself up like that, and do such work, they give him
a palace for it, and plenty of thousands a year. And then
they cry out—'The Church is in danger,'—'the poor man's
Church.' And why is it the poor man's Church? Because
he can have a seat for nothing. I think it *is* for nothing; for
it would be hard to tell what he gets by it. If the poor man
had a vote in the matter, I think he'd choose a different sort
of a Church to what that is. But do you think the aristocrats
will ever alter it if the belly doesn't pinch them? Not they.
It's part of their monopoly. They'll supply us with our religion like everything else, and get a profit on it. They'll give
us plenty of heaven. We may have land *there*. That's the
sort of religion they like—a religion that gives us working men
heaven, and nothing else. But we'll offer to change with 'em.
We'll give them back some of their heaven, and take it out in
something for us and our children in this world. They don't

seem to care so much about heaven themselves till they feel
the gout very bad; but you won't get them to give up anything else if you don't pinch 'em for it. And to pinch them
enough, we must get the suffrage, we must get votes, that we
may send the men to Parliament who will do our work for us;
and we must have Parliament dissolved every year, that we
may change our man if he doesn't do what we want him to do;
and we must have the country divided so that the little kings
of the counties can't do as they like, but must be shaken up in
one bag with us. I say, if we working men are ever to get a
man's share, we must have universal suffrage, and annual Parliaments, and the vote by ballot, and electoral districts."

"No!—something else before all that," said Felix, again
startling the audience into looking at him. But the speaker
glanced coldly at him and went on.

"That's what Sir Francis Burdett went in for fifteen years
ago; and it's the right thing for us, if it was Tomfool who
went in for it. You must lay hold of such handles as you
can. I don't believe much in liberal aristocrats; but if there's
any fine carved gold-headed stick of an aristocrat will make a
broomstick of himself, I'll lose no time but I'll sweep with
him. And that's what I think about Transome. And if any
of you have acquaintance among county voters, give 'em a hint
that you wish 'em to vote for Transome."

At the last word, the speaker stepped down from his slight
eminence, and walked away rapidly, like a man whose leisure
was exhausted, and who must go about his business. But he
had left an appetite in his audience for further oratory, and
one of them seemed to express a general sentiment as he turned
immediately to Felix, and said: "Come, sir, what do you
say?"

Felix did at once what he would very likely have done without being asked—he stepped on to the stone, and took off his
cap by an instinctive prompting that always led him to speak
uncovered. The effect of his figure in relief against the stone
background was unlike that of the previous speaker. He was
considerably taller, his head and neck were more massive, and
the expression of his mouth and eyes was something very
different from the mere acuteness and rather hard-lipped an-

tagonism of the trades-union man. Felix Holt's face had the look of habitual meditative abstraction from objects of mere personal vanity or desire which is the peculiar stamp of culture, and makes a very roughly cut face worthy to be called "the human face divine." Even lions and dogs know a distinction between men's glances; and doubtless those Duffield men, in the expectation with which they looked up at Felix, were unconsciously influenced by the grandeur of his full yet firm mouth, and the calm clearness of his gray eyes, which were somehow unlike what they were accustomed to see along with an old brown velveteen coat and an absence of chin-propping. When he began to speak, the contrast of voice was still stronger than that of appearance. The man in the flannel shirt had not been heard—had probably not cared to be heard —beyond the immediate group of listeners. But Felix at once drew the attention of persons comparatively at a distance.

"In my opinion," he said, almost the moment after he was addressed, "that was a true word spoken by your friend when he said the great question was how to give every man a man's share in life. But I think he expects voting to do more toward it than I do. I want the working men to have power. I'm a working man myself, and I don't want to be anything else. But there are two sorts of power. There's a power to do mischief— to undo what has been done with great expense and labor, to waste and destroy, to be cruel to the weak, to lie and quarrel, and to talk poisonous nonsense. That's the sort of power that ignorant numbers have. It never made a joint stool or planted a potato. Do you think it's likely to do much toward governing a great country, and making wise laws, and giving shelter, food, and clothes to millions of men? Ignorant power comes in the end to the same thing as wicked power; it makes misery. It's another sort of power that I want us working men to have, and I can see plainly enough that our all having votes will do little toward it at present. I hope we, or the children that come after us, will get plenty of political power some time. I tell everybody plainly, I hope there will be great changes, and that some time, whether we live to see it or not, men will have come to be ashamed of things they're proud of now. But I should like to convince you that votes would never give you political power worth having while things are as they are now, and that if you go the right way to work you may get power sooner without votes. Perhaps all you who hear me are sober men, who try to learn as much of the nature of things as you can, and to be as little like fools as possible. A fool or idiot is one who expects things to happen that never can happen; he pours milk into a can without a bottom, and expects the milk to stay there. The more of such vain expectations a man has, the more he is of a fool or idiot. And if any working man expects a vote to do for him what it never can do, he's foolish to that amount, if no more. I think that's clear enough, eh?"

"Hear, hear," said several voices, but they were not those of the original group; they belonged to some strollers who had been attracted by Felix Holt's vibrating voice, and were Tories from the Crown. Among them was Christian, who was smoking a cigar with a pleasure he always felt in being among people who did not know him, and doubtless took him to be something higher than he really was. Hearers from the Fox and Hounds also were slowly adding themselves to the nucleus. Felix, accessible to the pleasure of being listened to, went on with more and more animation:—

"The way to get rid of folly is to get rid of vain expectations, and of thoughts that don't agree with the nature of things. The men who have had true thoughts about water, and what it will do when it is turned into steam and under all sorts of circumstances, have made themselves a great power in the world: they are turning the wheels of engines that will help to change most things. But no engines would have done if there had been false notions about the way water would act. Now, all the schemes about voting, and districts, and annual Parliaments, and the rest, are engines, and the water or steam —the force that is to work them—must come out of human nature—out of men's passions, feelings, desires. Whether the engines will do good work or bad depends on these feelings; and if we have false expectations about men's characters, we are very much like the idiot who thinks he'll carry milk in a can without a bottom. In my opinion, the notions about what mere voting will do are very much of that sort."

"That's very fine," said a man in dirty fustian, with a scornful laugh. "But how are we to get the power without votes?"

"I'll tell you what's the greatest power under heaven," said Felix, "and that is public opinion—the ruling belief in society about what is right and what is wrong, what is honorable and what is shameful. That's the steam that is to work the engines. How can political freedom make us better, any more than a religion we don't believe in, if people laugh and wink when they see men abuse and defile it? And while public opinion is what it is—while men have no better beliefs about public duty—while corruption is not felt to be a damning disgrace—while men are not ashamed in Parliament and out of it to make public questions which concern the welfare of millions a mere screen for their own petty private ends,—I say, no fresh scheme of voting will much mend our condition. For take us working men of all sorts. Suppose out of every hundred who had a vote there were thirty who had some soberness, some sense to choose with, some good feeling to make them wish the right thing for all. And suppose there were seventy out of the hundred who were, half of them, not sober, who had no sense to choose one thing in politics more than another, and who had so little good feeling in them that they wasted on their own drinking the money that should have helped to feed and clothe their wives and children; and another half of them who, if they didn't drink, were too ignorant or mean or stupid to see any good for themselves better than pocketing a five-shilling piece when it was offered them. Where would be the political power of the thirty sober men? The power would lie with the seventy drunken and stupid votes; and I'll tell you what sort of men would get the power—what sort of men would end by returning whom they pleased to Parliament."

Felix had seen every face around him, and had particularly noticed a recent addition to his audience; but now he looked before him without appearing to fix his glance on any one. In spite of his cooling meditations an hour ago, his pulse was getting quickened by indignation, and the desire to crush what he hated was likely to vent itself in articulation. His tone became more biting.

"They would be men who would undertake to do the business for a candidate, and return him: men who have no real opinions, but who pilfer the words of every opinion, and turn them into a cant which will serve their purpose at the moment; men who look out for dirty work to make their fortunes by, because dirty work wants little talent and no conscience; men who know all the ins and outs of bribery, because there is not a cranny in their own souls where a bribe can't enter. Such men as these will be the masters wherever there's a majority of others who care more for money, more for drink, more for some mean little end which is their own and nobody else's, than for anything that has ever been called Right in the world. For suppose there's a poor voter named Jack, who has seven children, and twelve or fifteen shillings a week wages, perhaps less. Jack can't read—I don't say whose fault that is—he never had the chance to learn; he knows so little that he perhaps thinks God made the poor-laws, and if anybody said the pattern of the workhouse was laid down in the Testament he wouldn't be able to contradict them. What is poor Jack likely to do when he sees a smart stranger coming to him, who happens to be just one of those men that I say will be the masters till public opinion gets too hot for them? He's a middle-sized man, we'll say; stout, with coat upon coat of fine broadcloth, open enough to show a fine gold chain: none of your dark, scowling men, but one with an innocent pink-and-white skin and very smooth light hair—a most respectable man, who calls himself by a good, sound, well-known English name—as Green, or Baker, or Wilson, or, let us say, Johnson——"

Felix was interrupted by an explosion of laughter from a majority of the bystanders. Some eyes had been turned on Johnson, who stood on the right hand of Felix, at the very beginning of the description, and these were gradually followed by others, till at last every hearer's attention was fixed on him, and the first burst of laughter from the two or three who knew the attorney's name let every one sufficiently into the secret to make the amusement common. Johnson, who had kept his ground till his name was mentioned, now turned away, looking unusually white after being unusually red, and feeling by an attorney's instinct for his pocket-book, as if he felt it was a case for taking down the names of witnesses.

All the well-dressed hearers turned away too, thinking they had had the cream of the speech in the joke against Johnson, which, as a thing worth telling, helped to recall them to the scene of dinner.

" Who is this Johnson? " said Christian to a young man who had been standing near him, and had been one of the first to laugh. Christian's curiosity had naturally been awakened by what might prove a golden opportunity.

" Oh—a London attorney. He acts for Transome. That tremendous fellow at the corner there is some red-hot Radical demagogue, and Johnson has offended him, I suppose; else he wouldn't have turned in that way on a man of their own party."

" I had heard there was a Johnson who was an understrapper of Jermyn's," said Christian.

" Well, so this man may have been for what I know. But he's a London man now—a very busy fellow—on his own legs in Bedford Row. Ha! ha! It's capital, though, when these Liberals get a slap in the face from the working men they're so very fond of."

Another turn along the street enabled Christian to come to a resolution. Having seen Jermyn drive away an hour before, he was in no fear: he walked at once to the Fox and Hounds and asked to speak to Mr. Johnson. A brief interview, in which Christian ascertained that he had before him the Johnson mentioned by the bill-sticker, issued in the appointment of a longer one at a later hour; and before they left Duffield they had come not exactly to a mutual understanding, but to an exchange of information mutually welcome.

Christian had been very cautious in the commencement, only intimating that he knew something important which some chance hints had induced him to think might be interesting to Mr. Johnson, but that this entirely depended on how far he had a common interest with Mr. Jermyn. Johnson replied that he had much business in which that gentleman was not concerned, but that to a certain extent they had a common interest. Probably, then, Christian observed, the affairs of the Transome estate were part of the business in which Mr. Jermyn and Mr. Johnson might be understood to represent each other—in which case he need not detain Mr. Johnson? At this hint Johnson could not conceal that he was becoming eager. He had no idea what Christian's information was, but there were many grounds on which Johnson desired to know as much as he could about the Transome affairs independently of Jermyn. By little and little an understanding was arrived at. Christian told of his interview with Tommy Trounsem, and stated that if Johnson could show him whether the knowledge could have any legal value he could bring evidence that a legitimate child of Bycliffe's existed: he felt certain of his fact, and of his proof. Johnson explained that in this case the death of the old bill-sticker would give the child the first valid claim to the Bycliffe heirship; that for his own part he should be glad to further a true claim, but that caution must be observed. How did Christian know that Jermyn was informed on this subject? Christian, more and more convinced that Johnson would be glad to counteract Jermyn, at length became explicit about Esther, but still withheld his own real name, and the nature of his relations with Bycliffe. He said he would bring the rest of his information when Mr. Johnson took the case up seriously, and place it in the hands of Bycliffe's old lawyers—of course he would do that? Johnson replied that he would certainly do that; but that there were legal niceties which Mr. Christian was probably not acquainted with; that Esther's claim had not yet accrued; and that hurry was useless.

The two men parted, each in distrust of the other, but each well pleased to have learned something. Johnson was not at all sure how he should act, but thought it likely that events would soon guide him. Christian was beginning to meditate a way of securing his own ends without depending in the least on Johnson's procedure. It was enough for him that he was now assured of Esther's legal claim on the Transome estates.

CHAPTER XXXI.

"In the copia of the factious language the word Tory was entertained, . . . and being a vocal clever-sounding word, readily pronounced, it kept its hold, and took possession of the foul mouths of the faction. . . . The Loyalists began to cheer up and to take heart of grace, and in the working of this crisis, according to the common laws of scolding, they considered which way to make payment for so much of Tory as they had been treated with, to clear scores. . . . Immediately the train took, and ran like wildfire and became general. And so the account of Tory was balanced, and soon began to run up a sharp score on the other side."—NORTH'S *Examen*, p. 321.

AT last the great epoch of the election for North Loamshire had arrived. The roads approaching Treby were early traversed by a larger number of vehicles, horsemen, and also foot-passengers than were ever seen there at the annual fair. Treby was the polling-place for many voters whose faces were quite strange in the town; and if there were some strangers who did not come to poll, though they had business not unconnected with the election, they were not liable to be regarded with suspicion or especial curiosity. It was understood that no division of a county had ever been more thoroughly canvassed, and that there would be a hard run between Garstin and Transome. Mr. Johnson's headquarters were at Duffield; but it was a maxim which he repeated after the great Putty that a capable agent makes himself omnipresent; and quite apart from the express between him and Jermyn, Mr. John Johnson's presence in the universe had potent effects on this December day at Treby Magna.

A slight drizzling rain which was observed by some Tories who looked out of their bedroom windows before six o'clock made them hope that, after all, the day might pass off better than alarmists had expected. The rain was felt to be somehow on the side of quiet and Conservatism; but soon the breaking of the clouds and the mild gleams of a December sun brought back previous apprehensions. As there were already precedents for riot at a Reformed election, and as the Trebian district had had its confidence in the natural course of things somewhat shaken by a landed proprietor with an old name offering himself as a Radical candidate, the election had been looked forward to by many with a vague sense that it would

be an occasion something like a fighting-match, when bad characters would probably assemble, and there might be struggles
and alarms for respectable men, which would make it expedient for them to take a little neat brandy as a precaution beforehand and a restorative afterward. The tenants on the Transome estate were comparatively fearless: poor Mr. Goffe, of
Rabbit's End, considered that "one thing was as mauling as
another," and that an election was no worse than the sheep-
rot; while Mr. Dibbs, taking the more cheerful view of a prosperous man, reflected that if the Radicals were dangerous it
was safer to be on their side. It was the voters for Debarry
and Garstin who considered that they alone had the right to
regard themselves as targets for evil-minded men; and Mr.
Crowder, if he could have got his ideas countenanced, would
have recommended a muster of farm-servants with defensive
pitchforks on the side of Church and King. But the bolder
men were rather gratified by the prospect of being groaned at,
so that they might face about and groan in return.

Mr. Crow, the high constable of Treby, inwardly rehearsed
a brief address to a riotous crowd in case it should be wanted,
having been warned by the Rector that it was a primary duty
on these occasions to keep a watch against provocation as well
as violence. The Rector, with a brother magistrate who was
on the spot, had thought it desirable to swear in some special
constables, but the presence of loyal men not absolutely
required for the polling was not looked at in the light of a
provocation. The Benefit Clubs from various quarters made a
show, some with the orange-colored ribbons and streamers of
the true Tory candidate, some with the mazarine of the Whig.
The orange-colored bands played "Auld Langsyne," and a
louder mazarine band came across them with "Oh, whistle and
I will come to thee, my lad"—probably as the tune the most
symbolical of Liberalism which their repertory would furnish.
There was not a single club bearing the Radical blue: the Sproxton Club members wore the mazarine, and Mr. Chubb wore so
much of it that he looked (at a sufficient distance) like a very
large gentianella. It was generally understood that "these
brave fellows," representing the fine institution of Benefit
Clubs, and holding aloft the motto, "Let brotherly love con-

tinue," were a civil force calculated to encourage voters of sound opinions and keep up their spirits. But a considerable number of unadorned heavy navvies, colliers, and stone-pit men, who used their freedom as British subjects to be present in Treby on this great occasion, looked like a possibly uncivil force whose politics were dubious until it was clearly seen for whom they cheered and for whom they groaned.

Thus the way up to the polling-booths was variously lined, and those who walked it, to whatever side they belonged, had the advantage of hearing from the opposite side what were the most marked defects or excesses in their personal appearance; for the Trebians of that day held, without being aware that they had Cicero's authority for it, that the bodily blemishes of an opponent were a legitimate ground for ridicule; but if the voter frustrated wit by being handsome, he was groaned at and satirized according to a formula, in which the adjective was Tory, Whig, or Radical, as the case might be, and the substantive a blank to be filled up after the taste of the speaker.

Some of the more timid had chosen to go through this ordeal as early as possible in the morning. One of the earliest was Mr. Timothy Rose, the gentleman farmer from Leek Malton. He had left home with some foreboding, having swathed his more vital parts in layers of flannel, and put on two greatcoats as a soft kind of armor. But reflecting with some trepidation that there were no resources for protecting his head, he once more wavered in his intention to vote; he once more observed to Mrs. Rose that these were hard times when a man of independent property was expected to vote "willy-nilly"; but finally, coerced by the sense that he should be looked ill on "in these times" if he did not stand by the gentlemen round about, he set out in his gig, taking with him a powerful wagoner, whom he ordered to keep him in sight as he went to the polling-booth. It was hardly more than nine o'clock when Mr. Rose, having thus come up to the level of his times, cheered himself with a little cherry brandy at the Marquis, drove away in a much more courageous spirit, and got down at Mr. Nolan's, just outside the town. The retired Londoner, he considered, was a man of experience, who would estimate properly the judicious course he had taken, and could make it known to others. Mr. Nolan was superintending the removal of some shrubs in his garden.

"Well, Mr. Nolan," said Rose, twinkling a self-complacent look over the red prominence of his cheeks, "have you been to give your vote yet?"

"No; all in good time. I shall go presently."

"Well, I wouldn't lose an hour, I wouldn't. I said to my-self, if I've got to do gentlemen a favor, I'll do it at once. You see, I've got no landlord, Nolan—I'm in that position o' life that I can be independent."

"Just so, my dear sir," said the wiry-faced Nolan, pinch-ing his under lip between his thumb and finger, and giving one of those wonderful universal shrugs, by which he seemed to be recalling all his garments from a tendency to disperse them-selves. "Come in and see Mrs. Nolan?"

"No, no, thankye. Mrs. Rose expects me back. But, as I was saying, I'm a independent man, and I consider it's not my part to show favor to one more than another, but to make things as even as I can. If I'd been a tenant to anybody, well, in course I must have voted for my landlord—that stands to sense. But I wish everybody well; and if one's returned to Parliament more than another, nobody can say it's my do-ing; for when you can vote for two, you can make things even. So I gave one to Debarry and one to Transome; and I wish Garstin no ill, but I can't help the odd number, and he hangs on to Debarry, they say."

"God bless me, sir," said Mr. Nolan, coughing down a laugh, "don't you perceive that you might as well have stayed at home and not voted at all, unless you would rather send a Radical to Parliament than a sober Whig?"

"Well, I'm sorry you should have anything to say against what I've done, Nolan," said Mr. Rose, rather crestfallen, though sustained by inward warmth. "I thought you'd agree with me, as you're a sensible man. But the most a independ-ent man can do is to try and please all; and if he hasn't the luck—here's wishing I may do it another time," added Mr. Rose, apparently confounding a toast with a salutation, for he put out his hand for a passing shake, and then stepped into his gig again.

At the time that Mr. Timothy Rose left the town, the crowd in King Street and in the market-place, where the polling-booths stood, was fluctuating. Voters as yet were scanty, and brave fellows who had come from any distance this morning, or who had sat up late drinking the night before, required some reinforcement of their strength and spirits. Every public-house in Treby, not excepting the venerable and sombre Cross-Keys, was lively with changing and numerous company. Not, of course, that there was any treating: treating necessarily had stopped, from moral scruples, when once "the writs were out"; but there was drinking, which did equally well under any name.

Poor Tommy Trounsem, breakfasting here on Falstaff's proportion of bread, and something which, for gentility's sake, I will call sack, was more than usually victorious over the ills of life, and felt himself one of the heroes of the day. He had an immense light-blue cockade in his hat, and an amount of silver in a dirty little canvas bag which astonished himself. For some reason, at first inscrutable to him, he had been paid for his bill-sticking with great liberality at Mr. Jermyn's office, in spite of his having been the victim of a trick by which he had once lost his own bills and pasted up Debarry's; but he soon saw that this was simply a recognition of his merit as "an old family kept out of its rights," and also of his peculiar share in an occasion when the family was to get into Parliament. Under these circumstances, it was due from him that he should show himself prominently where business was going forward, and give additional value by his presence to every vote for Transome. With this view he got a half-pint bottle filled with his peculiar kind of "sack," and hastened back to the market-place, feeling good-natured and patronizing toward all political parties, and only so far partial as his family bound him to be.

But a disposition to concentrate at that extremity of King Street which issued in the market-place was not universal among the increasing crowd. Some of them seemed attracted toward another nucleus at the other extremity of King Street, near the Seven Stars. This was Garstin's chief house, where his committee sat, and it was also a point which must neces-

20

sarily be passed by many voters entering the town on the eastern side. It seemed natural that the mazarine colors should be visible here, and that Pack, the tall "shepherd" of the Sproxton men, should be seen moving to and fro where there would be a frequent opportunity of cheering the voters for a gentleman who had the chief share in the Sproxton mines. But the side lanes and entries out of King Street were numerous enough to relieve any pressure if there was need to make way. The lanes had a distinguished reputation. Two of them had odors of brewing; one had a side entrance to Mr. Tiliot's wine and spirit vaults; up another Mr. Muscat's cheeses were frequently being unloaded; and even some of the entries had those cheerful suggestions of plentiful provision which were among the characteristics of Treby.

Between ten and eleven the voters came in more rapid succession, and the whole scene became spirited. Cheers, sarcasms, and oaths, which seemed to have a flavor of wit for many hearers, were beginning to be reinforced by more practical demonstrations, dubiously jocose. There was a disposition in the crowd to close and hem in the way for voters, either going or coming, until they had paid some kind of toll. It was difficult to see who set the example in the transition from words to deeds. Some thought it was due to Jacob Cuff, a Tory charity man, who was a well-known ornament of the pothouse, and gave his mind much leisure for amusing devices; but questions of origination in stirring periods are notoriously hard to settle. It is by no means necessary in human things that there should be only one beginner. This, however, is certain—that Mr. Chubb, who wished it to be noticed that he voted for Garstin solely, was one of the first to get rather more notice than he wished, and that he had his hat knocked off and crushed in the interest of Debarry by Tories opposed to coalition. On the other hand, some said it was at the same time that Mr. Pink, the saddler, being stopped on his way and made to declare that he was going to vote for Debarry, got himself well chalked as to his coat, and pushed up an entry, where he remained the prisoner of terror combined with the want of any back outlet, and never gave his vote that day.

The second Tory joke was performed with much gusto. The

majority of the Transome tenants came in a body from the Ram Inn, with Mr. Banks the bailiff leading them. Poor Goffe was the last of them, and his worn melancholy look and forward-leaning gait gave the jocose Cuff the notion that the farmer was not what he called "compus." Mr. Goffe was cut off from his companions and hemmed in; asked, by voices with hot breath close to his ear, how many horses he had, how many cows, how many fat pigs; then jostled from one to another, who made trumpets with their hands, and deafened him by telling him to vote for Debarry. In this way the melancholy Goffe was hustled on till he was at the polling-booth—filled with confused alarms, the immediate alarm being that of having to go back in still worse fashion than he had come. Arriving in this way after the other tenants had left, he astonished all hearers who knew him for a tenant of the Transomes by saying "Debarry," and was jostled back trembling amid shouts of laughter.

By stages of this kind the fun grew faster, and was in danger of getting rather serious. The Tories began to feel that their jokes were returned by others of a heavier sort, and that the main strength of the crowd was not on the side of sound opinion, but might come to be on the side of sound cudgelling and kicking. The navvies and pitmen in dishabille seemed to be multiplying, and to be clearly not belonging to the party of Order. The shops were freely resorted to for various forms of playful missiles and weapons; and news came to the magistrates, watching from the large window of the Marquis, that a gentleman coming in on horseback at the other end of the street to vote for Garstin had had his horse turned round and frightened into a headlong gallop out of it again.

Mr. Crow and his subordinates, and all the special constables, felt that it was necessary to make some energetic effort, or else every voter would be intimidated and the poll must be adjourned. The Rector determined to get on horseback and go amidst the crowd with the constables; and he sent a message to Mr. Lingon, who was at the Ram, calling on him to do the same. "Sporting Jack" was sure the good fellows meant no harm, but he was courageous enough to face any bodily dangers, and rode out in his brown leggings and colored bandanna, speaking persuasively.

It was nearly twelve o'clock when this sally was made: the constables and magistrates tried the most pacific measures, and they seemed to succeed. There was a rapid thinning of the crowd: the most boisterous disappeared, or seemed to do so by becoming quiet; missiles ceased to fly, and a sufficient way was cleared for voters along King Street. The magistrates returned to their quarters, and the constables took convenient posts of observation. Mr. Wace, who was one of Debarry's committee, had suggested to the Rector that it might be wise to send for the military from Duffield, with orders that they should station themselves at Hathercote, three miles off: there was so much property in the town that it would be better to make it secure against risks. But the Rector felt that this was not the part of a moderate and wise magistrate, unless the signs of riot recurred. He was a brave man, and fond of thinking that his own authority sufficed for the maintenance of the general good in Treby.

CHAPTER XXXII.

> Go from me. Yet I feel that I shall stand
> Henceforward in thy shadow. Never more
> Alone upon the threshold of my door
> Of individual life, I shall command
> The uses of my soul, nor lift my hand
> Serenely in the sunshine as before
> Without the sense of that which I forbore—
> Thy touch upon the palm. The widest land
> Doom takes to part us, leaves thy heart in mine
> With pulses that beat double. What I do
> And what I dream include thee, as the wine
> Must taste of its own grapes. And when I sue
> God for myself, He hears that name of thine,
> And sees within my eyes the tears of two.
> MRS. BROWNING.

FELIX HOLT, seated at his work without his pupils, who had asked for a holiday with a notion that the wooden booths promised some sort of show, noticed about eleven o'clock that the noises which reached him from the main street were getting more and more tumultuous. He had long seen bad auguries for this election, but, like all people who dread the prophetic wisdom that ends in desiring the fulfilment of its own evil forebodings, he had checked himself with remembering that, though many conditions were possible which might bring on violence, there were just as many which might avert it. There would, perhaps, be no other mischief than what he was already certain of. With these thoughts he had sat down quietly to his work, meaning not to vex his soul by going to look on at things he would fain have made different if he could. But he was of a fibre that vibrated too strongly to the life around him to shut himself away in quiet, even from suffering and irremediable wrong. As the noises grew louder, and wrought more and more strongly on his imagination, he was obliged to lay down his delicate wheel-work. His mother came from her turnip-paring in the kitchen, where little Job was her companion, to observe that they must be killing everybody in the High Street, and that the election, which had never been before at Treby, must have come for a judgment; that there were mercies where you didn't look for them, and that she thanked God in His wisdom for making her live up a back street.

Felix snatched his cap and rushed out. But when he got to the turning into the market-place the magistrates were already on horseback there, the constables were moving about, and Felix observed that there was no strong spirit of resistance to them. He stayed long enough to see the partial dispersion of the crowd and the restoration of tolerable quiet, and then went back to Mrs. Holt to tell her that there was nothing to fear now; he was going out again, and she must not be in any anxiety at his absence. She might set by his dinner for him.

Felix had been thinking of Esther and her probable alarm at the noises that must have reached her more distinctly than they had reached him, for Malthouse Yard was removed but a little way from the main street. Mr. Lyon was away from home, having been called to preach charity sermons and attend meetings in a distant town; and Esther, with the plaintive Lyddy for her sole companion, was not cheerfully circumstanced. Felix had not been to see her yet since her father's departure, but to-day he gave way to new reasons.

"Miss Esther was in the garret," Lyddy said, trying to see what was going on. But before she was fetched she came running down the stairs, drawn by the knock at the door, which had shaken the small dwelling.

"I am so thankful to see you," she said, eagerly. "Pray come in."

When she had shut the parlor door behind them, Felix said, "I suspected that you might have been made anxious by the noises. I came to tell you that things are quiet now. Though, indeed, you can hear that they are."

"I *was* frightened," said Esther. "The shouting and roaring of rude men is so hideous. It is a relief to me that my father is not at home—that he is out of the reach of any danger he might have fallen into if he had been here. But I gave you credit for being in the midst of the danger," she added, smiling, with a determination not to show much feeling. "Sit down and tell me what has happened."

They sat down at the extremities of the old black sofa, and Felix said,—

"To tell you the truth, I had shut myself up, and tried to be as indifferent to the election as if I'd been one of the fishes in the Lapp, till the noises got too strong for me. But I only saw the tail end of the disturbance. The poor noisy simpletons seemed to give way before the magistrates and the constables. I hope nobody has been much hurt. The fear is that they may turn out again by and by; their giving way so soon may not be altogether a good sign. There's a great number of heavy fellows in the town. If they go and drink more, the last end may be worse than the first. However——"

Felix broke off, as if this talk were futile, clasped his hands behind his head, and, leaning backward, looked at Esther, who was looking at him.

"May I stay here a little while?" he said, after a moment, which seemed long.

"Pray do," said Esther, coloring. To relieve herself she took some work and bowed her head over her stitching. It was in reality a little heaven to her that Felix was there, but she saw beyond it—saw that by and by he would be gone, and that they should be farther on their way, not toward meeting, but parting. His will was impregnable. He was a rock, and she was no more to him than the white clinging mist-cloud.

"I wish I could be sure that you see things just as I do," he said, abruptly, after a minute's silence.

"I am sure you see them much more wisely than I do," said Esther, almost bitterly, without looking up.

"There are some people one must wish to judge one truly. Not to wish it would be mere hardness. I know you think I am a man without feeling—at least, without strong affections. You think I love nothing but my own resolutions."

"Suppose I reply in the same sort of strain?" said Esther, with a little toss of the head.

"How?"

"Why, that you think me a shallow woman, incapable of believing what is best in you, setting down everything that is too high for me as a deficiency."

"Don't parry what I say. Answer me." There was an expression of painful beseeching in the tone with which Felix said this. Esther let her work fall on her lap and looked at him, but she was unable to speak.

"I want you to tell me—once—that you know it would be easier to me to give myself up to loving and being loved, as other men do, when they can, than to——"

This breaking off in speech was something quite new in Felix. For the first time he had lost his self-possession, and turned his eyes away. He was at variance with himself. He had begun what he felt that he ought not to finish.

Esther, like a woman as she was—a woman waiting for love, never able to ask for it—had her joy in these signs of her power; but they made her generous, not chary, as they might have done if she had had a pettier disposition. She said, with deep yet timid earnestness,—

"What you have chosen to do has only convinced me that your love would be the better worth having."

All the finest part of Esther's nature trembled in those words. To be right in great memorable moments is perhaps the thing we need most desire for ourselves.

Felix as quick as lightning turned his look upon her again, and, leaning forward, took her sweet hand and held it to his lips some moments before he let it fall again and raised his head.

"We shall always be the better for thinking of each other," he said, leaning his elbow on the back of the sofa, and supporting his head as he looked at her with calm sadness. "This thing can never come to me twice over. It is my knighthood. That was always a business of great cost."

He smiled at her, but she sat biting her inner lip, and pressing her hands together. She desired to be worthy of what she reverenced in Felix, but the inevitable renunciation was too difficult. She saw herself wandering through the future weak and forsaken. The charming sauciness was all gone from her face, but the memory of it made this childlike dependent sorrow all the more touching.

"Tell me what you would——" Felix burst out, leaning nearer to her; but the next instant he started up, went to the table, took his cap in his hand, and came in front of her.

"Good-by," he said, very gently, not daring to put out his hand. But Esther put up hers instead of speaking. He just pressed it and then went away.

She heard the doors close behind him, and felt free to be miserable. She cried bitterly. If she might have married Felix Holt, she could have been a good woman. She felt no trust that she could ever be good without him.

Felix reproached himself. He would have done better not to speak in that way. But the prompting to which he had chiefly listened had been the desire to prove to Esther that he set a high value on her feelings. He could not help seeing that he was very important to her; and he was too simple and sincere a man to ape a sort of humility which would not have made him any the better if he had possessed it. Such pretences turn our lives into sorry dramas. And Felix wished Esther to know that her love was dear to him as the beloved dead are dear. He felt that they must not marry—that they would ruin each other's lives. But he had longed for her to know fully that his will to be always apart from her was renunciation, not an easy preference. In this he was thoroughly generous; and yet, now some subtle, mysterious conjuncture of impressions and circumstances had made him speak, he questioned the wisdom of what he had done. Express confessions give definiteness to memories that might more easily melt away without them; and Felix felt for Esther's pain as the strong soldier, who can march on hungering without fear that he shall faint, feels for the young brother—the maiden-cheeked conscript whose load is too heavy for him.

———————◆———————

CHAPTER XXXIII.

Mischief, thou art afoot.
Julius Cæsar.

FELIX could not go home again immediately after quitting Esther. He got out of the town, skirted it a little while, looking across the December stillness of the fields, and then re-entered it by the main road into the market-place, thinking that, after all, it would be better for him to look at the busy doings of men than to listen in solitude to the voices within him; and he wished to know how things were going on.

It was now nearly half-past one, and Felix perceived that the street was filling with more than the previous crowd. By the time he got in front of the booths, he was himself so surrounded by men who were being thrust hither and thither that retreat would have been impossible; and he went where he was obliged to go, although his height and strength were above the average even in a crowd where there were so many heavy-armed workmen used to the pickaxe. Almost all shabby-coated Trebians must have been there, but the entries and back streets of the town did not supply the mass of the crowd; and besides the rural incomers, both of the more decent and the rougher sort, Felix, as he was pushed along, thought he discerned here and there men of that keener aspect which is only common in manufacturing towns.

But at present there was no evidence of any distinctly mischievous design. There was only evidence that the majority of the crowd were excited with drink, and that their actions could hardly be calculated on more than those of oxen and pigs congregated amidst hootings and pushings. The confused deafening shouts, the incidental fighting, the knocking over, pulling, and scuffling, seemed to increase every moment. Such of the constables as were mixed with the crowd were quite helpless; and if an official staff was seen above the heads, it moved about fitfully, showing as little sign of a guiding hand as the summit of a buoy on the waves. Doubtless many hurts and bruises had been received, but no one could know the amount of injuries that were widely scattered.

It was clear that no more voting could be done, and the poll had been adjourned. The probabilities of serious mischief had grown strong enough to prevail over the Rector's objection to getting military aid within reach; and when Felix re-entered the town, a galloping messenger had already been despatched to Duffield. The Rector wished to ride out again, and read the Riot Act from a point where he could be better heard than from the window of the Marquis; but Mr. Crow, the high constable, who had returned from closer observation, insisted that the risk would be too great. New special constables had been sworn in, but Mr. Crow said prophetically that if once mischief began the mob was past caring for constables.

But the Rector's voice was ringing and penetrating, and when he appeared on the narrow balcony and read the formula, commanding all men to go to their homes or about their lawful business, there was a strong transient effect. Every one within hearing listened, and for a few moments after the final words, "God save the King!" the comparative silence continued. Then the people began to move, the buzz rose again, and grew, and grew, till it turned to shouts and roaring as before. The movement was that of a flood hemmed in; it carried nobody away. Whether the crowd would obey the order to disperse themselves within an hour was a doubt that approached nearer to a negative certainty.

Presently Mr. Crow, who held himself a tactician, took a well-intentioned step, which went far to fulfil his own prophecy. He had arrived with the magistrates by a back way at the Seven Stars, and here again the Riot Act was read from a window, with much the same result as before. The Rector had returned by the same way to the Marquis, as the headquarters most suited for administration, but Mr. Crow remained at the other extremity of King Street, where some awe-striking presence was certainly needed. Seeing that the time was passing, and all effect from the voice of law had disappeared, he showed himself at an upper window, and addressed the crowd, telling them that the soldiers had been sent for, and that if they did not disperse they would have cavalry upon them instead of constables.

Mr. Crow, like some other high constables more celebrated in history, "enjoyed a bad reputation"; that is to say, he enjoyed many things which caused his reputation to be bad, and he was anything but popular in Treby. It is probable that a pleasant message would have lost something from his lips, and what he actually said was so unpleasant that, instead of persuading the crowd, it appeared to enrage them. Some one, snatching a raw potato from a sack in the greengrocer's shop behind him, threw it at the constable and hit him on the mouth. Straightway raw potatoes and turnips were flying by twenties at the windows of the Seven Stars, and the panes were smashed. Felix, who was half-way up the street, heard the voices turning to a savage roar, and saw a rush toward the hardware shop, which furnished more effective weapons and missiles than turnips and potatoes. Then a cry ran along that the Tories had sent for the soldiers, and if those among the mob who called themselves Tories as willingly as anything else were disposed to take whatever called itself the Tory side, they only helped the main result of reckless disorder.

But there were proofs that the predominant will of the crowd was against "Debarry's men," and in favor of Transome. Several shops were invaded, and they were all of them "Tory shops." The tradesmen who could do so now locked their doors and barricaded their windows within. There was a panic among the householders of this hitherto peaceful town, and a general anxiety for the military to arrive. The Rector was in painful anxiety on this head: he had sent out two messengers as secretly as he could toward Hathercote to order the soldiers to ride straight to the town; but he feared that these messengers had been somehow intercepted.

It was three o'clock: more than an hour had elapsed since the reading of the Riot Act. The Rector of Treby Magna

wrote an indignant message and sent it to the Ram, to Mr.
Lingon, the Rector of Little Treby, saying that there was evidently a Radical animus in the mob, and that Mr. Transome's
party should hold themselves peculiarly responsible. Where
was Mr. Jermyn?

Mr. Lingon replied that he was going himself out toward
Duffield to see after the soldiers. As for Jermyn, he was not
that attorney's sponsor: he believed that Jermyn was gone
away somewhere on business—to fetch voters.

A serious effort was now being made by all the civil force
at command. The December day would soon be passing into
evening, and all disorder would be aggravated by obscurity.
The horrors of fire were as likely to happen as any minor evil.
The constables, as many of them as could do so, armed themselves with carbines and sabres: all the respectable inhabitants
who had any courage prepared themselves to struggle for order;
and many felt with Mr. Wace and Mr. Tiliot that the nearest
duty was to defend the breweries and the spirit- and wine-
vaults, where the property was of a sort at once most likely to
be threatened and most dangerous in its effects. The Rector,
with fine determination, got on horseback again, as the best
mode of leading the constables, who could only act efficiently
in a close body. By his direction the column of armed men
avoided the main street, and made their way along a back road,
that they might occupy the two chief lanes leading to the wine-
vaults and the brewery, and bear down on the crowd from
these openings, which it was especially desirable to guard.

Meanwhile Felix Holt had been hotly occupied in King
Street. After the first window-smashing at the Seven Stars,
there was a sufficient reason for damaging that inn to the utmost. The destructive spirit tends toward completeness; and
any object once maimed or otherwise injured is as readily
doomed by unreasoning men as by unreasoning boys. Also
the Seven Stars sheltered Spratt; and to some Sproxton men
in front of that inn it was exasperating that Spratt should be
safe and sound on a day when blows were going, and justice
might be rendered. And again, there was the general desir-
ableness of being inside a public-house.

Felix had at last been willingly urged on to this spot. Hitherto swayed by the crowd, he had been able to do nothing but defend himself and keep on his legs; but he foresaw that the people would burst into the inn; he heard cries of "Spratt!" "Fetch him out!" "We'll pitch him out!" "Pummel him!" It was not unlikely that lives might be sacrificed; and it was intolerable to Felix to be witnessing the blind outrages of this mad crowd, and yet be doing nothing to counteract them. Even some vain effort would satisfy him better than mere gazing. Within the walls of the inn he might save some one. He went in with a miscellaneous set, who dispersed themselves with different objects—some to the tap-room, and to search for the cellar; some upstairs to search in all rooms for Spratt, or any one else, perhaps, as a temporary scapegoat for Spratt. Guided by the screams of women, Felix at last got to a high upstairs passage, where the landlady and some of her servants were running away in helpless terror from two or three half-tipsy men, who had been emptying a spirit-decanter in the bar. Assuming the tone of a mob leader, he cried out, "Here, boys, here's better fun this way—come with me!" and drew the men back with him along the passage. They reached the lower staircase in time to see the unhappy Spratt being dragged, coatless and screaming, down the steps. No one at present was striking or kicking him; it seemed as if he were being reserved for punishment on some wider area, where the satisfaction might be more generally shared. Felix followed close, determined, if he could, to rescue both assailers and assaulted from the worst consequences. His mind was busy with possible devices.

Down the stairs, out along the stones through the gateway, Spratt was dragged as a mere heap of linen and cloth rags. When he was got outside the gateway, there was an immense hooting and roaring, though many there had no grudge against him, and only guessed that others had the grudge. But this was the narrower part of the street; it widened as it went onward, and Spratt was dragged on, his enemies crying, "We'll make a ring—we'll see how frightened he looks!"

"Kick him, and have done with him," Felix heard another say. "Let's go to Tiliot's vaults—there's more gin there!"

Here were two hideous threats. In dragging Spratt onward

the people were getting very near to the lane leading up to Tiliot's. Felix kept as close as he could to the threatened victim. He had thrown away his own stick, and carried a bludg-
eon which had escaped from the hands of an invader at the
Seven Stars; his head was bare; he looked, to undiscerning
eyes, like a leading spirit of the mob. In this condition he
was observed by several persons looking anxiously from their
upper windows, and finally observed to push himself, by vio-
lent efforts, close behind the dragged man.

Meanwhile the foremost among the constables, who, coming
by the back way, had now reached the opening of Tiliot's
Lane, discerned that the crowd had a victim amongst them.
One spirited fellow, named Tucker, who was a regular constable, feeling that no time was to be lost in meditation, called
on his neighbor to follow him, and with the sabre that had
happened to be his weapon got a way for himself where he
was not expected, by dint of quick resolution. At this moment
Spratt had been let go—had been dropped, in fact, almost life-
less with terror, on the street stones, and the men round him
had retreated for a little space, as if to amuse themselves with
looking at him. Felix had taken his opportunity; and seeing
the first step toward a plan he was bent on, he sprang forward
close to the cowering Spratt. As he did this, Tucker had cut
his way to the spot, and imagining Felix to be the destined ex-
ecutioner of Spratt—for any discrimination of Tucker's lay in
his muscles rather than his eyes—he rushed up to Felix, meaning to collar him and throw him down. But Felix had rapid
senses and quick thoughts; he discerned the situation; he
chose between two evils. Quick as lightning he frustrated the
constable, fell upon him, and tried to master his weapon. In
the struggle, which was watched without interference, the constable fell undermost, and Felix got his weapon. He started
up with the bare sabre in his hand. The crowd round him
cried "Hurray!" with a sense that he was on their side against
the constable. Tucker did not rise immediately; but Felix
did not imagine that he was much hurt.

"Don't touch him!" said Felix. "Let him go. Here,
bring Spratt, and follow me."

Felix was perfectly conscious that he was in the midst of a

tangled business. But he had chiefly before his imagination
the horrors that might come if the mass of wild chaotic desires
and impulses around him were not diverted from any further
attack on places where they would get in the midst of intoxicating and inflammable materials. It was not a moment in
which a spirit like his could calculate the effect of misunderstanding as to himself: nature never makes men who are at
once energetically sympathetic and minutely calculating. He
believed he had the power, and he was resolved to try, to carry
the dangerous mass out of mischief till the military came to
awe them—which he supposed, from Mr. Crow's announcement
long ago, must be a near event.

He was followed the more willingly because Tiliot's Lane
was seen by the hindmost to be now defended by constables,
some of whom had firearms; and where there is no strong
counter-movement, any proposition to do something unspecified
stimulates stupid curiosity. To many of the Sproxton men
who were within sight of him Felix was known personally, and
vaguely believed to be a man who meant many queer things,
not at all of an every-day kind. Pressing along like a leader,
with the sabre in his hand, and inviting them to bring on
Spratt, there seemed a better reason for following him than
for doing anything else. A man with a definite will and an
energetic personality acts as a sort of flag to draw and bind
together the foolish units of a mob. It was on this sort of
influence over men whose mental state was a mere medley of
appetites and confused impressions that Felix had dared to
count. He hurried them along with words of invitation, telling them to hold up Spratt and not drag him; and those behind
followed him, with a growing belief that he had some design
worth knowing, while those in front were urged along partly
by the same notion, partly by the sense that there was a motive in those behind them, not knowing what the motive was.
It was that mixture of pushing forward and being pushed forward which is a brief history of most human things.

What Felix really intended to do was to get the crowd by
the nearest way out of the town, and induce them to skirt it
on the north side with him, keeping up in them the idea that
he was leading them to execute some stratagem by which they

would surprise something worth attacking, and circumvent the constables who were defending the lanes. In the mean time he trusted that the soldiers would have arrived, and with this sort of mob, which was animated by no real political passion or fury against social distinctions, it was in the highest degree unlikely that there would be any resistance to a military force. The presence of fifty soldiers would probably be enough to scatter the rioting hundreds. How numerous the mob was no one ever knew: many inhabitants afterward were ready to swear that there must have been at least two thousand rioters. Felix knew he was incurring great risks; but "his blood was up": we hardly allow enough in common life for the results of that enkindled passionate enthusiasm which, under other conditions, makes world-famous deeds.

He was making for a point where the street branched off on one side toward a speedy opening between hedgerows, on the other toward the shabby wideness of Pollard's End. At this forking of the street there was a large space, in the centre of which there was a small stone platform, mounting by three steps, with an old green finger-post upon it. Felix went straight to this platform and stepped upon it, crying "Halt!" in a loud voice to the men behind and before him, and calling to those who held Spratt to bring him there. All came to a stand with faces toward the finger-post, and perhaps for the first time the extremities of the crowd got a definite idea that a man with a sabre in his hand was taking the command.

"Now!" said Felix, when Spratt had been brought on to the stone platform, faint and trembling, "has anybody got cord? if not, handkerchiefs knotted fast; give them to me."

He drew out his own handkerchief, and two or three others were mustered and handed to him. He ordered them to be knotted together, while curious eyes were fixed on him. Was he going to have Spratt hanged? Felix kept fast hold of his weapon, and ordered others to act.

"Now, put it round his waist, wind his arms in, draw them a little backward—so! and tie it fast on the other side of the post."

When that was done, Felix said, imperatively,—

"Leave him there—we shall come back to him; let us make

haste; march along, lads!   Up Park Street and down Hobb's Lane."

It was the best chance he could think of for saving Spratt's life.   And he succeeded.   The pleasure of seeing the helpless man tied up sufficed for the moment, if there were any who had ferocity enough to count much on coming back to him. Nobody's imagination represented the certainty that some one out of the houses at hand would soon come and untie him when he was left alone.

And the rioters pushed up Park Street, a noisy stream, with Felix still in the midst of them, though he was laboring hard to get his way to the front.   He wished to determine the course of the crowd along a by-road called Hobb's Lane, which would have taken them to the other—the Duffield—end of the town.   He urged several of the men round him, one of whom was no less a person than the big Dredge, our old Sproxton acquaintance, to get forward, and be sure that all the fellows would go down the lane, else they would spoil sport.   Hitherto Felix had been successful, and he had gone along with an un-broken impulse.   But soon something occurred which brought with a terrible shock the sense that his plan might turn out to be as mad as all bold projects are seen to be when they have failed.

Mingled with the more headlong and half-drunken crowd there were some sharp-visaged men who loved the irrationality of riots for something else than its own sake, and who at pres-ent were not so much the richer as they desired to be for the pains they had taken in coming to the Treby election, induced by certain prognostics gathered at Duffield on the nomination day that there might be the conditions favorable to that con-fusion which was always a harvest-time.   It was known to some of these sharp men that Park Street led out toward the grand house of Treby Manor, which was as good—nay, better for their purpose than the bank.   While Felix was entertaining his ardent purpose, these other sons of Adam were entertaining another ardent purpose of their peculiar sort, and the moment was come when they were to have their triumph.

From the front ranks backward toward Felix there ran a new summons—a new invitation.

21

"Let us go to Treby Manor!"

From that moment Felix was powerless; a new definite suggestion overrode his vaguer influence. There was a determined rush past Hobb's Lane, and not down it. Felix was carried along too. He did not know whether to wish the contrary. Once on the road, out of the town, with openings into fields and with the wide park at hand, it would have been easy for him to liberate himself from the crowd. At first it seemed to him the better part to do this, and to get back to the town as fast as he could, in the hope of finding the military and getting a detachment to come and save the Manor. But he reflected that the course of the mob had been sufficiently seen, and that there were plenty of people in Park Street to carry the information faster than he could. It seemed more necessary that he should secure the presence of some help for the family at the Manor by going there himself.

The Debarrys were not of the class he was wont to be anxious about; but Felix Holt's conscience was alive to the accusation that any danger they might be in now was brought on by a deed of his. In these moments of bitter vexation and disappointment, it did occur to him that very unpleasant consequences might be hanging over him of a kind quite different from inward dissatisfaction; but it was useless now to think of averting such consequences. As he was pressed along with the multitude into Treby Park, his very movement seemed to him only an image of the day's fatalities, in which the multitudinous small wickednesses of small selfish ends, really undirected toward any larger result, had issued in widely shared mischief that might yet be hideous.

The light was declining: already the candles shone through many windows of the Manor. Already the foremost part of the crowd had burst into the offices, and adroit men were busy in the right places to find plate, after setting others to force the butler into unlocking the cellars; and Felix had only just been able to force his way on to the front terrace, with the hope of getting to the rooms where he would find the ladies of the household and comfort them with the assurance that rescue must soon come, when the sound of horses' feet convinced him that the rescue was nearer than he had expected. Just as he heard the horses, he had approached the large window of a room, where a brilliant light suspended from the ceiling showed him a group of women clinging together in terror. Others of the crowd were pushing their way up the terrace steps and gravel slopes at various points. Hearing the horses, he kept his post in front of the window, and, motioning with his sabre, cried out to the oncomers: "Keep back! I hear the soldiers coming." Some scrambled back, some paused automatically.

The louder and louder sound of the hoofs changed its pace and distribution. "Halt! Fire!" Bang! bang! bang!— came deafening the ears of the men on the terrace.

Before they had time or nerve to move, there was a rushing sound closer to them—again "Fire!" a bullet whizzed, and passed through Felix Holt's shoulder—the shoulder of the arm that held the naked weapon which shone in the light from the window.

Felix fell. The rioters ran confusedly, like terrified sheep. Some of the soldiers, turning, drove them along with the flat of their swords. The greater difficulty was to clear the invaded offices.

The Rector, who with another magistrate and several other gentlemen on horseback had accompanied the soldiers, now jumped on to the terrace, and hurried to the ladies of the family.

Presently there was a group round Felix, who had fainted, and, reviving, had fainted again. He had had little food during the day, and had been overwrought. Two of the group were civilians, but only one of them knew Felix, the other being a magistrate not resident in Treby. The one who knew Felix was Mr. John Johnson, whose zeal for the public peace had brought him from Duffield when he heard that the soldiers were summoned.

"I know this man very well," said Mr. Johnson. "He is a dangerous character—quite revolutionary."

It was a weary night; and the next day, Felix, whose wound was declared trivial, was lodged in Loamford Jail. There were three charges against him: that he had assaulted a constable, that he had committed manslaughter (Tucker was dead from spinal concussion), and that he had led a riotous on-slaught on a dwelling-house.

Four other men were committed: one of them for possessing himself of a gold cup with the Debarry arms on it; the three others, one of whom was the collier Dredge, for riot and assault.

That morning Treby town was no longer in terror; but it was in much sadness. Other men, more innocent than the hated Spratt, were groaning under severe bodily injuries. And poor Tucker's corpse was not the only one that had been lifted from the pavement. It is true that none grieved much for the other dead man, unless it be grief to say, "Poor old fellow!" He had been trampled upon, doubtless, where he fell drunkenly, near the entrance of the Seven Stars. This second corpse was old Tommy Trounsem, the bill-sticker—otherwise Thomas Transome, the last of a very old family line.

———◆———

CHAPTER XXXIV.

> The fields are hoary with December's frost.
> I too am hoary with the chills of age.
> But through the fields and through the untrodden woods
> Is rest and stillness—only in my heart
> The pall of winter shrouds a throbbing life.

A WEEK after that Treby riot, Harold Transome was at Transome Court. He had returned from a hasty visit to town to keep his Christmas at this delightful country home, not in the best Christmas spirits. He had lost the election; but if that had been his only annoyance, he had good humor and good sense enough to have borne it as well as most men, and to have paid the eight or nine thousand, which had been the price of ascertaining that he was not to sit in the next Parliament, without useless grumbling. But the disappointments of life can never, any more than its pleasures, be estimated singly; and the healthiest and most agreeable of men is exposed to that coincidence of various vexations, each heightening the effect of the other, which may produce in him something corresponding to the spontaneous and externally unaccountable moodiness of the morbid and disagreeable.

Harold might not have grieved much at a small riot in
Treby, even if it had caused some expenses to fall on the
county; but the turn which the riot had actually taken was a
bitter morsel for rumination on more grounds than one. However the disturbances had arisen and been aggravated—and
probably no one knew the whole truth on these points—the
conspicuous, gravest incidents had all tended to throw the
blame on the Radical party, that is to say, on Transome and
on Transome's agents; and so far the candidateship and its
results had done Harold dishonor in the county: precisely the
opposite effect to that which was a dear object of his ambition.
More than this, Harold's conscience was active enough to be
very unpleasantly affected by what had befallen Felix Holt.
His memory, always good, was particularly vivid in its reten-
tion of Felix Holt's complaint to him about the treating of the
Sproxton men, and of the subsequent irritating scene in Jermyn's office, when the personage with the inauspicious name
of Johnson had expounded to him the impossibility of revising
an electioneering scheme once begun, and of turning your vehicle back when it had already begun to roll downhill. Remembering Felix Holt's words of indignant warning about hiring men with drink in them to make a noise, Harold could not
resist the urgent impression that the offences for which Felix
was committed were fatalities, not brought about by any willing co-operation of his with the rioters, but arising probably
from some ill-judged efforts to counteract their violence. And
this impression, which insisted on growing into a conviction,
became in one of its phases an uneasy sense that he held evidence which would at once tend to exonerate Felix and to place
himself and his agents in anything but a desirable light. It
was likely that some one else could give equivalent evidence in
favor of Felix—the little talkative Dissenting preacher, for
example; but, anyhow, the affair with the Sproxton men would
be ripped open and made the worst of by the opposite parties.
The man who has failed in the use of some indirectness is
helped very little by the fact that his rivals are men to whom
that indirectness is a something human, very far from being
alien. There remains this grand distinction, that he has failed,
and that the jet of light is thrown entirely on his misdoings.

In this matter Harold felt himself a victim. Could he hinder the tricks of his agents? In this particular case he had tried to hinder them, and had tried in vain. He had not loved the two agents in question, to begin with; and now at this later stage of events he was more innocent than ever of bearing them anything but the most sincere ill-will. He was more utterly exasperated with them than he would probably have been if his one great passion had been for public virtue. Jermyn, with his John Johnson, had added this ugly dirty business of the Treby election to all the long-accumulating list of offences, which Harold was resolved to visit on him to the utmost. He had seen some handbills carrying the insinuation that there was a discreditable indebtedness to Jermyn on the part of the Transomes. If any such notions existed apart from electioneering slander, there was all the more reason for letting the world see Jermyn severely punished for abusing his power over the family affairs and tampering with the family property. And the world certainly should see this with as little delay as possible. The cool confident assuming fellow should be bled to the last drop in compensation, and all connection with him be finally got rid of. Now that the election was done with, Harold meant to devote himself to private affairs, till everything lay in complete order under his own supervision.

This morning he was seated as usual in his private room, which had now been handsomely fitted up for him. It was but the third morning after the first Christmas he had spent in his English home for fifteen years, and the home looked like an eminently desirable one. The white frost lay on the broad lawn, on the many-formed leaves of the evergreens, and on the giant trees at a distance. Logs of dry oak blazed on the hearth; the carpet was like warm moss under his feet; he had breakfasted just according to his taste, and he had the interesting occupations of a large proprietor to fill the morning. All through the house now steps were noiseless on carpets or on fine matting; there was warmth in hall and corridors; there were servants enough to do everything, and to do it at the right time. Skilful Dominic was always at hand to meet his master's demands, and his bland presence diffused itself like a smile over the household, infecting the gloomy English mind with the belief that life was easy, and making his real predominance seem as soft and light as a down quilt. Old Mr. Transome had gathered new courage and strength since little Harry and Dominic had come, and since Harold had insisted on his taking drives. Mrs. Transome herself was seen on a fresh background with a gown of rich new stuff. And if, in spite of this, she did not seem happy, Harold either did not observe it, or kindly ignored it as the necessary frailty of elderly women whose lives have had too much of dulness and privation. Our minds get tricks and attitudes as our bodies do, thought Harold, and age stiffens them into unalterableness. "Poor mother! I confess I should not like to be an elderly woman myself. One requires a good deal of the purring cat for that, or else of the loving grandame. I wish she would take more to little Harry. I suppose she has her suspicions about the lad's mother, and is as rigid in those matters as in her Toryism. However, I do what I can; it would be difficult to say what there is wanting to her in the way of indulgence and luxury to make up for the old niggardly life."

And certainly Transome Court was now such a home as many women would covet. Yet even Harold's own satisfaction in the midst of its elegant comfort needed at present to be sustained by the expectation of gratified resentment. He was obviously less bright and enjoying than usual, and his mother, who watched him closely without daring to ask questions, had gathered hints and drawn inferences enough to make her feel sure that there was some storm gathering between him and Jermyn. She did not dare to ask questions, and yet she had not resisted the temptation to say something bitter about Harold's failure to get returned as a Radical, helping, with feminine self-defeat, to exclude herself more completely from any consultation by him. In this way poor women, whose power lies solely in their influence, make themselves like music out of tune, and only move men to run away.

This morning Harold had ordered his letters to be brought to him at the breakfast-table, which was not his usual practice. His mother could see that there were London business letters about which he was eager, and she had found out that the let-

ter brought by a clerk the day before was to make an appoint
ment with Harold for Jermyn to come to Transome Court at
eleven this morning. She observed Harold swallow his coffee
and push away his plate with an early abstraction from the
business of breakfast which was not at all after his usual
manner. She herself ate nothing: her sips of tea seemed to
excite her; her cheeks flushed, and her hands were cold. She
was still young and ardent in her terrors; the passions of the
past were living in her dread.

When Harold left the table she went into the long drawing-
room, where she might relieve her restlessness by walking up
and down, and catch the sound of Jermyn's entrance into Harold's room, which was close by. Here she moved to and fro
amongst the rose-colored satin of chairs and curtains—the great
story of this world reduced for her to the little tale of her own
existence—dull obscurity everywhere, except where the keen
light fell on the narrow track of her own lot, wide only for a
woman's anguish. At last she heard the expected ring and
footstep, and the opening and closing door. Unable to walk
about any longer, she sank into a large cushioned chair, helpless and prayerless. She was not thinking of God's anger or
mercy, but of her son's. She was thinking of what might be
brought, not by death, but by life.

CHAPTER XXXV.

M. Check to your queen!
N.　　　　　　　　　　Nay, your own king is bare,
　　And moving so, you give yourself checkmate.

WHEN Jermyn entered the room, Harold, who was seated
at his library-table examining papers, with his back toward
the light and his face toward the door, moved his head coldly.
Jermyn said an ungracious " Good-morning "—as little as possible like a salutation to one who might regard himself as a
patron. On the attorney's handsome face there was a black
cloud of defiant determination slightly startling to Harold,
who had expected to feel that the overpowering weight of

temper in the interview was on his own side. Nobody was ever prepared beforehand for this expression of Jermyn's face, which seemed as strongly contrasted with the cold impenetrableness which he preserved under the ordinary annoyances of business as with the bland radiance of his lighter moments.

Harold himself did not look amiable just then, but his anger was of the sort that seeks a vent without waiting to give a fatal blow; it was that of a nature more subtly mixed than Jermyn's—less animally forcible, less unwavering in selfishness, and with more of high-bred pride. He looked at Jermyn with increased disgust and secret wonder.

"Sit down," he said, curtly.

Jermyn seated himself in silence, opened his greatcoat, and took some papers from a side pocket.

"I have written to Makepeace," said Harold, "to tell him to take the entire management of the election expenses. So you will transmit your accounts to him."

"Very well. I am come this morning on other business."

"If it's about the riot and the prisoners, I have only to say that I shall enter into no plans. If I am called on, I shall say what I know about that young fellow Felix Holt. People may prove what they can about Johnson's damnable tricks, or yours either."

"I am not come to speak about the riot. I agree with you in thinking that quite a subordinate subject." (When Jermyn had the black cloud over his face, he never hesitated or drawled, and made no Latin quotations.)

"Be so good, then, as to open your business at once," said Harold, in a tone of imperious indifference.

"That is precisely what I wish to do. I have here information from a London correspondent that you are about to file a bill against me in Chancery." Jermyn, as he spoke, laid his hand on the papers before him, and looked straight at Harold.

"In that case, the question for you is, how far your conduct as the family solicitor will bear investigation. But it is a question which you will consider quite apart from me."

"Doubtless. But prior to that there is a question which we must consider together."

The tone in which Jermyn said this gave an unpleasant shock to Harold's sense of mastery. Was it possible that he should have the weapon wrenched out of his hand?

"I shall know what to think of that," he replied, as haughtily as ever, "when you have stated what the question is."

"Simply, whether you will choose to retain the family estates, or lay yourself open to be forthwith legally deprived of them."

"I presume you refer to some underhand scheme of your own, on a par with the annuities you have drained us by in the name of Johnson," said Harold, feeling a new movement of anger. "If so, you had better state your scheme to my lawyers, Dymock and Halliwell."

"No. I think you will approve of my stating in your own ear first of all that it depends on my will whether you remain an important landed proprietor in North Loamshire, or whether you retire from the county with the remainder of the fortune you have acquired in trade."

Jermyn paused, as if to leave time for this morsel to be tasted.

"What do you mean?" said Harold, sharply.

"Not any scheme of mine; but a state of the facts, resulting from the settlement of the estate made in 1729: a state of the facts which renders your father's title and your own title to the family estates utterly worthless as soon as the true claimant is made aware of his right."

"And you intend to inform him?"

"That depends. I am the only person who has the requisite knowledge. It rests with you to decide whether I shall use that knowledge against you; or whether I shall use it in your favor—by putting an end to the evidence that would serve to oust you in spite of your 'robust title of occupancy.'"

Jermyn paused again. He had been speaking slowly, but without the least hesitation, and with a bitter definiteness of enunciation. There was a moment or two before Harold answered, and then he said abruptly,—

"I don't believe you."

"I thought you were more shrewd," said Jermyn, with a touch of scorn. "I thought you understood that I had had too much experience to waste my time in telling fables to persuade a man who has put himself into the attitude of my deadly enemy."

"Well, then, say at once what your proofs are," said Harold, shaking in spite of himself, and getting nervous.

"I have no inclination to be lengthy. It is not more than a few weeks since I ascertained that there is in existence an heir of the Bycliffes, the old adversaries of your family. More curiously, it is only a few days ago—in fact, only since the day of the riot—that the Bycliffe claim has become valid, and that the right of remainder accrues to the heir in question."

"And how, pray?" said Harold, rising from his chair, and making a turn in the room, with his hands thrust in his pockets. Jermyn rose too, and stood near the hearth, facing Harold as he moved to and fro.

"By the death of an old fellow who got drunk, and was trampled to death in the riot. He was the last of that Thomas Transome's line by the purchase of whose interest your family got its title to the estate. Your title died with him. It was supposed that the line had become extinct before—and on that supposition the old Bycliffes founded their claim. But I hunted up this man just about the time the last suit was closed. His death would have been of no consequence to you if there had not been a Bycliffe in existence; but I happen to know that there is, and that the fact can be legally proved."

For a minute or two Harold did not speak, but continued to pace the room, while Jermyn kept his position, holding his hands behind him. At last Harold said, from the other end of the room, speaking in a scornful tone,—

"That sounds alarming. But it is not to be proved simply by your statement."

"Clearly. I have here a document, with a copy which will back my statement. It is the opinion given on the case more than twenty years ago, and it bears the signature of the Attorney-General and the first conveyancer of the day."

Jermyn took up the papers he had laid on the table, opening them slowly and coolly as he went on speaking, and as Harold advanced toward him.

"You may suppose that we spared no pains to ascertain the

state of the title in the last suit against Maurice Christian By-cliffe, which threatened to be a hard run. This document is the result of a consultation; it gives an opinion which must be taken as a final authority. You may cast your eyes over that, if you please; I will wait your time. Or you may read the summing up here," Jermyn ended, holding out one of the papers to Harold, and pointing to a final passage.

Harold took the paper, with a slight gesture of impatience. He did not choose to obey Jermyn's indication, and confine himself to the summing up. He ran through the document. But in truth he was too much excited really to follow the details, and was rather acting than reading, till at length he threw himself into his chair and consented to bend his attention on the passage to which Jermyn had pointed. The attorney watched him as he read and twice re-read:—

"To sum up . . . we are of opinion that the title of the present possessors of the Transome estates can be strictly proved to rest solely upon a base fee created under the original settlement of 1729, and to be good so long only as issue exists of the tenant in tail by whom that base fee was created. We feel satisfied by the evidence that such issue exists in the person of Thomas Transome, otherwise Trounsem, of Littleshaw. But upon his decease without issue we are of opinion that the right in remainder of the Bycliffe family will arise, which right would not be barred by any statute of limitation."

When Harold's eyes were on the signatures to this document for the third time, Jermyn said,—

"As it turned out, the case being closed by the death of the claimant, we had no occasion for producing Thomas Transome, who was the old fellow I tell you of. The inquiries about him set him agog, and after they were dropped he came into this neighborhood, thinking there was something fine in store for him. Here, if you like to take it, is a memorandum about him. I repeat that he died in the riot. The proof is ready. And I repeat that, to my knowledge, and mine only, there is a Bycliffe in existence; and that I know how the proof can be made out."

Harold rose from his chair again, and again paced the room. He was not prepared with any defiance.

"And where is he—this Bycliffe?" he said at last, stopping in his walk, and facing round toward Jermyn.

"I decline to say more till you promise to suspend proceedings against me."

Harold turned again, and looked out of the window, without speaking, for a moment or two. It was impossible that there should not be a conflict within him, and at present it was a very confused one. At last he said, —

"This person is in ignorance of his claim?"

"Yes."

"Has been brought up in an inferior station?"

"Yes," said Jermyn, keen enough to guess part of what was going on in Harold's mind. "There is no harm in leaving him in ignorance. The question is a purely legal one. And, as I said before, the complete knowledge of the case, as one of evidence, lies exclusively with me. I can nullify the evidence, or I can make it tell with certainty against you. The choice lies with you."

"I must have time to think of this," said Harold, conscious of a terrible pressure.

"I can give you no time unless you promise me to suspend proceedings."

"And then, when I ask you, you will lay the details before me?"

"Not without a thorough understanding beforehand. If I engage not to use my knowledge against you, you must engage in writing that on being satisfied by the details you will cancel all hostile proceedings against me, and will not institute fresh ones on the strength of any occurrences now past."

"Well, I must have time," said Harold, more than ever inclined to thrash the attorney, but feeling bound hand and foot with knots that he was not sure he could ever unfasten.

"That is to say," said Jermyn, with his black-browed persistence, "you will write to suspend proceedings."

Again Harold paused. He was more than ever exasperated, but he was threatened, mortified, and confounded by the necessity for an immediate decision between alternatives almost equally hateful to him. It was with difficulty that he could prevail on himself to speak any conclusive words. He walked as far as he could from Jermyn—to the other end of the room—then walked back to his chair and threw himself into it. At last he said, without looking at Jermyn, "I agree—I must have time."

"Very well. It is a bargain."

"No further than this," said Harold, hastily, flashing a look at Jermyn—"no further than this, that I require time, and therefore I give it to you."

"Of course. You require time to consider whether the pleasure of trying to ruin me—me to whom you are really indebted—is worth the loss of the Transome estates. I shall wish you good-morning."

Harold did not speak to him or look at him again, and Jermyn walked out of the room. As he appeared outside the door and closed it behind him, Mrs. Transome showed her white face at another door which opened on a level with Harold's in such a way that it was just possible for Jermyn not to see her. He availed himself of that possibility, and walked straight across the hall, where there was no servant in attendance to let him out, as if he believed that no one was looking at him who could expect recognition. He did not want to speak to Mrs. Transome at present; he had nothing to ask from her, and one disagreeable interview had been enough for him this morning.

She was convinced that he had avoided her, and she was too proud to arrest him. She was as insignificant now in his eyes as in her son's. "Men have no memories in their hearts," she said to herself, bitterly. Turning into her sitting-room, she heard the voices of Mr. Transome and little Harry at play together. She would have given a great deal at this moment if her feeble husband had not always lived in dread of her temper and her tyranny, so that he might have been fond of her now. She felt herself loveless; if she was important to any one, it was only to her old waiting-woman Denner.

CHAPTER XXXVI.

Are these things then necessities?
Then let us meet them like necessities.
SHAKESPEARE: *Henry IV.*

See now the virtue living in a word!
Hobson will think of swearing it was noon
When he saw Dobson at the May-day fair,
To prove poor Dobson did not rob the mail.
'Tis neighborly to save a neighbor's neck.
What harm in lying when you mean no harm?
But say 'tis perjury, then Hobson quakes—
He'll none of perjury.
　　　　　　　Thus words embalm
The conscience of mankind ; and Roman laws
Bring still a conscience to poor Hobson's aid.

FEW men would have felt otherwise than Harold Transome felt if, having a reversion tantamount to possession of a fine estate, carrying an association with an old name and considerable social importance, they were suddenly informed that there was a person who had a legal right to deprive them of these advantages; that person's right having never been contemplated by any one as more than a chance, and being quite unknown to himself. In ordinary cases a shorter possession than Harold's family had enjoyed was allowed by the law to constitute an indefeasible right; and if in rare and peculiar instances the law left the possessor of a long inheritance exposed to deprivation as a consequence of old obscure transactions, the moral reasons for giving legal validity to the title of long occupancy were not the less strong. Nobody would have said that Harold was bound to hunt out this alleged remainder-man and urge his rights upon him; on the contrary, all the world would have laughed at such conduct, and he would have been thought an interesting patient for a mad-doctor. The unconscious remainder-man was probably much better off left in his original station: Harold would not have been called upon to consider his existence if it had not been presented to him in the shape of a threat from one who had power to execute the threat.

In fact, what he would have done had the circumstances been different was much clearer than what he should choose to do or feel himself compelled to do in the actual crisis. He would not have been disgraced if, on a valid claim being urged, he had got his lawyers to fight it out for him on the chance of eluding the claim by some adroit technical management. Nobody off the stage could be sentimental about these things, or pretend to shed tears of joy because an estate was handed over from a gentleman to a mendicant sailor with a wooden leg. And this chance remainder-man was perhaps some such specimen of inheritance as the drunken fellow killed in the riot. All the world would think the actual Transomes in the right to contest any adverse claim to the utmost. But then—it was not certain that they would win in the contest; and not winning, they would incur other loss besides that of the estate. There had been a little too much of such loss already.

But why, if it were not wrong to contest the claim, should he feel the most uncomfortable scruples about robbing the claim of its sting by getting rid of its evidence? It was a mortal disappointment—it was a sacrifice of indemnification— to abstain from punishing Jermyn. But even if he brought his mind to contemplate that as the wiser course, he still shrank from what looked like complicity with Jermyn; he still shrank from the secret nullification of a just legal claim. If he had only known the details, if he had known who this alleged heir was, he might have seen his way to some course that would not have grated on his sense of honor and dignity. But Jermyn had been too acute to let Harold know this: he had even carefully kept to the masculine pronoun. And he believed that there was no one besides himself who would or could make Harold any wiser. He went home persuaded that between this interview and the next which they would have together Harold would be left to an inward debate, founded entirely on the information he himself had given. And he had not much doubt that the result would be what he˙ desired. Harold was no fool: there were many good things he liked better in life than an irrational vindictiveness.

And it did happen that, after writing to London in fulfilment of his pledge, Harold spent many hours over that inward debate, which was not very different from what Jermyn imagined. He took it everywhere with him, on foot and on horseback, and it was his companion through a great deal of the night. His nature was not of a kind given to internal conflict, and he had never before been long undecided and puzzled. This unaccustomed state of mind was so painfully irksome to him—he rebelled so impatiently against the oppression of circumstances in which his quick temperament and habitual decision could not help him—that it added tenfold to his hatred of Jermyn, who was the cause of it. And thus, as the temptation to avoid all risk of losing the estate grew and grew till scruples looked minute by the side of it, the difficulty of bringing himself to make a compact with Jermyn seemed more and more insurmountable.

But we have seen that the attorney was much too confident in his calculations. And while Harold was being gulled by his subjection to Jermyn's knowledge, independent information was on its way to him. The messenger was Christian, who, after as complete a survey of probabilities as he was capable of, had come to the conclusion that the most profitable investment he could make of his peculiar experience and testimony in relation to Bycliffe and Bycliffe's daughter was to place them at the disposal of Harold Transome. He was afraid of Jermyn; he utterly distrusted Johnson; but he thought he was secure in relying on Harold Transome's care for his own interest; and he preferred above all issues the prospect of forthwith leaving the country with a sum that at least for a good while would put him at his ease.

When, only three mornings after the interview with Jermyn, Dominic opened the door of Harold's sitting-room, and said that "Meester Chreestian," Mr. Philip Debarry's courier and an acquaintance of his own at Naples, requested to be admitted on business of importance, Harold's immediate thought was that the business referred to the so-called political affairs which were just now his chief association with the name of Debarry, though it seemed an oddness requiring explanation that a servant should be personally an intermediary. He assented, expecting something rather disagreeable than otherwise.

Christian wore this morning those perfect manners of a sub-

22

ordinate who is not servile which he always adopted toward
his unquestionable superiors.   Mr. Debarry, who preferred
having some one about him with as little resemblance as possible to a regular servant, had a singular liking for the adroit,
quiet-mannered Christian, and would have been amazed to
see the insolent assumption he was capable of in the presence
of people like Mr. Lyon, who were of no account in society.
Christian had that sort of cleverness which is said to "know
the world"—that is to say, he knew the price-current of most
things.

Aware that he was looked at as a messenger while he remained standing near the door with his hat in his hand, he
said, with respectful ease,—

"You will probably be surprised, sir, at my coming to speak
to you on my own account; and, in fact, I could not have
thought of doing so if my business did not happen to be
something of more importance to you than to any one
else."

"You don't come from Mr. Debarry, then?" said Harold,
with some surprise.

"No, sir.   My business is a secret; and, if you please, must
remain so."

"Is it a pledge you are demanding from me?" said Harold,
rather suspiciously, having no ground for confidence in a man
of Christian's position.

"Yes, sir; I am obliged to ask no less than that you will
pledge yourself not to take Mr. Jermyn into confidence concerning what passes between us."

"With all my heart," said Harold, something like a gleam
passing over his face.   His circulation had become more rapid.
"But what have you had to do with Jermyn?"

"He has not mentioned me to you, then—has he, sir?"

"No; certainly not—never."

Christian thought, "Aha, Mr. Jermyn! you are keeping the
secret well, are you?"   He said, aloud,—

"Then Mr. Jermyn has never mentioned to you, sir, what
I believe he is aware of—that there is danger of a new suit
being raised against you on the part of a Bycliffe, to get the
estate?"

"Ah!" said Harold, starting up, and placing himself with his back against the mantelpiece. He was electrified by surprise at the quarter from which this information was coming. Any fresh alarm was counteracted by the flashing thought that he might be enabled to act independently of Jermyn; and in the rush of feelings he could utter no more than an interjection. Christian concluded that Harold had had no previous hint.

"It is this fact, sir, that I came to tell you of."

"From some other motive than kindness to me, I presume," said Harold, with a slight approach to a smile.

"Certainly," said Christian, as quietly as if he had been stating yesterday's weather. "I should not have the folly to use any affectation with you, Mr. Transome. I lost considerable property early in life, and am now in the receipt of a salary simply. In the affair I have just mentioned to you I can give evidence which will turn the scale against you. I have no wish to do so, if you will make it worth my while to leave the country."

Harold listened as if he had been a legendary hero, selected for peculiar solicitation by the Evil One. Here was temptation in a more alluring form than before, because it was sweetened by the prospect of eluding Jermyn. But the desire to gain time served all the purposes of caution and resistance, and his indifference to the speaker in this case helped him to preserve perfect self-command.

"You are aware," he said, coolly, "that silence is not a commodity worth purchasing unless it is loaded. There are many persons, I dare say, who would like me to pay their travelling expenses for them. But they might hardly be able to show me that it was worth my while."

"You wish me to state what I know?"

"Well, that is a necessary preliminary to any further conversation."

"I think you will see, Mr. Transome, that, as a matter of justice, the knowledge I can give is worth something, quite apart from my future appearance or non-appearance as a witness. I must take care of my own interest, and if anything should hinder you from choosing to satisfy me for taking an essential witness out of the way, I must at least be paid for bringing you the information."

"Can you tell me who and where this Bycliffe is?"

"I can."

"—And give me a notion of the whole affair?"

"Yes: I have talked to a lawyer—not Jermyn—who is at the bottom of the law in the affair."

"You must not count on any wish of mine to suppress evidence or remove a witness. But name your price for the information."

"In that case I must be paid the higher for my information. Say, two thousand pounds."

"Two thousand devils!" burst out Harold, throwing himself into his chair again, and turning his shoulder toward Christian. New thoughts crowded upon him. "This fellow may want to decamp for some reason or other," he said to himself. "More people besides Jermyn know about his evidence, it seems. The whole thing may look black for me if it comes out. I shall be believed to have bribed him to run away, whether or not." Thus the outside conscience came in aid of the inner.

"I will not give you one sixpence for your information," he said, resolutely, "until time has made it clear that you do not intend to decamp, but will be forthcoming when you are called for. On those terms I have no objection to give you a note, specifying that after the fulfilment of that condition—that is, after the occurrence of a suit, or the understanding that no suit is to occur—I will pay you a certain sum in consideration of the information you now give me!"

Christian felt himself caught in a vice. In the first instance he had counted confidently on Harold's ready seizure of his offer to disappear; and after some words had seemed to cast a doubt on this presupposition, he had inwardly determined to go away, whether Harold wished it or not, if he could get a sufficient sum. He did not reply immediately, and Harold waited in silence, inwardly anxious to know what Christian could tell, but with a vision at present so far cleared that he was determined not to risk incurring the imputation of having anything to do with scoundrelism. We are very much indebted to such a linking of events as makes a doubtful action look wrong.

Christian was reflecting that if he stayed, and faced some possible inconveniences of being known publicly as Henry Scaddon for the sake of what he might get from Esther, it would at least be wise to be certain of some money from Harold Transome, since he turned out to be of so peculiar a disposition as to insist on a punctilious honesty to his own disadvantage. Did he think of making a bargain with the other side? If so, he might be content to wait for the knowledge till it came in some other way. Christian was beginning to be afraid lest he should get nothing by this clever move of coming to Transome Court. At last he said, —

"I think, sir, two thousand would not be an unreasonable sum, on those conditions."

"I will not give two thousand."

"Allow me to say, sir, you must consider that there is no one whose interest it is to tell you as much as I shall, even if they could; since Mr. Jermyn, who knows it, has not thought fit to tell you. There may be use you don't think of in getting the information at once."

"Well?"

"I think a gentleman should act liberally under such circumstances."

"So I will."

"I could not take less than a thousand pounds. It really would not be worth my while. If Mr. Jermyn knew I gave you the information, he would endeavor to injure me."

"I will give you a thousand," said Harold, immediately, for Christian had unconsciously touched a sure spring. "At least, I'll give you a note to the effect I spoke of."

He wrote as he had promised, and gave the paper to Christian.

"Now, don't be circuitous," said Harold. "You seem to have a business-like gift of speech. Who and where is this Bycliffe?"

"You will be surprised to hear, sir, that she is supposed to be the daughter of the old preacher, Lyon, in Malthouse Yard."

"Good God! How can that be?" said Harold. At once the first occasion on which he had seen Esther rose in his memory—the little dark parlor—the graceful girl in blue, with the surprisingly distinguished manners and appearance.

"In this way. Old Lyon, by some strange means or other, married Bycliffe's widow when this girl was a baby. And the preacher didn't want the girl to know that he was not her real father: he told me that himself. But she is the image of Bycliffe, whom I knew well—an uncommonly fine woman—steps like a queen."

"I have seen her," said Harold, more than ever glad to have purchased this knowledge. "But now, go on."

Christian proceeded to tell all he knew, including his conversation with Jermyn, except so far as it had an unpleasant relation to himself.

"Then," said Harold, as the details seemed to have come to a close, "you believe that Miss Lyon and her supposed father are at present unaware of the claims that might be urged for her on the strength of her birth?"

"I believe so. But I need not tell you that where the lawyers are on the scent you can never be sure of anything long together. I must remind you, sir, that you have promised to protect me from Mr. Jermyn by keeping my confidence."

"Never fear. Depend upon it, I shall betray nothing to Mr. Jermyn."

Christian was dismissed with a "Good-morning"; and while he cultivated some friendly reminiscences with Dominic, Harold sat chewing the cud of his new knowledge, and finding it not altogether so bitter as he had expected.

From the first, after his interview with Jermyn, the recoil of Harold's mind from the idea of strangling a legal right threw him on the alternative of attempting a compromise. Some middle course might be possible, which would be a less evil than a costly lawsuit, or than the total renunciation of the estates. And now he had learned that the new claimant was a woman—a young woman, brought up under circumstances that would make the fourth of the Transome property seem to her an immense fortune. Both the sex and the social condition were of the sort that lies open to many softening influences. And having seen Esther, it was inevitable that, amongst the various issues, agreeable and disagreeable, depicted by Harold's imagination, there should present itself a possibility that would unite the two claims—his own, which he felt to be the rational, and Esther's, which apparently was the legal claim.

Harold, as he had constantly said to his mother, was "not a marrying man"; he did not contemplate bringing a wife to Transome Court for many years to come, if at all. Having little Harry as an heir, he preferred freedom. Western women were not to his taste: they showed a transition from the feebly animal to the thinking being which was simply troublesome. Harold preferred a slow-witted large-eyed woman, silent and affectionate, with a load of black hair weighing much more heavily than her brains. He had seen no such woman in England, except one whom he had brought with him from the East.

Therefore Harold did not care to be married until or unless some surprising chance presented itself; and now that such a chance had occurred to suggest marriage to him, he would not admit to himself that he contemplated marrying Esther as a plan; he was only obliged to see that such an issue was not inconceivable. He was not going to take any step expressly directed toward that end! what he had made up his mind to, as the course most satisfactory to his nature under present urgencies, was to behave to Esther with a frank gentlemanliness, which must win her good-will, and incline her to save his family interest as much as possible. He was helped to this determination by the pleasure of frustrating Jermyn's contrivance to shield himself from punishment; and his most distinct and cheering prospect was, that within a very short space of time he should not only have effected a satisfactory compromise with Esther, but should have made Jermyn aware, by a very disagreeable form of announcement, that Harold Transome was no longer afraid of him. Jermyn should bite the dust.

At the end of these meditations he felt satisfied with himself and light-hearted. He had rejected two dishonest propositions, and he was going to do something that seemed eminently graceful. But he needed his mother's assistance, and it was necessary that he should both confide in her and persuade her.

Within two hours 'after Christian left him, Harold begged his mother to come into his private room, and there he told her the strange and startling story, omitting, however, any particulars which would involve the identification of Christian as his informant. Harold felt that his engagement demanded his reticence; and he told his mother that he was bound to conceal the source of that knowledge which he had got independently of Jermyn.

Mrs. Transome said little in the course of the story: she made no exclamations, but she listened with close attention, and asked a few questions so much to the point as to surprise Harold. When he showed her the copy of the legal opinion which Jermyn had left with him, she said she knew it very well; she had a copy herself. The particulars of that last lawsuit were too well engraven on her mind: it happened at a time when there was no one to supersede her, and she was the virtual head of the family affairs. She was prepared to understand how the estate might be in danger; but nothing had prepared her for the strange details—for the way in which the new claimant had been reared and brought within the range of converging motives that had led to this revelation, least of all' for the part Jermyn had come to play in the revelation. Mrs. Transome saw these things through the medium of certain dominant emotions that made them seem like a long-ripening retribution. Harold perceived that she was painfully agitated, that she trembled, and that her white lips would not readily lend themselves to speech. And this was hardly more than he expected. He had not liked the revelation himself when it had first come to him.

But he did not guess what it was in his narrative which had most pierced his mother. It was something that made the threat about the estate only a secondary alarm. Now, for the first time, she heard of the intended proceedings against Jermyn. Harold had not chosen to speak of them before; but having at last called his mother into consultation, there was nothing in his mind to hinder him from speaking without reserve of his determination to visit on the attorney his shameful maladministration of the family affairs.

Harold went through the whole narrative—of what he called Jermyn's scheme to catch him in a vice, and his power of triumphantly frustrating that scheme—in his usual rapid way, speaking with a final decisiveness of tone: and his mother felt that if she urged any counter-consideration at all, she could only do so when he had no more to say.

"Now, what I want you to do, mother, if you can see this matter as I see it," Harold said in conclusion, "is to go with me to call on this girl in Malthouse Yard. I will open the affair to her; it appears she is not likely to have been informed yet; and you will invite her to visit you here at once, that all scandal, all hatching of law-mischief, may be avoided, and the thing may be brought to an amicable conclusion."

"It seems almost incredible—extraordinary—a girl in her position," said Mrs. Transome, with difficulty. It would have seemed the bitterest humiliating penance if another sort of suffering had left any room in her heart.

"I assure you she is a lady; I saw her when I was canvassing, and was amazed at the time. You will be quite struck with her. It is no indignity for you to invite her."

"Oh," said Mrs. Transome, with low-toned bitterness, "I must put up with all things as they are determined for me. When shall we go?"

"Well," said Harold, looking at his watch, "it is hardly two yet. We could really go to-day, when you have lunched. It is better to lose no time. I'll order the carriage."

"Stay," said Mrs. Transome, making a desperate effort. "There is plenty of time. I shall not lunch. I have a word to say."

Harold withdrew his hand from the bell, and leaned against the mantelpiece to listen.

"You see I comply with your wish at once, Harold?"

"Yes, mother, I'm much obliged to you for making no difficulties."

"You ought to listen to me in return."

"Pray go on," said Harold, expecting to be annoyed.

"What is the good of having these Chancery proceedings against Jermyn?"

"Good? This good: that fellow has burdened the estate with annuities and mortgages to the extent of three thousand a year; and the bulk of them, I am certain, he holds himself under the name of another man. And the advances this yearly interest represents have not been much more than twenty thousand. Of course he has hoodwinked you, and my father never gave attention to these things. He has been up to all sorts of devil's work with the deeds; he didn't count on my coming back from Smyrna to fill poor Durfey's place. He shall feel the difference. And the good will be, that I shall save almost all the annuities for the rest of my father's life, which may be ten years or more, and I shall get back some of the money, and I shall punish a scoundrel. That is the good."

"He will be ruined."

"That's what I intend," said Harold, sharply.

"He exerted himself a great deal for us in the old suits: every one said he had wonderful zeal and ability," said Mrs. Transome, getting courage and warmth as she went on. Her temper was rising.

"What he did, he did for his own sake, you may depend on that," said Harold, with a scornful laugh.

"There were very painful things in that last suit. You seem anxious about this young woman, to avoid all further scandal and contests in the family. Why don't you wish to do it in this case? Jermyn might be willing to arrange things amicably—to make restitution as far as he can—if he has done anything wrong."

"I will arrange nothing amicably with him," said Harold, decisively. "If he has ever done anything scandalous as our agent, let him bear the infamy. And the right way to throw the infamy on him is to show the world that he has robbed us, and that I mean to punish him. Why do you wish to shield such a fellow, mother? It has been chiefly through him that you have had to lead such a thrifty miserable life— you who used to make as brilliant a figure as a woman need wish."

Mrs. Transome's rising temper was turned into a horrible sensation, as painful as a sudden concussion from something hard and immovable when we have struck out with our fist, intending to hit something warm, soft, and breathing, like ourselves. Poor Mrs. Transome's strokes were sent jarring back on her by a hard unalterable past. She did not speak in answer to Harold, but rose from the chair as if she gave up the debate.

"Women are frightened at everything, I know," said Harold, kindly, feeling that he had been a little harsh after his mother's compliance. "And you have been used for so many years to think Jermyn a law of nature. Come, mother," he went on, looking at her gently, and resting his hands on her shoulders, "look cheerful. We shall get through all these difficulties. And this girl—I dare say she will be quite an interesting visitor for you. You have not had any young girl about you for a long while. Who knows? she may fall deeply in love with me, and I may be obliged to marry her."

He spoke laughingly, only thinking how he could make his mother smile. But she looked at him seriously and said, "Do you mean that, Harold?"

"Am I not capable of making a conquest? Not too fat yet—a handsome, well-rounded youth of thirty-four!"

She was forced to look straight at the beaming face, with its rich dark color, just bent a little over her. Why could she not be happy in this son whose future she had once dreamed of, and who had been as fortunate as she had ever hoped? The tears came, not plenteously, but making her dark eyes as large and bright as youth had once made them without tears.

"There, there!" said Harold, coaxingly. "Don't be afraid. You shall not have a daughter-in-law unless she is a pearl. Now we will get ready to go."

In half an hour from that time Mrs. Transome came down, looking majestic in sables and velvet, ready to call on "the girl in Malthouse Yard." She had composed herself to go through this task. She saw there was nothing better to be done. After the resolutions Harold had taken, some sort of compromise with this oddly placed heiress was the result most to be hoped for; if the compromise turned out to be a marriage—well, she had no reason to care much: she was already powerless. It remained to be seen what this girl was.

The carriage was to be driven round the back way, to avoid too much observation. But the late election affairs might account for Mr. Lyon's receiving a visit from the unsuccessful Radical candidate.

CHAPTER XXXVII.

I also could speak as ye do; if your soul were in my soul's stead, I could heap up words against you, and shake mine head at you.—*Book of Job.*

In the interval since Esther parted with Felix Holt on the day of the riot, she had gone through so much emotion, and had already had so strong a shock of surprise, that she was prepared to receive any new incident of an unwonted kind with comparative equanimity.

When Mr. Lyon had got home again from his preaching excursion, Felix was already on his way to Loamford Jail. The little minister was terribly shaken by the news. He saw no clear explanation of Felix Holt's conduct; for the statements Esther had heard were so conflicting that she had not been able to gather distinctly what had come out in the examination by the magistrates. But Mr. Lyon felt confident that Felix was innocent of any wish to abet a riot or the infliction of injuries; what he chiefly feared was that in the fatal encounter with Tucker he had been moved by a rash temper, not sufficiently guarded against by a prayerful and humble spirit.

"My poor young friend is being taught with mysterious severity the evil of a too-confident self-reliance," he said to Esther, as they sat opposite to each other, listening and speaking sadly.

"You will go and see him, father?"

"Verily will I. But I must straightway go and see that poor afflicted woman, whose soul is doubtless whirled about in this trouble like a shapeless and unstable thing driven by divided winds." Mr. Lyon rose and took his hat hastily, ready to walk out, with his greatcoat flying open and exposing his small person to the keen air.

"Stay, father, pray, till you have had some food," said Esther, putting her hand on his arm. " You look quite weary and shattered."

"Child, I cannot stay. I can neither eat bread nor drink water till I have learned more about this young man's deeds, what can be proved and what cannot be proved against him. I fear he has none to stand by him in this town, for even by the friends of our church I have been ofttimes rebuked because he seemed dear to me. But, Esther, my beloved child——"

Here Mr. Lyon grasped her arm, and seemed in the need of speech to forget his previous haste. "I bear in mind this: the Lord knoweth them that are His; but we—we are left to judge by uncertain signs, that so we may learn to exercise hope and faith toward one another; and in this uncertainty I cling with awful hope to those whom the world loves not because their conscience, albeit mistakenly, is at war with the habits of the world. Our great faith, my Esther, is the faith of martyrs: I will not lightly turn away from any man who endures harshness because he will not lie; nay, though I would not wantonly grasp at ease of mind through an arbitrary choice of doctrine, I cannot but believe that the merits of the Divine Sacrifice are wider than our utmost charity. I once believed otherwise—but not now, not now."

The minister paused, and seemed to be abstractedly gazing at some memory: he was always liable to be snatched away by thoughts from the pursuit of a purpose which had seemed pressing. Esther seized the opportunity and prevailed on him to fortify himself with some of Lyddy's porridge before he went out on his tiring task of seeking definite trustworthy knowledge from the lips of various witnesses, beginning with that feminine darkener of counsel, poor Mrs. Holt.

She, regarding all her trouble about Felix in the light of a fulfilment of her own prophecies, treated the sad history with a preference for edification above accuracy, and for mystery above relevance, worthy of a commentator on the Apocalypse. She insisted chiefly, not on the important facts that Felix had sat at his work till after eleven, like a deaf man, had rushed out in surprise and alarm, had come back to report with satisfaction that things were quiet, and had asked her to set by

his dinner for him—facts which would tell as evidence that
Felix was disconnected with any project of disturbances, and
was averse to them. These things came out incidentally in
her long plaint to the minister; but what Mrs. Holt felt it
essential to state was, that long before Michaelmas was
turned, sitting in her chair, she had said to Felix that there
would be a judgment on him for being so certain sure about
the Pills and the Elixir.

"And now, Mr. Lyon," said the poor woman, who had
dressed herself in a gown previously cast off, a front all out
of curl, and a cap with no starch in it, while she held little
coughing Job on her knee,—"and now you see—my words
have come true sooner than I thought they would. Felix
may contradict me if he will; but there he is in prison, and
here am I, with nothing in the world to bless myself with but
half a crown a week as I've saved by my own scraping, and
this house I've got to pay rent for. It's not me has done
wrong, Mr. Lyon: there's nobody can say it of me—not the
orphan child on me knee is more innicent o' riot and murder
and anything else as is bad. But when you've got a son so
masterful and stopping medicines as Providence has sent, and
his betters have been taking up and down the country since
before he was a baby, it's o' no use being good here below.
But he *was* a baby, Mr. Lyon, and I gave him the breast,"
—here poor Mrs. Holt's motherly love overcame her exposi-
tory eagerness, and she fell more and more to crying as she
spoke—"And to think there's folks saying now as he'll be
transported, and his hair shaved off, and the treadmill, and
everything. Oh, dear!"

As Mrs. Holt broke off into sobbing, little Job also, who
had got a confused yet profound sense of sorrow, and of Felix
being hurt and gone away, set up a little wail of wondering
misery.

"Nay, Mistress Holt," said the minister, soothingly, "en-
large not your grief by more than warrantable grounds. I
have good hope that my young friend, your son, will be delivered from any severe consequences beyond the death of the
man Tucker, which I fear will ever be a sore burthen on his
memory. I feel confident that a jury of his countrymen will

discern between misfortune, or it may be misjudgment, and an evil will, and that he will be acquitted of any grave offence."

"He never stole anything in his life, Mr. Lyon," said Mrs. Holt, reviving. "Nobody can throw it in my face as my son ran away with money like the young man at the bank—though he looked most respectable, and far different on a Sunday to what Felix ever did. And I know it's very hard fighting with constables; but they say Tucker's wife'll be a deal better off than she was before, for the great folks'll pension her, and she'll be put on all the charities, and her children at the Free School, and everything. Your trouble's easy borne when everybody gives it a lift for you; and if judge and jury wants to do right by Felix, they'll think of his poor mother, with the bread took out of her mouth, all but half a crown a week and furniture—which, to be sure, is most excellent, and of my own buying—and got to keep this orphin child as Felix himself brought on me. And I might send him back to his old grandfather on parish pay, but I'm not that woman, Mr. Lyon: I've a tender heart. And here's his little feet and toes, like marbil; do but look"—here Mrs. Holt drew off Job's sock and shoe, and showed a well-washed little foot— "and you'll perhaps say I might take a lodger; but it's easy talking; it isn't everybody at a loose-end wants a parlor and a bedroom; and if anything bad happens to Felix, I may as well go and sit in the parish Pound, and nobody to buy me out; for it's beyond everything how the church-members find fault with my son. But I think they might leave his mother to find fault; for queer and masterful he might be, and flying in the face of the very Scripture about the physic, but he was most clever beyond anything—that I *will* say—and was his own father's lawful child, and me his mother, that was Mary Wall thirty years before ever I married his father." Here Mrs. Holt's feelings again became too much for her, but she struggled on to say, sobbingly, "And if they're to transport him, I should like to go to the prison and take the orphin child; for he was most fond of having him on his lap, and said he'd never marry; and there was One above overheard him, for he's been took at his word."

Mr. Lyon listened with low groans, and then tried to comfort her by saying that he would himself go to Loamford as soon as possible, and would give his soul no rest till he had done all he could do for Felix.

On one point Mrs. Holt's plaint tallied with his own forebodings, and he found them verified: the state of feeling in Treby among the Liberal Dissenting flock was unfavorable to Felix. None who had observed his conduct from the windows saw anything tending to excuse him, and his own account of his motives, given on his examination, was spoken of with head-shaking; if it had not been for his habit of always thinking himself wiser than other people, he would never have entertained such a wild scheme. He had set himself up for something extraordinary, and had spoken ill of respectable tradespeople. He had put a stop to the making of salable drugs, contrary to the nature of buying and selling, and to a due reliance on what Providence might effect in the human inside through the instrumentality of remedies unsuitable to the stomach, looked at in a merely secular light; and the result was what might have been expected. He had brought his mother to poverty, and himself into trouble. And what for? He had done no good to "the cause"; if he had fought about Church rates, or had been worsted in some struggle in which he was distinctly the champion of Dissent and Liberalism, his case would have been one for gold, silver, and copper subscriptions, in order to procure the best defence; sermons might have been preached on him, and his name might have floated on flags from Newcastle to Dorchester. But there seemed to be no edification in what had befallen Felix. The riot at Treby, "turn it which way you would," as Mr. Muscat observed, was no great credit to Liberalism; and what Mr. Lyon had to testify as to Felix Holt's conduct in the matter of the Sproxton men only made it clear that the defence of Felix was the accusation of his party. The whole affair, Mr. Nuttwood said, was dark and inscrutable, and seemed not to be one in which the interference of God's servants would tend to give the glory where the glory was due. That a candidate for whom the richer church-members had all voted should have his name associated with the encouragement of drunkenness, riot, and plunder was an occasion for the enemy to blaspheme; and it was not clear how the enemy's mouth would be stopped by exertions in favor of a rash young man, whose interference had made things worse instead of better. Mr. Lyon was warned lest his human partialities should blind him to the interests of truth: it was God's cause that was endangered in this matter.

The little minister's soul was bruised; he himself was keenly alive to the complication of public and private regards in this affair, and suffered a good deal at the thought of Tory triumph in the demonstration that, excepting the attack on the Seven Stars, which called itself a Whig house, all damage to property had been borne by Tories. He cared intensely for his opinions, and would have liked events to speak for them in a sort of picture-writing that everybody could understand. The enthusiasms of the world are not to be stimulated by a commentary in small and subtle characters which alone can tell the whole truth; and the picture-writing in Felix Holt's troubles was of an entirely puzzling kind: if he were a martyr, neither side wanted to claim him. Yet the minister, as we have seen, found in his Christian faith a reason for clinging the more to one who had not a large party to back him. That little man's heart was heroic; he was not one of those Liberals who make their anxiety for "the cause" of Liberalism a plea for cowardly desertion.

Besides himself, he believed there was no one who could bear testimony to the remonstrances of Felix concerning the treating of the Sproxton men, except Jermyn, Johnson, and Harold Transome. Though he had the vaguest idea of what could be done in the case, he fixed his mind on the probability that Mr. Transome would be moved to the utmost exertion, if only as an atonement; but he dared not take any step until he had consulted Felix, who he foresaw was likely to have a very strong determination as to the help he would accept or not accept.

This last expectation was fulfilled. Mr. Lyon returned to Esther, after his day's journey to Loamford and back, with less of trouble and perplexity in his mind: he had at least got a definite course marked out, to which he must resign himself. Felix had declared that he would receive no aid from Harold

23

Transome, except the aid he might give as an honest witness. There was nothing to be done for him but what was perfectly simple and direct. Even if the pleading of counsel had been permitted (and at that time it was not) on behalf of a prisoner on trial for felony, Felix would have declined it: he would in any case have spoken in his own defence. He had a perfectly simple account to give, and needed not to avail himself of any legal adroitness. He consented to accept the services of a respectable solicitor in Loamford, who offered to conduct his case without any fees. The work was plain and easy, Felix said. The only witnesses who had to be hunted up at all were some who could testify that he had tried to take the crowd down Hobb's Lane, and that they had gone to the Manor in spite of him.

"Then he is not so much cast down as you feared, father?" said Esther.

"No, child; albeit he is pale and much shaken for one so stalwart. He hath no grief, he says, save for the poor man Tucker, and for his mother; otherwise his heart is without a burthen. We discoursed greatly on the sad effect of all this for his mother, and on the perplexed condition of human things, whereby even right action seems to bring evil consequences, if we have respect only to our own brief lives, and not to that larger rule whereby we are stewards of the eternal dealings, and not contrivers of our own success."

"Did he say nothing about me, father?" said Esther, trembling a little, but unable to repress her egoism.

"Yea; he asked if you were well, and sent his affectionate regards. Nay, he bade me say something which appears to refer to your discourse together when I was not present. 'Tell her,' he said, 'whatever they sentence me to, she knows they can't rob me of my vocation. With poverty for my bride, and preaching and pedagogy for my business, I am sure of a handsome establishment.' He laughed—doubtless bearing in mind some playfulness of thine."

Mr. Lyon seemed to be looking at Esther as he smiled, but she was not near enough for him to discern the expression of her face. Just then it seemed made for melancholy rather than for playfulness. Hers was not a childish beauty; and when the sparkle of mischief, wit, and vanity was out of her eyes, and the large look of abstracted sorrow was there, you would have been surprised by a certain grandeur which the smiles had hidden. That changing face was the perfect symbol of her mixed susceptible nature, in which battle was inevitable, and the side of victory uncertain.

She began to look on all that had passed between herself and Felix as something not buried, but embalmed and kept as a relic in a private sanctuary. The very entireness of her preoccupation about him, the perpetual repetition in her memory of all that had passed between them, tended to produce this effect. She lived with him in the past; in the future she seemed shut out from him. He was an influence above her life, rather than a part of it; some time or other, perhaps, he would be to her as if he belonged to the solemn admonishing skies, checking her self-satisfied pettiness with the suggestion of a wider life.

But not yet—not while her trouble was so fresh. For it was still *her* trouble, and not Felix Holt's. Perhaps it was a subtraction from his power over her that she could never think of him with pity, because he always seemed to her too great and strong to be pitied: he wanted nothing. He evaded calamity by choosing privation. The best part of a woman's love is worship; but it is hard to her to be sent away with her precious spikenard rejected, and her long tresses too, that were let fall ready to soothe the wearied feet.

While Esther was carrying these things in her heart, the January days were beginning to pass by with their wonted wintry monotony, except that there was rather more of good cheer than usual remaining from the feast of Twelfth Night among the triumphant Tories, and rather more scandal than usual excited among the mortified Dissenters by the wilfulness of their minister. He had actually mentioned Felix Holt by name in his evening sermon, and offered up a petition for him in the evening prayer, also by name—not as "a young Ishmaelite, whom we would fain see brought back from the lawless life of the desert, and seated in the same fold even with the sons of Judah and of Benjamin," a suitable periphrasis which Brother Kemp threw off without any effort,

and with all the felicity of a suggestive critic. Poor Mrs.
Holt, indeed, even in the midst of her grief, experienced a
proud satisfaction that, though not a church-member, she was
now an object of congregational remark and ministerial allusion.
Feeling herself a spotless character standing out in relief on a
dark background of affliction, and a practical contradiction to
that extreme doctrine of human depravity which she had
never "given in to," she was naturally gratified and soothed
by a notice which must be a recognition. But more influen-
tial hearers were of opinion that in a man who had so many
long sentences at command as Mr. Lyon, so many parentheses
and modifying clauses, this naked use of a non-scriptural Treby
name in an address to the Almighty was all the more offensive.
In a low unlettered local preacher of the Wesleyan persuasion such things might pass; but a certain style in prayer
was demanded from Independents, the most educated body in
the ranks of orthodox Dissent. To Mr. Lyon such notions
seemed painfully perverse, and the next morning he was declaring to Esther his resolution stoutly to withstand them, and
to count nothing common or unclean on which a blessing could
be asked, when the tenor of his thoughts was completely
changed by a great shock of surprise which made both himself and Esther sit looking at each other in speechless amaze-
ment.

The cause was a letter brought by a special messenger from
Duffield; a heavy letter addressed to Esther in a business-like
manner, quite unexampled in her correspondence. And the
contents of the letter were more startling than its exterior.
It began :—

MADAM,—Herewith we send you a brief abstract of evidence which
has come within our knowledge, that the right of remainder whereby
the lineal issue of Edward Bycliffe can claim possession of the estates
of which the entail was settled by John Justus Transome in 1729, now
first accrues to you as the sole and lawful issue of Maurice Christian
Bycliffe. We are confident of success in the prosecution of this claim,
which will result to you in the possession of estates to the value, at the
lowest, of from five to six thousand per annum——

It was at this point that Esther, who was reading aloud, let
her hand fall with the letter on her lap, and with a palpitat-

ing heart looked at her father, who looked again, in silence that lasted for two or three minutes. A certain terror was upon them both, though the thoughts that laid that weight on the tongue of each were different.

It was Mr. Lyon who spoke first.

"This, then, is what the man named Christian referred to. I distrusted him, yet it seems he spoke truly."

"But," said Esther, whose imagination ran necessarily to those conditions of wealth which she could best appreciate, "do they mean that the Transomes would be turned out of Transome Court, and that I should go and live there? It seems quite an impossible thing."

"Nay, child, I know not. I am ignorant in these things, and the thought of worldly grandeur for you hath more of terror than of gladness for me. Nevertheless we must duly weigh all things, not considering aught that befalls us as a bare event, but rather as an occasion for faithful stewardship. Let us go to my study and consider this writing further."

How this announcement, which to Esther seemed as unprepared as if it had fallen from the skies, came to be made to her by solicitors other than Batt & Cowley, the old lawyers of the Bycliffes, was by a sequence as natural, that is to say, as legally natural, as any in the world. The secret worker of the apparent wonder was Mr. Johnson, who, on the very day when he wrote to give his patron, Mr. Jermyn, the serious warning that a bill was likely to be filed in Chancery against him, had carried forward with added zeal the business already commenced, of arranging with another firm his share in the profits likely to result from the prosecution of Esther Bycliffe's claim.

Jermyn's star was certainly going down, and Johnson did not feel an unmitigated grief. Beyond some troublesome declarations as to his actual share in transactions in which his name had been used, Johnson saw nothing formidable in prospect for himself. He was not going to be ruined, though Jermyn probably was: he was not a high-flyer, but a mere climbing-bird, who could hold on and get his livelihood just as well if his wings were clipped a little. And, in the mean time, here was something to be gained in this Bycliffe business, which, it was not unpleasant to think, was a nut that Jermyn had intended to keep for his own particular cracking, and which would be rather a severe astonishment to Mr. Harold Transome, whose manners toward respectable agents were such as leave a smart in a man of spirit.

Under the stimulus of small many-mixed motives like these, a great deal of business has been done in the world by well-clad and, in 1833, clean-shaven men, whose names are on charity lists, and who do not know that they are base. Mr. Johnson's character was not much more exceptional than his double chin.

No system, religious or political, I believe, has laid it down as a principle that all men are alike virtuous, or even that all the people rated for £80 houses are an honor to their species.

CHAPTER XXXVIII.

The down we rest on in our aëry dreams
Has not been plucked from birds that live and smart:
'Tis but warm snow, that melts not.

THE story and the prospect revealed to Esther by the lawyer's letter, which she and her father studied together, had made an impression on her very different from what she had been used to figure to herself in her many day-dreams as to the effect of a sudden elevation in rank and fortune. In her day-dreams she had not traced out the means by which such a change could be brought about; in fact, the change had seemed impossible to her, except in her little private Utopia, which, like other Utopias, was filled with delightful results, independent of processes. But her mind had fixed itself habitually on the signs and luxuries of ladyhood, for which she had the keenest perception. She had seen the very mat in her carriage, had scented the dried rose-leaves in her corridors, had felt the soft carpets under her pretty feet, and seen herself, as she rose from her sofa cushions, in the crystal panel that reflected a long drawing-room, where the conservatory flowers and the pictures of fair women left her still with the supremacy of charm. She had trodden the marble-firm gravel of her garden-walks and the soft deep turf of her lawn; she had had her servants about her filled with adoring respect because of her kindness as well as her grace and beauty; and she had had several accomplished cavaliers all at once suing for her hand—one of whom, uniting very high birth with long dark eyelashes and the most distinguished talents, she secretly preferred, though his pride and hers hindered an avowal, and supplied the inestimable interest of retardation. The glimpses she had had in her brief life as a family governess supplied her ready faculty with details enough of delightful still life to furnish her day-dreams; and no one who has not, like Esther, a strong natural prompting and susceptibility toward such things, and has at the same time suffered from the presence of opposite conditions, can understand how powerfully those minor accidents of rank which please the fastidious sense can preoccupy the imagination.

It seemed that almost everything in her day-dreams—cavaliers apart—must be found at Transome Court. But now that fancy was becoming real, and the impossible appeared possible, Esther found the balance of her attention reversed: now that her ladyhood was not simply in Utopia, she found herself arrested and painfully grasped by the means through which the ladyhood was to be obtained. To her inexperience this strange story of an alienated inheritance, of such a last representative of pure-blooded lineage as old Thomas Transome the bill-sticker, above all of the dispossession hanging over those who actually held, and had expected always to hold, the wealth and position which were suddenly announced to be rightly hers—all these things made a picture, not for her own tastes and fancies to float in with Elysian indulgence, but in which she was compelled to gaze on the degrading hard experience of other human beings, and on a humiliating loss which was the obverse of her own proud gain. Even in her times of most untroubled egoism Esther shrank from anything ungenerous; and the fact that she had a very lively image of Harold Transome and his gypsy-eyed boy in her mind gave additional distinctness to the thought that if she entered they must depart. Of the elder Transomes she had a dimmer vi-

sion, and they were necessarily in the background to her sympathy.

She and her father sat with their hands locked, as they
might have done if they had been listening to a solemn oracle
in the days of old, revealing unknown kinship and rightful
heirdom.   It was not that Esther had any thought of renouncing her fortune; she was incapable, in these moments, of con-
densing her vague ideas and feelings into any distinct plan of
action, nor indeed did it seem that she was called upon to act
with any promptitude.   It was only that she was conscious of
being strangely awed by something that was called good fortune; and the awe shut out any scheme of rejection as much
as any triumphant joy in acceptance.   Her first father, she
learned, had died disappointed and in wrongful imprisonment,
and an undefined sense of Nemesis seemed half to sanctify her
inheritance and counteract its apparent arbitrariness.

Felix Holt was present in her mind throughout: what he
would say was an imaginary commentary that she was constantly framing, and the words that she most frequently gave
him—for she dramatized under the inspiration of a sadness
slightly bitter—were of this kind: "That is clearly your destiny—to be aristocratic, to be rich. I always saw that our
lots lay widely apart. You are not fit for poverty, or any
work of difficulty. But remember what I once said to you
about a vision of consequences; take care where your fortune
leads you."

Her father had not spoken since they had ended their study
and discussion of the story and the evidence as it was presented to them.   Into this he had entered with his usual penetrating activity; but he was so accustomed to the impersonal
study of narrative that even in these exceptional moments
the habit of half a century asserted itself, and he seemed
sometimes not to distinguish the case of Esther's inheritance
from a story in ancient history, until some detail recalled him
to the profound feeling that a great, great change might be
coming over the life of this child who was so close to him.
At last he relapsed into total silence, and for some time Esther was not moved to interrupt it.   He had sunk back in his
chair, with his hand locked in hers, and was pursuing a sort

of prayerful meditation: he lifted up no formal petition, but it was as if his soul travelled again over the facts he had been considering in the company of a guide ready to inspire and correct him. He was striving to purify his feeling in this matter from selfish or worldly dross—a striving which is that prayer without ceasing, sure to wrest an answer by its sublime importunity.

There is no knowing how long they might have sat in this way, if it had not been for the inevitable Lyddy reminding them dismally of dinner.

"Yes, Lyddy, we come," said Esther; and then, before moving,—

"Is there any advice you have in your mind for me, father?" The sense of awe was growing in Esther. Her intensest life was no longer in her dreams, where she made things to her own mind: she was moving in a world charged with forces.

"Not yet, my dear—save this: that you will seek special illumination in this juncture, and, above all, be watchful that your soul be not lifted up within you by what, rightly considered, is rather an increase of charge, and a call upon you to walk along a path which is indeed easy to the flesh, but dangerous to the spirit."

"You would always live with me, father?" Esther spoke under a strong impulse—partly affection, partly the need to grasp at some moral help. But she had no sooner uttered the words than they raised a vision, showing, as by a flash of lightning, the incongruity of that past which had created the sanctities and affections of her life with that future which was coming to her. . . . The little rusty old minister, with the one luxury of his Sunday-evening pipe, smoked up the kitchen chimney, coming to live in the midst of grandeur . . . but no! her father, with the grandeur of his past sorrow and his long struggling labors, forsaking his vocation, and vulgarly accepting an existence unsuited to him. . . . Esther's face flushed with the excitement of this vision and its reversed interpretation, which five months ago she would have been incapable of seeing. Her question to her father seemed like a mockery; she was ashamed. He answered slowly,—

"Touch not that chord yet, child. I must learn to think of

thy lot according to the demands of Providence. We will rest
a while from the subject; and I will seek calmness in my
ordinary duties."

The next morning nothing more was said. Mr. Lyon was
absorbed in his sermon-making, for it was near the end of the
week, and Esther was obliged to attend to her pupils. Mrs.
Holt came by invitation with little Job to share their dinner
of roast meat; and, after much of what the minister called
unprofitable discourse, she was quitting the house when she
hastened back with an astonished face, to tell Mr. Lyon and
Esther, who were already in wonder at crashing, thundering
sounds on the pavement, that there was a carriage stopping
and stamping at the entry into Malthouse Yard, with "all
sorts of fine liveries," and a lady and gentleman inside. Mr.
Lyon and Esther looked at each other, both having the same
name in their minds.

"If it's Mr. Transome or somebody else as is great, Mr.
Lyon," urged Mrs. Holt, "you'll remember my son, and say
he's got a mother with a character they may inquire into as
much as they like. And never mind what Felix says, for
he's so masterful he'd stay in prison and be transported
whether or no, only to have his own way. For it's not to
be thought but what the great people could get him off if
they would; and it's very hard with a King in the country
and all the texts in Proverbs about the King's countenance,
and Solomon and the live baby——"

Mr. Lyon lifted up his hand deprecatingly, and Mrs. Holt
retreated from the parlor door to a corner of the kitchen, the
outer door-way being occupied by Dominic, who was inquiring
if Mr. and Miss Lyon were at home, and could receive Mrs.
Transome and Mr. Harold Transome. While Dominic went
back to the carriage, Mrs. Holt escaped with her tiny companion to Zachary's, the pew-opener, observing to Lyddy that
she knew herself, and was not that woman to stay where she
might not be wanted; whereupon Lyddy, differing funda-
mentally, admonished her parting ear that it was well if she
knew herself to be dust and ashes—silently extending the
application of this remark to Mrs. Transome as she saw the
tall lady sweep in, arrayed in her rich black and fur, with that

fine gentleman behind her whose thick topknot of wavy hair, sparkling ring, dark complexion, and general air of worldly exaltation unconnected with chapel were painfully suggestive to Lyddy of Herod, Pontius Pilate, or the much-quoted Gallio.

Harold Transome, greeting Esther gracefully, presented his mother, whose eagle-like glance, fixed on her from the first moment of entering, seemed to Esther to pierce her through. Mrs. Transome hardly noticed Mr. Lyon, not from studied haughtiness, but from sheer mental inability to consider him —as a person ignorant of natural history is unable to consider a fresh-water polyp otherwise than as a sort of animated weed, certainly not fit for table. But Harold saw that his mother was agreeably struck by Esther, who indeed showed to much advantage. She was not at all taken by surprise, and maintained a dignified quietude; but her previous knowledge and reflection about the possible dispossession of these Transomes gave her a softened feeling toward them which tinged her manners very agreeably.

Harold was carefully polite to the minister, throwing out a word to make him understand that he had an important part in the important business which had brought this unannounced visit; and the four made a group seated not far off each other near the window, Mrs. Transome and Esther being on the sofa.

"You must be astonished at a visit from me, Miss Lyon," Mrs. Transome began; "I seldom come to Treby Magna. Now I see you, the visit is an unexpected pleasure; but the cause of my coming is business of a serious nature, which my son will communicate to you."

"I ought to begin by saying that what I have to announce to you is the reverse of disagreeable, Miss Lyon," said Harold, with lively ease. "I don't suppose the world would consider it very good news for me; but a rejected candidate, Mr. Lyon," Harold went on, turning graciously to the minister, "begins to be inured to loss and misfortune."

"Truly, sir," said Mr. Lyon, with a rather sad solemnity, "your allusion hath a grievous bearing for me, but I will not retard your present purpose by further remark."

"You will never guess what I have to disclose," said Harold, again looking at Esther, "unless, indeed, you have had some previous intimation of it."

"Does it refer to law and inheritance?" said Esther, with a smile. She was already brightened by Harold's manner. The news seemed to be losing its chillness, and to be something really belonging to warm, comfortable, interesting life.

"Then you have already heard of it?" said Harold, inwardly vexed, but sufficiently prepared not to seem so.

"Only yesterday," said Esther, quite simply. "I received a letter from some lawyers with a statement of many surprising things, showing that I was an heiress"—here she turned very prettily to address Mrs. Transome—"which, as you may imagine, is one of the last things I could have supposed myself to be."

"My dear," said Mrs. Transome with elderly grace, just laying her hand for an instant on Esther's, "it is a lot that would become you admirably."

Esther blushed, and said playfully,—

"Oh, I know what to buy with fifty pounds a year, but I know the price of nothing beyond that."

Her father sat looking at her through his spectacles, stroking his chin. It was amazing to herself that she was taking so lightly now what had caused her such deep emotion yesterday.

"I dare say, then," said Harold, "you are more fully possessed of particulars than I am. So that my mother and I need only tell you what no one else can tell you—that is, what are her and my feelings and wishes under these new and unexpected circumstances."

"I am most anxious," said Esther, with a grave beautiful look of respect to Mrs. Transome—"most anxious on that point. Indeed, being of course in uncertainty about it, I have not yet known whether I could rejoice." Mrs. Transome's glance had softened. She liked Esther to look at her.

"Our chief anxiety," she said, knowing what Harold wished her to say, "is, that there may be no contest, no useless expenditure of money. Of course we will surrender what can be rightfully claimed."

"My mother expresses our feeling precisely, Miss Lyon,"

said Harold. "And I'm sure, Mr. Lyon, you will understand our desire."

"Assuredly, sir. My daughter would in any case have had my advice to seek a conclusion which would involve no strife. We endeavor, sir, in our body, to hold to the apostolic rule that one Christian brother should not go to law with another; and I, for my part, would extend this rule to all my fellow-men, apprehending that the practice of our courts is little consistent with the simplicity that is in Christ."

"If it is to depend on my will," said Esther, "there is nothing that would be more repugnant to me than any struggle on such a subject. But can't the lawyers go on doing what they will in spite of me? It seems that this is what they mean."

"Not exactly," said Harold, smiling. "Of course they live by such struggles as you dislike. But we can thwart them by determining not to quarrel. It is desirable that we should consider the affair together, and put it into the hands of honorable solicitors. I assure you we Transomes will not contend for what is not our own."

"And this is what I have come to beg of you," said Mrs. Transome. "It is that you will come to Transome Court—and let us take full time to arrange matters. Do oblige me: you shall not be teased more than you like by an old woman: you shall do just as you please, and become acquainted with your future home, since it is to be yours. I can tell you a world of things that you will want to know; and the business can proceed properly."

"Do consent," said Harold, with winning brevity.

Esther was flushed, and her eyes were bright. It was impossible for her not to feel that the proposal was a more tempting step toward her change of condition than she could have thought of beforehand. She had forgotten that she was in any trouble. But she looked toward her father, who was again stroking his chin, as was his habit when he was doubting and deliberating.

"I hope you do not disapprove of Miss Lyon's granting us this favor?" said Harold to the minister.

"I have nothing to oppose to it, sir, if my daughter's own mind is clear as to her course."

"You will come—now—with us," said Mrs. Transome, persuasively. "You will go back with us in the carriage."

Harold was highly gratified with the perfection of his mother's manner on this occasion, which he had looked forward to as difficult. Since he had come home again he had never seen her so much at her ease, or with so much benignancy in her face. The secret lay in the charm of Esther's sweet young deference, a sort of charm that had not before entered into Mrs. Transome's elderly life. Esther's pretty behavior, it must be confessed, was not fed entirely from lofty moral sources: over and above her really generous feeling, she enjoyed Mrs. Transome's accent, the high-bred quietness of her speech, the delicate odor of her drapery. She had always thought that life must be particularly easy if one could pass it among refined people; and so it seemed at this moment. She wished, unmixedly, to go to Transome Court.

"Since my father has no objection," she said, "and you urge me so kindly. But I must beg for time to pack up a few clothes."

"By all means," said Mrs. Transome. "We are not at all pressed."

When Esther had left the room, Harold said, "Apart from our immediate reason for coming, Mr. Lyon, I could have wished to see you about these unhappy consequences of the election contest. But you will understand that I have been much preoccupied with private affairs."

"You have well said that the consequences are unhappy, sir. And but for a reliance on something more than human calculation, I know not which I should most bewail—the scandal which wrong-dealing has brought on right principles, or the snares which it laid for the feet of a young man who is dear to me. 'One soweth, and another reapeth,' is a verity that applies to evil as well as good."

"You are referring to Felix Holt. I have not neglected steps to secure the best legal help for the prisoners; but I am given to understand that Holt refuses any aid from me. I hope he will not go rashly to work in speaking in his own defence without any legal instruction. It is an opprobrium of our law that no counsel is allowed to plead for the prisoner in cases of felony. A ready tongue may do a man as much harm as good in a court of justice. He piques himself on making a display, and displays a little too much."

"Sir, you know him not," said the little minister, in his deeper tone. "He would not accept, even if it were accorded, a defence wherein the truth was screened or avoided,—not from a vainglorious spirit of self-exhibition, for he hath a singular directness and simplicity of speech; but from an averseness to a profession wherein a man may without shame seek to justify the wicked for reward, and take away the righteousness of the righteous from him."

"It's a pity a fine young fellow should do himself harm by fanatical notions of that sort. I could at least have procured the advantage of first-rate consultation. He didn't look to me like a dreamy personage."

"Nor is he dreamy; rather, his excess lies in being too practical."

"Well, I hope you will not encourage him in such irrationality: the question is not one of misrepresentation, but of adjusting fact, so as to raise it to the power of evidence. Don't you see that?"

"I do, I do. But I distrust not Felix Holt's discernment in regard to his own case. He builds not on doubtful things, and hath no illusory hopes; on the contrary, he is of a too-scornful incredulity where I would fain see a more childish faith. But he will hold no belief without action corresponding thereto; and the occasion of his return to this his native place at a time which has proved fatal was no other than his resolve to hinder the sale of some drugs, which had chiefly supported his mother, but which his better knowledge showed him to be pernicious to the human frame. He undertook to support her by his own labor: but, sir, I pray you to mark —and, old as I am, I will not deny that this young man instructs me herein—I pray you to mark the poisonous confusion of good and evil which is the widespreading effect of vicious practices. Through the use of undue electioneering means— concerning which, however, I do not accuse you farther than of having acted the part of him who washes his hands when he delivers up to others the exercise of an iniquitous power—

Felix Holt is, I will not scruple to say, the innocent victim of a riot; and that deed of strict honesty, whereby he took on himself the charge of his aged mother, seems now to have deprived her of sufficient bread, and is even an occasion of reproach to him from the weaker brethren."

"I shall be proud to supply her as amply as you think desirable," said Harold, not enjoying this lecture.

"I will pray you to speak of this question with my daughter, who, it appears, may herself have large means at command, and would desire to minister to Mrs. Holt's needs with all friendship and delicacy. For the present, I can take care that she lacks nothing essential."

As Mr. Lyon was speaking, Esther re-entered, equipped for her drive. She laid her hand on her father's arm, and said, "You will let my pupils know at once, will you, father?"

"Doubtless, my dear," said the old man, trembling a little under the feeling that this departure of Esther's was a crisis. Nothing again would be as it had been in their mutual life. But he feared that he was being mastered by a too-tender self-regard, and struggled to keep himself calm.

Mrs. Transome and Harold had both risen.

"If you are quite ready, Miss Lyon," said Harold, divining that the father and daughter would like to have an unobserved moment, "I will take my mother to the carriage, and come back for you."

When they were alone, Esther put her hands on her father's shoulders and kissed him.

"This will not be a grief to you, I hope, father? You think it is better that I should go?"

"Nay, child, I am weak. But I would fain be capable of a joy quite apart from the accidents of my aged earthly existence, which, indeed, is a petty and almost dried-up fountain, —whereas to the receptive soul the river of life pauseth not, nor is diminished."

"Perhaps you will see Felix Holt again and tell him everything?"

"Shall I say aught to him for you?"

"Oh, no; only that Job Tudge has a little flannel shirt and a box of lozenges," said Esther, smiling. "Ah, I hear Mr.

Transome coming back. I must say good-by to Lyddy, else she will cry over my hard heart."

In spite of all the grave thoughts that had been, Esther felt it a very pleasant as well as new experience to be led to the carriage by Harold Transome, to be seated on soft cushions, and bowled along, looked at admiringly and deferentially by a person opposite whom it was agreeable to look at in return, and talked to with suavity and liveliness. Toward what prospect was that easy carriage really leading her? She could not be always asking herself Mentor-like questions. Her young bright nature was rather weary of the sadness that had grown heavier in these last weeks, like a chill white mist hopelessly veiling the day. Her fortune was beginning to appear worthy of being called good fortune. She had come to a new stage in her journey; a new day had arisen on new scenes, and her young untried spirit was full of curiosity.

CHAPTER XXXIX.

No man believes that many-textured knowledge and skill—as a just idea of the solar system, or the power of painting flesh, or of reading written harmonies—can come late and of a sudden; yet many will not stick at believing that happiness can come at any day and hour solely by a new disposition of events; though there is nought least capable of a magical production than a mortal's happiness, which is mainly a complex of habitual relations and dispositions not to be wrought by news from foreign parts, or any whirling of fortune's wheel for one on whose brow Time has written legibly.

Some days after Esther's arrival at Transome Court, Denner, coming to dress Mrs. Transome before dinner—a labor of love for which she had ample leisure now—found her mistress seated with more than ever of that marble aspect of self-absorbed suffering which to the waiting-woman's keen observation had been gradually intensifying itself during the past week. She had tapped at the door without having been summoned, and she had ventured to enter, though she had heard no voice saying "Come in."

Mrs. Transome had on a dark warm dressing-gown, hanging in thick folds about her, and she was seated before a mirror, which filled a panel from the floor to the ceiling. The

24

room was bright with the light of the fire and of wax candles. For some reason, contrary to her usual practice, Mrs. Transome had herself unfastened her abundant gray hair, which rolled backward in a pale sunless stream over her dark dress. She was seated before the mirror apparently looking at herself, her brow knit in one deep furrow, and her jewelled hands laid one above the other on her knee. Probably she had ceased to see the reflection in the mirror, for her eyes had the fixed wide-open look that belongs not to examination, but to revery. Motionless in that way, her clear-cut features keeping distinct record of past beauty, she looked like an image faded, dried, and bleached by uncounted suns, rather than a breathing woman who had numbered the years as they passed, and had a consciousness within her which was the slow deposit of those ceaseless rolling years.

Denner, with all her ingrained and systematic reserve, could not help showing signs that she was startled when, peering from between her half-closed eyelids, she saw the motionless image in the mirror opposite to her as she entered. Her gentle opening of the door had not roused her mistress, to whom the sensations produced by Denner's presence were as little disturbing as those of a favorite cat. But the slight cry, and the start reflected in the glass, were unusual enough to break the revery: Mrs. Transome moved, leaned back in her chair, and said,—

"So you're come at last, Denner?"

"Yes, madam; it is not late. I'm sorry you should have undone your hair yourself."

"I undid it to see what an old hag I am. These fine clothes you put on me, Denner, are only a smart shroud."

"Pray don't talk so, madam. If there's anybody doesn't think it pleasant to look at you, so much the worse for them. For my part, I've seen no young ones fit to hold up your train. Look at your likeness down below; and though you're older now, what signifies? I wouldn't be Letty in the scullery because she's got red cheeks. She mayn't know she's a poor creature, but I know it, and that's enough for me: I know what sort of a dowdy draggletail she'll be in ten years' time. I would change with nobody, madam. And if troubles were put up to market, I'd sooner buy old than new. It's something to have seen the worst."

"A woman never has seen the worst till she is old, Denner," said Mrs. Transome, bitterly.

The keen little waiting-woman was not clear as to the cause of her mistress's added bitterness; but she rarely brought herself to ask questions when Mrs. Transome did not authorize them by beginning to give her information. Banks the bailiff and the head servant had nodded and winked a good deal over the certainty that Mr. Harold was "none so fond" of Jermyn, but this was a subject on which Mrs. Transome had never made up her mind to speak, and Denner knew nothing definite. Again, she felt quite sure that there was some important secret connected with Esther's presence in the house; she suspected that the close Dominic knew the secret, and was more trusted than she was, in spite of her forty years' service; but any resentment on this ground would have been an entertained reproach against her mistress, inconsistent with Denner's creed and character. She inclined to the belief that Esther was the immediate cause of the new discontent.

"If there's anything worse coming to you, I should like to know what it is, madam," she said, after a moment's silence, speaking always in the same low quick way, and keeping up her quiet labors. "When I awake at cock-crow, I'd sooner have one real grief on my mind than twenty false. It's better to know one's robbed than to think one's going to be murdered."

"I believe you are the creature in the world that loves me best, Denner; yet you will never understand what I suffer. It's of no use telling you. There's no folly in you, and no heartache. You are made of iron. You have never had any trouble."

"I've had some of your trouble, madam."

"Yes, you good thing. But as a sick-nurse, that never caught the fever. You never even had a child."

"I can feel for things I never went through. I used to be sorry for the poor French Queen when I was young: I'd have lain cold for her to lie warm. I know people have feelings according to their birth and station. And you always took things to heart, madam, beyond anybody else. But I hope there's nothing new, to make you talk of the worst."

"Yes, Denner, there is—there is," said Mrs. Transome, speaking in a low tone of misery, while she bent for her head-dress to be pinned on.

"Is it this young lady?"

"Why, what do you think about her, Denner?" said Mrs. Transome, in a tone of more spirit, rather curious to hear what the old woman would say.

"I don't deny she's graceful, and she has a pretty smile and very good manners: it's quite unaccountable by what Banks says about her father. I know nothing of those Treby townsfolk myself, but for my part I'm puzzled. I'm fond of Mr. Harold. I always shall be, madam. I was at his bringing into the world, and nothing but his doing wrong by you would turn me against him. But the servants all say he's in love with Miss Lyon."

"I wish it were true, Denner," said Mrs. Transome, ener-getically. "I wish he were in love with her, so that she could master him, and make him do what she pleased."

"Then it is not true—what they say?"

"Not true that she will ever master him. No woman ever will. He will make her fond of him, and afraid of him. That's one of the things you have never gone through, Den-ner. A woman's love is always freezing into fear. She wants everything, she is secure of nothing. This girl has a fine spirit—plenty of fire and pride and wit. Men like such captives, as they like horses that champ the bit and paw the ground: they feel more triumph in their mastery. What is the use of a woman's will?—if she tries, she doesn't get it, and she ceases to be loved. God was cruel when He made women."

Denner was used to such outbursts as this. Her mistress's rhetoric and temper belonged to her superior rank, her grand person, and her piercing black eyes. Mrs. Transome had a sense of impiety in her words which made them all the more tempting to her impotent anger. The waiting-woman had none of that awe which could be turned into defiance: the Sacred Grove was a common thicket to her.

"It mayn't be good luck to be a woman," she said. "But one begins with it from a baby: one gets used to it. And I shouldn't like to be a man—to cough so loud, and stand straddling about on a wet day, and be so wasteful with meat and drink. They're a coarse lot, I think. Then I needn't make a trouble of this young lady, madam," she added, after a moment's pause.

"No, Denner. I like her. If that were all—I should like Harold to marry her. It would be the best thing. If the truth were known—and it will be known soon—the estate is hers by law—such law as it is. It's a strange story: she's a Bycliffe really."

Denner did not look amazed, but went on fastening her mistress's dress, as she said,—

"Well, madam, I was sure there was something wonderful at the bottom of it. And turning the old lawsuits and everything else over in my mind, I thought the law might have something to do with it. Then she is a born lady?"

"Yes; she has good blood in her veins."

"We talked that over in the housekeeper's room—what a hand and an instep she has, and how her head is set on her shoulders—almost like your own, madam. But her lightish complexion spoils her, to my thinking. And Dominic said Mr. Harold never admired that sort of woman before. There's nothing that smooth fellow couldn't tell you if he would: he knows the answers to riddles before they're made. However, he knows how to hold his tongue; I'll say that for him. And so do I, madam."

"Yes, yes; you will not talk of it till other people are talking of it."

"And so, if Mr. Harold married her, it would save all fuss and mischief?"

"Yes—about the estate."

"And he seems inclined; and she'll not refuse him, I'll answer for it. And you like her, madam. There's everything to set your mind at rest."

Denner was putting the finishing touch to Mrs. Transome's dress by throwing an Indian scarf over her shoulders, and so completing the contrast between the majestic lady in costume and the dishevelled Hecuba-like woman whom she had found half an hour before.

"I am not at rest!" Mrs. Transome said, with slow distinctness, moving from the mirror to the window, where the blind was not drawn down, and she could see the chill white landscape and the far-off unheeding stars.

Denner, more distressed by her mistress's suffering than she could have been by anything else, took up with the instinct of affection a gold vinaigrette which Mrs. Transome often liked to carry with her, and, going up to her, put it into her hand gently. Mrs. Transome grasped the little woman's hand hard, and held it so.

"Denner," she said, in a low tone, "if I could choose at this moment, I would choose that Harold should never have been born."

"Nay, my dear" (Denner had only once before in her life said "my dear" to her mistress), "it was a happiness to you then."

"I don't believe I felt the happiness then as I feel the misery now. It is foolish to say people can't feel much when they are getting old. Not pleasure, perhaps—little comes. But they can feel they are forsaken—why, every fibre in me seems to be a memory that makes a pang. They can feel that all the love in their lives is turned to hatred or contempt."

"Not mine, madam, not mine. Let what would be, I should want to live for your sake, for fear you should have nobody to do for you as I would."

"Ah, then, you are a happy woman, Denner; you have loved somebody for forty years who is old and weak now, and can't do without you."

The sound of the dinner-gong resounded below, and Mrs. Transome let the faithful hand fall again.

CHAPTER XL.

"She's beautiful; and therefore to be wooed:
She is a woman; therefore to be won."

Henry VI.

IF Denner had had a suspicion that Esther's presence at
Transome Court was not agreeable to her mistress, it was
impossible to entertain such a suspicion with regard to the
other members of the family. Between her and little Harry
there was an extraordinary fascination. This creature, with
the soft broad brown cheeks, low forehead, great black eyes,
tiny well-defined nose, fierce biting tricks toward every person
and thing he disliked, and insistence on entirely occupying
those he liked, was a human specimen such as Esther had
never seen before, and she seemed to be equally original in
Harry's experience. At first sight her light complexion and
her blue gown, probably also her sunny smile and her hands
stretched out toward him, seemed to make a show for him as
of a new sort of bird: he threw himself backward against his
"Gappa," as he called old Mr. Transome, and stared at this
newcomer with the gravity of a wild animal. But she had
no sooner sat down on the sofa in the library than he climbed
up to her, and began to treat her as an attractive object in
natural history, snatched up her curls with his brown fist,
and, discovering that there was a little ear under them,
pinched it and blew into it, pulled at her coronet of plaits,
and seemed to discover with satisfaction that it did not grow
at the summit of her head, but could be dragged down and
altogether undone. Then, finding that she laughed, tossed
him back, kissed, and pretended to bite him—in fact, was an
animal that understood fun—he rushed off and made Dominic
bring a small menagerie of white mice, squirrels, and birds,
with Moro, the black spaniel, to make her acquaintance.
Whomsoever Harry liked, it followed that Mr. Transome
must like: "Gappa," along with Nimrod the retriever, was
part of the menagerie, and perhaps endured more than all the
other live creatures in the way of being tumbled about. See-

ing that Esther bore having her hair pulled down quite merrily, and that she was willing to be harnessed and beaten, the old man began to confide to her, in his feeble, smiling, and rather jerking fashion, Harry's remarkable feats: how he had one day, when Gappa was asleep, unpinned a whole drawerful of beetles, to see if they would fly away; then, disgusted with their stupidity, was about to throw them all on the ground and stamp on them, when Dominic came in and rescued these valuable specimens; also, how he had subtly watched Mrs. Transome at the cabinet where she kept her medicines, and, when she had left it for a little while without locking it, had gone to the drawers and scattered half the contents on the floor. But what old Mr. Transome thought the most wonderful proof of an almost preternatural cleverness was, that Harry would hardly ever talk, but preferred making inarticulate noises, or combining syllables after a method of his own.

"He can talk well enough if he likes," said Gappa, evidently thinking that Harry, like the monkeys, had deep reasons for his reticence.

"You mind him," he added, nodding at Esther, and shaking with low-toned laughter. "You'll hear: he knows the right names of things well enough, but he likes to make his own. He'll give you one all to yourself before long."

And when Harry seemed to have made up his mind distinctly that Esther's name was "Boo," Mr. Transome nodded at her with triumphant satisfaction, and then told her in a low whisper, looking round cautiously beforehand, that Harry would never call Mrs. Transome "Gamma," but always "Bite."

"It's wonderful!" said he, laughing slyly.

The old man seemed so happy now in the new world created for him by Dominic and Harry that he would perhaps have made a holocaust of his flies and beetles if it had been necessary in order to keep this living, lively kindness about him. He no longer confined himself to the library, but shuffled along from room to room, staying and looking on at what was going forward wherever he did not find Mrs. Transome alone.

To Esther the sight of this feeble-minded, timid, paralytic man, who had long abdicated all mastery over the things that were his, was something piteous. Certainly this had never been part of the furniture she had imagined for the delightful aristocratic dwelling in her Utopia; and the sad irony of such a lot impressed her the more because in her father she was accustomed to age accompanied with mental acumen and activity. Her thoughts went back in conjecture over the past life of Mr. and Mrs. Transome, a couple so strangely different from each other. She found it impossible to arrange their existence in the seclusion of this fine park and in this lofty large-roomed house, where it seemed quite ridiculous to be anything so small as a human being without finding it rather dull. Mr. Transome had always had his beetles, but Mrs. Transome——? It was not easy to conceive that the husband and wife had ever been very fond of each other.

Esther felt at her ease with Mrs. Transome: she was gratified by the consciousness—for on this point Esther was very quick—that Mrs. Transome admired her, and looked at her with satisfied eyes. But when they were together in the early days of her stay, the conversation turned chiefly on what happened in Mrs. Transome's youth—what she wore when she was presented at Court—who were the most distinguished and beautiful women at that time—the terrible excitement of the French Revolution—the emigrants she had known, and the history of various titled members of the Lingon family. And Esther, from native delicacy, did not lead to more recent topics of a personal kind. She was copiously instructed that the Lingon family was better than that even of the elder Transomes, and was privileged with an explanation of the various quarterings, which proved that the Lingon blood had been continually enriched. Poor Mrs. Transome, with her secret bitterness and dread, still found a flavor in this sort of pride; none the less because certain deeds of her own life had been in fatal inconsistency with it. Besides, genealogies entered into her stock of ideas, and her talk on such subjects was as necessary as the notes of the linnet or the blackbird. She had no ultimate analysis of things that went beyond blood and family—the Herons of Fenshore or the Badgers of Hillbury. She had never seen behind the canvas with which her life was hung. In the dim background there was the burning mount

and the tables of the law; in the foreground there was Lady
Debarry privately gossiping about her, and Lady Wyvern
finally deciding not to send her invitations to dinner. Unlike that Semiramis who made laws to suit her practical license, she lived, poor soul, in the midst of desecrated sanctities, and of honors that looked tarnished in the light of
monotonous and weary suns. Glimpses of the Lingon her-
aldry in their freshness were interesting to Esther; but it occurred to her that when she had known about them a good
while they would cease to be succulent themes of converse or
meditation, and Mrs. Transome, having known them all along,
might have felt a vacuum in spite of them.

Nevertheless it was entertaining at present to be seated on
soft cushions with her netting before her, while Mrs. Transome went on with her embroidery, and told in that easy
phrase, and with that refined high-bred tone and accent which
she possessed in perfection, family stories that to Esther were
like so many novelettes: what diamonds were in the Earl's
family, own cousins to Mrs. Transome; how poor Lady Sara's
husband went off into jealous madness only a month after
their marriage, and dragged that sweet blue-eyed thing by the
hair; and how the brilliant Fanny, having married a country
parson, became so niggardly that she had gone about almost
begging for fresh eggs from the farmers' wives, though she
had done very well with her six sons, as there was a bishop
and no end of interest in the family, and two of them got
appointments in India.

At present Mrs. Transome did not touch at all on her own
time of privation, or her troubles with her eldest son, or on
anything that lay very close to her heart. She conversed with
Esther, and acted the part of hostess as she performed her
toilet and went on with her embroidery: these things were to
be done whether one were happy or miserable. Even the pa-
triarch Job, if he had been a gentleman of the modern West,
would have avoided picturesque disorder and poetical laments;
and the friends who called on him, though not less disposed
than Bildad the Shuhite to hint that their unfortunate friend
was in the wrong, would have sat on chairs and held their hats
in their hands. The harder problems of our life have changed

less than our manners; we wrestle with the old sorrows, but more decorously. Esther's inexperience prevented her from divining much about this fine gray-haired woman, whom she could not help perceiving to stand apart from the family group, as if there were some cause of isolation for her both within and without. To her young heart there was a peculiar interest in Mrs. Transome. An elderly woman, whose beauty, position, and graceful kindness toward herself made deference to her spontaneous, was a new figure in Esther's experience. Her quick light movement was always ready to anticipate what Mrs. Transome wanted; her bright apprehension and silvery speech were always ready to cap Mrs. Transome's narratives or instructions, even about doses and liniments, with some lively commentary. She must have behaved charmingly; for one day when she had tripped across the room to put the screen just in the right place, Mrs. Transome said, taking her hand, " My dear, you make me wish I had a daughter! "

That was pleasant; and so it was to be decked by Mrs. Transome's own hands in a set of turquoise ornaments, which became her wonderfully, worn with a white cashmere dress which was also insisted on. Esther never reflected that there was a double intention in these pretty ways toward her; with young generosity, she was rather preoccupied by the desire to prove that she herself entertained no low triumph in the fact that she had rights prejudicial to this family whose life she was learning. And besides, through all Mrs. Transome's perfect manners there pierced some undefinable indications of a hidden anxiety much deeper than anything she could feel about this affair of the estate—to which she often alluded slightly as a reason for informing Esther of something. It was impossible to mistake her for a happy woman; and young speculation is always stirred by discontent for which there is no obvious cause. When we are older, we take the uneasy eyes and the bitter lips more as a matter of course.

But Harold Transome was more communicative about recent years than his mother was. He thought it well that Esther should know how the fortune of his family had been drained by law expenses, owing to suits mistakenly urged by her family; he spoke of his mother's lonely life and pinched circumstances, of her lack of comfort in her elder son, and of the habit she had consequently acquired of looking at the gloomy side of things. He hinted that she had been accustomed to dictate, and that, as he had left her when he was a boy, she had perhaps indulged the dream that he would come back a boy. She was still sore on the point of his politics. These things could not be helped; but, so far as he could, he wished to make the rest of her life as cheerful as possible.

Esther listened eagerly, and took these things to heart. The claim to an inheritance, the sudden discovery of a right to a fortune held by others, was acquiring a very distinct and unexpected meaning for her. Every day she was getting more clearly into her imagination what it would be to abandon her own past, and what she would enter into in exchange for it; what it would be to disturb a long possession, and how difficult it was to fix a point at which the disturbance might begin, so as to be contemplated without pain.

Harold Transome's thoughts turned on the same subject, but accompanied by a different state of feeling and with more definite resolutions. He saw a mode of reconciling all difficulties, which looked pleasanter to him the longer he looked at Esther. When she had been hardly a week in the house, he had made up his mind to marry her; and it had never entered into that mind that the decision did not rest entirely with his inclination. It was not that he thought slightly of Esther's demands; he saw that she would require considerable attractions to please her, and that there were difficulties to be overcome. She was clearly a girl who must be wooed; but Harold did not despair of presenting the requisite attractions, and the difficulties gave more interest to the wooing than he could have believed. When he had said that he would not marry an Englishwoman, he had always made a mental reservation in favor of peculiar circumstances; and now the peculiar circumstances were come. To be deeply in love was a catastrophe not likely to happen to him; but he was readily amorous. No woman could make him miserable, but he was sensitive to the presence of women, and was kind to them; not with grimaces, like a man of mere gallantry, but beamingly, easily, like a man of genuine good nature. And each day that he was near Esther the solution of all difficulties by marriage became a more pleasing prospect; though he had to confess to himself that the difficulties did not diminish on a nearer view, in spite of the flattering sense that she brightened at his approach.

Harold was not one to fail in a purpose for want of assiduity. After an hour or two devoted to business in the morning, he went to look for Esther, and if he did not find her at play with Harry and old Mr. Transome, or chatting with his mother, he went into the drawing-room, where she was usually either seated with a book on her knee and "making a bed for her cheek" with one little hand, while she looked out of the window, or else standing in front of one of the full-length family portraits with an air of rumination. Esther found it impossible to read in these days; her life was a book which she seemed herself to be constructing—trying to make character clear before her, and looking into the ways of destiny.

The active Harold had almost always something definite to propose by way of filling the time: if it were fine, she must walk out with him and see the grounds; and when the snow melted and it was no longer slippery, she must get on horseback and learn to ride. If they stayed indoors, she must learn to play at billiards, or she must go over the house and see the pictures he had had hung anew, or the costumes he had brought from the East, or come into his study and look at the map of the estate, and hear what—if it had remained in his family—he had intended to do in every corner of it in order to make the most of its capabilities.

About a certain time in the morning Esther had learned to expect him. Let every wooer make himself strongly expected; he may succeed by dint of being absent, but hardly in the first instance. One morning Harold found her in the drawing-room, leaning against a console-table, and looking at the full-length portrait of a certain Lady Betty Transome, who had lived a century and a half before, and had the usual charm of ladies in Sir Peter Lely's style.

"Don't move, pray," he said on entering; "you look as if you were standing for your own portrait."

"I take that as an insinuation," said Esther, laughing, and

moving toward her seat on an ottoman near the fire, "for I notice almost all the portraits are in a conscious, affected attitude. That fair Lady Betty looks as if she had been drilled into that posture, and had not will enough of her own ever to move again unless she had a little push given to her."

"She brightens up that panel well with her long satin skirt," said Harold, as he followed Esther, "but alive I dare say she would have been less cheerful company."

"One would certainly think that she had just been unpacked from silver paper. Ah, how chivalrous you are!" said Esther, as Harold, kneeling on one knee, held her silken netting-stirrup for her to put her foot through. She had often fancied pleasant scenes in which such homage was rendered to her, and the homage was not disagreeable now it was really come; but, strangely enough, a little darting sensation at that moment was accompanied by the vivid remembrance of some one who had never paid the least attention to her foot. There had been a slight blush, such as often came and went rapidly, and she was silent a moment. Harold naturally believed that it was he himself who was filling the field of vision. He would have liked to place himself on the ottoman near Esther, and behave very much more like a lover; but he took a chair opposite to her at a circumspect distance. He dared not do otherwise. Along with Esther's playful charm she conveyed an impression of personal pride and high spirit which warned Harold's acuteness that in the delicacy of their present position he might easily make a false move and offend her. A woman was likely to be credulous about adoration, and to find no difficulty in referring it to her intrinsic attractions; but Esther was too dangerously quick and critical not to discern the least awkwardness that looked like offering her marriage as a convenient compromise for himself. Beforehand, he might have said that such characteristics as hers were not lovable in a woman; but, as it was, he found that the hope of pleasing her had a piquancy quite new to him.

"I wonder," said Esther, breaking her silence in her usual light silvery tones—"I wonder whether the woman who looked in that way ever felt any troubles. I see there are two old ones upstairs in the billiard-room who have only got fat; the expression of their faces is just of the same sort."

"A woman ought never to have any trouble. There should always be a man to guard her from it." (Harold Transome was masculine and fallible; he had incautiously sat down this morning to pay his addresses by talk about nothing in particular; and, clever experienced man as he was, he fell into nonsense.)

"But suppose the man himself got into trouble—you would wish her to mind about that. Or suppose," added Esther, suddenly looking up merrily at Harold, "the man himself was troublesome?"

"Oh, you must not strain probabilities in that way. The generality of men are perfect. Take me, for example."

"You are a perfect judge of sauces," said Esther, who had her triumphs in letting Harold know that she was capable of taking notes.

"That is perfection number one. Pray go on."

"Oh, the catalogue is too long—I should be tired before I got to your magnificent ruby ring and your gloves always of the right color."

"If you would let me tell you your perfections, I should not be tired."

"That is not complimentary; it means that the list is short."

"No; it means that the list is pleasant to dwell upon."

"Pray don't begin," said Esther, with her pretty toss of the head; "it would be dangerous to our good understanding. The person I liked best in the world was one who did nothing but scold me and tell me of my faults."

When Esther began to speak, she meant to do no more than make a remote, unintelligible allusion, feeling, it must be owned, a naughty will to flirt and be saucy, and thwart Harold's attempts to be felicitous in compliment. But she had no sooner uttered the words than they seemed to her like a confession. A deep flush spread itself over her face and neck, and the sense that she was blushing went on deepening her color. Harold felt himself unpleasantly illuminated as to a possibility that had never yet occurred to him. His surprise made an uncomfortable pause, in which Esther had time to feel much vexation.

"You speak in the past tense," said Harold, at last; "yet I am rather envious of that person. I shall never be able to win your regard in the same way. Is it any one at Treby? Because in that case I can inquire about your faults."

"Oh, you know I have always lived among grave people," said Esther, more able to recover herself now she was spoken to. "Before I came home to be with my father I was nothing but a schoolgirl first, and then a teacher in different stages of growth. People in those circumstances are not usually flattered. But there are varieties in fault-finding. At our Paris school the master I liked best was an old man who stormed at me terribly when I read Racine, but yet showed that he was proud of me."

Esther was getting quite cool again. But Harold was not entirely satisfied; if there was any obstacle in his way, he wished to know exactly what it was.

"That must have been a wretched life for you at Treby," he said,—"a person of your accomplishments."

"I used to be dreadfully discontented," said Esther, much occupied with mistakes she had made in her netting. "But I was becoming less so. I have had time to get rather wise, you know; I am two-and-twenty."

"Yes," said Harold, rising and walking a few paces backward and forward, "you are past your majority; you are empress of your own fortunes—and more besides."

"Dear me," said Esther, letting her work fall, and leaning back against the cushions; "I don't think I know very well what to do with my empire."

"Well," said Harold, pausing in front of her, leaning one arm on the mantelpiece, and speaking very gravely, "I hope that in any case, since you appear to have no near relative who understands affairs, you will confide in me, and trust me with all your intentions as if I had no other personal concern in the matter than a regard for you. I hope you believe me capable of acting as the guardian of your interest, even where it turns out to be inevitably opposed to my own."

"I am sure you have given me reason to believe it," said

Esther, with seriousness, putting out her hand to Harold. She had not been left in ignorance that he had had opportunities twice offered of stifling her claims.

Harold raised the hand to his lips, but dared not retain it more than an instant. Still the sweet reliance in Esther's manner made an irresistible temptation to him. After standing still a moment or two, while she bent over her work, he glided to the ottoman and seated himself close by her, looking at her busy hands.

"I see you have made mistakes in your work," he said, bending still nearer, for he saw that she was conscious, yet not angry.

"Nonsense! you know nothing about it," said Esther, laughing and crushing up the soft silk under her palms. "Those blunders have a design in them."

She looked round, and saw a handsome face very near her. Harold was looking, as he felt, thoroughly enamoured of this bright woman, who was not at all to his preconceived taste. Perhaps a touch of hypothetic jealousy now helped to heighten the effect. But he mastered all indiscretion, and only looked at her as he said,—

"I am wondering whether you have any deep wishes and secrets that I can't guess."

"Pray don't speak of my wishes," said Esther, quite overmastered by this new and apparently involuntary manifestation in Harold; "I could not possibly tell you one at this moment—I think I shall never find them out again. Oh, yes," she said, abruptly, struggling to relieve herself from the oppression of unintelligible feelings—"I do know one wish distinctly. I want to go and see my father. He writes me word that all is well with him, but still I want to see him."

"You shall be driven there when you like."

"May I go now—I mean as soon as it is convenient?" said Esther, rising.

"I will give the order immediately, if you wish it," said Harold, understanding that the audience was broken up.

25

CHAPTER XLI.

He rates me as the merchant does the wares
He will not purchase—" quality not high !—
'Twill lose its color opened to the sun,
Has no aroma, and, in fine, is naught—
I barter not for such commodities—
There is no ratio betwixt sand and gems."
'Tis wicked judgment ! for the soul can grow,
As embryos, that live and move but blindly,
Burst from the dark, emerge regenerate,
And lead a life of vision and of choice.

ESTHER did not take the carriage into Malthouse Lane, but
left it to wait for her outside the town; and when she entered
the house she put her finger on her lip to Lyddy and ran
lightly upstairs. She wished to surprise her father by this
visit, and she succeeded. The little minister was just then
almost surrounded by a wall of books, with merely his head
peeping above them, being much embarrassed to find a substitute for tables and desks on which to arrange the volumes he
kept open for reference. He was absorbed in mastering all
those painstaking interpretations of the Book of Daniel which
are by this time well gone to the limbo of mistaken criticism;
and Esther, as she opened the door softly, heard him rehears-
ing aloud a passage in which he declared, with some paren-
thetic provisos, that he conceived not how a perverse ingenuity could blunt the edge of prophetic explicitness, or how an
open mind could fail to see in the chronology of " the little
horn " the resplendent lamp of an inspired symbol searching
out the germinal growth of an antichristian power.

"You will not like me to interrupt you, father?" said
Esther, slyly.

"Ah, my beloved child!" he exclaimed, upsetting a pile of
books, and thus unintentionally making a convenient breach
in his wall, through which Esther could get up to him and
kiss him. "Thy appearing is as a joy despaired of. I had
thought of thee as the blinded think of the daylight—which
indeed is a thing to rejoice in, like all other good, though we
see it not nigh."

"Are you sure you have been as well and comfortable as you

said you were in your letters?" said Esther, seating herself close in front of her father, and laying her hand on his shoulder.

"I wrote truly, my dear, according to my knowledge at the time. But to an old memory like mine the present days are but as a little water poured on the deep. It seems now that all has been as usual, except my studies, which have gone somewhat curiously into prophetic history. But I fear you will rebuke me for my negligent apparel," said the little man, feeling in front of Esther's brightness like a bat overtaken by the morning.

"That is Lyddy's fault, who sits crying over her want of Christian assurance instead of brushing your clothes and putting out your clean cravat. She is always saying her righteousness is filthy rags, and really I don't think that is a very strong expression for it. I'm sure it is dusty clothes and furniture."

"Nay, my dear, your playfulness glances too severely on our faithful Lyddy. Doubtless I am myself deficient, in that I do not aid her infirm memory by admonition. But now tell me aught that you have left untold about yourself. Your heart has gone out somewhat toward this family—the old man and the child, whom I had not reckoned of?"

"Yes, father. It is more and more difficult to me to see how I can make up my mind to disturb these people at all."

"Something should doubtless be devised to lighten the loss and the change to the aged father and mother. I would have you in any case seek to temper a vicissitude, which is nevertheless a providential arrangement not to be wholly set aside."

"Do you think, father—do you feel assured that a case of inheritance like this of mine is a sort of providential arrangement that makes a command?"

"I have so held it," said Mr. Lyon, solemnly; "in all my meditations I have so held it. For you have to consider, my dear, that you have been led by a peculiar path, and into experience which is not ordinarily the lot of those who are seated in high places; and what I have hinted to you already in my letters on this head I shall wish on a future opportunity to enter into more at large."

Esther was uneasily silent. On this great question of her lot she saw doubts and difficulties, in which it seemed as if her father could not help her. There was no illumination for her in this theory of providential arrangement. She said suddenly (what she had not thought of at all suddenly)—

"Have you been again to see Felix Holt, father? You have not mentioned him in your letters."

"I have been since I last wrote, my dear, and I took his mother with me, who, I fear, made the time heavy to him with her plaints. But afterward I carried her away to the house of a brother minister at Loamford, and returned to Felix, and then we had much discourse."

"Did you tell him of everything that has happened—I mean about me—about the Transomes?"

"Assuredly I told him, and he listened as one astonished. For he had much to hear, knowing nought of your birth, and that you had any other father than Rufus Lyon. 'Tis a narrative I trust I shall not be called on to give to others; but I was not without satisfaction in unfolding the truth to this young man, who hath wrought himself into my affection strangely—I would fain hope for ends that will be a visible good in his less wayworn life, when mine shall be no longer."

"And you told him how the Transomes had come, and that I was staying at Transome Court?"

"Yes, I told these things with some particularity, as is my wont concerning what hath imprinted itself on my mind."

"What did Felix say?"

"Truly, my dear, nothing desirable to recite," said Mr. Lyon, rubbing his hand over his brow.

"Dear father, he did say something, and you always remember what people say. Pray tell me; I want to know."

"It was a hasty remark, and rather escaped him than was consciously framed. He said, 'Then she will marry Transome; that is what Transome means.'"

"That was all?" said Esther, turning rather pale, and biting her lip with the determination that the tears should not start.

"Yes, we did not go further into that branch of the subject. I apprehend there is no warrant for his seeming prognostic, and I should not be without disquiet if I thought otherwise. For I confess that in your accession to this great position and property I contemplate with hopeful satisfaction your remaining attached to that body of congregational Dissent which, as I hold, hath retained most of pure and primitive discipline. Your education and peculiar history would thus be seen to have coincided with a long train of events in making this family property a means of honoring and illustrating a purer form of Christianity than that which hath unhappily obtained the pre-eminence in this land. I speak, my child, as you know, always in the hope that you will fully join our communion; and this dear wish of my heart—nay, this urgent prayer—would seem to be frustrated by your marriage with a man of whom there is at least no visible indication that he would unite himself to our body."

If Esther had been less agitated, she would hardly have helped smiling at the picture her father's words suggested of Harold Transome "joining the church" in Malthouse Yard. But she was too seriously preoccupied with what Felix had said, which hurt her in a two-edged fashion that was highly significant. First, she was angry with him for daring to say positively whom she would marry; secondly, she was angry at the implication that there was from the first a cool deliberate design in Harold Transome to marry her. Esther said to herself that she was quite capable of discerning Harold Transome's disposition, and judging of his conduct. She felt sure he was generous and open. It did not lower him in her opinion that since circumstances had brought them together he evidently admired her—was in love with her—in short, desired to marry her; and she thought that she discerned the delicacy which hindered him from being more explicit. There is no point on which young women are more easily piqued than this of their sufficiency to judge the men who make love to them. And Esther's generous nature delighted to believe in generosity. All these thoughts were making a tumult in her mind while her father was suggesting the radiance her lot might cast on the cause of congregational Dissent. She heard what he said, and remembered it afterward, but she made no reply at present, and chose rather to start up in search of a brush—

an action which would seem to her father quite a usual sequence with her. It served the purpose of diverting him from a lengthy subject.

"Have you yet spoken with Mr. Transome concerning Mrs. Holt, my dear?" he said, as Esther was moving about the room. "I hinted to him that you would best decide how assistance should be tendered to her."

"No, father, we have not approached the subject. Mr. Transome may have forgotten it, and, for several reasons, I would rather not talk of this—of money matters to him at present. There is money due to me from the Lukyns and the Pendrells."

"They have paid it," said Mr. Lyon, opening his desk. "I have it here ready to deliver to you."

"Keep it, father, and pay Mrs. Holt's rent with it, and do anything else that is wanted for her. We must consider everything temporary now," said Esther, enveloping her father in a towel, and beginning to brush his auburn fringe of hair, while he shut his eyes in preparation for this pleasant passivity. "Everything is uncertain—what may become of Felix—what may become of us all. Oh, dear," she went on, changing suddenly to laughing merriment, "I am beginning to talk like Lyddy, I think."

"Truly," said Mr. Lyon, smiling, "the uncertainty of things is a text rather too wide and obvious for fruitful application; and to discourse of it is, as one may say, to bottle up the air, and make a present of it to those who are already standing out of doors."

"Do you think," said Esther, in the course of their chat, "that the Treby people know at all about the reasons of my being at Transome Court?"

"I have had no sign thereof; and indeed there is no one, as it appears, who could make the story public. The man Christian is away in London with Mr. Debarry, Parliament now beginning; and Mr. Jermyn would doubtless respect the confidence of the Transomes. I have not seen him lately. I know nothing of his movements. And so far as my own speech is concerned, and my strict command to Lyddy, I have withheld the means of information even as to your having returned to Transome Court in the carriage, not wishing to give any occasion to solicitous questioning till time hath somewhat inured me. But it hath got abroad that you are there, and is the subject of conjectures, whereof, I imagine, the chief is, that you are gone as companion to Mistress Transome; for some of our friends have already hinted a rebuke to me that I should permit your taking a position so little likely to further your spiritual welfare."

"Now, father, I think I shall be obliged to run away from you, not to keep the carriage too long," said Esther, as she finished her reforms on the minister's toilet. "You look beautiful now, and I must give Lyddy a little lecture before I go."

"Yes, my dear; I would not detain you, seeing that my duties demand me. But take with you this Treatise, which I have purposely selected. It concerns all the main questions between ourselves and the Establishment—government, discipline, State support. It is seasonable that you should give a nearer attention to these polemics, lest you be drawn aside by the fallacious association of a State Church with elevated rank."

Esther chose to take the volume submissively, rather than to adopt the ungraceful sincerity of saying that she was unable at present to give her mind to the original functions of a bishop, or the comparative merit of Endowments and Voluntaryism. But she did not run her eyes over the pages during her solitary drive to get a foretaste of the argument, for she was entirely occupied with Felix Holt's prophecy that she would marry Harold Transome.

CHAPTER XLII.

Thou sayst it, and not I ; for thou hast done
The ugly deed that made these ugly words.
                    SOPHOCLES: *Electra.*

Yea, it becomes a man
To cherish memory, where he had delight.
For kindness is the natural birth of kindness.
Whose soul records not the great debt of joy,
Is stamped forever an ignoble man.
                    SOPHOCLES: *Ajax.*

IT so happened that, on the morning of the day when Esther went to see her father, Jermyn had not yet heard of her
presence at Transome Court.   One fact conducing to keep
him in this ignorance was, that some days after his critical
interview with Harold -days during which he had been wondering how long it would be before Harold made up his mind
to sacrifice the luxury of satisfied anger for the solid advantage of securing fortune and position—he was peremptorily
called away by business to the south of England, and was
obliged to inform Harold by letter of his absence.   He took
care also to notify his return; but Harold made no sign in
reply.   The days passed without bringing him any gossip concerning Esther's visit, for such gossip was almost confined
to Mr. Lyon's congregation; her Church pupils, Miss Louisa
Jermyn among them, having been satisfied by her father's
written statement that she was gone on a visit of uncertain
duration.   But on this day of Esther's call in Malthouse
Yard, the Miss Jermyns in their walk saw her getting into
the Transomes' carriage, which they had previously observed
to be waiting, and which they now saw bowled along on the
road toward Little Treby.   It followed that only a few hours
later the news reached the astonished ears of Matthew Jermyn.

Entirely ignorant of those converging indications and small
links of incident which had raised Christian's conjectures, and
had gradually contributed to put him in possession of the
facts; ignorant, too, of some busy motives in the mind of his
obliged servant Johnson,—Jermyn was not likely to see at
once how the momentous information that Esther was the

surviving Bycliffe could possibly have reached Harold. His daughters naturally leaped, as others had done, to the conclusion that the Transomes, seeking a governess for little Harry, had had their choice directed to Esther, and observed that they must have attracted her by a high salary to induce her to take charge of such a small pupil; though of course it was important that his English and French should be carefully attended to from the first. Jermyn, hearing this suggestion, was not without a momentary hope that it might be true, and that Harold was still safely unconscious of having under the same roof with him the legal claimant of the family estate.

But a mind in the grasp of a terrible anxiety is not credulous of easy solutions. The one stay that bears up our hopes is sure to appear frail, and if looked at long will seem to totter. Too much depended on that unconsciousness of Harold's; and although Jermyn did not see the course of things that could have disclosed and combined the various items of knowledge which he had imagined to be his own secret, and therefore his safeguard, he saw quite clearly what was likely to be the result of the disclosure. Not only would Harold Transome be no longer afraid of him, but also, by marrying Esther (and Jermyn at once felt sure of this issue), he would be triumphantly freed from any unpleasant consequences, and could pursue much at his ease the gratification of ruining Matthew Jermyn. The prevision of an enemy's triumphant ease is in any case sufficiently irritating to hatred, and there were reasons why it was peculiarly exasperating here; but Jermyn had not the leisure now for mere fruitless emotion : he had to think of a possible device which might save him from imminent ruin—not an indefinite adversity, but a ruin in detail, which his thoughts painted out with the sharpest, ugliest intensity. A man of sixty, with an unsuspicious wife and daughters capable of shrieking and fainting at a sudden revelation, and of looking at him reproachfully in their daily misery under a shabby lot to which he had reduced them—with a mind and with habits dried hard by the years—with no glimpse of an endurable standing-ground except where he could domineer and be prosperous according to the ambitions of pushing middle-class gentility,—such a man is likely to find the prospect

of worldly ruin ghastly enough to drive him to the most unin-
viting means of escape. He will probably prefer any private
scorn that will save him from public infamy or that will leave
him money in his pocket, to the humiliation and hardship of
new servitude in old age, a shabby hat and a melancholy
hearth, where the firing must be used charily and the wom-
en look sad. But though a man may be willing to escape
through a sewer, a sewer with an outlet into the dry air is not
always at hand. Running away, especially when spoken of
as absconding, seems at a distance to offer a good modern substitute for the right of sanctuary; but seen closely it is often
found inconvenient and scarcely possible.

Jermyn, on thoroughly considering his position, saw that he
had no very agreeable resources at command. But he soon
made up his mind what he would do next. He wrote to Mrs.
Transome, requesting her to appoint an hour in which he could
see her privately : he knew she would understand that it was
to be an hour when Harold was not at home. As he sealed
the letter, he indulged a faint hope that in this interview he
might be assured of Esther's birth being unknown at Transome Court; but, in the worst case, perhaps some help might
be found in Mrs. Transome. To such uses may tender relations come when they have ceased to be tender! The Hazaels
of our world who are pushed on quickly against their preconceived confidence in themselves to do doglike actions by the
sudden suggestion of a wicked ambition are much fewer than
those who are led on through the years by the gradual demands of a selfishness which has spread its fibres far and wide
through the intricate vanities and sordid cares of an every-day
existence.

In consequence of that letter to Mrs. Transome, Jermyn
was two days afterward ushered into the smaller drawing-
room at Transome Court. It was a charming little room in
its refurbished condition : it had two pretty inlaid cabinets,
great china vases with contents that sent forth odors of paradise, groups of flowers in oval frames on the walls, and Mrs.
Transome's own portrait in the evening costume of 1800, with
a garden in the background. That brilliant young woman
looked smilingly down on Mr. Jermyn as he passed in front

of the fire; and at present hers was the only gaze in the room. He could not help meeting the gaze as he waited, holding his hat behind him—could not help seeing many memories lit up by it; but the strong bent of his mind was to go on arguing each memory into a claim, and to see in the regard others had for him a merit of his own. There had been plenty of roads open to him when he was a young man; perhaps if he had not allowed himself to be determined (chiefly, of course, by the feelings of others, for of what effect would his own feelings have been without them?) into the road he actually took, he might have done better for himself. At any rate, he was likely at last to get the worst of it, and it was he who had most reason to complain. The fortunate Jason, as we know from Euripides, piously thanked the goddess, and saw clearly that he was not at all obliged to Medea: Jermyn was perhaps not aware of the precedent, but thought out his own freedom from obligation and the indebtedness of others toward him with a native faculty not inferior to Jason's.

Before three minutes had passed, however, as if by some sorcery, the brilliant smiling young woman above the mantel-piece seemed to be appearing at the door-way withered and frosted by many winters, and with lips and eyes from which the smile had departed. Jermyn advanced, and they shook hands, but neither of them said anything by way of greeting. Mrs. Transome seated herself, and pointed to a chair opposite and near her.

"Harold has gone to Loamford," she said, in a subdued tone. "You had something particular to say to me?"

"Yes," said Jermyn, with his soft and deferential air. "The last time I was here I could not take the opportunity of speaking to you. But I am anxious to know whether you are aware of what has passed between me and Harold?"

"Yes, he has told me everything."

"About his proceedings against me? and the reason he stopped them?"

"Yes: have you had notice that he has begun them again?"

"No," said Jermyn, with a very unpleasant sensation.

"Of course he will now," said Mrs. Transome. "There is no reason in his mind why he should not."

"Has he resolved to risk the estate, then?"

"He feels in no danger on that score. And if there were, the danger doesn't depend on you. The most likely thing is, that he will marry this girl."

"He knows everything, then?" said Jermyn, the expression of his face getting clouded.

"Everything. It's of no use for you to think of mastering him: you can't do it. I used to wish Harold to be fortunate —and he is fortunate," said Mrs. Transome, with intense bitterness. "It's not my star that he inherits."

"Do you know how he came by the information about this girl?"

"No; but she knew it all before we spoke to her. It's no secret."

Jermyn was confounded by this hopeless frustration to which he had no key. Though he thought of Christian, the thought shed no light; but the more fatal point was clear: he held no secret that could help him.

"You are aware that these Chancery proceedings may ruin me?"

"He told me they would. But if you are imagining that I can do anything, dismiss the notion. I have told him as plainly as I dare that I wish him to drop all public quarrel with you, and that you could make an arrangement without scandal. I can do no more. He will not listen to me; he doesn't mind about my feelings. He cares more for Mr. Transome than he does for me. He will not listen to me any more than if I were an old ballad-singer."

"It's very hard on *me*, I know," said Jermyn, in the tone with which a man flings out a reproach.

"I besought you three months ago to bear anything rather than quarrel with him."

"I have not quarrelled with him. It is he who has been always seeking a quarrel with me. I have borne a good deal —more than any one else would. He set his teeth against me from the first."

"He saw things that annoyed him; and men are not like women," said Mrs. Transome. There was a bitter innuendo in that truism.

"It's very hard on me—I know that," said Jermyn, with an intensification of his previous tone, rising and walking a step or two, then turning and laying his hand on the back of the chair. "Of course the law in this case can't in the least represent the justice of the matter. I made a good many sacrifices in times past. I gave up a great deal of fine business for the sake of attending to the family affairs, and in that lawsuit they would have gone to rack and ruin if it hadn't been for me."

He moved away again, laid down his hat, which he had been previously holding, and thrust his hands into his pockets as he returned. Mrs. Transome sat motionless as marble, and almost as pale. Her hands lay crossed on her knees. This man, young, slim, and graceful, with a selfishness which then took the form of homage to her, had at one time kneeled to her and kissed those hands fervently; and she had thought there was a poetry in such passion beyond any to be found in every-day domesticity.

"I stretched my conscience a good deal in that affair of Bycliffe, as you know perfectly well. I told you everything at the time. I told you I was very uneasy about those witnesses, and about getting him thrown into prison. I know it's the blackest thing anybody could charge me with, if they knew my life from beginning to end; and I should never have done it if I had not been under an infatuation such as makes a man do anything. What did it signify to me about the loss of the lawsuit? I was a young bachelor—I had the world before me."

"Yes," said Mrs. Transome, in a low tone. "It was a pity you didn't make another choice."

"What would have become of you?" said Jermyn, carried along a climax, like other self-justifiers. "I had to think of you. You would not have liked me to make another choice then."

"Clearly," said Mrs. Transome, with concentrated bitterness, but still quietly; "the greater mistake was mine."

Egoism is usually stupid in a dialogue; but Jermyn's did not make him so stupid that he did not feel the edge of Mrs. Transome's words. They increased his irritation.

"I hardly see that," he replied, with a slight laugh of scorn. "You had an estate and a position to save, to go no farther. I remember very well what you said to me—'A clever lawyer can do anything if he has the will; if it's impossible, he will make it possible. And the property is sure to be Harold's some day.' He was a baby then."

"I remember most things a little too well: you had better say at once what is your object in recalling them."

"An object that is nothing more than justice. With the relation I stood in, it was not likely I should think myself bound by all the forms that are made to bind strangers. I had often immense trouble to raise the money necessary to pay off debts and carry on the affairs; and, as I said before, I had given up other lines of advancement which would have been open to me if I had not stayed in this neighborhood at a critical time when I was fresh to the world. Anybody who knew the whole circumstances would say that my being hunted and run down on the score of my past transactions with regard to the family affairs is an abominably unjust and unnatural thing."

Jermyn paused a moment, and then added, "At my time of life . . . and with a family about me—and after what has passed . . . I should have thought there was nothing you would care more to prevent."

"I do care. It makes me miserable. That is the extent of my power—to feel miserable."

"No, it is not the extent of your power. You could save me if you would. It is not to be supposed that Harold would go on against me . . . if he knew the whole truth."

Jermyn had sat down before he uttered the last words. He had lowered his voice slightly. He had the air of one who thought that he had prepared the way for an understanding. That a man with so much sharpness, with so much suavity at command—a man who piqued himself on his persuasiveness toward women,—should behave just as Jermyn did on this occasion would be surprising but for the constant experience that temper and selfish insensibility will defeat excellent gifts —will make a sensible person shout when shouting is out of place, and will make a polished man rude when his polish might be of eminent use to him.

As Jermyn, sitting down and leaning forward with an elbow on his knee, uttered his last words—"if he knew the whole truth"—a slight shock seemed to pass through Mrs. Transome's hitherto motionless body, followed by a sudden light in her eyes, as in an animal's about to spring.

"And you expect me to tell him?" she said, not loudly, but yet with a clear metallic ring in her voice.

"Would it not be right for him to know?" said Jermyn, in a more bland and persuasive tone than he had yet used.

Perhaps some of the most terrible irony of the human lot is this of a deep truth coming to be uttered by lips that have no right to it.

"I will never tell him!" said Mrs. Transome, starting up, her whole frame thrilled with a passion that seemed almost to make her young again. Her hands hung beside her, clinched tightly, her eyes and lips lost the helpless repressed bitterness of discontent, and seemed suddenly fed with energy. "You reckon up your sacrifices for me: you have kept a good account of them, and it is needful; they are some of them what no one else could guess or find out. But you made your sacrifices when they seemed pleasant to you; when you told me they were your happiness; when you told me that it was I who stooped, and I who bestowed favors."

Jermyn rose too, and laid his hand on the back of the chair. He had grown visibly paler, but seemed about to speak.

"Don't speak!" Mrs. Transome said peremptorily. "Don't open your lips again. You have said enough; I will speak now. I have made sacrifices too, but it was when I knew that they were not my happiness. It was after I saw that I *had* stooped—after I saw that your tenderness had turned into calculation—after I saw that you cared for yourself only, and not for me. I heard your explanations—of your duty in life—of our mutual reputation—of a virtuous young lady attached to you. I bore it; I let everything go; I shut my eyes; I might almost have let myself starve, rather than have scenes of quarrel with the man I had loved, in which I must accuse him of turning my love into a good bargain." There was a slight tremor in Mrs. Transome's voice in the last words, and for a moment she paused; but when she spoke again it seemed as if the tremor had frozen into a cutting icicle. "I suppose if a lover picked one's pocket, there's no woman would like to own it. I don't say I was not afraid of you; I *was* afraid of you, and I know now I was right."

"Mrs. Transome," said Jermyn, white to the lips, "it is needless to say more. I withdraw any words that have offended you."

"You can't withdraw them. Can a man apologize for being a dastard? . . . And I have caused you to strain your conscience, have I?—it is I who have sullied your purity? I should think the demons have more honor—they are not so impudent to one another. I would not lose the misery of being a woman, now I see what can be the baseness of a man. One must be a man—first to tell a woman that her love has made her your debtor, and then ask her to pay you by breaking the last poor threads between her and her son."

"I do not ask it," said Jermyn, with a certain asperity. He was beginning to find this intolerable. The mere brute strength of a masculine creature rebelled. He felt almost inclined to throttle the voice out of this woman.

"You do ask it: it is what you would like. I have had a terror on me lest evil should happen to you. From the first, after Harold came home, I had a horrible dread. It seemed as if murder might come between you—I didn't know what. I felt the horror of his not knowing the truth. I might have been dragged at last, by my own feeling—by my own memory —to tell him all, and make him as well as myself miserable, to save you."

Again there was a slight tremor, as if at the remembrance of womanly tenderness and pity. But immediately she launched forth again.

"But, now you have asked me, I will never tell him! Be ruined—no—do something more dastardly to save yourself. If I sinned, my judgment went beforehand—that I should sin for a man like you."

Swiftly upon those last words Mrs. Transome passed out of

the room. The softly padded door closed behind her, making no noise, and Jermyn found himself alone.

For a brief space he stood still. Human beings in moments of passionate reproach and denunciation, especially when their anger is on their own account, are never so wholly in the right that the person who has to wince cannot possibly protest against some unreasonableness or unfairness in their outburst. And if Jermyn had been capable of feeling that he had thoroughly merited this infliction, he would not have uttered the words that drew it down on him. Men do not become penitent and learn to abhor themselves by having their backs cut open with the lash; rather, they learn to abhor the lash. What Jermyn felt about Mrs. Transome when she disappeared was that she was a furious woman—who would not do what he wanted her to do. And he was supported as to his justifiableness by the inward repetition of what he had already said to her; it was right that Harold should know the truth. He did not take into account (how should he?) the exasperation and loathing excited by his daring to urge the plea of right. A man who had stolen the pyx, and got frightened when justice was at his heels, might feel the sort of penitence which would induce him to run back in the dark and lay the pyx where the sexton might find it; but if in doing so he whispered to the Blessed Virgin that he was moved by considering the sacredness of all property, and the peculiar sacredness of the pyx, it is not to be believed that she would like him the better for it. Indeed, one often seems to see why the saints should prefer candles to words, especially from penitents whose skin is in danger. Some salt of generosity would have made Jermyn conscious that he had lost the citizenship which authorized him to plead the right; still more, that his self-vindication to Mrs. Transome would be like the exhibition of a brand-mark, and only show that he was shame-proof. There is heroism even in the circles of hell for fellow-sinners who cling to each other in the fiery whirlwind and never recriminate. But these things, which are easy to discern when they are painted for us on the large canvas of poetic story, become confused and obscure even for well-read gentlemen when their affection for themselves is alarmed by pressing details of

26

actual experience. If their comparison of instances is active
at such times, it is chiefly in showing them that their own
case has subtle distinctions from all other cases, which should
free them from unmitigated condemnation.

And it was in this way with Matthew Jermyn. So many
things were more distinctly visible to him, and touched him
more acutely, than the effect of his acts or words on Mrs.
Transome's feelings! In fact—he asked, with a touch of
something that makes us all akin—was it not preposterous,
this excess of feeling on points which he himself did not find
powerfully moving? She had treated him most unreasonably.
It would have been right for her to do what he had—not
asked, but only hinted at in a mild and interrogatory manner.
But the clearest and most unpleasant result of the interview
was that this right thing which he desired so much would
certainly not be done for him by Mrs. Transome.

As he was moving his arm from the chair-back, and turning
to take his hat, there was a boisterous noise in the entrance
hall; the door of the small drawing-room, which had closed
without latching, was pushed open, and old Mr. Transome
appeared with a face of feeble delight, playing horse to little Harry, who roared and flogged behind him, while Moro
yapped in a puppy voice at their heels. But when Mr. Transome saw Jermyn in the room he stood still in the door-way,
as if he did not know whether entrance were permissible.
The majority of his thoughts were but ravelled threads of the
past. The attorney came forward to shake hands with due
politeness, but the old man said, with a bewildered look, and
in a hesitating way,—

"Mr. Jermyn?—why—why—where is Mrs. Transome?"

Jermyn smiled his way out past the unexpected group; and
little Harry, thinking he had an eligible opportunity, turned
round to give a parting stroke on the stranger's coat-tails.

CHAPTER XLIII.

Whichever way my days decline,
  I felt and feel, though left alone,
  His being working in mine own,
The footsteps of his life in mine.
. . . .

Dear friend, far off, my lost desire,
  So far, so near, in woe and weal;
  Oh, loved the most when most I fee
There is a lower and a higher !
             TENNYSON: *In Memoriam.*

AFTER that morning on which Esther found herself reddened and confused by the sense of having made a distant allusion to Felix Holt, she felt it impossible that she should even, as she had sometimes intended, speak of him explicitly to Harold, in order to discuss the probabilities as to the issue of his trial. She was certain she could not do it without betraying emotion, and there were very complex reasons in Esther's mind why she could not bear that Harold should detect her sensibility on this subject. It was not only all the fibres of maidenly pride and reserve, of a bashfulness undefinably peculiar toward this man, who, while much older than herself, and bearing the stamp of an experience quite hidden from her imagination, was taking strongly the aspect of a lover—it was not only this exquisite kind of shame which was at work within her: there was another sort of susceptibility in Esther which her present circumstances tended to encourage, though she had come to regard it as not at all lofty, but rather as something which condemned her to littleness in comparison with a mind she had learned to venerate. She knew quite well that, to Harold Transome, Felix Holt was one of the common people who could come into question in no other than a public light. She had a native capability for discerning that the sense of ranks and degrees has its repulsions corresponding to the repulsions dependent on difference of race and color; and she remembered her own impressions too well not to foresee that it would come on Harold Transome as a shock if he suspected there had been any love-passages between her and this young man, who to him was of course no more than any other intelligent member of the working class. "To him," said Esther to herself, with a reaction of her newer, better pride, "who has not had the sort of intercourse in which Felix Holt's cultured nature would have asserted its superiority." And in her fluctuations on this matter she found herself mentally protesting that, whatever Harold might think, there was a light in which he was vulgar compared with Felix. Felix had ideas and motives which she did not believe that Harold could understand. More than all, there was this test: she herself had no sense of inferiority and just subjection when she was with Harold Transome; there were even points in him for which she felt a touch not of angry but of playful scorn; whereas with Felix she had always a sense of dependence and possible illumination. In those large, grave, candid gray eyes of his love seemed something that belonged to the high enthusiasm of life, such as might now be forever shut out from her.

All the same, her vanity winced at the idea that Harold should discern what, from his point of view, would seem like a degradation of her taste and refinement. She could not help being gratified by all the manifestations from those around her that she was thought thoroughly fitted for a high position; could not help enjoying, with more or less keenness, a rehearsal of that demeanor amongst luxuries and dignities which had often been a part of her day-dreams, and the rehearsal included the reception of more and more emphatic attentions from Harold, and of an effusiveness in his manners which, in proportion as it would have been offensive if it had appeared earlier, became flattering as the effect of a growing acquaintance and daily contact. It comes in so many forms in this life of ours—the knowledge that there is something sweetest and noblest of which we despair, and the sense of something present that solicits us with an immediate and easy indulgence. And there is a pernicious falsity in the pretence that a woman's love lies above the range of such temptations.

Day after day Esther had an arm offered her, had very beaming looks upon her, had opportunities for a great deal of light, airy talk, in which she knew herself to be charming, and had the attractive interest of noticing Harold's practical cleverness—the masculine ease with which he governed every-

body and administered everything about him, without the
least harshness, and with a facile good nature which yet was
not weak. In the background, too, there was the ever-present
consideration that if Harold Transome wished to marry her,
and she accepted him, the problem of her lot would be more
easily solved than in any other way. It was difficult by any
theory of Providence, or consideration of results, to see a
course which she could call duty: if something would come
and urge itself strongly as pleasure, and save her from the
effort to find a clew of principle amid the labyrinthine confu-
sions of right and possession, the promise could not but seem
alluring. And yet this life at Transome Court was *not* the
life of her day-dreams: there was dulness already in its ease,
and in the absence of high demand; and there was a vague
consciousness that the love of this not unfascinating man who
hovered about her gave an air of moral mediocrity to all her
prospects. She would not have been able perhaps to define
this impression; but somehow or other by this elevation of
fortune it seemed that the higher ambition which had begun
to spring in her was forever nullified. All life seemed cheap-
ened; as it might seem to a young student who, having believed that to gain a certain degree he must write a thesis
in which he would bring his powers to bear with memorable
effect, suddenly ascertained that no thesis was expected, but
the sum (in English money) of twenty-seven pounds ten shillings and sixpence.

After all, she was a woman, and could not make her own
lot. As she had once said to Felix, "A woman must choose
meaner things, because only meaner things are offered to her."
Her lot is made for her by the love she accepts. And Esther
began to think that her lot was being made for her by the
love that was surrounding her with the influence of a garden
on a summer morning.

Harold, on his side, was conscious that the interest of his
wooing was not standing still. He was beginning to think it
a conquest in which it would be disappointing to fail, even if
this fair nymph had no claim to the estate. He would have
liked—and yet he would not have liked—that just a slight
shadow of doubt as to his success should be removed. There

was something about Esther that he did not altogether understand. She was clearly a woman that could be governed; she was too charming for him to fear that she would ever be obstinate or interfering. Yet there was a lightning that shot out of her now and then, which seemed the sign of a dangerous judgment; as if she inwardly saw something more admirable than Harold Transome. Now, to be perfectly charming, a woman should not see this.

One fine February day, when already the golden and purple crocuses were out on the terrace—one of those flattering days which sometimes precede the northeast winds of March, and make believe that the coming spring will be enjoyable—a very striking group, of whom Esther and Harold made a part, came out at mid-day to walk upon the gravel at Transome Court. They did not, as usual, go toward the pleasure-grounds on the eastern side, because Mr. Lingon, who was one of them, was going home, and his road lay through the stone gateway into the park.

Uncle Lingon, who disliked painful confidences, and preferred knowing "no mischief of anybody," had not objected to being let into the important secret about Esther, and was sure at once that the whole affair, instead of being a misfortune, was a piece of excellent luck. For himself, he did not profess to be a judge of women, but she seemed to have all the "points," and to carry herself as well as Arabella did, which was saying a good deal. Honest Jack Lingon's first impressions quickly became traditions which no subsequent evidence could disturb. He was fond of his sister, and seemed never to be conscious of any change for the worse in her since their early time. He considered that man a beast who said anything unpleasant about the persons to whom he was attached. It was not that he winked; his wide-open eyes saw nothing but what his easy disposition inclined him to see. Harold was a good fellow; a clever chap; and Esther's peculiar fitness for him, under all the circumstances, was extraordinary: it reminded him of something in the classics, though he couldn't think exactly what—in fact, a memory was a nasty uneasy thing. Esther was always glad when the old Rector came. With an odd contrariety to her former niceties she liked his rough attire and careless frank speech; they were something not point device that seemed to connect the life of Transome Court with that rougher, commoner world where her home had been.

She and Harold were walking a little in advance of the rest of the party, who were retarded by various causes. Old Mr. Transome, wrapped in a cloth cloak trimmed with sable, and with a soft warm cap also trimmed with fur on his head, had a shuffling uncertain walk. Little Harry was dragging a toy vehicle, on the seat of which he had insisted on tying Moro, with a piece of scarlet drapery round him, making him look like a barbaric prince in a chariot. Moro, having little imagination, objected to this, and barked with feeble snappishness as the tyrannous lad ran forward, then whirled the chariot round and ran back to "Gappa," then came to a dead stop, which overset the chariot, that he might watch Uncle Lingon's water-spaniel run for the hurled stick and bring it in his mouth. Nimrod kept close to his old master's legs, glancing with much indifference at this youthful ardor about sticks— he had "gone through all that"; and Dominic walked by, looking on blandly, and taking care both of young and old. Mrs. Transome was not there.

Looking back and seeing that they were a good deal in advance of the rest, Esther and Harold paused.

"What do you think about thinning the trees over there?" said Harold, pointing with his stick. "I have a bit of a notion that if they were divided into clumps so as to show the oaks beyond it would be a great improvement. It would give an idea of extent that is lost now. And there might be some very pretty clumps got out of those mixed trees. What do you think?"

"I should think it would be an improvement. One likes a 'beyond' everywhere. But I never heard you express yourself so dubiously," said Esther, looking at him rather archly: "you generally see things so clearly, and are so convinced, that I shall begin to feel quite tottering if I find you in uncertainty. Pray don't begin to be doubtful; it is so infectious."

"You think me a great deal too sure—too confident?" said Harold.

"Not at all. It is an immense advantage to know your own will when you always mean to have it."

"But suppose I couldn't get it, in spite of meaning?" said Harold, with a beaming inquiry in his eyes.

"Oh, then," said Esther, turning her head aside, carelessly, as if she were considering the distant birch-stems, "you would bear it quite easily, as you did your not getting into Parliament. You would know you could get it another time—or get something else as good."

"The fact is," said Harold, moving on a little, as if he did not want to be quite overtaken by the others, "you consider me a fat, fatuous, self-satisfied fellow."

"Oh, there are degrees," said Esther, with a silvery laugh; "you have just as much of those qualities as is becoming. There are different styles. You are perfect in your own."

"But you prefer another style, I suspect. A more submissive, tearful, devout worshipper, who would offer his incense with more trembling."

"You are quite mistaken," said Esther, still lightly. "I find I am very wayward. When anything is offered to me, it seems that I prize it less, and don't want to have it."

Here was a very balky answer, but in spite of it Harold could not help believing that Esther was very far from objecting to the sort of incense he had been offering just then.

"I have often read that that is in human nature," she went on, "yet it takes me by surprise in myself. I suppose," she added, smiling, "I didn't think of myself as human nature."

"I don't confess to the same waywardness," said Harold. "I am very fond of things that I can get. And I never longed much for anything out of my reach. Whatever I feel sure of getting I like all the better. I think half those priggish maxims about human nature in the lump are no more to be relied on than universal remedies. There are different sorts of human nature. Some are given to discontent and longing, others to securing and enjoying. And let me tell you, the discontented, longing style is unpleasant to live with."

Harold nodded with a meaning smile at Esther.

"Oh, I assure you I have abjured all admiration for it," she said, smiling up at him in return.

She was remembering the schooling Felix had given her about her Byronic heroes, and was inwardly adding a third sort of human nature to those varieties which Harold had mentioned. He naturally supposed that he might take the abjuration to be entirely in his own favor. And his face did look very pleasant; she could not help liking him, although he was certainly too particular about sauces, gravies, and wines, and had a way of virtually measuring the value of everything by the contribution it made to his own pleasure. His very good nature was unsympathetic: it never came from any thorough understanding or deep respect for what was in the mind of the person he obliged or indulged; it was like his kindness to his mother—an arrangement of his for the happiness of others, which, if they were sensible, ought to succeed. And an inevitable comparison which haunted her showed her the same quality in his political views: the utmost enjoyment of his own advantages was the solvent that blended pride in his family and position with the adhesion to changes that were to obliterate tradition and melt down enchased gold heirlooms into plating for the egg-spoons of "the people." It is terrible—the keen bright eye of a woman when it has once been turned with admiration on what is severely true; but then the severely true rarely comes within its range of vision. Esther had had an unusual illumination; Harold did not know how, but he discerned enough of the effect to make him more cautious than he had ever been in his life before. That caution would have prevented him just then from following up the question as to the style of person Esther would think pleasant to live with, even if Uncle Lingon had not joined them, as he did, to talk about soughing tiles; saying presently that he should turn across the grass and get on to the Home Farm, to have a look at the improvements that Harold was making with such racing speed.

"But you know, lad," said the Rector, as they paused at the expected parting, "you can't do everything in a hurry. The wheat must have time to grow, even when you've reformed all us old Tories off the face of the ground. Dash it!

now the election's over, I'm an old Tory again. You see, Harold, a Radical won't do for the county. At another election you must be on the lookout for a borough where they want a bit of blood. I should have liked you uncommonly to stand for the county; and a Radical of good family squares well enough with a new-fashioned Tory like young Debarry; but, you see, these riots—it's been a nasty business; I shall have my hair combed at the sessions for a year to come. But, hey-day! What dame is this, with a small boy?—not one of my parishioners?"

Harold and Esther turned, and saw an elderly woman advancing with a tiny red-haired boy, scantily attired as to his jacket, which merged into a small sparrow-tail a little higher than his waist, but muffled as to his throat with a blue woollen comforter. Esther recognized the pair too well, and felt very uncomfortable. We are so pitiably in subjection to all sorts of vanity—even the very vanities we are practically renouncing! And in spite of the almost solemn memories connected with Mrs. Holt, Esther's first shudder was raised by the idea of what things this woman would say, and by the mortification of having Felix in any way represented by his mother.

As Mrs. Holt advanced into closer observation, it became more evident that she was attired with a view not to charm the eye, but rather to afflict it with all that expression of woe which belongs to very rusty bombazine and the limpest state of false hair. Still, she was not a woman to lose the sense of her own value, or become abject in her manners under any circumstances of depression; and she had a peculiar sense on the present occasion that she was justly relying on the force of her own character and judgment, in independence of anything that Mr. Lyon or the masterful Felix would have said, if she had thought them worthy to know of her undertaking. She courtesied once, as if to the entire group, now including even the dogs, who showed various degrees of curiosity, especially as to what kind of game the smaller animal Job might prove to be after due investigation; and then she proceeded at once toward Esther, who, in spite of her annoyance, took her arm from Harold's, said, "How do you do, Mrs. Holt?" very kindly, and stooped to pat little Job.

"Yes—you know him, Miss Lyon," said Mrs. Holt in that tone which implies that the conversation is intended for the edification of the company generally; "you know the orphin child, as Felix brought home for me that am his mother to take care of. And it's what I've done—nobody more so—though it's trouble is my reward."

Esther had raised herself again, to stand in helpless endurance of whatever might be coming. But by this time young Harry, struck even more than the dogs by the appearance of Job Tudge, had come round dragging his chariot, and placed himself close to the pale child, whom he exceeded in height and breadth, as well as in depth of coloring. He looked into Job's eyes, peeped round at the tail of his jacket, and pulled it a little, and then, taking off the tiny cloth cap, observed with much interest the tight red curls which had been hidden underneath it. Job looked at his inspector with the round blue eyes of astonishment, until Harry, purely by way of experiment, took a bon-bon from a fantastic wallet which hung over his shoulder and applied the test to Job's lips. The result was satisfactory to both. Every one had been watching this small comedy, and when Job crunched the bon-bon while Harry looked down at him inquiringly and patted his back, there was general laughter except on the part of Mrs. Holt, who was shaking her head slowly, and slapping the back of her left hand with the painful patience of a tragedian whose part is in abeyance to an ill-timed introduction of the humorous.

"I hope Job's cough has been better lately," said Esther, in mere uncertainty as to what it would be desirable to say or do.

"I dare say you hope so, Miss Lyon," said Mrs. Holt, looking at the distant landscape. "I've no reason to disbelieve but what you wish well to the child, and to Felix, and to me. I'm sure nobody has any occasion to wish me otherways. My character will bear inquiry, and what you, as are young, don't know, others can tell you. That was what I said to myself when I made up my mind to come here and see you, and ask you to get me the freedom to speak to Mr. Transome. I said, whatever Miss Lyon may be now, in the way of being lifted

up among great people, she's our minister's daughter, and
was not above coming to my house and walking with my son
Felix—though I'll not deny he made that figure on the Lord's
Day that'll perhaps go against him with the judge, if anybody thinks well to tell him."

Here Mrs. Holt paused a moment, as with a mind arrested
by the painful image it had called up.

Esther's face was glowing, when Harold glanced at her;
and, seeing this, he was considerate enough to address Mrs.
Holt instead of her.

"You are then the mother of the unfortunate young man
who is in prison?"

"Indeed I am, sir," said Mrs. Holt, feeling that she was
now in deep water. "It's not likely I should claim him if
he wasn't my own; though it's not by my will, nor my advice, sir, that he ever walked; for I gave him none but good.
But if everybody's son was guided by their mothers, the
world 'ud be different; my son is not worse than many another woman's son, and that in Treby, whatever they may
say as haven't got their sons in prison. And as to his giving
up the doctoring, and then stopping his father's medicines, I
know it's bad—that I know—but it's me has had to suffer,
and it's me a king and Parliament 'ud consider, if they meant
to do the right thing, and had anybody to make it known to
'em. And as for the rioting and killing the constable—my
son said most plain to me he never meant it, and there was
his bit of potato-pie for his dinner getting dry by the fire, the
whole blessed time as I sat and never knew what was coming
on me. And it's my opinion as if great people make elections
to get themselves into Parliament, and there's riot and murder to do it, they ought to see it as the widow and the
widow's son doesn't suffer for it. I well know my duty:
and I read my Bible; and I know in Jude, where it's been
stained with the dried tulip-leaves this many a year, as you're
told not to rail at your betters if they was the devil himself;
nor will I; but this I do say, if it's three Mr. Transomes instead of one as is listening to me, as there's them ought to
go to the king and get him to let off my son Felix."

This speech, in its chief points, had been deliberately prepared. Mrs. Holt had set her face like a flint, to make the gentry know their duty as she knew hers: her defiant defensive tone was due to the consciousness, not only that she was braving a powerful audience, but that she was daring to stand on the strong basis of her own judgment in opposition to her son's. Her proposals had been waived off by Mr. Lyon and Felix: but she had long had the feminine conviction that if she could "get to speak" in the right quarter, things might be different. The daring bit of impromptu about the three Mr. Transomes was immediately suggested by a movement of old Mr. Transome to the foreground in a line with Mr. Lingon and Harold; his furred and unusual costume appearing to indicate a mysterious dignity which she must hasten to include in her appeal.

And there were reasons that none could have foreseen which made Mrs. Holt's remonstrance immediately effective. While old Mr. Transome stared, very much like a waxen image in which the expression is a failure, and the Rector, accustomed to female parishioners and complainants, looked on with a smile in his eyes, Harold said at once, with cordial kindness, —

"I think you are quite right, Mrs. Holt. And for my part, I am determined to do my best for your son, both in the witness-box and elsewhere. Take comfort; if it is necessary, the king shall be appealed to. And rely upon it, I shall bear you in mind as Felix Holt's mother."

Rapid thoughts had convinced Harold that in this way he was best commending himself to Esther.

"Well, sir," said Mrs. Holt, who was not going to pour forth disproportionate thanks, "I am glad to hear you speak so becoming; and if you had been the king himself, I should have made free to tell you my opinion. For the Bible says, the king's favor is toward a wise servant; and it's reasonable to think he'd make all the more account of them as have never been in service, or took wage, which I never did, and never thought of my son doing; and his father left money, meaning otherways, so as he might have been a doctor on horseback at this very minute, instead of being in prison."

"What! was he regularly apprenticed to a doctor?" said Mr. Lingon, who had not understood this before.

"Sir, he was, and most clever, like his father before him, only he turned contrairy. But as for harming anybody, Felix never meant to harm anybody but himself and his mother, which he certainly did in respect of his clothes, and taking to be a low working man, and stopping my living respectable, more particular by the pills, which had a sale, as you may be sure they suited people's insides. And what folks can never have boxes enough of to swallow, I should think you have a right to sell. And there's many and many a text for it, as I've opened on without ever thinking; for if it's true, 'Ask, and you shall have,' I should think it's truer when you're willing to pay for what you have."

This was a little too much for Mr. Lingon's gravity; he exploded, and Harold could not help following him. Mrs. Holt fixed her eyes on the distance, and slapped the back of her left hand again: it might be that this kind of mirth was the peculiar effect produced by forcible truth on high and worldly people who were neither in the Independent nor the General Baptist connection.

"I'm sure you must be tired with your long walk, and little Job too," said Esther, by way of breaking this awkward scene. "Aren't you, Job?" she added, stooping to caress the child, who was timidly shrinking from Harry's invitation to him to pull the little chariot—Harry's view being that Job would make a good horse for him to beat, and would run faster than Gappa.

"It's well you can feel for the orphin child, Miss Lyon," said Mrs. Holt, choosing an indirect answer rather than to humble herself by confessing fatigue before gentlemen who seemed to be taking her too lightly. "I didn't believe but what you'd behave pretty, as you always did to me, though everybody used to say you held yourself high. But I'm sure you never did to Felix, for you let him sit by you at the Free School before all the town, and him with never a bit of stock round his neck. And it shows you saw *that* in him worth taking notice of;—and it is but right, if you know my words are true, as you should speak for him to the gentlemen."

"I assure you, Mrs. Holt," said Harold, coming to the rescue—"I assure you that enough has been said to make me use

my best efforts for your son. And now, pray, go on to the
house with the little boy and take some rest. Dominic, show
Mrs. Holt the way, and ask Mrs. Hickes to make her comfortable, and see that somebody takes her back to Treby in the
buggy."

"I will go back with Mrs. Holt," said Esther, making an
effort against herself.

"No, pray," said Harold, with that kind of entreaty which
is really a decision. "Let Mrs. Holt have time to rest. We
shall have returned, and you can see her before she goes. We
will say good-by for the present, Mrs. Holt."

The poor woman was not sorry to have the prospect of rest
and food, especially for "the orphin child," of whom she was
tenderly careful. Like many women who appear to others to
have a masculine decisiveness of tone, and to themselves to
have a masculine force of mind, and who come into severe
collision with sons arrived at the masterful stage, she had the
maternal cord vibrating strongly within her toward all tiny
children. And when she saw Dominic pick up Job and hoist
him on his arm for a little while, by way of making acquaintance, she regarded him with an approval which she had not
thought it possible to extend to a foreigner. Since Dominic
was going, Harry and old Mr. Transome chose to follow.
Uncle Lingon shook hands and turned off across the grass, and
thus Esther was left alone with Harold.

But there was a new consciousness between them. Harold's
quick perception was least likely to be slow in seizing indications of anything that might affect his position with regard to
Esther. Some time before, his jealousy had been awakened
to the possibility that before she had known him she had been
deeply interested in some one else. Jealousy of all sorts—
whether for our fortune or our love—is ready at combinations,
and likely even to outstrip the fact. And Esther's renewed
confusion, united with her silence about Felix, which now first
seemed noteworthy, and with Mrs. Holt's graphic details as
to her walking with him and letting him sit by her before all
the town, were grounds not merely for a suspicion, but for a
conclusion in Harold's mind. The effect of this, which he at
once regarded as a discovery, was rather different from what

Esther had anticipated. It seemed to him that Felix was the least formidable person that he could have found out as an object of interest antecedent to himself. A young workman who had got himself thrown into prison, whatever recommendations he might have had for a girl at a romantic age in the dreariness of Dissenting society at Treby, could hardly be considered by Harold in the light of a rival. Esther was too clever and tasteful a woman to make a ballad heroine of herself by bestowing her beauty and her lands on this lowly lover. Besides, Harold cherished the belief that, at the present time, Esther was more wisely disposed to bestow these things on another lover in every way eligible. But in two directions this discovery had a determining effect on him: his curiosity was stirred to know exactly what the relation with Felix had been, and he was solicitous that his behavior with regard to this young man should be such as to enhance his own merit in Esther's eyes. At the same time he was not inclined to any euphemisms that would seem by any possibility to bring Felix into the lists with himself.

Naturally, when they were left alone, it was Harold who spoke first. "I should think there's a good deal of worth in this young fellow—this Holt, notwithstanding the mistakes he has made. A little queer and conceited, perhaps; but that is usually the case with men of his class when they are at all superior to their fellows."

"Felix Holt is a highly cultivated man; he is not at all conceited," said Esther. The different kinds of pride within her were coalescing now. She was aware that there had been a betrayal.

"Ah?" said Harold, not quite liking the tone of this answer. "This eccentricity is a sort of fanaticism, then?— this giving up being a doctor on horseback, as the old woman calls it, and taking to—let me see—watchmaking, isn't it?"

"If it is eccentricity to be very much better than other men, he is certainly eccentric; and fanatical too, if it is fanatical to renounce all small selfish motives for the sake of a great and unselfish one. I never knew what nobleness of character really was before I knew Felix Holt."

It seemed to Esther as if, in the excitement of this moment, her own words were bringing her a clearer revelation.

"God bless me!" said Harold, in a tone of surprised yet thorough belief, and looking in Esther's face. "I wish you had talked to me about this before."

Esther at that moment looked perfectly beautiful, with an expression which Harold had never hitherto seen. All the confusion which had depended on personal feeling had given way before the sense that she had to speak the truth about the man whom she felt to be admirable.

"I think I didn't see the meaning of anything fine—I didn't even see the value of my father's character, until I had been taught a little by hearing what Felix Holt said, and seeing that his life was like his words."

Harold looked and listened, and felt his slight jealousy allayed rather than heightened. "This is not like love," he said to himself, with some satisfaction. With all due regard to Harold Transome, he was one of those men who are liable to make the greater mistakes about a particular woman's feelings because they pique themselves on a power of interpretation derived from much experience. Experience is enlightening, but with a difference. Experiments on live animals may go on for a long period, and yet the fauna on which they are made may be limited. There may be a passion in the mind of a woman which precipitates her, not along the path of easy beguilement, but into a great leap away from it. Harold's experience had not taught him this; and Esther's enthusiasm about Felix Holt did not seem to him to be dangerous.

"He's quite an apostolic sort of fellow, then," was the self-quieting answer he gave to her last words. "He didn't look like that; but I had only a short interview with him, and I was given to understand that he refused to see me in prison. I believe he's not very well inclined toward me. But you saw a great deal of him, I suppose; and your testimony to any one is enough for me," said Harold, lowering his voice rather tenderly. "Now I know what your opinion is, I shall spare no effort on behalf of such a young man. In fact, I had come to the same resolution before, but your wish would make difficult things easy."

27

After that energetic speech of Esther's, as often happens, the tears had just suffused her eyes. It was nothing more than might have been expected in a tender-hearted woman, considering Felix Holt's circumstances, and the tears only made more lovely the look with which she met Harold's when he spoke so kindly. She felt pleased with him; she was open to the fallacious delight of being assured that she had power over him to make him do what she liked, and quite forgot the many impressions which had convinced her that Harold had a padded yoke ready for the neck of every man, woman, and child that depended on him.

After a short silence, they were getting near the stone gateway, and Harold said, with an air of intimate consultation,—

"What could we do for this young man, supposing he were let off? I shall send a letter with fifty pounds to the old woman to-morrow. I ought to have done it before, but it really slipped my memory, amongst the many things that have occupied me lately. But this young man—what do you think would be the best thing we could do for him, if he gets at large again? He should be put in a position where his qualities could be more telling."

Esther was recovering her liveliness a little, and was disposed to encourage it for the sake of veiling other feelings, about which she felt renewed reticence, now that the overpowering influence of her enthusiasm was past. She was rather wickedly amused and scornful at Harold's misconceptions and ill-placed intentions of patronage.

"You are hopelessly in the dark," she said, with a light laugh and toss of her head. "What would you offer Felix Holt? a place in the Excise? You might as well think of offering it to John the Baptist. Felix has chosen his lot. He means always to be a poor man."

"Means? Yes," said Harold, slightly piqued, "but what a man means usually depends on what happens. I mean to be a commoner; but a peerage might present itself under acceptable circumstances."

"Oh, there is no sum in proportion to be done there," said

Esther, again gayly. "As you are to a peerage, so is *not* Felix Holt to any offer of advantage that you could imagine for him."

"You must think him fit for any position—the first in the county."

"No, I don't," said Esther, shaking her head mischievously. "I think him too high for it."

"I see you can be ardent in your admiration."

"Yes, it is my champagne; you know I don't like the other kind."

"That would be satisfactory if one were sure of getting your admiration," said Harold, leading her up to the terrace, and amongst the crocuses, from whence they had a fine view of the park and river. They stood still near the east parapet, and saw the dash of light on the water, and the pencilled shadows of the trees on the grassy lawn.

"Would it do as well to admire you, instead of being worthy to be admired?" said Harold, turning his eyes from that land-scape to Esther's face.

"It would be a thing to be put up with," said Esther, smiling at him rather roguishly. "But you are not in that state of self-despair."

"Well, I am conscious of not having those severe virtues that you have been praising."

"That is true. You are quite in another *genre*."

"A woman would not find me a tragic hero."

"Oh, no! She must dress for genteel comedy—such as your mother once described to me—where the most thrilling event is the drawing of a handsome check."

"You are a naughty fairy," said Harold, daring to press Esther's hand a little more closely to him, and drawing her down the eastern steps into the pleasure-ground, as if he were unwilling to give up the conversation. "Confess that you are disgusted with my want of romance."

"I shall not confess to being disgusted. I shall ask you to confess that you are not a romantic figure."

"I am a little too stout."

"For romance—yes. At least you must find security for not getting stouter."

"And I don't look languishing enough?"

"Oh, yes—rather too much so—at a fine cigar."

"And I am not in danger of committing suicide?"

"No; you are a widower."

Harold did not reply immediately to this last thrust of Esther's. She had uttered it with innocent thoughtlessness from the playful suggestions of the moment; but it was a fact that Harold's previous married life had entered strongly into her impressions about him. The presence of Harry made it inevitable. Harold took this allusion of Esther's as an indication that his quality of widower was a point that made against him; and after a brief silence he said, in an altered, more serious tone,—

"You don't suppose, I hope, that any other woman has ever held the place that you could hold in my life?"

Esther began to tremble a little, as she always did when the love-talk between them seemed getting serious. She only gave the rather stumbling answer, "How so?"

"Harry's mother had been a slave—was bought, in fact."

It was impossible for Harold to preconceive the effect this had on Esther. His natural disqualification for judging of a girl's feelings was heightened by the blinding effect of an exclusive object—which was to assure her that her own place was peculiar and supreme. Hitherto Esther's acquaintance with Oriental love was derived chiefly from Byronic poems, and this had not sufficed to adjust her mind to a new story, where the Giaour concerned was giving her his arm. She was unable to speak; and Harold went on,—

"Though I am close on thirty-five, I never met with a woman at all like you before. There are new eras in one's life that are equivalent to youth—are something better than youth. I was never an aspirant till I knew you."

Esther was still silent.

"Not that I dare to call myself that. I am not so confident a, personage as you imagine. I am necessarily in a painful position for a man who has any feeling."

Here at last Harold had stirred the right fibre. Esther's generosity seized at once the whole meaning implied in that last sentence. She had a fine sensibility to the line at which flirtation must cease; and she was now pale, and shaking with feelings she had not yet defined for herself.

"Do not let us speak of difficult things any more now," she said, with gentle seriousness. "I am come into a new world of late, and have to learn life all over again. Let us go in. I must see poor Mrs. Holt again, and my little friend Job."

She paused at the glass door that opened on the terrace, and entered there, while Harold went round to the stables.

When Esther had been upstairs and descended again into the large entrance hall, she found its stony spaciousness made lively by human figures extremely unlike the statues. Since Harry insisted on playing with Job again, Mrs. Holt and her orphan, after dining, had just been brought to this delightful scene for a game of hide-and-seek, and for exhibiting the climbing powers of the two pet squirrels. Mrs. Holt sat on a stool, in singular relief against the pedestal of the Apollo, while Dominic and Denner (otherwise Mrs. Hickes) bore her company; Harry, in his bright red and purple, flitted about like a great tropic bird after the sparrow-tailed Job, who hid himself with much intelligence behind the scagliola pillars and the pedestals; while one of the squirrels perched itself on the head of the tallest statue, and the other was already peeping down from among the heavy stuccoed angels on the ceiling. near the summit of a pillar.

Mrs. Holt held on her lap a basket filled with good things for Job, and seemed much soothed by pleasant company and excellent treatment. As Esther, descending softly and unobserved, leaned over the stone banisters and looked at the scene for a minute or two, she saw that Mrs. Holt's attention, having been directed to the squirrel which had scampered on to the head of the Silenus carrying the infant Bacchus, had been drawn downward to the tiny babe looked at with so much affection by the rather ugly and hairy gentleman, of whom she nevertheless spoke with reserve as of one who possibly belonged to the Transome family.

"It's most pretty to see its little limbs, and the gentleman holding it. I should think he was amiable by his look; but it was odd he should have his likeness took without any clothes.

Was he Transome by name?" (Mrs. Holt suspected that there might be a mild madness in the family.)

Denner, peering and smiling quietly, was about to reply, when she was prevented by the appearance of old Mr. Transome, who since his walk had been having "forty winks" on the sofa in the library, and now came out to look for Harry. He had doffed his fur cap and cloak, but in lying down to sleep he had thrown over his shoulders a soft Oriental scarf which Harold had given him, and this still hung over his scanty white hair and down to his knees, held fast by his wooden-looking arms and laxly clasped hands, which fell in front of him.

This singular appearance of an undoubted Transome fitted exactly into Mrs. Holt's thought at the moment. It lay in the probabilities of things that gentry's intellects should be peculiar: since they had not to get their own living, the good Lord might have economized in their case that common sense which others were so much more in need of; and in the shuffling figure before her she saw a descendant of the gentleman who had chosen to be represented without his clothes—all the more eccentric where there were the means of buying the best. But these oddities "said nothing" in great folks, who were powerful in high quarters all the same. And Mrs. Holt rose and courtesied with a proud respect, precisely as she would have done if Mr. Transome had looked as wise as Lord Burleigh.

"I hope I'm in no way taking a liberty, sir," she began, while the old gentleman looked at her with bland feebleness; "I'm not that woman to sit anywhere out of my own home without inviting and pressing too. But I was brought here to wait, because the little gentleman wanted to play with the orphin child."

"Very glad, my good woman—sit down—sit down," said Mr. Transome, nodding and smiling between his clauses. "Nice little boy. Your grandchild?"

"Indeed, sir, no," said Mrs. Holt, continuing to stand. Quite apart from any awe of Mr. Transome, sitting down, she felt, would be a too great familiarity with her own pathetic importance on this extra and unlooked-for occasion.

"It's not me has any grandchild, nor ever shall have, though most fit. But with my only son saying he'll never be married, and in prison besides, and some saying he'll be transported, you may see yourself—though a gentleman—as there isn't much chance of my having grandchildren of my own. And this is old Master Tudge's grandchild, as my own Felix took to for pity because he was sickly and clemm'd, and I was noways against it, being of a tender heart. For I'm a widow myself, and my son Felix, though big, is fatherless, and I know my duty in consequence. And it's to be wished, sir, as others should know it as are more in power and live in great houses, and can ride in a carriage where they will. And if you're tho gentleman as is the head of everything—and it's not to be thought you'd give up to your son as a poor widow's been forced to do—it behooves you to take the part of them as are deserving; for the Bible says, gray hairs should speak."

"Yes, yes—poor woman—what shall I say?" said old Mr. Transome, feeling himself scolded, and as usual desirous of mollifying displeasure.

"Sir, I can tell you what to say fast enough; for it's what I should say myself if I could get to speak to the king. For I've asked them that know, and they say it's the truth both out of the Bible and in as the king can pardon anything and anybody. And judging by his countenance on the new signs, and the talk there was a while ago about his being the people's friend, as the minister once said it from the very pulpit—if there's any meaning in words, he'll do the right thing by me and my son, if he's asked proper."

"Yes—a very good man—he'll do anything right," said Mr. Transome, whose own ideas about the king just then were somewhat misty, consisting chiefly in broken reminiscences of George the Third. "I'll ask him anything you like," he added, with a pressing desire to satisfy Mrs. Holt, who alarmed him slightly.

"Then, sir, if you'll go in your carriage and say, This young man, Felix Holt by name, as his father was known the country round, and his mother most respectable—he never meant harm to anybody, and so far from bloody murder and fighting would part with his victual to them that needed it more—and if you'd get other gentlemen to say the same, and if they're not satisfied to inquire—I'll not believe but what the king 'ud let my son out of prison. Or if it's true he must stand his trial, the king 'ud take care no mischief happened to him. I've got my senses, and I'll never believe as in a country where there's a God above and a king below the right thing can't be done if great people was willing to do it."

Mrs. Holt, like all orators, had waxed louder and more energetic, ceasing to propel her arguments, and being propelled by them. Poor old Mr. Transome, getting more and more frightened at this severe-spoken woman, who had the horrible possibility to his mind of being a novelty that was to become permanent, seemed to be fascinated by fear, and stood helplessly forgetful that if he liked he might turn round and walk away.

Little Harry, alive to anything that had relation to "Gappa," had paused in his game, and, discerning what he thought a hostile aspect in this naughty black old woman, rushed toward her, and proceeded first to beat her with his mimic jockey's whip, and then, suspecting that her bombazine was not sensitive, to set his teeth in her arm. While Dominic rebuked him and pulled him off, Nimrod began to bark anxiously, and the scene was become alarming even to the squirrels, which scrambled as far off as possible.

Esther, who had been waiting for an opportunity of intervention, now came up to Mrs. Holt, to speak some soothing words; and old Mr. Transome, seeing a sufficient screen between himself and his formidable suppliant, at last gathered courage to turn round and shuffle away with unusual swiftness into the library.

"Dear Mrs. Holt," said Esther, "do rest comforted. I assure you you have done the utmost that can be done by your words. Your visit has not been thrown away. See how the children have enjoyed it! I saw little Job actually laughing. I think I never saw him do more than smile before." Then, turning round to Dominic, she said, "Will the buggy come round to this door?"

This hint was sufficient. Dominic went to see if the vehicle was ready, and Denner, remarking that Mrs. Holt would like to mount it in the inner court, invited her to go back into the housekeeper's room. But there was a fresh resistance raised in Harry by the threatened departure of Job, who had seemed an invaluable addition to the menagerie of tamed creatures; and it was barely in time that Esther had the relief of seeing the entrance hall cleared so as to prevent any further encounter of Mrs. Holt with Harold, who was now coming up the flight of steps at the entrance.

CHAPTER XLIV.

I'm sick at heart. The eye of day,
The insistent summer noon, seems pitiless,
Shining in all the barren crevices
Of weary life, leaving no shade, no dark,
Where I may dream that hidden waters lie.

SHORTLY after Mrs. Holt's striking presentation of herself at Transome Court, Esther went on a second visit to her father. The Loamford Assizes were approaching; it was expected that in about ten days Felix Holt's trial would come on, and some hints in her father's letters had given Esther the impression that he was taking a melancholy view of the result. Harold Transome had once or twice mentioned the subject with a facile hopefulness as to "the young fellow's coming off easily," which, in her anxious mind, was not a counterpoise to disquieting suggestions, and she had not chosen to introduce another conversation about Felix Holt by questioning Harold concerning the probabilities he relied on. Since those moments on the terrace Harold had daily become more of the solicitous and indirectly beseeching lover; and Esther, from the very fact that she was weighed on by thoughts that were painfully bewildering to her—by thoughts which, in their newness to her young mind, seemed to shake her belief that life could be anything else than a compromise with things repugnant to the moral taste—had become more passive to his attentions at the very time that she had begun to feel more profoundly that in accepting Harold Transome she left the high mountain air, the passionate serenity, of perfect love forever behind her, and must adjust her wishes to a life of

middling delights, overhung with the languorous haziness of
motiveless ease, where poetry was only literature, and the fine
ideas had to be taken down from the shelves of the library
when her husband's back was turned. But it seemed as if all
outward conditions concurred, along with her generous sympathy for the Transomes, and with those native tendencies
against which she had once begun to struggle, to make this
middling lot the best she could attain to. She was in this
half-sad half-satisfied resignation to something like what is
called worldly wisdom when she went to see her father, and
learn what she could from him about Felix.

The little minister was much depressed, unable to resign
himself to the dread which had begun to haunt him, that
Felix might have to endure the odious penalty of transportation for the manslaughter, which was the offence that no evidence in his favor could disprove.

"I had been encouraged by the assurances of men instructed
in this regard," said Mr. Lyon, while Esther sat on the stool
near him, and listened anxiously, "that, though he were pronounced guilty in regard to this deed whereinto he hath ca-
lamitously fallen, yet that a judge mildly disposed, and with
a due sense of that invisible activity of the soul whereby the
deeds which are the same in outward appearance and effect
yet differ as the knife-stroke of the surgeon, even though it
kill, differs from the knife-stroke of a wanton mutilator, might
use his discretion in tempering the punishment so that it would
not be very evil to bear. But now it is said that the judge
who cometh is a severe man, and one nourishing a prejudice
against the bolder spirits who stand not in the old paths."

"I am going to be present at the trial, father," said Esther,
who was preparing the way to express a wish which she was
timid about even with her father. "I mentioned to Mrs.
Transome that I should like to do so, and she said that she
used in old days always to attend the assizes, and that she
would take me. You will be there, father?"

"Assuredly I shall be there, having been summoned to bear
witness to Felix's character, and to his having uttered remonstrances and warnings long beforehand whereby he proved
himself an enemy to riot. In our ears, who know him, it

sounds strangely that aught else should be credible; but he hath few to speak for him, though I trust that Mr. Harold Transome's testimony will go far, if, as you say, he is disposed to set aside all minor regards, and not to speak the truth grudgingly and reluctantly. For the very truth hath a color from the disposition of the utterer."

"He is kind; he is capable of being generous," said Esther.

"It is well. For I verily believe that evil-minded men have been at work against Felix. The *Duffield Watchman* hath written continually in allusion to him as one of those mischievous men who seek to elevate themselves through the dishonor of their party; and as one of those who go not heart and soul with the needs of the people, but seek only to get a hearing for themselves by raising their voices in crotchety discord. It is these things that cause me heaviness of spirit: the dark secret of this young man's lot is a cross I carry daily."

"Father," said Esther, timidly, while the eyes of both were filling with tears, "I should like to see him again before his trial. Might I? Will you ask him? Will you take me?"

The minister raised his suffused eyes to hers, and did not speak for a moment or two. A new thought had visited him. But his delicate tenderness shrank even from an inward inquiry that was too curious—that seemed like an effort to peep at sacred secrets.

"I see nought against it, my dear child, if you arrived early enough, and would take the elderly lady into your confidence, so that you might descend from the carriage at some suitable place—the house of the Independent minister, for example—where I could meet and accompany you. I would forewarn Felix, who would doubtless delight to see your face again; seeing that he may go away, and be, as it were, buried from you, even though it may be only in prison, and not——"

This was too much for Esther. She threw her arms round her father's neck and sobbed like a child. It was an unspeakable relief to her after all the pent-up, stifling experience, all the inward, incommunicable debate, of the last few weeks. The old man was deeply moved, too, and held his arm close round the dear child, praying silently.

No word was spoken for some minutes, till Esther raised herself, dried her eyes, and with an action that seemed playful, though there was no smile on her face, pressed her handkerchief against her father's cheeks. Then, when she had put her hand in his, he said, solemnly,—

"'Tis a great and mysterious gift, this clinging of the heart, my Esther, whereby it hath often seemed to me that even in the very moment of suffering our souls have the keenest foretaste of heaven. I speak not lightly, but as one who hath endured. And 'tis a strange truth that only in the agony of parting we look into the depths of love."

So the interview ended, without any question from Mr. Lyon concerning what Esther contemplated as the ultimate arrangement between herself and the Transomes.

After this conversation, which showed him that what happened to Felix touched Esther more closely than he had supposed, the minister felt no impulse to raise the images of a future so unlike anything that Felix would share. And Esther would have been unable to answer any such questions. The successive weeks, instead of bringing her nearer to clearness and decision, had only brought that state of disenchantment belonging to the actual presence of things which have long dwelt in the imagination with all the factitious charms of arbitrary arrangement. Her imaginary mansion had not been inhabited just as Transome Court was; her imaginary fortune had not been attended with circumstances which she was unable to sweep away. She herself, in her Utopia, had never been what she was now—a woman whose heart was divided and oppressed. The first spontaneous offering of her woman's devotion, the first great inspiration of her life, was a sort of vanished ecstasy which had left its wounds. It seemed to her a cruel misfortune of her young life that her best feeling, her most precious dependence, had been called forth just where the conditions were hardest, and that all the easy invitations of circumstance were toward something which that previous consecration of her longing had made a moral descent for her. It was characteristic of her that she scarcely at all entertained the alternative of such a compromise as would have given her the larger portion of the fortune to which she had a legal claim, and yet have satisfied her sympathy by leaving the Transomes in possession of their old home. Her domestication with this family had brought them into the foreground of her imagination; the gradual wooing of Harold had acted on her with a constant immediate influence that predominated over all indefinite prospects; and a solitary elevation to wealth, which out of Utopia she had no notion how she should manage, looked as chill and dreary as the offer of dignities in an unknown country.

In the ages since Adam's marriage it has been good for some men to be alone, and for some women also. But Esther was not one of these women: she was intensely of the feminine type, verging neither toward the saint nor the angel. She was "a fair divided excellence, whose fulness of perfection" must be in marriage. And, like all youthful creatures, she felt as if the present conditions of choice were final. It belonged to the freshness of her heart that, having had her emotions strongly stirred by real objects, she never speculated on possible relations yet to come. It seemed to her that she stood at the first and last parting of the ways. And, in one sense, she was under no illusion. It is only in that freshness of our time that the choice is possible which gives unity to life, and makes the memory a temple where all relics and all votive offerings, all worship and all grateful joy, are an unbroken history sanctified by one religion.

CHAPTER XLV.

We may not make this world a paradise
By walking it together with clasped hands
And eyes that meeting feed a double strength.
We must be only joined by pains divine,
Of spirits blent in mutual memories.

IT was a consequence of that interview with her father that when Esther stepped early on a gray March morning into the carriage with Mrs. Transome, to go to the Loamford Assizes, she was full of an expectation that held her lips in trembling silence, and gave her eyes that sightless beauty which tells that the vision is all within.

Mrs. Transome did not disturb her with unnecessary speech. Of late Esther's anxious observation had been drawn to a change in Mrs. Transome, shown in many small ways which only women notice. It was not only that when they sat together the talk seemed more of an effort to her: that might have come from the gradual draining away of matter for discourse pertaining to most sorts of companionship, in which repetition is not felt to be as desirable as novelty. But while Mrs. Transome was dressed just as usual, took her seat as usual, trifled with her drugs and had her embroidery before her as usual, and still made her morning greetings with that finished easy politeness and consideration of tone which to rougher people seems like affection, Esther noticed a strange fitfulness in her movements. Sometimes the stitches of her embroidery went on with silent unbroken swiftness for a quarter of an hour, as if she had to work out her deliverance from bondage by finishing a scroll-patterned border; then her hands dropped suddenly and her gaze fell blankly on the table before her, and she would sit in that way motionless as a seated statue, apparently unconscious of Esther's presence, till some thought darting within her seemed to have the effect of an external shock and roused her with a start, when she looked round hastily like a person ashamed of having slept. Esther, touched with wondering pity at signs of unhappiness that were new in her experience, took the most delicate care to appear inobservant, and only tried to increase the gentle attention that might help to soothe or gratify this uneasy woman. But, one morning, Mrs. Transome had said, breaking rather a long silence,—

"My dear, I shall make this house dull for you. You sit with me like an embodied patience. I am unendurable; I am getting into a melancholy dotage. A fidgety old woman like me is as unpleasant to see as a rook with its wing broken. Don't mind me, my dear. Run away from me without ceremony. Every one else does, you see. I am part of the old furniture with new drapery."

"Dear Mrs. Transome," said Esther, gliding to the low ottoman close by the basket of embroidery, "do you dislike my sitting with you?"

"Only for your own sake, my fairy," said Mrs. Transome, smiling faintly, and putting her hand under Esther's chin. "Doesn't it make you shudder to look at me?"

"Why will you say such naughty things?" said Esther affectionately. "If you had had a daughter, she would have desired to be with you most when you most wanted cheering. And surely every young woman has something of a daughter's feeling toward an older one who has been kind to her."

"I should like you to be really my daughter," said Mrs. Transome, rousing herself to look a little brighter. "That is something still for an old woman to hope for."

Esther blushed: she had not foreseen this application of words that came from pitying tenderness. To divert the train of thought as quickly as possible, she at once asked what she had previously had in her mind to ask. Before her blush had disappeared she said,—

"Oh, you are so good; I shall ask you to indulge me very much. It is to let us set out very early to Loamford on Wednesday, and put me down at a particular house, that I may keep an engagement with my father. It is a private matter, that I wish no one to know about, if possible. And he will bring me back to you whenever you appoint."

In that way Esther won her end without needing to betray it; and as Harold was already away at Loamford, she was the more secure.

The Independent minister's house, at which she was set down, and where she was received by her father, was in a quiet street not far from the jail. Esther had thrown a dark cloak over the handsomer coverings which Denner had assured her were absolutely required of ladies who sat anywhere near the judge at a great trial; and as the bonnet of that day did not throw the face into high relief, but rather into perspective, a veil drawn down gave her a sufficiently inconspicuous appearance.

"I have arranged all things, my dear," said Mr. Lyon, "and Felix expects us. We will lose no time."

They walked away at once, Esther not asking a question. She had no consciousness of the road along which they passed; she could never remember anything but a dim sense of entering within high walls and going along passages, till they were ushered into a larger space than she expected, and her father said,—

"It is here that we are permitted to see Felix, my Esther. He will presently appear."

Esther automatically took off her gloves and bonnet, as if she had entered the house after a walk. She had lost the complete consciousness of everything except that she was going to see Felix. She trembled. It seemed to her as if he too would look altered after her new life—as if even the past would change for her and be no longer a steadfast remembrance, but something she had been mistaken about, as she had been about the new life. Perhaps she was growing out of that childhood to which common things have rareness, and all objects look larger. Perhaps from henceforth the whole world was to be meaner for her. The dread concentrated in those moments seemed worse than anything she had known before. It was what the dread of the pilgrim might be who has it whispered to him that the holy places are a delusion, or that he will see them with a soul unstirred and unbelieving. Every minute that passes may be charged with some such crisis in the little inner world of man or woman.

But soon the door opened slightly; some one looked in; then it opened wide and Felix Holt entered.

"Miss Lyon—Esther!" and her hand was in his grasp.

He was just the same—no, something inexpressibly better, because of the distance and separation, and the half-weary novelties, which made him like the return of morning.

"Take no heed of me, children," said Mr. Lyon. "I have some notes to make, and my time is precious. We may remain here only a quarter of an hour." And the old man sat down at a window with his back to them, writing with his head bent close to the paper.

"You are very pale; you look ill, compared with your old self," said Esther. She had taken her hand away, but they stood still near each other, she looking up at him.

"The fact is, I'm not fond of prison," said Felix, smiling; "but I suppose the best I can hope for is to have a good deal more of it."

"It is thought that in the worst case a pardon may be obtained," said Esther, avoiding Harold Transome's name.

"I don't rely on that," said Felix, shaking his head. "My wisest course is to make up my mind to the very ugliest penalty they can condemn me to. If I can face that, anything less will seem easy. But you know," he went on, smiling at her brightly, "I never went in for fine company and cushions. I can't be very heavily disappointed in that way."

"Do you see things just as you used to do?" said Esther, turning pale as she said it—"I mean—about poverty, and the people you will live among. Has all the misunderstanding and sadness left you just as obstinate?" She tried to smile, but could not succeed.

"What—about the sort of life I should lead if I were free again?" said Felix.

"Yes. I can't help being discouraged for you by all these things that have happened. See how you may fail!" Esther spoke timidly. She saw a peculiar smile, which she knew well, gathering in his eyes. "Ah, I dare say I am silly," she said, deprecatingly

"No, you are dreadfully inspired," said Felix. "When the wicked Tempter is tired of snarling that word failure in a man's cell, he sends a voice like a thrush to say it for him. See now what a messenger of darkness you are!" He smiled, and took her two hands between his, pressed together as children hold them up in prayer. Both of them felt too solemnly to be bashful. They looked straight into each other's eyes, as angels do when they tell some truth. And they stood in that way while he went on speaking.

"But I'm proof against that word failure. I've seen behind it. The only failure a man ought to fear is failure in cleaving to the purpose he sees to be best. As to just the amount of result he may see from his particular work—that's a tremendous uncertainty: the universe has not been arranged for the gratification of his feelings. As long as a man sees and believes in some great good, he'll prefer working toward that in the way he's best fit for, come what may. I put effects at their minimum, but I'd rather have the minimum of effect, if it's of the sort I care for, than the maximum of

28

effect I don't care for—a lot of fine things that are not to my taste—and if they were, the conditions of holding them while the world is what it is are such as would jar on me like grating metal."

"Yes," said Esther, in a low tone, "I think I understand that now better than I used to do." The words of Felix at last seemed strangely to fit her own experience. But she said no more, though he seemed to wait for it a moment or two, looking at her. But then he went on,—

"I don't mean to be illustrious, you know, and make a new era, else it would be kind of you to get a raven and teach it to croak 'failure' in my ears. Where great things can't happen, I care for very small things, such as will never be known beyond a few garrets and workshops. And then, as to one thing I believe in, I don't think I can altogether fail. If there's anything our people want convincing of, it is that there's some dignity and happiness for a man other than changing his station. That's one of the beliefs I choose to consecrate my life to. If anybody could demonstrate to me that I was a flat for it, I shouldn't think it would follow that I must borrow money to set up genteelly and order new clothes. That's not a vigorous consequence to my understanding."

They smiled at each other, with the old sense of amusement they had so often had together.

"You are just the same," said Esther.

"And you?" said Felix. "My affairs have been settled long ago. But yours—a great change has come in them—magic at work."

"Yes," said Esther, rather falteringly.

"Well," said Felix, looking at her gravely again, "it's a case of fitness that seems to give a chance sanction to that musty law. The first time I saw you your birth was an immense puzzle to me. However, the appropriate conditions are come at last."

These words seemed cruel to Esther. But Felix could not know all the reasons for their seeming so. She could not speak; she was turning cold and feeling her heart beat painfully.

"All your tastes are gratified now," he went on innocently. "But you'll remember the old pedagogue and his lectures?"

One thought in the mind of Felix was that Esther was sure to marry Harold Transome. Men readily believe these things of the women who love them. But he could not allude to the marriage more directly. He was afraid of this destiny for her, without having any very distinct knowledge by which to justify his fear to the mind of another. It did not satisfy him that Esther should marry Harold Transome.

"My children," said Mr. Lyon at this moment, not looking round, but only looking close at his watch, "we have just two minutes more." Then he went on writing.

Esther did not speak, but Felix could not help observing now that her hands had turned to a deathly coldness, and that she was trembling. He believed, he knew, that whatever prospects she had this feeling was for his sake. An overpowering impulse from mingled love, gratitude, and anxiety urged him to say,—

"I had a horrible struggle, Esther. But you see I was right. There was a fitting lot in reserve for you. But remember you have cost a great price—don't throw what is precious away. I shall want the news that you have a happiness worthy of you."

Esther felt too miserable for tears to come. She looked helplessly at Felix for a moment, then took her hands from his, and, turning away mutely, walked dreamily toward her father, and said, "Father, I am ready—there is no more to say."

She turned back again, toward the chair where her bonnet lay, with a face quite corpse-like above her dark garment.

"Esther!"

She heard Felix say the word, with an entreating cry, and went toward him with the swift movement of a frightened child toward its protector. He clasped her, and they kissed each other.

She never could recall anything else that happened till she was in the carriage again with Mrs. Transome.

CHAPTER XLVI.

Why, there are maidens of heroic touch,
And yet they seem like things of gossamer
You'd pinch the life out of, as out of moths.
Oh, it is not loud tones and mouthingness,
'Tis not the arms akimbo and large strides,
That make a woman's force. The tiniest birds,
With softest downy breasts, have passions in them
And are brave with love.

ESTHER was so placed in the Court, under Mrs. Transome's
wing, as to see and hear everything without effort. Harold
had received them at the hotel, and had observed that Esther
looked ill, and was unusually abstracted in her manner; but
this seemed to be sufficiently accounted for by her sympathetic
anxiety about the result of a trial in which the prisoner at the
bar was a friend, and in which both her father and himself
were important witnesses. Mrs. Transome had no reluctance
to keep a small secret from her son, and no betrayal was made
of that previous "engagement" of Esther's with her father.
Harold was particularly delicate and unobtrusive in his attentions to-day: he had the consciousness that he was going to
behave in a way that would gratify Esther and win her admiration, and we are all of us made more graceful by the inward
presence of what we believe to be a generous purpose; our
actions move to a hidden music—"a melody that's sweetly
played in tune."

If Esther had been less absorbed by supreme feelings, she
would have been aware that she was an object of special notice. In the bare squareness of a public hall, where there was
not one jutting angle to hang a guess or a thought upon, not
an image or a bit of color to stir the fancy, and where the only
objects of speculation, of admiration, or of any interest whatever were human beings, and especially the human beings
that occupied positions indicating some importance, the notice bestowed on Esther would not have been surprising, even
if it had been merely a tribute to her youthful charm, which
was well companioned by Mrs. Transome's elderly majesty.
But it was due also to whisperings that she was an hereditary

claimant of the Transome estates, whom Harold Transome was about to marry. Harold himself had of late not cared to conceal either the fact or the probability : they both tended rather to his honor than his dishonor. And to-day, when there was a good proportion of Trebians present, the whisperings spread rapidly.

The Court was still more crowded than on the previous day, when our poor acquaintance Dredge and his two collier companions were sentenced to a year's imprisonment with hard labor, and the more enlightened prisoner, who stole the De-barry's plate, to transportation for life. Poor Dredge had cried, had wished he'd "never heared of a 'lection," and in spite of sermons from the jail chaplain fell back on the explanation that this was a world in which Spratt and Old Nick were sure to get the best of it; so that in Dredge's case, at least, most observers must have had the melancholy conviction that there had been no enhancement of public spirit and faith in progress from that wave of political agitation which had reached the Sproxton Pits.

But curiosity was necessarily at a higher pitch to-day, when the character of the prisoner and the circumstances of his offence were of a highly unusual kind. As soon as Felix appeared at the bar, a murmur rose and spread into a loud buzz, which continued until there had been repeated authoritative calls for silence in the Court. Rather singularly, it was now for the first time that Esther had a feeling of pride in him on the ground simply of his appearance. At this moment, when he was the centre of a multitudinous gaze, which seemed to act on her own vision like a broad unmitigated daylight, she felt that there was something pre-eminent in him, notwithstanding the vicinity of numerous gentlemen. No apple-woman would have admired him; not only to feminine minds like Mrs. Tiliot's, but to many minds in coat and waistcoat, there was something dangerous and perhaps unprincipled in his bare throat and great Gothic head; and his somewhat massive person would doubtless have come out very oddly from the hands of a fashionable tailor of that time. But as Esther saw his large gray eyes looking round calmly and undefiantly, first at the audience generally, and then with a more observant expression at the lawyers and other persons immediately around him, she felt that he bore the outward stamp of a distinguished nature. Forgive her if she needed this satisfaction: all of us—whether men or women—are liable to this weakness of liking to have our preference justified before others as well as ourselves. Esther said inwardly, with a certain triumph, that Felix Holt looked as worthy to be chosen in the midst of this large assembly as he had ever looked in their *tête-à-tête* under the sombre light of the little parlor in Malthouse Yard.

Esther had felt some relief in hearing from her father that Felix had insisted on doing without his mother's presence; and since to Mrs. Holt's imagination, notwithstanding her general desire to have her character inquired into, there was no greatly consolatory difference between being a witness and a criminal, and an appearance of any kind "before the judge" could hardly be made to suggest anything definite that would overcome the dim sense of unalleviated disgrace, she had been less inclined than usual to complain of her son's decision. Esther had shuddered beforehand at the inevitable farce there would be in Mrs. Holt's testimony. But surely Felix would lose something for want of a witness who could testify to his behavior in the morning before he became involved in the tumult?

"He is really a fine young fellow," said Harold, coming to speak to Esther after a colloquy with the prisoner's solicitor. "I hope he will not make a blunder in defending himself."

"He is not likely to make a blunder," said Esther. She had recovered her color a little, and was brighter than she had been all the morning before.

Felix had seemed to include her in his general glance, but had avoided looking at her particularly. She understood how delicate feeling for her would prevent this, and that she might safely look at him, and toward her father, whom she could see in the same direction. Turning to Harold, to make an observation, she saw that he was looking toward the same point, but with an expression on his face that surprised her.

"Dear me," she said, prompted to speak without any reflection; "how angry you look! I never saw you look so angry before. It is not my father you are looking at?"

"Oh, no! I am angry at something I'm looking away from," said Harold, making an effort to drive back the troublesome demon who would stare out at window. "It's that Jermyn," he added, glancing at his mother as well as Esther. "He will thrust himself under my eyes everywhere since I refused him an interview and returned his letter. I'm determined never to speak to him directly again, if I can help it."

Mrs. Transome heard with a changeless face. She had for some time been watching, and had taken on her marble look of immobility. She said an inward bitter "Of course!" to everything that was unpleasant.

After this Esther soon became impatient of all speech: her attention was riveted on the proceedings of the Court, and on the mode in which Felix bore himself. In the case for the prosecution there was nothing more than a reproduction, with irrelevancies added by witnesses, of the facts already known to us. Spratt had retained consciousness enough, in the midst of his terror, to swear that, when he was tied to the finger-post, Felix was presiding over the actions of the mob. The landlady of the Seven Stars, who was indebted to Felix for rescue from pursuit by some drunken rioters, gave evidence that went to prove his assumption of leadership prior to the assault on Spratt,—remembering only that he had called away her pursuers to "better sport." Various respectable witnesses swore to Felix's "encouragement" of the rioters who were dragging Spratt in King Street; to his fatal assault on Tucker; and to his attitude in front of the drawing-room window at the Manor.

Three other witnesses gave evidence of expressions used by the prisoner, tending to show the character of the acts with which he was charged. Two were Treby tradesmen, the third was a clerk from Duffield. The clerk had heard Felix speak at Duffield; the Treby men had frequently heard him declare himself on public matters; and they all quoted expressions which tended to show that he had a virulent feeling against the respectable shopkeeping class, and that nothing was likely to be more congenial to him than the gutting of retailers'

shops. No one else knew—the witnesses themselves did not
know fully—how far their strong perception and memory on
these points was due to a fourth mind, namely, that of Mr.
John Johnson, the attorney, who was nearly related to one of
the Treby witnesses, and a familiar acquaintance of the Duffield clerk. Man cannot be defined as an evidence-giving
animal; and in the difficulty of getting up evidence on any
subject there is room for much unrecognized action of diligent persons who have the extra stimulus of some private
motive. Mr. Johnson was present in Court to-day, but in a
modest, retired situation. He had come down to give information to Mr. Jermyn, and to gather information in other
quarters, which was well illuminated by the appearance of
Esther in company with the Transomes.

When the case for the prosecution closed, all strangers
thought that it looked very black for the prisoner. In two
instances only Felix had chosen to put a cross-examining
question. The first was to ask Spratt if he did not believe
that his having been tied to the post had saved him from a
probably mortal injury. The second was to ask the tradesman who swore to his having heard Felix tell the rioters to
leave Tucker alone and come along with him whether he had
not, shortly before, heard cries among the mob summoning to
an attack on the wine-vaults and brewery.

Esther had hitherto listened closely, but calmly. She knew
that there would be this strong adverse testimony; and all her
hopes and fears were bent on what was to come beyond it.
It was when the prisoner was asked what he had to adduce in
reply that she felt herself in the grasp of that tremor which
does not disable the mind, but rather gives keener consciousness of a mind having a penalty of body attached to it.

There was a silence as of night when Felix Holt began to
speak. His voice was firm and clear: he spoke with simple
gravity, and evidently without any enjoyment of the occasion.
Esther had never seen his face look so weary.

"My Lord, I am not going to occupy the time of the Court
with unnecessary words. I believe the witnesses for the prosecution have spoken the truth as far as a superficial observation would enable them to do it; and I see nothing that can

weigh with the jury in my favor, unless they believe my statement of my own motives, and the testimony that certain witnesses will give to my character and purposes as being inconsistent with my willingly abetting disorder. I will tell the Court in as few words as I can how I got entangled in the mob, how I came to attack the constable, and how I was led to take a course which seems rather mad to myself, now I look back upon it."

Felix then gave a concise narrative of his motives and conduct on the day of the riot from the moment when he was startled into quitting his work by the earlier uproar of the morning. He omitted, of course, his visit to Malthouse Yard, and merely said that he went out to walk again after returning to quiet his mother's mind. He got warmed by the story of his experience, which moved him more strongly than ever, now he recalled it in vibrating words before a large audience of his fellow-men. The sublime delight of truthful speech to one who has the great gift of uttering it will make itself felt even through the pangs of sorrow.

"That is all I have to say for myself, my Lord. I pleaded 'Not guilty' to the charge of Manslaughter because I know that word may carry a meaning which would not fairly apply to my act. When I threw Tucker down, I did not see the possibility that he would die from a sort of attack which ordinarily occurs in fighting without any fatal effect. As to my assaulting a constable, it was a quick choice between two evils: I should else have been disabled. And he attacked me under a mistake about my intentions. I'm not prepared to say I never would assault a constable where I had more chance of deliberation. I certainly should assault him if I saw him doing anything that made my blood boil: I reverence the law, but not where it is a pretext for wrong, which it should be the very object of law to hinder. I consider that I should be making an unworthy defence if I let the Court infer from what I say myself, or from what is said by my witnesses, that because I am a man who hate drunken motiveless disorder, or any wanton harm, therefore I am a man who would never fight against authority: I hold it blasphemy to say that a man ought not to fight against authority: there is no great religion and no great freedom that has not done it, in the beginning. It would be impertinent for me to speak of this now if I did not need to say in my own defence that I should hold myself the worst sort of traitor if I put my hand either to fighting or disorder—which must mean injury to somebody—if I were not urged to it by what I hold to be sacred feelings, making a sacred duty either to my own manhood or to my fellow-man. And certainly," Felix ended with a strong ring of scorn in his voice, "I never held it a sacred duty to try and get a Radical candidate returned for North Loamshire by willingly heading a drunken howling mob, whose public action must consist in breaking windows, destroying hard-got produce, and endangering the lives of men and women. I have no more to say, my Lord."

"I foresaw he would make a blunder," said Harold, in a low voice to Esther. Then, seeing her shrink a little, he feared she might suspect him of being merely stung by the allusion to himself. "I don't mean what he said about the Radical candidate," he added hastily, in correction. "I don't mean the last sentence. I mean that whole peroration of his, which he ought to have left unsaid. It has done him harm with the jury—they won't understand it, or rather will misunderstand it. And I'll answer for it, it has soured the judge. It remains to be seen what we witnesses can say for him to nullify the effect of what he has said for himself. I hope the attorney has done his best in collecting the evidence: I understand the expense of the witnesses is undertaken by some Liberals at Glasgow and in Lancashire, friends of Holt's. But I suppose your father has told you."

The first witness called for the defence was Mr. Lyon. The gist of his statements was that from the beginning of September last until the day of election he was in very frequent intercourse with the prisoner: that he had become intimately acquainted with his character and views of life, and his conduct with respect to the election, and that these were totally inconsistent with any other supposition than that his being involved in the riot, and his fatal encounter with the constable, were due to the calamitous failure of a bold but good purpose. He stated further that he had been present when an interview had occurred in his own house between the prisoner and Mr. Harold Transome, who was then canvassing for the representation of North Loamshire. That the object of the prisoner in seeking this interview had been to inform Mr. Transome of treating given in his name to the workmen in the pits and on the canal at Sproxton, and to remonstrate against its continuance; the prisoner fearing that disturbance and mischief might result from what he believed to be the end toward which this treating was directed—namely, the presence of these men on the occasions of the nomination and polling. Several times after this interview, Mr. Lyon said, he had heard Felix Holt recur to the subject therein discussed with expressions of grief and anxiety. He himself was in the habit of visiting Sproxton in his ministerial capacity: he knew fully what the prisoner had done there in order to found a night-school, and was certain that the prisoner's interest in the working men of that district turned entirely on the possibility of converting them somewhat to habits of soberness and to a due care for the instruction of their children. Finally, he stated that the prisoner, in compliance with his request, had been present at Duffield on the day of the nomination, and had on his return expressed himself with strong indignation concerning the employment of the Sproxton men on that occasion, and what he called the wickedness of hiring blind violence.

The quaint appearance and manner of the little Dissenting minister could not fail to stimulate the peculiar wit of the bar. He was subjected to a troublesome cross-examination, which he bore with wide-eyed short-sighted quietude and absorption in the duty of truthful response. On being asked, rather sneeringly, if the prisoner was not one of his flock, he answered, in that deeper tone which made one of the most effective transitions of his varying voice,—

"Nay—would to God he were! I should then feel that the great virtues and the pure life I have beheld in him were a witness to the efficacy of the faith I believe in and the discipline of the Church whereunto I belong."

Perhaps it required a larger power of comparison than was possessed by any of that audience to appreciate the moral elevation of an Independent minister who could utter those words.

Nevertheless there was a murmur, which was clearly one of sympathy.

The next witness, and the one on whom the interest of the spectators was chiefly concentrated, was Harold Transome. There was a decided predominance of Tory feeling in the Court, and the human disposition to enjoy the infliction of a little punishment on an opposite party was, in this instance, of a Tory complexion. Harold was keenly alive to this, and to everything else that might prove disagreeable to him in his having to appear in the witness-box. But he was not likely to lose his self-possession, or to fail in adjusting himself gracefully, under conditions which most men would find it difficult to carry without awkwardness. He had generosity and candor enough to bear Felix Holt's proud rejection of his advances without any petty resentment; he had all the susceptibilities of a gentleman; and these moral qualities gave the right direction to his acumen in judging of the behavior that would best secure his dignity. Everything requiring self-command was easier to him because of Esther's presence; for her admiration was just then the object which this well-tanned man of the world had it most at heart to secure.

When he entered the witness-box he was much admired by the ladies amongst the audience, many of whom sighed a little at the thought of his wrong course in politics. He certainly looked like a handsome portrait by Sir Thomas Lawrence, in which that remarkable artist had happily omitted the usual excess of honeyed blandness mixed with alert intelligence, which is hardly compatible with the state of man out of paradise. He stood not far off Felix; and the two Radicals certainly made a striking contrast. Felix might have come from the hands of a sculptor in the later Roman period, when the plastic impulse was stirred by the grandeur of barbaric forms —when rolled collars were not yet conceived, and satin stocks were not.

Harold Transome declared that he had had only one interview with the prisoner: it was the interview referred to by the previous witness, in whose presence and in whose house it was begun. The interview, however, was continued beyond the observation of Mr. Lyon. The prisoner and himself quitted the Dissenting minister's house in Malthouse Yard together, and proceeded to the office of Mr. Jermyn, who was then conducting electioneering business on his behalf. His object was to comply with Holt's remonstrance by inquiring into the alleged proceedings at Sproxton, and, if possible, to put a stop to them. Holt's language, both in Malthouse Yard and in the attorney's office, was strong: he was evidently indignant, and his indignation turned on the danger of employing ignorant men excited by drink on an occasion of popular concourse. He believed that Holt's sole motive was the prevention of disorder, and what he considered the demoralization of the workmen by treating. The event had certainly justified his remonstrances. He had not had any subsequent opportunities of observing the prisoner; but if any reliance was to be placed on a rational conclusion, it must, he thought, be plain that the anxiety thus manifested by Holt was a guaranty of the statement he had made as to his motives on the day of the riot. His entire impression from Holt's manner in that single interview was that he was a moral and political enthusiast, who, if he sought to coerce others, would seek to coerce them into a difficult, and perhaps impracticable, scrupulosity.

Harold spoke with as noticeable a directness and emphasis as if what he said could have no reaction on himself. He had of course not entered unnecessarily into what occurred in Jermyn's office. But now he was subjected to a cross-examination on this subject which gave rise to some subdued shrugs, smiles, and winks among county gentlemen.

The questions were directed so as to bring out, if possible, some indication that Felix Holt was moved to his remonstrance by personal resentment against the political agents concerned in setting on foot the treating at Sproxton, but such questioning is a sort of target-shooting that sometimes hits about widely. The cross-examining counsel had close connections among the Tories of Loamshire, and enjoyed his business to-day. Under the fire of various questions about Jermyn and the agent employed by him at Sproxton, Harold got warm, and in one of his replies said, with his rapid sharpness, —

"Mr. Jermyn was my agent then, not now: I have no longer any but hostile relations with him."

The sense that he had shown a slight heat would have vexed Harold more if he had not got some satisfaction out of the thought that Jermyn heard those words. He recovered his good temper quickly, and when, subsequently, the question came,—

"You acquiesced in the treating of the Sproxton men as necessary to the efficient working of the reformed constituency?" Harold replied, with quiet fluency,—

"Yes; on my return to England, before I put up for North Loamshire, I got the best advice from practised agents, both Whig and Tory. They all agreed as to electioneering measures."

The next witness was Michael Brincey, otherwise Mike Brindle, who gave evidence of the sayings and doings of the prisoner amongst the Sproxton men. Mike declared that Felix went "uncommon again' drink, and pitch-and-toss, and quarrelling, and sich," and was "all for schooling and bringing up the little chaps"; but on being cross-examined he admitted that he "couldn't give much account"; that Felix did talk again' idle folks, whether poor or rich, and that most like he meant the rich, who had "a rights to be idle," which was what he, Mike, liked himself sometimes, though for the most part he was "a hard-working butty." On being checked for this superfluous allegation of his own theory and practice, Mike became timidly conscious that answering was a great mystery beyond the reaches of a butty's soul, and began to err from defect instead of excess. However, he reasserted that what Felix most wanted was "to get 'em to set up a school for the little chaps."

With the two succeeding witnesses, who swore to the fact that Felix had tried to lead the mob along Hobb's Lane instead of toward the Manor, and to the violently threatening character of Tucker's attack on him, the case for the defence was understood to close.

Meanwhile Esther had been looking on and listening with growing misery, in the sense that all had not been said which might have been said on behalf of Felix. If it was the jury who were to be acted on, she argued to herself, there might have been an impression made on their feeling which would determine their verdict. Was it not constantly said and seen that juries pronounced Guilty or Not Guilty from sympathy for or against the accused? She was too inexperienced to check her own argument by thoroughly representing to herself the course of things: how the counsel for the prosecution would reply, and how the judge would sum up, with the object of cooling down sympathy into deliberation. What she had painfully pressing on her inward vision was that the trial was coming to an end, and that the voice of right and truth had not been strong enough.

When a woman feels purely and nobly, that ardor of hers which breaks through formulas too rigorously urged on men by daily practical needs makes one of her most precious influences: she is the added impulse that shatters the stiffening crust of cautious experience. Her inspired ignorance gives a sublimity to actions so incongruously simple that otherwise they would make men smile. Some of that ardor which has flashed out and illuminated all poetry and history was burning to-day in the bosom of sweet Esther Lyon. In this, at least, her woman's lot was perfect: that the man she loved was her hero; that her woman's passion and her reverence for rarest goodness rushed together in an undivided current. And to-day they were making one danger, one terror, one irresistible impulse for her heart. Her feelings were growing into a necessity for action rather than a resolve to act. She could not support the thought that the trial would come to an end, that sentence would be passed on Felix, and that all the while something had been omitted which might have been said for him. There had been no witness to tell what had been his behavior and state of mind just before the riot. She must do it. It was possible. There was time. But not too much time. All other agitation became merged in eagerness not to let the moment escape. The last witness was being called. Harold Transome had not been able to get back to her on leaving the witness-box, but Mr. Lingon was close by her. With firm quickness she said to him, —

"Pray tell the attorney that I have evidence to give for the prisoner—lose no time."

"Do you know what you are going to say, my dear?" said Mr. Lingon, looking at her in astonishment.

"Yes—I entreat you, for God's sake," said Esther, in that low tone of urgent beseeching which is equivalent to a cry; and with a look of appeal more penetrating still, "I would rather die than not do it."

The old Rector, always leaning to the good-natured view of things, felt chiefly that there seemed to be an additional chance for the poor fellow who had got himself into trouble. He disputed no farther, but went to the attorney.

Before Harold was aware of Esther's intention she was on her way to the witness-box. When she appeared there, it was as if a vibration, quick as light, had gone through the Court and had shaken Felix himself, who had hitherto seemed impassive. A sort of gleam seemed to shoot across his face, and any one close to him would have seen that his hand, which lay on the edge of the dock, trembled.

At the first moment Harold was startled and alarmed; the next, he felt delight in Esther's beautiful aspect, and in the admiration of the Court. There was no blush on her face: she stood divested of all personal considerations, whether of vanity or shyness. Her clear voice sounded as it might have done if she had been making a confession of faith. She began and went on without query or interruption. Every face looked grave and respectful.

"I am Esther Lyon, the daughter of Mr. Lyon, the Independent minister at Treby, who has been one of the witnesses for the prisoner. I know Felix Holt well. On the day of the election at Treby, when I had been much alarmed by the noises that reached me from the main street, Felix Holt came to call upon me. He knew that my father was away, and he thought that I should be alarmed by the sounds of disturbance. It was about the middle of the day, and he came to tell me that the disturbance was quieted, and that the streets were nearly emptied. But he said he feared that the men would collect again after drinking, and that something worse might happen later in the day. And he was in much sadness at this thought. He stayed a little while and then he left me. He was very melancholy. His mind was full of great resolutions that came from his kind feeling toward others. It was the last thing he would have done to join in riot or to hurt any man, if he could have helped it. His nature is very noble; he is tender-hearted; he could never have had any intention that was not brave and good."

There was something so naïve and beautiful in this action of Esther's that it conquered every low or petty suggestion even in the commonest minds. The three men in that assembly who knew her best—even her father and Felix Holt—felt a thrill of surprise mingling with their admiration. This bright, delicate, beautiful-shaped thing that seemed most like a toy or ornament—some hand had touched the chords, and there came forth music that brought tears. Half a year before, Esther's dread of being ridiculous spread over the surface of her life; but the depth below was sleeping.

Harold Transome was ready to give her his hand and lead her back to her place. When she was there, Felix, for the first time, could not help looking toward her, and their eyes met in one solemn glance.

Afterward Esther found herself unable to listen so as to form any judgment on what she heard. The acting out of that strong impulse had exhausted her energy. There was a brief pause, filled with a murmur, a buzz, and much coughing. The audience generally felt as if dull weather was setting in again. And under those auspices the counsel for the prosecution got up to make his reply. Esther's deed had its effect beyond the momentary one, but the effect was not visible in the rigid necessities of legal procedure. The counsel's duty of restoring all unfavorable facts to due prominence in the minds of the jurors had its effect altogether reinforced by the summing up of the judge. Even the bare discernment of facts, much more their arrangement with a view to inferences, must carry a bias: human impartiality, whether judicial or not, can hardly escape being more or less loaded. It was not that the judge had severe intentions; it was only that he saw with severity. The conduct of Felix was not such as inclined him to indulgent consideration, and, in his directions to the jury, that mental attitude necessarily told on the light in which he placed the homicide. Even to many in the Court

29

who were not constrained by judicial duty, it seemed that, though this high regard felt for the prisoner by his friends, and especially by a generous-hearted woman, was very pretty, such conduct as his was not the less dangerous and foolish, and assaulting and killing a constable was not the less an offence to be regarded without leniency.

Esther seemed now so tremulous, and looked so ill, that Harold begged her to leave the Court with his mother and Mr. Lingon. He would come and tell her the issue. But she said, quietly, that she would rather stay; she was only a little overcome by the exertion of speaking. She was inwardly resolved to see Felix to the last moment before he left the Court.

Though she could not follow the address of the counsel or the judge, she had a keen ear for what was brief and decisive. She heard the verdict, "Guilty of manslaughter." And every word uttered by the judge in pronouncing sentence fell upon her like an unforgetable sound that would come back in dreaming and in waking. She had her eyes on Felix, and at the words, "Imprisonment for four years," she saw his lip tremble. But otherwise he stood firm and calm.

Esther gave a start from her seat. Her heart swelled with a horrible sensation of pain; but, alarmed lest she should lose her self-command, she grasped Mrs. Transome's hand, getting some strength from that human contact.

Esther saw that Felix had turned. She could no longer see his face. "Yes," she said, drawing down her veil, "let us go."

CHAPTER XLVII.

The devil tempts us not — 'tis we tempt him,
Beckoning his skill with opportunity.

THE more permanent effect of Esther's action in the trial was visible in a meeting which took place the next day in the principal room of the White Hart at Loamford. To the magistrates and other county gentlemen who were drawn together about noon some of the necessary impulse might have been lacking but for that stirring of heart in certain just-spirited men and good fathers among them, which had been raised to a high pitch of emotion by Esther's maidenly fervor. Among these one of the foremost was Sir Maximus Debarry, who had come to the assizes with a mind, as usual, slightly rebellious under an influence which he never ultimately resisted—the influence of his son. Philip Debarry himself was detained in London, but in his correspondence with his father he had urged him, as well as his uncle Augustus, to keep eyes and interest awake on the subject of Felix Holt, whom, from all the knowledge of the case he had been able to obtain, he was inclined to believe peculiarly unfortunate rather than guilty. Philip had said he was the more anxious that his family should intervene benevolently in this affair, if it were possible, because he understood that Mr. Lyon took the young man's case particularly to heart, and he should always regard himself as obliged to the old preacher. At this superfineness of consideration Sir Maximus had vented a few " pshaws!" and, in relation to the whole affair, had grumbled that Phil was always setting him to do he didn't know what—always seeming to turn nothing into something by dint of words which hadn't so much substance as a mote behind them. Nevertheless he was coerced; and in reality he was willing to do anything fair or good-natured which had a handle that his understanding could lay hold of. His brother, the Rector, desired to be rigorously just; but he had come to Loamford with a severe opinion concerning Felix, thinking that some sharp punishment might be a wholesome check on the career of a young man disposed to rely too much on his own crude devices.

Before the trial commenced, Sir Maximus had naturally been one of those who had observed Esther with curiosity, owing to the report of her inheritance, and her probable marriage to his once-welcome but now exasperating neighbor, Harold Transome; and he had made the emphatic comment— "A fine girl! something thoroughbred in the look of her. Too good for a Radical; that's all I have to say." But during the trial Sir Maximus was wrought into a state of sympathetic ardor that needed no fanning. As soon as he could take his brother by the button-hole, he said,—

"I tell you what, Gus! we must exert ourselves to get a pardon for this young fellow. Confound it! what's the use of mewing him up for four years? Example? Nonsense. Will there be a man knocked down the less for it? That girl made me cry. Depend upon it, whether she's going to marry Transome or not, she's been fond of Holt—in her poverty, you know. She's a modest, brave, beautiful woman. I'd ride a steeplechase, old as I am, to gratify her feelings. Hang it! the fellow's a good fellow if she thinks so. And he threw out a fine sneer, I thought, at the Radical candidate. Depend upon it, he's a good fellow at bottom."

The Rector had not exactly the same kind of ardor, nor was he open to precisely that process of proof which appeared to have convinced Sir Maximus; but he had been so far influenced as to be inclined to unite in an effort on the side of mercy, observing, also, that he "knew Phil would be on that side." And by the co-operation of similar movements in the minds of other men whose names were of weight a meeting had been determined on to consult about getting up a memorial to the Home Secretary on behalf of Felix Holt. His case had never had the sort of significance that could rouse political partisanship; and such interest as was now felt in him was still more unmixed with that inducement. The gentlemen who gathered in the room at the White Hart were—not, as the large imagination of the *North Loamshire Herald* suggested, "of all shades of political opinion," but—of as many shades as were to be found among the gentlemen of that county.

Harold Transome had been energetically active in bringing about this meeting. Over and above the stings of conscience and a determination to act up to the level of all recognized honorableness, he had the powerful motive of desiring to do what would satisfy Esther. His gradually heightened perception that she had a strong feeling toward Felix Holt had not made him uneasy. Harold had a conviction that might have seemed like fatuity if it had not been that he saw the effect he produced on Esther by the light of his opinions about women in general. The conviction was that Felix Holt could not be his rival in any formidable sense: Esther's admiration for this eccentric young man was, he thought, a moral enthusiasm, a romantic fervor, which was one among those many attractions quite novel in his own experience; her distress about the trouble of one who had been a familiar object in her former home was no more than naturally followed from a tender woman's compassion. The place young Holt had held in her regard had necessarily changed its relations now that her lot was so widely changed. It is undeniable that what most conduced to the quieting nature of Harold's conclusions was the influence on his imagination of the more or less detailed reasons that Felix Holt was a watchmaker, that his home and dress were of a certain quality, that his person and manners—that, in short (for Harold, like the rest of us, had many impressions which saved him the trouble of distinct ideas), Felix Holt was not the sort of man a woman would be likely to be in love with when she was wooed by Harold Transome.

Thus he was sufficiently at rest on this point not to be exercising any painful self-conquest in acting as the zealous advocate of Felix Holt's cause with all persons worth influencing; but it was by no direct intercourse between him and Sir Maximus that they found themselves in co-operation, for the old Baronet would not recognize Harold by more than the faintest bow, and Harold was not a man to expose himself to a rebuff. Whatever he in his inmost soul regarded as nothing more than a narrow prejudice he could defy, not with airs of importance, but with easy indifference. He could bear most things good-humoredly where he felt that he had the superiority. The object of the meeting was discussed, and the memorial agreed upon without any clashing. Mr. Lingon was gone home, but it was expected that his concurrence and signature would be given, as well as those of other gentlemen who were absent. The business gradually reached that stage at which the concentration of interest ceases—when the attention of all but a few who are more practically concerned drops off and disperses itself in private chat, and there is no longer any particular reason why everybody stays except that everybody is there. The room was rather a long one, and invited to a little movement: one gentleman drew another aside to speak in an undertone about Scotch bullocks; another had something to say about the North Loamshire Hunt to a friend who was the reverse of good-looking, but who, nevertheless, while listening, showed his strength of mind by giving a severe attention also to his full-length reflection in the handsome tall mirror that filled the space between two windows. And in this way the groups were continually shifting.

But in the mean time there were moving toward this room at the White Hart the footsteps of a person whose presence had not been invited, and who, very far from being drawn thither by the belief that he would be welcome, knew well that his entrance would, to one person at least, be bitterly disagreeable. They were the footsteps of Mr. Jermyn, whose appearance that morning was not less comely and less carefully tended than usual, but who was suffering the torment of a compressed rage, which, if not impotent to inflict pain on another, was impotent to avert evil from himself. After his interview with Mrs. Transome there had been for some reasons a delay of positive procedures against him by Harold, of which delay Jermyn had twice availed himself; first, to seek an interview with Harold, and then to send him a letter. The interview had been refused; and the letter had been returned, with the statement that no communication could take place except through Harold's lawyers. And yesterday Johnson had brought Jermyn the information that he would quickly hear of the proceedings in Chancery being resumed: the watch Johnson kept in town had given him secure knowledge on this head. A doomed animal, with every issue earthed up except that where its enemy stands, must, if it has teeth and fierceness, try its one chance without delay. And a man may reach a point in his life in which his impulses are not distinguished from those of a hunted brute by any capability of scruples. Our selfishness is so robust and many-clutching that, well encouraged, it easily devours all sustenance away from our poor little scruples.

Since Harold would not give Jermyn access to him, that vigorous attorney was resolved to take it. He knew all about the meeting at the White Hart, and he was going thither with the determination of accosting Harold. He thought he knew what he should say, and the tone in which he should say it. It would be a vague intimation, carrying the effect of a threat, which should compel Harold to give him a private interview. To any counter-consideration that presented itself in his mind —to anything that an imagined voice might say—the imagined answer arose, "That's all very fine, but I'm not going to be ruined if I can help it—least of all, ruined in that way." Shall we call it degeneration or gradual development—this effect of thirty additional winters on the soft-glancing, versifying young Jermyn?

When Jermyn entered the room at the White Hart he did not immediately see Harold. The door was at the extremity of the room, and the view was obstructed by groups of gentlemen with figures broadened by overcoats. His entrance excited no peculiar observation: several persons had come in late. Only one or two, who knew Jermyn well, were not too much preoccupied to have a glancing remembrance of what had been chatted about freely the day before—Harold's irritated reply about his agent from the witness-box. Receiving and giving a slight nod here and there, Jermyn pushed his way, looking round keenly, until he saw Harold standing near the other end of the room. The solicitor who had acted for Felix was just then speaking to him, but having put a paper into his hand turned away; and Harold, standing isolated, though at no great distance from others, bent his eyes on the paper. He looked brilliant that morning; his blood was flowing prosperously. He had come in after a ride, and was additionally brightened by rapid talk and the excitement of seeking to impress himself favorably, or at least powerfully, on the minds of neighbors nearer or more remote. He had just that amount of flush which indicates that life is more enjoyable than usual; and as he stood with his left hand caressing his whisker, and his right holding the paper and his riding-whip, his dark eyes running rapidly along the written lines, and his lips reposing in a curve of good humor which had more happiness in it than a smile, all beholders might have seen that his mind was at ease.

Jermyn walked quickly and quietly close up to him. The two men were of the same height, and before Harold looked round Jermyn's voice was saying close to his ear, not in a whisper, but in a hard, incisive, disrespectful, and yet not loud tone,—

"Mr Transome, I must speak to you in private."

The sound jarred through Harold with a sensation all the more insufferable because of the revulsion from the satisfied, almost elated, state in which it had seized him. He started and looked round into Jermyn's eyes. For an instant, which seemed long, there was no sound between them, but only angry hatred gathering in the two faces. Harold felt himself going to crush this insolence: Jermyn felt that he had words within him that were fangs to clutch this obstinate strength, and wring forth the blood and compel submission. And Jermyn's impulse was the more urgent. He said, in a tone that was rather lower, but yet harder and more biting,—

"You will repent else—for your mother's sake."

At that sound, quick as a leaping flame, Harold had struck Jermyn across the face with his whip. The brim of the hat had been a defence. Jermyn, a powerful man, had instantly thrust out his hand and clutched Harold hard by the clothes just below the throat, pushing him slightly so as to make him stagger.

By this time everybody's attention had been called to this end of the room, but both Jermyn and Harold were beyond being arrested by any consciousness of spectators.

"Let me go, you scoundrel!" said Harold, fiercely, "or I'll be the death of you."

"Do," said Jermyn, in a grating voice; "*I am your father.*"

In the thrust by which Harold had been made to stagger backward a little the two men had got very near the long mirror. They were both white; both had anger and hatred in their faces; the hands of both were upraised. As Harold heard the last terrible words he started at a leaping throb that went through him, and in the start turned his eyes away from Jermyn's face. He turned them on the same face in the glass with his own beside it, and saw the hated fatherhood reasserted.

The young strong man reeled with a sick faintness. But in the same moment Jermyn released his hold, and Harold felt himself supported by the arm. It was Sir Maximus Debarry who had taken hold of him.

"Leave the room, sir!" the Baronet said to Jermyn, in a voice of imperious scorn. "This is a meeting of gentlemen.

"Come, Harold," he said, in the old friendly voice, "come away with me."

———◆———

CHAPTER XLVIII.

'Tis law as steadfast as the throne of Zeus —
Our days are heritors of days gone by.
ÆSCHYLUS: *Agamemnon.*

A LITTLE after five o'clock that day Harold arrived at Transome Court. As he was winding along the broad road of the park, some parting gleams of the March sun pierced the trees here and there, and threw on the grass a long shadow of himself and the groom riding, and illuminated a window or two of the home he was approaching. But the bitterness in his mind made these sunny gleams almost as odious as an artificial smile. He wished he had never come back to this pale English sunshine.

In the course of his eighteen miles' drive he had made up his mind what he would do. He understood now, as he had never understood before, the neglected solitariness of his mother's life, the allusions and innuendoes which had come out during the election. But with a proud insurrection against the hardship of an ignominy which was not of his own making, he inwardly said that if the circumstances of his birth were such as to warrant any man in regarding his character of gentleman with ready suspicion, that character should be the more strongly asserted in his conduct. No one should be able to allege with any show of proof that he had inherited meanness.

As he stepped from the carriage and entered the hall, there were the voice and the trotting feet of little Harry as usual, and the rush to clasp his father's leg and make his joyful puppy-like noises. Harold just touched the boy's head, and then said to Dominic in a weary voice, —

"Take the child away. Ask where my mother is."

Mrs. Transome, Dominic said, was upstairs. He had seen her go up after coming in from her walk with Miss Lyon, and she had not come down again.

Harold, throwing off his hat and greatcoat, went straight to his mother's dressing-room. There was still a hope in his mind. He might be suffering simply from a lie. There is much misery created in the world by mere mistake or slander, and he might have been stunned by a lie suggested by such slander. He rapped at his mother's door.

Her voice said immediately, "Come in."

Mrs. Transome was resting in her easy-chair, as she often did between an afternoon walk and dinner. She had taken off her walking-dress and wrapped herself in a soft dressing-gown. She was neither more nor less empty of joy than usual. But when she saw Harold, a dreadful certainty took possession of her. It was as if a long-expected letter, with a black seal, had come at last.

Harold's face told her what to fear the more decisively because she had never before seen it express a man's deep agitation. Since the time of its pouting childhood and careless youth she had seen only the confident strength and good-humored imperiousness of maturity. The last five hours had made a change as great as illness makes. Harold looked as if he had been wrestling, and had had some terrible blow. His eyes had that sunken look which, because it is unusual, seems to intensify expression.

He looked at his mother as he entered, and her eyes followed him as he moved, till he came and stood in front of her, she looking up at him with white lips.

"Mother," he said, speaking with a distinct slowness, in strange contrast with his habitual manner, "tell me the truth, that I may know how to act."

He paused a moment, and then said, "Who is my father?"

She was mute: her lips only trembled. Harold stood silent for a few moments, as if waiting. Then he spoke again.

"*He* has said—said it before others—that *he* is my father."

He looked still at his mother. She seemed as if age were

striking her with a sudden wand—as if her trembling face were getting haggard before him. She was mute. But her eyes had not fallen; they looked up in helpless misery at her son.

Her son turned away his eyes from her, and left her. In that moment Harold felt hard: he could show no pity. All the pride of his nature rebelled against his sonship.

CHAPTER XLIX.

Nay, falter not—'tis an assured good
To seek the noblest—'tis your only good
Now you have seen it ; for that higher vision
Poisons all meaner choice for ever more.

THAT day Esther dined with old Mr. Transome only. Harold sent word that he was engaged and had already dined, and Mrs. Transome that she was feeling ill. Esther was much disappointed that any tidings Harold might have brought relating to Felix were deferred in this way; and, her anxiety making her fearful, she was haunted by the thought that if there had been anything cheering to tell he would have found time to tell it without delay. Old Mr. Transome went as usual to his sofa in the library to sleep after dinner, and Esther had to seat herself in the small drawing-room, in a well-lit solitude that was unusually dispiriting to her. Pretty as this room was, she did not like it. Mrs. Transome's full-length portrait, being the only picture there, urged itself too strongly on her attention: the youthful brilliancy it represented saddened Esther by its inevitable association with what she daily saw had come instead of it—a joyless, embittered age. The sense that Mrs. Transome was unhappy affected Esther more and more deeply as the growing familiarity which relaxed the efforts of the hostess revealed more and more the threadbare tissue of this majestic lady's life. Even the flowers and the pure sunshine and the sweet waters of paradise would have been spoiled for a young heart if the bowered walks had been haunted by an Eve gone gray with bitter memories of an Adam who had complained, "The woman . . . she gave me of the tree, and I did eat." And many of us know how, even in our childhood, some blank discontented face on the background of our home has marred our summer mornings. Why was it, when the birds were singing, when the fields were a garden, and when we were clasping another little hand just larger than our own, there was somebody who found it hard to smile? Esther had got far beyond that childhood to a time and circumstances when this daily presence of elderly dissatisfaction amidst such outward things as she had always thought must greatly help to satisfy awaked not merely vague questioning emotion, but strong determining thought. And now, in these hours since her return from Loamford, her mind was in that state of highly wrought activity, that large discourse, in which we seem to stand aloof from our own life—weighing impartially our own temptations and the weak desires that most habitually solicit us. "I think I am getting that power Felix wished me to have: I shall soon see strong visions," she said to herself, with a melancholy smile flitting across her face, as she put out the wax-lights that she might get rid of the oppressive urgency of walls and upholstery and that portrait smiling with deluded brightness, unwitting of the future.

Just then Dominic came to say that Mr. Harold sent his compliments, and begged that she would grant him an interview in his study. He disliked the small drawing-room: if she would oblige him by going to the study at once, he would join her very soon. Esther went, in some wonder and anxiety. What she most feared or hoped in these moments related to Felix Holt, and it did not occur to her that Harold could have anything special to say to her that evening on other subjects.

Certainly the study was pleasanter than the small drawing-room. A quiet light shone on nothing but greenness and dark wood, and Dominic had placed a delightful chair for her opposite to his master's, which was still empty. All the little objects of luxury around indicated Harold's habitual occupancy; and as Esther sat opposite all these things along with the empty chair which suggested the coming presence, the expectation of his beseeching homage brought with it an impatience and repugnance which she had never felt before. While these feelings were strongly upon her, the door opened and Harold appeared.

He had recovered his self-possession since his interview with his mother: he had dressed and was perfectly calm. He had been occupied with resolute thoughts, determining to do what he knew that perfect honor demanded, let it cost him what it would. It is true he had a tacit hope behind that it might not cost him what he prized most highly: it is true he had a glimpse even of reward; but it was not less true that he would have acted as he did without that hope or glimpse. It was the most serious moment in Harold Transome's life: for the first time the iron had entered into his soul, and he felt the hard pressure of our common lot, the yoke of that mighty resistless destiny laid upon us by the acts of other men as well as our own.

When Esther looked at him she relented, and felt ashamed of her gratuitous impatience. She saw that his mind was in some way burdened. But then immediately sprang the dread that he had to say something hopeless about Felix.

They shook hands in silence, Esther looking at him with anxious surprise. He released her hand, but it did not occur to her to sit down, and they both continued standing on the hearth.

"Don't let me alarm you," said Harold, seeing that her face gathered solemnity from his. "I suppose I carry the marks of a past agitation. It relates entirely to troubles of my own—of my own family. No one beyond is involved in them."

Esther wondered still more, and felt still more relenting.

"But," said Harold, after a slight pause, and in a voice that was weighted with new feeling, "it involves a difference in my position with regard to you; and it is on this point that I wished to speak to you at once. When a man sees what ought to be done, he had better do it forthwith. He can't answer for himself to-morrow."

While Esther continued to look at him, with eyes widened by anxious expectation, Harold turned a little, leaned on the mantelpiece, and ceased to look at her as he spoke.

"My feelings drag me another way. I need not tell you that your regard has become very important to me—that if our mutual position had been different—that, in short, you must have seen—if it had not seemed to be a matter of worldly interest, I should have told you plainly already that I loved you, and that my happiness could be complete only if you would consent to marry me."

Esther felt her heart beginning to beat painfully. Harold's voice and words moved her so much that her own task seemed more difficult than she had before imagined. It seemed as if the silence, unbroken by anything but the clicking of the fire, had been long before Harold turned round toward her again and said,—

"But to-day I have heard something that affects my own position. I cannot tell you what it is. There is no need. It is not any culpability of my own. But I have not just the same unsullied name and fame in the eyes of the world around us as I believed that I had when I allowed myself to entertain that wish about you. You are very young, entering on a fresh life with bright prospects—you are worthy of everything that is best. I may be too vain in thinking it was at all necessary; but I take this precaution against myself. I shut myself out from the chance of trying, after to-day, to induce you to accept anything which others may regard as specked and stained by any obloquy, however slight."

Esther was keenly touched. With a paradoxical longing, such as often happens to us, she wished at that moment that she could have loved this man with her whole heart. The tears came into her eyes; she did not speak, but, with an angel's tenderness in her face, she laid her hand on his sleeve. Harold commanded himself strongly, and said,—

"What is to be done now is that we should proceed at once to the necessary legal measures for putting you in possession of your own, and arranging mutual claims. After that I shall probably leave England."

Esther was oppressed by an overpowering difficulty. Her sympathy with Harold at this moment was so strong that it spread itself like a mist over all previous thought and resolve.

It was impossible now to wound him afresh. With her hand still resting on his arm, she said, timidly,—

"Should you be urged—obliged to go—in any case?"

"Not in every case, perhaps," Harold said, with an evident movement of the blood toward his face; "at least not for long, not for always."

Esther was conscious of the gleam in his eyes. With terror at herself, she said, in difficult haste, "I can't speak. I can't say anything to-night. A great decision has to be made: I must wait—till to-morrow."

She was moving her hand from his arm, when Harold took it reverentially and raised it to his lips. She turned toward her chair, and as he released her hand she sank down on the seat with a sense that she needed that support. She did not want to go away from Harold yet. All the while there was something she needed to know, and yet she could not bring herself to ask it. She must resign herself to depend entirely on his recollection of anything beyond his own immediate trial. She sat helpless under contending sympathies, while Harold stood at some distance from her, feeling more harassed by weariness and uncertainty, now that he had fulfilled his resolve, and was no longer under the excitement of actually fulfilling it.

Esther's last words had forbidden his revival of the subject that was necessarily supreme with him. But still she sat there, and his mind, busy as to the probabilities of her feeling, glanced over all she had done and said in the later days of their intercourse. It was this retrospect that led him to say at last,—

"You will be glad to hear that we shall get a very powerfully signed memorial to the Home Secretary about young Holt. I think your speaking for him helped a great deal. You made all the men wish what you wished."

This was what Esther had been yearning to hear and dared not ask, as well from respect for Harold's absorption in his own sorrow as from the shrinking that belongs to our dearest need. The intense relief of hearing what she longed to hear affected her whole frame: her color, her expression, changed as if she had been suddenly freed from some torturing constraint. But we interpret signs of emotion as we interpret other signs—often quite erroneously, unless we have the right key to what they signify. Harold did not gather that this was what Esther had waited for, or that the change in her indicated more than he had expected her to feel at this allusion to an unusual act which she had done under a strong impulse.

Besides, the introduction of a new subject after very momentous words have passed, and are still dwelling on the mind, is necessarily a sort of concussion, shaking us into a new adjustment of ourselves.

It seemed natural that soon afterward Esther put out her hand and said, "Good-night."

Harold went to his bedroom on the same level with his study, thinking of the morning with an uncertainty that dipped on the side of hope. This sweet woman for whom he felt a passion newer than any he had expected to feel might possibly make some hard things more bearable—if she loved him. If not—well, he had acted so that he could defy any one to say he was not a gentleman.

Esther went upstairs to her bedroom, thinking that she should not sleep that night. She set her light on a high stand, and did not touch her dress. What she desired to see with undisturbed clearness were things not present: the rest she needed was the rest of a final choice. It was difficult. On each side there was renunciation.

She drew up her blinds, liking to see the gray sky, where there were some veiled glimmerings of moonlight, and the lines of the forever-running river, and the bending movement of the black trees. She wanted the largeness of the world to help her thought. This young creature, who trod lightly backward and forward, and leaned against the window-frame, and shook back her brown curls as she looked at something not visible, had lived hardly more than six months since she saw Felix Holt for the first time. But life is measured by the rapidity of change, the succession of influences that modify the being; and Esther had undergone something little short of an inward revolution. The revolutionary struggle, however, was not quite at an end.

There was something which she now felt profoundly to be

the best thing that life could give her. But—if it was to be had at all—it was not to be had without paying a heavy price for it, such as we must pay for all that is greatly good. A supreme love, a motive that gives a sublime rhythm to a woman's life, and exalts habit into partnership with the soul's highest needs, is not to be had where and how she wills: to know that high initiation she must often tread where it is hard to tread, and feel the chill air, and watch through darkness. It is not true that love makes all things easy: it makes us choose what is difficult. Esther's previous life had brought her into close acquaintance with many negations, and with many positive ills, too, not of the acutely painful but of the distasteful sort. What if she chose the hardship, and had to bear it alone, with no strength to lean upon—no other better self to make a place for trust and joy? Her past experience saved her from illusions. She knew the dim life of the back street, the contact with sordid vulgarity, the lack of refinement for the senses, the summons to a daily task; and the gain that was to make that life of privation something on which she dreaded to turn her back as if it were heaven—the presence and the love of Felix Holt—was only a quivering hope, not a certainty. It was not in her woman's nature that the hope should not spring within her and make a strong impulse. She knew that he loved her: had he not said how a woman might help a man if she were worthy? and if she proved herself worthy? But still there was the dread that after all she might find herself on the stony road alone, and faint and be weary. Even with the fulfilment of her hope, she knew that she pledged herself to meet high demands.

And on the other side there was a lot where everything seemed easy—but for the fatal absence of those feelings which, now she had once known them, it seemed nothing less than a fall and a degradation to do without. With a terrible prescience which a multitude of impressions during her stay at Transome Court had contributed to form, she saw herself in a silken bondage that arrested all motive, and was nothing better than a well-cushioned despair. To be restless amidst ease, to be languid among all appliances for pleasure, was a possibility that seemed to haunt the rooms of this house, and

30

wander with her under the oaks and elms of the park. And Harold Transome's love, no longer a hovering fancy with which she played, but become a serious fact, seemed to threaten her with a stifling oppression. The homage of a man may be delightful until he asks straight for love, by which a woman renders homage. Since she and Felix had kissed each other in the prison, she felt as if she had vowed herself away, as if memory lay on her lips like a seal of possession. Yet what had happened that very evening had strengthened her liking for Harold, and her care for all that regarded him: it had increased her repugnance to turning him out of anything he had expected to be his, or to snatching anything from him on the ground of an arbitrary claim. It had even made her dread, as a coming pain, the task of saying anything to him that was not a promise of the utmost comfort under this newly disclosed trouble of his.

It was already near midnight, but with these thoughts succeeding and returning in her mind like scenes through which she was living, Esther had a more intense wakefulness than any she had known by day. All had been stillness hitherto, except the fitful wind outside. But her ears now caught a sound within—slight, but sudden. She moved near her door, and heard the sweep of something on the matting outside. It came closer, and paused. Then it began again, and seemed to sweep away from her. Then it approached, and paused as it had done before. Esther listened, wondering. The same thing happened again and again, till she could bear it no longer. She opened her door, and in the dim light of the corridor, where the glass above seemed to make a glimmering sky, she saw Mrs. Transome's tall figure pacing slowly, with her cheek upon her hand.

CHAPTER L.

The great question in life is the suffering we cause; and the utmost ingenuity of meta-physics cannot justify the man who has pierced the heart that loved him.—BENJAMIN CONSTANT.

WHEN Denner had gone up to her mistress's room to dress her for dinner, she had found her seated just as Harold had found her, only with eyelids drooping and trembling over slowly rolling tears—nay, with a face in which every sensitive feature, every muscle, seemed to be quivering with a silent endurance of some agony.

Denner went and stood by the chair a minute without speaking, only laying her hand gently on Mrs. Transome's. At last she said, beseechingly, "Pray speak, madam. What has happened?"

"The worst, Denner—the worst."

"You are ill. Let me undress you, and put you to bed."

"No, I am not ill. I am not going to die! I shall live—I shall live!"

"What may I do?"

"Go and say I shall not dine. Then you may come back, if you will."

The patient waiting-woman came back and sat by her mistress in motionless silence. Mrs. Transome would not let her dress be touched, and waved away all proffers with a slight movement of her hand. Denner dared not even light a candle without being told. At last, when the evening was far gone, Mrs. Transome said,—

"Go down, Denner, and find out where Harold is, and come back and tell me."

"Shall I ask him to come to you, madam?"

"No; don't dare to do it, if you love me. Come back."

Denner brought word that Mr. Harold was in his study, and that Miss Lyon was with him. He had not dined, but had sent later to ask Miss Lyon to go into his study.

"Light the candles and leave me."

"Mayn't I come again?"

"No. It may be that my son will come to me."

"Mayn't I sleep on the little bed in your bedroom?"

"No, good Denner; I am not ill. You can't help me."

"That's the hardest word of all, madam."

"The time will come—but not now. Kiss me. Now go."

The small quiet old woman obeyed, as she had always done. She shrank from seeming to claim an equal's share in her mistress's sorrow.

For two hours Mrs. Transome's mind hung on what was hardly a hope—hardly more than the listening for a bare possibility. She began to create the sounds that her anguish craved to hear—began to imagine a footfall, and a hand upon the door. Then, checked by continual disappointment, she tried to rouse a truer consciousness by rising from her seat and walking to her window, where she saw streaks of light moving and disappearing on the grass, and heard the sound of bolts and closing doors. She hurried away and threw herself into her seat again, and buried her head in the deafening down of the cushions. There was no sound of comfort for her.

Then her heart cried out within her against the cruelty of this son. When he turned from her in the first moment, he had not had time to feel anything but the blow that had fallen on himself. But afterward—was it possible that he should not be touched with a son's pity—was it possible that he should not have been visited by some thought of the long years through which she had suffered? The memory of those years came back to her now with a protest against the cruelty that had all fallen on *her*. She started up with a new restlessness from this spirit of resistance. She was not penitent. She had borne too hard a punishment. Always the edge of calamity had fallen on *her*. Who had felt for her? She was desolate. God had no pity, else her son would not have been so hard. What dreary future was there after this dreary past? She, too, looked out into the dim night; but the black boundary of trees and the long line of the river seemed only part of the loneliness and monotony of her life.

Suddenly she saw a light on the stone balustrades of the balcony that projected in front of Esther's window, and the flash of a moving candle falling on a shrub below. Esther was still awake and up. What had Harold told her—what had passed between them? Harold was fond of this young creature, who had been always sweet and reverential to her. There was mercy in her young heart; she might be a daughter who had no impulse to punish and to strike her whom fate had stricken. On the dim loneliness before her she seemed to see Esther's gentle look; it was possible still that the misery of this night might be broken by some comfort. The proud woman yearned for the caressing pity that must dwell in that young bosom. She opened her door gently, but when she had reached Esther's she hesitated. She had never yet in her life asked for compassion—had never thrown herself in faith on an unproffered love. And she might have gone on pacing the corridor like an uneasy spirit without a goal if Esther's thought, leaping toward her, had not saved her from her need to ask admission.

Mrs. Transome was walking toward the door when it opened. As Esther saw that image of restless misery, it blent itself by a rapid flash with all that Harold had said in the evening. She divined that the son's new trouble must be one with the mother's long sadness. But there was no waiting. In an instant Mrs. Transome felt Esther's arm round her neck, and a voice saying softly,—

"Oh, why didn't you call me before?"

They turned hand in hand into the room, and sat down together on a sofa at the foot of the bed. The disordered gray hair—the haggard face—the reddened eyelids under which the tears seemed to be coming again with pain, pierced Esther to the heart. A passionate desire to soothe this suffering woman came over her. She clung round her again, and kissed her poor quivering lips and eyelids, and laid her young cheek against the pale haggard one. Words could not be quick or strong enough to utter her yearning. As Mrs. Transome felt that soft clinging, she said,—

"God has some pity on me."

"Rest on my bed," said Esther. "You are so tired. I will cover you up warmly, and then you will sleep."

"No—tell me, dear—tell me what Harold said."

"That he has had some new trouble."

"He said nothing hard about me?"

"No—nothing.   He did not mention you."

"I have been an unhappy woman, dear."

"I feared it," said Esther, pressing her gently.

"Men are selfish.   They are selfish and cruel.   What they care for is their own pleasure and their own pride."

"Not all," said Esther, on whom these words fell with a painful jar.

"All I have ever loved," said Mrs. Transome.   She paused a moment or two, and then said, "For more than twenty years I have not had an hour's happiness.   Harold knows it, and yet he is hard to me."

"He will not be.   To-morrow he will not be.   I am sure he will be good," said Esther, pleadingly.   "Remember—he said to me his trouble was new—he has not had time."

"It is too hard to bear, dear," Mrs. Transome said, a new sob rising as she clung fast to Esther in return.   "I am old, and expect so little now—a very little thing would seem great. Why should I be punished any more?"

Esther found it difficult to speak.   The dimly suggested tragedy of this woman's life, the dreary waste of years empty of sweet trust and affection, afflicted her even to horror.   It seemed to have come as a last vision to urge her toward the life where the draughts of joy sprang from the unchanging fountains of reverence and devout love.

But all the more she longed to still the pain of this heart that beat against hers.

"Do let me go to your own room with you, and let me undress you, and let me tend upon you," she said, with a woman's gentle instinct.   "It will be a very great thing to me.   I shall seem to have a mother again.   Do let me."

Mrs. Transome yielded at last, and let Esther soothe her with a daughter's tendance.   She was undressed and went to bed; and at last dozed fitfully, with frequent starts.   But Esther watched by her till the chills of morning came, and then she only wrapped more warmth around her, and slept fast in the chair till Denner's movement in the room roused her.   She started out of a dream in which she was telling Felix what had happened to her that night.

Mrs. Transome was now in the sounder morning sleep which sometimes comes after a long night of misery. Esther beckoned Denner into the dressing-room, and said,—

"It is late, Mrs. Hickes. Do you think Mr. Harold is out of his room?"

"Yes, a long while; he was out earlier than usual."

"Will you ask him to come up here? Say I begged you."

When Harold entered, Esther was leaning against the back of the empty chair where yesterday he had seen his mother sitting. He was in a state of wonder and suspense, and when Esther approached him and gave him her hand he said, in a startled way,—

"Good God! how ill you look! Have you been sitting up with my mother?"

"Yes. She is asleep now," said Esther. They had merely pressed hands by way of greeting, and now stood apart looking at each other solemnly.

"Has she told you anything?" said Harold.

"No—only that she is wretched. Oh, I think I would bear a great deal of unhappiness to save her from having any more."

A painful thrill passed through Harold, and showed itself in his face with that pale rapid flash which can never be painted. Esther pressed her hands together, and said, timidly, though it was from an urgent prompting,—

"There is nothing in all this place—nothing since ever I came here—I could care for so much as that you should sit down by her now, and that she should see you when she wakes."

Then with delicate instinct she added, just laying her hand on his sleeve, "I know you would have come. I know you meant it. But she is asleep now. Go gently before she wakes."

Harold just laid his right hand for an instant on the back of Esther's as it rested on his sleeve, and then stepped softly to his mother's bedside.

An hour afterward, when Harold had laid his mother's pillow afresh, and sat down again by her, she said,—

"If that dear thing will marry you, Harold, it will make up to you for a great deal."

But before the day closed Harold knew that this was not to be. That young presence, which had flitted like a white new-winged dove over all the saddening relics and new finery of Transome Court, could not find its home there. Harold heard from Esther's lips that she loved some one else, and that she resigned all claim to the Transome estates.

She wished to go back to her father.

---◆---

CHAPTER LI.

The maiden said, I wis the londe
Is very fair to see,
But my true-love that is in bonde
Is fairer still to me.

ONE April day, when the sun shone on the lingering rain-drops, Lyddy was gone out, and Esther chose to sit in the kitchen, in the wicker chair against the white table, between the fire and the window. The kettle was singing, and the clock was ticking steadily toward four o'clock.

She was not reading, but stitching; and as her fingers moved nimbly something played about her parted lips like a ray. Suddenly she laid down her work, pressed her hands together on her knees, and bent forward a little. The next moment there came a loud rap at the door. She started up and opened it, but kept herself hidden behind it.

"Mr. Lyon at home?" said Felix, in his firm tones.

"No, sir," said Esther from behind her screen; "but Miss Lyon is if you'll please to walk in."

"Esther!" exclaimed Felix, amazed.

They held each other by both hands, and looked into each other's faces with delight.

"You are out of prison?"

"Yes, till I do something bad again. But you?—how is it all?"

"Oh, it is," said Esther, smiling brightly as she moved toward the wicker chair, and seated herself again, "that everything is as usual: my father is gone to see the sick; Lyddy is gone in deep despondency to buy the grocery; and

I am sitting here, with some vanity in me, needing to be scolded."

Felix had seated himself on a chair that happened to be near her, at the corner of the table. He looked at her still with questioning eyes—he grave, she mischievously smiling.

"Are you come back to live here, then?"

"Yes."

"You are not going to be married to Harold Transome, or to be rich?"

"No." Something made Esther take up her work again, and begin to stitch. The smiles were dying into a tremor.

"Why?" said Felix, in rather a low tone, leaning his elbow on the table, and resting his head on his hand while he looked at her.

"I did not wish to marry him, or to be rich."

"You have given it all up?" said Felix, leaning forward a little, and speaking in a still lower tone.

Esther did not speak. They heard the kettle singing and the clock loudly ticking. There was no knowing how it was: Esther's work fell, their eyes met; and the next instant their arms were round each other's necks, and once more they kissed each other.

When their hands fell again, their eyes were bright with tears. Felix laid his hand on her shoulder.

"Could you share the life of a poor man, then, Esther?"

"If I thought well enough of him," she said, the smile coming again, with the pretty saucy movement of her head.

"Have you considered well what it would be?—that it would be a very bare and simple life?"

"Yes—without attar of roses."

Felix suddenly removed his hand from her shoulder, rose from his chair, and walked a step or two; then he turned round and said, with deep gravity,—

"And the people I shall live among, Esther? They have not just the same follies and vices as the rich, but they have their own forms of folly and vice; and they have not what are called the refinements of the rich to make their faults more bearable. I don't say more bearable to me—I'm not fond of those refinements; but you are."

Felix paused an instant, and then added,—

"It is very serious, Esther."

"I know it is serious," said Esther, looking up at him. "Since I have been at Transome Court I have seen many things very seriously. If I had not, I should not have left what I did leave. I made a deliberate choice."

Felix stood a moment or two, dwelling on her with a face where the gravity gathered tenderness.

"And these curls?" he said, with a sort of relenting, seating himself again, and putting his hand on them.

"They cost nothing—they are natural."

"You are such a delicate creature."

"I am very healthy. Poor women, I think, are healthier than the rich. Besides," Esther went on, with a mischievous meaning, "I think of having some wealth."

"How?" said Felix, with an anxious start. "What do you mean?"

"I think even of two pounds a week: one needn't live up to the splendor of all that, you know; we might live as simply as you liked: there would be money to spare, and you could do wonders, and be obliged to work too, only not if sickness came. And then I think of a little income for your mother, enough for her to live as she has been used to live; and a little income for my father, to save him from being dependent when he is no longer able to preach."

Esther said all this in a playful tone, but she ended with a grave look of appealing submission,—

"I mean—if you approve. I wish to do what you think it will be right to do."

Felix put his hand on her shoulder again and reflected a little while, looking on the hearth: then he said, lifting up his eyes, with a smile at her,—

"Why, I shall be able to set up a great library, and lend the books to be dog's-eared and marked with bread-crumbs."

Esther said, laughing, "You think you are to do everything. You don't know how clever I am. I mean to go on teaching a great many things."

"Teaching me?"

"Oh, yes," she said, with a little toss; "I shall improve your French accent."

"You won't want me to wear a stock," said Felix, with a defiant shake of the head.

"No; and you will not attribute stupid thoughts to me before I've uttered them."

They laughed merrily, each holding the other's arms, like girl and boy. There was the ineffable sense of youth in common.

Then Felix leaned forward, that their lips might meet again, and after that his eyes roved tenderly over her face and curls.

"I'm a rough, severe fellow, Esther. Shall you never repent?—never be inwardly reproaching me that I was not a man who could have shared your wealth? Are you quite sure?"

"Quite sure!" said Esther, shaking her head; "for then I should have honored you less. I am weak—my husband must be greater and nobler than I am."

"Oh, I tell you what, though," said Felix, starting up, thrusting his hands into his pockets, and creasing his brow, playfully, "if you take me in that way I shall be forced to be a much better fellow than I ever thought of being."

"I call that retribution," said Esther, with a laugh as sweet as the morning thrush.

———————◆———————

EPILOGUE.

Our finest hope is finest memory ;
And those who love in age think youth is happy
Because it has a life to fill with love.

THE very next May, Felix and Esther were married. Every one in those days was married at the parish church; but Mr. Lyon was not satisfied without an additional private solemnity, "wherein there was no bondage to questionable forms, so that he might have a more enlarged utterance of joy and supplication."

It was a very simple wedding; but no wedding, even the gayest, ever raised so much interest and debate in Treby

Magna. Even very great people, like Sir Maximus and his family, went to the church to look at this bride, who had renounced wealth, and chosen to be the wife of a man who said he would always be poor.

Some few shook their heads; could not quite believe it; and thought there was "more behind." But the majority of honest Trebians were affected somewhat in the same way as happy-looking Mr. Wace was, who observed to his wife, as they walked from under the churchyard chestnuts: "It's wonderful how things go through you—you don't know how. I feel somehow as if I believed more in everything that's good."

Mrs. Holt, that day, said she felt herself to be receiving "some reward," implying that justice certainly had much more in reserve. Little Job Tudge had an entirely new suit, of which he fingered every separate brass button in a way that threatened an arithmetical mania; and Mrs. Holt had out her best tea-trays and put down her carpet again, with the satisfaction of thinking that there would no more be boys coming in all weathers with dirty shoes.

For Felix and Esther did not take up their abode in Treby Magna; and after a while Mr. Lyon left the town too, and joined them where they dwelt. On his resignation the church in Malthouse Yard chose a successor to him whose doctrine was rather higher.

There were other departures from Treby. Mr. Jermyn's establishment was broken up, and he was understood to have gone to reside at a great distance: some said "abroad," that large home of ruined reputations. Mr. Johnson continued blond and sufficiently prosperous till he got gray and rather more prosperous. Some persons, who did not think highly of him, held that his prosperity was a fact to be kept in the background, as being dangerous to the morals of the young; judging that it was not altogether creditable to the Divine Providence that anything but virtue should be rewarded by a front and back drawing-room in Bedford Row.

As for Mr. Christian, he had no more profitable secrets at his disposal. But he got his thousand pounds from Harold Transome.

The Transome family were absent for some time from

Transome Court. The place was kept up and shown to visitors, but not by Denner, who was away with her mistress. After a while the family came back, and Mrs. Transome died there. Sir Maximus was at her funeral, and throughout that neighborhood there was silence about the past.

Uncle Lingon continued to watch over the shooting on the Manor and the covers until that event occurred which he had predicted as a part of Church reform sure to come. Little Treby had a new rector, but others were sorry besides the old pointers.

As to all that wide parish of Treby Magna, it has since prospered as the rest of England has prospered. Doubtless there is more enlightenment now. Whether the farmers are all public-spirited, the shopkeepers nobly independent, the Sproxton men entirely sober and judicious, the Dissenters quite without narrowness or asperity in religion and politics, and the publicans all fit, like Gaius, to be the friends of an apostle —these things I have not heard, not having correspondence in those parts. Whether any presumption may be drawn from the fact that North Loamshire does not yet return a Radical candidate I leave to the all-wise—I mean the newspapers.

As to the town in which Felix Holt now resides, I will keep that a secret, lest he should be troubled by any visitor having the insufferable motive of curiosity.

I will only say that Esther has never repented. Felix, however, grumbles a little that she has made his life too easy, and that, if it were not for much walking, he should be a sleek dog.

There is a young Felix, who has a great deal more science than his father, but not much more money.

THE END.